The Archaeology
of City-States

Smithsonian Series in Archaeological Inquiry

Robert McC. Adams and Bruce D. Smith, Series Editors

The Smithsonian Series in Archaeological Inquiry presents original case studies that address important general research problems and demonstrate the values of particular theoretical and/or methodological approaches. Titles include well-focused edited collections as well as works by individual authors. The series is open to all subject areas, geographical regions, and theoretical modes.

Advisory Board

The Archaeology of City-States

Cross-Cultural Approaches

Edited by Deborah L. Nichols
and Thomas H. Charlton

SMITHSONIAN INSTITUTION PRESS
Washington and London

In memoriam

Mary G. Hodge

1946–1996

Copy editor: Peter Donovan
Production editor: Duke Johns
Designer: Linda McKnight

Library of Congress Cataloging-in-Publication Data
The archaeology of city-states : cross-cultural approaches /
   edited by Deborah L. Nichols and Thomas H. Charlton.
      p.   cm.
   Includes bibliographical references (p.   ) and index.
   ISBN 1-56098-746-4 (alk. paper). —
   ISBN 1-56098-722-7 (pbk. : alk. paper)
   1. Ethnoarchaeology—Congresses. 2. Civilization,
Ancient—Cross-cultural studies—Congresses. 3. City-
states—Cross-cultural studies—Congresses. I. Nichols,
Deborah L. II. Charlton, Thomas H.
   CC79.E85A76   1998
   930.1—dc21   97-8283

British Library Cataloguing-in-Publication Data is available

Manufactured in the United States of America
04 03 02 01 00 99 98 97   5 4 3 2 1

♾ The paper used in this publication meets the minimum
requirements of the American National Standard for
Information Sciences—Permanence of Paper for Printed
Library Materials ANSI Z39.48-1984.

Contents

Illustrations

Tables

Contributors

Thomas H. Charlton, professor of anthropology, Department of Anthropology, University of Iowa, Iowa City, Iowa.

Mary G. Hodge, associate professor of anthropology, School of Human Sciences and Humanities, University of Houston Clear Lake, Houston, Texas, deceased.

Jonathan Mark Kenoyer, associate professor, Department of Anthropology, University of Wisconsin, Madison, Wisconsin.

Alan L. Kolata, professor of anthropology, director, Center for Latin American Studies, Department of Anthropology, University of Chicago, Chicago, Illinois.

Ian Morris, professor of classics and history, Department of Classics, Stanford University, Stanford, California.

Deborah L. Nichols, professor of anthropology, Department of Anthropology, Dartmouth College, Hanover, New Hampshire.

Richard Pearson, professor of anthropology, Department of Anthropology and Sociology, University of British Columbia, Vancouver, British Columbia.

K. Anne Pyburn, associate professor of anthropology, Department of Anthropology, Indiana University, Bloomington, Indiana.

David B. Small, associate professor of anthropology, Department of Sociology and Anthropology, Lehigh University, Bethlehem, Pennsylvania.

Elizabeth Stone, professor of anthropology, Department of Anthropology, State University of New York at Stony Brook, Stony Brook, New York.

David Webster, professor of anthropology, Department of Anthropology, Pennsylvania State University, University Park, Pennsylvania.

Robert J. Wenke, professor of anthropology, Department of Anthropology, University of Washington, Seattle, Washington.

David J. Wilson, associate professor of anthropology, Department of Anthropology, Southern Methodist University, Dallas, Texas.

Robin D. S. Yates, professor of history and East Asian studies, McGill University, Montréal, Québec.

Norman Yoffee, professor of anthropology and
Near Eastern studies, curator, Museum of
Anthropology, Department of Near Eastern Studies,
University of Michigan, Ann Arbor, Michigan.

Preface

The roots for this volume run deep. Thomas Charlton has regularly taught a course on the comparative evolution of early civilizations since 1966 and had concluded that the city-state, although not completely universal, did have a large degree of cross-cultural validity. Our collaborative research, beginning in 1988 and still continuing, with a focus on the Late Aztec city-state of Otumba, emphasized the need for a systematic examination of the extent to which the city-state was a regularly recurring form of organization in primary and secondary civilizations. In 1991 Charlton suggested organizing a symposium on the city-state for the 1992 Annual Meeting of the American Anthropological Association. For most of 1992 Charlton was in Mexico overseeing analysis of materials from the Otumba Project and, despite the wonders of facsimile machines, the bulk of the organizational details fell to Nichols.

With the encouragement and support of those scholars who prepared papers for the symposium—Ian Morris, Richard Pearson, K. Anne Pyburn, David Small, Elizabeth Stone, Robert Wenke, David Wilson, and Robin Yates—and the discussants—Mary Hodge and Norman Yoffee—we proposed incorporating revised and expanded versions of the papers into an edited volume. In order to expand coverage of the earliest civilizations, we invited Mark Kenoyer, Alan Kolata, and David Webster to contribute papers to the volume. We developed a paper on central Mexico, while Mary Hodge moved from discussant to preparing a paper on Aztec city-states.

The history, formation, and development of Aztec city-states were central themes of Mary Hodge's research. As in her paper for this volume, throughout her career as an anthropologist she combined original studies in both ethnohistory and archaeology. When she started her research in the 1970s as a graduate student at the University of Michigan, studies of Aztec society, although numerous, generally followed a top-down approach and reflected the perspectives of the imperial capitals—most especially Tenochtitlán-Tlatelolco and the Mexica and their Spanish conquerors. Mary, however, took a different approach (Hodge 1984).

Using Nahuatl and Spanish colonial documents, supplemented by archaeological data where available, she focused her analysis on the city-state, *altepetl*, and examined the history and organization of five city-states in the Basin of Mexico both before and after their incorporation into the Triple Alliance or Aztec empire (Hodge 1984). She emphasized the diversity of these city-states' political organization and the different ways such organization was adapted to suit the imperial structure of the Triple Alliance. Viewed from the perspective of individual city-states, the political hierarchy of the Triple Alliance was less centralized than the imperial tribute hierarchy and each city-state retained "its political identity" (Hodge 1984:150).

This research led Mary to further consider what effect the development of the Triple Alliance had on market and exchange systems, especially those involving utilitarian goods. To address this issue, she and Leah Minc (Hodge and Minc 1990, 1991) turned to the archaeological record to examine the spatial distribution of decorated Early and Late Aztec pottery collected by settlement-pattern surveys in the eastern and southern Basin of Mexico. Collaborating with M. James Blackman (Smithsonian Institution Conservation Laboratory), and Hector Neff (Missouri University Research Reactor), they also undertook the first large-scale neutron-activation analysis of Aztec pottery and clays to identify production areas.

Mary and her colleagues analyzed decorated serving vessels that were distributed through the market system but not as tribute items. They concluded that, although Aztec pottery is highly standardized, ceramic production was multicentric. Decorated serving vessels were generally exchanged at the level of confederacies of city-states (Hodge 1992; Hodge et al. 1992, 1993; Hodge and Neff 1994; Minc et al. 1994; Neff and Hodge 1996). Although individual city-states retained their political identities under the Aztec empire, the growth of Tenochtitlán-Tlatelolco as the imperial capital and largest city and commercial center in Mesoamerica led to a restructuring of the economies of city-states in the core of the Basin of Mexico immediately around Tenochtitlán. Mary with Hector Neff (Hodge and Neff 1994) proposed a decline in Late Aztec pottery manufacturing at Xaltocán (a city-state capital in the northwestern Basin) as Tenochtitlán became an important production center. They (Neff and Hodge 1996) also found a similar pattern using data from excavations that Mary had directed at the city-state center of Chalco (Hodge, in press).

Mary (1994, 1996) also developed methods to integrate documentary sources and archaeological settlement pattern data which she used to reconstruct Aztec political geography and to show the continued concentration of political and religious activities in city-state capitals even after their incorporation into the Aztec empire. Thus, she concluded that by employing the existing city-state organization, the Triple Alliance was able "to control large populations using few new administrative functions" (Hodge 1994:61). Such an approach allowed Mary to define details of city-state organization and interactions not available from either the written or archaeological record alone.

Mary Hodge helped to begin a new era of city-state archaeology in central Mexico. Her contribution to this volume, which she revised less than two months before her death, was to be Mary's last paper devoted to the subject of city-states. The approaches she applied to Aztec city-states have broad applicability. To move forward with the methods and ideas presented by her and the other authors will require us to look at city-state organization from multiple perspectives, ranging from the humble potsherd to royal stelae and local documentary sources to regional settlement patterns.

Acknowledgments

We are grateful to all the authors for their individual contributions and for their patience and responsiveness throughout the long process of preparing this volume. Bruce Trigger encouraged the development of the symposium. Jeremy Rutter and Michael Smith made useful suggestions as we were putting together the symposium that led to the book. Deborah Hodges assisted in the initial phase of editing and formatting the volume and brought her considerable experience to the task of compiling the index. Joyce Marcus carefully read and commented on our introductory chapter. Ridie Ghezzi (Baker Library, Dartmouth College) helped track down details of references. Elizabeth Landy and Ed Vicente, with patience and perseverance, checked citations yet one more time. Nathan Somers sent faxes and made photocopies that kept the manuscript on schedule. Cynthia L. Otis Charlton prepared the maps and tables in our introduction and one figure in our central Mexico chapter. The University of Iowa Photographic Service and Medical Illustrations of Dartmouth College reproduced numerous maps and drawings in their final form.

A grant from the Claire Garber Goodman Fund (Dartmouth College) helped cover costs incurred in preparing the volume and we acknowledge that support. Nichols completed much of the editing while on sabbatical leave from Dartmouth in 1995–96; she thanks the Dean of Faculty Office and James Wright for the computer upgrade and their continued support. Charlton, while on Developmental Assignment from the University of Iowa in 1993, refined many of the perspectives included in the introductory chapter and the chapter on central Mexico. He thanks the University of Iowa for that assignment, as well as the National Endowment for the Humanities who supported the ongoing Otumba analyses with grant RO-22268-91, 1992–93. Although continuing with the Otumba analysis, he participated in the editing process by reading papers, commenting, and acting as a sounding board for Nichols's suggestions.

In particular we thank Daniel Goodwin and Bruce Smith for their support and encouragement from the outset. Robert Lockhart assisted Daniel Goodwin. Peter Donovan's and Duke Johns's careful editing at the Smithsonian Institution Press turned a manuscript into a book.

Our most important support comes from our families. John Watanabe has patiently listened and commented on Nichols's musings about archaeology and ancient states while fixing the daily ration of a peanut-butter-and-jelly sandwich for our son Aaron, who has made our lives busier and better in ways we never imagined. Thanks to the children of the Dartmouth Child Care Center, some of the stacks of paper produced in the course of editing the volume have been recycled into "decorative art."

Cynthia Otis Charlton provided an artistic counterpart to Charlton's discussions on the intricacies and opaqueness of nineteenth-century German texts on ancient social, political, and economic systems and thought as seen through a romantic filter. Our five cats, Cocoa, Xochipilli, Xochiquetzal, Ce Acatl, and Ome Tochtli, were singularly unimpressed with the work but relentlessly fascinated with the piles of paper. Cyndi translates their comments as "Certainly there must be something for cats here!" Certainly!

1

The City-State Concept

Development and Applications

In our ongoing research into the political and economic dynamics of the Late Aztec period of the Basin of Mexico (A.D. 1350–1521) we quite readily view our archaeological data within the context of an indigenous system of interrelated small polities. These small polities or small states in the Basin and elsewhere in Mesoamerica have been referred to variously as *altepetl, señorios, cacicazgos,* kingdoms, petty kingdoms, principalities, and city-states, terms often used interchangeably.

The term *city-state* links the phenomenon of the state and a particular kind of settlement pattern (cf. Rihll and Wilson 1991:60). In general we understand city-states to be small, territorially based, politically independent state systems, characterized by a capital city or town, with an economically and socially integrated adjacent hinterland. The whole unit, city plus hinterlands, is relatively self-sufficient economically and perceived as being ethnically distinct from other similar city-state systems (cf. Burke 1986; Griffeth and Thomas 1981a:xiii–xx, 1981b:186, 188; J. Marcus 1989:201; Raaflaub 1991:567–568; Trigger 1993:8–14). City-states frequently, but not inevitably, occur in groups of fairly evenly spaced units of approximately equivalent size (Renfrew 1975:12–20).

Small polities, with apparently similar political structure and organization along with associated economic, ideological, and settlement pattern components, were widely distributed throughout Mesoamerica in the early sixteenth century. In many areas they had persisted from the earliest beginnings of state-level societies. In others, after periods of subjugation by or incorporation into larger state systems (Cowgill 1988: 265), city-states reappeared or reformed when those systems broke down (see Charlton 1973, 1975; Charlton and Nichols, this volume; Griffeth and Thomas 1981a:xix; Hodge 1984, this volume; J. Marcus 1989, 1992a; Pyburn, this volume; Webster, this volume).

The phenomenon of the small polity as city-state is present in areas other than Mesoamerica both as an early and a recurrent form of political organization. Similar phenomena occur and reoccur at different periods in many parts of the world, beginning with the earliest Near Eastern civilization (Stone, this volume) and continuing until the dominance of the nation-state during the nineteenth century.[1]

In a recent work on economic development in the United States during the late twentieth century, Peirce argues that new forms of city-states are presently emerging here and in other nation-states as part of

THOMAS H. CHARLTON
AND DEBORAH L. NICHOLS

local and worldwide political and economic realities (1993:1–37). He bases his discussion on the city-state concept as it has been defined and applied to ancient, classical, medieval, and Renaissance cultures (1993: 6–11). However, Peirce styles his concept "citistate" as applied to contemporary phenomena to reflect the newly present worldwide context of "citistate" emergence, and the late-twentieth-century structural differences of transglobal connectedness and increasing domination by a world population (1993:x). In such a context, "across America and across the globe, citistates are emerging as a critical focus of economic activity, of governance, of social organization of the 1990s and the century to come" (1993:1).

Peirce's emerging "citistates" notwithstanding, there are few, if any, contemporary city-states. To the best of our knowledge all have special functions such as religion (Vatican City), trade and finance (Hong Kong and Singapore), and energy resources (Abu Dhabi, Qatar, and Kuwait). As special-function sites or polities, all are inextricably integrated into a worldwide economic and political system (cf. Griffeth and Thomas 1981a:xiv).

Their settlement systems emphasize the urban center to such an extent that the state and the city are virtually coterminous. These characteristics, the worldwide economic system, the equivalency between city and state, and the absence or reduced importance of socially and economically integrated supporting hinterlands clearly differentiate these contemporary city-states from earlier examples and raise the issue of their even being structurally and functionally present-day examples of the earlier form.

The City-State Concept: A Brief Historical Review

It has been stated that a country, a nation-state, seeking to defend all (lands, resources, industries, and settlements) by deploying its military forces just inside and along the entire length of its borders, spreads its defenses so thin that it defends nothing. Similarly it might well be suggested that the term *city-state*, referring to phenomena so diverse, so chronologically and spatially dispersed, is analogous to wide but shallow defenses, spread so thin that it refers to everything and thereby to nothing. If this were the case, then an argument could be made to replace *city-state* and to adopt a more neutral term to be used to describe small polities of a particular kind.

We are concerned with a particular organizational structure that for historical reasons is called a city-state, which today is the most widely and most commonly used term in English to refer to such similarly structured small polities of all areas and at all times. The term *city-state* carries a lot of baggage in Western scholarship and we might be better off with a more neutral term; however, it is embedded in the literature and rather than add more jargon we will use it to refer to a particular organizational structure.

The term *city-state*, so far as we can determine, appeared in the late nineteenth century. It referred to a concept of governance consciously discussed by European scholars, and others, with reference to Greek and Roman classical writers. The ancient Greeks themselves discussed it (Dover 1992; de Romilly 1977). Finley, disclaiming any knowledge of its origin, suggests that *city-state* is a convention to translate the Greek *polis* in order to avoid confusion in meaning since *polis* in antiquity could mean both city or town *and* city-state (1977a:306). Burke and Gawantka cite classicist William Warde Fowler's 1893 book, The *City-State of the Greeks and Romans,* as containing the earliest appearance in print in English of the term *city-state* (Burke 1986:139; Gawantka 1985:205). *City-state* has become well-established in English-speaking contexts dealing with ancient Greek civilization (e.g. Burke 1986:139; Donlan 1994; Finley 1977a, 1982; Grant 1987; Halliday 1967 [1923]; Jeffery 1976; Sealey 1976; Thomas 1981). *Polis* still appears, sometimes as a synonym for city-state (e.g. Starr 1977), and sometimes to differentiate in a subtle manner the Greek city-states from those found elsewhere (e.g. Owens 1991:28; Sakellariou 1989).

The German equivalent is *Stadtstaat* (Finley 1977a:306), the French term *Etat-ville* or *cité-Etat*, the Italian term *stato-città* or *città-Stato* (Burke 1986: 139; Gawantka 1985:73–75, note 17 and Appendix 4, 204–206), and the Spanish term in Mexico *ciudad-estado*. Burke suggests that the French and Italian terms are much less popular than city-state. In Mexico *ciudad-estado* is not commonly used. Finley states that the "French and Italians have not adopted the 'city-state' convention so that *cité* (or *città*), like *polis*, can mean either [urban center or city-state]" (1977a:311). Burke and Gawantka, however, do suggest that terms equivalent to the English *city-state* do exist in late-twentieth century French and Italian, and they are occasionally used.

Although the German term *Stadtstaat* first appeared in print by 1860, many other terms used earlier continued to be employed to refer, apparently, to the same or similar phenomena (Chittolini 1994:32; Gawantka 1985:192, 204–206; Glatz 1960:107). In 1898 Jacob Burckhardt defined and applied the classical Greek term *die Polis* for *Stadtstaat* in his work *Griechische Kulturgeschichte* (1898) thus formalizing the use of a loan word present in German writing since at least 1845 and providing an ostensibly strong ideological connection between the ancient Greek *polis* and the city-state concept (Gawantka 1985:31, 190). Are German Romanticism and idealization of the nineteenth-century constructed *polis* (as seen in Burckhardt's work of the last half of the nineteenth century; cf. Morris 1994a:15–20, this volume), our only concerns about the conceptual bases of city-state definition?

Certainly our current concept or idea of a particular form of state, the city-state, regardless of the term used, developed within the context of late-eighteenth and early-nineteenth-century Hellenistic studies. These were affected by German political nationalism and by a more general European scholarly context, heavily influenced by German scholars and German Romanticism (Gawantka 1985:192; Morris 1994a: 14–19; Friedman 1992:838–841; Grafton 1992; Kardulias 1994:42; Wohlleben 1992). One result, relevant to our topic, was the ostensible attachment of some strong conceptual content to the idea of the city-state, supposedly from detailed considerations of the Greek *poleis,* but in fact derived from many other interwoven strands contained in the late-eighteenth-century and nineteenth-century recreation of the Greek State, the Idea of the Greek State, or *die Polis.*

Those strands involved not only views on the Greek *poleis,* especially Athens, but also included views on the medieval and Renaissance city-states of northern Italy, especially the Florentine and Venetian city-states.[2] In other words, the development of a general concept of city-state was informed by specific European examples of city-states: those of Greece in classical antiquity, and those of Renaissance Italy.

This matrix of interaction, a two-way street along which flowed in both directions ideas of Greek city-states and ideas of Renaissance Italian city-states, affected the concept of the city-state in general. Morris (1994a:15–16), citing Frank M. Turner's *The Greek Heritage in Victorian Britain* (1981), does argue that the influence of classical civilizations on western Europe involved only Roman influences until the late eighteenth century, at which time significant influence from ancient Greek sources began to be felt there. Dionisotti (1992) and Burke (1992) support this position.

Nevertheless, there are some intriguing indications to support our position that some classical Greek influence on Italian thinking about Renaissance Italian city-states and the reciprocal influence of considerations of Renaissance Italian city-states on thinking about classical Greek *poleis* went back at least to the fourteenth century, when "intellectuals turned to the surviving literature of the classical era to provide a glorious past for the emerging Italian city states and to justify the increasing secularization of Italian culture" (Trigger 1989a:35; see also Burke 1992:140; Rowe 1965; Slotkin 1965:x). Such intellectual interaction, extending back at least to the Renaissance, probably formed part of "the cultural tradition of Greece and Rome [that] continued unbroken into the Middle Ages" (Rowe 1965:8) and was not solely a late-eighteenth or nineteenth-century development (see also Chittolini 1991; Griffiths 1981; Grubb 1991 on the emergence of medieval Italian city-states; and Wickham 1989:9–28 for a discussion of political developments between A.D. 400 and 1000).

Martines cites numerous instances of Renaissance Italian city-states, especially Florence, as being described in terms of, or compared with, both Roman and Greek predecessors as understood through written sources (1979:116–117, 126–127, 198; see also Burke 1992:140). He does note that the Greek sources were usually accessed through Latin translations (1979:192–193; cf. Morris 1994a:16). Brown, also writing about Florence, noted the influence of rediscovered Greek texts on the development of comparisons between Italian and classical Greek city-states in the fifteenth century, although the "most appropriate—and easily accessible—analogy for Italian communes" was republican Rome (1991:97; see also Rowe 1965:10). Ciappelli points out that "classical precedents were used as models in contemporary political discourse" and mentions both Roman and Greek sources (1991:125). Brown discusses the self-conscious analogies medieval city-states drew with Rome and Athens: "It was at the level of politics that the analogy between classical and medieval Italian city-states was felt most keenly" (1991:95).

Thus we propose that there had been an ongoing dialogue between Italian city-states (medieval and Renaissance) on the one hand, and ideas of and about city-states in classical antiquity on the other, with analogies drawn to enhance Italian city-states, well before scholars of the late eighteenth century and the nineteenth century turned their attention to the same city-states. Undoubtedly some of the ideas and concepts that developed in attempts at self-definition and self-enhancement by the Italian city-states were also incorporated as concepts into the nineteenth-century definition of city-state.

Burke points out that publications by two nineteenth-century scholars, J. C. L. Simonde de Sismondi's (1826) *Histoire des républiques italiennes du moyenâge* (16 volumes 1807–1818), and Jacob Burckhardt's *Die Kultur der Renaissance in Italien* (1937 [1860]), were influential treatises on Renaissance Italian city-states ("republics" according to both authors; Burke 1986:139). Their formulations in turn came to influence perceptions not only of Renaissance Italian city-states, but also of the classical Greek *poleis*. Burke argues that both Sismondi and Burckhardt were involved, through their studies, in a "nineteenth century invention of tradition" contributing to the "cult of the Renaissance city-state" and possibly establishing the favorable image of the city-state in general (Burke 1986:138). Both Sismondi and Burckhardt were attracted to the Italian city-states for personal reasons. For Sismondi, who "set out to do for the Italian republics what had already been done for ancient Greece and medieval Switzerland" (Burke 1986:138), this was the theme of liberty or the history of liberty (Waley 1988:154–175). For Burckhardt it was a nostalgia for Basel as a city-state (see also Gawantka 1985:16, note 14).

These developments are of interest for two main reasons. First was the creation of a glorified or idealized romantic image of Renaissance Italian city-states placed within or against a long-standing tradition of referencing them against constructs of Roman and Greek predecessors (Burke 1986; Friedman 1992; Gawantka 1985; Grafton 1992:241). Second, Burckhardt later replaced *Stadtstaat* with *Polis* in Volume 1 of his 1898 *Griechische Kulturgeschichte* and applied his romantic notions about Renaissance Italian city-states to the ancient Greek city-state (Burckhardt 1898; Gawantka 1985:12–13; Morris 1993, personal communication; Raaflaub 1991:566).

Obviously the nineteenth-century creation of ancient Greece, even as it pertains only to the *polis* or city-state concept, is much too complex a web to untangle here. We shall endeavor, however, to develop and apply a definition of city-state that is not as culture specific or culture bound and that will be useful and valid in a comparative cross-cultural sense, not merely as a label but also as a model (see Burke 1986:140 ff. for a current example of a model derived from Renaissance Italian examples and Maisels 1987:324 for one derived from the other "classic" example of city-states, ancient Greece).

As we have discussed, among Western scholars the idea of the Greek *polis*, based primarily on the writings of Greek philosophers but with some aspects of Renaissance city-states included, became a significant component of the concepts state, city, and city-state. By reexamining the *polis* more critically from a comparative perspective (see chapters by Morris, Small, and Stone, this volume), and not as an ideal type of city-state, it is possible to see similarities and differences between the *polis* as a city-state and examples of city-states in other places and times. Although the *polis* figured strongly in the development of the city-state concept by nineteenth-century Western scholars, it is no longer justified to treat the *polis* in general, and Athens in particular, as the prototypical city-state, given the evidence for substantial variation in the *poleis* of classical Greece and the independent development of city-states in many other areas of the world (Pounds 1969). Hodge, Kenoyer, Stone, and Yates draw extensively on conceptualizations of city-state organization known from historical and ethnohistorical sources from other parts of the world outside of the European/Near Eastern tradition.

The City-State Concept: Definitional Details

We want to strip the concept down to fighting weight for use in the comparative cross-cultural approach to which we are committed. Our theoretical position in this matter is a middle ground that lies between the extremes of neoevolutionism and historical particularism, described so well by Trigger in his recent synthesis of archaeological thought (1989a:400–407). Our position most closely approximates Steward's multilinear model of evolution which sought evidence for cross-cultural regularities in those limited areas of the world where early civilizations developed autochthonously (1949, 1955). As Trigger points out: "More order is observable in cross-cultural perspective than would be the case if each culture were the product of purely fortuitous circumstances. Yet there is sufficient diversity to rule out any simple, strongly deterministic causality" (1989a:403). We are trying to differentiate the patterns of cultural order from the background noise of cultural diversity (see also Drennan 1996:30). The city-state is one of those cross-cultural regularities.

In practice, for most archaeologists the essential criteria defining a small state system as a city-state are: a state system centered in a capital city or town; a small integrated territory or hinterland; a small overall population; political independence; relative economic self-sufficiency; and perceived ethnic distinctiveness. These criteria conform to those in definitions put forward by Griffeth and Thomas (1981a: xiii–xx), Maisels (1987:332–337, 1990:10–13); J. Marcus (1989:201) and Trigger (1993:8–14) in comparative studies, by Burke on Renaissance Italian city-states (1989:140–143), and by Raaflaub on ancient Greece (1991:567–568).

Previous comparative studies of city-states include the pioneering work *The City-State in Five Cultures* (Griffeth and Thomas 1981c) with a focus on a diachronic examination of city-states in the Near Eastern and European cultural traditions (Sumer, ancient Greece, Italy, Switzerland, and Germany) and in one area of West Africa (Hausa-Nigeria). More recently Molho and his colleagues in their book, *City-States in Classical Antiquity and Medieval Italy,* consciously selected Athens, Rome, Florence, and Venice as historically well-known city-states in order to develop a basis for comparisons to be expanded later (1991b: 16). In both of these previous works comparing city-states, the data were primarily historical, and, with the exception of Sumer, all are examples of city-states within secondary civilizations—civilizations that formed from preexisting civilizations or states.

Working with *both* textual *and* archaeological data, most contributors to the volume recognize the city-state as being one of two or three major forms of early states. Two of these early state forms, the city-state and the village state (Maisels 1987:332, 354, 1990:xvi), or the city-state and the territorial state (Trigger 1993:8–14), have been proposed as recurring contrasting forms of political organization that resulted from alternate developmental trajectories and economic systems, and which characterize numerous pristine and secondary civilizations. Territorial states (Trigger 1993:8–9) or village states (Maisels 1987: 332–337, 1990:10–13) integrate large areas through a hierarchy of administrative centers, which are small,

decentralized, urban centers, with ideological and political functions, with primarily rulers, administrators, craft specialists, and retainers in residence, and most farmers in homesteads and villages. The economy is two-tiered with little economic integration aside from the paying of taxes to the rulers (Maisels 1990:10–13; Trigger 1993:10–11). Although Maisels and Trigger differ about the placement of the Classic Maya,[3] the criteria included in their definitions of these state forms are comparable to each other and to our definition. Maisels, in fact, makes direct reference to the city-state as defined or measured by the ancient Greek *polis* as described by Aristotle and modern scholars (1987:354–355, 1990:11–13; see also chapters by Morris, Small, and Stone, this volume).

In this volume we have extended the previous comparative studies of city-states by expanding coverage to additional cultural and geographical areas outside of Europe, by including primary civilizations of the Near East, southwest and East Asia, and the Americas that together represent a time range from 4000 B.C. to A.D. 1600, and by encouraging a major emphasis on archaeological data (Figs. 1.1 and 1.2). Our intent is to represent each area of the world in which primary civilizations emerged and to include selected regions where there have been sufficient archaeological investigations, which we are emphasizing to provide comparative data from additional secondary civilizations.

Archaeological Manifestations

The development and expansion of the settlement-pattern approach in archaeology provided a data base against which ideas of state organization, including city-states, could be studied (Willey 1953). City-state organization, including the size of territories and urban settlements and the nature of urban-hinterland integration, is reflected in many levels of the archaeological settlement-pattern record ranging from patterns of artifact distributions to regional settlement patterns.

Regional settlement-pattern data are critical to defining city-state size and organization, and for understanding processes of formation and termination (Charlton and Nichols, this volume; Wilson, this volume). Hodge, using such data, along with artifact distribution studies, is able to examine archaeological correlates of the city-state in considerable detail (this volume). She also discusses the problem of defining

Figure 1.1. Schematic map showing location of states discussed in this volume. Drawn by Cynthia L. Otis Charlton.

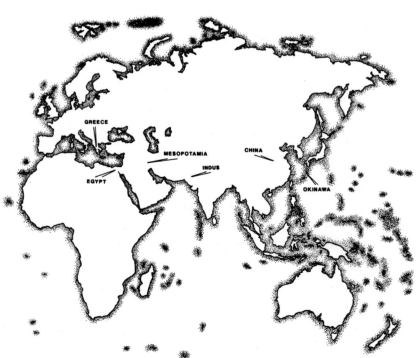

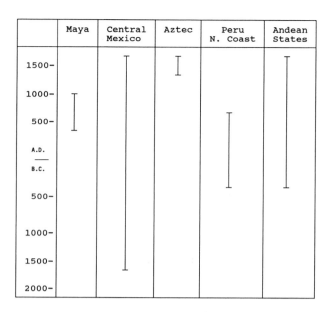

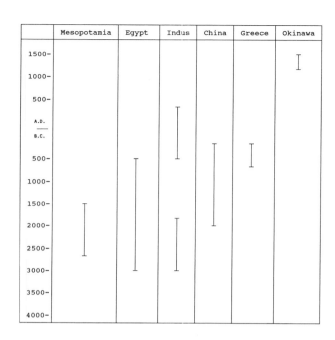

Figure 1.2. Chronology of states discussed in this volume. Prepared by Cynthia L. Otis Charlton.

boundaries of city-states and confederations in the archaeological record, a problem that partly stems from the fluidity of political boundaries. Nonetheless, she shows that the Early Aztec settlement pattern in the Basin of Mexico conforms well to a city-state model.

The fragmentation of power among factions within a city-state, as well as between city-states, can be examined archaeologically in a number of ways: at the regional level in settlement hierarchies (Charlton and Nichols, this volume), and in defensive site locations and/or defensive architecture (Pearson, this volume). Recent work at Classic Maya sites like Copán demonstrates how organizations based on lineages can be identified (Hendon 1991; Webster, this volume). Pyburn considers the archaeological manifestations of different sources of elite power (this volume). Social and political differences within city-states might be viewed through evidence for factional competition that involves the manipulation of symbols as part of the construction of alliances and coalitions. Factions can be reflected in artifact patterning—for example in stylistic differences in the artifacts used in competitive ritual displays, including feasting (Brumfiel 1994).

Criteria for defining city-state organization are also reflected in the types of structures, their organization, distribution, and layout within the capital town or city. Stone, Kenoyer, Pearson, Webster, and Kolata illustrate how the form and composition of cities reflect various aspects of city-state organization. In the urban settlements of city-states, administrative and religious complexes are separate from each other and

separate from the marketplace(s). Members of the upper and lower classes reside in the same residential districts where manufacturing workshops are located.

In very urbanized societies—those with more than one urban center—not all cities are city-state capitals. Capitals, because of their role as political and economic centers, often contain public open places (e.g., plazas, *agora*) and remains of other types of places for the "exercise of public power" (Frézouls 1991:449). Capital cities are also likely to have more monumental public symbols, and the city-state center is also likely to be the locus for convergence of roads and other transportation arteries (Ackerman 1991), the "all roads lead to Rome" syndrome.

Through trace-element studies of artifacts it is possible to reconstruct the areas throughout which the goods produced in the workshops of the city-state center were distributed. This helps us better understand operation of the political economy, or the political and economic integration of the population throughout the city-state (Hodge, this volume; Pearson, this volume). Hodge finds that ceramic exchange was most intense in the Basin of Mexico between those Early Aztec city-states that were members of the same confederation. She examines how the expansion of confederations and the formation of the Triple Alliance (Aztec empire) altered the political economies of city-states as reflected in the ceramic-artifact distribution networks.

Ethnicity, an important aspect of city-state definition when written records are available, is one aspect of city-state definition that needs to be explored in more depth in terms of its archaeological manifestations. We would expect to find evidence for regional city-state differences in the worship of different patron deities—metaphors of cosmic forces (Trigger 1993:88)—at various levels ranging from temples in capitals to household shrines. Ritual paraphernalia may exhibit stylistic and symbolic differences that are related to expressions of ethnicity by city-states. Ethnicity is often also expressed in clothing, ornamentation and, while these items may not themselves always remain in the archaeological record, depictions of them in a less perishable medium, such as pottery, may be recovered.

City-State Size

Compactness or small size is a defining criterion of a city-state, going back to Aristotle (as quoted by Maisels 1990:11; see also Vilatte 1995). Some see the compactness of the city-state, its resultant "territorial integrity," as its most distinctive feature (Cornell 1991:67). Size and compactness relate to technological and ecological factors. Although city-states within any particular civilization varied in size, usually in relation to ecological and topographical dimensions, generally the boundaries of most city-states lay within a radius of one-day's walk from the central town or city (10 kilometers to no more than 30 kilometers; Hodge, this volume; Hassig 1988:66–67).

The technology of transportation—the friction of distance (Hassig 1992:33)—limited the size of the area that a ruler could effectively integrate (Wenke, this volume). Thus transportation technology affects the size of the territory, the size of the urban and hinterland populations, and the integration of both. These in turn form the basis for the typical organic solidarity of city-state organization.

Morris, Small, Stone, Yoffee point out in this volume that the very structure of city-state organization is substantially based on small size. They suggest that the integrity, the organic solidarity, and the consensual political arrangements developing from contests for control of economic, political, and ideological sources of power, in turn inhibit the ability of the ruling group of any individual city-state to expand to include a broader territory on a permanent or stable basis to any significant degree. Phases of political integration, either when one group of elites is able to dominate others, or when elites in one city-state cooperate with elites in another city-state in some type of alliance, therefore tend to be short-lived. City-states that became long-lived territorial states should have undergone significant reorganization and, in some cases, have acquired new transportation technology. The fact that the political unification of Indus city-states did not occur until the development of an expansive military organization that employed the horse and elephant for transport, along with iron weapons for battle, nicely illustrates this point. We do suggest, however, that the integrative periods of Teotihuacán and Tula in central Mexico might be exceptions to the usually small size of city-states, because of the need to reorganize for territorial control. Teotihuacán's longevity was also exceptional. Hodge (this volume) argues conversely that the compactness of Aztec city-states contributed to their persistence during the Colonial period in Mexico despite their incorporation into a worldwide Spanish Empire by an elite with a sophisticated military technology and including horses, a new transportation technology.

In Egypt, the Nile facilitated integration with its relative ease of transportation and communication along with a substantially homogeneous resource distribution. From the outset Egypt was a territorial state (Trigger 1993:10–11). Under very different ecological circumstances, Kolata argues that territorial states were also the norm in the pre-Columbian Andean highlands (Kolata, this volume; cf. Trigger 1993:13–14). Setting aside the issue of urbanism for the moment, Andean systems of vertical ecological integration involving colonization and direct control of different ecological zones apparently favored territorial states rather than small polities. Kolata suggests city-states might have developed as a consequence of the fragmentation of the highland empires of Tiwanaku and Huari similar to the situation J. Marcus (1989) describes for Postclassic Mesoamerica (Charlton and Nichols, this volume; Graffam 1992).

If we exclude the small polities of the late Protodynastic and the early Dynastic (Wenke, this volume), the closest approximation to city-states in Egypt appeared during the first centuries A.D., *not* from the fragmentation of an empire but from the expansion of first Greek, and then Roman, imperial rule to Egypt. Although the center of an empire, Athens retained the structure of the *polis* throughout its imperial expansion (Molho et al. 1991a:10). Rome, another city-state that became the center of an empire, did change to some extent. Rome exceeded the size of a city-state early in its growth. However, its city-state ideology, internal structure, and self-perception persisted and influenced its imperial administration (Molho et al. 1991a:10–11).

At their empire's greatest extent, the Romans promoted local government. They continued to regard the city state, the archetypal government of early Rome and of its neighbours, as the fundamental unit of political organization. Because of this, they undertook at great effort and cost to transform tribal areas that they conquered (such as southern England) into a mosaic of what appeared to them (if not to the conquered peoples) to be city states. (Trigger 1978:207)

Wilson also does not find the city-state concept applicable to the earliest states of the Peruvian coast and he argues against defining types of states in favor of a systemic approach (this volume). To clarify multicausal explanations he proposes a hierarchic systemic model of infrastructure, structure, and superstructure. In contrast to early neoevolutionary models, this model does not preclude top-down causality (see Flannery 1972). He sees the essential factors in the development of state organization on the coast to have been: (1) circumscribed environment, (2) canal-based agriculture, (3) settlements situated up-valley for defense, (4) intervalley warfare, and (5) an ideology that fostered cooperation within and between some valleys and hostility towards others.

Wilson places the earliest development of state organization on the north coast to between 350 B.C. and A.D. 1 in the Casma Valley. At this time the Casma Valley held an estimated total population of 40,000 people distributed in a three-tiered hierarchy of settlements, rural villages, and local centers, with a main center at Pampa Rosario. The small size of Pampa Rosario (2,000 persons) and the generally low degree of urbanism lead Wilson to conclude that the city-state form is not applicable to the early phases of state evolution on the Coast, a position similar to Kolata's view on the later coastal state centered at Chan Chan (this volume). Thus, there seems to be a lower boundary or population threshold for the "city" of the "city-state" that none of the early large coastal settlements surpassed (Trigger 1993).

The City

Cities cannot be understood apart from the larger societal structure in which they are embedded. Although urbanism was associated with city-state organization, even very urbanized societies such as Mesopotamia (Stone, this volume), the Harappan pe-riod of the Indus Valley (Kenoyer, this volume), the early-sixteenth-century Basin of Mexico (Charlton and Nichols, this volume; Hodge, this volume), classical Greece and Rome, and the late medieval and Renaissance European city-states (Molho et al. 1991b) display substantial variation in the size of city-state capitals, in the size of rural or dependent settlements (Schwartz and Falconer 1994), and in the degree of functional differentiation found between them.

In this volume Wilson and Kolata argue that a much lower degree of urbanism prevailed among early states in the Andean highlands and on the coast of Peru than in city-states, and that the use of *city-state* to characterize these systems is not appropriate. This pattern is similar to that described for Dynastic Egypt and early China (Wenke, this volume; Trigger 1993; Maisels 1990:12–13; Yates, this volume). The concept of the "territorial state" (Trigger 1993) or "village-state" (Maisels 1987, 1990) would apply here. Small polities, referred to as kingdoms, *cura-cazgos,* and *señorios* (Moseley 1992:48, 231–262), however, formed following the breakup of large Andean states during the Late Intermediate and Colonial periods.

Kolata argues that the cities of Andean territorial states were ritual-regal centers characterized by low population size and "intense development of social control." He points to similarities between Egypt and the expansionist patrimonial states of the Andes: capitals as cosmograms, low diversity in types of cities, frequent movement of king and court throughout realm, strong vertical relationships between king and provincial rulers, but weakly developed horizontal structures. In addition to Egypt, Kolata also notes strong parallels to Classic Maya cities, which Webster (this volume) and Sanders and Webster (1988, 1989; cf. Smith 1989) have also characterized as ritual-regal centers. In contrast to the Egyptian or the Andean territorial states, however, the cities of the Classic period Maya were enmeshed in a less centralized political structure.

Kolata attributes the low degree of urbanism in Andean territorial states to the lack of merchants and marketplace exchange, a point also made by Wenke for Egypt and Webster for the Classic Maya (see also Brumfiel and Earle 1987:4). Kolata's contention is generally supported by the states examined in this volume. Wenke relates the weak development of urbanism and functional differentiation to the homogeneous resource distribution of Egypt and an ideology that encouraged uniformity and order within the boundaries of the state. Webster also thinks that a relatively low degree of environmental diversity inhibited the development of craft specialization and marketplace exchange in Classic Maya cities, although others see more functional differentiation in Maya settlements than does Webster (e.g. Hester and Shafer 1994; Marcus 1993:163). In contrast, evidence that merchants and the marketplace exchange of basic commodities, as well as prestige goods, were significant in the economy of city-states is evident in archaeological remains from the urban center and from the hinterland (Hodge, this volume; Pearson, this volume). In terms of the political economy, the compactness of city-states, and the presence of a central place—the urban center—created a situation well suited initially to economic integration of urban center and rural hinterland through exchange of a variety of products.

Stone argues that the highly urban character of the city-state also relates to the important role of the city in providing a place to develop consensus among competing segments. The layout of city-state capitals, while often a symbolic representation of religious and cosmological precepts, also mirrors the political form: political segmentation and fragmentation among competing factions are associated with a physical separation of administrative, religious, and market centers. Residential zones contain both upper-class and commoner households (reflecting the vertical structure of kinship groups or political factions). Most manufacturing takes place in residential districts since it is not under the direct control of the ruler. Large plazas, monumental religious complexes, and assembly halls, for example, were arenas for forging consensus among competing factions and institutions. Stone concludes that most Mesopotamian cities follow the expected pattern: political and religious institutions are separated and residential districts contain most manufacturing workshops and a heterogeneous composition of elites and commoners. Contrary to Wheeler's model of a citadel and town that has dominated thinking about Harappan cities (1972 [1966]), Kenoyer shows that each city consisted of a series of mounds, each of which replicates upper-class and commoner residences and industrial areas that produced both elite and utilitarian goods (this volume).

Not only were the cities of city-states loci for contests of power where "priests, councils, and military leaders often competed for power openly" (Trigger 1978:209), but in bringing together in close physical proximity members of all classes and diverse occupations, Trigger argues they radically transformed society: the city of early Mesopotamian city-states was a veritable

> pressure cooker that transformed the totality of Mesopotamian life. By contrast, the Egyptian and Peruvian peasant lived most of his life in nearly total isolation from such forces. It was the very alienness of the upper classes to his everyday experience that made credible royal claims of divine status such as no ruler of a city-state was able to establish. (Trigger 1978:209)

The capitals of Aztec city-states in the Basin of Mexico, according to Hodge (this volume), show a gradation in wealth from the center to the edge of the city, which perhaps reflects greater political centralization than that found among the earlier city-states of Mesopotamia or the Indus. Most manufacturing, however, took place in household workshops outside the elite nucleated core of the capital city/town of Aztec city-states, at least in the examples for which we have good archaeological data (Charlton 1994; Charlton et al. 1991; Nichols 1994; Otis Charlton et al. 1993). Teotihuacán exhibits some of the features described for city-state capitals: separation of marketplace, pyramid-temples, and palace, upper-class residences scattered in all parts of the city, evidence of corporate kinship groups, and a predominance of workshops in residential areas—although there is evidence that Teotihuacán's rulers were actively involved in long-distance trade in obsidian (Millon 1992). Moreover, Teotihuacán's rulers were sufficiently powerful (at least after the destruction of their major competitor, Cuicuilco) to aggregate at one time nearly 80 percent of the entire population of the Basin into the city and to reorganize the city itself (Charlton and Nichols, this volume).

City-State Organization

The compactness and small size often seen as defining features of the city-state are to some extent functionally related, as we have indicated, to an internal political condition of diffuse or fragmented power. Stone argues that resolution of such a situation is often carried out through the development of consensual political arrangements among competing elites and factions (this volume). Consensual arrangements such as assemblies, she argues, were common features of city-state governance in many places, not just classical Greece. She and Morris (this volume) find such a characteristic difficult to reconcile with the neoevolutionary state models of Fried (1967) and Service (1962). Those models envisioned a small minority of elites in control of state institutions, including writing, with religion supporting the social structure. To resolve this dilemma she and Morris propose a continuum of political forms among early states: at one end lies the neoevolutionary (or Gellner's [1988] agro-literate) state, while at the other end are city-states characterized by segmentation and fragmentation, consensual arrangements, and in some cases, an ideology of citizen participation in government. Individual states also may oscillate over time along this continuum as Morris illustrates for classic Greek city-states.

In our chapter on central Mexico, we argue that the development of city-states exhibited a cyclic pattern. Each cycle began with an initial period of numerous competitive small city-states and was followed by a period dominated by a single, large integrative city-state that subsequently fragmented into numerous small city-states. The one exception occurs during the last cycle when the imperial structure created by the Spanish during the early Colonial period (A.D. 1521–1620) prevented the competitiveness characteristic of prehispanic city-states. The first large integrative city-state system, Teotihuacán, lacking any nearby competitors, held its position of dominance for an unusually long time; the fragmentation of the later integrative city-states of Toltec Tula and Aztec Tenochtitlán-Tlatelolco took place more quickly. The integrative city-state system of Tenochtitlán, however, remained relatively decentralized because of the considerably larger population and market dynamic greater than that of any previous period in Mesoamerica (Blanton 1976:194, 1996; Blanton et al. 1993:156–157; Kowalewski et al. 1989:307). Although Teotihuacán, Tula, and Tenochtitlán dominated relatively large territories and populations, like imperial Athens and Rome, their hegemonies retained many elements of city-state organization. Marcus also emphasizes cyclic processes in the growth and contraction of early states, but she concludes that no initial state was a city-state; in her view city-states occur as a product of the breakdown polities of centralized states (1992a:394–399; 1993:164–170).

Equality of political opportunity for citizens has long been viewed as one of the defining features of the Athenian *polis* (Ferguson 1991:172). Citizenship in Athens was based not on wealth or occupation, but on residence, gender (male), age (adult), and nonslave status. To be a citizen meant the opportunity to participate in the political system, "to have an equal share of masculine status" (Morris, this volume). Concepts of citizen participation and even assemblies, however, were not unique to classical Greece and can be found among earlier city-states, like those of Mesopotamia (Stone, this volume) and the Indo-Gangetic Tradition (Kenoyer, this volume). In early states however, these political arrangements were embedded in hierarchical social systems where inequality was understood as a "natural order established by the gods at the time of creation" (Trigger 1993:53). The *polis* and the much vaunted "democracy" of Athens were by comparison later developments in the history of preindustrial states and represent *in relative terms* a more broadly based system of citizen governance than that found among earlier city-states.

In her essay Stone argues that the segmentation of power often characteristic of city-state organization occurs when control over labor, not land or resources, is the key element of agricultural production "where agricultural land is essentially temporary and mutable—slash-and-burn agriculture and fragile irrigation systems are examples—so that the key feature of agriculture is not land ownership but control over the labor needed to bring land under cultivation." Under these conditions no hereditary aristocratic minority is able to monopolize the means of production. Political power is fragmented and diffuse and vertical structures of integration, for example lineal kinship groups, may be as important as horizontal class divisions. Small, for example, argues that a lineage-based mode of production and distribution was a central feature of classical Greek economies and one that made it difficult for political elites to control the economy (this volume).

Ranked kinship groups also remained significant in the early stages of state formation in Mesoamerica (Pyburn, this volume) and "co-existed with specialized institutions of political power" (Sanders 1992: 279). In Postclassic Maya polities that were dominated by a hereditary nobility in which there existed "significant differences in rank, role, and profession," a vertical system of lineages that included nobles and commoners cut across horizontal socioeconomic classes (Marcus 1992b:221; Webster, this volume). In his consideration of Classic Maya polities, Webster broadens the concept of the city-state to include stratified societies that may not exhibit a full range of state institutions, such as an administrative bureaucracy (Webster, this volume; see also Fried 1967:185–

226; Houston 1992; Mathews and Willey 1991; Sabloff 1996). He does so because he does not see evidence of state institutions among most Classic Maya polities of a complexity comparable to those of autochthonous states in Mesopotamia, or in other parts of Mesoamerica such as Teotihuacán. Ranked lineages were also important among Classic Maya city-states like Copán (Hendon 1991); however, at Tikal, the largest Classic Maya city, even though lineage organization was present, socioeconomic class divisions became more important over time and by the Late Classic period (A.D. 650–900) Haviland finds little evidence for ranking within lineages (1992).

Maya archaeologists agree that the Classic Maya lowland civilization was never politically unified into a single state; however, they differ over the scale of Maya polities: the so-called "small polity versus big polity" debate. Webster's position is an intermediate one that sees twenty to thirty independent city-states coexisting at any one time. Real differences existed among Maya states in their size and degree of integration; however, some of this debate stems from the lack of regional settlement-pattern studies in large areas of the lowlands (Nichols 1996; Sabloff 1996). The study of the formation of any ancient state, most especially the earliest ones, must involve a methodology that incorporates settlement-pattern studies, "in order to have at hand as complete a sample as possible of all the kinds of settlements that constituted its postulated hierarchical organization" (Wilson, this volume). The expanding corpus of deciphered Classic Maya writing provides an opportunity to better understand the world view of the elite Maya as recorded by their scribes for a Maya audience. These texts alone will not resolve debates about Maya political organization. Webster feels that the jury is still out concerning the existence of large regional states in Classic Maya civilization. If such existed, they were probably short-lived and unstable. Like J. Marcus (1989), Webster sees the city-state as the fundamental unit of Maya society during the Postclassic period (A.D. 900–1519) and persisting into the early Colonial period after the Spanish conquest.

Yates also notes the importance of lineage and family structure in the early Chinese state (this volume). He argues that the city-state concept is useful to understanding early Chinese civilizations, but with modifications. These modifications take into account Chinese conceptualizations that, in addition to the importance of lineage and family structure, emphasize ancestor worship, the ruler as "gift-giver" rather than as administrator, and a holistic cosmology. Yates suggests that Tambiah's (1985) model of the galactic polity may actually represent a widespread Asiatic cosmology where ritual plays a critical role in the political process and settlement hierarchies represent ritual replications of sacred space manifested by walled settlements.

The Harappan civilization of the Indus Valley, like the lowland Classic Maya, was never unified politically (Kenoyer, this volume). Rather, the similarity of material culture across the Indus Valley reflects a shared elite culture and ideology (a "Great Tradition"), that cuts across independent city-states, and "that required specific symbols and artifacts for ritual purposes as well as for defining class affiliations." Kenoyer makes a strong case for much greater continuity between the Harappan phase of the Indus Valley and the Early Historic period of the Indo-Gangetic Tradition than had previously been thought. He argues that the city-states of the Harappan phase were similar to the *gana* city-states of the Early Historic period governed by a council and whose definition of citizenship extended to nonslaves in the hinterland as well as the city.

The *raja dhikna* of the Early Historic period of the Indo-Gangetic Tradition was ruled by a monarchy (Kenoyer, this volume), and thus appears to represent a more centralized form of city-state governance, similar to the city-states of Postclassic Mesoamerica (Hodge, this volume) and the Chuzan Kingdom of Okinawa (Pearson, this volume). Webster (this volume), like Sanders (1992) and Marcus (1992b; but cf. Chase and Chase 1992:313), sees the prehispanic states of Mesoamerica as stratified into essentially two major classes: a hereditary nobility and commoners or peasants, with a small intermediary class of merchants and luxury artisans. Among the Aztec city-states of central Mexico, for example, a small council of hereditary nobles usually selected the city-state ruler, the *tlatoani*, (or rulers as some city-states had two or more *tlatoque*) from a royal lineage. The upper class was organized into a system of ranked lineages and noble houses.

On Okinawa, the consolidation of power by the king of Chuzan, who had previously shared it with his counselors, involved separating the *anji* from their hereditary estates, their traditional power base, and the eventual takeover of the *anji* estates by royal overseers, which reinforced "the division of social class over local kin groups" (Pearson, this volume). The consolidation of political and military power by the king coincided with the establishment of his sister as the chief *noro,* or priestess. The king's court was also directly involved in a complex maritime trade network that relayed goods from Japan and Southeast Asia to China, and even though Okinawa was surrounded by powerful states it for the most part "lay outside their direct grasp" (Pearson, this volume).

Trigger (1993) and Wolf (1982) find this class hierarchy, based on a tributary relationship through which the upper class appropriated surpluses, to be a near-universal feature of early civilizations even though the degree of stratification and status differentiation within classes and the complexity of state institutions varied considerably. Although the ruler of a city-state, such as an Aztec *tlatoani,* might be "head of the political, religious, and economic structure of his domain" (Hicks 1986:40), the institution of ruler existed alongside political factions that cut across social classes, and linked together members of the upper class and commoners in patron-client relations, even in those city-states where ranked kinship groups were no longer important (Brumfiel 1989, 1994; Brumfiel and Fox 1994).

Ideology

While the capitals of city-states symbolize elite power, political autonomy, ethnicity, and religious ideology, city-states are conceived of as tightly integrated units of city and hinterland (Adams 1966; Ehlers 1992: 103–104; Fox 1977; Frézouls 1991; Hannerz 1980: 76–91; Sanders and Webster 1988, 1989; Sjoberg 1960; Smith 1989; Wheatley 1971). In the case of the *polis,* the Nahua (or Aztec) *altepetl,* and the Indian *gana,* for example, the concept of citizenship extended to male nonslave residents of the hinterland. The integration of city and hinterland stems from the agrarian foundation of the city-state. As autonomous entities, individual city-states seek to distinguish themselves from others through expressions of ethnicity, through origin accounts that serve as the city-state's mythic charter (Brumfiel 1994), and through worship of patron deities.

Trigger in his recent review of early civilizations (1993, also 1995:451–452), notes many parallels in symbolism often recognizable in the archaeological record, such as the elevation of rulers on thrones and mats, in ideology such as the concept of the foreign king or nobles who claim descent from outsiders (Kolata, this volume), and in religious beliefs and activities. The monumentality of religious architecture in early city-states bespeaks the importance of a shared ideology or, at least, the attempt to foster one in a fragmented milieu (Adams 1992:216; Trigger 1990a). In all early states rulers were mediators between the supernatural and humanity. Trigger suggests that, compared to territorial states, rulers in city-states perhaps need less divine attribution or have "a much harder time establishing claims of omnipotence" (1978:202) because of their closer physical proximity to their subjects. The elaborateness of the funerary cults of the Egyptian pharaohs (Wenke, this volume) and the Inka bears out this point (Kolata, this volume). In contrast, the development of classical Greek city-states was associated with a changing cosmological order that began to separate the human, natural, and supernatural realms (Trigger 1993:93).

Religious rituals ranging from the level of the household to city-state temple, on the one hand, foster unity and social cohesion (Millon 1992:13), while on the other hand, the worship of patron deities and the expression of political struggles in religious metaphors mirror the fragmentation of power (Trigger 1993:88). The ideological transformation of loyalty to kin groups to loyalty to the city-state, although important in city-state evolution, was "often incomplete" (Ferguson 1991:172). The ideology of an integrated city-hinterland may break down when city-states are integrated into larger city-state systems or into more centralized territorial or national states as eventually happened to the prehispanic city-states of Mesoamerica, even though initially the Spanish imperial system reinforced many aspects of city-state organization (Lockhart 1992). In Europe, the growth of mercantilism and manufacturing in medieval cities led to greater distinctions between urban and rural dwellers and to the notion of the dominance of the city, and the eventual replacement of the city-state ideology with an ideology of the nation-state (Molho et al. 1991a).

Notes

1. The papers in this volume together cover a time-span, albeit with gaps, from about 4000 B.C. to about A.D. 1600 in both the Old and the New Worlds; see also Blockmans 1994; Burke 1986; Cherry and Renfrew 1986; Crone 1989; Griffeth and Thomas 1981a, 1981b, 1981c; Kochakova 1978; Maisels 1987, 1990; J. Marcus 1989, 1992a; Martines 1979; Molho et al. 1991a, 1991b; Price 1977; Renfrew 1975, 1986a; Tilly and Blockmans 1994; Trigger 1993; Wickham 1989.

2. See Burke 1986:137–140 1992:140, Klapisch-Zuber 1991:241, Molho et al. 1991a:17, and Morris, this volume, for discussion and a continuation of emphasis on the study of what might be considered atypical city-states such as Rome, Athens, Florence, and Venice.

3. Maisels includes the Classic Maya as village (territorial) states (1987:337; 1990:13, 254, 304; Pyburn, this volume) while Trigger counts them among the city-states (1993:9; see also Webster, this volume; Houston 1992; Mathews and Willey 1991; Sabloff 1996).

2

City-States and Their Centers

The Mesopotamian Example

ELIZABETH STONE

The city-state, as a distinctive category of state-organized society, was originally defined in reference to the Greek *polis,* with emphasis on concepts of active citizenship and participatory democracy. The horizons of scholarship have subsequently broadened to the point where now it is generally recognized that the earliest city-states were in Mesopotamia, not Greece, and that an ethos of "primitive democracy" and concepts of citizenry predate Solon's Athens by almost two millennia (Jacobsen 1970:132–172).[1] But if democracy and an egalitarian ideology are characteristic of both Mesopotamia and Greece, how are these compatible with models used by anthropologists to describe state society that stress coercion as the primary source of social cohesion? These forces of coercion are seen in the monopoly on absolute power—control of the army—and on the means of production—ownership and control of productive agricultural land—which permitted a minority to organize and manage a subordinate majority.

In this chapter, I argue that data from Mesopotamia and elsewhere require a more flexible approach to state societies—an approach that uses a continuum of subtypes, including states that fit the standard model and those based on more consensual arrangements among differently defined segments of society. Many—perhaps all—of the more consensual societies are associated with city-states. This chapter explores the coincidence between a political structure based on city-states and a tendency toward democracy by posing the following questions about Mesopotamia: Why was Mesopotamian society so urban? In what ways did urban centers dominate the hinterland? Why were imperial episodes so short-lived? How were royal and elite power kept in check?

Following a description of the role of consensus in two different preindustrial city-state societies—the Yoruba of West Africa and late medieval Islam—I discuss the causative factors involved in the development and maintenance of such consensual relationships and link this descriptive model to what we know of ancient Mesopotamia. The body of the paper describes the nature and organization of Mesopotamian city-states. Due to the limitations of our sources from nonurban sites, however, the emphasis is on the cities as microcosms of Mesopotamian city-states, especially those of the southern alluvium, where city-state organization was most pronounced (Steinkeller 1993).

Consensus in Preindustrial States

Two exceptionally well-documented preindustrial city-state societies are the Yoruba, primarily in the nineteenth century, and late medieval Islam.[2] If they were situated along a continuum between consensual and coercive poles, they would both fall near the consensual end. These societies do not, of course, replicate ancient Mesopotamian society—or, indeed, any other city-state society—but they illustrate the fact that models of state society should not focus exclusively on coercion.

The deviation of Yoruba and medieval Islamic city-states from standard models has led to the introduction of new terms to define them—for example, the "tribal kingdom" (Lloyd 1971:1), the "congruent state" (Eisenstadt et al. 1988), and the "Islamic city" (Hourani and Stern 1970; Serjeant 1980). Especially in the case of Africa, the societies have been considered "unstable" (Fortes 1953), due to the apparent incompatibility between lineage and state norms (Fallers 1956:16). In some cases, they have been excluded from the general category of state society (Fortes and Evans-Pritchard 1940; Mair 1977), in spite of their similarity to, say, classical Greece. However, few today would deny that they represent state societies (Eisenstadt et al. 1988).

The key difference between these societies and traditionally defined state societies is that they exhibit vertical divisions based on kinship or other forms of affiliation, which, as structuring elements, are more important than the horizontal divisions represented by classes. Status differences exist within these vertical groups, with elites dependent on the support of lower echelons of the social segments to which they belong. Since this support is to a certain extent voluntary and maintained only by a high level of generosity, elite status can rarely be held by any one family for more than a generation or two. All segments of society have the potential to rise to elite status in the future, and consequently they are imbued with a strongly egalitarian ideology.

The close ties between insecure elites and their subordinates appear to coexist with two other features—power sharing by the different groups that make up the city, and sovereignty, nominally in the hands of an individual (usually a king) who is isolated from the rest of society.[3] The separation of the king is seen in his reliance on slaves, rather than citizens, to run the palace, while his lack of autocratic power is reflected in the importance of the city council, which rep-resents all interests in the city. Offices that are normally thought to concentrate political power in the hands of the ruler—control of religious institutions and even of the army—are also largely in the hands of the local elites. The king, nevertheless, plays a key role as a unifying symbol in these otherwise highly segmented societies and as the representative of the state in such external relations as trade, diplomacy, and war.

Under what circumstances do these more consensual state societies develop, and how are the data from Yorubaland and late medieval Islam relevant to the case of Mesopotamia? I propose that the underlying causes of the pattern are similar in all three examples and probably in many other city-states as well. Let us consider a basic question about consensual societies—why are elite and royal power so restricted? The answer, I think, lies in the economy. These states are found in areas where agricultural land is essentially temporary and mutable—slash-and-burn agriculture and fragile irrigation systems are examples—so that the key feature of agriculture is not land ownership but control over the labor needed to bring land under cultivation. Moreover, the societies are not in full control of their subsistence base and rely on exchange with groups living outside the purview of the state (pastoral nomads, marsh dwellers, hunters, etc.) for part of their food. Since such societies have large areas of potentially cultivable wasteland in their vicinity to provide refuge for the disaffected, the main challenge to urban leadership is that of maintaining the labor force.

A second question is why these societies are so urban. Cities play many of the same roles in consensual societies as they do in their more coercive counterparts, but they are probably most important in this instance as places where the communication necessary to forge consensus among all groups in a non-autocratic society can take place. Long ago, Adams suggested that an important factor in the genesis of Mesopotamian urban centers in the fourth millennium B.C. lay in the need for coordination between the different residents of the area—the farmers, herders, and fishermen (1966). Here I take the argument one step further and argue that the continued need for coordination established the urban character of this and similar consensual societies.

Finally, we need to look at the reasons underlying the limitations on the political authority of the king. The societies under consideration obviously could not be considered consensual if they were dominated by an autocratic king with unchallenged political power. I would argue that that kind of power is only possible where it is supported by a hereditary aristocracy—where a minority has succeeded in monopolizing the means of production—something not possible in the circumstances under discussion here. This begs the key question of why, under these circumstances, there was a king at all.

While some consensual state societies, such as classical Athens, did not have kings, in most instances—including earlier passages in Athenian history—a tendency toward factionalism required some unifying agent. Factionalism typifies organizations without clear hierarchical structures, whether they are academic departments or ancient societies (Landé 1977: xxxiii), and it was a major problem in many Islamic cities (Bodman 1963)—most notably at Nishapur, where it resulted in the destruction of the city (Bulliet 1972). It has also been documented among the Yoruba (Falola 1984:18–19; Smith 1988:113–117). The solution to factional strife in Athens and in Renaissance Florence was the imposition of tyranny (Eder 1991)—and in the case of Florence, leaders were brought in from outside (Brucker 1969:132–133). Thus, in addition to its role in military affairs, the position of king in consensual societies should be seen as a unifying symbol, one who is above the political fray. In order for this to be successful, however, the king cannot be associated with any local sources of authority—those represented in the council—and cannot rely on them for part of his administration. Among the Yoruba, the king is chosen from a lineage that has little to do with the affairs of the city. Late medieval Islamic cities were ruled first by Mamluks (descendants of royal slaves) and then by Ottoman Turks—in both cases, outsiders with little knowledge of local conditions.

The king also plays an important symbolic, unifying role. Among the Yoruba he is considered divine. This divinity limits his freedom of action, but it also makes him a potent symbol of the unity of the city-state. The unity of Islamic cities was also expressed in religious terms, but here it was Islamic law that held the key. During Ottoman rule, the most important office was that of the *Qadi*—or judge—who was appointed for a single year in a location far from his place of origin. Thus, while the power of Islamic law unified the city, the actual officeholder was always an outsider.

Mesopotamia

How does this model of a consensual state society fit with the data from Mesopotamia? I would argue that the rich textual and archaeological sources of the area present a picture that is consistent with this model. Mesopotamia was a highly urban civilization in an environment where the temporary nature of irrigated fields—caused by shifting watercourses, high evaporation, and consequent salinization (Jacobsen 1982; Powell 1985; Poyck 1962)—resulted in an agricultural system dependent more on the control over labor than on land ownership. The literature is also replete with discussions of the importance of vertical divisions in Mesopotamian society, not only between the kinship and ethnic groups that made up the "private sector" of the cities, but also between these groups and groups tied to the major urban institutions.[4] In contrast, class distinctions seem of much less importance, and the evidence suggests that social mobility was high (Steinkeller 1987:100–101).

City councils that represented all these interests were probably the key political institution during the first few centuries of Mesopotamian civilization, the Protoliterate period, and perhaps even the beginning of the Early Dynastic period (Jacobsen 1970:132–172). When the institution of kingship was added, the king's power was still tempered by a city council and by the other, separate urban institutions, the temples (Evans 1958; Postgate 1992:268–270). Moreover, as in other consensual state societies, the king was quite isolated and often ethnically distinct from much of the rest of the city, to the extent that some scholars have chosen—erroneously, I think—to see Mesopotamian history in terms of continued conflict between different ethnic groups (Roux 1980).

Thus I would argue that the textual record of Mesopotamian society indicates clear similarities with the consensual states described above. Moreover, since much of the evidence for ancient Mesopotamian society is archaeological in nature, we have an opportunity to determine the archaeological hallmarks of such societies and to explore how these societies are related to the city-state form of organization.

Mesopotamian cities in the southern alluvium, 2700–1600 B.C.

I will restrict my analysis to the best-documented area and period of Mesopotamian history. To minimize distortions that might stem from environmental dif-

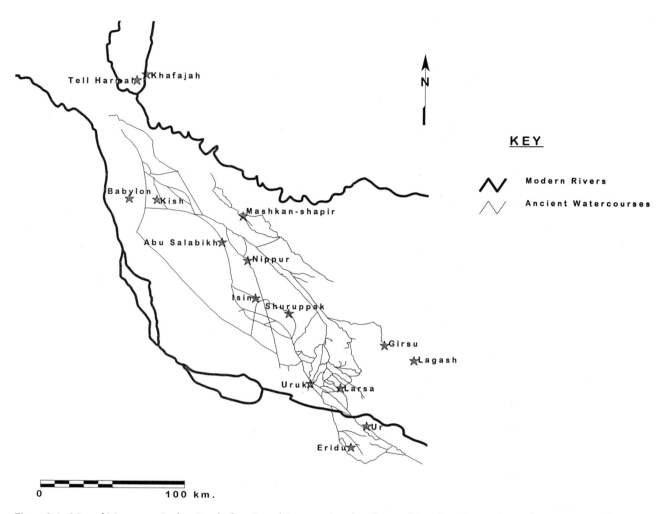

Figure 2.1. Map of Mesopotamia showing the location of sites mentioned in the text. Note that Mari and Haradum are omitted from this illustration due to their location far up on the Euphrates, far from the other sites. After R. McC. Adams (1965:figure 3, 1981:figure 28). Additional details of ancient canals derived from an analysis of SPOT imagery of the area.

ferences, I will concentrate on Mesopotamian sites in the southern alluvium (Fig. 2.1), all of which depended on irrigation agriculture. I will focus on the period from around 2700 B.C.—when the full institutional complexity of Mesopotamian cities had been established—to around 1600 B.C., a date that marks the beginning of a long dark age. Two types of archaeological data can be brought to bear on the problem at hand: detailed excavation and survey data on the intrasite organization of Mesopotamian urban centers—the settlements lying at the heart of the city-states, and broad-scale surface surveys, which provide a picture of the overall settlement system. Since the more reliable evidence from controlled excavations comes almost entirely from large urban sites, I begin with an assessment of Mesopotamian urban organization.

It has long been argued by urban geographers that the distribution of people and institutions within cities reflects the overall structure of the society as a whole (e.g. Clark 1982:141). If this is true, the distribution of elites and major civic institutions should make city-states formed on a more consensual basis distinguishable from cities with more coercive political environments. In the consensual societies under discussion here, a key point of separation was between the isolated king and the religious focus of the city. In Islamic cities, the Friday Mosque lay at the heart of the economic center of the city—the *suq*— while the citadel—the focus of political power—was located on the periphery (Sauvaget 1941). This distinction is even clearer in Yoruba cities, where the palace, as the major central institution, was an inner, walled compound, while the religious shrines lay between the densely settled residential districts and the city wall (Krapf-Askari 1969). Thus the separation of centers of administration and religion characteristic of these societies is mirrored in their physical location within the city.

The reliance of elites on the groups they represent dictated that (*contra* Sjoberg 1960:97–98) they be embedded within the residential districts housing those they represented as evidenced in both Yoruba and medieval Islamic cities (David 1975). Thus these cities do not have elite and commoner districts but a broad distribution of elites within an urban space segmented into residential districts that reflect vertical divisions based on affiliation. It is within these districts that much of the economic activity of the city—manufacturing—took place. Once again, these activities were not under the control of the palace or a hereditary aristocracy, and this is reflected in their spatial distribution. Even in Islamic cities, where the institution of the *suq* concentrated much of the manufacturing in the central area, important centers of production were located in the residential neighborhoods, and the artisans who worked by day in the *suq* spent their nights in districts that often concentrated members of their trade (David 1975).

Thus when we examine the plans of Mesopotamian cities—and the centers of other consensual city-states—we should expect to find a segmented urban space, with foci of administration, religion, manufacturing, and marketing physically separated for the most part. Residential districts, on the other hand, should not exhibit major differences in the status of their residents; rather, each should have a mixture of rich and poor dwellings.

Mesopotamian cities were large, varying in size from 40 to 400 hectares, and their location at the center of the irrigated zone, where land was most valuable, created a crowded urban environment. Canals flowing through the city formed the basic subdivisions. This is clearly illustrated by the Mashkan-shapir survey, where functionally distinct classes of artifacts were recovered from the surface of each sector, and at Larsa, where canals delimit the administrative/religious and habitation zones (Stone 1990; Stone and Zimansky 1992, 1994; Huot et al. 1989:19–52). These channels limited intercourse between different parts of the city and served as the main source of fresh water. Where they extended into the hinterland, they provided major routes of communication.

At Ur (Woolley and Mallowan 1976:10), at Mashkan-shapir (Stone and Zimansky 1992, 1994), and perhaps at Larsa (Huot 1989:figure 2a; Stone 1993: 238), we can identify broad harbors attached to the intramural watercourses. Cuneiform sources identify "the quay" as the center of external trade and exchange and home to a distinct guild of merchants, but it is not clear whether the term refers to these harbors or to more substantial ports beyond the city walls. In any event, these intramural havens clearly played an important economic role, and it is noteworthy that they are located away from the large political and religious institutions—the temple and the palace.

The street pattern reinforced the role of the canals. At Larsa (Huot 1989:Figure 9a; Stone 1993:238) and Mashkan-shapir (Stone and Zimansky 1992, 1994), streets run both parallel to the canals and at right angles to them, cutting the city into blocks of about 1 hectare. To a certain extent, streets—as they crossed the canals by bridges or ferries—linked those parts of the city divided by water, but they may also have delimited residential districts.

Walls too served as both unifying and dividing features. All major Mesopotamian cities were surrounded by fortifications that separated the city from its hinterland, but major walls have also been encountered within the cities, subdividing the larger units marked off by water. The religious quarter at Ur (Woolley 1974:55), the administrative and cemetery areas at Mashkan-shapir (Stone and Zimansky 1992, 1994), and a residential sector at Khafajah (Delougaz et al. 1967:17) are examples of areas isolated from the rest of the city by substantial walls.

The positioning of major urban institutions within this segmented urban space is of crucial importance to our inquiry. The Mesopotamian institution most readily identifiable archaeologically is the main temple, whose location on a high platform made it a visual focus for miles around. These temples were usually situated on the periphery, beside the city wall, not in the center. Even in the few instances where this is not the case, temple placement was decidedly asymmetrical.

Excavated palaces are quite rare. Since they were not elevated, they are difficult to identify without excavation. In the majority of cases, they too have been found on the periphery, far from the center of religious activities. With the exception of Larsa, where the palace is next to the main temple, the locations of temples and administrative centers in Mesopotamia appear to reflect a pattern of opposition, symbolizing the parallel but conflicting functions of the two main institutions.

The key to the consensual basis of Mesopotamian city-states lies in the structuring of the habitation zone, where both elites and manufacturing were firmly embedded in residential neighborhoods. Cuneiform records are not as clear about the structuring of the residential zone as they are about temples and palaces. Unfortunately, archaeological evidence on the subject is also limited, but by combining the two sources, we can form a tentative picture. It is clear, for example, that the cities were divided into a number of residential neighborhoods, although we do not know the specifics of their size and location. There are textual indications that some had recognized leadership structures, but it is clear that the residential neighborhoods were not defined on the basis of class. Both tablets and archaeological data indicate that an important official could live beside a humble fisherman and that large, well-appointed houses were nestled alongside small, poor structures (Steinkeller n.d.:4–5; Stone 1987:125). It has been suggested that some of the other basic divisions in Mesopotamian society—between people attached to large institutions and the more independent small landowners—might be reflected in the divisions between neighborhoods (Stone 1987), but thus far no unequivocal archaeological evidence of this pattern has been found.

It is within residential zones that we find evidence for workshops. Textual data on the organization of production is very limited, but archaeological surveys have identified concentrations of manufacturing debris and their distribution. At Mashkan-shapir our survey indicates that production was concentrated in particular areas (Stone and Zimansky 1992, 1994). Near the most extensive ceramic area—that located in the leeward part of the site—was a possible lapidary area, marked by small grinders and exotic pebbles. Small copper and cuprous slag deposits—representing the locations of the smithies that produced finished goods—were located in the center of the city along a major street, and in one or two scattered locations. At Abu Salabikh, ceramic production seems to have been located at the edge of the site (Postgate 1990:103–104), and a similar situation may have existed at Larsa (Huot et al. 1989:34–36) and at Lagash (Carter 1993). These data suggest that while "smokestack" industries were concentrated where their fumes would disturb the inhabitants the least, other, less noxious manufacturing took place in many locations within the residential zone.

Together the data suggest a pattern of manufacturing embedded in residential neighborhoods, with some areas specializing in certain crafts. However, minor scatters of manufacturing debris throughout the residential area suggest that each district may have had its own potter, smith, and lapidary worker who supplied local needs. We should add to this picture the small-scale workshops located within the palace and temple precincts—seen most clearly in the palace at Mari—that supplied these institutions (Parrot 1958:280–305).

Comparison: north and south alluvium

Mesopotamian cities exhibit the physical separation of political and religious institutions predicted for consensual societies, as well as a neighborhood structure that reflects social segmentation based on affiliation rather than class. Ancient Mesopotamia also provides a unique laboratory for the elements that differentiate city-states, nation-states, and imperial structures—the issues of central concern in this volume. Not only did it have a turbulent political history, characterized by imperial episodes that alternated with periods when independent city-states were dominant, but, as Steinkeller has argued (1993), differences in organization between the northern and southern alluvium appear to have transcended the patterns of cyclical change and allow us to explore variations within a single consensual society.

There were subtle differences in the external environment between the north and south alluvium. The greatest instability of watercourses was in the wide, flat southern sector, which also had—and has—the largest concentration of marshlands. Farther north, where the third-millennium-B.C. population was more Semitic and less Sumerian, the valley was quite narrow (narrower even than today), the watercourses more permanent, and the vast, unbroken desert—suitable only for seasonal grazing—at closer proximity. When the south was characterized by numerous small city-states, the northern area, Steinkeller argues (1993:115), saw Mesopotamia's first large political entity—the Early Dynastic kingdom ruled from Kish.

Located in the center of the narrow flood plain, Kish was the dominant city in the north, and it apparently had a somewhat more centralized political structure than southern polities, with enhanced power in the hands of the king. Where the southern city-states were imbued with a communal ideology centered on temples, in the north there was more emphasis on the building of consensus between rival kin groups. Whether the kingdom controlled by Kish should be considered a city-state remains moot. Griffeth and Thomas argue that city-states are primarily defined on the basis of size, with an area of a few hundred square miles as the upper boundary (1981b:185). Kish, although much larger than the largest southern city-state, probably did not exceed this.

Although there is no evidence for a hereditary aristocracy at Kish or for a king with full autocratic powers, the early Kish kingdom does indicate that some variability existed, both in the political organization of the southern Mesopotamian alluvium and in the size, scope, and perhaps even the structure of the Mesopotamian polities. That the Mesopotamians were aware of this variability is clear from the title "King of Kish," which was used by southern kings who wished to enhance their authority (Steinkeller 1993:120).

It can be argued that this variability reflects a tension between ideologies of small, competing city-states dominated by the temple of the city god and those of a larger imperial structure ruled by a king. During the period under discussion, ancient Mesopotamian political organization vacillated between the two models. Some scholars view the variation as an alternation between centralization and collapse (Gibson 1973) or maximization and resilience (Adams 1978), while others see a continuity of the city-state structure punctuated by brief imperial episodes (Nissen 1988). Virtually all see the cyclical nature of Mesopotamian history as an inevitable process. This volatile political history, however, can elucidate how the consensual basis for Mesopotamian society served to perpetuate city-state organization in the face of competing political ideologies.

From 2700 to 1500 B.C., three separate empires were established in southern Mesopotamia, each with different characteristics. During the latter part of the Early Dynastic period, both the southern Mesopotamian city-states and the larger northern kingdom dominated by Kish were ruled by kings. But where the southern kings were weak, those in the north were strong. Where the southern city-states were small and confined by neighboring entities, the borders of the northern kingdom were delimited by the edges of the cultivated zone. Steinkeller argues that interaction between the two areas eventually strengthened the power of the southern kings and introduced the idea of hegemony, which led in turn to the intercity rivalry and warfare that characterized the end of the Early Dynastic period (1993:125). This came to an abrupt halt when Sargon of Akkad conquered southern Mesopotamia and then brought under his loose imperial mantle much of the remainder of the known world.

That the world's first empire arose in northern Babylonia is not surprising, but it did not mark the end of city-state organization in the south. City-states continued to be the basic building block of society, but they became provinces within a larger kingdom and were no longer independent. Kingship was personal and charismatic, not institutional, as exemplified by the rebellions that occurred with the accession of each new Akkadian king. Nevertheless, this first empire lasted for more than a century, collapsing during the rule of Sargon's great-grandson in the twenty-second century B.C. The ensuing period saw a return to city-state rule, with cities such as Girsu and Ur attempting to reassert hegemony. Ur proved the most successful, and by 2030 B.C. it controlled all of southern Mesopotamia. Perhaps learning from the failure of the unstructured system developed by his Akkadian predecessors, Shulgi attempted to unite the entire area under a single, bureaucratically run economy. At the same time—true to his southern origins—he worked to bring the powerful institution of the temple under his control. The city-states had always had to rely on trade and exchange both with their neighbors and outsiders to survive, but this interdependence increased during the Ur III period. But if the plaintive letters from the last king requesting shipments of grain are anything to go by (Jacobsen 1970:175–177), this very interdependence sowed the seeds for the demise of the kingdom less than a century after its establishment, paving the way for a new period of warring city-states.

During the Isin-Larsa period, the cities of Uruk, Isin, Larsa, and Babylon all vied for control. Babylon was ultimately successful, but the high point of the Old Babylonian period lasted for just two decades, ending with the collapse of the south's entire economy. With the dramatic depopulation of the cities that ensued, the Old Babylonian kings controlled only a small enclave of civilization near modern Baghdad. The south's collapse—the result of political and ecological mismanagement (Stone 1987:26–27)—illustrates the fragility of its agriculture as compared to the northern alluvium once dominated by Kish and then by Babylon.

There are some important conclusions to be drawn from this turbulent history. First, no one city in either the north or the south was seen as having an exclusive "right" to political leadership. Indeed, during this long period, no city achieved domination more than once. Second, although political centralization had clear economic benefits, it could not be maintained in the long run, irrespective of the effectiveness of the administration. Third, the kings who were able to establish hegemony—whether localized or more universal—were usually outsiders. The *Myth of Sargon* suggests that he was the ultimate outsider—the progeny of a priestess and a pastoral nomad. Ur-Nammu, founder of the Ur III dynasty, probably came from Uruk, while both Hammurabi and Rim-Sin—architects of the Babylonian and Larsa kingdoms respectively—were Amorites. Finally, with the exception of the general abandonment that occurred in the south during the Old Babylonian period, the collapse of political centralization led to the reassertion of independence by the city-states. We are less well informed on the political organization of northern Mesopotamia during the interregna.

To identify the differences between north and south, and the effects of the numerous political upheavals that characterized the period under consideration, it is necessary to go beyond the data on urban organization. While city planning reflects the basic organization of society, it does not directly reflect the organization of the polity as a whole. To explore the organization of Mesopotamia's city-states and their variation over time and space we need to turn to the extensive surface survey data collected by Adams and his students (R. McC. Adams 1965, 1972, 1981; Adams and Nissen 1972; Gibson 1972; Wright 1981). The Mesopotamian alluvium was divided among areas of intensive cultivation, intersected by numerous canals; marshes, which were sources of reeds, fish, and waterfowl; and wasteland, suitable only for grazing without new irrigation projects. In the southern part of this plain, cities were scattered at 20–25 kilometer intervals, each located in the midst of a belt of highly productive irrigated land that was studded with small towns and villages. Between them lay the desert and marshes. Although the cities tapped the resources of the marshes, the marshes sheltered disruptive elements hostile to state society. It seems likely that in Mesopotamia, as in the city-states of Yorubaland and the Islamic Middle East, political control was strongest at the center and weakest at the periphery. Obviously such a conclusion is tentative, since we do not yet have clear evidence for the location of the boundaries between city-states or for the relationship between these boundaries and the key geographic features of the plain—the canals and rivers.

This picture is also quite generalized, and there were variations over both time and space. By and large, cities were closer together in the south and farther apart in the north, with a transitional area in between—a pattern seen most clearly in the Early Dynastic period. After that, the south underwent a slow decrease in the number of large cities, as important early centers like Lagash, Shurupak, and Eridu became depopulated. A similar pattern can be seen in the data from central Babylonia, but it is not apparent in northern Babylonia—perhaps a symptom of the greater stability enjoyed in the north. But even as what were once separate states coalesced in the south, the city-state ideology was retained, and remnants of these original divisions often continued to structure the larger entities that emerged. A correlative trend, remarked on by Adams (R. McC. Adams 1981:138), was the slow increase in the number of small settlements following the "urban implosion" associated with the institutional complexity of the southern city-states in the latter part of the Early Dynastic period (Adams and Nissen 1972:11–21). The trend, clear in southern and central Babylonia, is absent in the north.[5]

A key question here is the relationship between the city and its hinterland. One of the features of city-states, for example, is their urban-centric character. Bonine has argued that Islamic cities—and perhaps, by extension, other city-states—exhibit a much greater degree of urban dominance than is found in the West—a pattern long ago noted by Arab geographers. In terms of settlement patterns this is reflected in the relative paucity of secondary centers. Bonine's data indicate that rural populations in the province of Yazd journeyed long distances to the primary city for goods and services available at much closer secondary centers, and the secondary centers, as a consequence, were poorly developed. In the case of Yazd, the main city is six times the size of the largest secondary center (Bonine 1980:192–196).

Such relationships are normally best illustrated by rank-size distribution graphs, where the weak development of secondary centers is reflected by a concave or primate graph (Johnson 1981:148–151), but in the case of Mesopotamia—given the probable low recovery rate of the smallest sites[6] and the difficulties involved in forming temporally precise judgments of the occupation area of large, multicomponent sites—it seems preferable to present only the raw data. These data (Figs. 2.2 and 2.3) indicate profound differences in settlement distribution between northern and southern Babylonia. In the Early Dynastic period, before the first attempt at unification under Sargon of

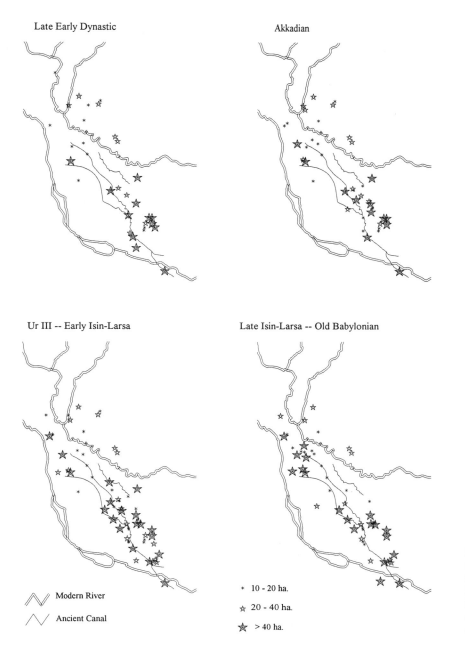

Late Early Dynastic

Akkadian

Ur III -- Early Isin-Larsa

Late Isin-Larsa -- Old Babylonian

Modern River

Ancient Canal

* 10 - 20 ha.
☆ 20 - 40 ha.
✬ > 40 ha.

Figure 2.2. Maps showing the distribution of medium and large sites in Babylonia from the Early Dynastic through Old Babylonian periods. Data derived from R. McC. Adams (1965, 1972, 1981), Adams and Nissen (1972), Gibson (1972), and Wright (1981).

Akkad, the south shows a well-developed primate pattern, with secondary centers of 10–40 hectares significantly underrepresented, a pattern almost identical to that of Yazd (Bonine 1980). A similar picture is presented by the data from Nippur in central Babylonia, but it is not as well developed. In contrast, the settlement pattern of Akkad and the Diyala region is similar to the settlement patterns of the dry-farming areas farther north (Wilkinson and Tucker 1995), which exhibit only limited urban development and a full complement of secondary centers. The archaeological evidence thus corresponds to the textual data presented by Steinkeller (1993), which suggests that in the early third millennium B.C., the north was a unified territory controlled by the city of Kish—the only truly urban center at the time—while the south was divided into numerous independent city-states.

Over time, two trends can be observed. In the south, although there is evidence of a slow increase in the number of secondary settlements to match a slight decrease in urban centers, it is insufficient to change the basic urban dominance of the area. In many instances, the later secondary settlements are merely old capitals reduced to minor religious centers (e.g., Eridu

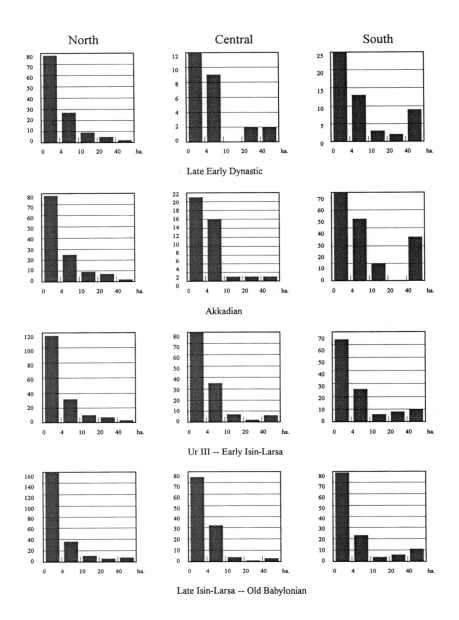

Figure 2.3. Graphs showing the distribution of sites of different size categories in northern, central, and southern Babylonia from the Early Dynastic through Old Babylonian periods. Data derived from R. McC. Adams (1965, 1972, 1981), Adams and Nissen (1972), Gibson (1972), and Wright (1981).

and Lagash), while in other cases, they are special-purpose sites (e.g., Drehem, the site of the centralized management of livestock during the Ur III period). While it is dangerous to argue from negative information, there is no evidence to suggest that these medium-sized sites played an intermediate role in the administration of the province or city-state. Moreover, the data recovered from the largest sites—from temples, administrative buildings, private houses with texts, and so on—are different only in scale than those recovered from sites smaller than 1 hectare in area, such as Tell Harmal (Baqir 1959) or Haradum (Kepinski-Lecomte 1992).

Although the settlement pattern in the south adds

some characteristics of the north without changing its basic organization, in the north we can see a dramatic increase in the number of urban centers over time. By the Old Babylonian period, the north is nearly as urbanized as the south—especially considering that at least two major urban centers (Dilbat and Borsippa) lie outside the survey zone. The increase in urban centers is also associated with a decrease in the number of secondary centers. By the Old Babylonian period, the heartland of northern Babylonia shows a decidedly primate distribution with secondary centers mostly in peripheral areas—especially along the Diyala River. Thus by the early second millennium B.C., the settlement pattern of the north resembles that of the city-states of the south, despite the centralized control exerted by Babylon and a history characterized by repeated periods of political unification.

Again there are caveats. Our chronological indicators are not sensitive enough to distinguish between northern Babylonian settlements that postdate the large-scale abandonment of urban settlement in the south that took place toward the end of the eighteenth century B.C., and settlements that predate this event. It is possible—even probable—that the increase in settlement in the north associated with the Old Babylonian period and the nature of that growth may have been the result of large-scale population movement from the south, a movement also reflected in the textual record (Charpin 1986:488–489; Black 1993:32–33; Finkelstein 1972:11–12).

Whatever the exact historical circumstances, the data suggest that in the competition between the city-state ideology of the south and the more unified state ideology of the north, the former came to dominate the overall organization of society, even as political unification became the norm rather than the exception. But there were no such things as bloodless coups. Empire-building was effected through conquest and war, with all but the most secure monarchs constantly threatened by the rebellion of subject city-states. Only the Ur III kings held sway for more than a generation without a major uprising. Their tactic was to develop a highly specialized economy, where each district was dependent on the redistribution of resources from other areas to survive. In the end, even this unified economy could not withstand the forces of fragmentation that characterized this city-state-based society. Indeed, Ur became so dependent on outside resources that in its last days the city almost starved to death (Jacobsen 1970:175–177), leaving other localities—especially Isin—more capable of marshaling the resources necessary for expansion.

The reasons for the instability of the larger Mesopotamian polities are to be sought in the argument made by Eisenstadt and his colleagues: without a distinguishable ruling elite, the most efficient means of imperial expansion—co-optation of hereditary aristocracies of neighboring states—is eliminated (Eisenstadt et al. 1988:186–192). Instead, an ambitious ruler has no choice but to rely on direct military conquest. And without the cooperation of local elites, full integration into a nation-state is impossible, so conquered territories tend to revert to their component parts at the slightest sign of weakness at the imperial center.

Eisenstadt and his colleagues focus on the process of expansion of state societies, but their analysis is also applicable to the internal organization of states. While settlements in city-states are integrated through consensual arrangements between competing groups and institutions, these arrangements apparently cannot be extended over large distances. I would argue that it is this geographic limitation that makes the city-state a legitimate unit of analysis, whether or not it is incorporated into a larger polity. No Mesopotamian ruler during the period under consideration was able to integrate the political order of the localities—based on consensus—with that of the larger territory based on conquest and coercion. Without an integrated political order, the instability illustrated by the volatile history of such city-state societies as the Yoruba and Mesopotamia is inevitable.

Conclusion

The hallmarks of the Greek *polis*—citizenship, egalitarianism, and consensus—were also features of ancient Mesopotamian city-states. They are found most developed in areas where the key feature of agriculture is not land ownership but control over labor. In areas where a permanent, land-based elite cannot develop, the persistence of consensus as the basis for political order on the local level required face-to-face communication, limiting the possibilities of geographic expansion. The "Sumerian League" (Jacobsen 1970:139–140) might have been such an attempt to extend such communication to the entire southern alluvium, but if so it was short-lived. In cases where the ideology of a nation-state was embraced and the city-states were united through conquest—as was the case for Mesopotamia—the persistence of consensus as the basis for political order clashed with the coercive structure of the nation-states of which they were a part. It was this clash that led to fragmentation at the end of each imperial episode and insured the persistence of Mesopotamian city-states. The value of working in Mesopotamia is that the variety of datasets that can be brought to bear on the problem of city-state organization—archaeological, surface survey, and textual—indicate features that can be tested on civilizations where only archaeological data are available.

I have argued that the consensual basis of these societies is mirrored in the dispersion of the centers of religion, administration, manufacture, and exchange within these cities and in a lack of social differentiation between residential neighborhoods. In addition, as has long been argued by geographers, city-states can be identified by their settlement patterns, where a "primate" distribution of site sizes, with a lower-than-expected number of secondary centers, marks this type of polity. For Mesopotamia, it is possible to demonstrate the persistence of city-state organization in the face of repeated attempts at political unification.

Notes

1. The concept of citizenry is seen most clearly in laws that forbid the sale of slaves beyond their native cities.
2. I consulted numerous sources to develop the composite picture of Yoruba and Islamic cities. Among the major sources used for the Yoruba are Kochakova 1978; Krapf-Askari 1969; Lloyd 1954, 1971; Ojo 1966; and Smith 1988. Major sources used for Islamic cities are Abdel-Nour 1982; Bouhdiba and Chevallier 1982; Hourani and Stern 1970; Lapidus 1969, 1984; A. Marcus 1989; Schilcher 1985; and Serjeant 1980.
3. Clearly in the case of both classic Greece and Renaissance Florence, this position did not exist, although under certain circumstances both resorted to introduced individual leadership. It is noteworthy, in this context, that the key attribute of Florentine "tyrants"

was that they originated from outside the city and were therefore isolated from the rest of society.
4. The most important discussions of these issues are found in Diakanoff 1971, 1972, 1974a, 1974b, 1982; Gelb 1967, 1972; and Oppenheim 1964:9.
5. Adams (R. McC. Adams 1981:Table 14) indicates a general lack of settlements dating to the Old Babylonian period for the Nippur area. This pattern is due to changes in the terms used to define particular ceramic types. Late Isin-Larsa and early Old Babylonian types are virtually indistinguishable—not surprisingly, since Babylonian domination of southern and central Babylonia lasted little more than two decades. The ceramic types used by Adams to identify Old Babylonian occupation in this area date to the later part of the Old Babylonian period—or are burial vessels (R. McC. Adams 1981:171). A number of sites have later Old Babylonian burials without any clear evidence of extensive occupation at that time.
6. An Ur III text from Umma listing all men from the province eligible for military service suggests the existence of a much larger number of small settlements than has been identified on survey (Steinkeller n.d.). In all probability, much of the rural population lived in reed-hut settlements whose remains have not withstood the millennia of wind erosion and alluviation, leaving only the more substantial mud-brick villages for contemporary archaeologists to observe.

3

City-States, Nation-States, and Territorial States

The Problem of Egypt

ROBERT J. WENKE

When John Wilson attempted to apply V. Gordon Childe's ideas about early urbanism to ancient Egypt, he came to the spectacularly tentative conclusion that "one may accept a truth in Childe's 'urban revolution' provided that it is understood that it was not 'urban' and was not a 'revolution'" (1951:34; Childe 1936: 158–201). Wilson argued that Egypt had been instead a nation-state that comprised a "civilization without cities" (Wilson 1960—a phrase that has since been cited in the literature on Egypt with a frequency approaching that of Herodotus's observation that "Egypt is the gift of the Nile").

Like most generalizations that achieve the status of clichés, Wilson's assessment is subject to numerous qualifications. He was astutely summarizing what was then known about settlements of the earlier Pharaonic periods, but he was doing so in the nearly complete absence of evidence (an absence that continues) about what may have been the largest and most city-like settlements of this era—third-millennium-B.C. Memphis, for example. Memphis, the presumed capital of third-millennium-B.C. Egypt, still lies largely untouched below later occupations and the water table. More important, Wilson was applying a definition of city derived in part from the Mesopotamian metropolises of antiquity, and he specifically restricted it to communities in which commerce replaced agriculture as the main economic activity. He concluded that until about 1500 B.C., most (perhaps all) Egyptian settlements were agriculturally based and thus not true cities (Wilson 1960).

Gideon Sjoberg, on the other hand, argued that because early Egyptian communities were different in some respects from Mesopotamian cities, "this does not mean they were not cities" (1960:40), and he included ancient Egypt in *The Preindustrial City*.

These differing interpretations illustrate the kind of typological debate that has characterized comparative studies of civilizations from their inception. Wilson and Sjoberg were insightful scholars, and their discussions of what constitutes a city are enlightening, but unless the necessary and sufficient conditions for class membership for such terms as *city, state,* and *city-state,* are specified, debates about whether ancient Egypt or some other archaeological record constitutes an example of one or another of these types are bound to be unresolvable (although not necessarily sterile).

Wilson's and Sjoberg's different interpretations illustrate another classic conundrum of comparative civilization studies—the "so what?" question. Unless

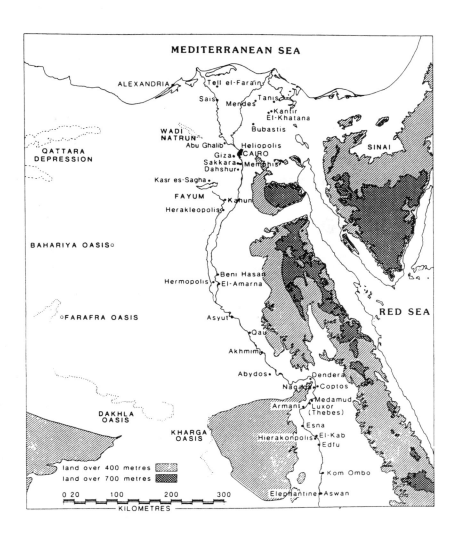

Figure 3.1. The northern Nile Valley and Delta, with principal ancient and modern settlements. From Barry Kemp, *Ancient Egypt: Anatomy of a Civilization* (1989: 8, figure 1). Reprinted with permission of Routledge.

classifications are derived from relevant theory, they tend to be descriptive, not analytical. Thus, if we stipulate the conditions to classify some segment of an archaeological record as a city-state or something else and then find examples of them, we must ask, "So what?" Is this simply analogous to butterfly collecting? Even if we grant that many early civilizations were interacting to a degree grossly underestimated by earlier analysts—perhaps forming "world systems" much earlier than has previously been thought (e.g., Frank 1993)—it is clear that many important similarities among early states (e.g., Old Kingdom Egypt and Aztec Mexico) are not the result of contact or of descent from a common culture.

But to what analytical purpose can we put such similarities? Scholars from many different positions on the spectrum of contemporary thought have criticized the notion that such similarities are the basic data of a science of history (as has been argued by Carneiro 1970; Childe 1934; Marx 1932; Service 1975; White 1949; Wittfogel 1957). Shanks and Tilley, for example, refer to the "sledge hammer of cross-cultural generalizations" (1987a:95) that pulverizes meaning and significance in history. They and like-minded scholars regard most traditional comparative analyses of ancient civilizations as fundamentally flawed by "causal reductionism" and weakened by the incorporation of inappropriate concepts, such as "spatialized time," with the result that, according to these scholars, such analyses are little more than manifestations of "ethnocentrism" and "colonialism" that obscure what should be the true focus of archaeological inquiry, specifically, the unique and individual histories and characteristics of ancient cultures, and that they also frustrate what should be a primary use of archaeological materials and interpretations, namely, to assist in bringing about "progressive" political changes in the contemporary world (Shanks and Tilley 1987a, 1987b, 1989).

Many of the theoretical issues raised by such differ-

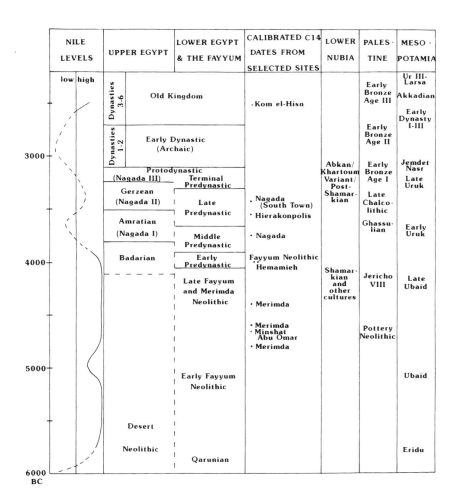

Figure 3.2. A cultural chronology of Egypt. From Trigger (1983a:figure 1.1). Reprinted with permission of Cambridge University Press.

ent perspectives are beyond the scope of this paper, but I discuss some of them below because they necessarily arise in the course of any attempt to evaluate the concept of ancient city-state.

The rich and varied cultural history of Egypt cannot even be outlined within the scope of this chapter, much less summarized. Thus I will focus on the origins and development of Egyptian community structure within the context of the evolving Egyptian state before it was transformed by Persian, Greek, and Roman influences (after about 600 B.C.). Figures 3.1 and 3.2 provide the geographical and chronological context for my review and analysis.

State and Community Structure and Functioning

Ancient Egypt exhibited great cultural continuity for so long and in so many core elements, ranging from agricultural techniques to cosmological principles, that it may be considered to exceed all other ancient civilizations in this respect. Nonetheless, it also showed great variability in other important elements—population densities and settlement size and functions, for example—and in many sociopolitical variables as well. I will focus here on variability in elements that are most directly related to changes in the basic organization of the early Egyptian state and its constituent communities.

But how should one define and select the cultural elements that are fundamental to the nature of cultural complexity, and to concepts such as civilization and city-state? Generations of scholars have debated this point and have come to vastly different conclusions (reviewed in Maisels 1990; Wenke 1989b).

Many scholars have assumed that functional differentiation and integration of economic and administrative elements are key analytical elements in comparisons of early civilizations. Trigger evaluates the attempts to place examples of the preindustrial city on a single continuum and concludes that, while we can identify key variables that link these examples, the variables combine "to shape an indefinite number of trajectories or paths of pre-industrial urban development, any one of which may be associated with a particular civilization" (1985:343). He identifies three variables of particular importance:

(1) The degree of economic complexity of the society in which the city is found, as measured in terms of the degree of division of labour in craft production, the increasing number of people divorced from food production . . . and the increasingly large areas and numbers of people that are effectively linked by routine economic interaction. . . ; (2) the different strategies by which urban dwellers obtain food from their hinterland . . . ; (3) The political context within which cities occur. (Trigger 1985:344–345)

Wright and Johnson focus on administrative hierarchies and their reflections in the archaeological record (Wright 1977, 1986; Wright and Johnson 1975; Johnson 1977, 1982). They argue that changing degrees of functional differentiation and integration, for example, can be measured archaeologically by determining changes over time and space in settlement-size hierarchies and spatial relationships, the location of craft production facilities, and so on.

Analyses of functional differentiation and integration have been recast by some scholars as studies of "power relationships" in which the functional elements were embedded in ancient societies (Haas 1982; Patterson and Gailey 1987; Preucel 1992). Crumley examines the concept of heterarchy—that is, differentiations of functional and other societal elements—and argues that our view of the elements of society as hierarchically arranged is based on largely unexamined assumptions (1987a).

From an evolutionary perspective, the difference between, for example, Neolithic Egypt and the Early Dynastic state represents a difference in the scale of selection. That is, the size and complexity of functional relationships of people and communities dependent on one another for existence and competitive success changed radically once societal functioning and competitive success depended on the integrated activities of professional soldiers, farmers, bakers, and the thousands of other individuals who performed the hundreds of specialized activities on which Early Dynastic Egyptian society depended.

These concepts of functional differentiation and integration cannot be restricted simply to modes and mechanisms of economic production and exchange. Baines (1990), for example, reviews the hierarchical

stratification of Pharaonic Egypt in relation to knowledge and shows how complex the distribution of information and knowledge was—and how access to information and knowledge reinforced the hierarchical arrangements of society. He notes that some restrictions on access to knowledge can stimulate social competition and divisiveness, but this is not true of religious knowledge: "It does not matter what the 'Eastern Souls' sing at sunrise; what is important is that the king knows it (and others do not)" (Baines 1990:22). Baines traces changes in restrictions on knowledge and relates them to evolving administrative institutions and other social aspects of Egypt in different Pharaonic eras.

Similarly, we must assume that the "symbolic capital" (Joffe n.d., 1991) represented by the imported timber and other products used in constructing the pyramids, for example, constituted an economically significant and direct impetus in mobilizing an organized work force to be used for many important purposes, a work force that was also used by elites to dominate the citizenry (Trigger 1990a). By the time there is a relatively full documentary record concerning administrative matters in Egypt, as existed in the Middle Kingdom, not only are there scores of important occupational specialties, but the administrative hierarchies that acted as control systems are also highly specialized and complexly integrated (Quirke 1990).

These concepts of functional differentiation and integration also entail problems in interpreting homological and analogical similarities and differences. Egypt appears to have evolved most of the functional elements associated with civilization and the administrative apparatus of a nation-state before any one settlement became a true urban metropolis (as traditionally defined) at the center of a state (also as traditionally defined); whereas in Mesopotamia, individual cities and their dependent towns and villages— fourth-millennium-B.C. Sumer, for example—developed most of the hallmarks of civilization before the city-states were combined into successively larger nation-states through competition and cooperation.

But what is the importance of such a difference? One can argue that early Egyptian and Mesopotamian civilizations both contained essentially the same functional elements, integrated in similar ways, but the elements were arranged in different spatial patterns. Thus throughout the early history of Egypt and Mesopotamia, the variability in sizes of settlements at any particular time seems to have been much greater in Mesopotamia than in the Nile Valley. At one level, this appears to be a simple and rather uninteresting function of differences in ecological, demographic, and historical factors. If so, then the city-state, as exemplified by those of Mesopotamia, might be considered one of several types of settlement patterns—dependent on particular ecological and historical circumstances—that a nation-state could exhibit during its development.

Differences of spatial arrangement are not necessarily unimportant or uninteresting: the histories, economic interactions, and sociopolitical relationships of Egypt and Mesopotamia—and other civilizations as well—shaped and were shaped by the spatial arrangements of their elements. Sjoberg refers to the city as a "dependent variable . . . shaped as it is by the enfolding sociocultural system" (1960:15). Patterson and Gailey assert that the accumulation of archaeological evidence in recent decades has "dispelled any notion that sociopolitical organization mirrored in a simple way subsistence and technological practices" (1987:4).

In this context, Trigger has come to an interesting conclusion about the results of his many years of study of early civilizations:

I expected to discover that, because of ecological constraints, the differences in economic systems [among early states] would be limited, and there would be more variation in sociopolitical organization, religious beliefs, and art styles. In fact, I have found that a wide variety of economic behavior was associated with early civilizations, the one constant being the production of surpluses that the upper classes appropriated through a tributary relationship. Yet I have been able to discover only one basic form of class hierarchy, two general forms of political organization, and a single basic religious paradigm. . . . I have documented significant variation from one early civilization to another only in terms of art styles and cultural values. (1993:110)

Trigger's perceptive conclusion is directly related to the questions I posed above with regard to the significance of the individual evolutionary sequences of early civilizations and the significance of their similarities and differences. It seems reasonable to assume, as Trigger does, that there is such little variation in some elements in these early civilizations because of their relative "efficiency" (Trigger 1993:110), and great variations in other elements because they have little effect on the adaptiveness and competitive success of the social organism of which they are a part.

If so, then one aspect of an archaeological analysis of ancient Egypt can be an examination of the specific factors that may have determined the adaptiveness and efficiency of Egyptian cultural elements, and changes in these variables over time and space. This kind of investigation does not require that one ignore the great extent to which the unique and specific values, ideas, and concepts of the ancient Egyptians (e.g., Divine Kingship, *ma'at*, etc.) formed the structure of this civilization and determined its history. It simply requires that one attempt to understand these in the specific and complex context of the entire civilization.

Initial Developmental Sequence

The central processes by which the first Egyptian nation-state formed have been summarized by Barry Kemp (1989), who envisions a three-stage developmental process occurring between 4000 and 3000 B.C. (Fig. 3.3). A chronology of early Egyptian cultural changes based on a recent recalibration of a large set of radiocarbon dates from Egypt is presented in Figure 3.4 (also see Hassan and Robinson 1987).

In this figure, the dates from Faiyum and Merimda are of the earliest known agricultural communities in Egypt, dating to the period of about 5000 to 4000 B.C. The Upper Egyptian Neolithic and early Predynastic sites of Omari and Qena/Sohag are from small settlements that appear to have had none of the elements traditionally associated with cultural complexity. The dates from Hierakonpolis encompass the period (ca. 3800–3200 B.C.) when the first elements of complexity appear in Egypt, in the form of increased variations in the "wealth" of individuals, nonresidential, public, monumental architecture, etc. The dates from Ma'adi are from occupations that show intensive cultural connections with Syro-Palestine, specialization in manufacture of stone, metal, and other artifacts, but at a time when the ceramics from Ma'adi are relatively different from those of Upper Egypt— suggesting only low-level cultural connections. The dates from Abydos are from occupations spanning the earliest period in which tombs and other data suggest this site was becoming a mortuary cult center for some of Egypt's earliest rulers. The dates from Minshat Abu Omar are from graves in a cemetery on the far eastern edge of the Delta, and the artifacts from this site are very similar in style to those in use all over Egypt at this time, and there are pot marks and other expressions of the symbols of the earliest rulers of the

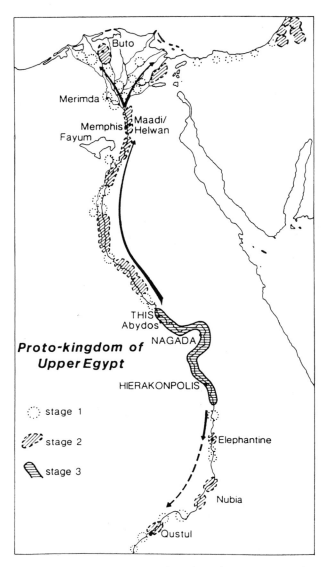

Figure 3.3. Barry Kemp's (1989) hypothetical reconstruction of early state formation in Egypt (ca. 3600–3200 B.C.). Kemp's model suggests that the earliest complex socioeconomic polities appeared in Upper (southern) Egypt, grew in size of the area they controlled until a "Proto-kingdom" appeared and began extending its influence northward. To Kemp's reconstruction can be added a Stage 4, in which the Delta and the Valley were integrated in a single polity (sometime between ca. 3400 and 3100 B.C.), and a Stage 5, in which the Egyptian state bureaucracy was in control of the entire area between northern Nubia and the Mediterranean coast. From Barry Kemp, *Ancient Egypt: Anatomy of a Civilization* (1989:34, figure 8). Reprinted with permission of Routledge.

Egyptian nation-state. The dates from Giza and Saqqara are from a variety of Old Kingdom tombs, temples, pyramids, and other structures and encompass the time when Egypt had become a highly centralized, functionally complex and integrated, powerful nation-state. For a review of the radiocarbon dates

on which this figure is based, see Hassan and Robinson (1987) and H. Haas et al. (1987).

Stage 1 involved small clusters of agricultural communities in the Delta and the Valley, although settlement density was probably greater and earlier in the south. Stage 2 entailed the formation of small polities, first in Upper Egypt around several sites such as Hierakonpolis and Abydos, and then, later perhaps, in the Delta around Buto and a few other communities. Stage 3 saw the appearance of a "proto-kingdom" in the area of Hierakonpolis, Nagada, and Abydos. It possessed modest expressions of monumental architecture, centralized craft production, and burials that may reflect significant wealth differences based on hereditary inequality (Eiwanger 1987). To Kemp's three-stage sequence could be added a Stage 4, involving the initial cultural integration, probably through military force, of Upper and Lower Egypt about 3100–2900 B.C.; and, also, a Stage 5, the formation of the first "mature" state during the Old Kingdom (ca. 2600 B.C.), which was marked by a northward shift of the demographic, economic, and administrative balance and the retraction of settlements in Sinai and Palestine to the eastern margins of the Delta, as Egypt's national borders became politically and culturally defined (Oren 1989:404). From this fifth stage onward, throughout most of the Pharaonic era, the area enclosed within Egypt's geographical boundaries remained approximately the same, and the northern Valley and Delta stayed the most densely populated and economically most important area of the country.

At what point in this sequence we can consider Egypt to have comprised a "city-state" or a "state" depends, of course, on how these terms are defined. Kemp has "used the term incipient city-state for territories in southern Upper Egypt. . . . 'Incipient' seems an appropriate word, since they cannot have matched the complexity of contemporary city-states in other parts of the Near East" (1989:52, 1977). We know comparatively little about the functional complexity of Egyptian polities in Kemp's Stages 2 and 3, but they lacked the size, monumental architecture, population density, and many other elements evident in—for example—late fourth-millennium-B.C. Sumer.

Redford (1992:8) notes that Egyptian writing may preserve a record of different kinds of settlements as they existed prior to and during the period when script was being developed. There are at least five terms describing settlements in early hieroglyphs: (1) a word usually translated as "city," whose root mean-

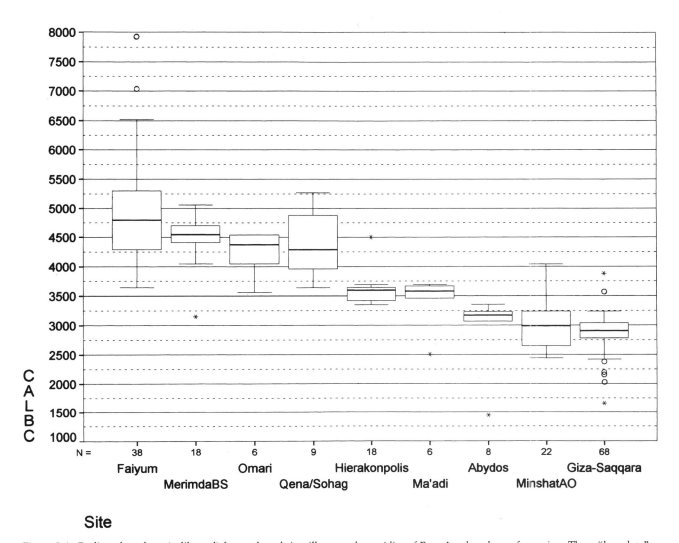

Figure 3.4. Radiocarbon dates (calibrated) from selected sites illustrate the rapidity of Egypt's cultural transformation. These "boxplots" are composed of three elements: a box (black rectangle) that encloses the half of the dates for a given site that fall around the median date (which is indicated by the line in the box); "whiskers," the lines that extend from the top and bottom of the box, and which indicate the spread of the dates between the upper quartile and the lower quartile; and, individual circles and asterisks that indicate the position of extreme ("outliers") dates—that is, dates that are relatively distant from the mean date.

ing is a collection of reed huts surrounded by a protective wall; (2) a word translated as "town," which actually means "to touch" and refers to locations on the riverbank where boats landed; (3) a word for "mound" that implies a settlement on a rise above the floodplain; (4) a word referring to "clan" or "family" that describes small hamlets of kin groups; and (5) a word meaning "seat" or "abode" of a god, which may imply some kind of temple within a community. Unfortunately, there is little evidence with which to evaluate the accuracy of these meanings as applied to individual settlements.

Toward the end of Kemp's Stage 3, however, about 3100 B.C., Egypt had: (1) a written language already in use for commodity control (e.g., inscribed mud-sealings on wine jars) and many other purposes; (2) uniform pottery styles that could be found in thousands of communities stretching from Palestine to Nubia; (3) craft production of a wide variety of artifacts, from metal needles to multiton architectural blocks of granite, which circulated throughout the Delta and Valley; (4) exchange networks capable of moving many commodities to and from Syro-Palestine and other foreign areas; (5) an emerging socioeconomic class stratification, already hierarchically arranged below the pharaoh; and (6) a national ideology that incorporated most of the ideas that fa- cilitated the functioning of the Egyptian state for 3,000 years thereafter.

The processes that transformed Egypt from a land- scape of hundreds of unlinked, "functionally redun- dant" subsistence agricultural villages into the Early Dynastic and Old Kingdom states can be summarized as follows.

South-to-north developmental process and sequence

The geographic sequence in which early complex pol- ities expanded may seem relatively unimportant, but in Egypt, it indicates some of the factors that were important in cultural evolution. The south-to-north process in Egypt is inferred primarily from the fact that Hierakonpolis, Abydos, and other southern com- munities (Fig. 3.1) are known to have had large popu- lations and productive economies shortly after 3800 B.C., whereas the earliest known sites in the Delta are 200–300 years later. Sites in the north (such as Ma'adi, near modern Cairo) that were contempor- aries of Hierakonpolis, Abydos, and other southern centers seem smaller and more simply organized, and monumental architecture—rock tombs, mudbrick tombs, massive nonmortuary mudbrick constructions (e.g., "forts"), and the earliest attempts at pyramid architecture—all seem to have appeared first in the south.

Finally, styles of ceramics in the south and north (especially in the Delta) are quite different in the last centuries of the fourth millennium B.C. About 3100 B.C., however, the distinctive local styles of pottery in the north, even on the northern and western fringes of the Delta (Fig. 3.1), appear to have been quickly replaced by styles that had been common in the south for centuries. Fourth-millennium-B.C. ceramics from Mendes and Ibrahim Awad in the Delta, for example, include many coarse, chaff-tempered forms that do not have close parallels in the south, but in the imme- diately succeeding levels several distinctive forms of ceramics, such as the "radial-burnished bowl," are found at these sites and throughout the Nile Valley, where they apparently originated. From the beginning of the third millennium B.C. and continuing through- out Egyptian antiquity, ceramic styles were similar in every region of the country, including Western Desert oases, the Nubian border, and the eastern and west- ern peripheries of the Delta.

The developmental priority of the south is, to some extent, counterintuitive. The Delta's greater agricul-

tural potential and proximity to the rapidly evolving states of western Asia and the Mediterranean raise the question of why it was not the initial area of develop- ment. Trigger has suggested that the flood basins along the banks of the Nile between Abydos and Hierakonpolis were more suitable for the irrigation and farming methods in use in the early fifth mil- lennium B.C. than the larger basins farther north (1983a:10; also see Bard and Carneiro 1989; Krzy- zaniak 1977). Hassan links some Neolithic and Predynastic developments to declining Nile floods, greater aridity, and increased variability in winter temperatures, all of which may have encouraged repo- sitioning settlements nearer the Nile (1986, 1988; Brewer 1991:299). But even severe fluctuations in the Nile apparently did not affect settlement size and composition in the way that climatic changes affected them in Southwest Asia (Weiss 1986). On the basis of chemical analyses of Nile sediments, Allen and his colleagues suggest that the appearance of agricultural economies and early Predynastic cultural develop- ments correspond to relatively high seasonal floods and sediment loads, but that the period preceding the cultural unification of the Delta and Valley (ca. 3600– 3100 B.C.) saw a significant lessening of flood levels (1993). They raise the issue of whether environmental stresses may have induced people in the southern Val- ley to intensify production through irrigation and then to expand to the large, fertile, and easily irri- gated farmlands of the Delta.

The presence of Mesopotamian artifacts and styles in the south in the mid-fourth millennium B.C. sug- gests that overland connections to Red Sea ports may have been a factor in the south's developmental prior- ity, and most of the important communities in the south (e.g., Abydos and Hierakonpolis) lie near a *wadi* (the bed of a Pleistocene river or stream) that connected them to the Red Sea or to Western Desert oases (Redford 1992:14).

Mechanisms of state formation

Evidence for the traditional assumption that the first Egyptian states evolved through warfare and competi- tion is almost entirely indirect and inferential. Textual references to the military campaigns of Menes or other semimythical kings appear centuries after the purported battles, and the (supposed) representations of these epic formative battles that appear on the Narmer Palette, the Libyan Palette, and other objects are of uncertain date and significance. Fairservis recently argued that the Narmer Palette, long thought to commemorate the conquest of Lower Egypt, instead refers to military campaigns in Nubia (1991; also see Millet 1990).

The abruptness of stylistic change in ceramics in the Delta, with local styles replaced by southern ones at the presumed time of conquest (Bakr 1988; van den Brink 1988), might be more secure evidence of the processes of state formation than ambiguous symbols on palettes and maceheads, but only a few Delta sites have been excavated at the level where these style changes occur, and none of them has been excavated extensively. Cemeteries dating to the late fourth and early third millennia B.C. have been found at numerous places in the Delta. Some contain artifacts in metal, alabaster, and pottery, distributed in patterns suggestive of minor wealth and sex/age differences (Kroeper 1988, 1989, 1990; Kroeper and Wildung 1985), but few of the associated settlements have been found (Krzyzaniak 1988). Thus there is little direct evidence about the processes whereby the Delta and Valley cultures were integrated.

There is, of course, reason to suppose that warfare was an important aspect of early Egyptian state formation, given the well-documented importance of warfare in the texts and archaeological records of later Egypt and in other early civilizations as well.

One of the most problematic elements in any model of initial Egyptian state formation is the degree to which these developments were influenced by contacts with western Asian and Mediterranean cultures—indeed, there is some evidence that Egypt and Mesopotamia represent a complex blend of homological and analogical similarities. The discovery at Buto in the northern Delta of a "port" settlement that contained Uruk-style clay wall cones of local manufacture and dated to about 3200 B.C. has given additional weight to the idea that Southwest Asia provided a great deal of cultural influence on Egypt's process of state formation (von der Way 1987, 1988, 1992). Recent excavations also suggest that there was a distinctive Lower Egyptian culture that shows few traces of interaction with the south before about 3100 B.C. The functional complexity of this Delta culture is largely unknown, although there was substantial commodity trade, probably overland via domesticated donkeys (Bokonyi 1985), between Lower Egypt sites such as Ma'adi and Syro-Palestine by about 3500 B.C. (Caneva et al. 1987, 1989).

Levy notes that recent radiocarbon dates from settlements in the Beersheva Valley indicate that they were contemporary with the early occupations at Ma'adi and suggests (citing Joffe 1991) that the expanding mid-fourth-millennium-B.C. Predynastic polities in Egypt may have given rise to "Chalcolithic entrepreneurs" in Palestine (1993a, 1993b). At the time Ma'adi was first occupied, the population of the Delta may have been small, but by the late fourth and early third millennium B.C., the area was densely occupied, at least in the eastern areas close to Syro-Palestine and probably in the north and west as well (Kroeper 1989). The Delta was considerably smaller in the early Pharaonic era than it is today because of subsidence and sea-level rise (Allen et al. 1993; Coutellier and Stanley 1987).

Buto is part of a growing body of evidence of early Egyptian/western Asian interactions, and the importance of these contacts on Egypt's formative processes involves both mechanisms and rate of cultural change.

Traditional interpretations of Egypt's history from the Gerzean Period through the 1st Dynasty argue a kind of *Drang nach Norden,* with the forces of political unification and expansion moving up the Nile Valley, engulfing the Delta, and expanding into Asia, increasing in force as the process proceeded. . . . There is one element that is particularly difficult to accommodate within this south-north sweep of Egyptian political evolution, and that is the clear evidence in Gerzean and later sites of artifacts and artifact (and architectural) styles that are Syro-Palestinian and Irano-Mesopotamian in origin. (Redford 1989:1–2)

Redford reviews the evidence on artifact styles, architectural styles, and seal impressions that indicates contact between Egypt and Syro-Palestine and Mesopotamia in the fourth millennium B.C. and notes that

although it is perhaps premature to arrive at conclusions, the evidence for contact with Mesopotamia is more extensive and specific than can be accommodated by a theory of intermittent and casual trade. It would seem that besides trade items, a human component of alien origin is to be sought in the Gerzean demography of Egypt. (1992:22)

Redford's allusion to a "human component of alien origin" is reminiscent of Petrie's idea of Egypt's formation through invasions by a "dynastic race" from Southwest Asia (1900). The physical anthropological evidence on this issue is a biased sample because many of the best-preserved skeletal remains are from southern Egyptian sites, as opposed to the Delta and northern Egypt, where preservation is not as good

(Angel 1972; Brace et al. 1993; Johnson and Lovell 1994), but the data do not support a sudden infusion into the Egyptian gene pool, either from the northwest or from the south. Brace and his colleagues' (1993) morphometrical analyses of a large sample of ancient Egyptian skeletal remains show very clearly the distinctiveness of ancient Egyptians as a physical type from the Pleistocene into the Pharaonic period, and they found ancient Egyptians to be most similar to European and circum-Mediterranean populations, not those to the south of Egypt (cf. Bernal 1987). If external cultures significantly influenced Egypt during its formative era, those most likely to have done so are Greater Mesopotamia, perhaps via Red Sea ports, and Syro-Palestine, probably by both land and sea. Egyptian artifacts from 2900–2700 B.C., including vessels from royal workshops, are found throughout the Negev and southern Palestine, which had a population at that time of perhaps 150,000 living in walled towns and villages (Joffe n.d., 1991; Redford 1992: 29–35). Egypt appears to have been dominant militarily and economically during this period, and Syro-Palestine was probably more influenced by Egypt than vice versa (Joffe 1991).

Redford emphasizes the apparent abruptness of Egyptian state formation: "Unlike the Tigris-Euphrates Valley, where the temples of Uruk presage the glories of Sumer centuries in advance, Egypt bounced overnight, as it were, out of the Stone Age and into urban culture" (1992:3). However, Wildung, whose excavations in the far eastern Delta at Minshat Abu Omar revealed numerous artifacts of Syro-Palestinian origins, suggests that:

The alleged 'cultural explosion' of Egypt in ca. 3100 B.C., with the foundation of the state, the 'discovery' of writing, and the canonization of arts did not take place. In Egypt, too, the 'higher culture' developed in a long organic process of evolution, which already in Nagada II and Nagada III covered the whole of Egypt, including the Nile Delta, and found its end several generations before the fictitious unification of the Kingdom. What is for us historically legible, are the very latest phases of a long-term natural growth. (1984:269; also see Kaiser 1964, 1985)

Additional evidence, especially from the Delta sites now known to date to this formative era, which is the focus of our own work in the Delta, is necessary for proper evaluation of these and other ideas about the evolution of Egyptian cultural complexity (Brewer and Wenke 1992; Redding 1992; Wenke 1986, 1989a, 1991; Wenke et al. 1988).

Geographic and Demographic Parameters of the Early Egyptian State

When we consider simple geographic size in the later periods of antiquity, Egypt seems to have been significantly smaller (about 34,000 square kilometers of occupied and farmed land) than some other early states. Also, the extent of the area settled, cultivated, and considered part of Egypt by its rulers and citizens was extremely stable. After a short period of rapid growth, its size stabilized and has remained effectively the same to the present day. As Kemp notes:

The 1st Dynasty began as a state which was territorially as large as most which were to occupy the lower Nile Valley until modern times. There was no long process of growth from the spread of a city-state, a common early political form which had a thriving history in, for example, Mesopotamia. (1989:52)

But the concept of "size" can have many definitions, and its analytical force is dependent on what is important in a given analysis, whether it be size as measured by stated national boundaries, size as measured by the volume and diversity of trade routes beyond national boundaries, or by other criteria. Egypt's links with Southwest Asia have already been noted; thus the size differential between Egypt and Mesopotamia may be more apparent than real if we view Egypt as also undergoing periodic expansions through external trade and warfare without a cultural homogenization of these distant areas. Yet even the direction and extent of these trade routes seem to have been remarkably stable throughout the Pharaonic era, at least until the Persian and Roman conquests.

Egypt's small size, compared to later Southwest Asian polities, seems largely a product of ecological and geographic differences. In Mesopotamia, polities seem to have expanded to a point where they overreached their control apparatus or suffered an evil conjunction of wars, salinization, and so on. States could expand in concentric circles of gradually increasing diameter, from the small city-states of Sumer to the Akkadian state, the Babylonian, Assyrian, and later empires, and so on. Egypt stands in sharp contrast to this pattern, for obvious reasons: desert borders and swamp lands on its northern periphery offered few incentives for the expansion cycles that occurred in Mesopotamia.

Like all states, ancient Egypt evolved mechanisms to promote stability in economic production. The uniformity of its agricultural potential and natural-resource distribution is such that stable agricultural production can be achieved if production comes from thousands of small communities that micromanage responses to variations in Nile floods and other determinants of production. Certainly there were times of stress caused by poor harvests, but regional differences in production and the government's role in taxation and redistribution mitigated fluctuations in economic production.

Egypt's overall geographical extent during its long periods of stability was largely determined by the Nile. "Size," in the sense of the distribution of functional elements that are systematically integrated, is strictly limited in preindustrial polities by the technology (and thereby the cost) of goods and information flow. From this perspective, the Nile makes Egypt much "smaller" in terms of transport costs than some of the earlier Southwest Asian states, despite the transport potential of the Tigris, Euphrates, and other rivers. Inferring these kinds of apparently causal correlations between geographic and culturally defined variables involves, of course, all the traditional limitations (e.g., equifinality) of functionalist explanations and ecological determinism.

One of the most important philosophical foundations of the early Egyptian state was containment of disorder: rulers were charged by the gods and their people to maintain order, and texts show that pharaohs recognized clear boundaries to Egypt and tried to fortify their borders. Within these borders, they encouraged uniformity and order (Badawy 1967). Geography set effective limits to early Egyptian polities, but the ideology that subsequently evolved to define Egypt's "size" was a potent determinant of the country's effective size long after Egypt had the military and political means to extend its power far beyond its original boundaries.

During the late Early Dynastic and Old Kingdom, when Egypt's state apparatus was enlarging, its periphery was actually contracting, as colonies in the southern Levant and eastern Delta were abandoned (Joffe 1991:29). It had the benefits of extensive size through its voluminous trade routes, without the costs of incorporating these areas culturally and protecting them against competitors—costs that appear to have been major factors in the expansion-collapse cycles of Mesopotamian states.

The concept of societal "collapse," a dominant theme in many analyses of Mesopotamia, China, and other early states (Yoffee 1979; Yoffee and Cowgill 1988), has some application to Egypt, but the peri-

odic partial disintegrations of Egyptian polities seem to have been quite different. When its central government weakened, there was a reversion to greater autonomy for the *nomes* (provinces) for brief periods. Even during the three "intermediate periods" that are taken as major divisions of Egypt's culture history, the level of disruption may have been less than originally estimated (Strudwick 1985). There was always a base level of expansion-collapse cycles as a result of variations in the Nile's annual flow. Various texts describe social disruptions that may be associated with flood-level fluctuations (Butzer 1984), but the Egyptian state evolved effective mechanisms to cope with these problems.

To some extent, Egypt's "intermediate periods" may have been periods of reorganization rather than of collapse. For example, the great decline in pyramid construction that marked the end of the Old Kingdom and the beginning of the First Intermediate period does not necessarily reflect catastrophe. In fact, there is evidence that any economic dislocations in these periods were short-lived and relatively minor (Strudwick 1985).

As powerful as the state apparatus was in Old Kingdom Egypt, it was nonetheless newly evolved and probably incorporated various instabilities. The resurgence of the state during the Middle Kingdom may have involved restructuring administrative relationships between the central government and provincial authorities—in other words an evolutionary change in response to a changing sociopolitical environment rather than the recovery of a temporarily weakened state apparatus.

Any sense of Egypt's "size" must also involve the size of its population at different times. Butzer's estimates of Egypt's demographic history probably contain significant errors (which he acknowledges), but they are based on reasonable estimates of site numbers and sizes and on textual and other evidence (1976). Figure 3.5 represents a revision of Butzer's data to reflect recent research, but the basic trends Butzer reconstructed appear to be supported by the data. Unless Figure 3.5 is grossly inaccurate, population growth in Egypt was slow, and densities were low in most areas until late in the Pharaonic era. The pattern is typical of long-term increase in total population as a result of small but consistent rates of growth. This supports Butzer's assessment that land shortages and other kinds of population stress were never a major determinant in Egypt's early cultural evolution. Some people probably starved when Nile floods were

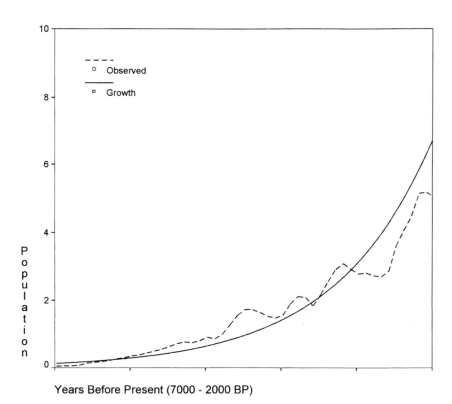

Years Before Present (7000 - 2000 BP)

Figure 3.5. A hypothetical demographic history of Pharaonic Egypt, based on a slightly revised version of Butzer's (1976) original estimates. "Population" is expressed here in millions of people. These estimates are speculative because most of the occupational communities of early Pharaonic Egypt have been destroyed or buried by alluvium and later occupations, but evidence from texts, cemeteries, and those communities that have been excavated suggest that the demographic history hypothesized in this figure is plausible. The growth rate indicated here by the solid line suggests that the population of ancient Egypt grew at a very slow but consistent rate ($R^2 = 0.917$, d.f. $= 51$, Sig. of F $= 0.000$, slope $= 0.0008$).

too high or low, according to the documentary evidence, but by preindustrial standards, Egypt was, as Kemp has shown (1989), a very rich and prosperous country.

The changes in Egypt's population densities seem to reflect the shift of Egypt's capital and administrative center. Southern Egypt was the most densely populated area of the country until the early phases of the Egyptian state, after which the demographic balance changed to Lower Egypt, especially the Delta. Butzer estimated that in the middle of the Old Kingdom period (2500 B.C.), there were about 1,040,000 people living in the Valley (including Giza and Memphis) and about half that many, about 540,000, living in the Delta (1976). But by 150 B.C., Butzer suggests, the population of the Delta and the Nile Valley may have been nearly equal (Fig. 3.5). If the developmental focus after about 3200 B.C. moved from Upper Egypt to Lower Egypt and the Delta, as is suggested by the

concentration of monumental architecture in the environs of Giza and Saqqara and the (presumed) rapid expansion of Memphis, then the rapid population growth in the Delta may be an indication of this shift. If so, the trend was well underway by 3000 B.C., as can be seen from the substantial Delta population densities at this time (Kroeper 1989).

General Developmental Sequence: Settlement-Pattern Variability and Functional Differentiation

Egypt contrasts sharply with Mesopotamia and some other early states in its basic socioeconomic and political unit.

The fundamental unit of Mesopotamian society is the city. The city is the basic economic unit and primary bearer and reproducer of the culture. . . . It is the building block

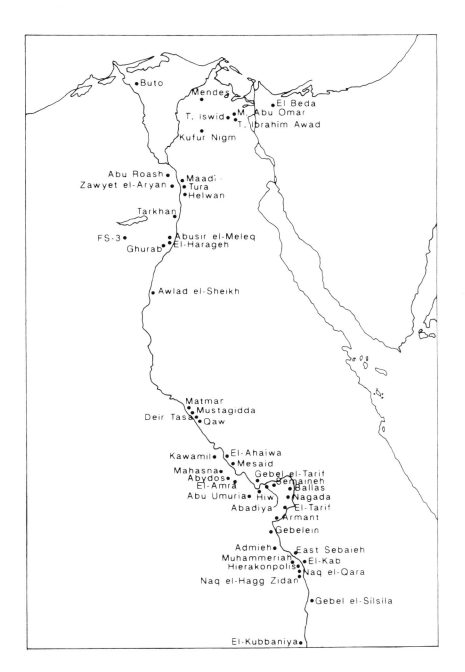

Figure 3.6. Some major Predynastic (4000–2900 B.C.) Egyptian sites. The relative sizes of these individual communities are difficult to estimate because most are either destroyed or buried beneath alluvium and later occupations.

of larger organizational forms, such as territorial states and empires, and it is the unit into which these forms collapse. . . . The city is the reference point for the culture, that unit or trait by which it understands 'inside' and 'outside' . . . and the starting point of repeated episodes of maximization along many scales. (Joffe 1991:35)

The basic socioeconomic and political "building block" in Egypt was not the city-state but the *nome*, the Greek word for the small provinces that were recognized as distinct administrative entities by successive Egyptian governments from Early Dynastic times through the medieval period. There appear to have been few (if any) settlements in Egypt with a populated area greater than 10 hectares until long after the Egyptian state was formed; and until about 500 B.C., when Persian, Greek, and Roman conquerors sequentially absorbed Egypt into their empires, there were only a few large towns.

Figures 3.6, 3.7, and 3.8 illustrate the changing patterns of settlements in three selected periods of Egyptian antiquity. Although the overall trend is toward a growing population and settlement of areas previously unoccupied, the extent to which this ex-

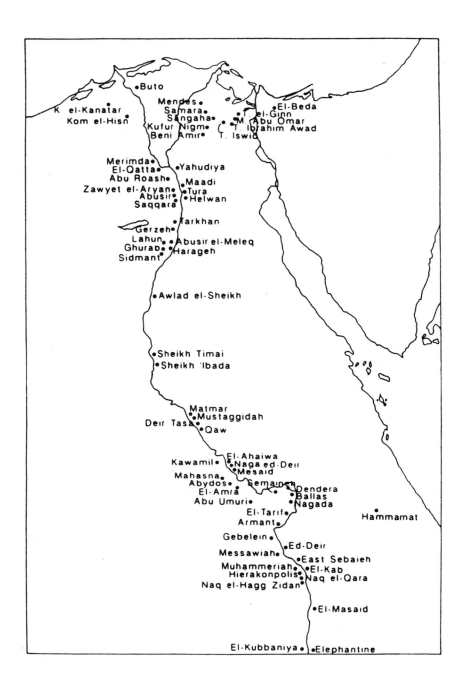

Figure 3.7. Some major Early Dynastic (ca. 2900–2600 B.C.) Egyptian sites. The relative sizes of these individual communities are difficult to estimate because most are either destroyed or buried beneath alluvium and later occupations.

pansion was a process of demographic accumulation, as opposed to a structural change in the functional apparatus of the Egyptian state, is uncertain. It is possible, for example, that much of the Delta's growth was multiplication of agricultural communities that were functionally redundant—that is, communities whose functions in the national economy were nearly identical. It is likely, however, that some of the Delta expansion was in the form of communities whose functional roles were unique and perhaps increasingly complex. Based on the sketchy evidence we have (Brewer and Wenke 1992), Mendes, for example, may

have grown, between 3100 and 2200 B.C., from a simple agricultural community like its neighbors into a port connecting the eastern Delta to Syro-Palestine, and also into a regional cult center.

Overall settlement patterns for Egypt are poorly known, given the destruction and obscuration of sites throughout the Valley and Delta, but results of the few attempts to estimate them would suggest a significant pattern of change in size variability and spatial arrangement. If accurate reconstructions could be made of settlement locations and sizes, I would expect rank-size plots (see Johnson 1977) to be convex

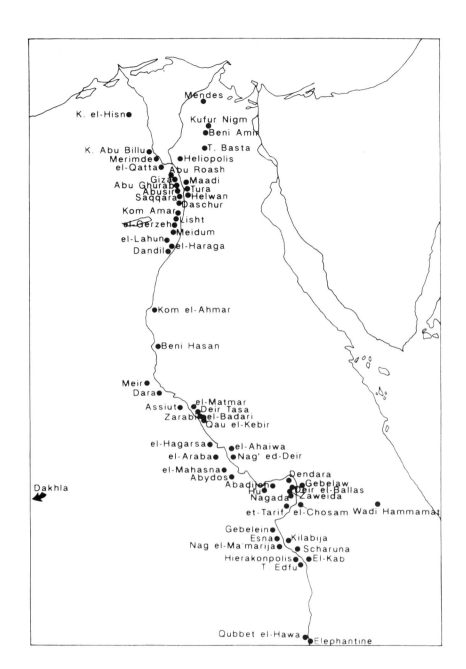

Figure 3.8. Some major Old Kingdom (ca. 2600–2000 B.C.) Egyptian sites. The relative sizes of these individual communities are difficult to estimate because most are either destroyed or buried beneath alluvium and later occupations.

during what might be termed the "proto-state period" (ca. 3600–3100 B.C.), as Hierakonpolis, Abydos, Naqada, and a few other centers grew and perhaps contended (Bard 1987; Hassan 1988). From about 3100 B.C. until well into the Middle Kingdom, the supposed predominance of Memphis may have produced a settlement pattern that approached a "primate" rank-size distribution, and in the Graeco-Roman period (ca. 3200–300 B.C.) these patterns may have at times reached a log-normal distribution, with the dominance of Alexandria and the appearance of many large cities throughout the Delta (e.g., Mendes) and in the Faiyum and the Valley as well. It

is interesting that if, as many suggest, Memphis did dominate the Egyptian settlement pattern in a "primate" fashion for centuries during the Old Kingdom, this same area is currently dominating it even more, in that Cairo is thought to be home to nearly 20 percent of all Egyptians.

Unfortunately, rank-size plots are difficult to interpret without knowledge of the functional composition of settlements and their economic relationships, and we have very little information about Egyptian communities before about 2000 B.C., by which time the state, by almost any definition, was already more than a millennium old. Some later cities were large.

Tell el-Amarna, for example, had a population of between 20,000 and 50,000 and had the diversity of craft production facilities, socioeconomic class hierarchies, and other elements comparable to an early Mesopotamian city (Kemp 1989:269). But overall, when one considers sites such as Hierakonpolis (Fairservis 1986; Hoffman 1982, 1989; Hoffman et al. 1986) and other excavated settlements (Kemp 1989; Trigger 1983a), most early Pharaonic Egyptian communities were small villages and towns.

Hierakonpolis, where some of the most impressive monuments and objects of imperial power were found, including the Narmer Palette, probably occupied no more than a few hectares in the Predynastic and Early Dynastic eras. In fact, Hierakonpolis and other southern communities appear to have become smaller in the Early Dynastic era than they were in the Predynastic period, perhaps, as Trigger has argued, because of the military conflicts and social unrest attendant in the process of state formation (1985). Trigger suggests that these stresses may have produced large walled communities at Hierakonpolis, Abydos, and other places, to which villagers would have migrated in periods of conflict (as R. McC. Adams [1981] suggested they did in Mesopotamia during the formative era), but that once political stability was achieved, settlement patterns reverted to the more efficient arrangement of hundreds of small agricultural villages and towns and a few larger settlements occupied primarily by administrators and craftsmen.

Memphis, for example, may have been more a royal and administrative center than a functionally diverse city like those of Sumer. Abydos is now known to contain some of the earliest attempts at pyramid architecture and the burials of "solar boats"—wooden boats intended apparently to transport the dead pharaoh in the afterlife (O'Connor 1989). Emery's excavations of Early Dynastic tombs at Saqqara revealed that this site was of great ceremonial significance. At the other end of the scale are small Early Dynastic agriculturally based villages, which have been found across the Delta and were probably densely distributed throughout the Valley.

The Old Kingdom, the earliest period for which we know a substantial amount about settlement types and functions, included at least five distinct types of settlements:

1. A national "capital" at Memphis. Memphis's status is known almost exclusively from textual in-

formation, since its early levels remain largely unexcavated (Jeffreys 1985; Smith and Jeffreys 1986). As noted above, it is not known if Old Kingdom Memphis was functionally more complex than other communities or just larger. It may have been established by an Early Dynastic period ruler, as ancient texts imply, but it probably grew extensively during the Old Kingdom, as the importance of Lower Egypt grew and the Giza Plateau became the main mortuary center for the nation. Old Kingdom remains have been found at many points deep below the surface of Memphis, so there is little doubt that it was a large settlement during this period, even if its characteristics are unknown. There seems little reason to doubt the traditional interpretation that Memphis's location, at the juncture of the Nile Valley and the Delta, was a major factor in its preeminence.

2. Large walled towns. Most major Old Kingdom Upper Egyptian settlements seem to have been walled complexes of tightly packed mudbrick houses. Hierakonpolis and Abydos both grew substantially during the Old Kingdom in comparison to their Early Dynastic occupations (Kemp 1983:98–100). The substantial enclosure walls at many Old Kingdom sites may imply some central planning and design, but most of them are not precise rectangles or squares, although some have long straight sections that sometimes form curvilinear patterns. Kemp suggests that the lack of uniformity in wall layout indicates that they were built on local initiative, not under the direction of the central government (1989:138). Few of the Old Kingdom sites in the Delta show evidence of large enclosing walls, but such walls would probably not have survived the *sebakhiin*—farmers who dig out old occupations and use the sediments for fertilizing and raising agricultural fields, as they have been doing for centuries.

3. Forts and trading entrepôts. Buhen, Elephantine, and similar sites seem to have marked the southern periphery of the Old Kingdom state. They appear to have been walled, medium-sized communities located at strategic points on the Nile or other trading routes.

4. Pyramid towns. At Abusir, Giza, and elsewhere are substantial Old Kingdom settlements directly associated with pyramid complexes (Kromer 1978; Lehner 1992). Although these communi-

ties might have been partly seasonal, some administrators, artisans, and others probably resided there on a permanent basis. A few of these communities eventually became permanent "fortified villages" (Kemp 1989:146–148).

5. Small provincial villages and towns. Van den Brink's surveys in the eastern Delta revealed scores of small settlements (1988), and there is reason to believe that similar densities would have been found in most areas of the Delta and Valley had they not been destroyed or buried by reoccupation and alluviation.

The degree of "urbanization" undoubtedly increased over time in early Pharaonic Egypt, in the sense that a greater percentage of the total population probably lived in larger communities (unfortunately, evidence is poor for later periods as well). However, there is no evidence that Egypt ever approached the degree of urbanization characteristic of early states in Mesopotamia, where approximately 80 percent of the population lived in cities at various times (Trigger 1985). Egyptian urbanization was uneven, both in terms of the number and size of communities, with a concentration in Lower Egypt. There were spectacular exceptions in the south, such as Thebes during both the New Kingdom and Late periods. True cities, by almost any definition, existed by the New Kingdom. Perhaps the best-known was Tell el-Amarna, Akhenaton's short-lived capital, where Kemp's extensive excavations revealed a large and functionally complex metropolis (1989). Although the archaeological evidence is unclear, there were probably many large towns in Egypt by the New Kingdom, including some that were functionally complex.

The closest approximations to an Athenian or Mesopotamian city-state in Egyptian history were the great towns, such as Karanis, of the first few centuries A.D. Egypt was totally transformed in this era by the introduction of Roman crops, crafts, religion, money, language, and even ethnic composition. Moreover, these towns and cities were not independent entities but elements in an administrative system that linked them to Alexandria and Persepolis and later to Athens and Rome (Porten and Yardeni 1993). Indeed, there are so many differences between Old Kingdom Egypt and Egypt in the third century A.D., for example, that these later forms of Egyptian civilization can be considered developmental outcomes of earlier trends only in an extremely limited sense.

Determinants of Egyptian Settlement Patterns

As in all early civilizations, variability over time in Egypt's settlements in terms of functional complexity, architectural arrangement, size, and spatial arrangements must be understood as products of complex interactions of ecological and cultural factors—interactions that are not easily resolvable into component elements that can be assigned relative importance.

As noted above, relatively simple and plausible correlations can be made between aspects of Egypt's settlement patterns and ecological factors. If we define urbanism, for example, so that it implies not only large relative size but also highly differentiated and coordinated function, then there seems to be little mystery about Egypt's largely nonurban history: given the ecological similarity of environments along the Nile Valley and into the Delta, as well as the rich concentrations of most important raw materials within Egypt's borders and the transport link provided by the Nile, urbanism, by the above definition, would seem to have few advantages in Egypt.

Unlike Mesopotamia, where regional and national political and economic factors were powerful determinants of settlement location, site location in Egypt for much of the Pharaonic era seems to have been largely determined by local ecological factors. The *nome* or provincial structure of the country is almost exactly defined by natural flood basins and river channels. Even Memphis, the largest settlement through most of the early Pharaonic era (which, according to texts, was built primarily for military and political purposes) is at the juncture of Egypt's main point of ecological diversity, the Valley and the Delta.

Nonetheless, the fact that the same environments of the Nile Valley produced at least two millennia of largely nonurban settlement patterns, giving way in the classical, medieval, and modern eras to extreme urbanism, should warn against facile ecological determinism. Tell el-Amarna, for example, is open to the same questions about locational theory that Monte Albán's location has spawned (Sanders and Nichols 1988). And the determining effects of some political factors are also evident. Delta settlements during the early period of state formation first appeared in number on routes to Syro-Palestine and the Mediterranean ports. In fact, the whole shift of the government center to Memphis and the associated ceremonial architecture of the pyramids is best understood as a response to the growing importance of the Delta, which was early and importantly tied to external relations.

Some analyses of the rise of the Mesopotamian city-state and state (Pollock 1992) have identified economic interactions between nomads and lowland agriculturalists as a key factor in the rise of urbanism and the control of craft production by managerial elites. The few nomads who lived on Egypt's desert borders did not offer a similar stimulus, and the overall sameness of the agricultural niche throughout Egypt made for very predictable and largely functionally redundant local economies. Although foreign and regional trade routes seem not to have stimulated urbanism in early Pharaonic Egypt to the extent that they did in Mesopotamia, much later, for example in the case of first-century-A.D. Alexandria, they did.

If we view urbanism as largely a response to economic relationships, we must consider that Egypt's highly centralized and state-dominated society did not require cities for effective functioning. Economic relationships in Pharaonic Egypt were complex, of course (Fattovich 1979), and while there was no real "private enterprise," private demand was a major factor. Kemp describes how in the midst of a state-run economy private demand was immense, a source of corruption and a major factor in national political changes, with the assertion of army rule to curb corruption (1989:246 ff.). Private demand was linked to burial goods (recycled through robbers), to "traders" whose job it was to exchange surpluses for other goods to the owners' profit, to nobles who built houses using funds derived from their official activities, and to other factors.

Small has stressed the importance of distinguishing between economic management by elites and management by the state apparatus, suggesting that separation of state formation from elite economic control can engender a heterarchical rather than a hierarchical social system within developing states (this volume). He reviews early Greek states from this perspective, and there are some Egyptian parallels in, for example, oscillations in the power of provincial nobles. But the Egyptian state-formation process tended much more toward the hierarchical than the heterarchical, and the power of the central government was, in most periods, pervasive and overwhelming. In any case, Egyptian economic activities and the economic relationships among elites and the central government's functionaries and institutions neither required nor resulted in urban centers in great numbers or of large size.

Warfare, too, has often been cited as a powerful stimulus to urbanism in Mesopotamia and elsewhere (R. McC. Adams 1981), but after unification, there are no indications that warfare provided any major stimulus to Egyptian urbanization until quite late. It would be difficult to measure with archaeological evidence, however, the effects of military threats—real or perceived—on settlement patterns and composition. The immense mudbrick walls of Delta sites such as Late period Mendes might well be a reflection of military threats from Syro-Palestine, but throughout the Pharaonic era, the vast majority of Egyptians appear to have lived in unwalled small villages.

Various scholars have argued that a key stimulus to urbanization in Mesopotamia and Egypt was the coercive power of elites who were able to compel farmers, soldiers, and others to live in and around settlements in which these elites were concentrated (e.g., R. McC. Adams 1981; Hassan 1993:359). The forcible relocation of farmers and craft specialists into relatively large, densely occupied settlements, as well as the noncoercive inducements of more urban centers, may well have been significant factors in the growth of early Egyptian towns and cities. The Nile, as noted above, may have counteracted some tendencies toward urbanism in that it offered to national command and control institutions easy access to the entire country, but the Nile also made it possible to transport the large volumes of food that would be required for a community that had grown larger than its adjacent agrarian resources could support.

Finally, with regard to assessing the significance of Egypt's unique settlement patterns and sociopolitical history, many scholars have argued for the creative role of urban life in shaping the character of a citizenry: that is, in fostering inventions, accelerating cultural change, producing feelings of alienation, class conflicts, and many other psychological conditions and cultural characteristics. Egypt's settlement pattern, seen from that point of view, was perhaps an important underlying factor in the static, uniform, ritualized qualities of Egyptian literature, arts, and religion. This cultural uniformity and stability could also be related to the near absence of urban life for most of Egypt's formative era, but there is no real indication that innovation in the arts and sciences suffered or that technological progress was stifled in comparison to, say, the rich urban landscape of Mesopotamia.

Some scholars have examined cities as mechanisms for encouraging innovation and efficient systems of information processing, storage, and control (Johnson 1982), or of "trait transmission" in evolutionary analyses (Boyd and Richerson 1985; Cavalli-Sforza and Feldman 1981). Craftsmen have to learn their craft and administrators and soldiers have to be trained, and there is no better venue in preindustrial polities than cities, if for no other reason than all commodities, even information, are subject to transport costs, and these are minimized in cities—provided, of course, that these urban populations can be efficiently supported by resources not necessarily directly produced locally. Though Egypt's great cultural uniformity and stability might be related to the near absence of urban life for most of its formative era, there is no indication that innovations in the arts and sciences were less than in other early civilizations.

In sum, urbanism, in the sense that I have discussed it, is simply one way of achieving a goal that early Egyptians reached in a different way: the early Egyptian state was able to do everything necessary for an advanced preindustrial civilization without large, functionally differentiated communities, simply by linking, via the Nile and an elaborate bureaucracy, the many functional elements one might find in a single Mesopotamian city-state. In Egypt these elements were distributed throughout the Nile Valley and Delta.

Ideological Foundations and Sociopolitical Structure and Functioning

In common with all other known ancient civilizations, Egypt had a national religious cult; extreme and heritable differences in access to wealth, power, and prestige; a grand elaboration of monumental public architecture; a long history of warfare, both civil and foreign; and many other characteristics associated with ancient states. But as with settlement patterns and economic institutions, it is the differences Egypt exhibits, in comparison to other ancient states, that are in some ways more interesting than the similarities.

History has no record of an early civilization that developed without a national religious cult. The inflexible, standard national religious systems found in all early states can only be explained on the basis of the functional advantages these systems conferred. The functional efficiency of cults and religions in uniting people for military and other group efforts, for legitimizing rulers and class stratification, and for facilitating all other operations necessary to preindustrial nation-states seems apparent. The central im-

portance of forms of religion in Egypt is manifestly evident from the earliest periods of agricultural life (Bard 1992) and throughout the Pharaonic era (Hassan 1988, 1992; Helck 1974; Quirke 1992; Shafer 1991).

Few scholars would suggest that every major feature of a specific religion helps to fulfill some functional need, but it is tempting to see many specifics of ancient Egyptian religion, and its contrasts with Mesopotamian religions as well, as reflections of specific features of geography, ecology, and socioeconomic and political structure. Knapp, for example, argues that

the rudimentary cosmologies of Egypt and Mesopotamia were similar inasmuch as both portrayed the gods creating order out of chaos. But the basic tenets of faith in the two countries were completely different. The Mesopotamians pessimistically viewed their universe as unpredictable, their gods as unstable, their afterlife as indistinct and undesirable. Egyptian religion, by contrast, inspired confidence in the eternal order and stability of the world, in the divinely guided rhythmic cycle of life and death, and in the belief that each individual Egyptian might share an eternal bliss. (1988:105)

Various scholars have suggested that Egypt differed from Mesopotamia in these ways because of the relative stability of Nile floods, and therefore of food, but such simple functional equations are difficult to substantiate. As rich and stable as Egypt was, comparatively speaking, Nile flood fluctuations did have some effect on political stability (Butzer 1984). Similarly, Egypt's concept of a king who was a god, compared to the Mesopotamian notion that the king was a human intercessor between his subjects and the gods, has been given considerable significance by some scholars (Frankfort 1956), but its ultimate importance is unclear. The Egyptians considered the pharaoh as divine, but they were not blind to the very human qualities of the occupants of this office.

Some changes in some features of Egyptian religion do seem to reflect directly political changes, such as variations in the relative rank of various gods in the pantheon. When Memphis became the preeminent settlement in Egypt, for example, its local god, Ptah, rose to the status of a state god, but he was later eclipsed by Re, as the power of the community at Heliopolis grew. This was followed by the ascendancy of Amon when Thebes became Egypt's capital (Knapp 1988:105).

Eisenstadt divides antiquity into eras defined in

terms of the relationship of the sacred and mundane in political and religious ideologies (1986). He describes civilizations where a sharp disjunction was made between the Transcendental and the Mundane as an "axial age." In early Egypt, the gods were imagined in human forms: each had many human characteristics, and there were a number of mundane elements throughout the religious ideology. Only in later civilizations did Christianity, Judaism, Islam, and Buddhism, for example, radically separate the Transcendental and the Mundane.

It is difficult to argue that a religion that makes a distinction between the Transcendental and the Mundane is in some way "superior." The supposed "monotheism" introduced by Akhenaton and the eventual monotheism of the Judeo-Christian and Islamic religions have been considered "advances" by generations of Western scholars, in the sense that all converged on what is supposed to be the central truth of a single omnipotent divinity. As Knapp and others have noted, however, the flexible polytheistic religion of Pharaonic Egypt had many functional virtues, in that it enmeshed Egyptians of all classes in a supportive cosmology that gave them a sense of being able to mitigate the world's ills and later to enjoy a pleasant afterlife (1988:102–108). "Axial age" civilizations may thus simply mark changes in the functional necessities of state polities, rather than adventitious or humanistically "progressive" innovations.

This relentlessly functional interpretation of religiosity reduces the richness and cultural significance of Egypt's ideologies to cost-benefit equations, and obviously, no religion can be accurately understood as a series of dependent variables that only *reflect* changes in other societal elements and conditions. Religions are strong causal agents, in a proximate sense, of cultures and their histories well. The proximate "causes" of many pivotal episodes in Egyptian history (e.g., Akhenaton's construction of Amarna) cannot be related simply to functional requirements, and there is the problem of "cultural lag," as well. It may well be that Egypt's settlement patterns in the first millennium of the Egyptian state were strongly and directly shaped by basic ecological and demographic factors, but that the relatively slow process of subsequent urbanization was both a function of these ecological factors and a "style" of living—a preference for village life and provincial systems of administration long after greater urbanization would have been, by strict cost-benefit calculations, increasingly "efficient."

Sociopolitical Stratification and Relationships

A number of scholars have argued that analyses of ancient civilizations should focus on the power relationships by which some members of the society dominated others (e.g., Patterson and Gailey 1987; Paynter 1989). The extremely hierarchical nature of Pharaonic Egyptian society from beginning to end is well documented (Baer 1960; Strudwick 1985), and in this, Egypt resembles most other early states. Many studies have considered the distribution of grave goods in burials dating from the earliest periods of agricultural life until well into the later Pharaonic era. If relative mortuary wealth truly reflects differences in access to wealth, power, and prestige, then Egypt was a hierarchically arranged society from the fifth millennium B.C. on (Anderson 1992; Atzler 1971–1972; Baer 1960; Bard 1992; Eiwanger 1987; Kanawati 1977; Kroeper and Wildung 1985; Kromer 1978; Seidlmayer 1987).

Any society operates most efficiently if its members do the "right thing," that is, perform conscientious civic labor, sacrifice one's life in battle, and do so because it is the "right" thing to do. In this sense, the ancient Egyptian concept of *ma'at* was undoubtedly a potent force. Although susceptible to differing interpretations, *ma'at* was the principal ethical standard that allowed petitioners to ask a court for justice, widows and orphans to expect alms from the wealthy, and people to anticipate fair treatment in ordinary commerce.

But even a society held together by the concept of *ma'at* did not extend its idea of fairness to an equitable and equal distribution of access to wealth, power, and prestige. Given the millions of years in which competition among individuals and groups may have been a major dynamic in human life, it is not surprising that even a powerful concept like *ma'at* was not sufficient to suppress the hierarchical nature of Egyptian society. In fact, *ma'at* justified the divisions.

Class-structured societies seem to have facilitated organizational integration and efficiency in all preindustrial civilizations, perhaps by making many decisions and activities highly predictable and by suppressing competition. Yet Egypt had a distinctive and unique form of social stratification. Slavery, for example, seems to have been different in Egypt. The concept of "slavery" is, of course, fundamental to

Marxist analyses of precapitalist social change, and some Marxists point to a word that can be read as "slave" in the earliest Egyptian documents (Vinogradov 1991:151). But as Emily Teeter notes (personal communication, 1995), the term *hm,* which is later used to denote slave, is a compound of priestly titles, *hm ntr* (literally, servant of the god), which had nothing to do with being free or unfree but referred instead to duty. So too the term *bɔk,* later used for slave, had different meanings, such as free retainer. Texts indicate that some people were in some ways legally tied to land in the early Old Kingdom, but they were not enslaved in the sense of being chattel who could be transferred without regard to their ties to land.

There seems to be some evidence for slavery of certain forms in the Sixth Dynasty, and a form of slavery existed by the late Middle Kingdom (Dynasty 13). The evidence comes from a text that lists seventy-nine slaves, thirty-three of whom have Egyptian names (Hayes 1955). Teeter notes that this text is particularly interesting because one side of it deals with a group of adults and children whose ownership (in the form of a deed of gift) is confirmed by a woman named Senebtisi (personal communication). The people, who belonged to her dead husband, are called *hmt.* They were apparently free-born, low-class Egyptians who were thrown into prison for evading the government corvée and then transferred to private family ownership. This transfer from the penal system to private ownership seems to have continued in the New Kingdom. Slaves acquired through military conquests are a common feature of most of the New Kingdom era.

In general, Egyptian slavery does not seem to have involved the enslavement for debt that became a potent factor in other societies. Moreover, slavery, as such, was seen as being of dubious morality: dedicatory inscriptions for royalty occasionally boasted of not having enslaved a single person. Considered in terms of the behavior and products of Egyptian society, however, we might apply the term *slave* to people taxed heavily or forced to labor on public construction projects, but there is no evidence that any of these forms of slavery created an underclass or proletariat in conflict with their oppressors.

The issue of the economic relationships embedded in ancient Egyptian culture is highly complex. The palace economy and the monumental mortuary cults created an enormous flow of exotic items whose labor costs were real and impressive but whose capital value must be regarded as largely symbolic—although a potent mechanism of social control, nevertheless (Joffe n.d.; Trigger 1990a). The majority of Egyptians in the Pharaonic age lived in a complex web of economic relationships that extended from the highest levels of the state, in the form of corvée labor performed by the ordinary populace, to small-scale exchange within the community in food and other commodities.

Observations on the Determinants and Evolutionary Trajectory of Egyptian Culture History

No epistemological position is easier to recommend than a holistic, synthetic, multilevel one in which all forms of inquiry and varieties of "knowledge" are equally valued, and Egypt seems the perfect illustration of the virtues of this approach. Even a Jungian analysis of Egyptian ideology offers some unexpected insights (Rice 1990:269–296). And anyone who aspires to a comprehensive understanding of the Egyptian past must master a wide range of data, from the hydrodynamics of Nile flood basins to the subtleties of the concept of *ma'at.* Amid all this multidisciplinary coherence and amity, however, remain some thorny problems of method, theory, and interpretation (see, for example, the discussion in volume 22 of *The Norwegian Archaeological Review* [1989]).

Contemporary scholars agree on few epistemological issues, but they are nearly unanimous in their view that the traditional concepts of cultural ecology and cultural evolution, which have long formed the foundations for comparative analyses of early civilizations, are extremely limited in their power to explain the past. There are many reasons for this rejectionist-revisionist climate. With regard to the notion of a theory of "cultural evolution," many scholars associate this term with the logical weaknesses of the functionalist arguments that comprise most cultural ecological and cultural evolutionary "explanations," and they also associate this term with the excesses of sociobiology and the tautologies and explanatory sterility of a direct analogy with Darwinian evolution.

On the other hand, the focus in contemporary anthropological archaeology on interpretations of power relationships, the nature of capital, and other sociological variables has been questioned by several scholars on a variety of grounds (e.g., Dunnell 1992). They argue that any analysis of the intentions of long-dead people (such as those who owned and administered the early Egyptian state) is beyond the bounds of empirical science because the intentions have no empirical existence and because they are known primarily from texts which do not reflect an accurate understanding of the physical and cultural world or may have been pure propaganda. In any case, these intentions are irrelevant to a science of the material record of the past, in that what actually happened—as is reflected in the material record—is what matters.

For most scholars of Egyptian antiquity, however, whether a particular form of inquiry is science, strictly speaking, is relatively unimportant. What is sought is a synthetic understanding of the past. To use Egypt as an example, it would be difficult to understand the changing settlement patterns of the Egyptian Delta in the early Pharaonic era without referring to the texts where various pharaohs record that they provided the money (in the form of tax breaks) to build settlements in the Delta, and they did so to protect their frontiers, to generate income to support religious cults, and for other eminently understandable reasons. These reasons may not constitute a scientific explanation, but they increase our comprehension of this segment of Egypt's past, as do the varying interpretations of ambiguous documents like the Narmer Palette.

However, a statistical analysis of changes in artifact styles in the Nile Valley and Delta showing the rate, direction, and intensity of the wave of homogenization of ceramic styles during this formative era would have a different scientific standing than that, for example, of the various interpretations of the Narmer Palette. Yet statistical evaluations of empirically measurable data (changing frequencies of artifact styles, for example) are often given little analytical importance unless they are linked to sociological variables (e.g., Shanks and Tilley 1989).

I have argued elsewhere that evolutionary theory may provide another way of analyzing the past, one that does not conflict with traditional and "postprocessual" methods of interpretation and may in fact complement them (Wenke 1981, 1991). The Egyptian pyramids provide a convenient example. We know nothing about the builders' motives because we have found no texts concerning them. Pyramid construction (and probably rates of per capita investments in monumental architecture) appears to have reached a peak at the critical formative point where centralized authority in Egypt had just succeeded in suppressing provincial autonomy. Once the elements of central-

ized government were in place, however, pyramid construction began to decrease dramatically, and artifacts lost most of their regional variation. It is also possible that the decline in pyramid construction coincided with the appearance of administrative and technical methods to integrate agricultural and craft production under the increasingly efficient control of the central government.

One might take the view that the rapid decline in pyramid construction toward the end of the third millennium B.C. was a reflection of what should be the true focus of analysis—the inferred power relations that may initially have been validated and reinforced by the expropriation of much labor and material which, in later periods, were validated and reinforced through other means (Trigger 1990a). The Temple at Karnak, for example, was built much later, but it required labor and materials on a scale that equaled the larger pyramids. Alternatively, one might view these data in an evolutionary context: at the same time the pyramids became a national focus of Egypt, the ceramics also changed from highly stylized, hand-painted, regionally specific forms to the rather drab, utilitarian, nationally distributed wares that were used almost exclusively for the remainder of the Pharaonic era (along with many highly decorated ceramics in later periods [Bourriau 1981]). Egypt, it should be noted, is not the only example of these kinds of changes. Two of the ugliest but most common pottery types ever produced in the ancient world were the Mesopotamian beveled-rim bowl and the Egyptian bread mold. In both areas, just as the first state societies were maturing, pottery styles, which had for the most part been highly and individually decorated, became simple, uniform, and utilitarian. Every Uruk-period site is littered with beveled-rim bowls; every Old Kingdom site is similarly strewn with bread molds, and the vessels look so much alike from one site to another that they were probably made through some form of mass production. If Egypt was a monolithic, relatively static society that valued conservatism and tradition, why was there such a radical change in something as obvious as pyramid construction and as basic as everyday ceramics?

Dunnell has argued that "waste," in the form of elaborate stylistic displays, including pyramid construction and highly stylized ceramic decoration, tends to diminish in cultural systems as major increases in carrying capacity occur, because these "wasteful" aspects of cultures are, in part, population-control mechanisms (1980, 1992, personal communication). He points to the "drab" Mesolithic period that followed the late Pleistocene cultures in Europe, to the decline of the Hopewell mound complexes and cults, and to other changes in the amount and form of societal investment in "waste," as new crops, new technologies, or new methods of organizing and integrating economic activities were fixed in evolutionary sequences.

Similarly, in all complex systemic entities, from the human body to ancient states, there are circumstances in which it is important that functional variability be suppressed. The great advantages of uniformity in various types of commodity production in industrial economies have long been recognized, and they apply to some extent to preindustrial commodities as well. It may, for example, have been advantageous for ancient states to reduce variability in such minor elements as pottery production and decoration for many reasons, reasons that go well beyond population control. After all, ceramic styles have long been known to represent "grammars" that reflect personal identities and ethnic affiliations. A look at the current world situation shows the evolutionary advantages of mechanisms that suppress expressions of ethnic identity (Bosnia-Herzegovina vis-à-vis Japan being a current object lesson on this point). We will probably never know the extent to which ethnic differences, wars, and conflict existed in Old Kingdom Egypt. But in Old Kingdom Egypt, as in all states, there is selective advantage to the suppression of potentially divisive expressions of individual and corporate distinctiveness, including such minor expressions as regional pottery styles, not to mention the economies of scale achieved by reducing pottery production to a limited range of vessels to meet predictable needs efficiently.

While such interpretations may appear to be simple, "functionalist" explanations and heir to all the ills these entail (e.g., equifinality), one could argue that this is not necessarily the case (R. N. Adams 1981; Dunnell 1980, 1992; Rindos 1984). Cultures, after all, don't *have* to evolve, and many did not. It is not even necessary to discuss these kinds of changes in terms of logical, positivistic "causes" or to obscure the unique aspects of individual ancient cultures.

Gould's celebration of the improbable, unpredictable, unique course of every evolutionary history demonstrates the need, when applying evolutionary principles to specific cases, to resist the notions of teleology that are so much a part of the literature on early civilizations (1989).

One of the fastest growing fields in research in many sciences, from biology to economics, concerns the "emergent" properties of complex systems. A wide range of complex systems, from colonies of bacteria to the international economic systems, appear to have inherent self-organizing potential. Attempts to analyze such systems, including ancient civilizations, on the basis of concepts and principles that link these many different kinds of systems may, at first glance, seem reminiscent of the "systems theory" popular in the archaeology of the 1970s, and subject to many of the same perceived faults (e.g., that systems theory was in essence a tautology and incapable of explaining change). Yet genuine advances in some sciences appear to have been made on the basis of contemporary theories about emergent properties and complex systems (reviewed in Waldrop 1992).

Moreover, as noted above, such evolutionary interpretations do not compete with, nor are they superseded by, Marxist or "postprocessual" analyses based on inferred intentions and sociopolitical relationships. We gain the best understanding of the past through a combination of archaeological excavation, ancient texts, and the constructs of modern social science, including assumptions about goal-directed behavior and applications of economic models. Neither would I dismiss in its entirety the Critical Postprocessual Archaeology inspired by Foucault (e.g., 1986) and Derrida (e.g., 1976). Despite the cogent critiques to which they have been subjected (Watson 1990; Renfrew 1989), such studies raise important issues (Trigger 1983b, 1989b, 1993). What I am suggesting is that evolutionary theory is not "cultural evolution," not simply a weak analogy to Darwinian theory, and not "biology" in any meaningful sense. Indeed, it has little to do with "sociobiology," as applied to complex cultures (Lewontin 1979), and it may offer an analytical perspective on archaeological problems that has been undeservedly neglected.

4

Early City-States in South Asia

Comparing the Harappan Phase and Early Historic Period

During the early to mid-third millennium B.C., the Harappan phase of the Indus Valley Tradition of Pakistan and western India developed one of the most extensive urban cultures in the Old World (Kenoyer 1991a; Shaffer 1991). Excavations have been carried out at numerous sites during the past seventy-five years and are still going on at the largest of the urban centers as well as at smaller regional settlements. While considerable advances are being made in understanding the origins and character of the Indus Valley Tradition through multidisciplinary archaeological research, no bilingual tablets or lengthy texts have yet been discovered, and the Indus Valley writing system remains undeciphered. The lack of ancient chronologies, king lists, economic texts, and sociopolitical and religious documents have made it difficult to resolve important questions about the time frame for the transition from pre-urban to urban forms and the nature of the political organization of these cities.

The degree to which these Harappan cities were integrated politically, socioeconomically, and ideologically is the focus of current research at three of the major cities.[1] Archaeological excavations and numerous problem-oriented studies, ranging from the analysis of architectural and craft technologies to subsistence, are providing scholars with considerable new data for reconstructing the growth and character of Harappan cities.[2]

This chapter will focus on new discoveries and interpretations about the physical structure and growth of three major Harappan-phase urban centers and how the organization of these cities can be correlated with general models of social and political organization. The first section will summarize the geographical context and chronology of the Indus Valley Tradition and provide some background on settlement patterns and urban organization. Following this is a discussion of the types of city-states represented in ancient Indian literature during the Early Historic period (600–300 B.C.). The final section focuses on the political organization of Harappan-phase cities and examines the applicability of the city-state model to this initial urbanism in South Asia.

Geographical Setting of the Indus Valley Tradition

A brief outline of the geographical setting of the Indus Valley Tradition and its cities is essential for understanding the environmental context for the development of early state-level society (Fig. 4.1). During the

JONATHAN MARK KENOYER

51

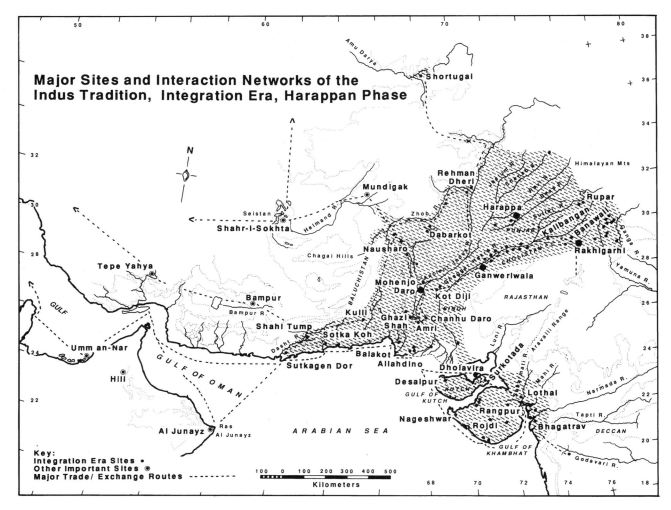

Major Sites and Interaction Networks of the Indus Tradition, Integration Era, Harappan Phase

Figure 4.1. Major sites and interaction networks of the Indus Valley Tradition.

mid-third millennium B.C., the greater Indus Valley was watered by two major river systems, the ancient Indus River and the now-dry Ghaggar-Hakra River (Flam 1986, 1991; Lambrick 1964). This second river is generally agreed to be the legendary Saraswati River, known from Vedic and later Sanskrit texts (Wilhemy 1969). Flowing parallel to each other, the rivers created a wide floodplain with extensive areas for grazing and agriculture. Surveys along the dry bed of the Ghaggar-Hakra indicate that it supported numerous settlements, including two extremely large cities, Ganweriwala and Rakhigarhi, comparable in size to the excavated sites of Mohenjo-daro and Harappa (Mughal 1990c, 1991). This archaeological data supports the textual information that proclaims the ancient Saraswati as a great river with many populous settlements along its course.

The combined alluvial plains of these two rivers are divided into two distinct regions, the Punjab (land of five rivers) in the north and Sindh in the south. To the northeast, the relatively flat plains of the Punjab merge into the drainage system of the modern Yamuna and Ganga rivers to the east, where numerous Harappan-phase settlements have been discovered.

The regions controlled by the cities of the Indus and Ghaggar-Hakra rivers were previously thought to have been limited to the floodplains, but current research indicates that there were numerous Harappan-phase settlements in the highlands to the west (Besenval 1992; Mughal 1992). Southeast of the combined delta of the two rivers lies the region of Kutch and the larger peninsula of Saurashtra, separated from the Indian subcontinent by the estuaries and shallow bays of the Rann of Kutch. Both regions appear to have been insular during the Harappan phase. A fifth major city of the Indus Valley Tradition, Dholavira, situated on a small island that commands access to the regions of Kutch and Saurashtra, has been recently excavated.

On either side of the alluvial plain were regions with localized agricultural and grazing land, as well as resource areas for important raw materials such as minerals and metals needed to supply the specialized industries of the cities. To the west were the piedmont and highland zones of Baluchistan and Afghanistan. In the east, the mineral-rich region of the Aravalli Mountains stretched from north to south, parallel to the Ghaggar-Hakra. Along the southern periphery, the rich marine coast extended from the Makran in the west across the delta to the coast of Gujarat. The total area encompassed during the Harappan phase was between 650,000 and 800,000 square kilometers (Kenoyer 1991a).

Two different weather systems dominated this vast geographical region, a winter cyclonic system in the western highlands and a summer monsoon system in the peninsular areas (Snead 1968). Studies of global climatic fluctuation do not support claims of significant climatic changes during the period of the Indus cities, although there is some evidence for a stronger summer monsoon and more seasonal fluctuation of temperatures from 7000 to 5000 B.C. (prior to the rise of cities; Kutzbach and COHMAP Members 1988:1049–1050). It appears that the overall climate has remained the same since at least 7000 B.C. (Raikes and Dyson 1961), which covers the period of the Indus Valley Tradition and the subsequent phases of the Indo-Gangetic Tradition. Any localized shifts in rainfall would have resulted from short-term climatic fluctuations in the two dominant weather systems. Documented environmental changes can be attributed to changing river-flow patterns and erosion from human activities, including overgrazing, deforestation, and irrigation (Misra 1984; Raikes and Dyson 1961).

The environmental and geographical context in which the first urban centers of the Indus Valley Tradition developed was vast and included diverse ecosystems juxtaposed in complementary patterns. Four large inland cities and numerous smaller regional towns dominated the floodplains of the major river systems as well as the highland regions to the west (most of Pakistan and northwestern India), while a fifth city and associated towns dominated the insular and coastal regions of what is now known as Kutch and Gujarat in western India.

Table 4.1

Selected Chronology of the Indus and Indo-Gangetic Traditions

Archaeological/Historical Events	General Dates
"Mesolithic" transition	10,000–6500 B.C.
Indus Valley Tradition	
Early Food-Producing Era, Neolithic/ Chalcolithic	ca. 6500–5000 B.C.
Regionalization Era, Early Harappan Phase	ca. 5000–2600 B.C.
Integration Era, Harappan Phase	2600–1900 B.C.
Localization Era, late Harappan Phase	1900–1300 B.C.
Post-Indus or Indo-Gangetic Tradition	
Regionalization Era	
Painted Grey Ware	+1200–800 B.C.
Northern Black Polished Ware	(?700) 500–300 B.C.
Early Historic Period begins ca. 600 B.C.	
Buddha (Siddartha Gautama)	563–483 B.C. (or 440–360 B.C.)
Panini (Sanskrit grammartian)	ca. 500–400 B.C.
Alexander of Macedon receives "submission" and becomes the "ally" of Ambhi, King of Taxila	326 B.C.
Integration Era	
Mauryan Empire	
Chandragupta Maurya	?317–298 B.C.
Kautilya (Minister of Chandragupta, possible author of *Arthashastra*)	
Bindusara	298–274 B.C.
Ashoka	274–232 B.C.

Chronology

On the basis of radiometric assays from a wide range of sites covering most of the region, the general chronology of the Indus Valley Tradition is firmly dated (Table 4.1). The earliest date for the rise of large urban centers is around 2600 B.C. during the Harappan phase, but there is some evidence for the presence of multitiered settlement patterns during the preceding Early Harappan phase (Mughal 1991), specifically the period from approximately 3300–2600 B.C. While most of the literature has emphasized the abandonment of cities at the end of the Harappan phase (1900 B.C.), current research at Harappa and other sites suggests that much of the greater Indus Valley continued to be dominated by localized polities with fairly large settlements (Kenoyer 1991b, 1994). Late Harappan settlements persisted until at least 1300 B.C., and there is no clear break in Gujarat or in the Ganga-Yamuna region between Late Harappan and subsequent cultural developments.

Some scholars feel that the transition from the Early Harappan to the Harappan phase occurred over 100–150 years (Jansen 1991, 1993; Possehl 1990). Others hold that it was a more gradual process over a longer period of time (Kenoyer 1991a, 1991b, 1994; Mughal 1990a, 1991), a view supported by recent excavations at Harappa, the only large urban center that has been extensively excavated. Preliminary reports from excavations at Dholavira in Kutch suggest that this site might also have begun its regional importance just prior to the Harappan phase (Bisht 1989, 1990), but the chronology and the cultural/stratigraphic sequence are not fully published. No Early Harappan-phase settlement has been established at Mohenjo-daro because there have been no excavations in the waterlogged lowest levels of the site. However, this site too will probably reveal an earlier phase of incipient urban development.

The other two large sites, Ganweriwala and Rakhigarhi, have not been excavated, but numerous Early Harappan sites (regionally identified as Kot Dijian, Sothi, or Hakra cultures) have been located in their hinterlands, suggesting that they too may have begun as regional centers during the Early Harappan phase and then gradually developed into major urban centers during the subsequent Harappan phase. When excavations are carried out at these sites, they will provide important comparative data for understanding whether the transition to major urban centers was gradual at all the settlements or only at Harappa. It would not be surprising to find that the transition occurred at different rates in the different environmental and geographical contexts of the vast Indus and Ghaggar-Hakra river systems.

Settlement Patterns

The organization and function of Harappan-phase cities is critical to understanding their political and economic role in specific geographical regions (Fig. 4.1). They represent the largest settlements within a multitiered settlement system, and their location can be correlated to a strategic position in terms of geographical and economic dominance.

At present it is possible to identify five settlements of greater than 50 hectares—Mohenjo-daro (+200 ha), Harappa (+150 ha), Ganweriwala and Rakhigarhi (+80 ha), and Dholavira (100 ha). The four inland centers are located at approximately equivalent distances in a zigzag pattern that covers the northern

Table 4.2

Distances between the Major Urban Centers

| Cities | Total Area (hectares) | Distances to Other Cities | | Hinterland (km²) |
		Cities	km	
Rakhigarhi (RKG)	+80	RKG–HAR	350	106,225
		RKG–GNW	407	
Harappa (HAR)	+150	HAR–GNW	280	128,800
Mohenjo-daro (MD)	+250	MD–GNW	308	169,260
		MD–HAR	570	
Ganweriwala (GNW)	+80	GNW–DLV	558	108,280
Dholavira (DLV)	100	DLV–MD	448	?
		DLV–GNW	523	

Ghaggar-Hakra and Gangetic plain, the Punjab, Cholistan, and Sindh (Table 4.2; Mughal 1991; Possehl 1990). Because we do not know how much of each city was occupied at a specific time, it is not possible to accurately estimate the population, although some scholars have proposed numbers ranging around 30,000–40,000 (e.g., Fairservis 1975).

The hinterland controlled by each city is difficult to estimate due to the lack of extensive regional studies, which have been hindered by the proximity of four of the largest cities to strategic international borders. A rough estimate of the hinterland for each of the inland cities can be derived by arbitrarily defining borders at a halfway mark between each of two or three cities and eliminating uninhabitable areas. On the basis of such calculations, the hinterland of each of the largest cities would range from approximately 100,000 to 170,000 square kilometers (Table 4.2).

Mohenjo-daro is located on a Pleistocene ridge that sits like an island in the floodplain of the Indus River. It is thought that the Indus flowed to the west of the site during the Harappan phase (Flam 1981), and this would have put Mohenjo-daro in a central position between the two river valleys, where it dominated trade routes leading to the passes in the Bolan Valley to the west and the north-south trade from the coast near modern Karachi.

Harappa is likewise situated on a ridge between the Ravi River and the modern Sutlej River. The Sutlej was probably captured by the Beas River, which in the past would have flowed east of Harappa. The Sutlej would have had a different watershed and joined the Ghaggar-Hakra system. Harappa would have dominated north-south movement along the river floodplains leading from Mohenjo-daro to the northwestern passes and east-west trade toward the resource areas of modern Rajasthan.

Rakhigarhi and Ganweriwala appear to have been located along the Ghaggar-Hakra (ancient Saraswati) River system, and, in addition to dominating the vast agricultural lands of this river, they would have controlled the movement of resources from the eastern desert regions and funneled goods upriver from the Rann of Kutch. Each of the inland cities was surrounded by a floodplain that had agricultural and grazing land, abundant wild game and fish, and considerable wild plant resources. In the absence of extensive irrigation systems, this diverse resource base and the economic networks linking the cities to regional production centers are thought to have been important in the rise and survival of such large cities (Kenoyer 1991a; Weber 1992).

The fifth site, Dholavira, was situated on an island in the Rann of Kutch, which has some alluvial patches that could have been cultivated and extensive grasslands that would have been suitable for grazing after the annual monsoon rains. Although the island has good underground water in sandstone aquifers, the extensive system of stone drains on the site were probably needed to catch and direct rainwater to reservoirs inside and at the edge of the city. The major support for the population probably derived from trade with Kutch, Saurashtra, and the core areas of the Indus Valley to the north. The island could have monitored shipping of raw materials and subsistence items between these regions, and it may also have had a role in external trade to the Arabian Gulf.

In contrast to the equidistant spacing of the major urban centers (except for the insular site of Dholavira), the distances from the major urban centers to smaller regional centers and rural settlements vary considerably (Fig. 4.1) and may reflect irregular networks that were defined by accessibility along rivers or overland routes as well as sociopolitical alliances.

The other levels of settlements range in size from 1–5 hectares, 5–10 hectares, and 10–50 hectares. Sites of less than 1 hectare are thought to reflect the temporary occupations characteristic of nomadic pastoralists or itinerant artisans. A final category of sites

invisible archaeologically would be communities that live on boats; they were essential for riverine commerce and communication (Kenoyer 1991a).

Although the size of settlements varies considerably and the settlements are scattered over a vast geographical area, the presence of distinctive seals with writing, chert weights for commerce and taxation, and a wide range of other artifacts indicate that the communities living in these settlements were integrated into a single cultural system. This integration would have been reinforced by the political, economic, and ideological dominance of the five major urban centers and their regional centers.

Harappan-Phase Urban Organization

The Harappan-phase cities have been featured in most anthropology and archaeology textbooks for decades, but the generalizations popularized by Piggott (1952) and Wheeler (1968) have become so distorted that it is necessary to correct some of the misconceptions.

Rather than a standard division of the cities into a high western "citadel" and a lower town to the east, each city is made up of a series of mounds oriented in different directions. Harappa (Fig. 4.2) and Mohenjo-daro (Fig. 4.3) both have a high rectangular mound on the west and extensive mounds to the north, south, and east. At Mohenjo-daro the other mounds are significantly lower, but at Harappa two of the eastern mounds (Mound E and the modern Harappa town) are almost as high as the western mound (Mound AB), and there are extensive low mounds to the west of Mound AB. At Dholavira (Fig. 4.4) there is a single walled mound that is internally subdivided into three or four walled sectors, which is highest in the southern sector, rather than the western sector, as at Mohenjo-daro and Harappa. To the west and northwest, outside the walled mound, are scattered low mounds with remains of Harappan houses that represent suburban areas of the city (Bisht 1989).

In all three cities, each mounded area or sector has a distinct layout of streets that can be characterized as an irregular grid network. Even though they are aligned in the same basic direction, the street plans for each mound at Harappa represent different episodes of city development. At Mohenjo-daro, where considerable documentation is available for different sectors of the city, there are significant differences in street alignment between the citadel and the lower

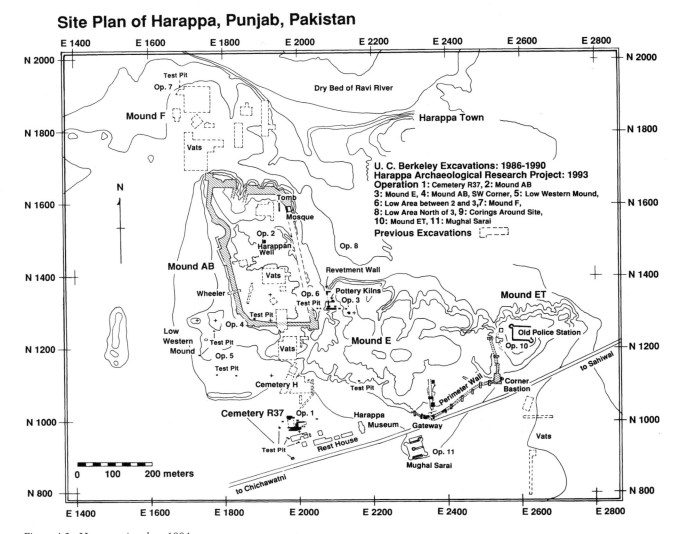

Figure 4.2. Harappa site plan, 1994.

town. Furthermore, changes in the alignment of streets and houses over time probably reflect gradual changes in the cardinal reference points (e.g., stellar east-west projections) used by the architects (Jansen 1978, 1980).

It had been assumed that the various mounds at Mohenjo-daro and Harappa were contemporaneous and that each city was divided into distinct functional sectors, the western mounds being administrative centers and the lower mounds representing habitation and industrial areas for the common populace. This simplistic interpretation is no longer supported by the available evidence, which indicates shifting centers of power within the city and the presence of habitation and industrial areas in each of the major mounds (Kenoyer 1991b; Pracchia et al. 1985; Vidale 1990). This irregular and dynamic process of city growth is

well documented in historical cities throughout the world and should not be discounted when looking at the first cities. When seen from this perspective, the various mounds that make up each of the Harappan cities come to have a very different significance, possibly reflecting changing centers of power among ruling elites and merchants.

City Walls and Foundation Platforms

The presence of walls around specific mounds and even entire settlements is significant for interpreting the role of different sectors of the city or of regional centers scattered around the larger cities. At present there is considerable debate about the function of these mud-brick structures (Jansen 1989; Kenoyer 1991b); some appear to have been freestanding walls

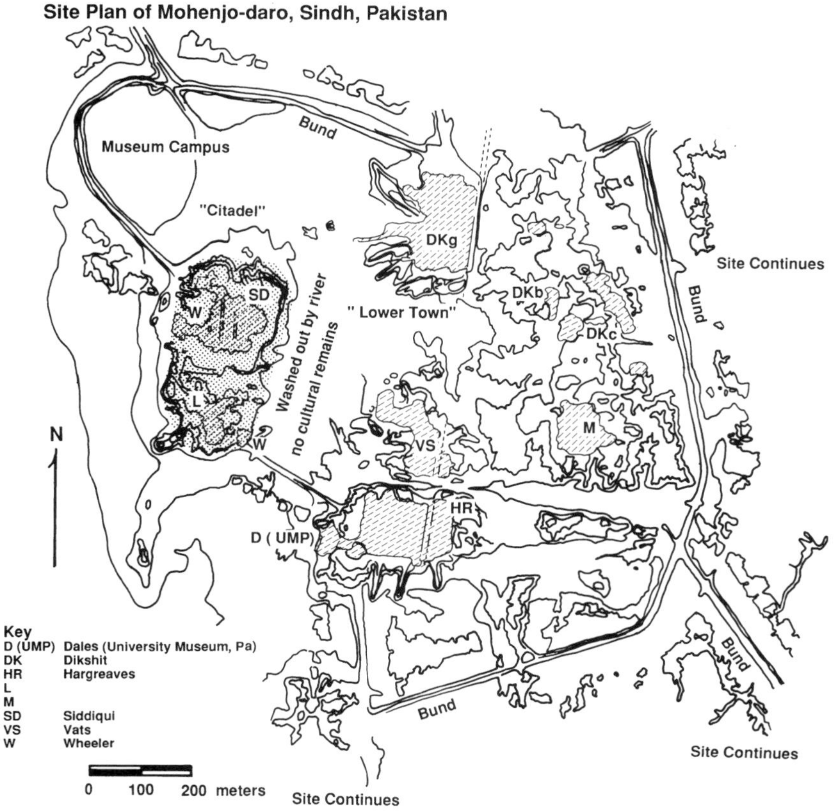

Site Plan of Mohenjo-daro, Sindh, Pakistan

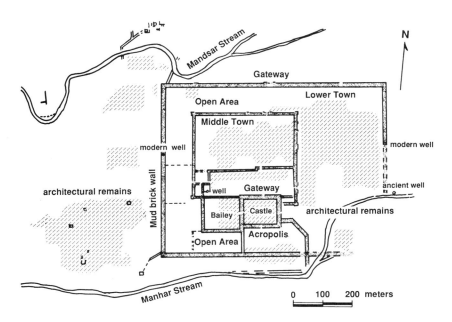

Bund

Museum Campus

"Citadel"

Site Continues

DKg

"Lower Town"

DKb

Washed out by river
no cultural remains

DKc

N

SD
W
L
W

M

VS

HR

D (UMP)

Bund

Bund

Key
D (UMP) Dales (University Museum, Pa)
DK   Dikshit
HR   Hargreaves
L
M
SD   Siddiqui
VS   Vats
W   Wheeler

0   100   200 meters

Site Continues

Site Continues

Figure 4.3. Mohenjo-daro site plan.
After Jansen (1984b:figure 8.2).

Site Plan of Dholavira, Gujarat, India

Mandsar Stream

N

Gateway

Open Area

Lower Town

Middle Town

modern well

modern well

Mud brick wall

well

Gateway

ancient well

architectural remains

Bailey   Castle

architectural remains

Open Area

Acropolis

Manhar Stream

0   100   200 meters

Figure 4.4. Dholavira site plan. After
Bisht (1989).

associated with large brick gateways, while others may have functioned primarily as revetments or foundation platforms.

The presence of massive walls around Harappa was noted by the earliest excavators (Vats 1940), but it was not until Wheeler's excavations at Harappa and Mohenjo-daro that the topic of walls became critical. Wheeler found a massive mud-brick wall around Mound AB at Harappa, which he labeled defensive (Wheeler 1947). At Mohenjo-daro he found a similar wall and gateway around the "citadel" mound (Wheeler 1972). Although Mackay tried to locate a wall around the Lower City at Mohenjo-daro, he was unsuccessful because of the high water table (Mackay 1938).

Massive mud-brick walls were subsequently identified at almost all the smaller sites—Lothal, Kalibangan, Surkotada, Sutkagendor (Wheeler 1972), Dholavira (Bisht 1989), Nausharo (Jarrige 1988), and Rehman Dheri (Durrani 1988; Durrani et al. 1991). With the exception of Kalibangan, these walled settlements consisted of a single outer wall; in some cases there was an internal dividing wall as well. At Kalibangan, a "citadel" in the west was subdivided into two sectors, while a large "lower town" in the east was surrounded by a single wall (Lal 1979; Thapar 1975).

These discoveries made it appear as if the larger sites had a walled citadel and an open lower town, while at the smaller sites, the entire city was walled. The most common interpretation of this pattern was that a ruling elite lived in defensive and administrative isolation, and the hinterland was dotted with smaller walled settlements or colonies (Wheeler 1972). This interpretation is proving incorrect at both Harappa and Mohenjo-daro. At Harappa, in addition to the well-known wall around Mound AB, there is evidence of a massive mud-brick wall around three sides of Mound E and along the southern edge of Mound ET. Traces of what appear to be a mud-brick wall have also been noted to the north of Mound F (Dales and Kenoyer 1993; Meadow and Kenoyer 1994), indicating that each of the major mounds might have been enclosed by mud-brick walls.

At Mohenjo-daro, research by a German and Italian team revealed the presence of a massive mud-brick platform/wall around the citadel mound (Jansen 1989) and a similar mud-brick structure along the southern edge of the Hr Area in the lower town (Leonardi 1988). The two mud-brick platform/walls are almost identical in construction and size to the city walls found around Mound E and Mound ET at Harappa. If they are walls rather than foundation platforms, as suggested by Jansen (Jansen 1987, 1989), then each of the major mounds at Mohenjo-daro would have been a separate entity encircled by massive mud-brick walls, as was the case at Harappa.

Harappa Site Plan and City Organization

Harappa is composed of several mounded areas that have different orientations and shapes (Fig. 4.2). The north-south parallelogram of Mound AB covers approximately 7 hectares and rises some 6–8 meters above the surrounding plain. To the north is a lower area, Mound F, covering approximately 10 hectares. Southeast of Mound AB is a long east-west mound that is over 13 hectares in area and, at its highest point, some 7 meters above the plain. To the east is a lower mound, Mound ET (Old Police Station Mound), which covers approximately 5.5 hectares. North of Mound E and ET is the modern town of Harappa, which is built on a mound of more than 20 hectares; its north-central portion is almost as high as Mound E and Mound AB (Fig. 4.2).

Mound AB is surrounded by a well-defined mud-brick wall or revetment that is more than 13.7 meters wide at the base and tapers to the top level of the mound on all but its eastern side. Mound AB has at least two sets of gateways, one in the west and one in the north. The mud-brick walls around Mound E are smaller, ranging from 4.5 to 9 meters wide, and they appear to have functioned as revetments along the western and eastern edges of the mound. They were freestanding along the southern perimeter. In the 1990 excavations, an impressive baked-brick gateway was found at the center of the southern wall (Kenoyer 1991b), and in 1994 a second gateway was discovered at the juncture of Mound E and Mound ET. The freestanding mud-brick wall continues along the southern perimeter of Mound ET, but further excavations are needed to determine if it encircles the mound. In 1997 traces of a mud-brick city wall were found along the north edge of Mound F, indicating that this suburb of Mound AB was also enclosed by a mud-brick wall.

Identical types of ceramics, figurines, inscribed seals, and terra-cotta and faience tablets (made from the same mold) have been found at the four major excavated mounds—E, ET, AB, and F. These artifacts demonstrate that the mounds were inhabited contemporaneously during the Harappan phase, but on the basis of deep stratigraphic sequences, it is clear that they were not all founded at the same time and that they grew at different rates.

Based on the most recent excavations in 1996 and 1997, the earliest settlement appears to have been spread out between the northern part of Mound AB and the northwestern corner of Mound E, dating from the Early Harappan period (3300 B.C.) (Period 1 and 2). This settlement gradually became larger and these areas continued to be inhabited through the Harappan (Period 3) and Late Harappan (Period 4 and 5) Phases (Kenoyer 1991b). The southern part of Mound AB and the eastern portion of Mound E appear to have been established later, at the end of the Early Harappan Phase or possibly at the beginning of the Harappan Phase (2600 B.C.). Mound ET is a suburb of Mound E and grew up outside of the eastern city wall of Mound E. Eventually it too was encircled by a massive mud-brick wall and a southern gateway was established. The lowest levels of Mound ET reveal habitation during the latest part of the Early Harappa (Period 2) and then it continued to be inhabited throughout the Harappan and Late Harappan Phases. In much the same way, Mound F appears to be a northern suburb of Mound AB that was founded slightly later than the other three mounds, but all were inhabited contemporaneously at the height of the Harappan phase (around 2000 B.C.). The area of modern Harappa also appears to have been occupied during the height of the Harappan phase and during the Late Harappan phase, but until excavations can be carried out in the core area, we will not be able to determine when this area was first inhabited.

The city wall and gateways around both Mound E and ET reveal three major episodes of rebuilding and repair that appear to cover the 700 years of the Harappan phase. A parallel sequence of repeated repairs and rebuilding was identified by Wheeler for Mound AB (1947). Both Mound AB and E/ET had gateways that led into the mound, but there is no evidence of a causeway or road that went from one mound to the other.

Studies are currently under way to correlate the wall repairs of the two mounds to determine if the repairs occurred simultaneously or at alternating times. If the repairs were undertaken simultaneously, it would suggest that the same civic authority maintained both walled mounds and that the city as a whole experienced cycles of growth and decay. An alternating sequence of repairs, however, would indicate that the mounds developed in a contrasting and competitive pattern, where one was being maintained

and developed while the other was falling into disrepair. The continuous and, at times, massive accumulations of garbage during phases of disrepair suggests that both mounds continued to be occupied by significant populations, even though one mound may have been better maintained at any one time.

The contemporaneity of these walled mounds raises the question of their function. Only 40 meters separates the high-walled northwestern corner of Mound E and the equally high-walled southeastern corner of Mound AB. At this distance it is possible to stand on one mound and shout greetings or insults to someone on the other mound. In between the two mounds is an eroded slope with traces of an open drain or road surface.

Three basic functions, which are not mutually exclusive, can be suggested for the walls at Harappa: military defense, flood protection, and economic/political control. If the walls surrounding the mounds were built for defense, then we should expect to see some evidence for conflict, such as weapons, projectiles, and burned or damaged structures. So far, no evidence of that nature has been found. The second possible function is protection from flooding, but the only ancient damage to the walls appears to derive exclusively from seasonal weathering and rainwater erosion. Flood deposits have been found at the site, but they are limited to the lower-lying habitation areas north of Mound E. Similar layers of alluvium have been found covering vast low-lying habitation areas at Mohenjo-daro, so it would appear that, while periodic flooding occurred at these sites, it did not erode or undermine the massive city walls. The remaining interpretation for the function of the walls is economic/political control. Evidence for this is less direct and is based on the presence of administrative and public buildings; workshops for specialized crafts; administrative devices such as seals, sealings, and weights; and distinctive patterns of elite artifacts such as ornaments, ceramics, and residences.

The generally poor preservation of architecture at Harappa has made it difficult to identify house plans and to define the function of specific buildings. The only large building found in excavations by Vats (1940) is the so-called Granary, located on Mound F, which is built on a massive mud-brick foundation (50 by 40 meters) that would have supported a substantial superstructure—a palace or temples, public meeting place, or public storeroom. Extensive excavations on the higher Mound AB to the south have not revealed any comparable administrative or public structures, and only limited areas have been exposed on Mound E and Mound ET. Because of the nature of the excavations and the poor preservation, architectural comparisons cannot be made between the mounds at Harappa. Mohenjo-daro and Dholavira, on the other hand, do have the appropriate architectural data and are discussed below.

Other types of evidence for economic and political control at Harappa are seen in the fluctuations in maintenance of city drains, walls, and gateways; the distribution of workshops and industrial areas; and artifact patterning. Each of the major excavated areas in Mounds AB, F, E, and ET reveal sequential phases of city maintenance and neglect of drains and street plans. Debris from workshops and industrial areas, many of which produced similar types of artifacts, have been located on all four mounds (Kenoyer 1991b). Important evidence for commercial or ritual interaction between communities on each mound is seen in the common types of ceramics, figurines, ornaments, and—most important—the common occurrence of sealings made from the same mold (Meadow and Kenoyer 1994). The fact that molded tablets with script and ritual motifs made from the same seal have been found on all four mounds indicates not only their contemporaneity but also commercial and/or ritual interactions between the inhabitants of these distinct sectors of the city. These different types of data suggest that, although the mounds were separated by walls and access was controlled by gateways, the sectors were integrated into a single large city.

Mohenjo-daro Site Plan and City Organization

The western "Citadel" mound is the highest at Mohenjo-daro, rising some 6 meters above the plain in the south and up to 12 meters above the plain in the north, where a Buddhist *stupa* and monastery of the historical period have been found (Fig. 4.3). The mound covers approximately 6.6 hectares and is encircled by a massive mud-brick wall/platform that has eroded down to the modern plain level. Many of the largest and most well-known buildings of the Harappan phase are located on this mound, such as the large colonnaded building with a specially designed water tank, usually referred to as the Great Bath. Adjacent to this is the foundation of a massive building that probably had a wooden superstructure. Often referred to as a granary, this building was probably a

large public structure, but it is not clear if it was a storehouse, a temple, or some form of administrative building. Two other major buildings with large open areas and colonnades have been labeled the Assembly Hall and the College. The rest of the mound is composed of smaller domestic units, with bathing platforms, wells, and small internal courtyards. While the large public structures may reflect "an aspect of combined or undiscriminated religious and secular administration" (Wheeler 1968:46–47), they appear to have been used at specific times as workshops by shell workers or leather workers, and the Granary was even truncated to construct the Great Bath. This pattern is significant because it indicates a distinct phase of urban decay on this mound—indeed, there were probably numerous such cycles during the life of this sector of the city.

To the north and south of the citadel mound and far to the east of the lower town are the scattered tops of small mounds buried more than 2 meters deep under sandy alluvium. In contrast to the small high mound, the lower town to the east consists of a series of low mounds covering more than 80 hectares. Four major north-south streets and four equally wide east-west streets divide the mounds into major blocks; there are also numerous smaller streets and alleyways (Jansen 1987).

The lower town has a very complex history that I will not discuss in detail here (see Jansen and Tosi 1988; Jansen and Urban 1984, 1987). Suffice it to say that numerous phases of rebuilding and reorganization are being identified in the context of both individual habitation units and entire neighborhoods. Most of the excavated architecture can be grouped into blocks of houses that represent periodic reconstruction and modifications of space and orientation.

Large building complexes have been identified in the various sectors of the lower town that compare in size to those found on the citadel mound to the west. None of these buildings has the type of colonnades seen in buildings on the citadel mound, but any one of them could have been used as an assembly area or public gathering place. One structure, House A1 in the Hr Area, is even thought to have been a temple, a palace, or the house of an elite family (Jansen 1985).

These large public and possibly ritual or administrative structures in the lower town may represent elite or administrative/ritual centers that competed with those found on the citadel mound. They could also reflect a shift of power to different areas of the city at different points in time. Attempts to relocate the artifacts from the different architectural units at the site may shed light on the internal chronology of Mohenjo-daro in the future (Jansen 1984a), but it is not possible to differentiate them chronologically at this time.

As at Harappa, workshops and industrial areas have been found in all the excavated sectors of Mohenjo-daro, indicating the dispersed distribution of specialized crafts throughout the city (Pracchia et al. 1985; Vidale 1990). Some workshops might have been established at different chronological periods, and in many cases they were located in abandoned buildings or administrative structures as the function of a neighborhood changed over time (Vidale 1990). Studies of street and building alignments, as well as artifact styles, indicate that many of the different sectors were inhabited contemporaneously, and studies currently under way will allow more detailed chronological correlation. An important indication of the contemporaneity of the Dk and Vs areas of the lower town is seen in the presence of two terra-cotta tablets with script and a rhinoceros motif made from the same mold.

Specific artifacts from Mohenjo-daro can be matched to identical objects found at Harappa. Many seals found at Harappa might have been produced at Mohenjo-daro and vice versa (Rissman 1989). More specifically, a terra-cotta tablet with script and a rhinoceros motif, made from the same mold as the tablets recovered at Mohenjo-daro, has been found at Harappa on Mound E (Meadow and Kenoyer 1994). This discovery relates both these major urban centers chronologically (during the Harappan phase) and demonstrates commercial or ritual interaction between individuals in both cities. Stoneware bangles (worn by elites) made with clays characteristic of Harappa have also been found at Mohenjo-daro and vice versa (Blackman and Vidale 1992), and similarities in lapidary work, shell work, ceramics, and numerous other well-known crafts indicate strong commercial and technological connections between the two cities.

Other categories of artifacts, however, suggest that certain social or ritual aspects of the two cites were distinct. Stone sculptures of seated male figures (such as the famous Priest King), copper tablets, and a wide variety of terra-cotta objects have been recovered at Mohenjo-daro but not at Harappa. Similarly, tiny rectangular inscribed tablets, female figurines, and composite animal and human figurines are common at Harappa but rare at Mohenjo-daro. These regional differences are also visible in ceramic styles (Dales

1991), architectural details, and general site layout (Jansen 1978, 1980; Kenoyer 1991b; Mughal 1990b).

This evidence suggests that, although certain general features of economic and social organization, as well as ritual practices, were shared, there were regional differences that served to distinguish some of the communities living in these two major cities. Such regional differences are even more pronounced at the island city of Dholavira in Kutch.

Dholavira Site Plan and City Organization

Dholavira (Kotada) is located on Kadir Island (Fig. 4.4) just north of the large island of Kutch (Bisht 1989:403). Kadir Island is only 196 square kilometers in area, but Dholavira would have been able to control shipping through the Rann between Saurashtra and the delta of the Indus and Ghaggar-Hakra Rivers. It is not possible to determine the hinterland of the city, but it probably controlled at least the island of Kutch (21,000 km^2) and the north coast of Saurashtra.

Originally it was thought that the initial occupation of Dholavira represented colonists from the Indus Valley, who brought with them a full-blown culture of the Harappan phase, but later excavations revealed ceramics identical to those of the Early Harappan (Kot Dijian) culture (Bisht, personal communication). At present, the details of the internal chronology have not been sorted out. There may have been an Early Harappan settlement, but the major period of expansion and occupation belongs to the Harappan and Late Harappan phases, after which the site appears to have been largely abandoned.

The city layout is very different from of Mohenjo-daro and Harappa, in that it consists of a series of three nested rectangular walls, with the highest area located to the south on the highest point of a low hill. The outer wall enclosed an area of approximately 47 hectares (Bisht 1994) and was constructed entirely of mud brick, with large square bastions and two major gateways located at the center of the northern and southern walls. Four gateways have been identified in the center of each of the walls of the middle town, as well as in the four walls of the acropolis (Bisht 1989). Like most sites in Kutch and Gujarat, the houses and drains are made with sandstone blocks (dressed and undressed) and clay mortar combined with some mud-brick superstructures.

Inside the outer wall is a fortified middle town (9 ha) and an acropolis (9 ha) which sits approximately

13 meters above the lower town (Bisht 1989). A large rectangular open area or plaza and an entrance ramp are situated directly below the major north gateway of the acropolis, and numerous large open spaces are found within the different walled areas. Some of these open spaces appear to have functioned as reservoirs that would have been filled with seasonal rainwater. The reservoirs account for 17 hectares (36 percent of the walled areas), and an additional reservoir has been identified outside the city wall (Bisht 1994). To the west, outside the walled city, are additional areas of habitation, which bring the total area of the site to approximately 100 hectares (Bisht 1989).

One of the most important discoveries at Dholavira is a large inscription found in a room associated with the northern gateway of the acropolis. This inscription, the largest example of writing ever discovered in the Indus cities, consists of ten symbols, each measuring approximately 37 centimeters high and 25–27 centimeters wide, is made from a white gypsum paste inlay that appears to have been set into a wooden plank. Bisht thinks the inscription is a signboard that would have been visible throughout the city if it had been mounted above the gateway or on top of the walls (1994).

Large buildings in the acropolis area may represent administrative or ritual structures, and some of the open areas in the city could have served as markets or public gathering places. Various types of craft activity areas have been located within the lower town, including agate bead making, shell working, and ceramic production. Habitation and craft activity areas in the lower sectors of the city are organized in blocks divided by north-south and east-west streets.

Artifacts found at Dholavira seem to reflect several source areas or spheres of influence. Some objects might have been produced in the core areas of the Indus Valley and brought to the site by colonists or traders. Other objects are clearly copies of Harappan-style ceramics and seals made from local materials by local artisans. A third category of objects represents the indigenous stylistic traditions of Kutch and Saurashtra (Bisht 1994, personal communication).

The presence of different types of artifacts suggests that the city was composed of a mixed population of Harappan elites and artisans from the inland regions, as well as local populations who maintained their own cultural traditions or a synthesis of Harappan and indigenous elements. Bisht feels that Dholavira represents a Harappan outpost or colony that was established to exploit resources needed by inland sites

in the core areas of the Indus Valley, and when the inland sites began to decline, the region was gradually abandoned (1989:406–407).

While this brief discussion does not do justice to the many important new discoveries at the site, it illustrates the features common to the other Indus cities—a walled settlement, similar planning of architecture, streets, and drainage systems; the use of sophisticated drainage systems; a common script, weights, ceramics; and other diagnostic artifact styles. The unique feature of the city plan is seen most clearly in the nested pattern of walled sectors instead of separate mounds enclosed by walls. Another important pattern is the small number of large buildings, all of them within the area of the acropolis. The influence of indigenous styles and the preference for local raw materials is considerably more prominent at Dholavira. This may reflect weaker cultural or ideological integration, since Dolavira is situated at the southeastern periphery of the greater Indus Valley.

Models for Defining Political Organization

Models of the political and socioeconomic aspects of Harappan-phase cities have been reconstructed almost exclusively from archaeological evidence and through comparisons with contemporaneous urban civilizations in West Asia (Kenoyer 1991a; Possehl 1990; Wheeler 1968). Additional sources of comparative information that have not been fully utilized are textual and archaeological data from subsequent historical developments in the South Asian subcontinent itself. Much of this latter information was ignored in previous discussions because of a misperception that there was a hiatus or Dark Age between the end of the Harappan phase (at about 1900 B.C.) and the subsequent Early Historic period (600 B.C.–A.D. 300; Fig. 4.5).

Through the concerted efforts of archaeologists, linguists, and historians (Kenoyer 1995; Shaffer 1993), it is now possible to identify significant technological and cultural continuities between the Harappan phase of the Indus Valley Tradition (2600–1900 B.C.) and the later Indo-Gangetic Tradition, where we see a new phase of urbanism and city-states emerging during the Early Historic period (600–300 B.C.). The continuities and derived developments in craft technologies, subsistence strategies, economic structures, weight systems, and settlement patterns between these two major urban phases indicate that the second phase of urbanism was influenced to some degree

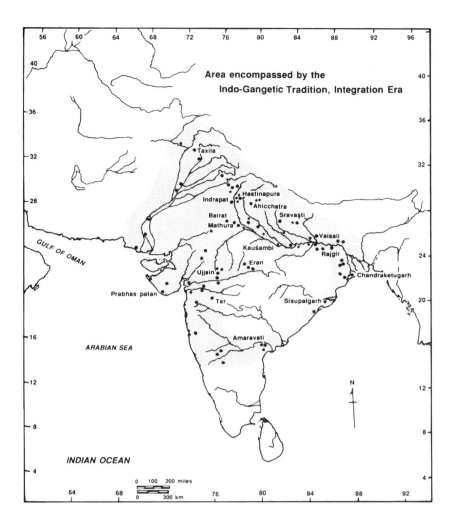

Figure 4.5. Area encompassed by the Indo-Gangetic Tradition, Integration Era.

by the legacy of the earlier urban culture. Because of these linkages, the extensive literature (Vedic and Epic texts, as well as later treatises) on the political and socioritual organization of the Early Historic city-states and empires can now be used to develop more appropriate working hypotheses and interpretive models for the political organization of the earlier cities of the Indus Valley Tradition.

Some of these South Asian models show general analogies with those being proposed for other early city-states, but I must emphasize the preliminary nature of the research and the need for further testing through archaeological studies of both the known city-states of the Early Historic period and the earlier Harappan-phase cities. In the following section, I outline some of the basic aspects of states and city-states, as reflected in the literary evidence from South Asia, and suggest how some of these patterns can be correlated to the archaeological evidence from Indus cities.

Early Historic States and City-States

Although most Western scholars derive the concept of the city-state from the Greek *polis,* I introduce here models of the state from ancient Indian literature. Most of the available texts remain untranslated from Sanskrit, Prakrit, and Pali, but fortunately, the few translated texts we have provide a fairly detailed account of the various categories of city-states found in the northern and northwestern subcontinent from the seventh to the fourth centuries B.C. The most important available texts include the *Arthashastra* of Kautilya, the *Astadhyayi* of Panini, and various Buddhist and Jaina texts (Ramachandran 1989).

The *Arthashastra* is a treatise on state organization attributed to Kautilya, a minister of Chandragupta Maurya who established the Mauryan Empire sometime between 326 and 313 B.C. The *Astadhyayi* is a grammatical treatise that includes lists of the early

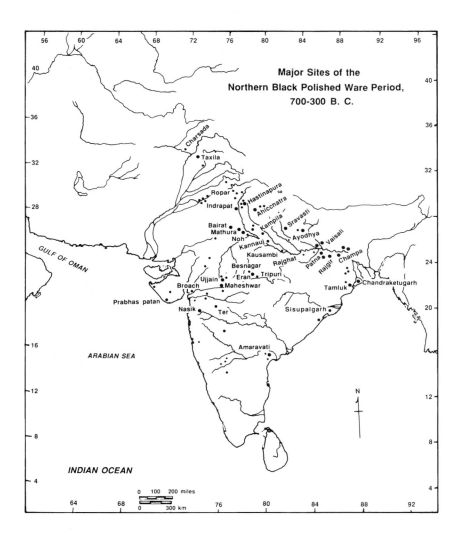

Figure 4.6. Major polities of the Indo-Gangetic Tradition, Integration Era ca. 500 B.C.

city-states. These texts, which were compiled from the fifth to the fourth centuries B.C., speak of the existence of as many as sixteen polities called *mahajanapada*, or great provinces, each dominated by a capital city and ruled by a centralized government (Fig. 4.6). Capital cities that have been identified and surveyed range from 50 to 200 hectares in size (Erdosy 1988), and with the rise of the Mauryan Empire they became even larger.

The size of each *mahajanapada* varied according to the geographical area and can only be approximated, but they appear to range from 80 square kilometers to an area "almost equal in size to the largest Greek *polis* of Sparta, which occupied an area of 3,360 square miles [168,000 km²]" (Sharma 1968:103). Together, these city-states encompassed the northern and northwestern portions of the subcontinent, from Bengal in the east to Afghanistan in the west and including the modern regions of Gujarat, Sindh, Punjab, and parts of Baluchistan.

The political organization of these city-states included both *raja dhina,* a country ruled by a king/monarch, and *gana dhina,* a country ruled by the *gana* council—that is, a nonmonarchical republic (Bongard-Levin 1986). Nonmonarchical states (*gana, sangha, vairajya, virat*) are contrasted with monarchical states ruled by young princes, single kings, two kings, two fighting kings, and kingdoms without a ruler that have fallen into anarchy (Altekar 1984; Bongard-Levin 1986). Smaller cities or towns were sometimes organized as oligarchies or tribes with hereditary leaders. It is clear that there is no distinct line dividing the various types of political organizations, and they represent a continuum from tyrannical rule to more democratic forms of government.

Many scholars feel that it is not useful to apply a narrowly defined Western concept of "state" to the political phenomena of the subcontinent (Basham 1964; Scharfe 1989). For example, the monarchical state, according to Kautilya's *Arthashastra,* is composed of seven components: king, officers, provinces, towns, treasury, army, allies. Scharfe suggests that "the Indian concept of state is wider than the one common in the West, because the ally (*mitra*) was regarded by Indian theorists as one of the seven constituents or factors of a state" (Scharfe 1989:2). However, as is evident in many chapters in this volume, although a city-state may aspire to independence, it is inextricably connected to other city-states through trade or political alliances at one time or another. A city-state does not evolve in isolation but is part of a larger landscape dotted with small and large settlements, some of which may be competing city-states.

According to several ancient texts, the Indian state was also responsible for the promotion of *dharma* (right action; fostering a feeling of piety and religiousness; encouraging virtue and morality), *artha* (wealth, through the encouragement of trade, industry, and agriculture; developing natural resources; bringing new land under cultivation; building dams; working of mines; etc.), *kama* (worldly pleasures; to be able to enjoy the good life and aesthetic culture through peace and order), and *moksha* (release from the cycle of rebirth through proper action, which includes pursuit of the previous three objectives; Altekar 1984; Ragaranjan 1992; Scharfe 1989). By encouraging these four principles, the state was able to grow strong and remain stable. These dynamic ideological and spiritual aspects of state rule are not unique to the Indian subcontinent and can be identified in many states throughout the world, both past and present.

Another important aspect of the Early Historic state is the contrasting role of aliens or foreigners within the state. On the one hand, there are references to noncitizens or foreigners holding important positions within the state administrative system. Altekar (1984:67) suggests that "the non-recognition of the aliens as a separate class was due partly to the catholic spirit of Hinduism and partly to its confidence of completely absorbing the foreigners in its body politic by means of its superior culture." On the other hand, Kautilya warns his king that strangers, whether foreigners or simply persons from outside the city, should be carefully monitored when they come into a city to insure the security of the city and protect the trade that sustained it (Ramachandran 1989:41). There were special rest houses set aside for travelers passing through the city, not only to facilitate their travels and attract their trade but presumably also so that they could be monitored more easily.

Geographical Context of Early Historic City-States

The geographical context of the Early Historic city-states in the subcontinent is also important to consider, not necessarily as a deterministic factor but as one that inhibited the formation of a strong centralized military or political authority over more than one region, thereby encouraging the development of regional political autonomy. Sharma goes so far as to suggest that states which evolved republican forms of government were situated in geographical locations with harsh climatic conditions—for example, hilly regions, marshy lands, deep forests—that inspired a martial zeal and democratic spirit in contrast to the docile subjects of monarchies (1968:241). While this takes environmental determinism to an extreme, his argument has some validity in that the nature of roads, transport, and communication systems made it difficult for a single monarch to subdue and maintain control over vast regions with inhospitable terrain. It was not until the Mauryan Empire, when roads and rest stops were built along major trade routes, that many of these areas were effectively united, with the support of a very large military organization that used the horse and elephant for transport and battle and had an impressive repertoire of iron weapons.

The vast plains of the Indus and the Ghaggar-Hakra river systems, as well as those of the Ganga-Yamuna rivers, provided an optimal setting for the development of large cities surrounded by a hinterland of smaller towns. The major cities appear to have been relatively self-sufficient in terms of basic subsistence needs but required strong intraregional trade networks to supply exotic raw materials and finished goods for defining and maintaining socioeconomic stratification and for ritual purposes. The most important settlements and the capitals of each *mahajanapada* were situated strategically along trade routes or controlled important resource areas (Fig. 4.2; Erdosy 1988; Lal 1986).

Early Historic Republics

The republican form of government is first revealed in the early Vedic period, which is generally dated from 1500–1000 or 800 B.C., and it is well documented in subsequent periods (600 B.C. and later), when each republic is clearly associated with an urban capital and numerous smaller cities and towns in the surrounding hinterland (Sharma 1968).

The population of these city-states was divided into

four *varna* or classes. The hierarchical relationships of the *varna* are defined in the literature, but the *jati* or occupational caste hierarchy is not well defined until hundreds of years later. In the republics, the highest ranking goes to the *kshatriya* (warrior aristocracy), followed by the *brahmana* (ritual specialists), the *vaisya* (merchant classes), and *shudra* (laborers). The *brahmana* held lower status in the *gana* than in monarchical states. Citizenship was available not only to the free inhabitants of the city but also to those in the areas annexed to the city.

Cities had differing numbers of assembly members. It is not possible to note all the variations here, but the main point is that there was a hierarchical organization of administration that involved a few elected leaders. They represented a larger body of free citizens who retained a critical role in governing the city-state.

City Organization

The capital city was a walled settlement with a rectangular or square plan, and some cities had a series of three concentric walls. A gate was located at the midpoint of each wall, and the walls were surrounded by moats. In a monarchical state, the capital contained, in addition to a palace for the king and his family, a council hall; the royal storehouse; public buildings for music, theater, and sports; merchant quarters and market areas; residences for various categories of inhabitants; and special rest houses for foreigners and travelers (Ramachandran 1989:41). Special meeting halls were constructed inside the city, where the assembly met on a daily basis. Large reservoirs or tanks for water storage and bathing were also constructed within or at the edge of the cities. These tanks were often used exclusively by elite classes, as is reported for Vaisali, where only the leading *kshatriya* families were allowed to bathe in a specific tank (Sharma 1968:105). Additional tanks or wells were constructed for the remainder of the population.

Cities were inhabited by classes defined by social status and material wealth. The ideal city, as defined by Kautilya, was divided into sixteen major sectors by three parallel streets running north-south and three running east-west. These major streets were approximately 8 meters wide, which would have allowed two-way traffic with ox carts and space for stalls along the edge of the streets. In Vaisali, there were three major sectors: high, middle, and low. In the high section were 7,000 houses topped with gold towers, while the middle and low sections had, respectively, 14,000 and 21,000 houses topped with silver and copper towers. Inhabitants in the low section included both free and slave laborers. Both private and state-owned slaves were used in agriculture and irrigation, but they also worked as laborers in the administrative center of the city.

Although there is no discussion of drainage or sanitation systems, excavations at many early cities have revealed drains and sump pits made with discarded storage jars or specially designed ceramic rings. These ceramic rings were also used to line wells. Large habitation units were made up of rooms surrounding a courtyard, with sheds for working and domestic activities and latrines/bathing areas (Ramachandran 1989:41).

The city had a heterogeneous population of many classes and ethnic groups, from rulers and administrators to merchants, laborers, and foreigners. In contrast, the villages in the hinterland were relatively homogeneous, consisting of agricultural settlements or settlements of specialized artisans—potters, mat-makers, salt-makers, and so on (Ramachandran 1989).

More than sixty different industries were present within the cities, and they have been grouped by into eleven basic categories:

(1) textiles, (2) carpentry and woodwork, (3) metalwork, including smiths and jewelers, (4) stonework, (5) glass industry, (6) bone and ivory work, (7) perfumery, (8) liquor and oil manufacture, (9) leather industry, (10) clay work, including pottery, terra-cotta figurine-making, modeling, and brick making, and (11) miscellaneous industries, such as making garlands, combs, baskets, musical instruments, and painting. (Ramachandran 1989:41–42)

The estimated total population for the entire Licchavi *janapada* is 200,000–300,000 (Sharma 1968), but not all would have been "Licchavi," and many of the occupational castes were probably ethnic minorities. The three related polities of the Licchavi, Naya, and Videha encompassed a long strip of land of greater than 168,000 square kilometers (Sharma 1968).

Agricultural land, grazing land, forests, and water resources were owned both privately and collectively by the *gana*-state. The army was made up of free men of various classes and directed by *kshatriya* leaders, who were elected to their positions by peers.

Trade and commerce were important for the well-being of the city and were controlled by the *kshatriya* (landed military aristocracy) and the *vaisya* (merchants). However, most of the important specialized crafts and occupations were organized as *nigama*, organizations of merchants, and *sreni*, groups of artisans. The term *sreni* has often been interpreted as a "guild," but it should be seen as a different form of organization because of the close association with hereditary occupational specialists, referred to as *jati* or caste.

It is thought that the *nigama* and *sreni* may have paid taxes directly to the state. Other taxes were collected from travelers bringing goods into the cities, and taxes were levied on agriculturalists. Each *gana* had its own coinage, with a specific symbol or set of symbols stamped onto the silver or copper coins. This type of monied economy is basically incompatible with simple clan or tribal organization (Bongard-Levin 1986).

Summary of Early Historic City-States

The leader of a *gana* republic (as well as a monarchy) was invariably a *kshatriya* who was appointed or elected by the *gana* and took the title of *raja* (king), *senapati* (general/leader of the troops), or *pramukh* (leader). There were no hereditary leaders, and they were servants of the *gana*. No royal marriages, alliances, or surrenders could be made without the approval and consensus of the *gana*. The *gana* assembly was open to all free inhabitants of the city, meaning the *kshatriya*, *brahmana*, and *vaisya*. There were regular meetings on a daily basis or sometimes even three times a day. The *gana* had explicit laws and legal codes for jurisdiction and punishment. They were not necessarily the same as those of monarchies. The *gana* had the power to kill, punish, banish, levy taxes and fines, control marriages and alliances, and it sent emissaries to monarchs. There was much rivalry within the *kshatriya* aristocracy and competition to acquire land, wealth, and power. In some cases, rivalries and alliances between small groups of *kshatriyas* led to the creation of oligarchies or even monarchies.

Within the *gana* we see the continued importance of *gotra* or clan affiliations, but they became less important over time and were eventually replaced or superseded by the *kula* or family ties. This is seen primarily in the leading political role of specific *kshatriya kula* (warrior families). There was continuous tension between the various *varna* and threat of revolt by slaves. *Kshatriya* leaders were repeatedly threatened by *brahmana* or *vaisya* who gained power through control of land and commerce. *Shudra* (laborer class) and slaves were often exploited and abused to the point of revolt.

One reason for looking closely at the sociopolitical structure of the *gana* and *sangha* republics is to see what makes them different from monarchies and to determine if the distinction could be identified archaeologically. In most aspects the two forms of state were very similar, though it is possible that the cities of the monarchical states were larger than those of the oligarchies or republics (Erdosy, personal communication). Both had centralized economies using standardized monetary and weight systems, army, taxes, local and international trade, and land ownership by the state. Archaeologically, the most distinctive difference would be the identification of a palace area or royal storehouse. It is possible that these could be distinguished from ordinary *kshatriya* elites, but other aspects of the architecture and layout of the cities would be similar. Both had a multitiered settlement pattern with the largest trade and urban centers being the administrative centers as well. Decentralized aspects of both state systems are seen in the private ownership of land and commerce. Similar languages and (later) writing systems were present throughout the northern subcontinent.

Both forms of state had hereditary classes of elites, retainers, administrators, craftsmen, laborers, slaves. The only major differences between the two appear to be the presence or absence of a hereditary ruler and the order of the *varna* hierarchy. In a monarchy the sequence from high to low is *brahmana*, *kshatriya*, *vaisya*, and *shudra*; while in the *gana* republic it is *kshatriya*, *brahmana*, *vaisya*, and *shudra*. In the monarchy the *brahmana* validated and legitimized the king though confirmation of his hereditary lineage, generally descended from the sun or the moon. In the *gana* republic, the leader was legitimized by the support of the *kshatriya* elites, and there was no need for additional *brahmana* validation.

It is important to note that the leadership in both forms of state was not reinforced by royal edicts or coins with the image of the king or elected leader. Consequently, without the aid of written documents, the differences between these two forms of state would not be visible archaeologically unless a palace area and royal storehouse could be identified.

Except for possible differences in the overall size of cities, there is very little to differentiate the two forms of city-state during the Early Historic period. This factor, combined with the textual evidence that identifies most of the oligarchies in the northwestern regions (northern Indus Valley), has great import for our investigation of the form of political organization during the Harappan phase. At this stage in our research it is not appropriate to focus on specific aspects of political organization but to devote our attention to the question of centralization and the organization of urban centers. We may never be able to differentiate between a monarchical state or a republican state during the Harappan phase, but it is possible to identify aspects of the Harappan cities that may be correlated to political and socioeconomic organization found in city-states during the subsequent Early Historic period. In identifying these similarities, I am not proposing that they result from identical cultural processes or that they are themselves identical but that they may reflect analogous political structures connected through direct historical/cultural links. These comparisons are necessary for building new research strategies to refine our interpretations of Harappan-phase cities.

Political Organization of Harappan-Phase Cities

All scholars actively involved in research on the Indus Valley Tradition agree that the largest cities were the focus of political and economic power for a period of more than 700 years. The cities were central places within a specific region. They appear to have used a shared script; they had a common material culture; there was a standardization of economic exchange that may reflect a form of taxation; and there is clear evidence for a common ideology (Kenoyer 1991a). We cannot at this time speak of citizenship laws, state policy on self-sufficiency, or independence, but on a general level, the definition of city-state proposed by Griffeth and Thomas (1981a) and that used by Charlton and Nichols (this volume) would include the cities of the Indus Valley Tradition as city-states.

Due to the nature of the data, previous discussions on the political organization of the Harappan phase have focused on the distinction between chiefdoms and state-level organization rather than on the specific issue of city-states. Some scholars have argued that the Indus cities do not represent a state-level society of the type found in Egypt or Mesopotamia (Fairservis 1989; Shaffer 1982, 1993), but there is a general consensus that they do reflect some form of centralized chiefdom or state-level organization (for summaries, see Kenoyer 1991a; Possehl 1990). On the basis of archaeological evidence alone, it would be difficult to differentiate a group of large village-based chiefdoms from a group of small city-states, but the scale of settlement hierarchy in the Indus does not seem compatible with most known chiefdoms.

The estimated hinterland of the largest Harappan-phase cities roughly corresponds to the larger city-states (both republican and monarchical) of the Early Historic period. This correlation probably results in part from the fact that city-states in both periods were located in similar geographical settings. However, it is culturally more significant to note that the technologies for communication, trade, and military coercion were at approximately the same scale and remained so until the advent of the Mauryan Empire, around 300 B.C. During the Early Historic period, the area encompassed by the various city-states included the previous region of the Harappan phase and additional territories in the Gangetic plain and peninsular India. The total area is more than twice that of the Harappan phase (Fig. 4.5), and it was integrated economically and ideologically but not politically.

Political integration of these city-states did not occur until the rise of the Mauryan Empire. It was achieved through military conquest, but it was maintained by the promotion of a new ideology and economic security. Emperor Ashoka, after defeating—and, in many cases, totally annihilating—his enemies, is said to have converted to Buddhism and proclaimed a reign of peace, nonviolence, and right action. Interestingly enough, however, his military force was never disbanded or disarmed.

The role of the Early Historic state in promoting *dharma* (right action), *artha* (wealth and trade), *kama* (the good life through peace and order), and *moksha* (release through the previous three objectives) emphasizes the ideological and economic benefits of integration. Integration of the numerous cities and smaller settlements in the greater Indus Valley could only have been maintained by the promotion of a shared ideology and economic benefits. If there was a period of military coercion, it was not reinforced by continued militarism but appears to have been replaced by ideological and economic coercion—a strategy that was later repeated by Ashoka.

The archaeological evidence for ideological and economic coercion is seen in the spatial organization of cities and the hierarchy in crafts and technology (Kenoyer 1989, 1992). In the Early Historic period these types of archaeologically visible evidence can be correlated to hierarchical political and socioeconomic organization, which in turn corresponds to social classes or *varna*. Walled sectors in the Early Historic cities served primarily to differentiate classes, provide security, and control economic interaction. Numerous different public or administrative buildings and the presence of separate water sources in the form of wells or tanks can also be seen to reflect hierarchical classes or distinct communities within the cities.

Separate walled mounds with associated suburbs at both Mohenjo-daro and Harappa suggest that these two cities had similar hierarchies of competing political and socioeconomic classes. While it is possible that a single community of elites with strong kin ties controlled both cities, it is highly unlikely that a ruler in one city dominated all the other cities. This type of centralized control does not appear until the time of Chandragupta Maurya, around 300 B.C.

The regional differences in artifact types and city layout suggest that each of the Harappan cities had an independent community of ruling elites. The fact that no single building or group of buildings dominates either site suggests that the political organization was probably not a hereditary monarchy, where one would expect to see palaces and royal storehouses. On the contrary, the presence of numerous large buildings and public spaces in the lower town at Mohenjo-daro and Mound F at Harappa would support the interpretation that there were several distinct elite groups living in each city. The exception to this pattern at Dholavira, with its nested walled areas, suggests that the political organization of this settlement may reflect the dominance of a single class. It is possible that this city was a small kingdom, but it also could represent a colony of one of the core-area cites.

In addition to the layout and organization of the cities, the presence of hierarchical classes in the Harappan-phase cities is supported by many other categories of evidence, such as "ritual" objects, ornaments, seals, and weights (Kenoyer 1991a). These types of objects continued to be used for differentiating classes during the Early Historic period and are the strongest evidence of ideological continuities between the two urban periods.

Earlier generalizations about uniformity in artifacts have stressed the authoritarian nature of Harappan culture, but most of the uniformity can be explained by the presence of a common belief system or conservative ideology that required specific symbols and artifacts for ritual purposes as well as for defining class affiliation (Fairservis 1984; Miller 1985). These symbolic objects also reinforced the hierarchy of the society and helped to legitimize the socioeconomic and political order (Miller 1985). The role of kin-related

learning processes and the diffusion of craft specialists from specific communities to all the major settlements is also an important mechanism for maintaining uniformity in technologies and style.

Unlike the later urban periods, where a rigid caste society was maintained, the Early Historic period was characterized by classes or *varna* whose ranking was flexible, depending on the economic power of a specific community. Supported by numerous craft specialists and service groups that also had the potential for gaining power, there was a continuous struggle for power between ritual specialists, military leaders or landowners, and merchants.

Harappan cities were undoubtedly composed of similar competing elites whose centers of power would have been within each of the separate walled mounds at Mohenjo-daro and Harappa or in the acropolis at Dholavira. These walled mounds would have reinforced the distinct communities of ruling elites and allowed total economic control of specialized goods being produced by artisans in a specific sector.

The ideal city defined by Kautilya had different sectors located in specific areas of the city. This placement of social and economic classes within a city reflects and reinforces the hierarchical organization of the society as a whole. It is probable that the strong similarities of layout and orientation between the western mounds at Harappa and Mohenjo-daro could represent a similar pattern. For example, the communities that lived in the walled western mound at Harappa may have had strong social or political connections with communities on the western (citadel) mound at Mohenjo-daro. The same could apply to other sectors of the cites. Current excavations at Harappa and proposed new excavations at Mohenjo-daro could begin to test such hypotheses.

Fluctuations in dominance between the communities on each of the mounds probably contributed to the economic development and the rapid buildup of the city as a whole. New suburbs with associated craft areas may have resulted from growing populations within the city and the agglomeration of new populations to the city. Similar patterns of competition between elites within a city-state are well documented in the Early Historic states. The competition between powerful *kshatriya* clans occasionally led to large-scale warfare (e.g., the Mahabharata battle), but more often it resulted in fission and the colonization of new regions such as South India and Sri Lanka (Thapar 1984). These colonial extensions in turn contributed to the spread of technologies, subsistence strategies, language, and ideology. The widespread distribution of Harappan-phase settlements may reflect a similar process of expansion and colonization through competition and fission among the ruling elites from the core regions of the Indus and Ghaggar-Hakra valleys. A site like Dholavira, or any of the smaller walled settlements in Gujarat, the Punjab, Baluchistan, or Afghanistan could represent such outposts or colonies. In contrast to the core-area cities, these outpost settlements may have supported only one dominant elite community, along with the necessary support classes of laborers or indigenous peoples.

Conclusion

The geographical setting and internal organization of the Harappan-phase cities, along with specific patterns of artifacts, indicates that these cities were most likely independent polities during much of their existence. As was common during the Early Historic period, we can envision several different types of city-states, with fluctuations from strong centralized control, dominated by single individuals or a small group of elites, to periods during which an entire class of people—for example, merchants, landowners, ritual specialists—were dominant. The nature of integrative control and alliances was probably just as stratified or ranked as was the society as a whole. Elites within each of the mounded areas of a site, or even between sites, may have been competing for power. Even though we cannot identify the specific mechanisms for their political control, the current evidence suggests that these larger cities can be identified as city-states.

The integration of this vast geographical area into a single cultural system was probably the result of economic strategies defined by ideology and social relations rather than overt military coercion. Competition between elites living in two or more of the Harappan-phase cities might have resulted in periods of greater or lesser integration, as one community or another came into power. Alliances between ruling elites living at two or more of the largest sites would have stimulated extensive colonization of resource areas by other communities to compete for power.

The literary evidence from the Early Historical period brings a new perspective to the mute archaeological patterns of the Harappan phase. There is no need to look outside the subcontinent to find analogies when we have such strong cultural and historical continuities in the actual region of study. Similar approaches have been the norm in Mesoamerica for generations, but only recently has it been possible to begin making the connections in the Indian subcontinent.

By utilizing this important body of data to refine our research strategies, we can collect and analyze the types of data needed to test specific questions about military action, ideology, and socioeconomic organization. The results of these studies will allow further refinement of the hypotheses and models of political organization that have been proposed for the Harappan phase.

Acknowledgments

I would first like to thank the editors, Deborah L. Nichols and Thomas H. Charlton, for their patience as I prepared this paper. The summary of results from excavations at Harappa include the most recent discoveries of the 1997 season, and I would like to thank the Department of Archaeology, Government of Pakistan, for allowing us to work at the site and to thank as well all my colleagues on the Harappa Archaeological Research Project—Richard H. Meadow, Rita P. Wright, Barbara Dales—and my American and Pakistani students for their contributions to the various seasons of work at the site. My excavations at Harappa and related projects have been generously supported by various funding agencies—the National Science Foundation, the National Endowment for the Humanities, the Smithsonian Institution, the National Geographic Society, the University of Wisconsin, Madison, and numerous private contributors.

Many of the ideas presented in this paper are the result of discussions with friends, colleagues, and students, who may or may not agree with some of my interpretations. I would like to thank R. S. Bisht, Kuldeep Bhan, Walter Fairservis, Rafique Mughal, Michael Jansen, J. F. Jarrige, Richard Meadow, Gregory Possehl, Jim Shaffer, Carla Sinopoli, Gil Stein, Massimo Vidale, Norman Yoffee, Rita P. Wright, Henry Wright, and many, many more for their stimulating interaction.

Notes

1. For the three major cities, see Bisht 1990; Dales and Kenoyer 1993; Jansen 1991; Kenoyer 1991b; Meadow 1991b. For the smaller sites see Besenval 1992; Biagi and Cremaschi 1990; Bisht 1982; Dikshit 1984; Durrani 1988; Durrani et al. 1991; Flam 1993; Jarrige 1986, 1990; Joshi 1973; and Joshi and Bala 1982.
2. For architectural analysis, see Jansen and Tosi 1988 and Jansen and Urban 1984, 1987. For craft technologies see Ardeleanu-Jansen 1992; Franke-Vogt 1992; Kenoyer 1992; Kenoyer and Miller in press; Vidale and Kenoyer 1992; and Wright 1989. For subsistence, see Belcher 1993; Costantini 1990; Meadow 1991a, 1993; and Reddy 1991.

5

The City-State in Ancient China

This chapter will analyze the appropriateness of the concept of city-state in relation to early China, an attempt which has not been made by Western scholars of the Middle Kingdom, but which has been suggested by the Chinese historian Tu Cheng-sheng (1986, 1987, 1992).[1] The idea of the city-state as *polis* first appeared in history in the secondary civilization of Greece after it emerged from the Dark Age that followed the collapse of the Mycenaean civilization around the eighth century B.C. But an important symposium edited by Griffeth and Thomas (1981a) suggested that city-states had appeared earlier in Sumer in the second half of the fourth millennium B.C. and could also be found in medieval and Renaissance Italy, later in Switzerland and Germany, as well as among the Hausa of West Africa from the mid-fifteenth to the early nineteenth century. While it is quite clear that Chinese cities had in later times very different administrative and legal arrangements from those in the West (cf. Weber 1958), could the Chinese have had a city-state system before the foundation of the empire in 221 B.C.? Not according to Trigger (1993), who claims that China is one of three prime examples of territorial states, the others being ancient Egypt and Inka Peru.

Wilson (this volume) offers a theoretical critique of Trigger's models and I will not repeat his strictures here. With regard to China in the Shang and Western Zhou (mid-second millennium B.C. to 771 B.C.; Table 5.1), however, the evidence is at present too scanty to support Trigger's categorization. It is not at all clear how much of the actual territory the Shang controlled at any one time: Keightley (1983a:548) sees the state in late Shang times as a "thin network of pathways and encampments" where the "network was laid over a hinterland that rarely saw or felt the king's presence and authority." This is not to say that elements of Shang culture were not widely dispersed in the north China plain and there were centers where Shang had greater influence (Fig. 5.1). A similar situation seems to have existed for the Western Zhou: the territory actually controlled and administered or directly exploited by the state apparatus was relatively limited along the middle and lower sections of the Yellow River (Shaughnessy 1989). The question of actual political unity of the Shang and Zhou polities, therefore, remains very much open, despite the fact that later Chinese traditional scholars assumed that these two dynasties, and the one that preceded them both, the Xia, were dynasties in the same mold as the centralized imperial states that those scholars were personally familiar with.

ROBIN D. S. YATES

Table 5.1

Time Line for the City-State in Early China

Date B.C.	Major Developments
7000	Beginnings of the Xianrendong culture in the Middle Yangzi Valley and of the Zengpiyan culture along the southeast coast
6500–5000	Cishan culture in Shanxi, Henan, and Hebei provinces, followed by the Laoguantai culture in Shaanxi and Shanxi and the Beixin in Shandong and Xinglongwa cultures in northern Hebei and Liaoning
5500–4000	Hemudu culture in the Lower Yangzi valley, south of Shanghai
5000–2500	Yangshao painted pottery culture in north and west China, followed slightly later by the Dawenkou culture in the east (Shandong) and the Hongshan culture in the northeast (Hebei and Liaoning); the Majiabang follows the Hemudu culture in the southeast and is succeeded by the Songze phase; in the central Yangzi, the Daxi, then the Qujialing cultures occupy the region where the Xianrendong flourished
2500–2000	Longshan interaction sphere
2000	Erlitou culture in central Henan, possibly the first of China's traditional dynasties, the Xia; beginnings of the Bronze Age
1750–1045	Shang dynasty in the Yellow River plain with its last capital at Anyang, northeast Henan
1045–770	Western Zhou dynasty with its capital located west of Xi'an in northwest China; establishment of many states subordinate to the Zhou, such as Lu at Qufu, Shandong
770	Beginning of the Eastern Zhou; the Zhou royal house forced to move its capital east to Luoyang, Henan province; Qin is enfeoffed as a full status lord; the official creation of the state of Qin
722	The beginning of the historical texts *Springs and Autumns Annals;* the beginning of the Springs and Autumns period
685–643	Rule of Duke Huan of Qi, the first hegemon; his main advisor is Guan Zhong, after whom important collection of early philosophical treatises, the *Guanzi,* is named
655	Jin conquers the small states of Guo and Yu, although the ruling houses are related to each other; beginning of the development of regional city-state systems
551–479	Life of Confucius; approximate beginnings of the use of iron
464	Last year of the *Zuo Commentary* on the *Springs and Autumns Annals;* beginning of the Warring States period
403	Heads of Han, Wei, and Zhao lineages invested as marquises, officially sanctioning the division of the territory of the ancient state of Jin
352	Wei Yang appointed chancellor of Qin; he institutes many legalist reforms in Qin and is later enfeoffed as Lord Shang
338	Death of Duke Xiao of Qin, and execution of Wei Yang, Lord Shang, his supporter and chancellor
256	Qin destroys Eastern Zhou
246	King Zheng, later the First Emperor, is enthroned at the age of 13 *sui* (years)
230–221	Campaigns by Qin to destroy all its rival city-states, starting with that of Han
221	Qin conquers Qi, unifies China, and establishes the empire; Zheng assumes the title of "First Emperor"
214	General Meng Tian is recorded as constructing the Great Wall
209	Huhai succeeds to the throne as the Second Emperor; rebellion against Qin oppression begins
207	Death of Second Emperor
206	January 11–February 9; the rebels attack and burn the First Emperor's mausoleum and capture Xianyang; the Qin dynasty collapses, succeeded after a bitter civil war by the Han

Source: Murowchick 1994.

Furthermore, it is impossible to estimate the percentage of the population that lived in the countryside in relation to that in the national capital or metropolitan areas, and so it is equally impossible to conclude that a two-tiered economy, urban and rural, had developed. As I show below, the bureaucracy in the Shang was minimal at best and so it cannot be asserted that the main economic link between the urban and rural sectors in early China was through the peasants paying taxes, rents, and corvée labor duties to the urban elite, or that this exploitation was monitored by a large administrative staff. As it has proved difficult for Chinese archaeologists to determine precise details of housing arrangements within the precincts of walled sites, it is also not possible to state categorically that farmers did not live there next to the expert artisans and craftsmen who were catering to the needs of the elite for luxury items, such as bronzes and jades. Later on, there is no question that farmers did not live within the walls of cities and towns. Finally, while certainly some centers of ritual activity do not appear to be walled, there were many

Figure 5.1. One view of the major regions (shaded) of the Late Shang state derived from oracle-bone inscriptions superimposed on a map of sites and finds of the Upper Erligang and Anyang stages. From Keightley, *The Origins of Chinese Civilization* (1983b:map 17.3). Reprinted with permission of the University of California Press.

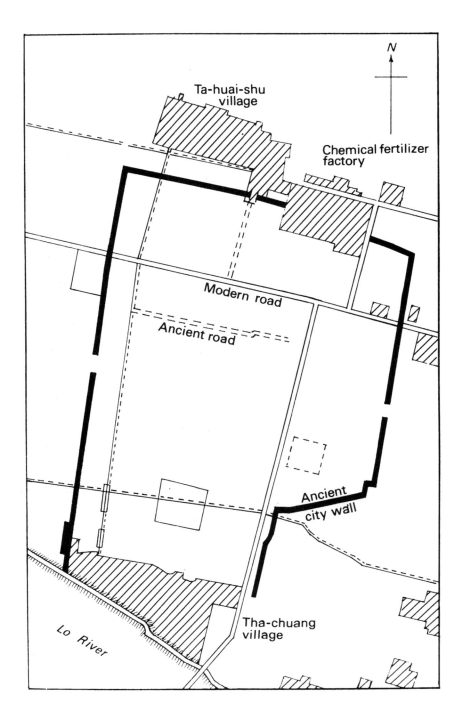

Figure 5.2. Ground plan of the Xia or Shang city at Shixianggou, Yanshi. After Zhongguo shehui kexueyuan kaogu yanjiusuo Luoyang Han Wei gucheng gongzuodui 1984:figure 2. From Needham and Yates (1994: 296:figure 140). Reprinted with permission of Cambridge University Press.

sites that were, and some unwalled sites should be examined in relation to nearby walled enceintes. For example, the twin sites in Yanshi, Henan province, where the one at Shixianggou is walled and the other, the Erlitou type site, predominantly containing palatial or ritual structures, is not, may have been the capital region of the Xia state, although this identification has been hotly contested among the specialists (Figs. 5.2–5.4; Chang 1986; Huber 1988; Needham and Yates 1994; Thorp 1991).

The Concept of the City-State

The subject of this volume, therefore, poses some difficulties for the archaeologist/historian of ancient China. The first of these difficulties is created by the nature of the theoretical positions that have been adopted over the years by scholars both inside and outside China for the study of the developmental sequence of Chinese civilization. Traditional Chinese scholars from the time of the first Chinese empire

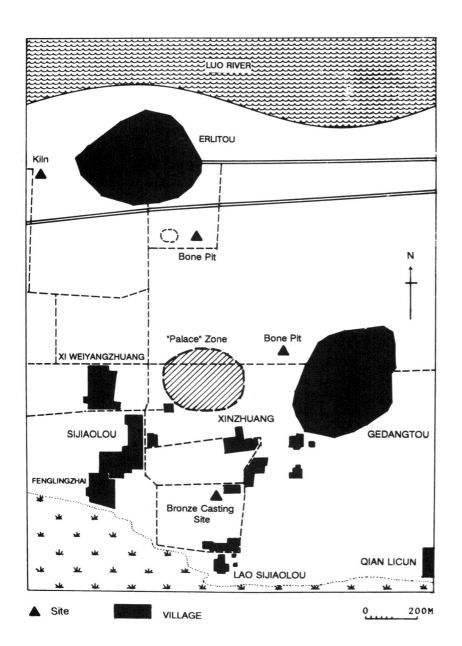

Figure 5.3. Sketch map of the Erlitou type site. Map by John A. Wysocki based on Chinese originals, from Thorp (1991:figure 1). Reprinted with permission of the author.

(third–second century B.C.) assumed that no fundamental distinction existed between the form of the political system in the three earliest dynasties, the Xia, Shang, and Zhou (the so-called Sandai or Three Dynasties, possibly late third to first millennium B.C.), and those of their own time. So they read back into the past the conditions and practices of their own day.

Marxist scholars on the mainland, on the other hand, adopted the simplistic formula of cultural evolution derived from Morgan (1877) as filtered through the work of Marx and Engels, especially Engels's *The Origin of the Family, Private Property and the State* (1972): namely that ancient China had passed through the stages of primitive communism

with patriarchy replacing the original matriarchy, slavery, and feudalism. Researchers in the west such as Creel (1970) and Hsu (1965) adopted a Weberian approach and were anxious to find a feudal empire as early as the eleventh century B.C. with the Zhou conquest of the Shang dynasty (ca. 1045 B.C.) which evolved into a rational-legal bureaucracy by the third century B.C. The apparent desire here was to demonstrate that China had not been as backward as nineteenth- and early-twentieth-century colonialist and imperialist scholars had thought: it had actually passed through the same evolutionary sequence as the West, but even earlier: the arrest in its evolutionary development came much later. However different

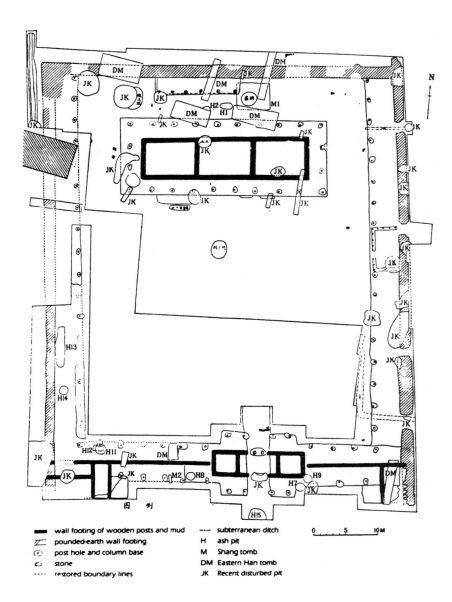

Figure 5.4. Plan of F2, Zone V, Erlitou.
From Thorp (1991:figure 3). Reprinted
with permission of the author.

▬ wall footing of wooden posts and mud	--- subterranean ditch	
⌇ pounded-earth wall footing	H ash pit	
⊙ post hole and column base	M Shang tomb	
◠ stone	DM Eastern Han tomb	
---- restored boundary lines	JK Recent disturbed pit	

0   5   10M

these positions are, all of them have more or less tended to encourage the practice of finding data in the Chinese record to match whatever theory was accepted a priori, rather than to stimulate the desire to generate hypotheses which could then be tested.[2] More recently, the paradigm adopted by scholars such as Kwang-chih Chang (1980), David Keightley (1983a), and Anne Underhill (1991) has been that of the chiefdom/state: I will discuss its application to the Chinese data below.

The second difficulty in studying city-states in early China is in analyzing potential candidates from the archaeological point of view. As there has been no access to the field by any scholars other than the Chinese since Liberation in 1949, the type of data that has been generated there has been produced with the sole aim of proving their accepted paradigm.[3] As the concept of the city-state has not been considered relevant by archaeologists in China, no effort has been expended to discover potential city-state sites or complexes and little data is available to analyze the formation of a potential city-state system or hierarchical settlement patterns (Tu Cheng-sheng 1986).[4]

If we take the Greek model of the city-state from the ideological point of view and posit that the city-state must be based on a free citizenry who possess legal rights through the ownership of land (cf. Weissleder 1978), it could well be argued that, since the Chinese never possessed a system of *individual* legal rights and landownership, as opposed to land possession, was always claimed by the state, the Chinese never could have had a system of city-states.[5]

On the other hand, Griffeth and Thomas suggest four criteria for the identification of city-states: a well-defined core surrounded by walls and/or a moat; economic self-sufficiency provided by the exploitation of a hinterland; a sense of common linguistic and cultural habits, and historical experience, shared with other city-states in the region; and political independence and de facto sovereignty, even though another polity might claim ultimate legal authority (1981a: xiii). These latter features I believe we can find in the Chinese record.

The third difficulty is related to the second. If the city state is indeed a "basic unit of state-level organization" as Charlton and Nichols suggest in Chapter 1, it is also important to determine when the state first appeared and what form(s) it took in the Chinese culture sphere. Since China has been convincingly proved to be one of the areas in which primary urban generation took place (Wheatley 1971), it is profitable to evaluate the theories on state formation that have been put forward by various scholars in the light of Chinese evidence and to try to clarify the nature of the early Chinese state in the light of these theories.

I will discuss first the problem of early state formation in China and then suggest that a city-state system did indeed develop there, and finally point out a few ways in which research into that system may help us interpret important features of the later mature traditional state of imperial times (post-221 B.C.).

The Chiefdom in the Longshan Phase

Unfortunately, the Chinese case has not featured in any significant way in recent, post-1980, studies of the state, such as those of Claessen and Skalník (1981), Claessen and van de Velde (1987b, 1991), and Johnson and Earle (1987), though Pokora (1978) contributed to the original symposium in Claessen and Skalník (1978). Nor has China generally been considered as having developed chiefdoms, whether of the simple or complex variety, possessing a staple or wealth mode of financing, or containing a group-oriented or individualizing structure (Earle 1987, 1989).

Among scholars of China, Underhill (1991, 1992) is alone, except for Wheatley (1971) and Liu (1994; see below), in explicitly using the chiefdom/state paradigm. She posits that the late Neolithic Longshan interaction sphere (third millennium B.C.) was at a stage of complex chiefdoms, though she does not argue for her interpretation,[6] and she suggests that the Xia may

have developed state organization, though she does not characterize the Xia as a city-state (1990).

Most recently, Yan Wenming has observed that nearly thirty walled sites dating from the Longshan period have been discovered (1994—not all of these have been published) and that the original black-pottery site of Chengziyai in Shandong has been reclassified as belonging to the Yueshi culture. Yan argues that the Longshan walled sites can be roughly divided into three groups. The first group is located in the middle and southern part of Inner Mongolia. Dating from early Longshan, the sites are generally small in area, from several thousands to several tens of thousands of square feet and are situated on mountains. He identifies three separate locations where groups of these enclosures have been discovered and the walls are constructed out of stone and mud. Kessler notes that the largest of these structures encloses an area of 10 hectares (1994:34). The greatest remaining height of the walls is between 2.1 and 3.5 meters and the largest width at the base is between 6 and 13 meters.

The second group is found in the middle reaches of the Yangzi River in central China. Dating from late Qujialing to early Shijiahe times in early Longshan, the walled sites here are very large. Shijiahe in Tianmenshi, Hubei, encloses nearly 100 hectares and Majiayuan in Jingmenshi, Hubei, covers almost 20 hectares. At Shijiahe, the roughly rectangular stamped-earth wall is 40–50 meters broad at the base and still stands to a height of 3 to 4 meters. It extends more than 1,000 meters north-south and more than 900 meters east-west. Outside the wall, the moat is several tens of meters wide. Inside, the foundations of several houses belonging to the elite have been discovered and to the northwest lie a cemetery and religious center. Here two pits with more than a thousand figurines of animals and humans have been excavated, including representations of pigs, dogs, oxen, sheep, chickens, monkeys, elephants, long-tailed birds, turtles, and fish; among the humans, there are figures wearing flat caps and long robes, and some are standing and some kneeling holding fish. Another three religious buildings have been identified in the southwest.

The third group is in the lower Yellow River region. The late Longshan sites here are also relatively large in area, ranging from several hectares to several tens of hectares, although Wangchenggang is an exception.[7] Notable, too, is the guardhouse at Pingliangtai in Henan (Fig. 5.5) with pottery drainpipes under the entrance gate. Another very significant discovery at

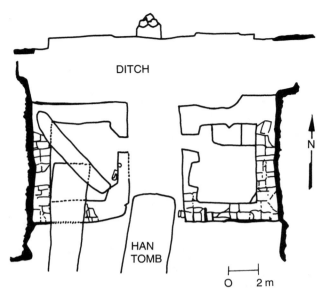

Figure 5.5. Ground plan of the Neolithic city of Pingliangtai (left); ground plan of the south gate and its flanking guard rooms (right). After Henan sheng wenwu yanjiusuo Zhoukou diqu wenhua qu wenwuke (1983 3: 27–28:figures 16 and 18). From Needham and Yates (1994:figure 138). Reprinted with permission of Cambridge University Press.

Wangchenggang was a fragment of black pottery, the flat base of a ceramic vessel which bore an inscription, carved before firing, of the single graph *gong* (Wang Zhenzhong 1992 vol. 2:234; Li Xiandeng 1984).

The exceptional size of the middle Yangzi sites suggests that the elite leaders of these communities were able to command the labor power of a considerable number of people to build the defensive fortifications, an indication that warfare had become an integral way of life for the inhabitants. Nonetheless, it seems correct to follow Underhill and conclude that these Longshan polities were still more or less comparable to the complex Mississippian chiefdoms of the southeastern United States such as Moundville discussed by Peebles and Kus (1977).[8]

The Early Bronze Age State

As mentioned above, the question of the historicity of the Xia dynasty is hotly contested and most Chinese scholars have attempted to correlate archaeological sites with the traditional historical record of there having been a dynastic state prior to the Shang (Huber 1988; Thorp 1991). Chang (1986) correlates Erlitou culture sites with traditional Xia dynastic capitals (Fig. 5.6), but Allan thinks that the Xia was an imaginary obverse of Shang existing only in the mythic thought of the Shang (1991). The area of Erli-

tou sites is quite prescribed, but it is too early yet to determine whether it is justifiable to interpret the cultural remains, which have been categorized into five subtypes based on the spatial distribution of pottery (Zou Heng 1980; Thorp 1991), as a regional system of city-states that in the course of their development learned the art of bronze making.[9]

We are better informed about the succeeding second-millennium Bronze Age culture of Shang, with which Chang and Keightley concern themselves, relying on the early discussions of the state in cross-cultural perspective. In an early formulation, Service claimed that

a true state is distinguishable from chiefdoms in particular, and all lower levels (of socio-cultural integration) in general, by the presence of that special form of control, the consistent threat of force by a body of persons legitimately constituted to use it. . . . Monopoly of force, as opposed to the power of the chief, for example, who might if necessary hold an *advantage* of force, is important; one of the simplest but most notable indices of a state's power lies in the degree to which personal (nongovernmental) use of force is outlawed and thereafter prevented. The presence of feud signifies the absence of state power at that time and place. (1971)

Wheatley (1977:544), in reviewing K. C. Chang's early studies on urbanism in China (Chang 1976), suggests that, because of the appearance of the conical clan in the Shang period (second millennium B.C.) as the basis of social and political structure, Shang was a chiefdom that "lacked a formal apparatus of forceful repression." Chang himself, however, in his illuminating study of Shang civilization (1980), quotes Flannery's characterization of the state as

a type of very strong, unusually highly centralized government with a professional ruling class, largely divorced from the bonds of kinship which characterize simpler societies. It is highly stratified and extremely diversified internally, with residential patterns often based on occupational specialization rather than blood or affinal relationship. The state attempts to maintain a monopoly of force, and is characterized by true law; almost any crime may be considered a crime against the state, in which case punishment is meted out by the state according to codified procedures rather than being the responsibility of the offended party or his kin, as in simpler societies. While individual citizens must forego violence, the state can wage war; it can also draft soldiers, levy taxes and exact tributes.

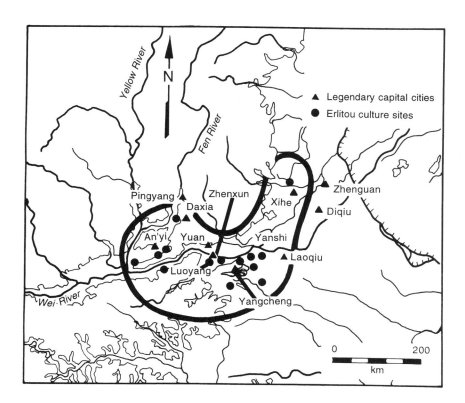

Figure 5.6. Major Erlitou culture sites and traditional Xia dynasty capitals. From Kwang-chih Chang, *The Archaeology of Ancient China,* 4th ed. (New Haven: Yale University Press, 1986), figure 272. © 1986 by Yale University. Reprinted with permission of Yale University Press.

Chang singles out the replacement of territorial bonds for kinship bonds and the monopoly of force as the criteria of state organization: Shang had a monopoly of force, but the replacement of territorial bonds did not occur. Since, however, Shang had social classes, a hierarchical ruling structure, and legitimate force, Shang must have been a state and it is necessary either to revise the criteria for statehood or consider the Chinese to be the anomalous case in the evolutionary sequence. More recent comparative work has, however, rejected the notion that lineage ceases to be an important feature in city-states (Griffeth and Thomas 1981a; Stone, this volume), and it is clear that earlier forms of association based on kinship continued to play an important integrating function throughout the life of the Greek city-states (Ferguson 1991; Small, this volume).[10]

Among the principal sources for the study of Shang history are the records of divinations scratched on cattle scapulae and turtle plastrons made by the Shang kings in the last 150 to 200 years of the dynasty from Wu Ding to the last king Zhou, Di Xin, who was attacked and killed by Wu Wang of the succeeding Zhou dynasty (probably mid-eleventh century B.C.). Inscriptions on bronze vessels provide supplementary information, but they are quite terse in contrast to those found on later Zhou examples. Further infor-

mation can be deduced from the archaeological record of residential sites and tomb furnishings found in excavations of sites such as the last capital of the Shang at Anyang, Henan province, and the small, fort-like, middle Shang outpost at Panlongcheng, Hubei (Chang 1980, 1986). Regrettably, Chinese archaeologists have not seen fit to expend much energy in determining settlement patterns, though I will provide some information below, so it is the oracle-bone records which have provided scholars with the richest source for the study of the question of the nature of the Shang polity.

It could be argued that it is really not very profitable to debate whether or not Shang was a complex chiefdom in Earle and others' formulation or a state in Service and Flannery's terms: what is more important is to try to see how the Shang and the Western Zhou actually operated their governments and how their societies were organized. But if we approach the data with the wrong conceptual framework, we will inevitably fall into numerous methodological mistakes as well as possible false interpretations of the often ambiguous data. This appears to be Herrlee Creel's mistake in his well-known study of the *Origins of Statecraft in China* (1970) in Western Zhou times. Creel bases his chapters on the analysis of putative institutions and titles his chapters "Finance," "Justice," and so on, even though there does not appear to *be* a concept of justice in Western Zhou times, and it has not yet been determined whether there was merely intermittent tribute or regular taxes sent from the subordinates of the Zhou to the center.

Exactly the same problem faces the researcher in the study of the Shang, if her concentration is focused upon institutions. What, for example, in Flannery's definition is meant by the term *true law* which he says characterizes the state? The terms *dian* and *ci* are usually adduced as evidence that the Shang had a code of laws (e.g., Chang 1980). *Dian,* however, means a document, as does *ci,* and refers rather to the records that were kept of the gifts that the king made, the original graph being a picture of bamboo or wooden slips being held by two hands.[11] It is only much later that *dian* came to mean what is normative by virtue of what was written down. Actual codes were only promulgated in the sixth century B.C., and the earliest extant systematic legal enactments are the Qin laws found at Yunmeng, which date possibly from the fourth century B.C. Actual regular or fixed procedures in legal proceedings only date from this time: the recent discoveries of disputes on late Western Zhou bronzes corroborate this view. Punishment of a broken obligation seems to have been a matter of bargaining between the two parties, not the imposition of a fixed penalty determined by the state.

With regard to the question of the control of force, it is clear from the oracle-bone inscriptions that the Shang could mobilize large numbers of persons for a military campaign, up to 13,000 in the case of Fu Hao, one of the principal wives of King Wu Ding, who led an expedition against the Qiang tribes.[12] The question of the Shang's *monopoly* of force, however, is in doubt: since we have only records of divinations from the Shang center, we cannot say whether segmented lineages had the right or the ability to mount campaigns on their own, without the permission or the help of the Shang king. This lack of independent documentary sources poses very serious difficulties for the student of the early Chinese state, for why should we accept at face value the claims of what are clearly ideologically biased religious records?

Nevertheless, much useful evidence can be gleaned from the oracle-bone inscriptions. Historical details of matters of daily concern to the Shang kings can be learned from them which cannot be gathered from other sources. Numerous inscriptions record questions about the harvest—whether, for example, it would be gathered in a specific place—and record the

theft by a certain *fang,* a term which appears to have designated groups on the periphery of the Shang who did not accept the Shang's claim to be the only legitimate authority and who were often the object of Shang attack. The Shang also seem to have sent groups of men called *zhongren,* who were organized in sections of one hundred men each, the largest number being three hundred, divided into an upper, middle, and lower section, to open up fields in the territory of those *fang.* There is scant evidence that the *fang* were states on the borders of the Shang, as K. C. Chang asserts, most of them could just as well have been hunting-gathering tribes with territories whose resources they exploited throughout but which lacked fixed borders. While some of these *fang* may indeed have possessed urban centers or citadels protected by stamped-earth walls, the Shang do not specify in their inscriptions the level of cultural sophistication of their opponents.[13]

In my opinion, the expeditions of *zhongren* organized along lineage and military lines were probably one of the most important means by which the Shang were able to incorporate more territory under their control.[14] Some locations are called *fang* in early records where the *zhongren* were agriculturally active. Later on the appellation *fang* is dropped, implying that the Shang had more permanent control over them. These *zhongren* engaged in other hard-labor activities apart from agricultural work and military operations: they also seem to have been responsible for building settlements (*yi*) and the rammed-earth foundations of the ritually significant buildings, and seem to have been under the direct supervision of lineage heads who participated in the Shang polity and who were subordinate to the Shang kings (cf. Zhu Fenghan 1990). The *zhongren,* together with the lowest level of the Shang population, were described linguistically as an undifferentiated mass. The heads of the lesser lineages were known by their lineage name, which was also the name of their town or settlement (*yi*).

Henry Wright has proposed a dynamic conceptualization of the state that suggests that

a *state* can be *recognized* as a society with specialized decision-making organizations that are receiving messages from many different sources, recoding their messages, supplementing them with previously stored data, making the actual decision, and conveying decisions back to other organizations. Such organizations are thus internally as well as externally specialized. Such societies contrast with those in which relations between the society's component organizations are mediated only by a generalized decision-maker and with those in which relations between component organizations are exclusively self-regulating. In contrast, a state can be *conceptualized* as a socio-cultural system in which there is a differentiated, internally specialized, decision-making sub-system that regulates varying exchanges among other sub-systems and with other systems. (1978:56)

Wright's formulation has, to be sure, received its share of criticism, especially for his somewhat arbitrary presumption that a state possesses at least three levels in its administrative hierarchy. Nevertheless, the fact that the Shang population was described as an undifferentiated mass suggests that Shang had not reached the kind of organizational level Wright proposes for a state.

David Keightley has proposed a series of thirty-nine criteria to judge whether a given group was a member of the Shang state, an ally, a dependency, or an enemy, or a nonmember of the state (1979–80).[15] These criteria are grouped under the subheadings Sovereignty, Territoriality, Religion and Kinship, Alliance, Warfare, and Exchange. Each group receives a state score calculated by multiplying the number of times the group appears in the inscriptions by the number of times it meets one of the criteria. While this is an admirable preliminary attempt to assess the importance of certain groups to the Shang, Keightley makes some important assumptions that cannot be verified. What justification is there, for example, to claim that the notion of sovereignty is appropriate as an analytic category for interpreting Shang ideas? This concept implies a well-defined sense of law, which we have just seen cannot be verified with evidence currently available. In addition, in the inscriptions only two levels in the hierarchy at most can be perceived. This suggests strongly that the Shang was not particularly internally differentiated and that the Shang was either a chiefdom or, at best, a minimal state, as Keightley himself points out. The divinations take these forms: "the Shang king orders X to do something" or "calls upon X to do something," or "the king orders X to lead the men of Y."

The king takes a personal and religious interest in the day-to-day activities of his subordinates, very much like the big-man of the egalitarian tribe; he is not so much the administrator of administrators, presiding over a large organization with internal specialization, as Wright suggests is necessary in a state system (1978; cf. Qi Wenxin 1991–92). But the evidence

may be misleading. It is quite possible that one of the uses of the oracle-bone divinations was to create a consensus as well as to validate a decision. The reading of the cracks must have involved considerable debate among the participants of the rite, especially since the answers, whether positive or negative, were not immediately clear from the cracks themselves as they appeared when the heat was applied to the bone.[16] Diviners, and possibly the shamans who assisted the king in his oracle-taking, most likely came from lineages allied to him by marriage, and so it was through the collective participation in the rite that bureaucratic and political decisions were made. Perhaps this was part of the religious heritage of the bureaucrats of imperial times, for they too were assistants to the emperor in keeping the cosmos in harmony.

I would suggest that the various policies aimed at segmenting and dividing the undifferentiated mass of the people that were proposed and implemented from Springs and Autumns times down to the Qin and Han empires (eighth to second centuries B.C.) were also attempts to reorganize and control geographical and social space. This was essentially an attempt to reorder the cosmos and the natural and human worlds (Yates 1994). Even the donation of grades of aristocratic or meritocratic rank (*jue*) to commoners for success in battle instituted by the legalist statesman Lord Shang in the fourth century B.C. in the northwestern state of Qin was an effort to draw into the ritual hierarchy all members of the community from Heaven on down through the ruler, the ministers, to the masses at the bottom of the social ladder.

In the light of the foregoing evidence, I would suggest that the definitions proposed by Western theorists of the state in the 1970s and their applications to the Chinese evidence, with their emphasis on Western-type institutions, fail to provide an adequate framework for analyzing both the early Chinese polity and the traditional Chinese state. The lineage and family structure of the Shang and Western Zhou became the basis of the social structure of traditional China (cf. Chun 1990), and this structure was preeminently a military one. The religion of the Shang, ancestor worship, became one of the most potent legitimizing forces for the imperial regime. The bureaucracy was always conceptualized as performing an essential religious and cosmic task (Yates 1994): of this we see the very small beginnings in the Shang (Keightley 1978), and it developed into one of the most permanent features of China's tradition of government. We must therefore make a new attempt to characterize the nature of the polity in Shang and Western Zhou times, one in which the king is seen rather in his role as gift-giver than as administrator, where his peregrinations are given their full cultural meaning (Keightley 1983a; Thorp 1985), and where the ancient Chinese people's own views of their world are taken into consideration.

While thus far I have emphasized the chiefdom-state paradigm, I recognize that some theorists have advanced cogent arguments criticizing the concept of the chiefdom, arguing that we should be looking for the characteristics of scale, level of integration, and complexity in any given society (Blanton et al. 1981: 17; Spencer 1987:379).

The City-State in China

In the light of the preceding discussion, it seems to me that the concept of the city-state is useful for the case of China, but in a particular way: it corresponds more closely to the Chinese notion of their settlements than do other models. Chang asserts that there is a fundamental difference between the Western and what he calls the "Asian-American" experience in the evolution of civilization, namely, that the Western experience is characterized by "rupture" with respect to man's relation to nature (the environment, the cosmos), whereas the Asian-American is characterized by "continuity" (1989). Chang argues that shamans were crucial to maintaining this "continuous" politico-religious system of the Neolithic and Shang cultures for they were able to communicate between the two spheres of existence, the lower world of earth and of humans and the upper world of heaven, deities, and ghosts. They could bring down the spirits to help humans, specifically to prophesy the future, and thus provide direction in everyday affairs such that "during the Shang period shamanism and political power were closely linked" (Chang 1994a:35; cf. Chang 1994b; Fung 1994; Mathieu 1987). I perceive some problems with Chang's interpretation of the pervasiveness and importance of shamanism in early China for I see no evidence that the kings themselves were shamans, no king is called "shaman-X", for example, the kings did not engage in cosmic flights, nor were they healers, although the later tradition does contain stories of archaic kings performing shaman-like rituals.[17] If shamans were so crucial to kingship in the early stages of the Bronze Age, Chang must explain how and why their position changed so radically in the later Bronze Age. From 700 B.C. on shamans

were located at the lower margins of society; they were outcasts, and subject to strict regulation and control by the political authorities.

In addition, I do not think that the archaic Chinese state was characterized by "true law" (Flannery's 1972 term). Here Chang has undercut his own argument about Asian or Chinese difference from the Western experience of evolution. This point is important, for many Western theorists stress the role of law. Max Weber is a notable example. According to Weber (1958), Chinese cities were primarily administrative centers. They had no separate legal existence as Western cities had from the later Middle Ages on, and thus their function in the Chinese political hierarchy was completely different. The structure and function of Chinese cities were not conducive for the emergence of the modern Western capitalist system in Weber's opinion; and yet, of course, from A.D. 1000 in the imperial period Chinese cities were far larger and more economically vibrant and culturally active than their counterparts in Western Europe. Donald V. Kurtz also stresses law in the development of states and his article, "The Legitimation of Early Inchoate States" (Kurtz 1981) is a classic example of orientalist thinking, with its uncritical assumption of the centrality of law in early states. One can have cities without them being separate legal entities, and one can have the legitimation of states without law.

A more appropriate approach to early Chinese chiefdom and state development is to be found through recognizing the validity of Chang's assertion that there was a profound difference between the Western and the Asian paradigms for the emergence of civilization: I leave the Americanists to debate its relevance to their data. This approach presumes that it is essential to analyze the Chinese people's own terminology and interpretation of their sociopolitical and cultural practices. In the Shang, all walled settlements were called *yi*, suggesting that they did not differentiate between settlements, no matter what their size or function. Before the construction of such settlements, divination frequently was resorted to, to ensure that the chosen site was auspicious (Peng Bangjiong 1982). In the Zhou, however, the state was the *guo*, and it is this that Tu Cheng-sheng (1986) has interpreted as a "feudal city-state." In turn, this "city-state" can be interpreted as close to the model that Tambiah has characterized as existing in a "galactic polity" (1977, 1985). Although Tambiah explained this model as deriving out of the concept of the *mandala*, implying that it was introduced into Southeast

Asia from India after the turn of the millennium, it may in fact represent a much more archaic Asian system of cosmic thinking or mode of being. A significant element of this model is the centrality of ritual to the political process and the principle of ritual replication of the center in the creation of the hierarchy of settlements or settlement clusters.

In the Chinese case, this is represented by the way in which all space, human and divine, secular and sacred, is incorporated into a system of nested hierarchies, boxes within boxes, compartmentalized and separated, yet each one being a template of the system as a whole (cf. Granet 1968; Yates 1994). The entire universe is therefore an organic whole (Chang 1989; Needham 1959) and humans are not categorically distinct from deities, nor are the dead in a state of alterity with respect to the living. This mode of thinking encourages inclusion, not exclusion, and emphasizes relationships, not individuation. Hence Flannery's point about the loosening of blood ties, of kinship structures in the state is irrelevant to the Asian/Chinese case.

On the ground in ancient China this patterning is represented by the formation of walled settlements (*yi*), although it would appear that it was by no means *necessary* that the settlement be walled (Keightley 1982). The ancient graph for this term *yi* seems to be a human beneath an enclosure made (ideally) of stamped earth. As few as ten households could be located within the wall, or it could be the state capital, as in the term Dayi Shang (Fig. 5.7), the great settlement of Shang, probably the last capital discovered at Anyang, northern Henan province.[18] Tu Cheng-sheng points out that the "area within the city wall was referred to as '*kuo (guo)*,*'* and the lands between the walls [*cheng*] and the borders of the fiefdom were known as '*yeh*' (*ye*) (or '*wilds*'). The entire territory within the limits of the fiefdom constituted the domain of the city-state, or in a general sense, of the *kuo* (state)" (1986).

In larger settlements, sometimes there were two or more walls. Cultivated fields could be found inside the walls of the inner enclosure. According to later written sources, partially confirmed by archaeological excavation, the position of the settlement in the hierarchy was signified by the type of religious buildings that were constructed inside. The capital held the altars of soil and grain of the entire state, as well as the ancestral temple of the dominant lineage, whereas the smallest village only contained the altar of the soil of the local deity. Regular sacrifices were required to feed both ancestors and soil-and-grain spirits. The latter enjoyed blood sacrifices provided by the slaughter of enemy in battle. Physically, the altars were mounds of earth with a tree planted on top and open to the sky. Covering over the altar would kill the spirits, because they would no longer receive the cosmic essences or ethers (*qi*), the material substance or lifeforce out of which the universe was created and which flowed through all things, animate and inanimate.

The outer boundary of the state was likewise marked by an earthen mound planted with trees. This was known as a *feng*. The establishment of the *feng*, with its symbolic representation of, and connection to, the altars of soil and grain at the center, expressed the creation of the state. Space was thereby ordered through the creation of relations of inner and outer spheres and thereby fitted into the cosmic whole. Virtually all, if not all, scholars claim that this *feng* system is the same as the feudal system of medieval Europe, and claim that China therefore had feudalism far earlier than the West (e.g., Creel 1970; Hsu 1965; Tu Cheng-sheng 1992). This is an error, for it completely disregards the symbolism that the Chinese were manipulating to give order to their world.[19]

What was the size of the average city-state (*guo*) in ancient China? Classical texts of the fifth to third centuries B.C. indicate that the largest were about 64 kilometers and the smallest about 19 kilometers per side of the outer boundaries and 32 kilometers would have been typical of the classical Chinese city-state (Tu Cheng-sheng 1986). The central enceinte may have been typically no larger than 250 meters long per side with a population of 3,000 households. This gives, according to Lin Yun (1986), on average a space of 158.7 square meters per household. He has shown that, from Neolithic times through the Bronze Age, this land-to-household ratio was approximately the same, 150–160 square meters per household, although, of course, the size of the *guo* state could vary tremendously.

One of the best-excavated Zhou city-state capitals is that of Lu, the home of Confucius, the famous philosopher, the present site of Qufu, Shandong province in eastern China (Fig. 5.8). Here an outer, roughly rectangular, defensive wall with a perimeter 11,771 meters in circumference protected large residential areas and many areas of workshops, including bronze, iron, bone, and pottery. The roads were constructed to cross at approximate right angles and the palace precincts were situated as a compound in the center of the entire enceinte. This latter form is what

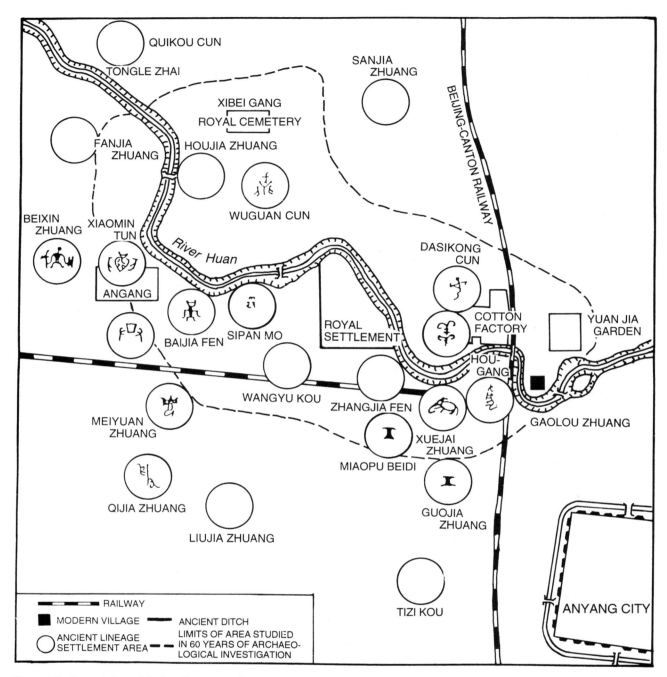

Figure 5.7. Ground plan of the late Shang capital, Dayi Shang, at Anyang. From Zheng Ruokui (1995:figure 2).

is recorded in the ancient texts, such as the *Zhou Li* (*Rites of Zhou*) as being the norm, although in fact there was considerable variation, depending on region and the physical environment (Ma Shizhi 1981, 1984, 1987; Needham and Yates 1994; Tu Cheng-sheng 1992). Much effort was expended by the excavators of Lu in determining the structure and layering of the city walls and obviously the defenses were repaired and improved many times over many centuries (Fig.

5.9). Presently, although there has been enormous damage inflicted upon them, the stamped-earth walls still stand to a considerable height. For example, the eastern side of the Eastern Gate on the southern wall is 7 meters high. The gate was 36 meters long and 10 meters wide (Tian An 1988), and probably originally topped with wooden towers (details in Needham and Yates 1994), the road running through it providing access to the important ritual structure, the Rain

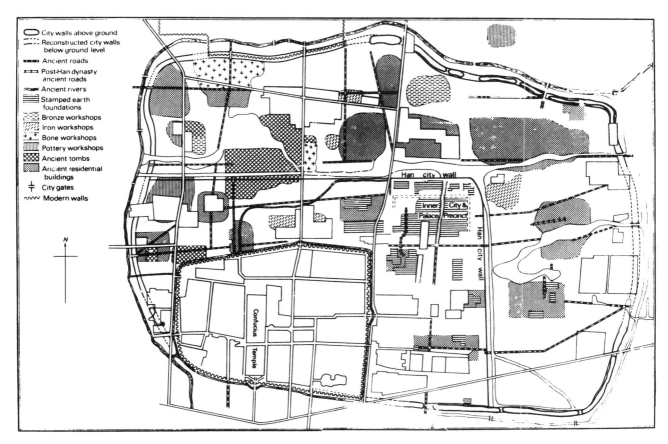

Figure 5.8. Plan of the capital of the state of Lu, Qufu, Shandong province. After Shandong sheng wenwu kaogu yanjiusuo (1982:figure 3). From Needham and Yates (1994:figure 141). Reprinted with permission of Cambridge University Press.

Dance Platform 1.7 kilometers to the south. Unfortunately, as in virtually all excavations in the Chinese heartland, the archaeologists were not able to determine precise details of the residential areas, and so the relative size of individual family compounds in this site is unknown.

Two other sites have been especially well excavated, the first at Jinan is the former capital of the very large state of Chu based in the middle Yangzi valley (Fig. 5.10) and another is the group of cities which formed the capital of the north-central state of Jin which was broken up into three smaller regional city-state systems at the beginning of the Warring States period (mid-fifth century B.C.). Given that the Jin cities are composed of walled enceintes in very close proximity to each other and given that it is known that Jin possessed very strong lineages, three of whom ultimately disposed of their rivals and divided the state, it is tempting to see this cluster of cities (Fig. 5.11) as similar to the "citadel" mounds at Mohenjo-daro discussed by Kenoyer (this volume): the headquarters at the state capital of powerful elite lineages.

The actual placement of smaller settlements in relation to the larger is not known at present because, as mentioned above, Chinese archaeologists have not invested much time in the study of settlement patterns.[20] Lin Yun (1986), however, has observed that clusters of *yi* settlements were differentiated into central capitals (*du*) and "appanages" (*bi*). The graph *bi* in the Shang oracle bones appears to depict a granary, which might suggest that the smaller settlements provided grain for the central capital that housed, in addition to farmers, specialized artisans, overseers of sacrifices, administrators, and merchants. Later on, in the time of the flowering of philosophical theorizing in the Warring States period (fifth to third centuries B.C.) when the states gradually came to be consolidated under new, more centralized regimes (Hsu 1965), the organization of the settlement hierarchy and the naming of the different parts exercised the minds of philosophers and statesmen alike. Many different proposals were made. The form of government also became the most intensely debated intellectual problem of the day as good order in the cosmos was

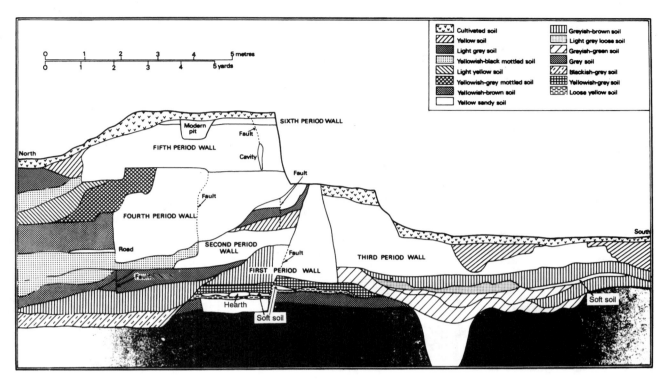

Figure 5.9. Cross-section of east wall, Qufu, site of the capital of the state of Lu at excavation site T505. After Shandong sheng wenwu kaogu yanjiusuo (1982:figure 18a). From Needham and Yates (1994:figure 143). Reprinted with permission of Cambridge University Press.

seen as dependent on good order in the human realm. A typical example is the section "Military Taxes" of the *Guanzi* translated by Rickett (1985:116, 119–120), which probably derives from the eastern state of Qi:

ON SITUATING THE CAPITAL (*Li Guo*)
Always situate the capital and urban centers (*du*) either at the foot of a great mountain or above [the bank of] a broad river. To insure sufficient water, avoid placing them so high as to approach the drought [level]. To conserve on [the need for] canals and embankments, avoid placing them so low as to approach the flood [level]. Take advantage of the resources of Heaven and adapt yourself to the strategic features of Earth. Hence city and suburban walls need not [rigidly] accord with the compass and square [i.e., need not be precisely square or rectangular and aligned to the cardinal points], nor roads with the level and marking line. . . .

ON THE GENTLEMEN, PEASANTS, ARTISANS, AND MERCHANTS
. . . An area six *li* [a *li* was approximately a third of a mile] square is called a village (*bao*). Five villages are called a section (*bu*), and five sections are called a subdistrict (*ju*). Each subdistrict should have a marketplace. If it does not, the people will suffer shortages. Five subdistricts are called

such and such a district (*xiang*). Four districts are called an area [*fang*, the same term that appears in the Shang oracle-bone inscriptions, see above]. This is the organization for administrations under direct rule (*guan*).

When [the organization of] administrations under direct rule has been completed, set up the areas administered through rural towns (*yi*). Five households (*jia*) form a group of five (*wu*), and ten households a group (*lian*). Five groups form a village (*bao*), and five villages a headquarters unit (*zhang*) known as such and such a district (*xiang*). Four districts are called a region (*du*). This is the organization of areas administered through rural towns.

When [the organization of] these areas has been completed, organize production. Four strips (*ju*) constitute a plot (*li*), and five plots a lot (*zhi*). Five lots constitute a field (*tian*), and two fields an individual tract (*fu*). Three such tracts constitute [the land] of a household. This is the organization for production.

With regard to the dating of the appearance of these "city-states," and to their termination, it seems as though the general patterning of the settlements began as early as the Yangshao (ca. 5000–3000 B.C.) Neolithic, with stamped-earth walls emerging in the Longshan interaction period (3000–2000 B.C.). From about 700 B.C., settlements were incorporated into

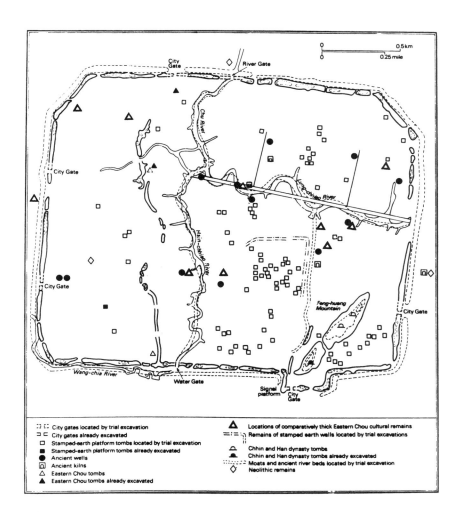

Figure 5.10. Ground plan of Jinan city, site of the capital of Chu. After Hubei sheng bowuguan (1982:figure 2). From Needham and Yates (1994:figure 146). Reprinted with permission of Cambridge University Press.

larger and larger systems through incessant warfare until in 221 B.C. a single empire was formed. While it is probably fair to posit that there was a "regional city-state system" in the later stages of this period, with each city ritually replicating the center in a galactic polity (cf. Tambiah 1977), the precise political, economic, and religious relationships between the central place and its surrounding hinterland cannot be determined in our present state of knowledge. The *pattern of settlement* I have described, however, remained intact. When central administrative control collapsed at the end of the second century A.D., the units of the galactic polity of the Han fragmented, some to be abandoned completely, others once again to be recombined into smaller polities until the Sui reunified the entire country in A.D. 589.

A few more comments on the economy of the Chinese city-states are in order. First of all, the states were based on self-sufficient agriculture. In the early period, control of long-distance trade does not seem to have played a significant role in their development,

although, of course, there was some circulation of, and trade in, prestige goods, such as cowry shells, jade, and turtle plastrons. As Chang has observed (1980), it was control over the labor force that provided state functionaries with the means to extract grain resources for their support and the means to create the stamped-earth constructions, such as walls and temple foundations, and large subterranean tombs, which displayed the power of the elite and their ritual preeminence. Trade, the regional specialization in products, metal currency, and an independent merchant class only appeared very late, after 700 B.C. (Hsu 1965), when the conquest of smaller states by the larger and the weaker by the stronger created larger and larger hierarchies, together with an increasing complexity of nested systems—in other words regional city-state or peer-polity systems, rather like the networks developed by Sparta and Athens. Nor does there appear to be very much evidence of redistribution of resources from the center in the early period, although perhaps it occurred. Resources cer-

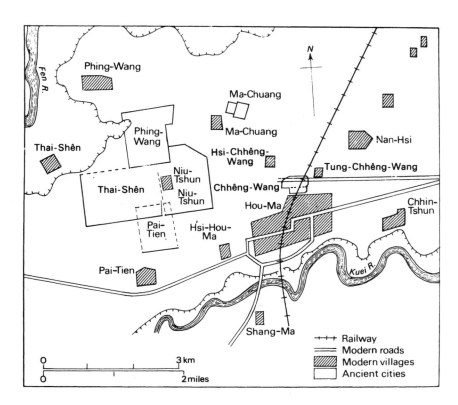

Figure 5.11. The ancient cities that made up Xintian, capital of the state of Jin. After Shansi sheng kaogu yanjiuso Houma gongzuo zhan (1988:figure 1). From Needham and Yates (1994:figure 89). Reprinted with permission of Cambridge University Press.

tainly were consumed by the elite, most notably in the form of the sacrifices made through the medium of the ritual bronzes so characteristic of the period 2000–200 B.C. As is well-known, these bronzes were used in the sacrifices to the ancestors, and it was in the sacrificial process that specialization of bureaucratic function first appeared (Keightley 1978). But though resources were consumed, they were not lost, for they provided the means by which the elite recreated and strengthened the bonds between the living and the dead and reaffirmed the continuity of being (Tu Wei-ming 1985:35–50).

Conclusion

Let me conclude briefly by saying that I find the concept of the city-state illuminating for the case of ancient China, not only because of the inadequacy of the feudal and imperial models that have been previously used to characterize the early Chinese political system, but also because the city-state corresponds far more closely to what the ancient Chinese understood as their model. However, the city-state in China was integrated into a model characterized by Tambiah (1985) as that of the galactic polity. Law was not essential, or significant, for the creation of the state,

but ritual and ritual replication was: each unit in the system was a representation of the ultimate unity of the cosmos, and over the centuries the units were combined and recombined into different configurations, but always based upon the same model. Thus when archaeologists study ancient city-states, it is essential for them also to take into consideration the "native's point of view" or the emic system to understand how the city-states were actually perceived to function in living reality.

When did the city-state emerge in China? Possibly with the Xia at Erlitou or the Shang at Zhengzhou. When were the last city-states incorporated into larger regional polities? Really only in the middle of the Warring States period when the various dominant states began to force all settlements into a state-controlled political hierarchy: when they were no longer politically independent and when they were forced to pay taxes into the central administration.[21] In other words, it is possible that the city-state period in China lasted longer, altogether approximately 1500 years, than in other parts of the world, although the individual city-states may have existed close to the five-hundred year maximum observed by Griffeth and Thomas (1981a).

Acknowledgment

I am most grateful to David N. Keightley who read the draft of this chapter with great care and made a number of suggestions for its improvement and for bibliographical additions.

Notes

1. Chang raises the suggestion that Shang was a city-state, but he does not develop or explore this possibility in his later research (1976:190). Peters intimates that if a Chinese state (*guo*) possessed only a single walled settlement, it might be considered a city-state. She does not push her suggestion further (1983:67). The nature of the *guo* will be examined below.

2. I realize I am being a little harsh here. Enormous strides have been made especially since 1949 in understanding Neolithic and Bronze Age China and undreamed-of discoveries have been made. Nevertheless, China has not been a source of models for cross-cultural theorizing and Chang has correctly observed that there was and is a strong tendency among Chinese scholars towards "dataism"; in other words, for scholars merely to report data without any conscious theoretical or conceptual models (1980). In the past five years or so, however, Chinese scholars have adopted a new approach and are now interested in developing theoretical models and applying them to data.

3. There is a strong possibility that this will change in the near future. K. C. Chang of Harvard University is engaged in a collaborative project to determine the location of the site of the earliest capital of the Shang dynasty, and scholars in China, such as Lin Yun of Jilin University and others, are adopting new theoretical models.

4. Tu Cheng-sheng points out that it was Hou Wailu who first suggested in 1941 that the concept of the "city-state" was valuable in reference to early China, and his initial formulation was taken up by two Japanese scholars. With the communist Liberation of China in 1949, however, the issue was dropped until Tu resurrected it.

5. Vitaly Rubin argues that there was a brief moment in the middle of the first millennium B.C. when at least one or two states in China moved towards the *polis* version of the city-state model, but this movement was quickly suppressed (1965, 1976).

6. Perhaps she would accept the following definition: the chiefdom or chieftaincy is characterized by the conical clan, and the units are ranked by the distance from the major lineage. People are therefore installed in societal positions and their authority comes from the organization rather than from their own efforts. Generally speaking, there are few or no classes in a chiefdom, for all members of the society are ultimately related to the common ancestor and so are related to each other. The paramount chief is the titular owner of his group's property, but it should be emphasized that he is rather the administrator of the property than the individual owner. He can, by appealing to his sacred power, direct the community's economic activities and thus intensify local production to support his own retinue. The paramount chief and his immediate relatives therefore consume far more than their needs for subsistence. Not only do they have the authority to command contribution from the lower-ranked members of their societies, but they have the means and the power to extract it. The resource flow therefore is characteristically centripetal. But it is not only centripetal, for the continuing obedience of the lesser lineages is largely dependent on the chief's activities as a redistributor of the resources (preciosities and/or staples) which flow to the center. A chiefdom, therefore, is a hierarchically organized society based on the conical clan which shows increasing economic specialization and division of labor.

7. The settlement seems to have consisted of two walled enclosures next to each other, but their exact dimensions remain unclear because erosion has heavily damaged the walls, especially those of the eastern enceinte. The western enceinte is roughly square, the western wall is 92 meters north-south slanting 5 degrees to the west, while the southern wall is 82.4 meters long (Chang 1986:273; Needham and Yates 1994:292, note C).

8. Liu Li has identified three different types of chiefdom systems in the middle and lower Yellow River valley in late Neolithic times; unified, competing, and underdeveloped (1994).

9. The most recent contribution to the debate is Dong Qi's (1995) essay, where Dong divides the historical development of Pre-Qin Chinese cities into three stages: (1) the period of castles (*chengbao*), from the beginnings in the Miaodigou culture phase to the end of the Longshan; (2) the period of capital settlements (*duyi*) from the Xia through the Western Zhou; and (3) the period of cities (*chengshi*), the Springs and Autumns and Warring States periods of the Eastern Zhou.

10. For much additional information on social and political organization in the Shang and Zhou, see Zhu Fenghan (1990).

11. Allan notes that sometimes a box or an altar is added to the graph (1991:16).

12. This indicates that the function and status of women in Bronze Age China was quite different from what they became under the influence of Confucian ideology.

13. A major discovery has been made in Guanghan, Sichuan, of a Bronze Age culture contemporaneous with the Shang. The capital was based on a walled city of considerable dimensions, but the surviving artifacts indicate that it possessed quite different traditions from those of the Shang. Whether this was the *fang* called Shu in the oracle-bone inscriptions has not been determined (cf. Bagley 1988).

14. Researchers generally agree that the lineage was a military organization in the Shang (cf. Wang Guimin 1983).

15. His essay was originally prepared as an appendix to Keightley (1982).

16. Allan points out that most of the inscriptions include only a charge or a proposition (followed frequently by a verification) and were not questions put to the ancestors or deities (1991:113–114; cf. "Forum" in *Early China* [1989:77–172]; Nivison 1989; Qiu Xigui 1989).

17. King Mu certainly is said to have engaged in cosmic flights later on in the tradition in Zhou times (cf. the *Mu tianzi zhuan*), but this text has no bearing on earlier beliefs. Chang provides a number of examples of kings performing shaman-like rituals (1994a; cf. Allan 1984; Yates 1990).

18. Chang observes that Shang remains have been retrieved from seventeen sites in the Anyang region within an area of approximately 24 square kilometers, but no walls have been confirmed in this region (1986:318). Zheng Ruokui has proposed that when Anyang was the last capital of the Shang, it was basically divided into two main units, the first comprising the royal palaces and tombs of the ruling Shang lineage and the second consisting of the twenty-two other sites occupied by lesser lineages closely allied to the Shang (Fig. 5.8; 1995). The middle Shang city at Zhengzhou, Henan, was discovered to have stamped-earth walls in a rough square, 1,690–1,870 meters per side (Chang 1980:263–288), and recently another wall adjacent to this enceinte has been found (Pei Mingxiang 1991; Henan sheng wenwu yanjiusuo 1993). Chang is leading an excavation team to locate the Dayi Shang that was the first capital of the Shang; he thinks the modern city of Shangqiu sits directly on top of the Shang capital that was later the capital of the Zhou state of Song (Chang, personal communication, 1996).

19. For a fascinating analysis of the symbolism of vassalage in the west with some very pertinent remarks on the Chinese ceremonies of so-called "enfeoffment," see Le Goff (1980).

20. Zhang Xuehai of the Cultural Relics Bureau, Shandong Province, told me in the summer of 1992 that he and his co-workers have been able to determine the settlement pattern in the late Neolithic period around the type site of the Longshan city at Chengziyai, first excavated in the 1930s (Li Chi, Liang Ssu-yung, et al. 1956). Zhang's report has just been published (1996), but the information contained in it arrived too late to be included in the body of the present chapter. Zhang concludes that there were two classes of cities in Neolithic Shandong, the first, although small in size, were capitals at the center of groups of settlements, the second were regional cities. He posits that there were at least three state systems, clustered round the sites of Chengziyai, Jiaochangpu, and Jingyanggang. But he concludes that these were not city-states, but rather "tribal ancient states" (*buluo guguo*). Anne Underhill is also preparing a settlement survey of Shandong (cf. Liu Li 1994).

21. It is interesting to observe that, in the internecine wars accompanying the consolidation of the city-states into larger and larger territories and the consequent decrease in the number of regional city-state systems, quite a few states were forced to move their capitals from one location to another. The relative ease with which the political elite were able to do this may well have been because they were able to move from one local city-state system to another, where each possessed its own local hinterland that provided its own basic economic means.

6

An Archaeology of Equalities?

The Greek City-States

IAN MORRIS

The central theme of this book is whether the city-state concept is important for archaeologists. In this chapter I focus on one aspect of it, the tendency of most textually documented city-states toward egalitarianism within a bounded citizen body. I concentrate on the roughly 750 city-states (*poleis*; sing., *polis*) of first-millennium B.C. Greece (Fig. 6.1). I suggest that one reason archaeologists have not paid much attention to city-states is because it is so difficult to fit this tendency into conventional models of social evolution. In this paper I try to integrate city-states into broader and more subtle approaches to early states—as ongoing processes rather than as static evolutionary stages.

The Agrarian State

Evolutionary theories of the state have been with us since antiquity, but most archaeologists only look back as far as 1960s neoevolutionism. Fried (1967) and Service (1962, 1975) identified four stages of increasing political centralization, culminating in the early state. Their great achievement was to simplify analysis of social change by concentrating on one or two indices, predicting other areas of behavior from them. Their models stimulated valuable analyses of archaeological data on a worldwide scale, but they also limited debate, since the only major controversy to develop within this perspective was whether elites were managerial or exploitative (see, for example, Cohen 1978a; Fried 1978; Haas 1982; Service 1978; B. Smith 1992).

But as with any universalizing theory, critics soon appeared. Some wanted a more biological approach (e.g., Dunnell 1980; 1989; Rindos 1985; Wenke 1981), while others were interested in dimensions of social life ignored by neoevolutionism (e.g., Blanton et al. 1981:12–29; Feinman and Neitzel 1984; Flannery and Marcus 1983; Steponaitis 1981). Denunciations of neoevolutionism are now standard fare (e.g., Barker and Pauketak 1992; Earle 1991; Upham 1990), but the successor theories have changed little (e.g., Claessen and van de Velde 1987b; Claessen et al. 1985; Gibson and Geselowitz 1988; Johnson and Earle 1987; Spencer 1987, 1990; Webster 1990).

Figure 6.2a represents Gellner's model of the "agroliterate state." It is closely based on Durkheim's century-old theory of mechanical solidarity, but it also effectively summarizes the postneoevolutionary consensus. Gellner claims that, in preindustrial complex societies, "the ruling class forms a small minor-

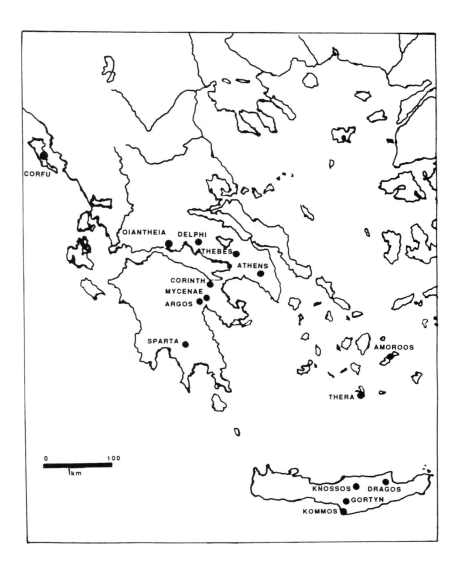

Figure 6.1. Sites and regions of Greece mentioned in the text.

ity of the population, rigidly separated from the great majority of direct agricultural producers, or peasants" (1983:9). Members of this class control state institutions, are internally stratified, and use cultural artifacts like writing (where it exists) and religion to underwrite social structure, thereby distancing themselves from nonelites. "Below the horizontally stratified minority at the top," Gellner continues, "there is another world, that of the laterally separated petty communities of the lay members of the society. . . . The state is interested in extracting taxes, maintaining the peace, and not much else" (1983:10).

Gellner contrasts the agro-literate state with "industrial society" (Durkheim's "organic solidarity"). Had he shown this too in a diagram, it probably would have looked like an empty rectangle. The essence of modern society in this model is the interchangeability of citizens—"no obstacle, of whatever

nature, prevents [people] from occupying the place in the social framework . . . compatible with their faculties" (Durkheim 1964:377). Durkheim constructed organic solidarity in conscious opposition to Marx, and he downplayed class stratification. Gellner recognizes the problem but argues that "the egalitarian, work- and career-oriented surface of industrial society is as significant as its inegalitarian hidden depths. Life, after all, is lived largely on the surface, even if important decisions are on occasion made deep down" (1983:37). This is unlikely to satisfy sociologists, Marxist or not (e.g., Giddens 1980), but in terms of this chapter, any shortcomings of organic solidarity are less important than the archaeological consensus in favor of mechanical solidarity.

Virtually all archaeologists have imagined social evolution as a process leading to the agro-literate state. Although some Mesoamericanists have drawn

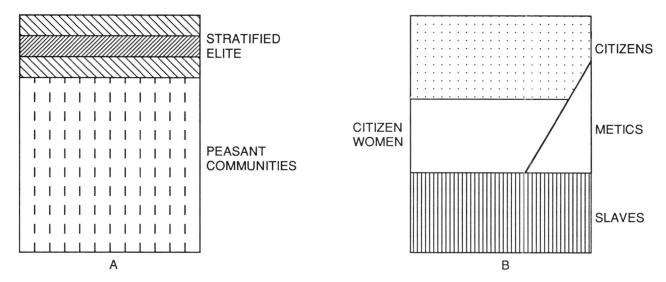

Figure 6.2. (a) Gellner's model of the agro-literate state. Stratified, horizontally segregated layers of the military, administrative, religious, and sometimes commercial ruling classes are rigidly divided from laterally insulated communities of agricultural producers. After Gellner (1983:figure 1).

(b) Ideal-type model of the extreme tendency of *polis* structure. A weakly stratified and slightly laterally insulated citizen group is rigidly divided from a strongly laterally insulated chattel slave population and highly fragmented groups of women and resident aliens.

on Durkheim to present alternatives (e.g., Coe 1961, 1965; de Montmollin 1989:25–26, 197–205, 225–226), they have used the mechanical/organic opposition to describe economic aspects of the division of labor, rather than using it as the totalizing model intended by Durkheim and Gellner. Thus, despite the emphasis on multilinear evolution, there is a single controlling model of "the" early state.

In an effort to fragment the notion of the chiefdom, for example, Kristiansen identifies two "variants of stratified society that seem to cover a majority of cases." In the first, the decentralized stratified society,

subsistence production is decentralized, with village communities or individual farms scattered across the landscape. Chiefs and kings set themselves apart from the agrarian substrate and rule through a retinue of warriors. Freed from kinship obligations, the warrior chiefs and king control, undermine, and exploit the farming communities through tribute and taxation. (Kristiansen 1991:19)

He suggests that these societies were common in prehistoric Europe, while in Asia, the centralized archaic state was more common. This second type of society

formalizes the tribal structure of the conical clan into a ruling elite, legitimized by controlled ritual access to the supernatural. . . . Through a formalized system of tribute, surplus production is converted into large-scale ritual ac-

tivities, building of ceremonial centers, organization of craft production, and centralized trade. Slave labor and a division of labor along lines of kinship evolves into new classes performing special activities. (Kristiansen 1991:21)

Life in Bronze Age Denmark was very different from life in Mari, but the two models are nevertheless relatively minor variations on Figure 6.2a. Only one historical trajectory can be imagined within this framework.

The same is true of the "archaeology of resistance" (e.g., Gailey and Patterson 1988; Gledhill 1988; McGuire and Paynter 1991; Miller et al. 1989; Patterson 1986; cf. Skalník 1989), which draws on postprocessualist critiques of neoevolutionism (e.g., Hodder 1982:152–157; Shanks and Tilley 1987a:143–165) and Marxism (e.g., Kohl 1984; McGuire 1983; Patterson and Gailey 1987; Paynter 1989) to examine how people "construct a terrain in which they seek to neutralize and negate the power of the state and the dominant classes" (Gailey and Patterson 1987:10). McGuire and Paynter rightly criticize neoevolutionism as a theory that "views the social world from the top . . . [and] assesses the control problems of those able to dominate others" (1991:10). Their approach is as innovative as was history-writing "from the bottom-up" (Kaye 1984:222–232) in the 1960s and '70s, and it differs significantly from top-down views (see McGuire 1992:145–177). However, Marx-

Table 6.1
Chronological Periods for Greece

Period	Dates
Mycenaean/Late Bronze Age	ca. 1650–1200 B.C.
Late Helladic IIIC	ca. 1200–1075 B.C.
Dark Age/Early Iron Age	ca. 1075–700 B.C.
Archaic	ca. 700–480 B.C.
Classical	480–323 B.C.
Hellenistic	323–31 B.C.

ist archaeologists continue to visualize evolution as being toward something like the agro-literate state (e.g., Friedman 1982; Friedman and Rowlands 1977; Gledhill and Rowlands 1982; Patterson 1991:21–41). In generalizing the agro-literate state, archaeologists naturalize it, as when Schiffer (1988:468) speaks of "the inevitability of social stratification in complex societies." Alternative social orders seem like speculative philosophy, as imaginary as the state of nature (see Zinn 1990:35–55).

Ancient Greece reveals some of the limitations of this view. Gellner observes that "the Agrarian Age was basically a period of stagnation, oppression, and superstition. Exceptions do occur, but we are all inclined, as in the case of classical Greece, to call them 'miracles'" (Gellner 1988:22). As so often, Gellner is speaking partly in jest; but taking refuge in miracles always reveals serious theoretical deficiencies. Archaeologists have had similar problems with Greece (e.g., Claessen and van de Velde 1987a:17; Cohen 1978b:13–14). Van der Vliet (1987:78) and Ferguson (1991) evade them by calling the *poleis* of the Archaic period (Table 6.1) chiefdoms. Only when tyrants seize power, they suggest, do *poleis* become states.

In examining the Pisistratid tyranny at Athens (546–510 B.C.), van der Vliet concludes that "one of the most obvious questions, which, as far as I know has never been asked by students of ancient history, is why the Athenian political system and state did not collapse as a consequence of the fall of the tyranny" (1987:80). The question has never been asked because it is nonsensical: van der Vliet's model forces him to distort the functions of the tyranny and what happened in Athens in 510–507 B.C. (see particularly Ober 1996:chapter 4). Similarly, Cohen notes that Aristotle did not see the state as a hierarchical organization. Instead of asking whether neoevolutionism is a useful framework, however, Cohen concludes that the philosopher had an "overgeneralized conception of social stratification" (1978b:14), which badly misrepresents Aristotle's social thought (Ober 1991). Neo-evolutionism and its heirs have become, as Kohl suggests, "a theoretical obsession that runs the risk of yielding no new insights and producing nothing more than hackneyed generalizations" (Kohl 1987:27).

Parameters of the Greek World

Natural environment

In southern Greece, ranges of hills divide up small plains, while farther north the plains tend to be larger. The northwest is mountainous and forested, with fertile upland valleys. Agricultural land can be just a few hours' walk from high pastures. Iron ore is widely distributed, but silver, copper, timber, and good building stone are restricted to a few areas (R. Osborne 1987:27–34; Sallares 1991:chapter 3). Beginning in the eighth century, emigrants from several parts of Greece set up new cities around the western Mediterranean and Black Sea. They generally favored ecological zones similar to those of their homeland.

Erosion may have changed the landscape since antiquity, but the climate has been stable. The south is typically "Mediterranean," with hot, dry summers and low rainfall in the winter; the north is more "Balkan," with cooler weather and higher, more evenly distributed precipitation. The south has high interannual variability in rainfall. Between 1931 and 1960, rainfall around Athens varied so much that barley failed one year in twenty, wheat one year in four, and legumes three years in four. Pollen, tree rings, and literary sources show that these figures are roughly applicable to antiquity (Garnsey 1988:8–16). According to a third-century B.C. proverb, "The year makes the crop, not the soil" (Theophrastus, *History of Plants* 8.7.6).

Agriculture and settlement

Dry-grain, sedentary, plow agriculture was the norm, with animal husbandry and fishing playing minor roles (Gallant 1985; Hodkinson 1988). Barley was the main crop, but those who could afford it probably preferred wheat (Foxhall and Forbes 1982). Yields rarely exceeded 650 kilograms per hectare (Garnsey 1992; Sallares 1991:372–389). Until recently, most historians agreed that localized climatic variability and partible inheritance encouraged fragmented landholdings, and this, in combination with fallow and a preference for nucleated settlement, kept productivity low (e.g., Gallant 1991:36–45; R. Osborne 1987:47–52). However, survey data suggest that in many areas there was a shift in the sixth century B.C. away from residence in nucleated villages toward dispersed settlement in rural farmsteads with catchments of 5–15 hectares. This pattern dominated until 200 B.C. (Alcock 1993:33–85). Bintliff and Snodgrass (1988; see also Snodgrass 1990a, 1991, 1994) argue that off-site sherd scatters indicate intensive manuring in this period, although this is disputed by Alcock and her colleagues (1994). Texts and ethnoarchaeology suggest a pattern of concentrated landholding and very intensive farming, with more production for the market than was posited in the older Chayanovian model (Garnsey 1988:93–101, 1992; Halstead 1987; Halstead and Jones 1989; Jameson 1978, 1992; Jameson et al. 1994:383–94).[1] Probably 80–90 percent of Greeks spent most of their lives in agricultural activities. Nearly all members of the *poleis* fed themselves when rainfall was good, but movement of food between communities dates back to prehistoric times (Halstead 1989).

Athens, the largest city-state, is the main exception. By the fifth century B.C., grain imports were required every year (Garnsey 1988:107–119; Sallares 1991:96–97). At its peak, in the 430s B.C., about 300,000 people lived in Attica—the 2,600 square kilometers surrounding Athens—and 10–15 percent of them lived in the city itself. Population declined after this, but it probably never fell below 150,000 in the fourth century B.C. (Hansen 1985, 1988:7–28). States varied greatly in size. Some had less than 100 square kilometers of territory, and Ruschenbusch (1984a, 1985) argues that a "Normalpolis" would have had fewer than 6,000 residents. Gehrke divides the states into six categories based on size and economic base (1986).

Robin Osborne (1991, 1992) and Foxhall (1992) argue that in fourth-century-B.C. Attica, 5–10 percent of the citizens held 30 percent of the arable land, and another 10–15 percent had no land at all. A "typical" farm would have been 3.6–5.4 hectares (Burford-Cooper 1978). Ruschenbusch suggests similar figures for Amorgos (1984b, 1989). The ease with which large estates could be built up varied. The largest known farm in Attica was only 40–50 hectares (de Ste. Croix 1966), and even 30 hectares was considered large (Burford-Cooper 1993:66–71). It is hard to document change in Attica, but in Sparta, the land that supported 8,000 citizens in 480 B.C. was owned by just 1,000 people in the 330s B.C. (Hodkinson 1986, 1989), and much larger properties were amassed in northern Greece. Meno of Thessaly, for example, is supposed to have raised 200–300 cavalrymen from his dependents in 476 B.C. (Demosthenes 13.23; 23.199).

State-level organization

By the seventh century B.C., much of Greece displayed features normally associated with early states (Snodgrass 1977, 1980). Writing reappeared around 750 B.C. (Jeffery 1990), and monumental stone temples by 700 B.C. (Mazarakis-Ainian 1985). Written law codes go back to the early seventh century B.C. (Gagarin 1986). A law code from late-seventh-century-B.C. Dreros limited the term of office of state magistrates (*kosmoi*) to ten years, and a contemporary inscription from Corfu mentions that Menekrates was the official representative (*proxenos*) of Oiantheia (Fornara 1983: numbers 11, 14). Around 600 B.C., states began minting their own coins (Kroll and Waggoner 1984), and in the sixth century B.C., states were competing in the scale of temple-building (Snodgrass 1986).

Political systems

Political independence was highly valued, but, as in many systems (Griffeth and Thomas 1981a:xiii), large city-states dominated smaller neighbors (Amit 1973). There was enormous institutional variation (Jones 1987) and frequent changes of regime (Gehrke 1985; Berger 1992). Aristotle identified three main political systems—monarchy, aristocracy, and democracy—and three degenerate forms—tyranny, oligarchy, and mob rule (Johnson 1990). Democracy is best known from Athens, where—apart from interruptions in 411 and 404–403 B.C.—it lasted from 507 until 322 B.C. (see M. Hansen 1991 on details). Forms of democracy appeared in several other *poleis* around 500 B.C. (Zimmermann 1975).

In fourth-century-B.C. Athens, where our sources are best, all free-born Athenian men over eighteen were citizens, regardless of occupation or wealth. They formed a distinct minority—probably no more than 30,000 out of a total population of 150,000. The proportion may have been higher in other states, but our information is scanty (Vatin 1984:35–54; Whitehead 1991). Athenian citizens monopolized landholding and made all important political decisions through direct votes in their assembly, which met roughly forty times each year. The assembly-place could accommodate no more than 6,000–8,000 citizens at one time.

The system rested on the belief that whatever this quorum agreed on in public discussion must be right (Ober 1989:156). Most offices were filled by lottery, with all citizens usually eligible, and the assembly's agenda was set by a council of 500—again chosen by lot from all citizens—which sat for one year. Virtually every citizen served on the council of 500 at least once. Athenians recognized a group of "politicians" (*rhetores*) who did most of the talking in the assembly, but ordinary citizens did speak, and the politicians never constituted a ruling elite or legal order (Hansen 1989:1–72, 93–125; Ober 1989:104–127). Those who spoke were vulnerable to the will of the citizens, and failure to conform to expectations could lead to fines, exile, or death (Finley 1985a:3–75; Sinclair 1988:136–190). Many wealthy Athenians were outraged at being answerable to the poor of their own city (Ober, in press).

Structures of citizenship

The core idea of fourth-century-B.C. Athenian citizen society was that the *polis* was a community of "middling citizens" (*metrioi*) characterized by their "like-mindedness" (*homonoia*; see Funke 1980: 13–26; Morris, in prep : chapter 2; Ober 1989:70–71, 297–299). The *metrios* was content with "a little" money and could be contrasted with both the rich and the poor, but wealth was not a major factor, and anyone could be called *metrios* if he lived properly—doing good for his family and for the community, having a strong sense of shame, and, above all, having his appetites under control (Ober 1989:257–259).

Citizens saw themselves as a group of *metrioi*, tied together by *philia*, an idea much like Sahlins's model of balanced reciprocity (Millett 1991:116–23; Sahlins 1972:192–230). They idealized the *polis* as a community under threat from marginal groups that lacked the virtues of the *metrioi*. A man judged to stand at any extreme was one who lacked control—he was "socially deviant in his entire being, whose deviance was principally observable in behavior that flagrantly violated or contravened the dominant social definition of masculinity. . . . The *kinaidos*, mentioned only with laughter or indignation, is the unreal, but dreaded, antitype behind every man's back" (Winkler 1990:177). The rich man, especially if young, was seen as prone to *hybris*, "serious assault on the hon-

our of another, which is likely to cause shame, and lead to anger and attempts at revenge" (Fisher 1992:1; cf. Ober 1989:208–210). From the eighth to the fourth century B.C., *hybris* was "constantly seen as a major crime, endangering the cohesion of the community as well as the essential self-esteem and identity of the individual" (Fisher 1992:493).

Poverty, on the other hand, forced a man to do undignified things, making him vulnerable to exploitation. Halperin suggests that, in popular thought, the poor, "deprived of their autonomy, assertiveness, and freedom of action—of their masculine dignity, in short—were in danger of being assimilated not only to slaves but to prostitutes, and so ultimately to women: they were at risk of being effeminized by poverty" (1990:99). The true *metrios* ought to be a self-sufficient farmer on his own land, head of a household, married with children, responsible, and self-controlled, standing his ground in the hoplite phalanx, a prominent metaphor for citizen solidarity.

We could dismiss this as false consciousness, with democracy blinding the poor to differences in wealth and power. For Cohen, democracy can only be a way for a traditional elite to control the lower classes (1988:9–10).[2] The emphasis on *homonoia* was clearly in large part a response to its scarcity (Loraux 1991), and many citizens were poor or even landless. But archaeologists are increasingly questioning absolute distinctions between "real" economics and "imaginary" ideology (e.g., Demarest 1989; Demarest and Conrad 1992; Hodder 1993:207–210), and in this case, belief systems were particularly important. By general agreement—a willing suspension of disbelief (Ober 1989:152–155)—citizens thought of each other as *metrioi* and *philoi*: "rich" and "poor" became categories of exclusion. The philosophy of the *metrios* was an essentialist democratic fiction, a powerful structuring principle that guided behavior.

A full share in the community, and therefore in its politics, flowed directly from the fact of being born a free male: as Halperin bluntly puts it (1990:103), "the symbolic language of democracy proclaimed on behalf of each citizen, 'I, too, have a phallus.'" The fact of being born an Athenian man, regardless of wealth, occupation, wisdom, or any other criterion, entitled a citizen to an equal share of masculine dignity and, through this, access to other social goods. As Finley (1985a:7–8) and Ober (1989:15–17, 334–335, n. 60) insist, in Athens, elitist political theory's "Iron Law of Oligarchy" breaks down. The mass of citizens limited the scope for elites of wealth, birth, or education to operate against their interests. Citizen society constructed a form of equality that cannot be explained by neoevolutionism and its successors.

Equality

Archaeologists usually identify equality with homogeneity (Paynter 1989). Lee, for example, complains that they "take an impossibly high, abstract definition of equality and then sit back and show that 'true' equality doesn't exist anywhere" (1990:236). For Marxists, Athens is an example of the Slave Mode of Production: "The class opposition on which the social and political institutions rested was no longer that of nobility and common people, but of slaves and free men" (Engels 1972:180–181). Some neo-Marxists change this emphasis (e.g., Vernant 1980: 1–18), but they have been met with scorn by orthodox Marxists (e.g., de Ste. Croix 1981:63–66). A large slave population—at least 30,000 in the fourth century B.C.—was subjected to systematic brutality (Patterson 1982:87–92). For feminists, the exclusion of women (Just 1989; Keuls 1985; Loraux 1993) makes Athens little different from most early states (e.g., Gailey 1985; Silverblatt 1988). As MacKinnon puts it, "Feminists do not argue that it means the same to women to be on the bottom in a feudal regime, a capitalist regime, and a socialist regime. The commonality is that, despite real changes, bottom is bottom" (1989:10).

Athens was a group of *metrioi*. Every *metrios* had a share in the community, and no one else had any share at all. Within the citizen group, equality cut across economic lines, forming a social structure unlike anything neoevolutionism predicts, while from the perspectives of women, slaves, or rich citizens, Athens was an unfair society in which poor male citizens tyrannized everyone else. We need a more sophisticated model of equality to interpret this.

In liberal thought, "equality" normally means equality of opportunity, the belief that everyone has an equal right to life's rewards through equal freedoms of speech, beliefs, and chances. Those who hold this view—the "commonsense" definition in most Western societies (Turner 1986)—accept that outcomes should be unequal and that the talented should be richer, more powerful, and more esteemed than failures. But critics point out that life's winners pass on economic and cultural capital to their children, making a mockery of the ideal of an even playing field. They suggest that the state should create equal-

ity of condition, helping the underprivileged by restricting the freedoms of the successful. Their policies—for example, affirmative action or banning private education and health care—generate opposition from proponents of equality of opportunity (Mulhall and Swift 1992:59–63; Rae 1981:55–59).

More radical socialists object that both these agendas assume that some people deserve larger shares of social goods than others. They argue instead for equality of outcome: "every human being, as such, deserves as much esteem as every other, because all share a common humanity. . . . Attributions of income and wealth can no longer be regarded as capable of justification. The condition of everyone should be the same, for lack of any reason why it should be different" (Phelps Brown 1988:5).

Depending on political choices, different "spaces" for equality appear obvious or natural. Sen observes that "critiques of egalitarianism tend to take the form of being—instead—egalitarian in some other space" (1992:15). Conflicts cluster around attempts to impose such choices on others, and challenges to norms generate backlashes (Dahrendorf 1988:25–47; Hirschman 1991). In most situations, some group imposes its view that a particular quality—wealth, birth, strength, education, beauty, or whatever—is *the* dominant good, and claims to monopolize it. Such "dominant ideologies" may convince few outside the ruling group (Abercrombie et al. 1980, 1990), but by a variety of means, the dominant group tries to convert its monopoly over one good into monopolies over others. Thus, in a plutocracy, equal rights to amass and dispose freely of money allow the rich to create inequalities in other spheres, such as politics, subsistence, or health. There will be pockets of nonconvertibility—it may not be possible, say, to buy divine grace or beauty—but the holders of the dominant good will struggle to breach these citadels of resistance.

Walzer observes that "since dominance is always incomplete and monopoly imperfect, the rule of every ruling class is unstable. It is continually challenged by other groups in the name of alternative patterns of conversion" (1983:11). The social order is constructed, not given. Thus, against the interests of plutocrats, a nobility might hold that certain goods—say, land, high office, dignity, and royal favor—cannot be bought. If they are successful in advancing their claims, plutocracy might gradually give way to aristocracy, with genealogical distance becoming the standard for judging equality, and wealth following in its train—"all good things come to those who have the one best thing" (Walzer 1983:11).

In Athens, the one best thing was male citizen birth. Other goods, even money, could only be converted into citizenship under extraordinary circumstances (M. J. Osborne 1983; Whitehead 1977). But dominance was imperfect and contested, and compromises had to be worked out with other visions of equality. Athenians did not insist that wealth, land, or influence strictly follow equal dignity, not because they only valued equality of political opportunity, as M. Hansen argues (1991:83–85), but because opposition from the rich made it difficult and because they did not need equality of resources to guarantee the basal dimension of "equality of attitude and respect between citizens" (Kerferd 1984:14). Some Archaic states did cancel debts, redistribute land, control inheritance, or even massacre the rich (Asheri 1963, 1966, 1969; Link 1991), but after 500 B.C. this only happened when states were already destabilized through war (Gehrke 1985).

Despite state-level organization, in some ways citizen society had more in common with the !Kung San than with agro-literate states. Lee notes that the !Kung have leaders and followers, but "their fierce adherence to egalitarianism [and] an abhorrence of the acceptance of status distinctions within them" are more important. Distinctions are undermined through "the remarkable institution of the leveling device"—above all, joking and gossip (Lee 1990:244; cf. Trigger 1990b:135). Common gossip was also the most effective way of bringing overprominent men down to size in Athens (Hunter 1994:96–119; Ober 1989:148–151). It was reinforced by ostracism, where each year the citizens could send into exile for ten years anyone who threatened democracy (Ober 1989:73–75). Fifth-century-B.C. Athens institutionalized joking in Old Comedy, performed in festivals and functioning partly to mock the prominent (Cartledge 1990; Rosen 1988). The tensions and anger these mechanisms aroused in would-be elite Athenians closely parallel those among the !Kung (Lee 1979: 458–461; Ober, in press).

Unlike the predictions of neoevolutionism, Athens was not dominated by a small wealthy elite lording it over peasant subjects. To the disgust of men like Plato, shoemakers, farmers, and the gilded youth all had equal shares in the community, regardless of education, wealth, or moral excellence. Only citizenship counted. The exclusion of women and slaves is to most of us as odious as the aristocracies of agro-literate states, but the important point is that Athens was *different*. The members of an ancient state could select a space for equality radically different from what evolutionary reconstructions would allot to them. Current theoretical assumptions impoverish our understandings of the past.

A Spectrum of Possibilities

I am not trying to make Athens into an archaeologists' nightmare, undermining cross-cultural studies. But its history does force us to think about what we mean by equality and inequality in social evolution. Faced by the tremendous institutional variations between Renaissance Italian city-states, which led Jones to deny the possibility of constructing a model of "the" Renaissance state (1965), Burke has responded by ranging the city-states along a spectrum, in which "some city-states . . . have less stateness or cityness than others" (1986:143). This approach can also help us locate the Greek city-states in a broader theory of social evolution. Gellner's agro-literate state (Fig. 6.2a) can stand at one end of a spectrum of possible state forms, and the citizen state (Fig. 6.2b) at the other. Each is an ideal type, which, "in its conceptual purity . . . can never be found empirically in reality" (Weber 1949:90). In the citizen state, the citizen body is weakly stratified by wealth and power and slightly laterally insulated by geographical distance and kinship. The major boundaries divide citizens from noncitizens, not rulers from subjects. Slaves are even more "laterally insulated" than Gellner's subjects and less capable of challenging the social order (Cartledge 1985; Vidal-Naquet 1986:159–167). Resident aliens, who were politically excluded, could be among the richest men in the state (Whitehead 1977).

We can locate different societies at different points along this spectrum, and describe their movement back and forth between the agro-literate state and the citizen state during their histories, according to the outcomes of specific social struggles. We thus avoid the tendency of both evolutionary archaeologists and Greek historians to impose static models.

In his standard work on *The Greek State,* Ehrenberg asked:

How far are we justified in speaking of 'the' Polis in general? We have to draw our picture of it from a number of states, and, to do so, we must recognize the unity that underlies the plurality. . . . Call it a compromise, if you will, but it is a compromise that is not only justified but absolutely necessary, if we are to win from the mass of detail a picture of the whole. (Ehrenberg 1969:xi–xii)

Ehrenberg identified "the" Greek state, but as Gawantka shows, he followed nineteenth-century scholarly traditions, which required that every *Volk* must have its own unique state (Gawantka 1985:14–15, 90–106). Gawantka suggests that this approach was firmly established by the publication in 1898 of Burckhardt's massively influential *History of Greek Culture* (Burckhardt 1963).

Burckhardt's thesis was that *Die Polis* was a hothouse of culture: "The Greek conception of the state completely subordinated the individual to the general polity, but . . . also developed the tendency of pushing him onward very forcefully" (Burckhardt 1963:16). He based this image on his 1860 model of Italian city-states (Burckhardt 1929). White explains that in his Italian study Burckhardt "supposes that an explanation of historical events is provided when the various strands that make up the tapestry of a historical era are discriminated and the linkages among the events, which make a 'fabric' of the historical field, are displayed" (White 1973:262). Burckhardt spoke of "the state as a work of art" (1929:21). By definition, every civilization had a unique spirit, and the historian's art was to weave an image of this deeper reality. The city-state was a work of art, to be recreated in a text which was another self-conscious work of art.

But Burckhardt's model of "the" Renaissance state as a work of art does not accommodate very much of the evidence, and early-modern Italian social history has for decades been dominated by debates over the usefulness of his concepts (Grubb 1988:ix–xvi). Until recently, Hellenists have been more comfortable with Burckhardt's transplant of his model to Greece, but Gawantka has now argued that we must reject Burckhardt's schematizations and go back to earlier compilations of the facts (1985:159–161). But this positivism has its own problems. Both Burckhardt and Gawantka take sides in a dispute going back to the eighteenth century between the liberal, historical humanists known as *Sachphilologen* and the positivist, "scientific" *Sprachphilologen* (Grafton 1991:214–243; Weintraub 1988). Gawantka offers not a disinterested, neutral commentary, but a continuation of this debate: there is no access to the past without a conscious act of representation in the present. Like the *Sachphilologen,* we may abstract an "essence" of *Die Polis,* or, like the *Sprachphilologen,* we may write histories

in which every statement or calculation to be found in an ancient text, every artifact finds a place. . . . The old problem of establishing canons of selection and of settling who determines them has been "solved" by abolishing selection altogether. Everything now goes in, as if in answer to the familiar question in children's examinations, "Tell all you know about X." (Finley 1985b:61)

The spectrum in Figure 6.2 preserves the distinctions emphasized by *Sprachphilologen* (e.g., Gehrke 1986; Ruschenbusch 1978) while still seeking regularities. In the fourth century B.C., Athens lay close to the citizen-state model; Thessaly, Macedon, and several other states were more like agro-literate states than citizen states; and Sparta and Gortyn were somewhere in the middle. Social relations within the citizen groups in states near the citizen-state end of the spectrum were more like Gellner's "industrial society" than his agro-literate state. Culture united citizens, rather than distinguishing great and little traditions. Writing was not monopolized for an elite. Only 5–10 percent of Athenians were literate (Harris 1989: 114), and then only in a restricted sense (Thomas 1992:15–28), but the public use of writing was crucial to democratic ideology.

Tragedy, performed in state festivals, contributed powerfully to civic consciousness (Winkler and Zeitlin 1990), which particularly annoyed Plato (Salkever 1986:337–343). Nearly all religious offices were open to all citizens by lot, and anyone could offer sacrifice (Burkert 1985:55–118). Juries of 500–2,500 citizens selected by lot judged lawsuits, without professional judges or lawyers. For Aristotle (*Constitution of Athens* 9.1), this freedom to interpret the law was fundamental to democracy. In these Athenian courts, the rich had to negotiate and compromise with the poor (Ober 1989). Athens also erected no political or legal barriers between city and country (Wood 1988: 101–110; Raaflaub 1991:567–570). The were no major boundaries within the citizen group, but those between it and noncitizens were fiercely defended (Davies 1978a).

As we move toward an agro-literate state, the pattern weakens. In Sparta and the Cretan cities,[3] citizens formed a smaller proportion of the population than in Athens; divisions within the group were stronger, and those between it and noncitizens were weaker. Equalities of condition and outcome were partly enforced through common educational systems and messes. Citizens contributed supplies to the mess, and any man who could not do so lost his status. In

Gortyn, serfs could inherit property and marry citizens' widows (*Gortyn Code* 5.25–27, 6.55–7.10; translated in Willetts 1967). As we move from a citizen state toward an agro-literate one, there is also a shift from permanently alienated, deracinated, purchased chattel-slave labor to serfs, with their own communities and customs (Cartledge 1988; Finley 1981:116–166; Hodkinson 1992).

In Sparta, restriction of literacy fragmented the citizens (Cartledge 1978). There is less evidence from Crete, but the existence of officials such as the "writer" and "rememberer," charged with interpreting laws, implies a similar situation (Thomas 1992: 69–71). Spartan law was famous for being oral and minimal, and it was easily manipulated by elite factions (MacDowell 1986). In both Sparta and Crete, specialists controlled many religious functions, and the Spartans were notorious for their deference to professional oracles (Hodkinson 1983:273–276). We know little about citizen settlements in Crete, but in Sparta, full citizens were concentrated in the main town and lower-status groups in the country (Shipley 1992). Restrictions on women's economic powers were also weaker in Sparta and Gortyn than in Athens (Schaps 1979).

Fourth-century-B.C. Macedon was still closer to an agro-literate state. Its kings developed a genuine elite culture through institutions such as the School of Royal Pages, which trained aristocratic boys to serve as the king's companions (Hammond 1990:53–58). The citizen/noncitizen distinction was less important than other status boundaries, and there were marked regional inequalities (Ellis 1976:21–40). In Epirus, two fourth-century-B.C. inscriptions even grant honorary citizenship to women (Vatin 1984:65–66).

Most historians distinguish between *poleis* and the *ethne* (lit., "tribes" or "peoples"; sing., *ethnos*), using *ethnos* to describe large, loose states like Thessaly and Macedon, which I place close to agro-literate states (e.g., Ehrenberg 1969:22–25). There is no warrant for this in the sources (Morgan 1991:132–133), however, and it creates more problems than it solves. For instance, sixth-century-B.C. Thessaly lay near the agro-literate end of the spectrum. It had a strong centralized aristocratic government with elected leaders ruling over weak local communities and a serf population. But by the 480s B.C., this structure had loosened, and individual cities became stronger. They extended citizenship, minted their own coins, acted more independently of the federal authorities, and sometimes even considered freeing their serfs. Had

Thessaly changed from an *ethnos* into several *poleis*? The question would have made little sense to a fifth-century-B.C. Greek. Thessaly had simply moved along the spectrum from the agro-literate toward the citizen state, although it never came very close to the Athenian position. By the 370s B.C., Thessaly's central government had recovered, and the cities lost many privileges. This was not a reconversion into an *ethnos*. Thessaly was moving back toward an agro-literate state (Larsen 1968:12–26).

This spectrum makes it easier to think about the histories of individual states and to relate them to broader theories. It also allows us to analyze the history of equalities in entire state systems. I argue below that around 700 B.C. and again around 500 B.C., most Greek states moved significantly toward the citizen-state model, and then began moving back toward the agro-literate end of the spectrum after 425 B.C. The process accelerated after 300 B.C. By the first century B.C., Greece resembled an agro-literate state, with the cities reduced to local communities ruled by a Mediterranean-wide Roman elite.

The Greek States

The Dark Age

The Late Bronze Age Aegean was dominated by redistributive palaces with political structures close to the agro-literate model (Laffineur and Niemeyer 1995; Rehak 1995). Around 1200 B.C., almost all the palaces were burned, and by 1100 B.C., the population may have been reduced by two-thirds. Monumental architecture, writing, and long-distance trade faded away, and there may have been invasions from the north (Rutter 1990; Small 1990). The changes were not wholly disastrous (Muhly 1992; Rutter 1992), but we should not minimize the chaos that marked the years from 1100 to 750 B.C., a period usually referred to as a Dark Age.

Most evidence is funerary. Homogeneous single burials generally replaced the Bronze Age multiple inhumations in chamber tombs. These graves have been seen as indicating egalitarian or tribal societies that lived in isolation and subsisted through pastoralism (e.g., Deger-Jalkotzy 1983; Hägg 1983; Musti 1991; Snodgrass 1971, 1987:170–210). A spectacular increase in the number of graves in eighth-century-B.C. central Greece has been explained as a population explosion, leading to state formation (Snodgrass 1977). I have argued against this view (Morris 1987, in prep.), proposing instead that a new ritual system emerged by 1000 B.C., which distinguished between elite and nonelite groups. The nonelite received informal burial, which archaeologists have only rarely detected. The social order was reconstructed relatively quickly after the Mycenaean collapse, but on different principles, with an elite that saw itself as a group of equals. Mazarakis-Ainian (1985, 1987, 1988) suggests that sacrificial rituals in central Greece also divided communities into elite and nonelite, with chiefs monopolizing cult rituals, holding ceremonies in their own houses, and restricting access. He suggests that, in the Dark Age, "'the chief's house' and 'the house where one honors the gods' could be used as synonyms" (1985:43).

This system weakened around 900 B.C., as central Greece became involved in wider economic networks. There was a huge increase in Phoenician activity (Röllig 1982), which had a major impact on the Aegean (Coldstream 1982; Gehrig and Niemeyer 1990). Greek settlement expanded into the Cyclades and the west coast of Turkey. There was growing competition within the elite and perhaps disputes over its definition. Imports began to appear in burials, and grave goods escalated until about 850 B.C. (Coldstream 1977:55–72). Ritual relationships between adults and children and the living and the dead all changed, and a few open-air sanctuaries appeared (Lambrinoudakis 1988; Morris 1987:179–183, in prep.:chapters 5, 6; Whitley 1991:136–137). Stability returned by 850/825 B.C., but the system was less homogeneous.

Patterns were different in other areas. On Crete, there was a shift toward mountain refuge sites after 1200 B.C., but Bronze Age house forms survived (see, for example, Hayden 1983; Nowicki 1987). Multiple tombs also continued in use, although cremation generally replaced inhumation in the tenth century B.C. (Snodgrass 1971:164–170). Rich grave goods continued, and the variability of Cretan tombs contrasts with the austere mainland rituals (Whitley 1991: 187). There was also much continuity in cult practice (see, for example, Lebessi 1981; Coldstream 1984). Crete seems to have been open to outside influence. Its south coast lay on the main Phoenician route to the West (Negbi 1992:607–609), and in the ninth century Phoenicians may have built a temple at Kommos (Shaw 1989) and settled at Knossos (Boardman 1967:63–67). Cretan social order probably remained near the agro-literate end of the spectrum and apparently did not go through an eleventh-century-B.C. reconstruction comparable to that of the Aegean area.

Crete appears to have had a more dynamic and open society, with its elites welcoming outside influences and combining them with a strong Bronze Age heritage.

In western Greece the picture of depopulation and small, mobile groups may be accurate, except for Messenia (Morgan 1990, 1991). Open-air sanctuaries were more common than in the Aegean, and Morgan suggests that hierarchy was organized in gatherings at remote shrines like Olympia (1990:29).

The Archaic period

There was an enormous transformation in the late eighth century B.C. (Morris, in prep.:chapter 8; Snodgrass 1980:15–84). In the early stages, we find an increase in both the number and the wealth of burials and the appearance of many open-air shrines, with abundant ceramic votives. During the second stage, large, homogeneous cemeteries outside settlements begin to take the place of rich graves. An escalation in votives, sometimes including much more metal, accompanies the building of temples. These changes often coincide with a reorganization of settlement space.

Parts of this package can be seen from Assyria to Iberia, indicating a demographic recovery, new trade links, more intense war, and state formation (Bartoloni and Rathje 1984; Gamito 1988; Lipinski 1987). We must seek explanations at this geographical scale, but so far none have been found. Yet it is also true that each part of the Mediterranean world—indeed, each part of Greece—reacted differently to the general process. The increase in social complexity in eighth-century-B.C. Greece was also a shift toward the citizen state, especially in the central Aegean area.

Since everyone now had access to similar burial customs, which partly explains the increase in the number of excavated graves, and since open-air sanctuaries proliferated, it is clear that exclusionary Dark Age rituals had collapsed. The old elites responded by using richer grave goods, but in the Aegean, this phase was brief. Snodgrass (1980:52–63, 99–100, 1990b) links the large increase in votives around 700 B.C. to the decline in grave goods, which he explains as a diversion of elite spending to communal ends, propitiating the gods for the whole *polis,* and de Polignac (1995) suggests that the emergence in most *poleis* of a "religious bipolarity"—one sanctuary in the main town and one near a border—defined the communal territory. We might measure movement toward a citizen state by how far a *polis* went in this two-stage transformation. States like Corinth and Argos, which had poor cemeteries and massive stone temples, went farthest.

It was a time of astounding cultural energy. Everything was open to challenge and experiment, and the results varied dramatically from place to place. House design went through a very rapid evolution; in the course of two generations, some houses were totally redesigned two or even three times (Morris, in prep.: chapter 7). People were building walls and knocking them down, digging pits and filling them in, and generally altering their physical environment at an unprecedented rate. Individual communities responded to this new atmosphere in tremendously varied ways. Some went through the first stage of transformations in the eighth century B.C. but continued to increase grave goods throughout the seventh century B.C., while at Athens, eighth-century-B.C. developments were reversed, and new burial and sacrificial rituals reinstated a division between elite and nonelite (Morris 1987; Houby-Nielsen 1992, 1995; Whitley 1991, 1994). Outside the central Aegean, the eighth-century-B.C. shift toward a citizen state was weaker. The Cretans, for example, adapted the new religious ideas to their older practices, which already included sanctuaries and rich votives (Beyer 1976:13–18, 66–70; Canciani 1970; Naumann 1976). The number, wealth, and variability of graves increased until about 625 B.C. We find virtually nothing in subsequent years; however, local sixth-century-B.C. pottery is hard to identify (Boardman 1962; Callaghan 1992:90–93; Coldstream 1973, 1992:85; Karetsou 1973), and Crete may have severed ties with Greece. There probably was a shift toward the citizen state around 750 B.C., but Crete then developed in unique ways. In Thessaly, on the other hand, the changes were weaker. The eighth-century-B.C. increase and seventh-century-B.C. decline in grave wealth were small, and only a handful of rich sanctuaries appeared. Still farther north, Macedon was affected very little. Grave goods may have declined after 700 B.C., but spectacular burials had returned by 550 B.C.

The shift toward a citizen state meant a major loss of prestige for would-be aristocrats. Many resisted it, while ordinary citizens struggled to move still closer to the citizen state, and this conflict became the driving force in Archaic history. The aristocrats created an oppositional social order in the interstices of the *polis* world. As Herman notes (1987:162–165), from this perspective Greece looked like the agro-literate state, but this interstate community was never more than an immanent elite, invoked in the self-consciously elitist contexts of the symposium, guest-friendship, and athletics at interstate sanctuaries. The imagined interstate community was vital to aristocratic consciousness, but it could only be converted into practice by carrying it back to the individual city-states.

In their poetry, the elitists gave themselves privileged links to the gods, the heroes of epic, and the mighty rulers of the East, and they valued these more highly than links to citizens in their own states. These links were created and demonstrated through "correct" use of luxury. This vision was contested by an equally strong "middling" poetic tradition, which mocked elitist pretensions and softness. Middling poetry was still produced by and for aristocrats, but by and for those who accepted the values of the citizen state and saw themselves as the leaders of a citizen community, not its rulers. This middling tradition denied all sources of authority external to the *polis* itself (Morris, in prep.:chapter 3).

Seen in this light, the shift from grave goods to votives could not have been unambiguously communal. In the fourth century, Xenophon (*Estate Manager* 2.5–7) and Aristotle (*Ethics* 1122 b 19–1123 a 4) defined lavish sacrifice as "magnificence," calling it spending "for the common good," but they also saw that it created a hierarchy of honor. Generosity to the gods was a true test of the correct use of luxury, and in the dedication of bronze tripods at panhellenic sanctuaries, the worlds of the gods, the heroes, Eastern rulers, and contemporary nobles collapsed into one another (Morris, 1996, 1997, in prep.:chapter 6).

The classical period

During the sixth and fifth centuries B.C., there was a shift from village settlement toward dispersed farmsteads, which must be linked with more intensive agricultural practices and a transfer of economic power toward the middling section of the communities (Morris 1994b, in prep.:chapter 8). The ability of the aristocracies to resist the middling ideology collapsed, and after 500 B.C., we hear no more of the Archaic elitist poetic traditions. They are replaced by the epinician form, which sought to accommodate aristocrats within the *polis* (Kurke 1991, 1992). The period was also marked by a massive archaeological transformation (I. Morris 1992:118–129, 145, 151–153, in prep.). From 500 to 425 B.C., there are virtually no rich graves or funerary monuments anywhere in Greece, and fifth-century-B.C. houses hardly vary in size, decoration, plan, or finds. Hoepfner and Schwandner (1986:1–26, 256–267; Hoepfner 1989) argue that in the 480s B.C., many cities began to build identical "Typenhäuser" to reflect a major social leveling. Rich votives all but disappeared by 500 B.C., and most major dedications were now made by states (Snodgrass 1990b). Literary sources indicate that aristocrats gave up expensive clothes, elaborate hairstyles, and jewelry.

The shift toward a citizen state was probably well under way by 480 B.C., when Persia attempted to conquer Greece. Greek writers interpreted this war as a clash between simple, homogeneous, restrained, and free *poleis* and rich, decadent, slavish Orientals (Hall 1989). In addition to contributing to the ideology of the citizen state, the Persian Wars left the Athenians at the head of a large military coalition. By the 450s B.C., if not earlier, they were using their position to promote a citizen-state model within member states, but when viewed from Athens, this imperialism was converting the Aegean as a whole into something more like an agro-literate state, as the Athenians tried to centralize administrative functions, levied tribute, and seized vital economic resources. The mid-fifth century B.C. was the zenith of the citizen state, but it contained the seeds of its own destruction. Attempting to expand their empire and to resist the Persians, the Athenians rapidly escalated the scale of warfare and the economic extraction needed to support it. To resist being drawn into the empire as subjected local communities, the Spartans and their allies increasingly did the same. The phalanx remained a symbol of citizen solidarity, but it was no longer the decisive military arm.

By 425 B.C., the shift back toward an agro-literate state had begun. During the last quarter of the century, rich men like the colorful Alcibiades began to attack the older austerity, dressing lavishly and spending huge sums on personal luxury (Millett 1991:67). By 400 B.C., monumental tombs had reappeared, grave goods were escalating, and a few large houses were being built, sometimes with mosaic floors or multiple courtyards. There are hints of an elite critique of state religion and a series of lawsuits at Athens over attempts to curtail public sacrifices. State spending on temple-building declined from 400 to 340 B.C. Some philosophers argued that there were

two kinds of equality—an "arithmetic" kind, in which each citizen carried equal weight, and a (preferable) "geometric" kind, in which each man had influence according to his innate worth (Harvey 1965).

Through most of the fifth century B.C., small, intensively organized city-states close to a citizen state were more politically effective than larger states nearer the agro-literate model, such as Thessaly or Macedon. These latter were weakened by the shift toward the citizen-state model and the consequent fragmentation of their power. But as the costs of war escalated and techniques of economic extraction improved, their central governments regained power. The defeat of Athens in 404 B.C. and Spartan inability to respond to the challenges of imperialism allowed charismatic rulers of large states to come to the fore (Davies 1978b:228–253). In 375 B.C., Jason of Pherai was elected *tagos* of the Thessalian league, and in 370 B.C. it looked as if he might become master of Greece; however, after his murder that year, no successor was able to preserve his gains.

In 356 B.C., the Phocians seized Delphi and used its treasures to hire a mercenary army, with which they held all the *poleis* at bay until crushed by Philip of Macedon in 346 B.C. As a boy, Philip had been a hostage in Thebes, but in 359 B.C. the Thebans sent him home to promote palace plots to keep Macedon weak. Instead, he revolutionized the state, and in 338 B.C., he succeeded where Jason had failed, imposing Macedonian control on most of Greece after the battle of Chaeronea. Had the battle gone the other way or had his son Alexander responded less ably after Philip's murder in 336 B.C., Macedonian power might have collapsed as Thessaly's had. But more challengers were coming along, and in responding to the escalation of military forces, the *poleis* were, in any case, accelerating their movement toward the agro-literate type of state.

Claims that the Macedonians destroyed democracy (e.g., de Ste. Croix 1981:283–300) may be exaggerated (cf. Bernhardt 1985; Gauthier 1985), but elites became more comfortable with lavish spending on monumental tombs (Fedak 1990) and spectacular houses (Hoepfner and Schwandner 1986:241–246). By 200 B.C., people were drifting back to the towns, breaking up the dispersed classical settlement pattern. Larger estates and magnificent villas appeared, and a demographic decline set in. By the first century A.D., few traces of the equalities of the classical *poleis* survived (Alcock 1993).

Conclusion

Some aspects of the city-state concept have already proved useful in archaeology. Renfrew's models of the early state module and peer-polity interaction (1982, 1984:94–116, 1986a) draw on both the small scale and clustering typical of city-state systems, and use Greek examples. But sociologically it is less obvious that there *is* a single city-state concept. I have emphasized egalitarian citizenship as crucial in ancient Greece. This can be seen in other systems (Griffeth and Thomas 1981b:191–192), but few city-state systems went far toward the citizen state. In medieval Italy, for example, lawyers and philosophers regularly cited Aristotle (Martines 1979:155–175; Riesenberg 1992:163–170), and developed notions of civic equality strikingly similar to those of Athens (Quaglioni 1991; Riesenberg 1992:155–157). But the Italian cities never gave citizenship to urban workers or peasants (Martines 1979:48), instead ruling as hegemonic centers over their hinterlands (Chittolini 1991). In states like Florence and Venice, wealth remained the dominant good, and all other social goods flowed from it (Herlihy 1991; Romano 1987).

Social structures close to the citizen-state model pose profound problems for archaeologists' theories of social evolution. I conclude from this that the comparative foundations of neoevolutionism are too narrow. Service (1975) and Johnson and Earle (1987) examined historical and ethnographic cases, but their conclusions nevertheless neglect the diversity of social arrangements documented in the historical record. To understand the variety of the past, archaeology must become more historical.

Processualists sometimes react that an historical archaeology cannot be scientific (e.g., Binford 1989), but such claims reflect ignorance of what historians do (Morris 1987:212–216) and set up false and unhelpful dichotomies (Wylie 1989, 1992). The Greek evidence does not undermine the possibility of a social-evolutionary archaeology, but it does show the need for a broader range of ideas and concepts.

Social structures shifted toward the citizen state in the eighth-century-B.C. Aegean because of the outcome of specific social conflicts. This was not "predictable" from a general model or covering law, but neither was it the chance result of purely contingent factors. In part, it depended on the existence of a power vacuum in the eastern Mediterranean. No larger state pressed into the Aegean between the thirteenth century B.C. and the late seventh century B.C.

It was not until about 500 B.C. that the Persians threatened the city-state system as a whole, and by then the *poleis* were strong enough to fight back.

The second decisive factor in the eighth century B.C. was the nature of the preexisting power structures. In the central area of Greece, an unusual ideology had taken shape around 1000 B.C., with an elite representing itself as a community of equals, and in this region, the main response to the economic and demographic transformations of the eighth century B.C. was to generalize that ideology to a broader citizen community. It was what Runciman has called an evolutionary turning point (1989:322), when one section of the community selects and imposes what is, for its members, an extremely successful adaptive strategy, but does so at the cost of the continued economic, military, and political expansion of the system as a whole.

Runciman suggests that the *polis* was an evolutionary dead end, "where institutional evolution stops although the environment is changing, and the type of society in question becomes extinct through incapacity to adapt to that change" (1990:349). The *poleis,* he argues, "permitted an alternation between 'oligarchy' and 'democracy' as the Greeks understood them but ruled out the possibility of effective and sustained concentration of power at the top" (1990:365). Runciman notes the changes of the fourth century B.C. but does not allow them to challenge the standard model of static and completely distinct *poleis* and *ethne*. *Poleis* near the citizen-state model were moving steadily toward the agro-literate model through the fourth century, and it is by no means clear that, given more time, they would not have converted themselves into a single larger state. Runciman rightly notes that the Athenian empire was less exploitative than Rome or Venice (1990:360; cf. Raaflaub 1991: 575–583), but again, there is every reason to suppose that, had the policies of the 440s and 430s B.C. continued, the Aegean would have been converted into something like a territorial state, with Athens as its capital.

The farther a state had moved toward the citizen state in the fifth century B.C., the more slowly it moved back toward the agro-literate in the fourth. Citizens defended their social order with tenacity, and it was states with weaker citizenship—Thessaly, Phocis, and Macedon—that profited most from the military revolution of the late fifth century B.C. In the Greek colonial foundations in Sicily, where citizenship had always been more fluid than in old Greece, the tyrants of Syracuse used drastic methods to create a large empire as early as the 480s B.C., and in the first half of the fourth century, Dionysius I created what was then the largest territorial state in the Greek world.

Griffeth and Thomas suggest that all city-state systems have a "half-life" and that after four or five centuries, they either tear themselves apart or attract conquest by a larger power (1981b:189–90, 201). The implication of this is that structures near the citizen-state model are not compatible with large, complex, and efficient political units. The Greek evidence certainly suggests that the more the *poleis* struggled to promote and defend the citizen state, particularly through the Athenian empire (created out of resistance to Persia) and the subsequent Spartan struggle against Athenian imperialism, the more they encouraged the kind of concentration of power discussed by Runciman: certain *poleis* became vastly stronger than others, and elites were increasingly able to promote alternative spaces for equality within states.

Organic solidarity within a citizen community, created by political means, was perhaps only possible on a very small scale. This idea of community depended on a high degree of ideological, economic, military, and political equality, and it favored the preservation of such equalities, but it was a fragile system, undermined by its own success in the fifth century B.C. Organic solidarity reemerged in the complex division of labor of the advanced industrial states of the nineteenth and twentieth centuries A.D., on the basis of very different economic principles. The surprising similarities between the citizen culture of city-states near the citizen-state end of the spectrum and modern industrial culture may explain why it has been so difficult to accommodate city-states within archaeological models of social evolution; and also why their study is so important.

Acknowledgments

I wrote most of this chapter during my tenure as visiting fellow at the Institute for Research in the Humanities at the University of Wisconsin-Madison. I would like to thank the Institute and the University of Chicago for their support.

Notes

1. Against this so-called new model, see Wood (1988: 42–80), Gallant (1991:30–33, 98–101), Isager and Skydsgaard (1992:108–114), Osborne (1985, 1988, 1991, 1992), and, more moderately, Burford-Cooper (1993).

2. Van der Vliet (1987:71; cf. Griffeth and Thomas 1981b:187) seizes on Thucydides's famous opinion (2.65.9) that Pericles virtually ruled Athens to claim that "during most of the fifth century BCE one man ruled the city." In fact, Thucydides's view only applies to the years 444–430, and other sources give a very different impression of Pericles's position (e.g., Fornara 1983:number 116). Thucydides's comments were part of a strategy of criticizing democracy by attributing everything good in Athens to Pericles (Connor 1984: 227, 239), and Pericles's repeated successes (and occasional failures) in the assembly are better explained through his skill in rejecting aristocratic ties and appealing directly to the people (Connor 1971:57–79; Ober 1989:86–91).

3. The idea of a uniform Cretan culture was a deliberate invention of fourth-century theorists (Perlman 1992), but there is rarely enough evidence to distinguish between the cities.

7

City-State Dynamics through a Greek Lens

Unlike many social and political structures, city-states exhibit varying degrees of centralization and hierarchy, oscillating internal organization, and democratic, egalitarian (Morris, this volume), or "consensual" (Stone, this volume) operating values. Consideration of the development of the city-state in ancient Greece can prove useful, not only in comparative studies of ancient states, but in future studies of city-state organization—indeed, Morris is correct in pointing out that Greek social constructions have unfortunately been kept out of the larger evolutionary debate. Although Greek examples appear to differ from other city-state formations, I argue that this difference is based on ecological and historical frameworks, and that the Greek state structure is similar to that of other city-states. What makes the Greek case important to city-state theorists is that it offers a well-documented example (archaeologically speaking), one that illuminates basic cross-cultural features as well as unique characteristics. I argue that city-states, in the process of their evolution, often fail to capture and transform regional lineage models of production and distribution and that a consequence of this is weak centralization, weak hierarchy, and internal instability.

My focus is on city-state formation in Archaic and classical (ca. 700–325 B.C.) Greece (Fig. 7.1). The object of study is the *polis*-state, a small independent territory with a dominant central polity that had the power to raise armies, enact laws, negotiate citizenship, conduct treaties, and establish state religion. By the classical period, Greece had about 750 of these polities, most with populations of 5,000 or less. Athens was an exception—if we include its hinterland of Attica, it had a population of 120,000–150,000 (Garnsey 1988:90). (The *ethnos*, or federated state, which was found in the northern regions of the Peloponnese and Thessaly, falls outside the limits of this study.)

Because I am trying to explain unusual features of social evolution, I focus my analysis on the political economy of Greece and use this lens to study the development of the small Greek state. In doing so, I follow the path of others who have sought to explain social process on a complex level through an economic focus.[1]

Greek Political Economies

Ancient Greece saw the development of two distinct political economies, one an elite economy operating on a regional scale and the other a city-state, whose

DAVID SMALL

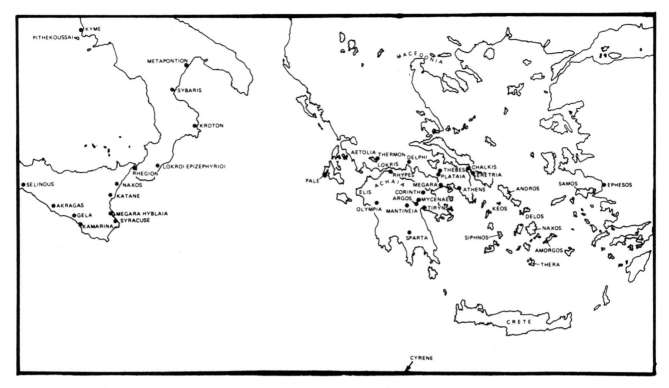

Figure 7.1. Map of Greek world. From Snodgrass (1986:figure 3.1). Reprinted with permission of Cambridge University Press.

goals were (often) neither coincident with nor as far-ranging as those of the elite.[2] I realize that this assertion challenges a basic assumption about the role of elite economies in cultural evolution. But, as I will show, this assumption does not fit the realities of city-state evolution.

The elite economic world

Ancient Greek economic elites amassed their wealth through ownership of estates, where they grew crops such as winter wheat, barley, broadbeans, lentils, olives, and grapes (Gallant 1989:396). Some also had an eye for the profit that could be made through interstate trade (Cartledge 1983; Small 1994), maritime loans (Millett 1983), and the ownership and command of trade ships (Humphreys 1978:167; Millett 1983), although they also worked through agents in foreign ports (Bravo 1974). Some engaged in the transportation of marble (Snodgrass 1983). Economic power, however, was relational and stemmed from interpersonal negotiation. Successful elites were able to transform their agricultural base into positions of power by building patron/client relationships with others from their own communities and by monopolizing the interstate trade of grain, primarily

through reciprocal family-centered relations with elites in other areas.

The ecological frame

Most of the eastern Mediterranean is characterized by low or marginal rainfall. Although dry farming was practiced in ancient Greece, major seed crops such as wheat and barley were often adversely affected by interannual fluctuations in precipitation (Gallant 1989, 1991; Halstead 1981, 1988, 1989; Halstead and O'Shea 1982), and the risk of agricultural failure was high. Gallant has shown that annual harvest production can vary as much as 30 to 50 percent from one region to another (1989). Data collected from Attica (the region around Athens) indicates that the frequency of shortfall in output for barley was one in twenty years, for wheat and legumes one in four (Garnsey and Morris 1989). Work by Halstead indicates that there might have been some difference in response to climatic fluctuation between different microenvironments (1981), but Gallant has demonstrated that the coefficient of variation between different regions of Greece was low, suggesting that large areas of Greece underwent similar agricultural responses to interannual climatic fluctuation (1989). The only areas that appear to have been different were Thessaly and the Pontus or Black Sea regions (Garnsey 1988; Garnsey et al. 1984). Although these areas were also subject to episodic agricultural shortfalls, they were also famous for supplying Greece with grain.

The social frame: alliance and its context

Elites sought economic power through the construction and manipulation of local patron/client relationships with nonelites and control of the commerce in interstate grain by alliances with other elites. In an argument that incorporates broad cross-cultural analysis with a study of Greek material, Gallant has demonstrated that a widespread patron/client system existed in ancient Greece (1991; see also Millett 1989).[3] It was based on the ability of elite houses to take advantage of nonelites trying to weather periods of agricultural shortfall. As Gallant concludes, "Elite-peasant dyads were a critical cog in ancient Greek risk-buffering strategies" (1991:162). These relationships existed on both an interpersonal level and between elites and entire communities. During a food crisis, elites obtained supplies of food from external sources, gave or sold grain to the community from their individual resources, sold grain and other supplies below the prevailing market price, gave or loaned money for the purchase of food, and/or interceded with external agencies on behalf of a community to procure grain and other supplies (Gallant 1991:183).

Epigraphic evidence documents how manipulative the elites were and how they used grain and money in power-building schemes. Gallant tells of Polykritos, a wealthy man in third-century-B.C. Erythrai in Ionia, who was appointed "grain official" by his community. He advanced money to the community to buy grain and then sold grain from his own stores to the community—no doubt at a hugely inflated price. In addition, he collected interest on the funds he had loaned. Polykritos was thus able to amass a huge profit *and* put the community in a position of clientage (Gallant 1991:184). Although a number of similar dealings between elites and communities have been recorded, the full extent of this type of operation must have been even greater.

Gallant argues that the case of Polykritos shows a community giving thanks to a "benefactor," even though Polykritos's manipulation and the huge profits he reaped are evident. Since these events were considered worthy of mention by the community, similar transactions between elites and communities elsewhere must have been less generous. Although Gallant's interest is in the operation of risk-buffering for nonelites, he recognizes that the dyadic relationship formed the basis for elite economic power: "Such a system, then, could easily slide from paternalism to exploitation, and the 'gifts' of patrons could turn into onerous debts" (1991:169).

Polykritos's dealings exemplify a patron/client relationship between elites and a community. Private relationships of clientage undoubtedly existed as well, but they are more difficult to document because historical sources are more likely to record elite/elite connections than elite/nonelite ones. Nevertheless, historians do not discount the presence of elite/nonelite interactions (Gallant 1991; Millett 1989). Gallant has shown that the interpersonal bonds of patron and client were widespread (1991:163–166). The telltale signs of private patron/client relationships in other cultures—sharecropping, seasonal wage labor, nonelite access to elite supplies, elite gifts of food, low- or no-interest loans—are seen as well in ancient Greece. The context for these private dyadic relationships probably lay in corporate groups, such as *genoi* (clans), *phratries, demes, thiasoi* (religious organizations), and so on (Gallant 1991:174). In such contexts, elites would meet periodically with commoners and form patron/client ties at a level above that of the village and below that of the state. An important feature of these groups was an obligation for elites to assist other members, but this did not lessen elites' opportunities for exploitation.

The essential economic tie between [elites and nonelites] was based on inequality and asymmetrical obligations. In short, associations helped foster the formation of patron-client bonds, but the precise nature of that tie was molded less by associational affinity than by socio-political accountability. For that reason, latent in the nature of patronage was the potential for exploitation. (Gallant 1991:162)

To keep their positions as patrons, it was vital that elites be able to loan grain to others in the community during periods of shortfall. If a shortage were extremely severe, however, or if it extended for more than a year, they were often unable to meet these requirements from their estates. In such cases, the patron was forced to acquire grain from outside the *polis.* We know that elites were engaged in a regional economy of grain production and distribution at least as early as the Archaic period (Garnsey and Morris 1989:101), and we know that their monopoly extended into the classical and Hellenistic eras, for written sources indicate that city-states looked to elites to furnish extra grain from outside the state in times of agricultural crisis. The *polis* states never developed a merchant fleet and relied instead on elite shipping. The *sitonia,* a liturgy placed upon the elite,[4] required them to obtain grain from foreign sources in response to a real or potential food crisis. The advantages of controlling the interstate flow of grain were evident to both the supplier and supplied. Herman has documented how Philip II and later Hellenistic monarchs gave grain and other natural products to elites in foreign polities to increase these rulers' influence (1987: 73–86).

The principal social institution for this acquisition of grain was ritualized friendship or *xenia.* Historical documents from the classical and Hellenistic periods show that elites did not seek grain from strangers but from *xenoi* (Herman 1987:82–88). Gallant agrees that "*xenia* gave wealthy men access to resources from outside their polity in times of crisis" (1991:168). *Xenia* was a form of fictive kinship that established a reciprocal bond of obligation between elite households in different Greek communities (Herman 1987). The salient features of *xenia* were its dependence on gift exchange between ritualized friends, its center within the *oikos* (noble house), and its ability to be passed on to male descendants. The power of an elite *oikos* increased with the growth in numbers of its *xenoi,* so houses were constantly attempting to form more ties with houses in other polities.

Information about which regions were experiencing a surplus or shortfall was as important as the means by which grain was exchanged. For example, how did Agathokles of Rhodes know that Ephesos was suffering a grain crisis around 300 B.C.? Since he brought 2,333 *medimnoi* (ca. 28,000 gallons) of grain to the market there (Gallant 1991:184), it is almost certain that he did so in response to news of a shortfall. Greece offered two formal contexts for the exchange of such information—funeral games and an athletic festival circuit. Both venues had features to attract the interest and participation of the wealthy (Kyle 1987).

With few exceptions, the expenses involved in training and the time necessary to travel to athletic competitions precluded any significant participation by nonelites. The ideology of agonistic competition was also ingrained in the institution of the noble *oikos,* which sought recognition in struggles with

other *oikoi* throughout Greece. The *oikos* was the central mediating social unit in athletic festivals, as well as between victors in the interstate festivals and the home *polis* (Kurke 1991). Additionally, athletic achievement and its recognition were closely tied to the concept of *xenia.* Athletic success was seen as a gift between divine and human *oikoi,* which were united by bonds of *xenia.* Like ritualized friendship, athletic success and its recognition was a hereditary feature within the *oikos,* and its celebration was the duty of ritualized friends. Athletic festivals, then, were the principal contexts for the activation and initiation of ritualized friendship.[5]

In Athens, funeral games gave way to civically sponsored sports events with the establishment of the Panathenaic festival in 556 B.C., and it is likely that other communities witnessed a similar shift. As the popularity of funeral games waned and as they were replaced by civic festivals, the interstate festival circuit apparently supplied the principal arenas for elite status negotiation. The shift may have coincided with the beginnings of state development, for private elite dedications in interstate sanctuaries also began to rise in the eighth century B.C. (Morgan 1990:203–204). By the fourth century B.C., interstate sanctuaries were the principal contexts for the identification of interstate *xenia.* Isokrates writes:

Having proclaimed a truce and resolved our pending quarrels, we come together in one place, where, as we make our prayers and sacrifices in common, we are reminded of the kinship which exists among us and are made to feel more kindly towards each other for the future, reviving old *xeniai* and establishing new ones. (quoted in Herman 1987:45)

I would suggest that interstate gatherings were also the principal contexts for the exchange of information on the success or failure of harvests in the Greek world, information that allowed elites to find sources of additional grain or customers for their surpluses. Several important physical and temporal features support this argument. The contests were essentially state-neutral: as Isokrates notes, a truce was often proclaimed for the festivals, allowing Greeks from warring polities to meet at the sanctuaries. In their panhellenic character, the gatherings provided an excellent opportunity for economic elites from all over the Greek world to meet on scheduled (and frequent) occasions. Olympia, Delphi, Nemea, and Isthmia formed the core of the *periodos* (athletic circuit) that by the fifth century included at least thirty and probably many more less visible athletic events in which athletes from different states participated (Morgan 1990, 1991; Pleket 1975). To this list should be added other major interstate festivals such as those at Dodona, Delos, and Mt. Mykale. Scheduling for Olympia, Delphi, Nemea, and Isthmia was carefully staggered (first year, Olympia and Isthmia; second year, Nemea; third year, Delphi and Isthmia; fourth year, Nemea again). When the schedule of these festivals is added to the less visible contests and the gatherings at other interstate sanctuaries, a wealthy man could easily have attended three or four festivals a year.

The timing of the festivals also meant that participants could assess the agricultural prospects of various regions in Greece. Major festivals appear to have been held after the summer's harvest. The Olympic games were scheduled for either the second or third full moon after the summer solstice—the exact time that Hesiod, a seventh-century poet, recommends for the initiation of overseas trading in agricultural goods (1982:80). This meant that elites came to the interstate sanctuaries after most of the harvest was in, and thus they could learn who had surpluses to sell and what areas were experiencing shortfalls.

Economic Goals of the *Polis*-State

With few exceptions, the economic goals of the city-states and those of their wealthy citizens were not coincident. The *polis* did little to further the local interests of its economic elite, and in foreign affairs the economic scope of the state was limited to short-term measures to alleviate subsistence crises.[6] This assertion challenges the common concept that management of the economic elite furthers social and political evolution (Johnson and Earle 1987), but the issue has been thoroughly aired by historians (Cartledge 1983; Hasebroek 1933). The state gathered revenue—in the case of Athens, at least—from ownership of mines, direct taxation of resident foreigners, use fees for harbors, imposition of tribute, and—in a reverse of what one might expect in a more conventional archaic state—from an indirect tax or liturgy (folk work) on wealthy citizens.

Although members of the economic elite were interested in profiting from interstate commerce, the city-states did little to favor them in the conduct of this trade. City-states even passed laws concerning the export of raw materials that hampered the trading ventures of their own elites—Solon's law prohibiting the export of all agricultural products except olive oil (Plutarch 1932:119) and similar prohibitions legis-

lated by the city-state of Teos are the best-known examples (Meiggs and Lewis 1969:50).

When thrust into a position of potential economic dominance, the city-state demonstrated a very limited economic vision. In the period after the Persian Wars, Athens secured a military hegemony over numerous other *poleis* in what is loosely termed the Athenian empire. But the Athenian economic elite did not benefit from Athens's control of the empire, as we would expect from the example of states such as the Aztec or Inca, which insured that wealthy citizens profited from the establishment of the empire. Athens imposed no navigation acts, no protective tariffs, no preferential treatment of Athenian shippers, and it made no attempt to remove commerce from the empire to Athens itself.[7] In fact, when Athens replaced the regular imperial tribute with a tax of 5 percent on all harbors in the empire, she levied the tax on all traders, foreign and Athenian alike.

Indeed, the Greek city-state essentially had no integrated economic policy. While economic issues were discussed in the public assembly, they dealt only with concerns generated in that context, such as the provision of grain to poorer citizens. There was no real relationship between the economic deliberations of the assembly and the interests of the marketplace. State economic policies were epiphenomenal reactions to internal crises. In securing grain, for example, the city-state did not expand its interests beyond the immediate goal of supplying grain for its citizens. Similarly, economic treaties with foreign states were limited to securing a supply of grain and other necessities; any further economic benefit was a secondary consideration (Garnsey 1988; Garnsey and Morris 1989).

In short, ancient Greece represents a culture where the goals of the economic elites and the *polis* states were very different. The states had a limited economic vision, and elites sought economic power, not through the state, but through the elite house, its clients, and fictive kin in other parts of the Greek world. They did so by manipulating food crises and controlling the flow of agricultural surplus through a network that centered upon the informational nodes of the panhellenic festivals.

Chronological Relationships between the City-State and the Economic Elite World: The Power of Context

It is probable that the elite economic household network predated the rise of the Greek city-state. Most of our information comes from the classical and Hellenistic periods, but there is good evidence that an elite *oikos*-based network existed in earlier phases of Greek history as well. The epic poems of Homer and Hesiod indicate that the power of the noble *oikos* in the eighth century was based on its ability to construct a retinue of nonelite retainers (clients) and to compete in a gift-exchange system with noble houses from other regions in Greece (Finley 1977b; Millett 1989; Morris 1989; Quiller 1981). The incipient features of gift exchange (and therefore *xenia*) can be found in the deposit of metals in burial and sanctuary dedications as early as the tenth century (Langdon 1987; Morgan 1990; Morris 1986, 1989). In the eighth century, the Homeric epics are evidence that gift exchange and the concept of *xenia* were quite familiar to elites of that period (Morris 1986). It is quite likely therefore that the regional elite economic network, based on the *oikos* and its nonstate contexts, existed prior to the development of states in ancient Greece.

The dual worlds of the elite household and the city-state existed—often at odds—from the establishment of the *polis* in the eighth century until the late Hellenistic period. The use of *xenia* by Hellenistic monarchs to empower individual elites boosted the strength of the elite house in the Hellenistic age and spelled the end of the viable city-state (Gallant 1989, 1991:187–196; Herman 1987:73–115). As noted above, the *polis* state never really developed any economic policies beyond the short term and often lost out to the economic power of the elites. By the Archaic period (Herman 1987:130–142), for example, the *polis* had begun to enter into economic relationships of *xenia* with different *proxenoi* (benefactors) as if they were individual *xenoi*. Instead of developing a lasting *polis*-generated means by which the state could obtain grain, the Greek city-state succumbed to the power of the elite houses.

Since the *polis* as a state began to develop in the eighth century, it developed within the preexisting network of elite economic power. But why was it that the goals of the economic elite and those of the state did not mesh, as we see in other archaic states? The most important reason lies in an inherent limitation of the Greek city-state. Unlike developing regional polities, the Greek city-state (with the exception of states such as Sparta or Syracuse) never expanded territorially to any great extent. The regional elite network, which best fits a lineage mode of production and distribution (albeit small, and identified with families and not clans), was never "captured" in the evolutionary process of the Greek city-state because a large part of its territorial definition stretched beyond the city-state itself. Unlike regional state-level polities, where much of the territorial definition of a preexisting elite regional network (minus limited examples of long-distance trade) becomes coterminous with the boundaries of the state, the Greek city-state did not transform this lineage mode of production into the political economy of the city-state (for a comparative analysis see Small 1995).

A second reason is more historical. The continued identification of the regional economy with the *oikos* was supported by the institution of the interstate festival circuit, which played a major role in constructing the underlying ideology of elite economics. This circuit emphasized the glory of the *oikos* and the institutions of *xenia* rather than the individual states. The state was not a mediating symbol for the negotiation of position between peers. In fact, a principal characteristic of Greek sanctuaries was their marginality to state interests. Even "state sanctuaries," such as that of Artemis at Ephesos or Hera at Samos, were separated from their associated *polis*. This loosened considerably their identification with the *polis* and fostered a more panhellenic character (Morgan 1990; also see Simon 1986 for a discussion of marginality). Negotiated positions at the festivals emphasized the aristocratic noble house and panhellenic qualities of the negotiators.

The usable context of these festivals—that is, the symbols and the structure for the negotiation of position between elites—did not recreate positions in the internal hierarchy of states. Olympia (Fig. 7.2) can serve as a model of some of the principal mediating symbols. It included an athletic stadium, temples to principal deities, treasure houses erected by individual *oikoi* on behalf of different states (Kurke 1991:189–190), athletic buildings for training, and hundreds of statues and honorific monuments that glorified the individual athlete and the *oikos* he represented. Personal athletic glory and the values of a private system of elite prestige were more dominant than the position the athlete held in his state.

Evolutionary Consequences for the Greek City-State

Since the Greek city-state developed parallel to this elite network, we must ask what effect the network had on its formation. To do so, we should first exam-

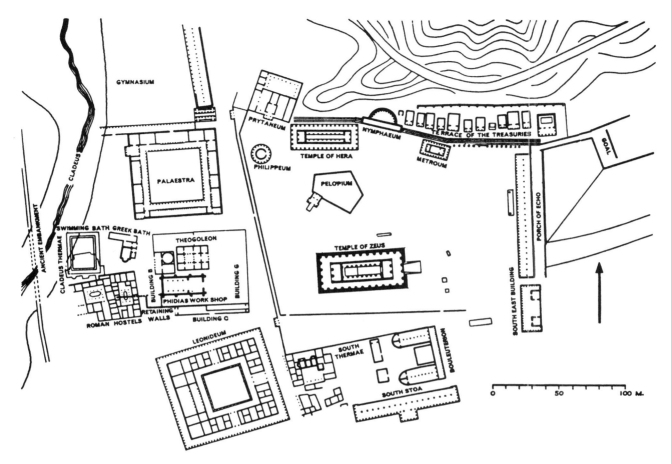

Figure 7.2. Plan of Olympia. From Renfrew (1986b:figure 1.16). Reprinted with permission of Cambridge University Press.

ine the structuring principles of Greek city-states and determine the characteristics that were produced by their separation from elite economics. The most perceptive analysis of Greek community evolution is that of Humphreys (1978). Her basic unit of analysis is the interaction context, which she identifies as a specified community context that contained separate norms, rules of behavior, symbolic settings, and a scheduling that separated it from other contexts within the community. These contexts included the council, the assembly, the law court, the military, the theater, the symposium, the gymnasium, and the funeral celebration.

Three features of the internal structure of the state are especially significant: a low level of integration between different social and political contexts within the states, a flexible ranking of these different contexts, and the importance of the intellectual or philosopher within the community. In reference to the first point, the evolutionary trajectory of the Greek city-state generates more from an increased articulation of roles and contexts rather than a developing inte-

gration of community contexts (Humphreys 1978: 242–275; see Morris, this volume, for a different conclusion), in what might be termed a contextual "involution" (see also Bargatzky 1988; Geertz 1963). We have already noted a lack of economic integration between the chief political contexts (the council and assembly) and economic contexts (such as the marketplace). There is evidence of a similar disjunction in the relationship between some aristocratic contexts (such as the symposium and the gymnasium, with their overtones of homosexuality) and political contexts (such as the council or public assembly). In general, the Greek city-state does not fit the customary paradigm of a complex state society, which presumes a high degree of organic integration.

Turning to our second point, the Greek city-state shows a flexible ranking of different community contexts, with no one context achieving dominance: during periods of democracy, the assembly was often emphasized; in times of oligarchy, the aristocratic contexts of the symposium, the gymnasium, or the funeral celebration; in times of tyranny, the military or public festival. Humphreys argues that this trend correlates with a generalized lack of ranking in roles and functions within the community (1978:252).

Our last point is the presence of intellectuals—Archaic poets such as Hesiod and lawgivers such as Solon—who played an important part in promoting values and reducing the tension between elites and nonelites. Humphreys argues that by the fifth and fourth centuries B.C., intellectuals had begun to distance themselves from the tensions of the community (1978:209–241), but this is only partially true. Both Plato and Aristotle, for example, addressed a fundamental problem of Greek city-states—civil strife. Plato suggested a utopian community, and Aristotle tried to tutor the Greeks with his *Politics*.

Although Humphreys bases her analysis chiefly upon Athens, I would argue that these features were inherent in many different *polis* states. The widespread distribution of the context for public assembly, the theater with its egalitarian symbols—whether under an oligarchy, a tyranny, or a monarchy—indicates that there was a disjunction between community contexts in a large number of Greek city-states, and weak integration seems to have been commonplace (Small 1987). Oscillating ranking of community contexts is also ubiquitous in Greece—indeed, a hallmark of the *polis* state was the internal instability occasioned by the struggle between rich and poor (Lintott 1982). Lastly, Greek intellectuals came from all states: Hesiod came from Boiotia; Theognis, who had a lot to say on social relations, was from Megara.

Examining Process

The unusual structure in most Greek city-states can be attributed directly to the separation of the state and the economic affairs of the wealthy. Since the familial house and its connection to a regional elite network formed the basis of elite economic power, the Greek city-state evolved without elite management of its political economy. To understand how this detachment could have such an effect, we need to reexamine the role that wealthy citizens normally play in the evolution of hierarchy and integration.

The most penetrating analysis of the development of hierarchy and centralization has been that of Johnson (1978, 1982, 1983, 1989), who argues that we should envision two types of hierarchy for decision making above the level of the household: sequential and simultaneous. Sequential hierarchies are the hallmark of small-scale egalitarian societies. They are

contexts of community individuals (perhaps family heads), where a temporary hierarchy is established within a specific context to meet the demands of community decision making. These hierarchies could be established for purposes relating to hunting, warfare, migrating, and so on. The existence of sequential hierarchies is determined by the interests of their constituent individuals. Ranking within these hierarchies is fluid, changing from time to time as new leaders are recognized as best for specific tasks. Ranking in one context does not necessarily equate with that of other contexts as well, as leadership is determined by the ability of the individual to handle the task at hand, rather than upon some fixed social position.

Simultaneous hierarchies are "simultaneous" in that they are more permanent decision-making contexts, seen in complex societies. Their internal structures are more crystallized than those of sequential, because leadership in these contexts is now tied to people with longer-lasting, more permanent positions of power, rather than falling on the recognized ability of an individual to perform well at a specific task. Indeed, the active involvement of the wealthy in furthering their economic positions is considered a major factor in the evolution from sequential to simultaneous hierarchies (Nassaney 1992:113). Because of these connections, simultaneous hierarchies are often ranked in importance vis-à-vis one another, as leaders evolve who can control several decision-making contexts at the same time. Hand in hand with this integration of decision-making contexts comes systemic centralization of the community, as well as ever increasingly more permanent differential accesses to resources.

Although Johnson makes a distinction between sequential hierarchy and hierarchy as displayed in ritual contexts, his differentiation may in fact be artificial. I would argue that the contexts of sequential hierarchies, whether an aggregation of household or clan leaders, are the same as those of ritual ceremony, although perhaps less obviously so. Furthermore, ceremonies and sequential hierarchies both function as mechanisms for decision making and integration in large groups, as Bargatzky has noted in his analysis of social and political organization in Safata (Samoa). In describing "occasional hierarchies," Bargatzky found that the ranking of different communities in Safata was negotiated in a meeting of the "houses of speakers," but the hierarchy existed only for the duration of the ceremony (1988).

Applying a sequential to simultaneous paradigm to

Greece, we can argue that the interstate, lineage-based network, which was supported by the establishment of an interstate festival circuit, turned the attention of wealthy Greeks away from the state and thereby created a sequential hierarchy on a complex level. Although the Greek situation does not mesh precisely with Johnson's definition, which equates sequential hierarchies with egalitarian societies, the concept of decentralization and multiple hierarchies need not, in fact, be limited to egalitarian societies. Indeed, Crumley suggests that "Johnson's difficulties would be eased if he abandoned the term egalitarian (implying, as it does, an equal distribution of resources and power) and substituted democratic, which maintains the value of egalitarianism while admitting the inequities of electoral praxis" (1990:5).

In sum, city-state evolution in ancient Greece presents an example of small states evolving within a large economic network centered on the *oikos* or elite-lineage mode of production and distribution. Its basis was the production and distribution of grain between different parts of the Greek world in accordance with annual microenvironmental harvest fluctuations. State monopoly over this type of commerce did not emerge because the Greek city-state was not large enough to incorporate both regions of surplus and regions of shortfall. The city-state's inability to mesh with the economy of its wealthy citizens was increased by the institution of the festival circuit, an "economic" context dominated by the values and ideologies of the elite houses. City-states thus could only react to economic crises as clients of this larger regional network. Conversely, the economic elite paid little attention to the developing city-state, except as a client, which meant that there was little impetus for evolving centralization and hierarchy. Greek city-states are instead notable for their weak centralization, temporary hierarchies, and internal oscillation.

Ancient Greece and Future Research into City-States

My reason for bringing the Greek example to this collection of studies on the city-state is to argue that the Greek experience, while exhibiting cultural singularities, suggests promising avenues for future archaeological research into city-states in general: (1) Greek city-states offer insights for a cross-cultural model for city-state evolution; (2) they force us to look at the nonmaterial aspects of interaction and their effect on city-state complexity; and (3) they suggest that future

analytical paradigms will have to develop scales of social complexity beyond our current measures of hierarchy.

Toward a cross-cultural model of city-state evolution

To an historian (Morris, this volume), the institutions of citizenship and values, like the egalitarianism that grew out of ancient Greece, proclaim the Greek city-state as a unique cultural achievement, best compared perhaps to the political institutions and values of Italian city-states (Molho et al. 1991b; Runciman 1990). To an archaeologist, considering the larger context of environment and the opportunities for developing political economies, the development of Greek city-states presents a model that could be useful in the study of city-states in other parts of the world.

The Greek example shows that when city-states evolve in a region dominated by elite-lineage modes of production and distribution, limited territorial control can hamper their capture of this economic sphere and preclude their transforming it—as larger, more expansive states can—into a state political economy (Small 1995). Of course each cultural region of city-state evolution will have its own historical and ecological frames, and some city-states will undoubtedly be more complex than others, but this model can have cross-cultural application.

Two of the better-known regions of small-state development, Mesopotamia and Mesoamerica, share many characteristics with ancient Greece, not only in the regional/small-state dichotomy but also in the resultant features of internal development. Mesopotamian city-states evolved within a preexisting network of interactive regional exchange in commodities such as grain, wool, copper, and textiles (Edens 1992; Larsen 1987; Yoffee 1979, 1981, 1991). Many Mesopotamian city-states failed to capture this economic production and distribution system, however, and much of their economy remained in the hands of wealthy families. Indeed, a major question in interpreting the character and development of the internal structure of many Mesopotamian cities was the degree and amount of involvement of the elite in developing internal political economies (Stone 1990, this volume; Stone and Zimansky 1994, 1995; Zagarell 1986). I would argue that many of the goods within this elite economy could have had immense political and economic importance within the evolving city-states, either in symbolizing access to status—which was not under the control of the state—or providing the means by which trade goods could be exchanged for increased land tenure. The removal of elite economics from city-state development has produced results within Mesopotamian states that are similar to those in Greece. Stone notes several unusual features of Mesopotamian city-state development—egalitarian ideology, consensual political operation, underdeveloped political economies—that do not fit the usual models for complex societies but are expected in a state where weak hierarchy and weak centralization is the norm (this volume).

The case for Mesoamerica is even more compelling. Maya city-states evolved within a larger regional economic network of trade in items such as cacao, obsidian, jade, pottery, stone vases, cotton, and salt (Graham 1987; Hirth 1992; Pyburn, this volume; Rathje 1972, 1975). The city-states were small, and their territories were not coterminous with the economic region. Excavation of the elite, nonroyal compound 9N-8 at Copán shows a continuation of the elite-lineage mode of production even at the height of the Copán state, suggesting the failure of the city-state to capture it (Sanders 1989; Webster and Abrams 1983). Courtyard D housed foreign craft specialists, who were attached to the elite household as clients. Copán's settlement pattern of small isolated farmsteads is also more indicative of a patron/client type of subordination than one of a central taxing authority (Sanders 1989; Willey and Leventhal 1979; Willey et al. 1978). Research in other areas of Maya settlement suggests that this lineage mode of production and distribution operated within other developed states as well (King and Potter 1994; Rice 1987). Specifically, ceramic production was not centralized but had production and distribution centers that were not coterminous with the city-states per se.

As with Greece and Mesopotamia, centralization was weak. This can be seen both economically and hierarchically (Webster, this volume). It appears, for example, that the royal family's right to power was challenged at Copán by other elites, for we find hieroglyphic propaganda by subelites—a use that would presumably be restricted to royalty alone. Most notable are the hieroglyphic bench in compound 9N-8 (Webster and Abrams 1983; Riese 1989; Fash and Stuart 1991), a hieroglyphic bench in area 9M-158 showing a ruler scattering his blood in a nonroyal context (Willey, Leventhal, and Fash 1978), and altars T and U in Group 9, which were erected by persons other than the paramount ruler. Indications

of weak central authority occur elsewhere as well: Sharer finds evidence for unstable, decentralized authority in states such as Tikal (1991), and Miller's analysis of the murals at Bonampak (1986), identifying the prominent role of nonroyal elites in the accession ceremony, would support the argument that weak centralization also appeared there.

The similarities that these cases of city-state evolution share with the better-documented example from ancient Greece provide strong support for application of this model of city-state evolution. If this assertion is correct, we are dealing with a type of evolutionary pattern wherein city-states stand outside the evolutionary processes we currently hold as valid. It is vital, then, that we understand city-states' immediate pre-state formations. If a city-state exhibits an inability to capture lineage modes of production, its pre-state formations must have shared this characteristic—contradicting the application of forms of chiefdom societies for their pre-state forms. The lack of internal taxes or tribute and the unusual system of liturgy or elite taxation in the Greek city-state argues against a system of tribute or taxation embedded within a political hierarchy in its pre-state forms. Ferguson has argued that ancient Greece displays overlapping forms of authority in its pre-state forms (1991), but I would argue that its composition was even more radical and lacked economic control and integration. We need new paradigms for city-states.

Interpreting interaction

This study elucidates some important methodological considerations, the first being an analysis of the effect of interaction. My conclusions fit well with recent work that argues that we need to understand the individuals and contexts of interaction in order to understand its effect on political structure (Schortman and Urban 1992). We cannot assume, as do Price (1977: 210) and Renfrew and Cherry (1986:8), that interaction between communities is an integral force in the development of greater hierarchical and integral complexity. The effect of interaction in Greece was that it impeded evolving centralization and hierarchy within the city-states. It would be more profitable if archaeologists were to consider the nonmaterial aspects of alliances, as Edens has done in his study of center-periphery networks in the third-millennium-B.C. Persian Gulf (1992).

It is also important that we understand the archaeological significance of focusing on contexts to determine the operational features of an alliance. The ideology of the interstate sanctuary was the most important factor in determining the effect of the network of elite power-seeking on the formation of the Greek states. Historical documentation has illuminated the connection between the sanctuaries and the Greek elite. Even without documentary evidence, however, these centers would have been strong candidates as vehicles for elite congregation because their attributes would correlate more closely with elites than nonelites—distance from many states; emphasis on athletics, especially events that required extensive training or, like horse-racing, events that required wealth; rich private dedications and the pan-state attributes that characterized many of the dedications.

If we have an understanding of the ecological frame, even for cultures that lack the substantial written record of ancient Greece, we might be able to use contextual analysis to supply concepts of the social frame as well. While we cannot always identify actors or their intentions, we can analyze the context of their interactions and suggest the components and constraints of their negotiation. I have argued elsewhere (Small 1992) that one channel of interaction between the classic Maya of the Petén was strongly affected by its principal context—the ritual ballcourt.

Adopting an analytical paradigm

One point of vital importance is the paradigm we select for the analysis of city-states. Several contributors to this volume (Morris, Stone, Pyburn) have argued that city-states do not fit into the current paradigms for the evolution of social structure. Limited political economies, weak centralization, oscillating internal poses, multiple internal power bases, and egalitarian values of social operation do not fit into our current models of social complexity. Like the poor fit between city-state and regional-state models of evolution, we are trying to define city-state complexity with models of hierarchy better suited to larger states. We need a broader analytical frame.

One approach that would be useful is based on heterarchy, a concept that was brought to the social sciences by Crumley from earlier studies of human and artificial intelligence (1987a, 1987b, 1990; Crumley and Marquadt 1987; see also Ehrenreich 1992), where heterarchy was used to argue that the brain does not operate in a hierarchical fashion but that different sections rise to dominance in reaction to different tasks. Heterarchy thus incorporates hierarchy as a

temporary process of problem-solving. She describes its features as

a system in which elements are unranked relative to one another or ranked in a variety of ways depending on conditions; the term is borrowed from cognitive psychology through artificial intelligence and refers explicitly to a heterarchy of values; an individual might ignore conflicting personal values (such as simultaneous opposition to abortion and support of the death penalty) or an awareness might precipitate a crisis. This is very similar to what Bateson refers to as the "double bind."

The implication for the values of an entire society is that an intricate net of power relations—counterpoised power—in which negotiating individuals operating in varying contexts play a critical role, cannot only support state apparatus but give rise to supra-state confederacies as well. To understand so-called complex societies, we must recognize that hierarchy is invariably a temporary solution to the problem of maintaining order; furthermore, generalized heterarchical structures—both cultural and environmental, and which are always present though not necessarily dominant—lend flexibility in the negotiation of power relations. Perhaps most importantly, the individuals who interpret, explain, and integrate values in a society (religious practitioners, lawgivers, philosophers) always play a pivotal role in maintaining order. (Crumley 1990:4–5)

This model of social structure fits well with our findings from ancient Greece.[8] Evidence from other city-states suggests that it would work in their analysis as well. King and Potter (1994) note that the great variety of internal "constitutions" of the numerous Maya polities, their extremely varied structures of interaction, and their weak political economies make them more amenable to a broader definition of structure than older hierarchical models. The same could be said of Mesopotamian city-states. Whether these states were based on state/temple leadership or more private means of production is too narrow a criterion. The greater question is why we have such variance, and this can only be addressed if we view hierarchy, as Nissen does (1982), as a temporary response to social crises within a larger heterarchical frame.

Conclusion

The city-state has been difficult for evolutionary theorists to envision. Its internal structure exhibits characteristics that we would not expect to find in our presumed models of complex societies. Looking at the city-state experience in ancient Greece has led to a better understanding of the city-state since its evolutionary pattern does not follow that of larger regional polities. We have been forced to develop a pattern of social change that stems distinctly from the city-state. This chapter is one step on such a path.

Notes

1. For example, control of irrigation (Sanders and Price 1968; Wittfogel 1957), tribute flow (Carneiro 1970), resource procurement (Rathje 1971; Haas 1982), agricultural intensification (Athens 1977), staple finance systems (D'Altroy and Earle 1985), and mercantile exchange (Johnson and Earle 1987).

2. Unless otherwise noted, I use the term *elite* to mean economic elite—the wealthy or well-to-do.

3. Gallant identifies nonvolunteeristic bonds as patron-client, while others would not. My own concern is with the construction of relationships of power. A good overview of patronage and its use by ancient historians can be found in Wallace-Hadrill (1989), with particular attention to the contribution of Johnson and Dandeker.

4. "The man whose wealth exceeded a certain sum had . . . to perform certain 'liturgies.' . . . He had to keep a warship in commission for one year . . . or finance the production of plays at the Festival, or equip a religious procession" (Kitto 1970:73–74).

5. This conclusion is at odds with Herman's (1987:45) argument that war provided the primary context for the initiation of *xenia*. I believe sanctuaries are more likely venues because of the greater mix of participants and their fixed scheduling, which would have provided a more reliable context than sporadic military encounters.

6. Other than the drought-inspired colonization of Cyrene by Thera or later colonizing movements by Athens in its empire, there is little evidence that colonization was directed by state economic interests, as we would expect in a more traditional archaic state. Current arguments for state direction are suspect: overpopulation and its correlative "land hunger" (Austin and Vidal-Naquet 1977; Snodgrass 1980:111–116) have not been identified archaeologically; commercial interests (Boardman 1980:44–46) are negated by Athens's lack of economic manipulation concerning its empire (see below). The general character of Greek overseas economic transactions appears to be private, as documented by the emporia of mixed Greek traders in famous outposts like Naucratis in Egypt and Al Mina in Syria.

7. De Ste. Croix argues for a direct relationship between the Athenian empire and elite profit through land acquisition and loans to subject communities (1981:290,

604–605). He confuses the issue by failing to separate secondary or epiphenomenal profit from state-directed action. Athens as a state made no move to benefit its elite in the governance of empire. What advantage the elite took of the empire was a private matter and better studied on the scale of elite interaction.

A strong case has been made (Finley 1978) that the real beneficiaries of imperialism were commoners. They would have been able to colonize confiscated territory, receive rent from confiscated lands, receive pay from the state for rowing in the navy, participate in empire-supported public offices, work in the dockyards, and gain relief from famine.

8. Although I have no wish to discredit work in Greek social structure, I do question the applicability of social models better suited to other hierarchical societies. Morris (1991; Garnsey and Morris 1989:101), for example, has adopted the conventional equation between population growth and the evolution of hierarchy put forward by Spencer (1896:449–450) and later pressed by Carneiro (1970), Forge (1972), and Johnson and Earle (1987). Unfortunately, this model fails to take account of different types of social decision-making processes, whether hierarchical or heterarchical, and the importance of contexts within Greek communities. Morris (1991) also adopted Flannery's (1972) early concept of linearization, which sees the state as an information-controlling hierarchy, to explain the development of the Greek *polis*. As we have seen, hierarchy in the *polis* was weakly constituted, temporary, and undermined by the lack of integration between contexts.

I also have reservations about the use of mortuary material to recreate Greek social structure (Morris 1987, 1992). The use of such data to explain the appearance of the Greek state has been keyed to historical models of rigid class distinctions, where the exclusion from formal burial is said to represent a division between elites and nonelites, but this overlooks the heterarchical basis of Greek political structure. Rather than being correlated with developing class distinctions, the variability in mortuary patterns in a heterarchical society is the result of numerous situationally invoked statuses (see White 1992 for similar conclusions for South Asia). Two distinctly different context-invoked statuses already noted in ancient Greece were those of citizen and client (Gallant 1989; Millet 1983). One might ask which status would be dominant in the mortuary record. There is not such a clean pancontextual distinction between elites and commoners or citizens and slaves or Greeks and foreigners as we assume. The issue is in need of reexamination.

8

The Chuzan Kingdom of Okinawa as a City-State

Okinawa could be likened to the city-states across the world in Europe which were flourishing then in maritime trade devoted in large part to the import and transshipment of exotic wares from the countries of Asia and Africa— spices, rare woods, jewels, textiles, and the curious substances needed by the alchemist and the pill-maker. The Shuri-Naha urban complex was supported by profitable traffic in luxury goods purchased in the Indies and the markets of Southeast Asia and moved through Naha for distribution to the ports of China, Korea, and Japan. Chuzan did not achieve the wealth of Genoa, the beauty of Venice, or the power of Lisbon, but the essential pattern of economic life was much the same.

(Kerr 1958:90)

RICHARD PEARSON

Between the twelfth and sixteenth centuries, a small secondary state gained ascendancy on Okinawa, the largest island (1,175 km²) in the Ryukyu Archipelago, which lies in the East China Sea southwest of Japan (Fig. 8.1). From A.D. 1372 to 1609, the island's Chuzan Kingdom maintained diplomatic ties with China, achieved superiority over other competing states on Okinawa, flourished as an independent trading entrê-pot with a distinctive culture, and then declined after its conquest in A.D. 1609 by the Satsuma fiefdom of Kagoshima in southern Kyushu, Japan. An unprecedented number of excavations and architectural reconstructions undertaken by the Japanese government, the Okinawan prefectural government, and local government agencies is bringing to light the archaeological record of state formation.

In this chapter, I discuss the processes leading to the emergence of the Chuzan Kingdom, the external factors that fostered development of the city-state and its palace center, and some details on its political and social organization. The focus of the discussion will be the main island of Okinawa, since the islands to the south lay outside the control of the central Ryukyus until about A.D. 1500.

The Archaeological Record

Humans have lived in the Ryukyu Islands since the Late Pleistocene; *Homo sapiens* fossils dating to ±18,000 years B.P. have been found at the Minato-gawa site in the southern part of Okinawa (Baba and Narasaki 1991). The Jomon culture extended as far south as Okinawa from 6000 to 400 B.C. It was followed by an Epi-Jomon culture (400 B.C. to A.D. 300), which was in relatively close contact with the Yayoi culture of Kyushu (Pearson 1990; Sasaki 1991: 352). Cultivation of rice and barley/wheat apparently began toward the end of the first millennium B.C. (Asato 1990:112–120).

Archaeological evidence for the development of the Chuzan or Ryukyu Kingdom is based primarily on the excavation of fortified castle sites (*gusuku* in the Okinawan dialect).[1] (*Gusuku* also denotes unfortified small religious sites, which are not treated in this paper.) Most of the sites occur in the southern portion of the island, which is composed of coral limestone. Along with the 223 castle sites recorded for Okinawa are a small number of village sites, such as Inafuku. Historical sources are also of some help in understanding Chuzan's development. They include accounts of Okinawan delegations to the Chinese Ming

Figure 8.1. Okinawa and surrounding region. Map by Joyce Johnson.

dynasty (A.D. 1368–1644) and the Korean Yi dynasty (A.D. 1392–1910), as well as other accounts from the seventeenth century on (Sakamaki 1963).

Castle sites are typically walled enclosures constructed of chunks of coral limestone, usually situated on rocky ridges or promontories that are easily defensible. In areas not underlain by coral limestone, as in the northern part of the island, defensive sites are created by digging ditches across ridges (Okinawa Kenritsu Hakubutsukan 1992).

Gusuku sites have been grouped by Asato Susumu into two types on the basis of size, although the spatial and functional interrelationships of the types are not clear (1990:97–107). Castles of less than 2,000 square meters have only a single enclosure and are found from the Early Gusuku period to the Final Gusuku period. Large structures, which range in size from 10,000 to 20,000 square meters, have multiple enclosures and are also found from the Early Gusuku period (A.D. 1200–1350) on. Some dating from the Final Gusuku period (A.D. 1550–1609) are more than 40,000 square meters in size. These large sites suggest rapid political change in which castle sites took on a range of functions and areas for different activities— residential, religious, and storage. The construction of castles also defined territories associated with local kin-based groups and their ancestors (cf. Earle 1991: 95) and asserted ownership over surrounding lands.

Figure 8.2. Katsuren Castle, located on the east coast of Okinawa Island. It was a center of vigorous trade during the fourteenth and fifteenth centuries, attested by the finding of Chinese coins and ceramics. The Lord of Katsuren, Amawari, was defeated by the forces of Sho Taikyu, King of Chuzan, in 1458. The castle consisted of several walled enclosures constructed on a high limestone ridge. The second enclosure from the top contained a large palace structure. From the original drawing published by Hisao Fujii in his *Chusei no Shiro to Kassen* [Castles and Battlefields of the Middle Ages]. Asahi Shimbunsha, Tokyo (1995). Reprinted with permission of the author.

While diagnostic sites do not actually appear until the twelfth and thirteenth centuries, changes leading to the Gusuku period are evident as early as the ninth century, with the appearance of trade goods, steatite (soapstone) cooking pots from Kyushu, and local gray stoneware made by emerging specialists (Asato 1990: 88, 89). Some unfortified sites from the Late Shellmound period (100 B.C.–A.D. 1200) appear in defensive locations, and some later fortified sites are underlain by shellmound layers.

Extensive excavations have taken place at Katsuren, the castle residence of Amawari, a local ruler who was killed by the forces of King Sho Taikyu of the Chuzan Kingdom in 1458. Asato's analysis of Katsuren (1990: 97), encompassing approximately 12,000 square meters (Fig. 8.2), indicates that its four enclosures had different functions. These have been interpreted from architectural remains, including roofing materials such as clay tiles, and associated objects. The smallest, most protected enclosure was the sacred precinct; the second, the residential palace. The third area was an enclosure in front of the residential palace used for assemblies, and the fourth area included storage, a work place for artisans, and a well.

Chinese ceramics are particularly abundant at castle sites. These artifacts include celadon (green glazed ceramic) vessels, usually in the form of plates, cups, shallow bowls, narrow-necked jars, and incense burners; white ware bowls, plates, cups, and wide-necked jars; and *temmoku* (oil spot glaze) bowls and black glazed tea containers. Black glazed wine containers have also been found (Toma 1985:15). Sherds of Korean Koryo celadons have been recovered from a small number of sites, and grayish roof tiles—probably made in Korea, but possibly produced on the northern part of the island—have been recovered from sites such as Urasoe. Special ridged mixing bowls (*suribachi*) have also been found, as well as pottery weights and spindle whorls.

The use of coinage is not entirely clear, although Chinese coins—primarily from the Song to the Ming periods—have been found. They are particularly abundant at Shuri and Katsuren. Dice for children's games have been recovered from Inafuku, Katsuren, and Urasoe; *saikoro*, bone gaming pieces, and *go* pieces have been found in the inner enclosure (*san no maru*) of Katsuren (Toma 1985:19, 20). Personal objects from Okinawan castles include beads, bronze hairpins (*kanzashi*), bone hairpins, metal tweezers, and finger rings. Small oil jars give evidence of the use of cosmetics, probably camellia oil, and a Chinese Song mirror was found at Inafuku.

Iron adzes, used for working both wood and stone, have been recovered, as well as iron knives, awls, sickles, and hooks. And there is clear evidence of how the tools were maintained—blacksmith shops, slag deposits, and whetstones. Objects associated with battle include iron and bone arrowheads, short sword blades and guards (*tsuba*), iron armor slats, gilded halters and bits, and decorative studs. Cow bones are the most common food remain; other food remains include carbonized rice and wheat/barley and the bones of wild boar, cats, dogs, birds, horses, dugongs, sea turtles, and fish. Some bone fragments show signs of cutting and shaping.

While many castle sites have been excavated and some have been restored, the excavation of a commoners' village from this time period is very rare. The only published case is Inafuku Iiutaki, a site located near Ozato village, which consisted of a cluster of five houses with a population of ten to twenty-five people (an extrapolation based on excavated portions of the site). The site was about 30 meters on each side. On the north side was a series of postholes and a hearth, while the south side contained a structure with six posts, thought to be for storage. To the east, archaeologists found a pavement, which may have been a ritual area, since many beads were found there, and south of this was a blacksmith area. The site is thought to have been an unfortified village from the thirteenth to fourteenth centuries.

The most abundant artifacts from the site were sherds of earthenware, followed by Chinese and Southeast Asian ceramics. Also found were *magatama* (nephrite comma-shaped beads) and green glass beads, knives, iron arrowheads, iron sickles for cut-

ting grain, clay weights, and carbonized rice and millet grains (Fujimoto and Naka 1980:303).

Asato calculated the ratio of domestic and foreign ceramics at Inafuku and at Katsuren (1980:335). The ratios were almost equal at both sites in the thirteenth century, but they changed dramatically over the next two hundred years at Katsuren, rising to about 3:1 in the fourteenth century and 15:1 in the fifteenth century. The ratios remained virtually unchanged at Inafuku.

The Subsistence Base

Irrigated wet rice cultivation, cattle raising, and dry cultivation of millet and wheat/barley formed the subsistence base. Iron tools—hand sickles and cultivating tools—were not in widespread use, and there is no archaeological evidence of iron plows or hoes, a lacuna substantiated by historical accounts (Asato 1990:116). Cattle were used for cultivation of both paddies and dry fields. Rice was sometimes treated as an annual, with two crops planted and harvested in one season; at other times it was treated as a perennial and harvested twice. The perennial types were in cultivation from Amami Oshima to Yaeyama, but the short-season variety was limited to Okinawa Island. It probably came to the island from China at the end of the fourteenth century.

Asato argues that the most reliable and productive system was a combination of upland wheat/barley and millet cultivation, with perennial rice cultivation

Table 8.1

Successive Rulers of Chuzan (Ryukyu)

Shunten Dynasty	Sho Shisho Dynasty
Shunten (A.D. 1187–1237)	Sho Shisho (A.D. 1406–1421)
Shunba Junki (A.D. 1238–1248)	Sho Hashi (A.D. 1422–1439)
Gihon (A.D. 1249–1258)	Sho Chu (A.D. 1440–1444)
	Sho Shitatsu (A.D. 1445–1449)
Eiso Dynasty	Sho Kinpuku (A.D. 1450–1453)
Eiso (A.D. 1260–1299)	Sho Taikyu (A.D. 1454–1460)
Taisei (A.D. 1300–1308)	Sho Toku (A.D. 1461–1469)
Eiji (A.D. 1309–1313)	Sho En Dynasty
Tamagusuku (A.D. 1314–1336)	Sho En (A.D. 1470–1476)
Sei-i (A.D. 1337–1349)	Sho Sen-i (A.D. 1477)
Satto Dynasty	Sho Shin (A.D. 1477–1526)
Satto (A.D. 1350–1395)	Sho Sei (A.D. 1527–1555)
Bunei (A.D. 1396–1405)	Sho Gen (A.D. 1556–1572)
	Sho Ei (A.D. 1573–1588)
	Sho Nei (A.D. 1589–1620)

in the valley bottoms and coastal areas (1990:116–120). Because agricultural activities were spread over several months, typhoons ruined very little of the total yield. The fact that the distribution of castle sites correlates well with the coral upland regions of the island seems to bear out Asato's argument.

Asato also suggests (1) that the castle sites form groupings on the raised coral limestone regions of southern Okinawa, (2) that the groupings derive from groupings of shellmounds at the end of the Late Shellmound period (A.D. 900; Figs. 8.3 and 8.4; Table 8.1), and (3) that the castle site groupings follow the boundaries of groups of sites recorded as political divisions (Okinawan, *shimajiri*) in the seventeenth century (1990:133–134). He also postulates that four types of domestic pottery can be distinguished on the

basis of inclusions in the paste and that pottery types may have been exchanged among groups of castles (1990:133).

Stages of Evolution of the Ryukyu Kingdom

The archaeological record can be correlated with the historical and political developments (Fig. 8.4) proposed by Asato (1987, 1988).

Early Gusuku period (A.D. 1200–1350)

During this period there were many large and small *gusuku* sites, but no powerful rulers or centers had yet emerged. Okinawan royal genealogies mention the

Figure 8.3. Site groupings on Okinawa (southern third of the island); (a) site groups in the Late Shellmound period (ca. A.D. 900), (b) site groups in the Gusuku period, (c) political subunits (*shimajiri*) of the seventeenth century A.D. and groups of castle sites of the Gusuku period. From Asato (1990:133). Reprinted with permission of the author.

Date	Okinawa	Japan	China
A.D. 1600	Final Gusuku A.D. 1550–1609	Momoyama A.D. 1573–1615	Ming A.D. 1368–1644
1500	Late Gusuku A.D. 1450–1550	Muromachi A.D. 1333–1573	
1400	Middle Gusuku A.D. 1350–1450		
1300	Early Gusuku A.D. 1200–1350	Kamakura A.D. 1185–1333	Yuan A.D. 1279–1368
1200			
1100		Heian A.D. 794–1185	Song A.D. 960–1279
1000	Late Shellmound period 100 B.C. – A.D. 1200		
900			Tang A.D. 618–960
800		Nara A.D. 710–794	
700		Asuka A.D. 600–710	
600			

Figure 8.4. Chronology of the Gusuku period.

union of a daughter of the lord of Ozato Castle and Tametomo, of the Minamoto family of Japan, one of the two rival factions at the end of the twelfth century, when main-island Japanese probably began to arrive on Okinawa. Sakihara points out that all over the Ryukyu Islands there are stories about the arrival of outsiders, often with little disturbance to the local communities (1987:49).

Middle Gusuku period (A.D. 1350–1450)

This is also called the Sanzan period, when three centers—Nakijin (north), Shuri (south-central), and Nanzan (south)—emerged preeminent from the many contending chiefdoms of the previous period. Related to these centers are the sites of confederates, the councilors of the ruler, for power was shared at this time by the king and his councilors. In the case of Nakijin, the King of Hokuzan subjugated the Motobu region, Kunigami, Haneji, Nago, Kin, and the Iheya and Izena islands, all in northern Okinawa.

Sakihara argues that trade with other areas must have been fully developed by this period (1987:144).

He notes that many of the goods taken by Sho Taiki, a powerful retainer of King Satto of Chuzan (r. A.D. 1350–1395), on tribute missions to China in A.D. 1373, 1374, 1376, and 1382 were transshipped items from Southeast Asia. The three principalities also sent missions to Korea in A.D. 1397 and to China in A.D. 1396 and 1397 (Kerr 1958:75–83). In A.D. 1403, Shuri apparently established relations with the Ashikaga shoguns (Kerr 1958:81). Eiso (r. A.D. 1260–1299) began to tax his subjects on Okinawa, as well as the people of the off-lying islands of Kume, Kerama, and Iheya, around A.D. 1264 (Kerr 1958:51; Sakihara 1987:140).

Sakihara also speaks of the role that rulers played in the distribution of iron agricultural implements purchased from Japanese and other foreign ships (1987:144). Satto and Sho Hashi (r. A.D. 1422–1439) were especially known for such activities. Iron slabs must have been imported to Okinawa as well, probably from China or Japan, for foundries and *tuyeres* have been found at some early *gusuku* sites, along with iron artifacts (Oshiro 1983). It is not clear whether iron artisans were attached to each *gusuku* or whether they functioned independently. Most likely they were attached to local *anji* (chiefs or nobles), since only the *anji* would have had the power to import the finished goods or iron slabs. By the fifteenth or sixteenth century, Okinawans had begun to obtain iron from ore-bearing sands.

Trade with Japan is also indicated, in Sakihara's view, in the *Omoro* Song of the Imported Folding Screen (Sakihara 1987:108–109). The *Omoro Soshi*, a collection of more than 1,000 poems from Okinawa and Amami Oshima, was compiled in the sixteenth and seventeenth centuries. Another *Omoro* mentions iron hammers and jewels from Japan, which Sakihara interprets as *magatama*, the comma-shaped jade beads that became the regalia of local spirit mediums (*noro*) (1987:110–111). They are similar in shape to beads from the Korean Three Kingdoms and the Japanese Kofun period (A.D. 250–600).

Late Gusuku period (A.D. 1450–1550)

This period overlaps with the end of the First Sho dynasty (A.D. 1406–1469) and the consolidation of power at Shuri, capital of Chuzan. Shuri is situated on a ridge inland and to the west of the main port of Naha. The first center of power during this period was Urasoe, which lies on a ridge 3 kilometers north of Shuri. From here, Satto, King of Chuzan, sent tribute to the Ming for the first time in A.D. 1372. In A.D. 1407, Sho Shisho (r. A.D. 1406–1421), *anji* of Sashiki, made himself King of Chuzan and started a line of rulers who resided at Shuri. In the consolidation process, Chuzan defeated Hokuzan and Nanzan in A.D. 1416 and 1429 respectively. In A.D. 1422, after the death of his father, Sho Hashi was acknowledged by the Chinese Emperor Yongle to be King of Ryukyu in recognition of the unification.

Wada Hisanori argues that the cessation of tribute from Hokuzan and Nanzan to China at this time does not necessarily signify the end of the two kingdoms, as has been generally assumed (1975:23). Their tribute missions had always been more sporadic than those of the more centrally located Chuzan Kingdom. Thus, throughout part of the fifteenth century—which saw the greatest flowering of the China trade and the development of Okinawan civilization—there may have been three kingdoms instead of one.

The second son of Sho Shisho became Hokuzan's governor in what has been termed the First Governorship (A.D. 1422–1469). There seem to have been lines of command at the time from Shuri to Nakijin and

from Shuri to the dependencies of Nakijin. Indeed, the position of Nakijin reflects the political structure of the period. The governor of Nakijin under the Second Sho Dynasty (begun in A.D. 1470) had the rank of a cabinet minister in the Shuri court. Sho Shin's third son, who was given this position, moved his residence to Nakijin, presumably to control the local nobles, who still maintained a good deal of power (Nakahara 1984:17).

Katsuren, situated on a peninsula on the central west coast, later became a rival of Shuri. Sakihara mentions that, prior to the open rivalry of the two centers, Princess Momoto Fumiagari, daughter of Sho Taikyu, was married to Amawari, ruler of Katsuren, an alliance doomed to failure, for Katsuren was destroyed in A.D. 1458 by Sho Taikyu (1987).

Final Gusuku period (A.D. 1550–1609)

During this period, especially during the reign of Sho Shin (r. A.D. 1477–1526), the structure of the state was consolidated. The king assumed greater power, forcing the *anji*, who had once been his equals, to reside permanently at Shuri with their families (Sakihara 1987:175). Until that time, most of the *anji* lived on their own hereditary estates (Kerr 1958:106), and the change in policy effectively separated them from the rural communities that had been their bases of power. Another effect of coercing the *anji* to move to the capital was to reinforce the divisions of social class over local kin groups. The Okinawan policy was more radical than that of the Japanese Tokugawa during the eighteenth and nineteenth centuries, for Japanese lords were allowed to reside in their own fiefs in alternate years.

The king increased his power in other ways as well. He no longer permitted swords to be worn as personal equipment, for example, and the *anji* were ordered to bring all weapons to a royal warehouse for storage. Gradually the outlying *anji* estates came under the control of royal overseers known as *jito dai*, and in A.D. 1477, the king's sister was established as chief *noro*, or priestess.

Within the aristocracy residing in Shuri, status distinctions based on six colors were introduced in A.D. 1506, apparently to rationalize the positions of various outlying local aristocrats into one unambiguous system at the center. Three years later, sumptuary rules were instituted, regulating dress and other manifestations of rank in Shuri (Kerr 1958:110).

Rebellions occurred in the outlying islands from

about the middle of the reign of Sho Shin, perhaps precipitated by harsh exploitation by the Shuri government as it became overextended. The Yaeyama Islands, located some 370 kilometers southwest of Okinawa, stopped sending tribute to Okinawa in A.D. 1496 or 1497 for which they were punished in A.D. 1500 by a force of 3,000 soldiers in 46 ships (Sakihara 1987:185).

In A.D. 1546, Shuri Castle was enlarged and strengthened. By this time, the only functioning castles remaining besides Shuri were Nakijin Castle, which protected the north under a governor appointed from Shuri, and the defensive castles for Naha Harbor, Yarazamori *gusuku,* and Mie *gusuku,* all built in A.D. 1554.

Okinawan Religion and the State

William Lebra (1966), noting that there are virtually no relevant written documents until the mid-seventeenth century, has reconstructed the processes by which religion was incorporated into the state organization in the Chuzan Kingdom. Revered figures from both the Japanese and Chinese legendary past were woven into the Okinawan state origin myth. In that origin myth, the legendary Tenson dynasty adopted the name and characters for Ninigi, grandson of the Japanese Sun Goddess and grandfather of the legendary emperor, Jimmu, who is said to have founded the Japanese state. The name of Shunten, the first historical ruler, who is dated to the twelfth century, seems to have been copied from Shun, the legendary Chinese ruler of ancient times.

During the time of the Chuzan Kingdom, its king and chief priestess were brother and sister. The priestess's shrine was located within the gates of Shuri Castle in the first half of the fifteenth century, and she may have played an active role in affairs of state (Lebra 1966:110). The priestess, source of power for the male ruler, was celibate and spent much of her life in seclusion. When state government and religion were centralized during the Sho Shin reign, the shrine of the chief priestess was moved to the opposite side of Shuri. The *anji,* now compelled to reside at Shuri, settled in three wards. Religious control of the wards and their outlying areas was in the hands of three high priestesses, one residing in each ward (Lebra 1966:113). The priestesses prayed for the health of the ruler and for the prosperity of their region.

In A.D. 1532, a system of local priestesses (*noro*) appointed by the central government was formalized.

These priestesses were not from the areas that they served, and they may in fact have limited the power of the villages' powerful families. Each *noro,* on attaining office, received a letter of investiture from the government and journeyed to Shuri to pray with the supervising priestess of her region. Thus religious practitioners owed their allegiance to the capital and, at least in the beginning, had no blood ties to the local community. At the same time, Shuri dispatched a lay official to administer the village; this office, unlike that of the *noro,* was not hereditary.

Okinawans venerated the southeastern corner of the island, where the first ancestors were thought to have arrived from the offshore island of Kudaka. In the fifteenth and sixteenth centuries, the entire court might have toured the southeastern part of the island to perform rites, subsequently crossing to Kudaka Island. After A.D. 1673, the king and court no longer participated directly, and a representative of the ruler traveled with the high priestesses.

Dual Subordination to China and Japan

As part of the tributary relationship with China, the Ryukyu kings were invested as vassals of the Chinese emperor. First, a mission reported the death of the ruler, and a second mission requested the investiture of the new ruler. When this request had been granted, Ryukyu sent an envoy to meet the investiture envoys, who went to Okinawa.[2] After the investiture, the king sent a messenger with special tribute to the Chinese court to express gratitude for the emperor's grace. Only the last mission went to Peking for an audience with the emperor. The others went to Fuzhou, Fujian province (Ch'en 1968).

In A.D. 1472, long before the invasion of Satsuma (A.D. 1587) and the subjugation of Okinawa (A.D. 1609), the lord of Satsuma attempted unsuccessfully to monopolize trade between Ryukyu and Japan. In A.D. 1588, the Japanese military ruler Hideyoshi, who had invaded Satsuma the previous year, requested—and received—a tribute mission from Okinawa. Three years later, Hideyoshi asked Okinawa to support the invasion of Korea, and the island reluctantly complied. In A.D. 1594 Hideyoshi ordered a land survey of the Ryukyu Islands, as an extension of the survey undertaken throughout the islands of Japan (Sakai 1968).

After its invasion of Okinawa in A.D. 1609, Satsuma considered the Ryukyu Islands a vassal state that should send annual tribute to the capital at Ka-

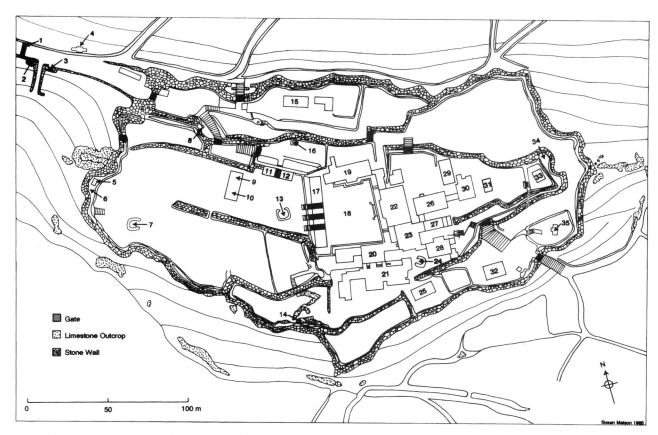

Figure 8.5. Plan of Shuri Castle (after Shuri Jo Fukugen Kiseikai, Naha Shuppankai Henshubu 1987:52–53). Late nineteenth century. (1) Ceremonial gate (*Shurei Mon*), first erected 1529, (2) Monument for beginning of stone paved road to Shikina summer residence (*Madamaminato Himon*), first erected 1522, (3) Monument dedicated to sixth Abbott, Enkakuji Temple, erected 1522, (4) Shrine (*Sonohyan Utaki*), (5) Bell tower, (6) Western parapet, (7) Shrine (*Madamamori Utaki*), (8) Dragon watercourse, (9) Royal records (*Keizuza*), (10) Foreign Relations Records, Protocol (*Yubutsuza*), (11) Administration of Sacred Places (*Jiinza*), (12) Registry of Births, Deaths, etc. (*Daiyoza*), (13) Shrine (*Shurimori Utaki*), (14) Watch tower, (15) Warehouse for ritual objects (*Zenigura*), (16) Sundial clock, (17) Storage of medicine, tobacco (*Naden*), (18) Plaza, (19) Reception hall for Chinese envoys (*Hokuden*), (20) Reception hall for Satsuma, Japanese envoys (*Nanden*), (21) Royal residence (*Shoin*), (22) Administrative palace (*Seiden*), (23) Sitting rooms for king, queen, (24) Shrine (*Kaimei Utaki*), (25) Kitchen, (26) Residence of queen mother, court ladies (*Yosoiodon*), (27) Royal refectory (*Yoriman*), (28) King's residence (*Nikai Den*), (29) Sitting rooms for court ladies, (30) Hall for king's succession rituals (*Yobokoriodon*), (31) Queen's residence (*Kogane Odon*), (32) Kitchen storage, (33) King's shrine (*Shinbyoden*), (34) East parapet, (35) Sashiki Palace (for queen's administrators). Prepared by Susan Matson.

goshima, as well as occasional missions to the *shogun* at Edo. Satsuma was the only Japanese *han* (fiefdom) to have control over a foreign king.

The Shuri Capital

The largest castle structure in the Ryukyus, Shuri Castle (Fig. 8.5), was built in the fourteenth century and enlarged over the succeeding two centuries. The original structure contained three major enclosures. The first, inner enclosure, in front of the palace, was an assembly area for chiefs and headmen. The second area was a space for the 200 members of the special militia that protected the palace and the king. In the third enclosure was a storage area and stables. State rituals took place in the palace gardens in front of the residential compound. The sixteenth-century *Omoro Soshi* songs also contain references to religious shrines (Okinawan *utaki*) at Shuri Castle.

Shuri Castle is situated on a limestone ridge 100 meters above sea level and commands a view over much of the southern part of the island, including the earlier capital of Urasoe to the north and the trading port of Naha to the west. Its dimensions are 400 meters east to west and 270 meters north to south, with a total area of 42,000 square meters (Fujimoto and Naka 1980:288). Beginning with the First Sho Dynasty, it has been the castle site of the king of Ryukyu.

The earliest phases of occupation and the initial phases of castle construction are not clear, and recent reconstruction of the castle may make it impossible to expose large areas of earlier strata. The castle itself may date from the reign of Satto (A.D. 1350–1395), but less complex elite residences probably preceded it. During the reigns of Sho Shin (r. A.D. 1477–1526) and Sho Sei (r. A.D. 1527–1555) in the Second Sho Dynasty, the stone wall on the east side was doubled in length during a major enlargement and reorganization, achieving a form that remained unchanged until the total destruction of the site during World War II in the Battle of Okinawa in 1945.

Along the outer periphery wall were four outer gates, and nine interior gates gave access to different divisions within the palace. With one exception, the inner walls were of cut limestone, 6–12 meters high, with wooden structures on top. The arched construction of the gates is of Chinese style. Administrative functions were carried out in three large buildings arranged around an open space; to the east were two buildings for the king and queen. The central administrative building, the *Seiden,* 16 meters in height, was the largest structure on Okinawa. By at least A.D. 1450, it was two stories high, and it was the seat of government. In front of the *Seiden* were two carved stone dragon pillars erected in A.D. 1508. The *Seiden* and other official buildings were set on a low platform (90 cm high) and all the buildings had tile roofs, wooden walls, and round pillars.

Flanking the *Seiden* were two buildings, the *Hokuden* (Northern Palace), used for receiving Chinese envoys, and the *Nanden* (Southern Palace), used by envoys from Satsuma. The *Hokuden* was constructed in Chinese Ming style. East of the *Nanden* was the *Uchibaru Shoin,* a residence for the king and queen connected to the *Seiden.* Behind this was the *Shoin,* a Japanese-style reception building with a tiled roof. Outside the main gate, at the western end of the castle, was the Sonohiyan Utaki shrine and the Enkakuji Buddhist temple.

Excavations at the time the *Seiden* was reconstructed revealed five different construction periods, but the actual forms of earlier buildings were not clear. Period I, known from only a small excavation sample, was marked by a brown soil layer. Japanese-style roof tiles were recovered and are thought to be from a building that preceded the *Seiden.* In Period II, a layer of cut stones was laid down, and its surface shows evidence of burning. On top of the cut stones was a building 16.36 meters by 9.09 meters (Kin et al. 1988:45–46). The western (front) portion of the building contained burned sherds of trade ceramics, armor slats, metal fittings, and fragments of burned charcoal, suggesting that the structure had suffered extensive burning. In Period III, the stonecutting and paving became extremely rough, as if refacing of the platform was done in a great hurry, perhaps because of some major event that occurred at this time. At least two more refacings occurred, in Periods IV and V, with the facing from Period V remaining until the twentieth century. The stratigraphy of the base platform of the *Seiden* has not been correlated to historical events.

Trade with China

The peculiar characteristics of the China trade were of crucial significance to Okinawan political and social development. Three kinds of trade existed—official tributary trade, private trade, and relaying or transshipping trade—with goods flowing from one type of trading arrangement into another. Chinese maritime trade can be traced to the Southern Song dynasty (A.D. 1127–1279), when Chinese merchants began to appear in the South China Sea and Indian Ocean (China Pictorial Publications 1989:206–227). Arabs and Malays had previously been the chief traders in the region. With the exception of territorially contiguous polities such as Korea and Vietnam, which were invaded by China, the relationship between China and its tributary subordinates was unusual, in that the flag did not follow trade. Outlying regions were not annexed or even defended when threatened or overcome by foreign powers. Gungwu Wang (1990) calls these Chinese traders "merchants without empire." They were at the bottom of the Chinese social scale. After the tenth century, even though they developed new roles with the expanding trade of the Song, they were not employed for imperial expansion. Unfortunately, despite the fact that trade generated great wealth, contemporary records are not very helpful (Wang 1990:402).

There was no official trade between China and Ryukyu until the Ming Dynasty (A.D. 1368–1644), but many Song ceramics have been found at Okinawan sites, and the first Okinawan polities emerged during the Song Dynasty (A.D. 960–1279). Thus it is important to understand the situation in that period. Maritime trade policy had been relatively liberal during the Song and Yuan (A.D. 1279–1368) dynasties (Chang 1991:24; Curtin 1984:125). In return for tributary gifts, the Chinese gave silver cash, luxury objects, textiles, and, on some occasions, horses and horse gear (Wong 1979). The Song government deliberately encouraged tributary and licensed trade, benefiting from the resale of tribute and the taxation of shipping and cargoes.

Payments in gold, silver, and copper coins became a drain on the Chinese economy, however, prompting the government in A.D. 1219 to issue an edict that only silk, textiles, porcelain, and lacquer wares could be used for trade with the countries of Southeast Asia. In the final decade of the thirteenth century, the government banned the export of gold and silver. Paper money was introduced into the international markets of the Yuan and Ming Dynasties, which not only helped to control the flow of precious metals abroad but also increased the dependence of foreign merchants on the Chinese government (Wicks 1992: 24, 25).

Between A.D. 1522 and 1644, the southeastern maritime provinces of China began to play a significant role in frontier policy, which had previously centered on the northern nomadic tribes. Unfortunately, the Ming Maritime Trade Ban (*haijin*), in effect from A.D. 1368 to 1567, made maritime trade with foreigners illegal, except for that conducted by tributary and investiture missions. The ban was intended to contain the losses from tributary trade. Under its provisions, private citizens were forbidden to sail overseas, and foreigners could enter China only on tribute missions.

Despite these restrictive government regulations, the south Fukienese, in the second half of the Ming Dynasty, embarked on an unprecedented participation in maritime business (Ng 1971:81). Seagoing trade yielded a tenfold profit, since the Ming Maritime Trade Ban was largely ineffective. Smuggling became a major part of the economic, social, and political life for inhabitants of Fujian and Zhejiang provinces in the fifteenth and sixteenth centuries. Chinese, Japanese, and Southeast Asian seafarers were hired by prominent mainland lineages to bring goods into Fujian. There was even a maritime quasi-kingdom in the A.D. 1540s. The Ming government tried unsuccessfully to subdue the smugglers for several decades—indeed, the pirates had grown so bold that 4,000 of them attacked two towns in southern Fujian in A.D. 1562 but were beaten back (Chang 1983:60, 242).

By A.D. 1517, because of falling revenues, the Ming government prepared to relax the prohibitions. Opinion was divided into three camps that Ng describes as the traditionalists (opposed to smuggling and foreign trade in general), the profiteers (in favor of opening trade), and the pragmatists (in favor of legalizing trade as a way to reduce piracy; Ng 1971:100). He argues that the government's restrictive policy had destroyed the development of a great maritime enterprise and failed to prevent substantial emigration. With a more favorable policy, the Fukien trade could have grown to the scale of Western maritime ventures instead of remaining a peddling trade.

The Ming ban was lifted in A.D. 1567, but the prohibition against trade with Japan remained in force, so the Japan-China trade was carried by the Portuguese from Kyushu to Macao (Wang 1990:416). Okinawa engaged in tributary trade with China and was a coveted source of Chinese goods. A total of eighty-eight licenses were given in A.D. 1589 from the ports of Fujian. Chang's analysis of two tax lists from this licensed trade, written in A.D. 1589 and 1615 and covering 115 commodities, found that items obtained from Ryukyu included unripe pepper seeds, sulfur, two varieties of conch shells, horse tails, ox and horse skins, and copper (1992:164–186). The pepper and copper were surely transshipped goods.

Atwell has noted two peaks of Ming prosperity that may be relevant to understanding political events and periods of intense construction activities in Okinawa (1977:25). The first, which occurred in the early fifteenth century, was a peak in the domestic mining of silver and the second, in the late sixteenth and early seventeenth centuries, was marked by the large-scale importation of silver. During the latter period, Okinawa was invaded by Satsuma, and its political independence came to an end. Okinawa's first appearance as a Chinese tributary state coincides with the Ming's first peak of prosperity, while Okinawa's subjugation by Satsuma and its demise as an independent entrepôt coincide with the second peak of prosperity. Japanese trading interests, formally shut out of China, were anxious to regain access to trade with China at the time of the second peak of Ming prosperity. Thus Ryukyu trade can be seen as a loop in a system linking China to the world economy.

Okinawa's relationship to the Quannan region of Fujian Province had a special effect on its development. The Quannan region was isolated from Chinese Han culture until the late Tang dynasty (A.D. 618–960), but during the tenth and eleventh centuries, its economy grew rapidly with the expansion of trade from Guangzhou to Quanzhou. Quanzhou had been the center of Fukienese maritime trade from the ninth century to the fifteenth century (Ng 1983). Although it had commercial ties with Korea and Japan throughout the Tang Dynasty (A.D. 618–960), it was only toward the end of that period that a large portion of the southern sea trade was directed to Quanzhou from Canton, primarily because Quanzhou could supply products from Korea and Japan more easily than Canton.

Quanzhou also had its own porcelain kilns, located outside the east gate of the city and dating from the Song Dynasty (A.D. 960–1279; Smith 1958). Kilns in the Quanzhou area made a variety of green (celadon) and white wares, as well as iron-spotted white wares (qingbai), which have been found in archaeological sites on the main islands of Japan, Okinawa, and Southeast Asia. Other kilns have been discovered in the past twenty years in Fujian and Guangdong provinces, and they undoubtedly supplemented the production of the well-known Longquan kilns of Zhejiang during the Song and Ming Dynasties (Kwan and Martin 1985).

By early in the eleventh century, unofficial trade in and out of Quanzhou had become substantial, but no revenue was collected by the state. Transshipment of goods from Southeast Asia made up a substantial part of this trade, and items from areas such as Fujian and Zhejiang, to which Quanzhou had access, were sent to Ryukyu. Clark notes a substantial drop in trade passing through the Quanzhou Trade Superintendency during the thirteenth century, occasioned by a variety of factors—piracy, corruption, and the enormous cost of supporting the Southern Branch of the Chinese imperial clan in Quanzhou and the Western Branch in Fuzhou (1991:175). Indeed, support of the court was an enormous drain on the economy in general. Clark thinks that some of the trade may have been diverted to local smuggling, in which case it would have disappeared from official statistics but not from the local economy. If this were the situation in Quanzhou, it is possible that the trade moved offshore—perhaps to places like Okinawa.

The Ming policy that halted private overseas trade affected Quanzhou very seriously. Quanzhou and other Fujian ports became imperial garrisons, with walled fortifications and flotillas of ships that controlled illegal shipping and piracy, whether by Chinese or foreigners. Fujian traders traveled along the coast, engaging in domestic trade and escaping to foreign ports whenever they encountered a chance to evade government surveillance (Wang 1990:406–408). It was economic growth in the coastal region, as

well as constant harassment from pirates and illegal traders, however, that led to the end of the Ming ban in A.D. 1567.

Late in the fifteenth century, Yuegang in Zhangzhou County began to replace Quanzhou as a center of trading importance. An important smuggling port, it was renamed Haicheng in A.D. 1567 and made an administrative seat—principally to control trade. The Zhangzhou area was known for its silk, crude porcelain, lacquered boxes, fans, salt, and iron pots and utensils, which were traded to Japan, the Ryukyus, and the Philippines. Ng reports that prominent Fujian families were able to monopolize the trade and minimize risk by sending out servants and managing partners for risky voyages (1971). Thus all aspects of trade were under the control of the family and its trusted employees. Families also adopted children to establish trading partners.

After the takeover of Okinawa by the Satsuma fiefdom of Kagoshima, Japan, in A.D. 1609, the Ming government was reluctant to engage in Ryukyu tributary trade because it compromised the ban on trade with Japan.

Tributary trade

Official tributary trade, which had developed in China during the Han dynasty (202 B.C. to A.D. 220), was based on the ideology of Chinese economic superiority that required states surrounding China to pay homage to the emperor, in return for which China provided lavish gifts. These tributary states were given privileges to trade at certain ports, and some goods given as gifts by the emperor to the representatives of the tributary rulers were carried home to be sold or distributed to political allies. At the level of state interaction, tributary trade was the official means of commerce. It legitimized and supported the Okinawan state and provided financing for public projects and maintenance of the royal family. Ryukyu was the last polity to enter the Chinese tributary system, which it did in the first years of the Ming Dynasty (A.D. 1368–1644). Other states from Southeast Asia—Srivijaya, for example—had been sending tribute to China for centuries. The Chinese system offered little or no military protection to tributary states, but neither did it interfere in their domestic affairs. At the beginning of the Ming (A.D. 1368) the designated port for tributary ships from Ryukyu was shifted from Quanzhou to Fuzhou but the Ryukyu-related customs office did not move officially until

A.D. 1472. Thus the Quannan area remained important for a long period. Thirty-six families from the Zhangzhou and Quanzhou region were sent to Naha by the first Ming emperor, Hongwu, as administrators and officials. They resided in a port area of Naha known as Kumemura.

In his study of the tributary trade system of the early Ming period, Kinjo notes two classes of tributary goods—luxury items and military items. Secret trade of military material was severely punished (Kinjo 1971:8). Native products sent as tribute were horses, sulfur, safflower dye, native silk floss padding, linen cloth, banana fiber, ramie, fans, white paper, and whetstones. Japanese products included short and long swords, spears, armor, gloves, shoulder and leg covers, helmets, horse armor and helmets, saddles, bridles, shields, fans, fruit boxes, small boxes, preserved plums, incense burners, vessels of gold and silver, lacquer objects, gold, and copper. Products from Southeast Asia included pepper, sandalwood, tin, ivory, sappanwood, incense wood, cloves, putchuk, incense, aloeswood, rhinoceros horns, and sea-otter skins.

To obtain goods for tributary trade and transshipment, Ryukyu ships went regularly to Japan and Southeast Asia carrying Chinese goods such as porcelain (Chang 1983:172–173). Sino-Ryukyu tribute trade was most active in the fourteenth and fifteenth centuries. It declined during the Jiaqing period (A.D. 1522–1566), when smuggling and piracy were at their peak on the Fujian coast. Ryukyu was given the monopoly to trade at Quanzhou during the Ming ban, while the Japanese traded at Ningbo until A.D. 1523, when they were excluded after disturbances caused by competing Japanese tribute missions. Prior to A.D. 1475, annual tribute missions often consisted of more than 200 persons who waited for months in Fujian while a small group proceeded to Peking. For investiture missions in the Hongwu period (A.D. 1368–1398), 500 individuals were involved, all carrying goods for private trading.

From A.D. 1385 to 1547, Ryukyu used Fujian-built ships for navigation, not only to China but also to Japan and Southeast Asia (Chang 1983:185). Chang has calculated that during the peak of tributary trading activity, an average of 1.58 ships per year traveled to China. This exchange was insignificant for Fujian Province, from which 100 ships a year sailed to Southeast Asia after A.D. 1567, but it was very important to Ryukyu (Chang 1983:193–197).

Sakamaki has suggested that Shuri gradually assumed control of exacting tribute from Okinawan communities, achieving, at the same time, a monopoly over the trade with China (1964). However, complete monopoly is not substantiated by the archaeological assemblages, which indicate that centers such as Nakijin and Katsuren had their own supplies of fine ceramics. The pattern of an upward movement of surpluses and a downward movement of trade goods seems to be far from perfect (cf. Wolf 1982:82), and it appears that during the Early and Middle Gusuku periods, no single political entity in Okinawa controlled the flow of goods from China.

Okinawans needed gifts of high prestige, as well as local raw materials, to present to the Ming authorities. To gain favor, these gifts had to appeal to the Chinese elite, necessitating the importation of a new technology to Okinawa to manufacture high-quality lacquer utensils and containers. Lacquer production in Ryukyu for use as tribute gifts offers an interesting example of elite sponsorship of craft production. Brumfiel notes that while elites presumably are able to impose their will on subordinates and to extract revenues from them for support of political superstructures, it is often the case that elites are unsuccessful in collecting taxes from kin-ordered commoner classes (1992). In such cases, they frequently establish enterprises to generate income, using the labor of individuals who are separated from the protection of kinship groups. Okinawan lacquer production represents a good example of this type of enterprise. It was begun in the fourteenth century, based on techniques imported from Fujian Province (Watt and Ford 1991: 330), and was sponsored by the Shuri court for tributary exchange with China. Most—if not all—of the raw materials were imported, since lacquer-producing trees grow poorly in the typhoon-prone climate of Okinawa (Ryukyu Shikki Jigyo Kyodo Kumiai 1991:30).

Relaying and private trade

The enormous number of traded ceramics found on Okinawa—and even more so on Southeast Asian sites—cannot be accounted for by tributary trade alone. Obviously, some derive from the private, unofficial trade and smuggling that proliferated (Chang 1983:225–250). Transshipment of elite goods is also well documented in the *Rekidai Hoan* (literally, Valuable Records of Successive Generations), a collection 269 volumes of diplomatic documents written in Chinese and dating from A.D. 1424 to 1867.

Although private trade is not well documented, it was probably more important than tributary trade, even in the Song (960–1279) and Early Ming (1368–1644) periods (Curtin 1984:125). During the Song and Yuan (1279–1368) dynasties, the trade port official collected tax; during the Ming, the tax, which was levied on goods coming into China for sale, was not levied against foreigners ("barbarians") as a good-will gesture.

The Chuzan court was most successful in relaying goods from Japan and Southeast Asia to China in the fourteenth and fifteenth centuries, when the Ming tributary system, coupled with the Ming ban, favored Okinawa and sealed off direct maritime exchanges between Chinese and other foreigners (Chang 1983:184). By the late fifteenth century, however, smuggling opened up chances for direct, unofficial contacts.

Through its trade with China, Okinawa also entered into the Chinese diaspora, socially interdependent but spatially distinct communities joined by kinship and sharing Confucian cultural and political values. China was in contact with the main islands of Japan from the time of the Han Dynasty (202 B.C. to A.D. 220), and considerable numbers of Chinese immigrated and became integrated into Japanese society in the sixth and seventh centuries (Pearson 1992:213, 263). Chinese contacts with the Ryukyus may have occurred, sporadically at first, as early as the first few centuries A.D., a speculation based on rare finds on Okinawa of Chinese knife coins and the occurrence of shell plaques, which appear to bear Chinese-derived decorative motifs (Pearson 1990:920). The overseas merchant diaspora from Fujian and Guandong provinces did not began to emerge until the fifteenth century, however. The diaspora consisted of permanently settled individuals as well as those who stayed for short periods or traveled on the junks. In the late fourteenth century, a group of Chinese families from Fujian was sent by the Ming government to live in Okinawa. They and their descendants, known as the Thirty-Six Families of Kume, were employed by the Chuzan rulers to establish and sustain maritime trade and a market network in East Asia.

The articulating units in the diaspora were three types of cities. The largest cities—those like Guangzhou or Quanzhou—were set in the political framework of a major empire. Next were ports of regionally strong states—Cambay and Ayudhya, for example—and the third were city-states like Malacca,

Aden, or Okinawa. The cities linked different levels of producers and consumers—producers of manufactured goods, trading ports, suppliers of raw materials, and groups on the edge of the system, such as pastoral nomads.

In summary, from the twelfth century, Chinese and Ryukyuans exchanged goods in private trade. During the fourteenth and fifteenth centuries, tributary trade existed as an official system parallel to private trade, while during the fifteenth and sixteenth centuries, exchange was primarily carried on through private trade and smuggling. The peculiar combination of a formalized tribute system, in which Okinawa held an established place in the Chinese imperial structure, and the commercial diaspora, in which transshipment was the main money-maker, created a special situation for the development of Okinawan society and culture.

Maritime archaeology and the trade

At least twelve sunken ships lying in East and Southeast Asian waters, dating from the twelfth to the sixteenth centuries, have been investigated by underwater archaeologists (Mainichi Shimbunsha 1993:107), and others have been looted. One of the richest, found at Sinan near Mokpo, Korea, dates to between A.D. 1308 and 1330 and was probably bound for Fukuoka, Japan. It contained more than 200,000 Chinese coins and 12,000 other artifacts, including a huge quantity of celadons (Keith 1980). Another, found in sand at Luoyang Bay east of Quanzhou, dates to about A.D. 1271. Considered to have been of average size, it was 24.2 meters long and 9.15 meters wide, with thirteen compartments. Apparently it sank on its first return voyage, for the hold contained precious woods, pepper, areca nuts, incense, ambergris, cinnabar, and mercury (Quanzhou Songdai Haichuan Fajue Baogao Banxiezu 1975; Salmon and Lombard 1979).

Discussion

Griffeth and Thomas have set forth a number of basic features that city-states have in common, including (1) a defined core, usually enclosed by walls or surrounded by water; (2) economic self-sufficiency, often achieved or promoted through the acquisition of an immediate and productive hinterland; and (3) political independence and self-government (1981a:xiii). Although the Chuzan Kingdom was small in scale, its political independence allowed it to dispose of its surplus on projects that directly benefited the city and its ruling groups. An impressive body of facilities and monuments was constructed in the palace complex and its surroundings and at the port of Naha.

Most city-states are dependent on trade and commerce with areas outside their control, their economies fluctuating in conjunction with trends in the larger economic system. The city-state comes to an end as a distinctive form of political association when the citizens' perception of their independence is forcefully changed, by whatever means (Griffeth and Thomas 1981a:xiii). Sometimes the wealth of a city-state was attractive to would-be conquerors, as was the case with Okinawa's conquest by Satsuma in A.D. 1609, which was seen as a way to gain access to a prosperous trading enterprise during the second of two peaks of prosperity during the Ming dynasty. After A.D. 1609, much of this wealth was passed on to the Satsuma rulers in Kagoshima.

City-states vary in their ability to produce food in the area immediately adjacent to the city. There were certainly open fields and agricultural communities surrounding Shuri and there seem to be no historical records delineating the importation of food, but we do not know precisely how food was secured and distributed by the state. Brumfiel and Earle point out that archaeologists have, in a number of instances, found that management of the production/distribution of subsistence goods was of little importance in the development of political centralization. They argue that "political elites often do not function as promoters of economic efficiency through redistribution or market management of subsistence goods, but that their wealth was acquired through long-distance trade and patronage of skilled craft specialists" (1987:6–8). In the case of Okinawa, the sample of commoner villages is too small to support generalizations, but the Inafuku excavation seems to indicate a lack of economic specialization at the village level (Fujimoto and Naka 1980:302–304). While the core of the city-state appears to have had well-developed markets, outlying regions did not have the secure supply of marketed goods that would have allowed them to become highly specialized.

Earle describes two basic types of finance for chiefdoms and emerging states—staple finance and wealth finance (1991:3). The first involves the mobilization and disbursement of food and technological goods as payment for services. Wealth finance entails the procurement of items of symbolic value, whether through long-distance exchange or patronized craft produc-

tion, and their bestowal on supporters. Gilman argues that any system of wealth finance must rest on some system of staple finance (1991:157). The construction of Okinawan *gusuku* appears to emphasize communal or kin-based ties and thus the production of staple finance. We do not find rich graves of the individuals who lived in the large structures, and there are few other signs of the display of individual wealth. The mobilization of trading ships to China and Southeast Asia seems to have been based on the activities of communities led by noble entrepreneurs.

Griffeth and Thomas argue that city-states develop when polities in the surrounding areas are relatively weak (1981a). While powerful states developed in the Chinese and Japanese regions, Okinawa lay outside their grasp. It engaged in trade—probably indirect—with the Yamato state of Japan from the eighth to the twelfth century, primarily in soapstone cooking vessels and other utilitarian goods. Okinawans are, of course, collateral relatives of main-island Japanese, with affinities in prehistoric ancestry and language, and finds from castle sites—for example, weapons and ornaments—show that they shared many customs with main-island Japanese. Yet Okinawa retained its political autonomy until A.D. 1609.

Geography played an important role in this autonomy, for the sea provided a measure of protection from the territorial expansion of both Japan and China. In addition, China's southeast coast, which lies only a few hundred miles west of the Ryukyus, was malarial and rather inaccessible. The fact that the island posed no threat to China but could be brought into its imperial system as a tributary state played a large role in the development of Okinawa's independent political system.

The diminutive size of Okinawa's city-states seems consistent with Mediterranean cases, in which the largest of the Greek city-states, Sparta, covered an area of 8,300 square kilometers, while other city-states ranged from 80 to 1,300 square kilometers. Populations ranged from 2,000–10,000 adult male citizens (Ferguson 1991:178). Ferguson notes that "the emerging *polis* not only had to widen the circle of governing elites but also had to overcome identities and ritual friendship patterns of behavior associated with Dark Age chiefdoms" (1991:181). This sounds similar to the consolidation processes of the Chuzan Kingdom.

The Chuzan Kingdom owed political allegiance only to the Chinese emperor, a fealty that brought many benefits and few costs. In exchange for political allegiance and tribute, Okinawans received extensive trading privileges and opportunities for education in China—at China's expense—as well as other cultural amenities (Ch'en 1968). Okinawans had a close relationship to Japan, it is true, through language and customs, but the Chuzan Kingdom is similar in size and economy to the small trading states of Southeast Asia such as the Sultanate of Brunei. These states relied primarily on the transshipment of luxury goods for a substantial part of their revenues. Okinawan music, traditional dress, and architecture display Southeast Asian cultural influences that reflect participation in this network.

Future Prospects for Research

Since city-states are defined in political terms and since part of their sources of wealth and energy often lie outside their immediate boundaries, they may be investigated in terms of their interaction with other polities. However, the fact that information as well as goods were exchanged makes it impossible to measure the sociopolitical significance of past contacts solely on the basis of preserved exotics found in excavated and surface collections (Schortman and Urban 1992:236). In their study of elite interactions, Schortman and Urban emphasize the placement of objects and styles within regional behavioral contexts, which suggests that a range of sites should be excavated (1992:237).

A city-state such as Okinawa seems best understood by the analysis of a social system or world system that cuts across culture, tribe, nation, state, and ethnic group (Santley and Alexander 1992:17). This perspective, in which a core and a periphery are identified, sheds light on the relationship of Okinawa and China. Southeast China during the Song (A.D. 960–1279), Yuan (A.D. 1279–1368), and Ming dynasties (A.D. 1368–1644) fits the model of a dendritic political economy dependent on demand from a periphery that was beyond its political control. In the six cases reviewed by Santley and Alexander (1992:33), there was evidence of an economic crisis at home at the time of expansion. In the case of Fujian, the crisis can be seen as an unfavorable balance between land and population, exacerbated by the suppression of economic opportunities through restrictive overseas trade policies and a ban on emigration.

Santley and Alexander note that dendritic political economies work well on a long-term basis only if (1) they can control demand on the periphery and (2) the

demand for luxury goods ("preciosities") does not change (1992). In the case of China, the appeal of Chinese trade ceramics and textiles was deeply ingrained in the culture of the surrounding regions—even assuming ritual and political significance—while the demand for exotic goods from the South Seas was also deeply institutionalized in Chinese culture (Guy 1984; Wong 1979:90). Archaeological research may provide some clues to the degree of access that lesser political leaders in Okinawa had to Chinese goods. If future research were to show a number of powerful centers, each with an amount of foreign prestige items comparable to Shuri's, rather than a regular distance fall-off pattern in the frequency of these goods, it might confirm that Chinese trade was not completely monopolized by the Shuri kings, despite their filial, tributary status to the Ming emperors.

From the perspective of political economy, Brumfiel (1992:557) notes that a state, by definition, always has boundaries beyond which political and economic control cannot be maintained. These regions, which may lie beyond the boundaries of the subsistence ecosystem, are important for understanding the political economy of interacting elites. Such a perspective is very useful in understanding the rise of competition and alliances in the history of the Chuzan state.

The way in which labor is controlled and the use of its products may also be fruitful areas for research. The construction of the castle sites' stone walls and ramparts involved substantial amounts of labor, given in exchange for foreign iron products, Chinese ceramics, and other goods, both utilitarian and prestigious. The flow of these goods and services at the local level and through intermediate centers has not yet been documented by the comparative analysis of archaeological assemblages, although many sites have been excavated and reported.

Acknowledgments

I wish to thank the University of British Columbia HSS Grants Committee for support of my 1992 project, "Okinawan Castle Sites and Overseas Trade, A.D. 1200–1600," under whose auspices this paper was prepared. I give thanks also to countless Okinawan colleagues.

Notes

1. Local terms and artifact names are given in Standard Japanese except where indicated. Japanese and Chinese proper names are given with surnames first.
2. Gerhard Mueller has prepared a detailed account of the investiture mission of 1534 (1991).

9

City-States of the Maya

A century ago, the great pioneer of Maya archaeology, Alfred Maudslay, lamented that the Spanish conquerors of the New World suffered from "the great disadvantage in having to explain the social, religious, and political systems of the New World in terminology suited only to the Old" (1974:2). Mesoamericanists in general, and Lowland Mayanists in particular, have continued this tradition. Widespread use of the term *city-state*, the central theme of this book, is a case in point. Given the derivation of the city-state concept from the Greek *polis* (Nichols and Charlton, this volume) and the early characterization of the Classic Maya as the "Greeks of the New World," such usage was probably inevitable. Generations of scholars have called Maya polities city-states. Probably the most influential Mayanist to do so was J. E. S. Thompson, who had a penchant for Old World—especially European—historical analogies (1954:78–82), and recent symposia and publications continue to do so (e.g., Benson 1986; J. Marcus 1989).

While Maudslay's remark is certainly apt in some regards, it is not entirely accurate. Uncritical use of concepts such as "feudal" or "city-state" can cloud our thinking. But there are regularities in the evolution and structures of ancient complex societies, and the particular origins of a concept need not preclude its wider application. Were they to do so, anthropologists would have to discard most of their general terminology.

The trick, of course, is to say exactly what we mean when we transplant or extend a concept such as city-state. I prefer not to speak of city-states in connection with the Maya, not because I believe that the concept lacks broad comparative utility, but because I doubt that the Maya generally had either cities or state-type institutions, as we think of them. The fact that these components of the city-state concept are variable is often ignored. Thompson, for example, attributed city-state organization to the Maya, but he also maintained that major Maya centers were vacant ceremonial places and not cities in the conventional sense of the word (1954:57). Moreover, his theocratic conception of Maya society did not accord closely with definitions of the state as a political form. More recent reconstructions agree that Maya polities were hierarchical and complex (e.g., Culbert 1991b), but glibly labeling them states is incautious—and probably incorrect. I long ago adopted the more neutral term *polity* for Maya political systems, thereby avoiding unnecessary evolutionary freight.

DAVID WEBSTER

Definition of the City-State

Given these caveats, Maya polities can be reasonably called city-states if we adopt a very broad definition: *A city-state is a polity organized around a single, large, autonomous central place that is differentiated from lesser places in its hinterland, over which it exerts political, economic, and cultural dominance. At least some forms of stratification must be present, even though true classes or the mature institutions that uphold an order of stratification need not be.*

Stratification means that there is differential access to basic resources among hierarchically ranked social subgroups and that advantaged groups can effectively deprive others of resources and thus use wealth as a political tool. This definition is flexible enough to cover a wide evolutionary range, including stratified societies or states—to use Fried's (1967) terminology—but it excludes complex ranked societies. Its analytical use implies that two sets of archaeological correlates can be identified—settlement-system features (which are easy to identify) and material or symbolic evidence for stratification (which is much less easy to discern).

Also inherent in the concept of city-state is the implication of political segmentation. We usually use the term to characterize individual polities in a network of autonomous, interacting polities, although there are exceptions—Teotihuacán, for example, of about A.D. 100 is usually considered a city-state, even though it had no nearby, remotely comparable neighbors. City-state political landscapes more commonly consisted of several similar, autonomous polities in close juxtaposition and interaction, as in classical Greece or southern Sumer. In such systems, the most fundamental and durable polity is the independent, dominant center and its hinterland settlements, territory, and population. Larger entities may be situationally created—by alliance or confederation or by the conquests of particularly able rulers—but they are fragile and short-lived.

Not only are individual city-states small polities, but there are also constraints—organizational or otherwise—on political expansion and effective consolidation of conquests. Cycles of coalescence and fragmentation may result, as noted by Marcus for the Maya (1993:164–168). City-states are also extremely diverse. Archaeological and historic information reveals that constituent interacting polities often have very different scales, histories, organization, and cultural prestige. This was the case in ancient Sumer, and the striking differences between Greek city-states (most notably Athens and Sparta) have long been recognized.

In this chapter, I will discuss the city-state concept with regard to Classic Maya polities from A.D. 300 to A.D. 900. Hundreds of large and small Classic Maya centers are known over the 250,000-square-kilometer region called the Maya Lowlands (Fig. 9.1). In the northeastern Petén of Guatemala, some imposing centers are located only 15–30 kilometers apart. Elsewhere, distances are greater, and some large centers are comparatively isolated by both distance and topography. I will also compare and contrast two centers that are particularly well known—Tikal in the northeastern Petén and Copán in western Honduras.

It is necessary to note at the outset that ancient Mesoamericans lacked domestic animals for traction or transportation. They also lacked energy-capturing devices like sails and water wheels. Human muscles did most of the work, unaided by metal tools, which would have increased muscular efficiency. Such energetic and technical constraints affected the development of Mesoamerican society in many ways, and this was especially true of its urban tradition (Sanders and Webster 1988).

The Ethnohistoric Maya

Sixteen polities, or "provinces," coexisted in the northern Yucatan Peninsula at the beginning of the sixteenth century, when they were first observed by Spanish explorers (de Landa 1941; Roys 1943, 1957). The Maya term for these polities, *cuchcabalob*, conveys a general sense of "jurisdiction" (J. Marcus 1989:203), which implies some measure of political integrity or independence. There was, in fact, considerable political fragmentation, although much of the region seems to have earlier been united under confederations centered on Chichén Itzá and Mayapán.

Extremely significant for our consideration of Classic society is the political variation among these provinces. Some were very large. Mani, for example, probably had a population of about 60,000. The town of Mani was the dominant central place, the establishment of the *halach uinic*, a hereditary territorial lord and member of the prestigious Xiu lineage. Subordinate governors called *batabob* (sing. *batab*) ruled lesser towns, and numerous smaller settlements or isolated farmsteads were widely dispersed over the countryside. In contrast to this type of politically centralized polity, other provinces consisted of networks

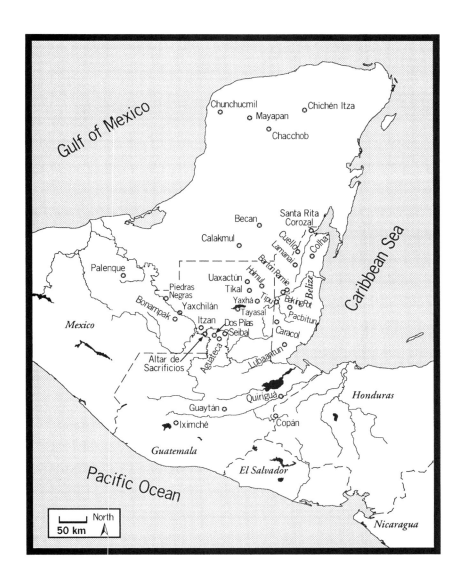

Figure 9.1. Map of the Maya Lowlands showing locations mentioned in the text, and other major Maya centers. The greatest concentration of Classic Lowland Maya centers is in the northeastern Petén, in the region around Tikal. Map courtesy of David M. Reed.

of elite centers, each with its own *batab*. These petty rulers shared common lineage affiliation, and their territories, though not dominated by a *halach uinic*, formed cohesive political units. Finally, some provinces were loose confederacies of independent towns whose *batabob* may or may not have shared common descent. These three variants are diagrammed in Figure 9.2. Warfare was common.

Although the general picture is one of considerable political variation, there is a great deal of dynamism as well, which suggests that the sixteenth-century Maya were in the fragmentation part of a larger cycle of political unification and breakdown.

The basic spatial and political unit of all these provinces was the town or central place where a lord resided, which was surrounded by outlying settlements or farmsteads. Where political centralization was pronounced, settlement hierarchies consisted of three

or more levels, dominated by a capital such as Mani. The ethnohistoric Maya thus conformed to what was apparently a general Mesoamerican concept of territory:

At the center of the territory was the place of residence of a ruler, usually a 'capital' or 'head town,' but sometimes just a royal palace or residence. The most meaningful political unit, however, was the entire territory controlled by that one ruler, including not only his capital but all secondary centers, tertiary centers, villages, hamlets, agricultural lands, and forested areas of his realm. (Marcus 1992c:189)

Note that the dominant central place need not be urban in configuration. It is simply the place where the paramount ruler maintains his establishment.

Some forms of stratification were present as well,

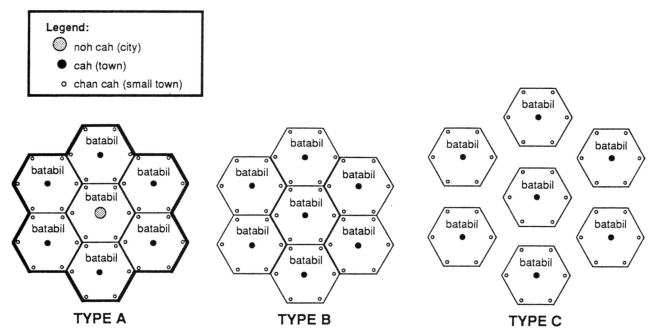

Figure 9.2. Schematic representations of Roys' three types of provinces (*cuchcabalob*):

Type A: A centralized polity with a territorial ruler (*halach uinic*) who resided in the *noh cah* or city (stippled circle) of the province. The *halach uinic* also ruled a series of dependencies (*batabil*) administered by local rulers (*batabob*). Each *batab*'s town is shown as a black dot; his villages are small white circles.

Type B: This type of province had no overall territorial ruler. Instead, the province was coadministered by related *batabob*, usually members of the same lineage, each of whose towns is shown as a black dot.

Type C: This type of province was administered by a loose affiliation of towns (black dots) headed by unrelated *batabob*, each of whom controlled a set of smaller villages (white circles).

From Marcus (1993: 119:figure 3). Reprinted with permission of Dumbarton Oaks Research Library and Collection.

especially in the more politically centralized provinces. Whether farmland was held in common is uncertain, but some powerful lords seem to have had privileged access to areas that produced valuable crops, such as cacao. Hereditary nobles emphasized separate descent from commoners and were further distinguished by a set of shared elite conventions and esoteric knowledge, including a special language. They collected taxes or tribute in the form of both labor and goods, owned slaves, and dominated long-distance trade. Towns where important lords lived had temples and other public buildings erected by communal labor, as well as impressive elite dwellings where the lords lived with their relatives, retainers, and slaves.

Cutting across these status distinctions was a system of vertical lineage organization that included both nobles and commoners (Roys 1943:35–36). About 250 patronymic names were widely distributed within and between provinces; in some provinces, large proportions of the inhabitants—nobles, commoners, and slaves—shared the same name and treated one another to some degree as kin, especially in terms of hospitality and marriage arrangements (rarely did two people of the same patronym marry). Because names were not localized, however, patronymic affiliation probably did not provide the general underpinnings of political structure except at the elite level.

Extensive swidden agriculture seems to have predominated, which is consistent with low population densities (the overall density of Mani, for example, was 6–12 people per square kilometer).

In summary, despite weakly developed patterns of urbanism and stratification, the ethnohistoric Maya clearly conform to our modified definition of city-state organization.

Preclassic Origins

How far back in time can we discern these patterns? Appropriate settlement correlates of the city-state appeared in the Maya Lowlands during the Late Preclassic period, or roughly between 400 B.C. and A.D. 300.

More specifically, several centers of large size were present by about 300 B.C., including Komchen in northeastern Yucatan (Ringle and Andrews 1990), El Mirador (Matheny 1986), Nakbé in the northern Petén of Guatemala (R. Hansen 1991), and Cerros in northern Belize (Robertson and Freidel 1986). All were of respectable size, and El Mirador was one of the largest centers in the Maya Lowlands. All featured impressive structures built by massed labor—most notably temples, but possibly elite residences (although the first clearly documented palace appears at Tikal only in the fourth century A.D. [Sharer 1994:178]). We know little about Late Preclassic settlement hierarchies, but there is no doubt that impressive central places dominated rural hinterlands that included lesser places, as they did in the sixteenth century.

The variation in architectural layout and iconography that characterize the Classic Maya Great Tradition also appeared about this time. Symbols associated with Classic Maya religion and rulership also have their roots in the Late Preclassic (Freidel and Schele 1988). Although written texts were inscribed on small objects by the end of the period (and possibly earlier), there are no lengthy inscriptions on large monuments until the erection of Stela 29 at Tikal in A.D. 292, which is considered the beginning of the Classic period. Inscriptions, along with their associated dates and iconography, provide important clues about political structure. Because of the absence of inscriptions (and for other reasons as well), Mayanists are divided on how Preclassic polities were organized and whether any forms of stratification were present. In my opinion, hierarchical sociopolitical structure is evident, but stratification appears to have been weak or nonexistent, with the possible exception of large centers such as El Mirador. Thus the settlement component of our definition is unambiguously present; unfortunately, the organizational component is not. Whether Late Preclassic polities were city-states is arguable.

The Classic Maya

The florescence of Classic Maya civilization occurred roughly between A.D. 300 and 900. Between about A.D. 650 and 850, regional populations peaked, centers became most numerous, and the Great Tradition of Classic art, architecture, calendrics, and written inscriptions was most far-flung, especially in the central and southern regions of the Lowlands. Although

more difficult to reconstruct from archaeological evidence, political variation may have been as pronounced in this mature Classic landscape as it was among the ethnohistoric Maya (Sharer 1991; Webster 1988). It is this mature stage of cultural development that we know best, and that we will examine most closely.

The heartland of the Classic Maya suffered severe depopulation after A.D. 800–900, and once-thriving Maya centers were engulfed by forest. Because large-scale masonry construction was used for public and elite buildings, material remains are conspicuous and well preserved. Stone monuments with inscriptions and iconography were also concentrated at these centers, so the sites attracted early archaeological interest. By the beginning of the nineteenth century, we were able to decipher Maya dates, and later breakthroughs in our understanding of texts and iconographic symbols have added political details. As a result, Maya scholarship has been heavily center-oriented, which is one reason why the city-state model gained wide acceptance. Before turning to the specific examples of Copán and Tikal, however, we must address several general issues pertaining to Classic political systems and their centers.

Nature and scale of centers

Without venturing into the theoretical thicket of what is urban and what is not, it is fair to say that Classic Maya centers were distinctly nonurban in comparison to centers in parts of the Old World—Europe, the Near East, and China—and elsewhere in Mesoamerica (e.g., Teotihuacán and Tenochtitlán). Most Mayanists believe that centers were essentially the establishments of rulers, a view that is consistent with Marcus's general Mesoamerican pattern (cited above). Sanders and Webster (1988), following a model of Richard Fox (1977), characterize them as regal-ritual centers. These centers lacked large, nucleated populations and were, in important respects, less differentiated from their rural hinterlands than many Old World cities, particularly in economic terms. They were essentially the households of hereditary Maya rulers or lesser nobles, architecturally dominated by masonry palaces, temples, and other ritual constructions (e.g., ballcourts), along with elaborate mortuary facilities for Maya lords. At some centers (e.g., Copán), the lesser, but still impressive households of subelite lords can also be identified.

In essence, the centers were places from which

Maya rulership emanated, dressed in an elaborate façade of royal status symbols and ritual display. Buildings were often decorated with ritual-political iconography and inscriptions, as were associated stone monuments, such as altars, thrones, and stelae. The displays were commissioned by rulers, and sometimes other lords, to project political messages to their subjects and to their peers in a complex mix of propaganda, history, and myth (Marcus 1992c). The hypertrophied ritual and symbolic dimension of Maya politics partly accounts for the monumentality and visual impressiveness of centers, but it also betrays the political fragility of rulership in the absence of institutions that effectively concentrated power and wealth in the hands of kings. Nevertheless, at some centers where inscriptions are abundant, we have clear evidence that royal titles were passed down through successive generations of dynastic rulers, as was the case at Tikal and Copán.

A few centers such as Tikal functioned as regal-ritual capitals for a millennium, and many others were occupied for hundreds of years. Strong rulers initiated ambitious building programs, burying old structures under later additions and erecting new temples and palaces. As a result, many capitals—and their constituent constructions—grew impressively large. Individual temples are often more than 30 meters high, and some are more than twice this height.

Measures of the comparative scale of Maya centers are common in the literature (e.g., Turner et al. 1981), but comparison is difficult because of differences in the configuration of architectural complexes from one site to another. One simple measure is the spatial extent of architectural complexes, including causeways and plazas, that form the regal-ritual cores of centers (bearing in mind that some centers grew over longer periods than others). My rough measures for the architectural cores of a range of Late Classic sites are as follows: Tikal: 400 hectares; Becán: 19 hectares; Quiriguá: 13 hectares; Copán: 22 hectares; Uaxactún: 16 hectares; Bonampak: 4 hectares.

While such crude comparisons can be misleading, they do provide gross contrasts. Tikal was unusually large (although my estimate is a very generous one); most centers were well under 100 hectares in area. Unlike many other preindustrial city-state centers, Maya regal-ritual cores were not heavily "built-up" with residential structures. Rather, major architectural complexes were grouped around large open plazas, often quite distant from one another, connected by wide artificial causeways.

Probably the most striking architectural contrast with many Old World city-states would be the lack of densely packed residences—as found, for example, in Sumerian cities. The 400-hectare central core of Tikal (Fig. 9.3) covers roughly the same area as Early Dynastic Uruk. Walking through Uruk, one would have been impressed by the rabbit warren of houses, relieved by a few open spaces and a core of ritual/palace architecture. The core of Tikal would have conveyed the opposite impression—a few small residences dominated by multiple complexes of temples, palaces, causeways, and open spaces. Its permanent population would have been minuscule compared to Uruk's. Mycenae—which, by our definition, would be a more comparable Old World city-state capital—had about the same area as Bonampak.

As many as 40,000–50,000 people lived in Early Dynastic Uruk, so the population density would have been about 100–125 people per hectare, or 10,000–12,500 per square kilometer. Such densities place Uruk well within the density range for preindustrial cities of 10,000–20,000 per square kilometer (see Storey 1992 for a useful recent review). We have no reliable way of estimating Tikal's core population, but it was probably on the order of 1,000–2,000 people, or an overall density of 2–5 people per hectare (I refer here to the 4-square-kilometer zone only). A similar guess for Copán's core population is 250 people (11 per hectare), and R. E. W. Adams (1974:294) reconstructed Uaxactún's palace population as 100–200 people.

We are, to some degree, comparing apples and oranges, however, because a substantial portion of Uruk's city-state population resided within the city walls, while Maya regal-ritual cores housed only rulers, nobles, and members of their households. Their spacious civic layouts were designed in part to accommodate large numbers of people from outlying settlements, who congregated around temples, ballcourts, and palaces for collective rituals or other public events.

Nature and scale of polities

There is no question that the Classic Maya Lowlands were fragmented into many independent polities, although, as we shall see, Mayanists disagree on their scales. A similar elite culture or Great Tradition cut across political boundaries, however, so that common ideological conventions are reflected in calendrics, art, ritual, and inscriptions. Some Mayanists believe

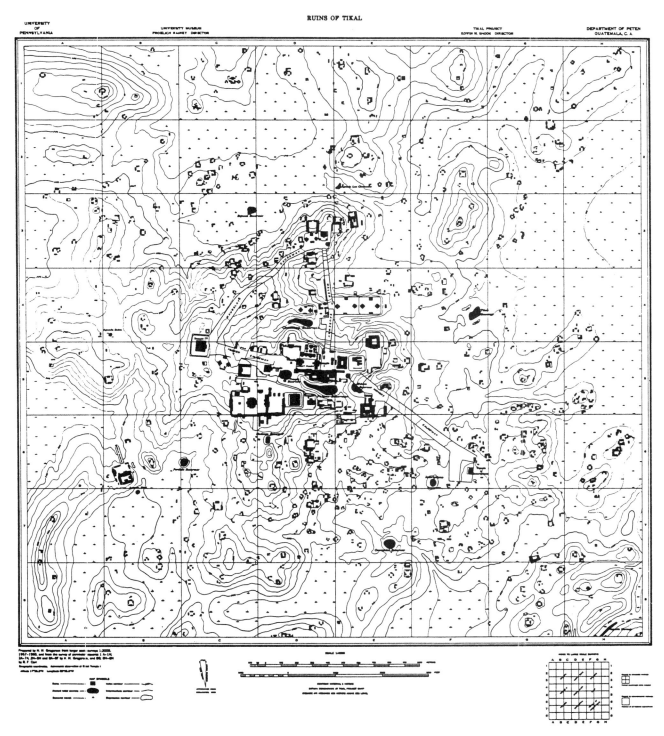

Figure 9.3. Map of the central 16 square kilometers of Tikal. From Carr and Hazard (1961). Reprinted with permission of the University of Pennsylvania Museum, Philadelphia.

Figure 9.4. Variants of emblem glyphs from (a) Copán and (b) Tikal.

that this shared ideology provided the framework for long-term, stable, "peer-polity" interactions during the Classic period (Freidel 1986). Elites intermarried, visited one another on ceremonial occasions, and exchanged status objects. They also warred with one another and formed military and political alliances. Independent centers, along with their immediate hinterlands and dependent populations, were the most basic components of the political landscape. The network of classical Greek or Sumerian city-states could be described in the much the same manner.

Much more controversial are issues involving the structure and scale of the largest Classic Maya polities. Most Mayanists fall into the "little-polity" school, but the "big-polity" position is vigorously defended (Culbert 1991b; Culbert et. al 1990; Marcus 1992a, 1992c; Martin and Grube 1996). The debate is fueled by the conviction that Tikal, with its long occupational history, hoary traditions of kingship, and early innovations in art, architecture, and writing, must have been, at least for long periods, politically preeminent.

The most important debates, however, concern the implications of emblem glyphs (Fig. 9.4). Emblem glyphs were first identified in the late 1950s; approximately forty are now known (Mathews 1991; Marcus 1992c). Although their exact meanings are not clear, we know they are not straightforward toponyms. Stuart has noted that they always occur as parts of titles that are also associated with personal names (1993: 325–326). When one center mentions the emblem glyph of another, the referent is not a place per se, but a "holy lord," presumably associated with a political unit identified by the main sign of the emblem glyph. They almost certainly were used at times to refer to whole polities rather than specific places, and Houston and Stuart believe they have identified other glyphs that name specific centers within such polities (Stuart 1993:328). Not all centers—even large ones—are associated with emblem glyphs. One center (Yaxchilán) has two glyphs, and other glyphs were used by more than one center. Inscriptions at many centers include glyphs associated with other places, thereby creating a complex network of political references that varies in time and space (Culbert 1991a:140–144).

Emblem glyphs appeared at a few sites before A.D. 435, but they proliferated after A.D. 650. Along with associated inscriptions and depictions, they have been used by Mayanists to infer political connections and hierarchical relationships between centers (Marcus 1976). In some cases, patterning of emblem glyphs and associated evidence for warfare are seen as evidence for regional political expansion and consolidation. An example is the expansive but short-lived Dos Pilas polity that emerged in the Pasion region of the western Maya Lowlands between A.D. 678 and 760 (Mathews and Willey 1991). However, many inscriptions record inconclusive wars with no such consequences, or interactions between independent (though perhaps allied) polities, such as the exchange of royal women as spouses.

Big-polity devotees believe that distributions of emblem glyphs and evidence such as variable forms of accession glyphs indicate the existence of large Classic states formed by conquest or other incorporative processes that extended over thousands of square kilometers. Culbert (1988, 1991a) and his colleagues, for example, have argued for the existence of a Tikal-centered regional state with a sustaining population of over 435,000, and smaller, but still impressive polities are held by some (e.g., Marcus 1992a; Martin and Grube 1996) to be centered on Palenque, Calakmul, Copán, Yaxchilán, Seibal, and other capitals at various times.

The small-polity perspective, which is more widely held, envisions sixty or seventy coexisting, independent polities at the end of the eighth century, each having territories of about 2,500 square kilometers (Mathews 1991). This perspective, which I share, does not deny occasional expansion by situationally vigorous centers, but it sees larger polities as very ephemeral, either in the sense that they do not last long or that the political relationships between centers are not highly centralized or hierarchical in power terms.

The sociopolitical implications of the two models are quite different. The big-polity model implies military and political institutions that allowed not only expansion but also the effective consolidation and administration of subordinated polities. It implies a much more complex settlement hierarchy, with one or more levels of formerly independent elite centers ruled by a dominant, autonomous central place or capital. Such rule would have presumably been based upon the retention of complaisant, formerly independent lords in positions of power or new subordinate governors who received their offices through delegation. Large, stable polities—if they existed—were clearly more state-like than small ones. Whether or not regional Classic polities existed, the general picture is consistent with our city-state definition. What seems certain, however, is that the most stable unit of organization was the individual center, dominated by a local lord and supported by an associated territory small enough to be crossed in a few days.

Stratification

The big-polity model implies considerable stratification, especially if conquest warfare was the mechanism that created large, regional states. Elites of dominant regional capitals subordinated lesser, formerly autonomous ruling lineages and their populations and extracted larger quantities of labor and tribute than were available in their own immediate hinterlands.

The implications for stratification are more problematic for the little-polity model. Marcus believes that all complex Mesoamerican societies had two classes—nobles and commoners (although each had internal gradations of status; Marcus 1992c). We have already seen that the ethnohistoric Maya can be broadly characterized this way. Even with the little-polity perspective, it is reasonable to assume that Classic Maya polities—especially mature ones of the seventh and eighth centuries—were at least as stratified as their sixteenth-century counterparts. Seen in the overall context of Mesoamerican political systems, however, patterns of Classic Maya stratification were quite weak, and they probably varied from polity to polity. We have no evidence for anything like the Aztec pattern, where a hereditary noble class enjoyed the fruits of an enormous tribute empire and owned personal estates farmed by serfs. Nor do the Maya seem to have had—aside from religion and ritual—mature state institutions that effectively upheld an order of stratification.

An alternative possibility is that some Classic Maya polities retained strong elements of ranked kinship organization—that is, they exhibited features of rank societies (Fried 1967). Ranking would be consistent with the comparatively small scale of many local Maya polities and their probable ethnic homogeneity (see below). Remember too that kinship cut across social boundaries to some degree among the ethnohistoric Maya. Retention of such kin organization, even as some forms of stratification developed, is characteristic of many societies that cannot be neatly labeled "chiefdoms" or "states."

I suspect that many large Classic Maya polities consisted of a mass of commoners truncated from a much smaller, dominant segment of lords and their families that itself retained complex patterns of kinship ranking. Ethnohistorically known Polynesian island societies conform to this pattern (Earle 1978; Hommon 1986; Kirch 1984), an economic correlate of which was well-developed economic stratification. In such systems, a set of variable terms (*arik'i, ari'i ali'i*) indicated high, inherited status—that is, a person of consequence—as opposed to the vast majority of the population, which lacked distinguished pedigrees and were not players in the political game. Quite possibly the Maya title *ahaw* (which has the general meaning of lord), inscribed on many Classic elite objects, conveyed much the same sense of rank, privilege, and social discontinuity with commoners.

Ethnicity and diversity

Many Old World city-states were quite cosmopolitan in ethnic and occupational terms. In some Sumerian cities, for example, speakers of at least two unrelated languages—Sumerian and Akkadian—would have lived side by side. Visitors or merchants from outside Sumer, slaves captured during military campaigns, and nonurban pastoralists or fisherfolk bringing their products to the city added diversity as well.

In contrast, Classic Maya polities were probably quite homogeneous. The twenty-eight existing Maya languages form a generally contiguous block with a rough linguistic divide in the middle of the Yucatan Peninsula. To the north are the languages of the Yucatecan family, while Cholan languages were probably spoken in the southern Lowlands during Classic times. At centers near this divide there may have been some intrapolity mingling of speakers of one or more of these language families, but they were closely related in any case. Although foreign visitors, such as diplomats or traders, would situationally have been present, most inhabitants of Maya polities probably were not often confronted by people ethnically unlike themselves or anyone of distant origins or with different ways of making a living. Centers on the frontiers of the Maya Lowlands might have been ethnically more complex, however, and there were Postclassic intrusions of non-Maya peoples that considerably altered the older Classic situation.

Tikal and Copán

It is useful to make a detailed comparison between two Classic polities that have already appeared in our discussion—those centered on Tikal and Copán. Both are extremely well known archaeologically, and both exhibit the range of variation that characterized the political landscape of the Maya Lowlands.

Tikal

Located in the tropical forests of northeastern Guatemala, Tikal is the largest Classic Maya center, with a regal-ritual core covering (at a generous estimate) about 4 square kilometers (Figure 9.3). The configuration of this core—several major complexes of buildings connected by causeways—is, in part, a product of the local landscape, with its limestone hills and depressions. The plan of the site, mature by A.D. 800, reflects roughly 1,200 years of ambitious, albeit intermittent, building projects (Jones 1991). During the eighth century, the political heart of Tikal was the imposing Great Plaza, filled with royal altars and stelae and bounded on the east and west by Temples I and II; the former is a mortuary monument to the Late Classic ruler Ah Cacua (Ruler A). To the north is the North Acropolis, an ancient complex of superimposed temples and platforms containing the tombs of earlier kings. To the south is the Central Acropolis, the royal palace since at least the fourth century. It includes residential quarters for rulers and their families as well as ritual buildings and storerooms (Harrison 1986). Three great causeways converge on the Great Plaza, linking it to the other major architectural complexes that form the site core.

Very close to the core lie the impressive residential complexes that housed some of Tikal's highest elite, along with their servants and retainers (Haviland 1992). Such groups had specialized ritual structures and rich burials in elaborate tombs. Apparently some complexes also had workshops where marine shell and obsidian were processed into finished ornaments or tools.

Unlike that of other most Maya centers, Tikal's core territory is clearly bounded by natural and cultural features that facilitate demographic reconstructions (Culbert et al. 1990; Rice and Rice 1990). On east and west are extensive *bajos,* or swampy depressions. Artificial earthworks, almost surely fortifications, link these *bajos* on the north and south respectively at 4.5 and 7 kilometers from the Great Plaza. Together these boundaries enclose an area of about 120 square kilometers, with an estimated 13,440 structures (Harrison 1986:47). Settlement density declines with distance from the regal-ritual core. In the central 9 square kilometers (Tikal's epicenter), overall density is at least 235 structures per square kilometer. A 7-square-kilometer area around the epicenter has an estimated structure density of 181 per square kilometer, which drops to 112 per square kilometer in the remainder of the zone within the boundaries. Outside the *bajos* and earthworks, densities drop still further to around 39 structures per square kilometer.

Reconstructing population densities is more difficult than counting structures. Rice and Puleston estimate the density for epicentral Tikal in the eighth century at 600–700 people per square kilometer (1981: 144). More recently, Culbert and his colleagues have suggested a figure of 922 people per square kilometer for this zone (1990:116). The peripheral 7 square kilometers, they argue, had a density of 711 people per square kilometer, which fell to 440 for the remainder of the bounded region. Beyond the *bajos* and earthworks, there were only about 153 people per square kilometer.

Regardless of whether one accepts these estimates as precise in absolute terms, they are informative in two ways. First, they indicate the relative densities of the site as a whole, graded from core to periphery. These crude densities are also, in order-of-magnitude terms, distinctly lower than urban densities for other preindustrial cities (compare, for example, the maximum epicentral Tikal estimate [922] with the 10,000–12,500 per square kilometer estimate for Sumerian Uruk).

Haviland reconstructs the total Late Classic population within the boundaries at 50,000 people (1992: 937), while Culbert and his colleagues think a figure of 62,000 is more appropriate (1990:116). They further calculate that about 120,000 people lived within a 12-kilometer radius of the Great Plaza. This core region of 452 square kilometers did not include any other major centers and had an overall density of 265 people per square kilometer. If these estimates are reasonably accurate, Tikal was a very large polity in demographic terms, even if its territory were restricted to the core region.

I doubt that overall densities of 265 people per square kilometer were achieved or sustainable over regions of this size. A useful area for comparison is the Late Postclassic Basin of Mexico, which, at the beginning of the sixteenth century, was one of the most densely settled regions ever to have existed in Mesoamerica. Maximum population is estimated at about 1,200,000 in a region of approximately 7,000 square kilometers (Sanders et al. 1979), with overall densities on the order of 170–300 people per square kilometer, depending on what proportion of production derived from the lake system that occupied much of the valley floor. Even the powerful Aztec tribute system was unable to import more than a tiny subsidy of bulk food energy from outside the Basin (enough to support about 25,000 people). Most of the Basin's food energy derived from internal production, which included widespread use of intensive techniques (drained fields, irrigation, terracing) and specialized crops (e.g., maguey).

I know of no models supported by archaeological data that would explain population densities in the Tikal core region comparable to or greater than those of the Postclassic Aztecs and so much in excess of Postclassic Maya estimates. If these densities did obtain, the only explanation is consistent with the big-polity perspective: very heavy subsidies of food energy must have been extracted by Tikal from more distant territories under its political control. But this explanation raises other questions: Were populations in these peripheries so low that sizable portions of the landscape could be devoted to production for Tikal? If so, who provided the labor to produce the surpluses? Finally, how did transport costs affect the feasibility of importing large subsidies of food energy from distant peripheries?

Even if we halve the highest estimate for Tikal's core to 60,000 people, we still wind up with a local polity with about the same number of inhabitants as sixteenth-century Mani, which, at about 10,000 square kilometers, was some twenty-two times larger. Overall densities for Postclassic Mani are calculated at 6–12 people per square kilometer, or about 2–4 percent of those postulated for Tikal. Clearly, the local Tikal polity was demographically larger, and probably much more organizationally complex, than any sixteenth-century Maya polity, but it was not necessarily as large and powerful as current estimates suggest.

We have seen that Culbert, among others, champions a regional state centered on Tikal much larger than the 452-square-kilometer core zone. Sharing this opinion, Marcus envisions an early Tikal state that unified an area of about 30,000 square kilometers, including other major centers like Yaxchilán, Dos Pilas, Naranjo, Uaxactún, Río Azul, and Caracol between A.D. 534 and 889 (1992a:406–407). She believes that this huge territory "was administered both through direct rule (placing male relatives of the ruler at provincial capitals) and indirect rule (sending female relatives of the ruler to marry the local lords of provincial capitals)" (Marcus 1992a:406). Tikal reached its greatest territorial extent early, Marcus believes, then was reduced to about 10,000 square kilometers by A.D. 700 as constituent polities, such as Caracol and Dos Pilas, asserted their independence through warfare.

The problem with such reconstructions (apart from their historical accuracy) is that we do not know what the interactions signaled by emblem glyphs and other inscriptions imply about political power (Hammond 1991a). Terms such as *administrative hierarchies, secondary* or *tertiary* centers, or *dependencies* are bandied about as though we understand details of political relationships, when in fact we do not. What we perceive are webs of political interactions between local polities of differing sizes and histories. Some rulers or some centers had more prestige than others, but the crucial question is how (or if) this translated into centralization of power by major capitals and loss of autonomy by lesser centers. For example, who paid tribute to whom? Could Tikal summon up labor from political dependencies? Could even strong Tikal kings meddle with impunity in the successions of "dependent" rulers? So far we have no good answers to such questions.

There seems little doubt that stable, hierarchical relationships existed between closely juxtaposed centers of markedly different size, such as Tikal and Uaxactún, and that ambitious rulers may have tried to create larger polities as well. But until better evidence is available, I remain skeptical of claims that Tikal, or any other center, dominated huge, stable, regional states. If such larger systems existed, they were probably short-term, ramshackle affairs with little effective institutional integration or political subordination, the claims of their paramount lords to the contrary.

Tikal has the longest dynastic record of any Classic center. Clearly its royal line was more prestigious than any other, many of which were cadet branches, and this is undoubtedly one reason why Tikal appears to have been so politically influential. Because of breaks in the record of inscriptions and building programs (which probably signal internal political problems), there is no complete list of Tikal kings, although roughly thirty-nine must have existed (Sharer 1994: 155), and the record ends with two poorly documented reigns at the end of the ninth century. The earliest ruler whose name has come down to us on a Tikal monument is Scroll Ahau Jaguar, who ruled about A.D. 290–300. He was not the first king, however, so the origins of the dynasty lie still farther back in time. Mathews places its inception at about A.D. 238 (1985), while Jones pushes it back to A.D. 170 (1991).

Tikal had not only the first monumental inscriptions but also one of the earliest-known emblem glyphs identifying it as a polity. Nearby smaller centers mention Tikal before A.D. 435 (the beginning of the ninth cycle of the Classic Maya Long Count calendar), reflecting some sort of political relationship and possibly subordination. Before A.D. 435, several other impressive centers within 100 kilometers of Tikal also adopted emblem glyphs (Culbert 1991b:130–131). Apparently Tikal and its dynasty were central to the spread of carved, inscribed monuments and emblem glyphs.

The processes by which Tikal's influence spread and the nature of its early political relationships with other large centers remain unclear, but certainly royal marriages were involved, as noted by Marcus. Some epigraphers believe that Tikal began its military and political expansion as early as the fourth century with the conquest of nearby Uaxactún (Schele 1991), although others express doubt about this incident (Stuart 1993). Wider Mesoamerican interaction took place as well. Recent excavations, for example, have revealed that some large Early Classic structures incorporated elements of Central Mexican Teotihuacán style (Laporte and Fialko 1990).

There were conspicuous ebbs and flows in Tikal's political fortunes as populations and autonomous centers multiplied elsewhere in the Lowlands. By the eighth century, Tikal was no longer preeminent, culturally or otherwise, but it still controlled a considerable population. Vigorous rulers sponsored massive building programs in the early to mid eighth century. These included construction of some of the largest temples and the causeways connecting them (Jones 1991; Morley and Brainerd 1983:188–119). Construction slackened off as rulership weakened, and the last inscribed monument has a date of A.D. 869.

Copán

Copán, where I have worked extensively since 1980, contrasts sharply with Tikal in many ways, most notably in its physical setting. At an elevation of 600 meters in the mountains of western Honduras, it is one of the highest Classic Maya centers, although its climatic regime is similar to that of the Lowlands. Copán is also one of the comparatively few large centers located in a river valley. A bird's-eye view of this general region of Honduras would show a narrow valley about 30 kilometers long, widening out here and there to form five expanses of alluvial bottom land, locally called *bolsas*, or pockets (Fig. 9.5). The largest of these, the Copán pocket, is about 24 square kilometers in area, but it has only about 700–1,000 hectares of cultivable bottomland. These five pockets, along with smaller ones in several tributary streams, are little islands of agricultural land in a vast upland sea of rugged, pine-covered mountains. Steeper slopes are agriculturally unattractive, and most of the modern population, like that of ancient Copán, lives on and farms the active alluvial soils and terraces of the valley floors or the low foothills adjacent to them (Wingard 1992).

While Tikal was situated in an extensive agricultural environment that came to be socially and politically circumscribed as populations grew and centers multiplied, the Copán polity was environmentally circumscribed from the beginning. Tikal is in the heartland of Classic Maya culture, but Copán is on its southeastern frontier. It has no near neighbors of comparable scale. The closest large Maya center is Quiriguá, 50 kilometers to the north in a direct line, but much farther by foot over rugged terrain. The main effect of this circumscription was to insulate Copán from the political competition and factionalism characteristic of the northeastern Petén. Another consequence was unusually close ties between Copán and the highland regions of Guatemala and El Salvador and with central Honduras. These are manifested most obviously in Copán's distinctive ceramic sequence (Viel 1983), which is quite different from contemporary sequences in the Maya heartland.

Although farmers occupied the Copán Valley by as early as 2300 B.C. as shown by recent palynological analysis (Webster et al. 1996), the population remained very small until about A.D. 400, at which time there were probably a few thousand people in the valley (Webster et al. 1992). Because Copán is located

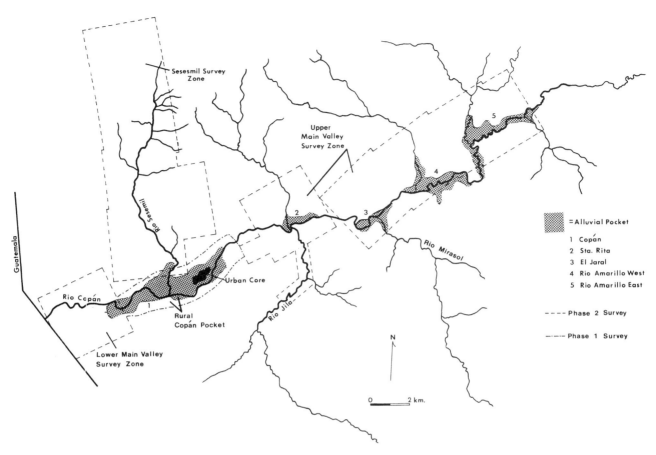

Figure 9.5. Map of Copán Valley showing alluvial pockets, survey zones, and location of the urban core.

on a linguistic frontier, opinion is divided about whether the original inhabitants were Maya speakers. If they were not, Copán would have been one of the most ethnically diverse Classic Maya polities. In any case, there is little that is characteristically Maya in the material culture of the region until shortly after A.D. 400, when the markers of the Maya Great Tradition make a rather abrupt appearance—presumably brought into the valley by intrusive elites from the northeast. Several later monuments record dates much earlier than A.D. 400; the earliest near-contemporaneous date (A.D. 376) appears on a carved bone from a tomb (Stuart 1992:171). From very early on, Copán had its own distinctive emblem glyph.

Because Copán's dynastic history was shorter than that of Tikal, copiously recorded on many monuments, and possibly more tranquil, it is possible to trace an unbroken line of rulers from the founder, K'inich Yax K'uk Mo' (who was in power by A.D. 435, according to the somewhat later Stela 63) to the sixteenth ruler, Yax Pac, who reigned from A.D. 763

to 820 or shortly thereafter. Yax Pac was the last (sixteenth) effective ruler, although in the first quarter of the ninth century, several shadowy claimants seem to have tried without success to perpetuate the royal line (Fash 1991; Stuart 1992, 1993). The last dated monument—significantly, unfinished—dates to A.D. 822.

The seat of the Copán kings was the Main Group, situated on an old terrace of the valley floor (Fig. 9.6). Recent excavations indicate that the first monumental constructions began in the fifth century (Sharer et al. 1992), although events during the reigns of the last five kings are best understood. Of particular importance were the twelfth king, Smoke Imix God K (A.D. 628–695), and his successor 18 Rabbit (A.D. 695–738). Smoke Imix's impressive valley stelae, marking the boundaries of the core Copán pocket, apparently reflect considerable political consolidation and centralization. He also carried out ceremonies at Quiriguá, then a comparatively unimpressive Maya center possibly linked to Copán in some dynastic fashion. 18 Rabbit raised more stelae and altars than any other

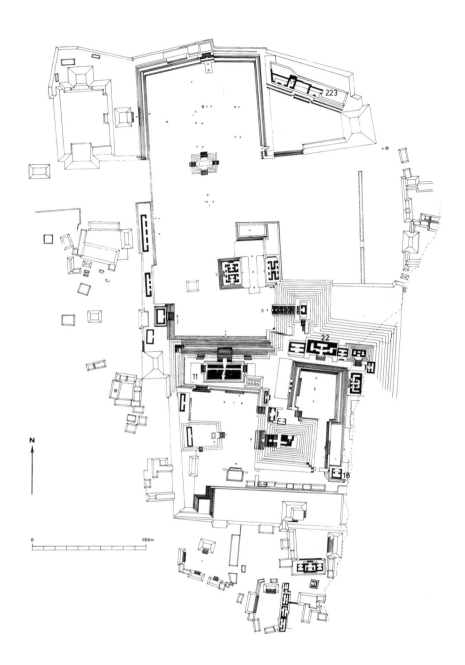

Figure 9.6. Plan of the Copán Main Group. The Acropolis is the elevated mass of structures in the southern half of the site. Redrawn by James Sheehy from an original provided by Hasso Hohman and Annegrete Vogerin (1982).

Copán king and was responsible for many of the most impressive plazas and buildings, including the first stage of the Hieroglyphic Stairway on Temple 26.

In its final form, the Main Group is more compact than the Tikal core. It consists of a series of structures surrounding large plazas on the north and a raised complex of courtyards, temples, palaces, and tombs, collectively called the Acropolis, on the south. Compared to Tikal, Copán's ritual-regal core is tiny, covering—at a generous estimate—about 22 hectares (an unknown amount has been washed away by the Copán River). Residential space in the Main Group is very limited, and the permanent population could not

have been more than several hundred people. I include in this estimate the residents of the impressive elite compound 10L-2 attached to the southern periphery of the Acropolis (Andrews and Fash 1992). Basic domestic facilities of the royal household during the last several reigns were probably concentrated there, with the Main Group itself representing the expanded regal-ritual facilities of the ruler.

Because of many years of settlement research at Copán (Baudez 1983; Freter 1988, 1992; Webster and Gonlin 1988; Webster et al. 1992), we know a great deal about its population history (Fig. 9.7). At the beginning of the seventh century, the whole valley had

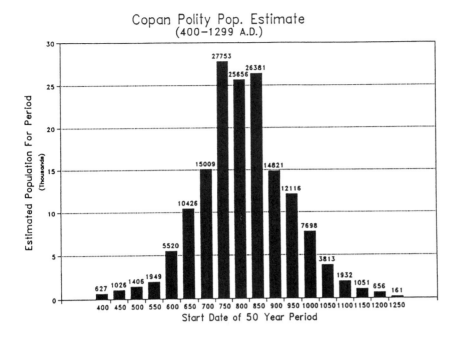

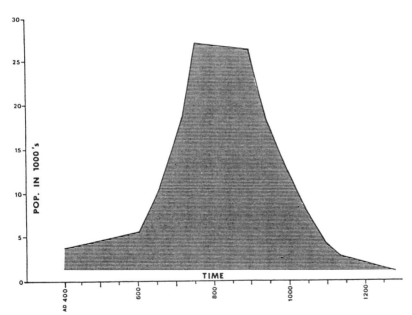

Figure 9.7. (a) Simulation of Copán population history from survey data and associated obsidian hydration dates; (b) smoothed population estimates, with pre-A.D. 600 levels inflated. From Webster et al. (1992:figures 3 and 6). Reprinted with permission of *Ancient Mesoamerica* 3:185–198, 1992.

an estimated 5,000–6,000 inhabitants. By A.D. 750, the population had increased to almost 28,000, an extremely rapid rate of growth that probably involved in-migration as well as internal increase. This peak population was maintained for 150–200 years. It then declined dramatically until, by A.D. 1200–1250, the valley was largely depopulated. Copán lost its royal lineage, its local elites, and ultimately its population over a period of 400 years (Webster and Freter 1990). During this time, the Copán alluvial pocket never contained less than 54 percent of the popula-

tion, and during most periods, it contained 70–80 percent of the population. This small zone was obviously the demographic and political heart of the polity.

Surrounding the Main Group and extending over an area of about 1 square kilometer is the Copán urban core, a dense concentration of impressive mound groups (Fig. 9.8). Structure density in the urban core is over 1,400 per square kilometer, and we estimate its maximum possible population at just under 12,000 during the Late Classic peak (A.D. 750–800). No

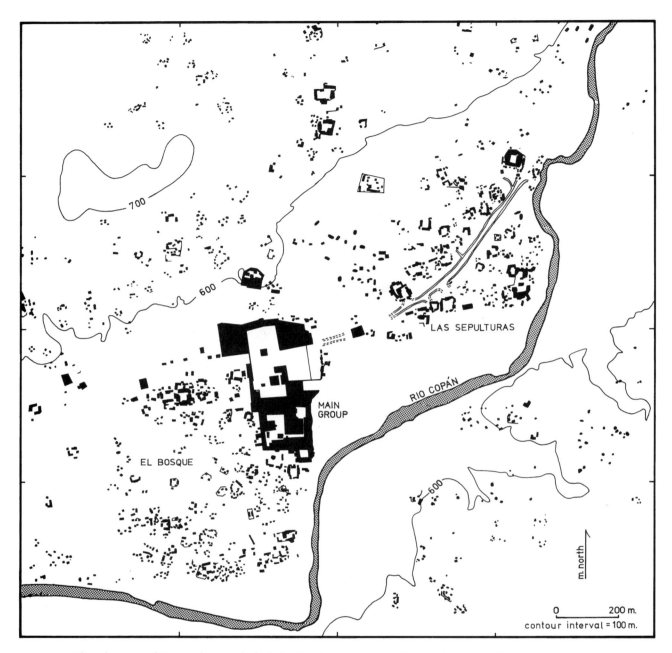

Figure 9.8. The urban core of Copán, showing the high density of structures in the Las Sepulturas and El Bosque residential enclaves.

other Classic Maya center had comparable concentrations of people and buildings. Although these densities fall into the comparative urban ranges discussed above, they are extremely localized. In contrast, Classic Teotihuacán in the Basin of Mexico had comparable densities over a much larger area and was distinctly more urban as a settlement and as a political capital.

There are twenty-eight impressive elite groups in the urban core. Some, such as those to the south and west, may have housed people closely related to the ruling lineage. Those to the northeast seem more independent of the Main Group, though linked to it by a causeway. Lords of both zones displayed impressive façade sculpture and carved monuments, such as thrones and altars, to a degree unusual for nonroyal Maya elites, especially after A.D. 750 (Webster 1989). Fash and other Copán researchers believe that such prerogatives signal weakness in the royal line vis-à-vis lesser lords during the last three reigns (1992). Interestingly, few major elite households were located more than a few kilometers from the Main Group, so the regional settlement pattern of the valley has no appreciable spatial hierarchical structure in administrative or economic terms.

Outside the urban core, the rural zone of the Copán pocket (an area of about 23 km²) had a maximum possible density of about 460 people per square kilometer, most of them farmers living in small farmsteads (Gonlin 1993). Food requirements for this dense population had to be supplemented from areas outside the pocket, where maximal densities were much lighter—around 100 per square kilometer (if all rural sites were indeed occupied all year round; see Webster et al. 1992:194–195; Webster and Kirker 1995). Such densities could not be long supported, and degradation of the agricultural landscape played an important role in the decline of the polity (Fash 1991; Webster and Freter 1990; Wingard 1992).

The issue of stratification at Copán is complicated. On the one hand, kings and lords, as the mature settlement system indicates, had impressive establishments by A.D. 700–800 and could obviously command considerable labor. On the other hand, the segmentary nature of Copán politics strongly suggests that lineage organization cut across status levels, creating more coherent political factions than it seems to have done in sixteenth-century Yucatan (Hendon 1991; Sanders 1989; Webster 1992). The core population was small and localized enough that kinship could have retained an important integrative role.

Stratification may have been stimulated by the nature of the agricultural landscape, which is highly variable in terms of both productivity and stability—much more so than at Tikal. From the earliest times, populations settled on the alluvial soils, and the bulk of the later elite establishments at Copán are situated there. Although lineage heads might have originally been stewards of collectively held lands, dramatic increases in population and colonization of more marginal land could have stimulated increasingly rigid land tenure and incipient economic stratification. In Copán today, local elites monopolize the best land on the valley floors, and this might well have been the situation by the end of the eighth century. An added factor is that some of the alluvial land is irrigable and suitable for commercial crops, offering further inducements to elite control (see Webster 1992:147–

150 for an extended discussion of this point). We have no direct evidence to substantiate these ideas, but in all probability, Copán society in the eighth century exhibited a complex and dynamic mix of kinship ranking and stratification.

When the Copán political system was at its peak (A.D. 750–800), we calculate that about 30 percent of the population resided in elite compounds (Webster et al. 1992). Many such residents were clearly of comparatively low status, however, and the actual titled, elite element of the polity was probably less than 10 percent (see Webster 1992 for a more complete discussion).

Haviland, although accepting the lineage model for Copán, argues that political institutions at Tikal were more stratified (1992). He is probably correct, but Tikal is the most atypical polity in the Maya Lowlands in terms of scale and dynastic history. The larger question is whether stratification, in the absence of effective lineage organization, dominated political traditions at the lesser Maya centers. Current evidence cannot answer this question, but I suspect Tikal was unique in this regard.

We are on firm ground in describing the mature Copán polity as a city-state, dominated by the kings of the Main Group, that incorporated several hundred square kilometers of mostly mountainous territory in western Honduras. Most of the population, however, was lineally concentrated on the more limited valley floors or adjacent foothills, an area only slightly larger than the bounded core of the Tikal polity. Seventy to 80 percent of those directly subordinate to the Copán kings lived within an hour's walk of the Main Group, most within sight of the royal compound. Virtually all of the rest resided within a day's walk.

But what of Copán's larger political relationships? The Copán emblem glyph, as well as the names of some of its rulers, are mentioned at other Maya centers (Grube 1990; Marcus 1992a, 1992c; Stuart 1992). Smoke Imix God K carried out rituals at Quiriguá, and the thirteenth ruler, 18 Rabbit, was captured and beheaded by the ruler of Quiriguá in A.D. 738. Yax Pac's mother was apparently a royal woman from the distant center of Palenque. Such ties clearly indicate Copán's participation in a wider sphere of elite Maya politics.

Marcus, primarily on the basis of her analysis of emblem glyphs and associated epigraphic and iconographic evidence, believes that Copán dominated a regional Classic state extending over an area of some

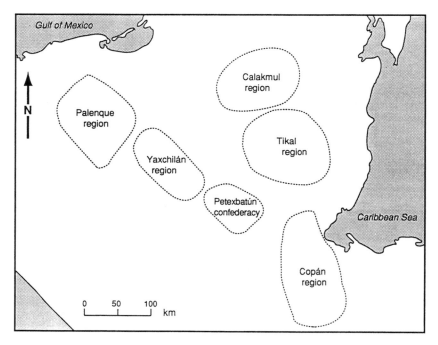

Figure 9.9. (a) Major Lowland Maya territorial states according to Marcus; (b) core region of the proposed Copán territorial polity. From Marcus (1992c): (a) from Figure 6.19, (b) from Figure 6.21. Reprinted with permission of Princeton University Press.

10,000 square kilometers (Fig. 9.9; Marcus 1992a, 1992c). Subsidiary centers included some close to Copán, but others were at linear distances of 50–60 kilometers. Unlike the landscapes of postulated large polities elsewhere in the Maya Lowlands, such a polity would have been fragmented by a rugged topography that had no navigable rivers. Only one of its

supposed dependencies, Quiriguá, was a major Classic Maya center in its own right, and eastern outliers (Los Higos) may not have had an ethnically Maya population. According to Marcus (1992a:407), the Copán state reached its maximum extent between A.D. 500–600, then diminished as its constituent units asserted their independence—Quiriguá did so in a spectacular manner by decapitating the hapless 18 Rabbit in A.D. 738.

I think that this reconstruction, with its implication of strong centralization of power by Copán, is incorrect for several reasons. First, recent iconographic studies question whether Copán ever meaningfully incorporated some of its ostensible dependencies (e.g., Los Higos; see Stuart 1992:174–175). Second, the Copán core polity had only about 6,000 people as late as A.D. 600, prior to the consolidations of Smoke Imix God K. It was probably both demographically and organizationally too feeble to project the political or military power necessary to disturb the autonomy of centers such as Quiriguá or Los Higos, especially over long distances on a fragmented landscape. Three of the purportedly "secondary" centers (El Jaral, Santa Rita, and Rio Amarillo) are all in the Copán drainage and were probably integral parts of Copán's core polity from their inception. It is likely that none was ever populous or distant enough to assert independence of the elite of the Copán pocket prior to the royal collapse.

Between A.D. 500 and 600, there were no unusually massive building programs at Copán to reflect regional political ascendancy. The most accelerated growth of the Main Group and the urban core occurred well after the proposed maximal extent of the regional state, and the labor investment necessary could easily have been provided by the local population (Webster et al. 1992:194–196). During its mature Late Classic phase, as we have seen, there is evidence of internal factionalism at Copán, and I believe the striking concentration of most of the hinterland population around the Main Group is symptomatic of political weakness rather than strength.

All this is not to deny the wider interactions of Copán's elites with those at Quiriguá and elsewhere, but the Copán city-state, in effective political terms, was almost certainly confined to the Honduran segments of the valley (although it might have extended somewhat into Guatemala). What the emblem glyphs and other inscriptions reveal is a complex web of political interactions, including competitive ones. What they do not reveal is the nature of these relationships. It seems premature to infer a regional state, in any meaningful sense of the term, or even—to use my much more cautious label—a regional polity. Although Copán and its rulers may have enjoyed heightened cultural and dynastic prestige on the southeastern frontier, nothing like an administrative or economic hierarchy, in my opinion, is clear from the inscriptions. The archaeological record strongly suggests that the little-polity model is most appropriate. An important lesson from the Copán research is that archaeological data often point to very different conclusions than inscriptional data.

Summary

From Preclassic times to the sixteenth century, the Lowland Maya political landscape was dominated by impressive centers, consistent with city-state organization, although they are better described as regal-ritual places instead of true cities. Stratification is more difficult to measure, but at least some forms of it must have been present by Classic times. From early on, Maya rulers and lords shared a common elite tradition, but polities also fought one another. Although some archaeologists believe that large regional states emerged by A.D. 400–500, smaller local polities were more stable and numerous, and there was never any overall political unification—again consistent with city-state organization.

Marcus, in a comparative study (J. Marcus 1989: 201), stresses the emergence of the city-state level of political organization out of the dissolution of larger regional polities. I believe it is clear in the Maya case that the individual city-state is usually the fundamental political unit from which such regional polities (such as they were) were assembled, and hence it is the most fundamental unit of archaeological analysis. During processes of dissolution, new forms of city-state organization may have appeared, as Marcus notes.

Settlement and demographic research indicates that a core Tikal state may have had as many as 120,000 inhabitants, but most other local city-states were smaller—for example, Copán with a population of 28,000. Comparisons between Tikal and Copán reveal considerable variation apart from scale, including differences in environment, dynastic history, settlement distribution, internal political organization, and stratification. Classic polities may thus have been as varied as their sixteenth-century counterparts.

The early phases of many ancient civilizations seem to be characterized by the emergence and interaction of numerous small polities that might reasonably be called city-states. Unfortunately, we usually lack the detailed information from either archaeology or inscriptions to reconstruct political structures and processes (e.g., for late Predynastic Egypt or Sumer before the Late Dynastic period). The uniquely accessible and detailed Maya archaeological record offers unparalleled comparative insights about such early complex systems. Provided that we bear in mind the distinctive features of Maya polities, we can usefully characterize them as city-states—similar to political systems elsewhere and essential to our broader understanding of this political form.

10

The Archaeological Signature of Complexity in the Maya Lowlands

K. ANNE PYBURN

The concept of the city-state is useful in exactly the same way that any typological category is useful: standardized descriptive terminology makes comparison possible. Even scholars who reject the concept on the basis of a specific data set that falls outside its boundaries have, in doing so, used the model to describe how their data are different. But the usefulness of typologies has a price, as numerous contributors to this volume have pointed out. By focusing on a set of categories derived from a description of one particular state (e.g., Greece or Rome), or even one particular type of state (e.g., an ancient European state), preconceived categories bias the perception and interpretation of new data. This is particularly acute with typologies based on lists of cultural traits and leads into such blind alleys of discussion as whether a culture without writing or defensive earthworks can qualify as a state, or how many people per square kilometer are required for true urbanism. Even worse, since a neoevolutionary perspective is part of the Western folk model of most archaeologists, the city-state becomes one end of a unilinear trajectory that extends from people "not like us" through developmental stages of people who are progressively "more like us" until finally civilization arises "just like ours." Alternatively, people who "were not like us" may have evolved to become "more like us" without ever developing states "just like ours" due to either environmental or ideological restrictions that prevented the rise of "mature institutions."

To avoid belaboring these issues, since they have already been elegantly treated by several authors in this volume, in this essay I take the position that any typology can be useful for comparative purposes, provided the author stipulates that no single typology (or comparison) is sufficient to characterize an entire civilization (Marcus 1983). A single cultural group (or group of people speaking related languages, such as the Maya) can be expected to employ strategies of political economy that varied over time and space. Ancient Maya groups may well have had both city-states and territorial states (*sensu* Trigger 1993) while functioning in some areas at some times more along the lines of complex chiefdoms (*sensu* Earle 1991). Examining particular data sets in the context of multiple typological frames can ameliorate the problem of typological preconceptions, by forcing us to recognize that some accuracies and biases exist in each.

Applying the city-state typology to the ancient Maya is an interesting reflexive exercise, since Western scholars traditionally argue that the Maya did not have either cities or states, unless we change the definition of city-states to include groups who were "not like us" (e.g., Webster, this volume). For Americanist scholars, the Maya have long functioned in our analyses as an exoticized other, dramatically "orientalized" (Said 1978) as mysterious and unique (Pyburn 1994, in press.) Although J. E. S. Thompson's characterization of the Maya as egalitarian, otherworldly number-worshippers is no longer accepted, a set of peculiar, almost magical qualities continues to imbue descriptions of the Maya. These include (1) the absence of an economically based political system during prehispanic times, despite long-distance trade, specialist production, intensive agriculture, chronic warfare, and a differential distribution of wealth shown in architecture (Sanders 1989), mortuary goods (Rathje 1970), and diet (Pohl 1994; White and Schwarcz 1989); (2) the ability to maintain a kinship and cosmological system over thousands of kilometers and through thousands of years despite conquest and domination; and (3) the lack of dense urban populations or organized neighborhoods.

This is actually a set of negatives: no economy beyond patrilineal kin relations, no change or variation over time or space, and no centralized populations, and negative evidence is always abundant to archaeologists. What is intriguing is that so few scholars have challenged these assumptions head-on. Most articles on Maya political organization begin with a summary of postconquest kin relations within a Maya speaking group, assert the primordial nature of patrilineal kin relations for the Maya, and proceed to exemplify a set of prior assumptions with data from a single site or from an amalgam of "representative" or "well-known" sites.

In this paper I take the position that despite the wealth of data now available on the ancient Maya, their political economy is still so poorly known that it is impossible to determine whether any particular site is representative. Furthermore, the possibility of complex intersite relations of both an economic and a political nature has begun to be suggested by some authors for some ancient Maya cities. If this is correct, then variation between sites ought to be the focus of our analysis, rather than the construction of an ideal type of Maya community. Variation between communities has been treated as the result of microenvironmental pressures and accidents of local history, which avoids the imponderable factor of human agency. But it is impossible to understand other cultures if we ignore the complexities of social process.

It is ethnocentric to interpret the accomplishments of other people (past or present) as constrained by nature and accident, but to explain our own as the result of cultural complexity and advance.

Neoevolutionary Baggage

Most reconstructions of ancient Maya civilization begin with the assumption that individual communities were economically self-sufficient and organizationally redundant. Data on local hydrology (McAnany 1990; Siemens 1982), soil types (Dunning 1991; Fedick 1989; Ford 1991a, 1991b), climate, sea-level changes (McKillop 1989; Pohl 1991), and crops are used to identify constraints on Maya community development. Technological practices are examined with pollen records, lake sediments, water-control features, and tools from the particular site under study to evaluate the sophistication and measure the sustainability of Maya cultural adaptation.

The emphasis on Maya communities, villages, towns or polities as independent and redundant political and economic entities often results in models of cultural evolution analogous to models of biological speciation. Biological evolution explains the origin of species as an adaptive response to local and physical environmental pressure. Unfortunately, complex societies cannot be understood solely as biological adaptations because they respond to both nonlocal resources and ideological stimuli as well as to their immediate physical environment. Most models of early state formation do acknowledge the impact of ideology or contact between groups (e.g., hostilities: Carneiro 1990; Haas 1982; Webster 1976; or commercial ventures: Flannery 1968; Rathje 1971, 1977; Sanders and Santley 1983). However, these models treat these factors as types of selective pressure affecting the exploitation of the local environment.

Culture separates sex from procreation, kinship from genetics, food from hunger, and violent aggression from survival instinct (Bourdieu 1984). So culture adapts to itself. Resource distribution may account for some long-term success of human adaptations, but the rise and fall of city-states are usually measured in centuries, rarely millennia. An evolutionary perspective focuses closely on the adaptation of an entity to its immediate environment, but the success or failure of a city-state is also related to its economic and historical relationships with other communities.

In this paper I argue that local subsistence patterns

and population densities are a product of intersite political economy as much as local resource availability. It is true that some types of social interaction are difficult to identify archaeologically, but even when we can account for trade in perishables, establish contemporaneity, and develop samples large enough to be representative, the quantity of nonlocal goods is not necessarily indicative of their political or economic impact (Schortman and Urban 1992). We lack a body of theory to help us understand what determines the goods and ideas that transfer between cultures and how the meanings of these goods and ideas change with transmission (Flannery 1968; Miller 1991; Mukerji 1983). Similarly, although warfare has loomed large in recent analyses (Chase 1988; Demarest 1978; Freidel 1986; Hassig 1992), we do not know if hostilities served as stimuli or impedimenta to cultural development.

The first step in considering the possibility that the Maya had economically as well as politically interdependent cities is to suspend traditional assumptions about the significance of continuities or contrasts in material culture. Homogeneity and variation in archaeological data do not necessarily correspond to mechanical and organic solidarity in ancient social systems. Homogeneity in the forms or distribution of material culture may indicate redundancy or be a cosmopolitan face put on cultural diversity, while heterogeneity may reflect a lack of integration or a multilevel division of labor in a highly integrated political economy.

In this context, it is worthwhile to recount recent arguments about whether the ancient Maya were a "two-class" society or a society with a "true middle class" (Chase and Chase 1992; Marcus 1992c). Marcus argues, on ethnohistoric grounds, that the Maya had a two-class political economy, with endogamous elites and endogamous peasants. This sounds unlikely, since elites do not go on long trips to get the obsidian they redistribute, even in "chiefdoms"; neither do they till their own fields nor train their own slaves nor clean their own houses nor make their own polychromes. Of course elites may not intermarry with service personnel, but those who perform special functions for them and thereby have access to luxuries, privileged information, and royal favors would necessarily be a bit elevated and likely to "put on airs." In fairly short order, such a group would be likely to also become endogamous in practice, if not by law.

Marcus has been criticized (and praised) by several authors who conflate the term *class* with the term *status*. These two concepts are not the same; I can think of no instance in which an ethnographer claimed the group under observation had only two economic or political statuses. Of course this is not at all what Marcus means; she has simply defined classes as endogamous social entities and allowed complex social stratification to occur within classes. The point she wishes to stress with her analysis is that heterogeneous groups may have homogeneous status in relation to some social norms, such as marriageability, but be highly stratified and differentiated in other ways, such as economic access or political opportunity. Even Marx believed that the dichotomy between the landed and the landless was smeared by the fact that not all land is equally good and not all masters are equally rotten.

Marcus's analysis points to the heart of one of the most egregious false dichotomies to nag Mayanists: the idea of the organizational gap between kin-based ranking systems and "truly" stratified societies. This is a holdover from Fried's (1967) and Service's (1962) "evolving cultural organism progressively modifying its adaptive strategy" model. Kinship is not a biological straitjacket that predetermines all social acts. It is a vocabulary that people use to talk about and negotiate social relations, whether a society is characterized as simple or complex. Not everyone can have the power of a Henry VIII to change the rules of kinship and marriage for their own purposes, but even among the lower classes of excessively rigid societies, the application of rules to particular situations shows them to be open to some interpretation. One need only look at Srinivas's description of the creative ways that Untouchables subvert the Hindu caste system to allow for the marriage and movement between castes that routinely occurs (1962). As he points out, it is not the rigidity, but the flexibility of the Hindu system that has allowed it to persist for millennia.

On the other hand, even the most capitalist society perpetually encounters complications caused by family ties. Hardly a day passes that some public figure from a developed nation is not skewered in the press for nepotism. The popularity of this social strategy within our own complex society is evidenced by the stiff penalties occasionally exacted on perpetrators. How can we forget the recent slogan, "Nobody elected Hilary Clinton"?

If people in all kinds of societies can be expected to do political and economic favors for relatives and if people routinely manipulate, subvert, or uphold kinship rules depending on the situation, then the dichotomy between kin-based and non–kin-based societies is either nonexistent or may be too subtle to be recoverable even with ethnohistoric data, much less by digging up temples and deciphering king lists. Maya scribes who expected to be paid obviously recorded that the ruler was following the highest moral interpretation of kinship rules, and informants of the Spanish would have explained "family values" in terms most likely to make sense to the Spanish and to justify local patterns. This does not mean that the scribes or the ethnohistoric informants were lying but that they were interpreting.

Trying to pigeonhole data on kinship into a pre-existing model of rigid norms assumes answers to the questions we most need to ask: Why is kinship used in this way in this instance? What can choices made in kin relations tell us about the political economy of the culture? How do these choices change over time? The evolutionary organismal model shows us culture from the outside, but we cannot assume that external events represent obvious motives.

One final point is relevant to the discussion of Maya centers in the context of a city-state model. When the ideas of Julian Steward held sway among archaeologists, environmental variation was thought to determine the appearance of civilization in a particular area. Areas requiring irrigation and having threatening neighbors were considered the most likely spots, whereas rain forests and tropical lowlands were not thought capable of supporting intensive agriculture, dense populations, or complex social organizations. Thus the Maya had "vacant ceremonial centers" and "immature" institutions.

The weight of data on population density has now forced modification of this model (Culbert and Rice 1990), but a few scholars continue to see Maya civilization as only marginally urban and marginally stratified. In fact, investigations have shown a wide variation in the organizational styles of independent complex societies, with densely stratified populations missing from many "cradles" from time to time. Furthermore, there is a growing body of evidence to suggest that the way we have traditionally calculated Maya population density is wrong. The usual procedure has been to count visible mounds, multiply them by some standard family size, and then divide the result by the estimated number of chronological periods represented (Rice and Culbert 1990). The technique has a flattening effect on the variations in configuration and density of individual communities over time.

Though we may question how tropical settings affect the rise of social complexity, the effect of a tropical biomass on preservation and archaeological visibility is profound. There is, for example, no reason to expect that wattle-and-daub structures would be as visible to archaeologists 1,000 years after abandonment as are large structures with stone foundations built on elevated platforms. Nor is there any reason to believe that such structures are impractical in the Maya Lowlands, since they are in use today (see Fig. 10.1). It is strange, in fact, that those who argue most forcefully for cultural continuity between past and present Maya take no account of the fact that the small perishable houses of many living Maya would leave almost no archaeological trace, especially without metal. Ethnoarchaeological studies have focussed on elevated houses.

Willey first noticed at Barton Ramie that he had potsherds from periods not represented by houses in his sample and that his architectural sample must therefore be incomplete (Willey et al. 1965). Direct evidence for ground-surface housing is now available from many sites, including Tikal (Bronson n.d.), Copán (Hendon 1987), Santa Rita (Chase 1990), Dzibilchaltún (Kurjack 1974), Cuello (Hammond 1991b; Wilk and Wilhite 1991), Pulltrouser (Harrison 1990), Cerros (Cliff 1982), Albion Island (Pyburn 1990b), and Nohmul (Pyburn 1988, 1989, 1990a). This probably means that the population densities of urban centers were greater than most estimates suggest, but there is a more important point to be made with these data. Studies outlining the distribution and character of ground-surface housing have shown that its distribution is not randomly associated with platform-based housing, that its distribution changes over time, and that economic differences may be signaled by the absence of a platform in an urban dwelling (Bronson n.d.; Hendon 1992; Pyburn 1989).

But further study of "invisible" architecture alone will not answer questions about state formation in the absence of comparative regional data. The key to understanding ancient Maya political economy and social organization will be found in the reconstruction of regional patterns of settlement and community development, rather than local patterns of kinship, population density, or ecological maps. Once data relevant to a regional scale of analysis are collected, guidelines for suitable ethnographic analogy can be developed. The current tendency among Mayanists to use Spanish ethnohistoric documents and modern Maya peasant strategies—to the exclusion of other possible analogues for explaining archaeological patterns from 1,000 years earlier—suggests a belief in

Figure 10.1. Nonmound Maya house, Belize, 1988. Photographed by the author.

race memory that cannot withstand intellectual scrutiny. To seek the causes of the collapse of ancient Maya civilization in the structure of modern Maya villages is to treat the Maya as a flawed race. The political implications of such an attitude are heinous (Arnold 1990; Pyburn 1992; Taylor 1992).

Although true regional analyses will not be available for many years, a close comparison of neighboring sites with contrasting histories would be extremely useful for testing propositions about political and economic relationships. Several recent studies develop the premise that elite behavior may provide a particularly good source of data on ancient Maya political economy (Chase and Chase 1992; Culbert 1991b). Elites, by definition, control the lion's share of goods and resources and benefit most from the display of symbols of power, and they have more impact on the archaeological record. Archaeological research has necessarily emphasized elite material culture, and elite behavior has come increasingly to be regarded as a kind of prime mover in cultural development; thus many researchers explain Maya cultural evolution on the basis of data collected exclusively from elite contexts. However, contradictory models of elite interaction coexist, partly because of the different perspectives of the investigators, but perhaps also because of variation in the strategies of elites over time and space. The site on which an investigator focuses and its state of preservation affect the resulting characterizations, which may be correct for the settlement in question, but may not be suitable for generalization or the construction of an ideal type.

A regional picture of elite representations would address the anomalies present in most settlement-pattern studies. Periods of low population visibility or increased building or agricultural intensification that appear autochthonous from a local perspective might fit into a regional structure. The archaeological record of Maya communities is so varied that many authors see a lack of regional interaction, but individual variation may indicate loose social integration or it may indicate very tight social control and orchestration. Uaxactún may be smaller than Tikal because it was a politically and economically independent community with a restricted resource base or it may be smaller because of the nature of its relationship to Tikal. Archaeologists are not in a strong enough position to be sure whether any Maya community was self-sufficient at any given time, since almost no regional syntheses have been done.

Maya Regional Environments and Settlement

The importance of regional data sets has been demonstrated for a variety of cultural contexts (Fish and Kowalewski 1990), especially when urban populations are involved (Kowalewski 1990; Parsons 1990). Although Maya population centers reached urban densities in some areas, we can only explain intraregional variation in terms of the limited types of regional data available: distribution of natural resources, such as soil types, microenvironmental zones, raw materials, or water sources (Dunning 1991; Fedick 1989; Ford 1986, 1991b; Graham 1987; Hester et al.1982; Rice and Rice 1990; Shafer and Hester 1983); or idiosyncratic historical events and ideological data derived from architecture, portable artifacts, monuments, and inscriptions (J. Marcus 1976, 1989; Schele and Freidel 1990; Schele and Miller 1986).

Much debate in Maya archaeology centers around methodological problems with the reconstruction of land-use patterns and uncertainty about theories that link subsistence strategies with specific modes of sociopolitical organization and economic interaction (Culbert and Rice 1990; Pohl 1990, 1991; Rice 1993, Sabloff 1990; Webster and Freter 1990). The quality and availability of natural resources are generally considered fundamental to both subsistence practices and cultural process. Ford has shown, for example, that "well-drained terrace alluvial valley zones and well-drained upland zones are the best agricultural areas and account for 87 percent of settlement in the Belize River area" (1991b:39). Nevertheless, shortfalls in environmental potential apparently led inhabitants of even these rural areas to seek economic interdependence through small-scale specialization.

Similarly, correlations have been noted between natural resources, such as raw materials or soil types (environmental zones), and settlement density in a variety of regions, including the Copán Valley (Webster and Freter 1990), the central Petén (Culbert and Rice 1990; D. Rice 1986; P. Rice 1986), coastal Yucatan (Andrews 1983; Andrews and Rovner 1973; Chase 1985; Jones 1982, 1983), central Belize (Fedick 1994; Ford 1990, 1991b; Willey et al. 1965), and the Pasion area (Willey 1973). These correlations have been used to suggest the limits of Maya sociopolitical integration. However, data from these areas also show some degree of intraregional interaction and such wide variation in settlement density and subsistence strategy between sites that prediction on the basis of local environmental variables is not possible (cf. Culbert and Rice 1990). New population centers continue to be discovered in "well known" areas (Pyburn 1991a).

Maya Elite Interaction

Elite material culture shows formal similarities throughout the Maya Lowlands (Willey et al. 1990). Most scholars assume that this denotes a uniform ideological power among Maya elites; in fact, Maya civilization has been seen as an ideological masterpiece, integrated by a pervasive religion that created a unified world view (Demarest 1992, Freidel 1983; Marcus 1976; Schele and Freidel 1990; Schele and Miller 1986). Other authors have put more emphasis on political prowess (Chase and Chase 1989; Demarest 1991; de Montmollin 1989) or economic factors

(Culbert 1988, Ford 1991a, 1991b, Hester et al. 1982, Rathje 1972, 1975, Rice and Rice 1984) in the formation of Maya civilization. In contrast to these approaches, Yoffee suggests that competition between Maya elites with different sources of power led to state formation, rather than successful domination through a particular strategy (1991).

Any complex society offers more than one source of power (Yoffee 1991), and elites compete for legitimacy and control by drawing on these different sources. Religious authorities may compete with politically powerful elites for control of economic resources and territory, as when the Renaissance papacy in Rome could successfully challenge the monarchy of any Catholic country in Europe. Conversely, an emerging middle class of traders may threaten an hereditary elite by developing new sources of economic power. "Thus it is in the nature of elites in ancient states, as much as in any environmental circumstances, that we find the important distinctions in the 'character' and socioeconomic stability of those polities" (Yoffee 1991:287). According to this model of early states, the style of elite interaction and competition indicates the nature and degree of social integration.

Data from Maya inscriptions support this idea. Schele and Mathews document several instances of anomalous inscriptions in which elite actors appear to be making a specific point, as when Pacal fails to mention his father on his ascension monument (Schele and Mathews 1991; Schele 1978), or when Yax Pac claims descent from a heroic king dead 333 years before Yax Pac's reign (Marcus 1995). These kinds of data undermine models of rigid religious formulae or total ideological unity. Our understanding of the politics of Maya rulership at major centers and how issues of power were related to interactions between sites has improved, as can be seen from the spate of recent publications (Chase and Chase 1989; Culbert 1991b; Demarest 1991; Fash 1988; Sanders 1989; Schele and Freidel 1990; Webster 1989). Nevertheless, it remains unclear how these machinations relate to the existence of lesser centers.

Settlement analysts have proposed several ways that hierarchical relationships between sites were codified in the relative locations and sizes of adjacent centers (Ball and Taschek 1991; N. Hammond 1972; Marcus 1976). Only a strong and rigid relationship involving ideological, economic, and political power at individual centers over long periods could result in such archaeologically detectable patterning. If the sources of elite power shifted over time and varied between sites, the coherence of settlements in a hierarchical pattern would be blurred and inconsistent in the archaeological record. However, although most scholars envision pan-Maya consistency in the sources of elite power, they differ about whether settlement hierarchies reflect an ancient system driven primarily by economics (Hester et al. 1982), politics (de Montmollin 1989), or ideology (Marcus 1983; Schele and Miller 1986).

The position that particular investigators take on this issue may be the result of valid assessments of individual sites or limited spans of time (Pyburn 1991b). Comparing the Maya with other early state societies (Adams and Jones 1981; Hammond 1991a; Yoffee 1991) shows that intercommunity/interelite strategies can be extremely versatile and volatile and are therefore difficult to characterize without tight chronological control. In ancient complex economies, one community often depended on the production of another (D'Altroy 1994; Kohl 1978; Wattenmaker 1994). In fact, surplus production and exchange are hallmarks of civilization in all parts of the world. Nevertheless, any Mayanist who fails to find evidence for intensive agriculture at a particular site feels justified in arguing for the lack of complexity on a pan-Lowland scale. For example, Puleston's proposition that the agricultural fields on Albion Island (and elsewhere, including Nohmul) were labor-intensive constructions designed for surplus production and the support of a specialized economic system (1977, 1978) has been challenged by Pohl (1990). She suggests that the lack of large-scale cooperative agricultural projects may have important implications for understanding Maya social complexity. But the question is not whether Maya organization involved intensive agricultural production strategies, but whether certain political and ideological configurations correlate in every instance with agricultural intensification or economic specialization. Whether a particular community can be shown to have a particular type of intensive agriculture at a particular point in time only has general ramifications for an extremely uniform system in which communities are economically independent but developmentally synchronized.

Data from Belize

Available evidence from adjacent Maya sites counters the idea of synchrony at the local level. In a recent comparison of elites at Lamanai and Altun Ha, communities 40 kilometers apart, Pendergast (1992) finds striking dissimilarity in both material culture and historical trajectory. Only one monumental structure at Altun Ha (B-4) is a "Lamanai style" construction, which Pendergast considers an architectural convention to "express in stone an ever-widening gulf between rulers and ruled" (1992:63). Elite residences are very different at the two sites. Lamanai has many huge structures, while those at Altun Ha have more elaborate decoration. Distribution of elite pottery, obsidian, and other exotic goods is much more uneven at Altun Ha than at Lamanai, perhaps as a result of Lamanai's more abundant agricultural land, an important factor in considering the rise and development of class relations at the two sites. Similarly, elite burials and offerings tend to be much more elaborate and sumptuous at Altun Ha than at Lamanai.

In the context of these differences, it is interesting to note that Altun Ha was depopulated in the ninth century, whereas Lamanai was occupied into the eighteenth century. Pendergast argues that the contrast in the relationship between elites and commoners at the two sites was shaped in part by the limitations and opportunities presented by local resource bases. This could account for the different fates of the two communities, which are close together but differ significantly.

Whether the proximity of Altun Ha and Lamanai denotes cooperative trade relations or a struggle between competitors is not yet known. Lamanai's participation in the central Petén cult suggests extra-regional influence, as well as a local emphasis on ideological and political integration. No evidence of fortification has been identified at either Lamanai or Altun Ha. Nevertheless, a jade plaque pendant from burial B-4/6 at Altun Ha refers to a conquest made in A.D. 569 by "the second chac pax of the west." The ruler who ascended to power in A.D. 584 was the son of a "Sky Lady," which suggests warfare and nonlocal interference from the "Sky" lineage, sometimes associated with Tikal (Molloy and Rathje 1974) or other cities of the central Petén (Schele and Miller 1986). Research at the intermediate site of Chau Hiix, 15 kilometers from Lamanai and 25 kilometers from Altun Ha, may ultimately clarify this relationship (Pyburn 1993).

Other research in northern Belize suggests profound variation between the economic strategy and political organizations of Nohmul and several nearby sites on Albion Island in the Hondo River. The population of Nohmul was spread over some 35 kilometers (Hammond 1985) along the east bank of the Hondo but was centered on a single large ceremonial and administrative complex throughout the life of the community. In contrast, the population of Albion Island, with an area of about 45 square kilometers, clustered around eight small centers. Both areas may have been involved in intensive agriculture (Hammond 1985; Siemens 1982), and both had easy access to each other and to other sites located along the Hondo River, which stretches from the coast to the central Petén. Though Nohmul, with its single large central precinct, may never have had more than 6,000 inhabitants (Pyburn 1989), by standard methods of estimation Albion Island's population was well over 50,000 (Culbert and Rice 1990; Pyburn 1996).

In both areas, there seems to have been a shift in the Early Classic from a scattered distribution of ordinary houses over the landscape to a tighter clustering of smaller houses around elite residences. This pattern is poorly defined at Nohmul, where there may have been a change in the archaeological visibility of the nonelite population or an actual population decline. Test excavations suggest that the Early Classic was the period with the greatest percentage of structures built off platforms, the structures most difficult to identify archaeologically at a riverine site like Nohmul (Pyburn 1989). The situation is different on Albion Island, since all habitations in the central upland area were constructed on bedrock outcrops, although many were no more elaborate than the simplest marl-floored, perishable houses at Nohmul. At both Nohmul and Albion Island sites, these small structures have disappeared down to their floors. At Nohmul they have to be located by posthole or shovel testing because they are concealed by 20 to 80 centimeters of overburden. But on Albion Island, nonplatform structures continue to be visible as lenses of rubble and living debris because their elevated bedrock base protects them from obliteration by most cultural and geological processes.

The Early Classic population density of Albion Island was probably not unique in northern Belize. The apparent difference in population size between Albion Island and other mainland sites is at least partly due to tropical site-formation processes and the nature of lower-class housing and material culture for the pre-Columbian Maya. Bronson drew similar conclusions from his nonplatform excavations at Tikal (Bronson n.d.), as did Hendon (1992) at Copán. Perhaps even more salient is the problem of assuming a standard family size for the ancient Maya as a whole, since ethnographic research has shown that economic factors affect decision making about household and residence patterns (Wilk and Netting 1984). Certainly the population densities of various sites were not uniform (Culbert and Rice 1990), and the population differences between Albion Island and Nohmul, although exaggerated by contrasting natural and cultural site-formation processes, were still substantial.

An important question to ask about these contrasting data sets is whether there are any discernible differences in the behavior of elites within these two closely situated areas. Were elites deriving their power strictly from the local landscape, or is there evidence of varied emphasis on ideological, political, and economic resources? Though the data sets are difficult to work with, preliminary analysis shows some surprising results.

Topographic contrasts between Nohmul and Albion Island make it impossible to compare a straightforward ratio of elites to nonelites, since the percentage of nonelites at Nohmul is unknown. Nevertheless, it is possible to compare elites at the two sites by testing the possibility that architecture and location may indicate differences in the sources of elite status. A second problem with the comparison is that the heaviest occupation of Albion Island occurred during the Early Classic, with a marked decline in architectural density during the Late and Terminal Classic. Consequently, the patterns revealed by the Albion Island maps are, for the most part, Early Classic patterns. At Nohmul, the densest occupation took place in the Terminal Classic. Thus, although all the structures considered in this analysis contained Early Classic material in building fill, the map of visible structures is a map of the last occupation of the site area and is therefore primarily a map of a Terminal Classic community. Further research on the collections from both settlements may make closer chronological control possible, but at present, I am comparing Early to Terminal Classic patterns as much as I am comparing Albion Island to Nohmul.

Bridging Arguments

Three basic sources of elite power are available: politics, economics, and ideology (Yoffee 1991). Although interrelated, these different types of power may occasionally have distinguishable archaeological signatures. Elites acquiring their power from political maneuvering in warfare and alliances will emphasize their position with commemorative monuments and large palaces. Elites with direct economic control amass large quantities of exotic goods, may be craft specialists or otherwise control the marketplace, or build storage structures. Elites with an agricultural power base are most likely to have palaces away from centralized ceremonial areas, in close proximity to arable land and agricultural laborers, or they might have both city and country estates. Either way, the pattern should show more rural elite structures. Elites dependent on esoteric knowledge and religious authority to establish and maintain their position in an ideological hierarchy are most likely to invest in schools, elaborate offerings, large temples, and sites for public ritual.

Because these sources of power are interrelated, there is no suggestion that elites manipulating a primarily economic power base, for example, may not participate in warfare or associate themselves with temples. No single type of data will occur to the exclusion of the others. Manifestations of all three types of power are likely to appear in sequence or at the same time at any particular site, but it is possible to test whether different emphases will appear and change over time in the archaeological record of related sites. The ratio of the different manifestations (e.g., palaces to temples, palaces to imported items, central to outlying palaces) may vary over time or between sites if there was variation in the locus of elite power. So, for example, a contrast in the ratio of temples to palaces at two sites in a region might indicate a contrast in the emphasis on secular authority. Even if palace dwellers control temples, or palaces are administrative buildings instead of residences, a contrast between sites in the ratio of one building type to another reflects some difference in decision making and the allocation of resources.

Multifaceted analysis at Copán has improved identifications of functions of structural types (Fash 1982, 1989, Sanders 1989; Webster and Freter 1990). Temples, for example, may be differentiated from palaces by the configuration of their superstructures. Although no one has yet proposed that elites residing away from urban areas might derive their status from different sources than elites located within centers, several authors have suggested that elite outliers are likely to have a reason for living away from other elites (Haviland 1981). Drennan (1988), for example, has proposed that subsistence patterns may have a centrifugal influence on settlement density, while other economic factors (specialist production and markets) or political factors (warfare and bureaucracy) tend to have a centripetal affect.

Structural Comparisons

For purposes of analysis, I have defined elite residences as mounds more than twice as long as they are wide (with apologies to Sabloff [1975]), and constructed atop secondary platforms (Fig. 10.2a). They are not usually vaulted in northern Belize, but, in contrast to nonplatform structures, they are labor-intensive and impressive enough to suggest that their residents were not the poorest class (Chase and Chase 1992). These structures occur singly, in multiples, and in conjunction with more modest structures or shrines and temples. Excavation in and around the structures has shown them to be frequently associated with modest caches and burials and occasionally decorated with painted walls or floors. The vaulted examples are much more elaborate in every respect, but I would argue that they represent the high end of the same economic scale as their unvaulted counterparts.

I have defined a temple as a square structure that is as tall or taller than it is wide with pyramidal sloping sides (Figure 10.2c). They are usually the tallest structures at a site and are unlikely to be residential, as the summit area is too small for familial activity. They usually contain the most elaborate caches and burials and are the first structures to be looted.

Shrines are similar to temples, but much smaller (Fig. 10.2d). They usually occur in the center of a platform that supports elite residences as well as an occasional temple. They cannot be interpreted as house bases, since they are too small to support a superstructure. They often contain multiple burials in northern Belize.

A residential platform (Fig. 10.2e) is defined as an artificial elevation on more than two sides of a house group that may or may not support visible evidence of superstructure(s). A residential terrace (Fig. 10.2f) is elevated on two sides only but supports a visible superstructure.

I also compared "infield" to "outfield" elites. At Nohmul, these are easy to distinguish because of a recognizable core settlement and a cluster of elite residences, but Albion Island has no single center. For Albion Island, I distinguished between elite residences that were clustered with other elite residences and temples and those that were surrounded by more modest houses. This is easy to do on Albion Island, since all the houses in rural areas of the island are visible.

For this analysis, I ignored nonplatform houses from both sites, since the sample from Nohmul is not

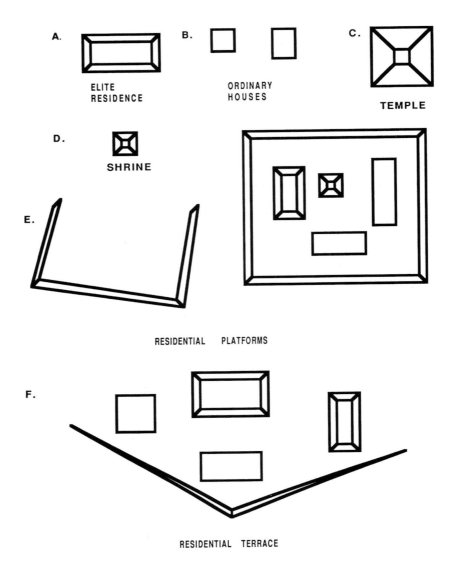

Figure 10.2. Types of structures.

reliable. This probably does not affect the count of elite structures, since the meager material culture associated with most of the nonplatform structures at Nohmul suggests that they were residences of poor people. The map of Nohmul covers the entire site; the map of Albion Island is a 5 percent sample of the island's surface, which means that absolute counts cannot be compared between the two loci. For this reason, I looked at the ratios of one type of structure to another in similar areas from both sites. Since all mapped areas of Albion Island were more densely settled than any part of Nohmul, I ended up comparing the mapped areas of the island to the most densely settled areas of Nohmul, but I did not lump structure counts from the center of Nohmul with other counts and ratios because nothing on the island compares with the massive architecture of Nohmul's center.

The results follow some expected patterns. Albion

Island has more visible remains of houses, more separate platforms, and more houses on each platform than Nohmul. If all possible architectural symbols of authority are lumped together (elite residences plus temples plus shrines), the ratio to ordinary platform-based houses is similar for both samples: about four houses to one "authority" structure, which might indicate that the control of ordinary people by elites of all kinds was similar.

When temples and palaces are distinguished, however, new patterns appear. There were significantly more shrines and temples on Albion Island than at Nohmul (Fig. 10.3). Even if only the most complex platforms are compared, significantly more shrines and temples occur on the island, where there is only one elite residence for every shrine or temple. At Nohmul, there are 2.6 elite residences for every shrine or temple. Similarly, there are only 8 residential plat-

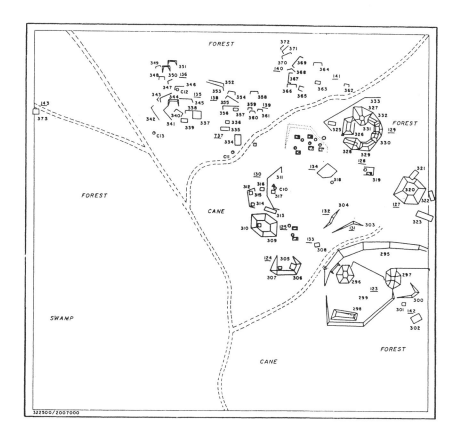

ALBION ISLAND

S.U. 93

1:2000

MARCH 1990

MICHAEL F. LANE

Figure 10.3. Minor ceremonial center on Albion Island, Baaxcamentic.

forms for every shrine or temple on the island, whereas there are 13 such houses for every shrine or temple at Nohmul. Separating shrines from temples shows the main difference to be in the frequency of shrines, which occur at a ratio of 2 shrines to 3 elite residences on the island and a ratio of 1:3 at Nohmul. There are 11 residential platforms for every shrine on Albion Island and 18 houses per shrine at Nohmul. There are 31 residential platforms for each temple on the island and 53 houses per temple at Nohmul.

Comparing Nohmul's center with the largest architectural concentration on Albion Island, the site of San Antonio, Rio Hondo (mapped by Lewenstein and Dahlin [1990] in 1974 and now largely destroyed) shows the same patterns. There are 3 elite residences for each shrine or temple at San Antonio and 7 elite residences for each shrine or temple in Nohmul's site center. If a cluster of shrines and temples that occurs just northwest of Nohmul's central precinct is in-

cluded, there are still 5 elite residences per temple or shrine at Nohmul.

About the same percentage of elite residences occurs in "infield" situations in both samples; that is, 3 out of 5 elite residences occur in nucleated areas. Temples are also more likely to occur in nucleated areas with elite structures and other temples or shrines. But on the island, 4 out of 5 shrines occur in outlying areas, at a rate of 1 per 30 outlying platform houses, as opposed to 1 per 50 outlying houses at Nohmul.

These figures may be interpreted in several ways. The increase in secular authority in later Maya history documented at several prominent sites may account for the differences between the two areas examined here, since the Albion Island pattern is Early Classic and Nohmul is mostly Terminal Classic. In fact, these data suggest something about the nature of the social mechanism that underlay this broad structural

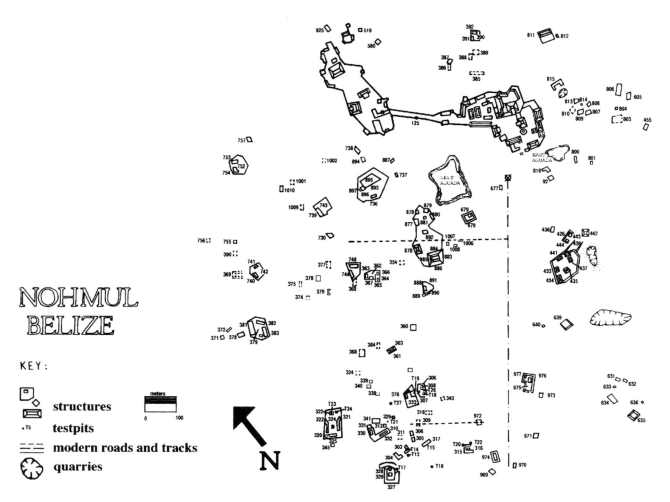

Figure 10.4. Map showing a portion of the northern sector of Nohmul. Redrawn based on Hammond et al. (1988:figure 3).

change. The shift in emphasis from household shrines to more centralized temples may indicate a shift to a more centralized religion and more government involvement, concomitant with the rise of more secular elites.

This inference is supported by several features of the Albion Island settlement system. First is the odd configuration of the minor center of Baaxcamentic (Fig. 10.4), which contains 5 large temples and only 7 palaces. Clustered in the central area between these large structures was a set of 6 *chultuns* (storage sites), with 7 others scattered closer to individual structures. No other settlement feature on the island or at Nohmul had such a concentration of storage features, and nowhere else at either site is there such a cluster of temples. Excavation showed that the area was continuously occupied from the Middle Preclassic into the Terminal Classic. If Baaxcamentic represents an association of storage facilities with religious authority, it contrasts sharply with the lack of similar concentra-

tions during this period at Nohmul and suggests a distinct difference in authority structure. Second, there are several instances of large pyramidal temples on Albion Island without secondary platforms and with few or no nearby elite residences. This pattern does not occur at Nohmul, where temples are always near (and almost always on the same platform with) elite residences, which suggests a closer tie between religious and secular authority at Nohmul.

Nohmul was probably not exclusively geared to production for local consumption, since despite its abundance of fertile riverine soil and use of intensive agriculture (Hammond et al. 1988), the community may never have been large (Pyburn 1989). The site's location on the Hondo River would have given its producers a water route to very near the center of the Maya political realm. The shift in the locus of non-platform occupation over time at Nohmul suggests the emergence of a group of specialist producers, since, by the Terminal Classic, these small houses were clustered on the edge of town, near areas of raised or riverine fields. I have argued elsewhere that this is the archaeological signature of an emerging class of agricultural laborers, such as existed in other complex societies around the world (Pyburn 1991b). The rise of a class of specialist producers within an economically isolated community of 6,000 people seems unlikely. Furthermore, Nohmul is the largest site in northern Belize with massive architecture and evidence of nucleation in the Terminal Classic, despite its modest population density (Pyburn 1989). Participation in a nonlocal political economy makes Nohmul's settlement trajectory comprehensible.

Like the inhabitants of Nohmul, the ancient population of Albion Island participated in a regional economy, but this participation had varied consequences at the local level. At Nohmul, a more elaborate and perhaps more secular local hierarchy was in place at a later time for a smaller number of people. On Albion Island, larger, denser populations correlate with greater numbers of temples and shrines. These tiny dwellings are not family households (see Fig. 10.4) but are more likely to be the dwellings of laborers working for someone else.

It seems clear that the quantity of food produced by Nohmul should not be estimated solely on the basis of intrasite population density, nor should Albion Island be understood as politically more marginal than Nohmul because it lacks massive architecture. With thousands of producers, the island must have been a great political prize. The decreased population of Albion Island may correlate with changes in production strategy and nonlocal control that were in place by the Terminal Classic period, since it may have been possible (or necessary) during this later period for fewer producers to produce more food. This is presumably what happened in the Basin of Mexico, when the strengthening of centralized control at Teotihuacán resulted in depopulation of smaller settlements at a time when population pressure on food resources would have been greatest (Sanders et al. 1979).

Conclusion

It is possible, of course, that pyramidal structures do not signal religious authority or that range structures (long, narrow, sometimes vaulted structures on large platforms often associated with other large buildings and elite material culture) were not secular palaces. Nevertheless, there are differences in the number and

distribution of architectural forms at most lowland sites. The tentative interpretation of the contrasts presented here is meant to serve as a guide in the selection of analogues and in the definition of future research designs.

In focusing on individual sites, we lose sight of significant variation in subsystems between Maya centers, as well as cross-cultural similarities in their ranges of variation. For example, it is possible for complex societies to include communities that are ideologically linked with other communities, but that are almost self-sufficient in political and economic terms (Flannery 1968). Classic-period settlements of the Belize River Valley may be an example (Ford 1991a, 1991b). A complex society may also contain communities that are politically, economically, or ideologically dominated by other communities, occasionally or continuously. This could characterize the situation at many centers in the central Petén during the Late Classic period (Culbert et al. 1990). The problem for archaeologists working in the Maya Lowlands is to determine where particular communities fall on this continuum of possibilities. In some cases, ancient Maya communities were self-sufficient, and links between subsystems were determined by local requirements. However, if communities were producing for nonlocal use, as I have argued was the case during some periods for Albion Island and Nohmul, the idea of a rigid link between population density, social organization, and subsistence strategy breaks down, and nothing less than a regional analysis can interpret the archaeological data.

This does not discount the possibility that elites sometimes become too powerful and create subsystems that are pathologically interdependent and doomed to systemic collapse. Flannery called this systemic "hypercoherence," and something like it may have affected some Maya regions during the Terminal Classic (Flannery 1972; Pyburn 1996). But inflexible linkages must be demonstrated and not simply assumed. Functional arguments based on the concept of total integration between subsystems such as economy, polity, and ideology ("bundles" [de Montmollin 1989] or "modules" [S. Gould 1992]) envision static systems that neither take in information from their environment nor change, except to fall apart. Even biological evolution involves uncoordinated change. In order for systems to evolve, subsystems must be separable: "Evolution does proceed (as it must) by dissociating complex systems into parts, or modules, made of a few correlated features, and by altering the various units at different rates and times" (S. Gould 1992:12).

The proposed correlations between architectural form, location, and size and competing sources of elite power are based solely on logic, which is an unreliable predictor of human behavior. Nevertheless, patterns in settlement data suggest that the correlations merit further investigation. Appropriate models must be sought, however, to identify and understand the type of data that would indicate elite competition. Ethnographic settings in which elite residence patterns are affected by competing bases of power would be relevant to further discussion, but societies that discourage ostentatious display of religious, political, or economic superiority would not provide useful analogues. This excludes most modern Maya groups and many societies in West Africa and Polynesia that overtly emphasize the redistribution of wealth, since ancient Maya strategies clearly revolved around conspicuous consumption.

At another level, regions themselves may be treated as subsystems or modules of a larger entity. Discussions of peer-polity interaction (Renfrew and Cherry 1986) and world systems (Kohl 1978; Wallerstein 1974) are attempts to come to grips with this level of systemic integration and its effects on the trajectories of smaller units, as well as the development of civilization as a whole. Though intraregional studies cannot control for the effects of such broad influences, they should ultimately provide the building blocks for a more robust analysis of cultural evolution, just as detailed investigations of individual sites will ultimately combine to construct effective regional analyses.

11

Diachronic Studies of City-States: Permutations on a Theme

Central Mexico from 1700 B.C. to A.D. 1600

THOMAS H. CHARLTON
AND DEBORAH L. NICHOLS

In central Mexico, a nuclear area for the evolution of ancient civilizations, the city-state has been most frequently used as an integrative and structural concept to describe and explain the dynamic social, political, and economic phenomena occurring between the fall of Teotihuacán (ca. A.D. 650/750) and the arrival of the Spaniards in A.D. 1519.[1] To a large extent this application was both encouraged and made possible by abundant ethnohistoric documents (Sanders et al. 1979:137–181), both native and Spanish, for the portion of this sequence from Tula (A.D. 900/950) to the conquest of the Aztec empire in A.D. 1521 (Table 11.1). The documentary and archaeological data support the existence of small political units, city-states, which alone or linked in confederacies, alliances, and tributary empires were important players in the post-Teotihuacán central Mexican political and economic scene. Similar archaeological and historical data support the persistence of city-states, albeit in somewhat attenuated forms, after the Spanish conquest (Charlton 1986; Gibson 1964; Lockhart 1991:23–24).

The late prehispanic central Mexican city-state was characterized by a small size, a recognized single ethnic identity (although often with a multiethnic composition), political and economic interdependence between settlements within the city-state territory, and varying degrees of political independence. The degree of political autonomy depended upon the nature and outcome of constantly fluctuating relationships—from peaceful to bellicose—between variably sized and structured city-state units linked within a regional matrix or network (Charlton, in press; Hirth 1989; Hodge 1996:20–23; Lockhart 1991:23; Marcus 1989, 1992a; Renfrew 1986a; Sanders 1970: 443–450; Smith 1992a:68). Such a city-state unit appears to have been the basic sociopolitical form for almost a millennium after the fall of Teotihuacán.

The extent to which the city-state system described above could apply to the increasingly complex sociopolitical units of the Formative period (1700–100 B.C.) antedating Teotihuacán in the Basin of Mexico or to Teotihuacán itself (100 B.C.–A.D. 650/750) is neither obvious nor readily agreed upon (see Webster, this volume, and Yoffee, this volume). The magnitude and uniqueness of Teotihuacán seem to overshadow our perceptions of all that went before, just as Teotihuacán, through the provision of images and models to emulate, influenced all succeeding cultures in central Mexico.

It is our position, however, that a city-state system did appear briefly in the Basin of Mexico prior to Teo-

Table 11.1

Archaeological Periods and Phase Names for the Basin of Mexico

Period	Phase Name	Approximate Dates
Postclassic period		A.D. 900/950–1521
Late Postclassic	Late Aztec	A.D. 1350/1430–1521
Middle Postclassic	Early Aztec	A.D. 1150/1200–1350/1430
Early Postclassic	Late Toltec	A.D. 900/950–1150
Epi-Teotihuacán/Classic	Early Toltec	A.D. 650/750–900/950
Classic period		A.D. 150–650/750
Late Classic		A.D. 500–650/750
	Metepec	A.D. 650–750
	Xolalpan	A.D. 500–650
Early Classic		A.D. 150–500
	Tlamimilolpa	A.D. 300–500
	Miccaotli	A.D. 150–300
Formative period		1500/1400 B.C.–A.D. 150
Late Terminal Formative	Tzacualli	100 B.C.–A.D. 150
Early Terminal Formative	Patlachique	300–100 B.C.
Late Formative	Cuanalán	650–300 B.C.
Late Middle Formative	Chiconauta	900–650 B.C.
Early Middle Formative	Altica	1150–900 B.C.
Early Formative		1500/1400–1100 B.C.
Initial Ceramic period		2000/1700–1500/1400 B.C.

Note: Cowgill (1996) has recently proposed a revised estimated chronology for Teotihuacán as follows: Cuanalán (650–200 B.C.), Patlachique (200–100 B.C.), Tzacualli (100 B.C.–A.D. 200), Miccaotli (A.D. 200–300), Early Xolalpan (A.D. 400–500), Late Xolalpan (A.D. 400–500), Metepec (A.D. 550–650), Early Toltec, Oxtotipac/Xometla (A.D. 650–800), Late Toltec, Mazapan/Atlatongo (A.D. 800–1000), Aztec I (A.D. 1000–1200), Aztec II (A.D. 1200–1350/1400), Aztec III (A.D. 1350/1400–1521+).

tihuacán's emergence as the sole state power. The earliest city-states were rapidly subordinated, first to the larger city-state systems of Cuicuilco and Teotihuacán and finally, through complete incorporation, to the macro state of Teotihuacán. Nevertheless they, along with less complex antecedent forms, participated in important successive peer-polity matrices (cf. Cherry and Renfrew 1986), the sociopolitical contexts out of which Teotihuacán emerged.

The development and evolution of the peer-polity matrix during the Formative period and the emergence of a single dominant state power, Teotihuacán, form two parts of a single cycle of political development. Similar cycles occurred twice before and once after the Spanish conquest (Table 11.2; Calnek 1982; Charlton 1973, 1975, in press; Marcus 1989, 1992a; Sanders 1981; Willey 1991). The second cycle began with the demise of Teotihuacán, followed by the appearance or reappearance of city-state systems that were subsequently integrated into the Tula Toltec state (Davies 1977; Diehl 1983; Healan 1989). The third and final preconquest cycle began with the collapse of Tula, and it too was followed by the appear-

ance or reappearance of city-state systems. These later fell under the hegemony of the Triple Alliance dominated by the Tenochtitlán city-state system. Subsequent to Cortés's conquest of Tenochtitlán, a fourth cycle emerged. City-state system units or modules reappeared and persisted in modified forms through the Colonial period, only to become integrated once again within a larger political structure, this time the nation-state.

Abundant archaeological and historical data from the Basin of Mexico and adjacent regions of the central highlands provide a basis for examining the changing nature of city-states during these four cycles of political evolution over a period of approximately three millennia. The cycles are marked by the differential operation of two dominant but opposing trends in political evolution: the extension of control by one "political unit" over increasingly larger territories and greater numbers of people, and the retraction or breakdown of control, accompanied by the appearance or reappearance of territorially and demographically restricted political units (see also Marcus 1992a). The tempo of change, from decentralization to cen-

Table 11.2

Cycles of City-State Development in the Basin of Mexico

Cycle	Approximate Dates
Cycle I: Initial development; Formative and classic periods	1700 B.C.–A.D. 650/750
Part 1: Initial Ceramic, Early Formative and Early Middle Formative periods	1700–900 B.C.
Part 2: Late Middle Formative, Late Formative, and Early Terminal Formative periods	900–100 B.C.
Part 3: The City-State of Teotihuacán; Late Terminal Formative, and Classic periods	100 B.C.–A.D. 650/750
Cycle II: Epi-Teotihuacán and Early Postclassic periods	A.D. 650/750–1150/1200
Part 1: Epi-Teotihuacán/Classic period	A.D. 650/750–900/950
Part 2: The City-State of Tula; Early Postclassic period	A.D. 900/950–1150/1200
Cycle III: Middle and Late Postclassic periods	A.D. 1150/1220–1521
Part 1: Middle Postclassic period	A.D. 1150/1200–1430
Part 2: The City-State of Tenochtitlán; Late Postclassic period	A.D. 1430–1521
Cycle IV: Spanish conquest to nation state	A.D. 1521–present
Part 1: Early Colonial period	A.D. 1521–1620

tralization and decentralization once again, accelerates through time. Associated changes include population growth, agricultural intensification, increasing urbanism, and the ubiquitous presence of the city-state form (Smith 1992a:68). Both the core areas and the dominated regions expand along with an increasing emphasis on militarism (Hassig 1992:171). Ideology emphasizes sacred places, cyclic time, and human sacrifice (Boone 1984; Conrad and Demarest 1984; Hirth 1989).

Of concern in this paper are the similarities and differences in city-states through time, in terms of their structure and function, prior to, during, and following cycles of regional sociopolitical integration. The fate of city-states during these cycles of integration, whether persistence or reformulation, varied according to the principles of integration adopted by the expansionist state. Although the basic structure of the city-state persisted, the city-states antedating Teotihuacán, Tula, or Tenochtitlán differed from those that postdate the incorporation or submergence of these city-states within the larger integrative states.

Research Background

Although pre- and postconquest documentary data have contributed much to our understanding of post-Teotihuacán, and especially post-Tula, central Mexican social, economic, and political structure, they are limited in periods, areas, and detail.[2] Some of these limitations are related to the nature of the recording systems used. "Simple pictograms and calendric signs" (Marcus 1992c:5), for example, occur at Teoti-

huacán (cf. Berlo 1989:19–23; Cowgill 1992; Langley 1992). Although subsequently elaborated in association with public art such as murals or low relief sculptures within the context of competitive small city-states (Berlo 1989:23, 44; cf. Marcus 1992c: 435–445), no fully developed writing system is known prior to that of the Aztecs (Marcus 1992c:35).

Pictograms and calendrical glyphs on public art, in Aztec Early Colonial codices (Dibble 1971; Marcus 1992c:46–57), along with descriptions of indigenous culture and history (e.g., Gibson 1964; Lockhart 1991; Sahagún 1950–1982) support the existence of competing social, economic, and political units in the form of city-states after the breakup of Tula. Those sources are generally consistent with the presence of such city-states in central Mexico for the entire period following the demise of Teotihuacán. For Teotihuacán and earlier periods, we have no historical data and must rely on archaeological investigations. To some degree, this also applies to the entire post-Teotihuacán period, and particularly to the last part just prior to the Aztec empire, for which texts are incomplete or consist of the surviving revisionist Late Aztec codices (Marcus 1992c:146–149).

The primary archaeological data on which we rely are regional settlement patterns derived from surveys carried out between 1960 and 1975 in the Basin of Mexico and adjacent areas.[3] This research consisted of ground surveys to locate sites and to assign them to culturally significant chronological periods, usually without the application of sampling procedures for site location or surface collections (Charlton 1984a: 198–202; Sanders et al. 1979:12–30).

Although the objective was complete ground coverage, this was not always possible in areas of dense modern occupation, especially in and around Mexico City, in its suburbs in the southwestern Basin, and in modern towns elsewhere in the Basin. The survey methods were extensive, designed to document long-term settlement, agricultural, and demographic trends, and thus they provide only limited information about the internal configuration and composition of individual sites (Charlton 1984a:202–204). The results of these initial surveys have been summarized on maps and in tables such as those included here from the synthesis by Sanders and his colleagues (Tables 11.3 and 11.4; Sanders et al. 1979). Excavations of varying scales have been undertaken in many of these projects and in others too numerous to summarize here. Areal and period coverage, however, are not uniform.[4]

Cycle I: Initial Development and Formation, 1700 B.C.–A.D. 650/750

This very long cycle of initial development of city-states within the Basin of Mexico can be subdivided into three parts.

Cycle I, Part 1: Initial Ceramic, Early Formative, and Early Middle Formative periods, 1700–900 B.C.

From the initial occupation of the Basin of Mexico by sedentary cultivators about 1500 B.C. (Tolstoy 1975, 1989a, 1989b; Tolstoy et al. 1977), but possibly as early as 2000 B.C. (McClung de Tapia and Zurita Noguera 1994; Niederberger 1976, 1979, 1987), until about 900 B.C. (see Table 11.1), population tripled from about 2,000 to 6,000 people (Sanders 1981:165; Sanders et al. 1979:218). By the early Middle Formative period, the growing population had expanded from the south of the Basin to the central-west and central-east areas (Figs. 11.1 and 11.2; Parsons 1989:166; Sanders 1981:164; Sanders et al. 1979:218; Tolstoy 1975:343). Between 1150 B.C. and 900 B.C., three sites—Tlatilco, Coapexco, and Tlapacoya—were quite large, "among the largest population concentrations of their time period in Mesoamerica" (Flannery and Marcus 1994:388). However, neither the settlement-pattern data (Sanders et al. 1979:94–95) nor the excavated materials from Coapexco, Tlapacoya, and Tlatilco indicate the presence of well-

developed site hierarchies, civic-ceremonial-elite architecture, strongly defined, highly restrictive status differences, or ranking systems (Blanton 1972:37–40a; Sanders et al. 1979:95; Tolstoy 1989a:97, 120–121, 1989b:293; Tolstoy and Paradis 1970).

Elaborations found in grave goods at Tlatilco (Tolstoy 1989a:101–119, 1989b:293) and the differential spatial distribution of artifacts within Coapexco (Tolstoy 1989a:87–101) and in ceramic and figurine styles at Tlapacoya (Tolstoy and Paradis 1970:347–348) have been interpreted as being due to: (1) strategic site location as related to efficient participation in Early Formative resource exploitation and trade with other regions (Charlton 1984b:23–29); (2) a combination of kinship, residence, ascribed and achieved status or rank principles as related to individuals (Tolstoy 1989a:97, 120, 1989b:293); and (3) the development of local ranked societies or chiefdoms in close contact and competition with similar societies in other areas (Flannery and Marcus 1994:385–390).

Given the data available, it is difficult, if not impossible, to determine with certainty the degree to which leadership was centralized during this period (cf. Earle 1987:289). The evident elaboration in artifact and burial complexes probably reflects a kinship-based village organization with some acquired and some inherited status or rank differentiation between lineages and between individuals.

Cycle I, Part 2: Late Middle Formative, Late Formative, and Early Terminal Formative periods, 900 B.C.–100 B.C.

Sanders describes this time period as "extraordinarily dynamic" (1981:165) with major increases in population, population expansion within the central Highlands, and changes in sociopolitical organization leading to increasing complexity, including the emergence of a chiefdom center at Chalcatzingo in Morelos (Grove 1981:384–385, 1987:439–440). Population increased from about 6,000 in 900 B.C. to 125,000 by 100 B.C. (Table 11.3; Parsons 1989:167, 171, 175; Sanders 1981:157, 165–166; Sanders et al. 1979:218).

During the Late Middle Formative period (Fig. 11.3), population growth occurred primarily within sites and zones previously occupied, resulting in the continued demographic dominance of the southern and western Basin. This pattern persisted through the

Table 11.3

Population and Distribution by Settlement Types[a] in the Basin of Mexico

Settlement Type	Cuicuilco	Chalco-Xochimilco	Ixtalpalapa	Texcoco	Teotihuacán Valley	Temascalapa	Tenayuca-Cuauhtitlán	Zumpango	Tacuba	Basin
Early Formative	2,500	1,600	480	—	—	—	173	—	1,500?	6,300
Hamlet	—	7%	56%	—	—	—	13%	—	unk.	6%
Small village	—	93%	44%	—	—	—	87%	—	unk.	30%
Large village	100%	—	—	—	—	—	—	—	100%?	64%
Middle Formative	5,000	7,000	855	2,520	683	—	4,088	—	unk.	20,000
Hamlet	—	7%	25%	4%	22%	—	11%	—	unk.	16%
Small village	—	18%	75%	—	78%	—	21%	—	unk.	20%
Large village	100%	75%	—	57%	—	—	68%	—	unk.	64%
Late Formative	10,000	29,100	9,864	10,800	6,994[b]	—	6,222	30	unk.	73,000
Hamlet	—	5%	5%	12%	35%	—	3%	100%	unk.	7%
Small village	—	12%	6%	9%	47%	—	27%	—	unk.	12%
Large village	—	48%	27%	40%	18%	—	70%	—	unk.	39%
Small center	—	36%	62%	39%	—	—	—	—	unk.	28%
Large center	100%	—	—	—	—	—	—	—	unk.	14%
E. T. Formative	20,000	22,400	8,886	24,150	43,601	—	4,060	900	unk.	124,000
Hamlet	—	8%	4%	5%	4%	—	5%	100%	unk.	5%
Small village	—	11%	7%	26%	1%	—	30%	—	unk.	9%
Large village	—	36%	42%	16%	1%	—	—	—	unk.	13%
Small center	—	45%	47%	53%	—	—	65%	—	unk.	24%
Large center	100%	—	—	—	94%	—	—	—	unk.	49%
L. T. Formative	5,000	—	—	—	93,792	675	1,368	900	unk.	101,800
Hamlet	—	—	—	—	2%	100%	54%	100%	unk.	4%
Large village	—	—	—	—	1%	—	44%	—	unk.	2%
Small center	100%	—	—	—	—	—	—	—	unk.	5%
Large center	—	—	—	—	—	—	—	—	unk.	—
Supraregional center	—	—	—	—	97%	—	—	—	—	89%
Classic	—	5,800	5,528	4,055	147,807	6,648	15,422	6,400	unk.	191,700
Hamlet	—	33%	22%	58%	2%	12%	7%	42%	unk.	7%
Small village	—	53%	30%	9%	3%	44%	23%	31%	unk.	9%
Large village	—	14%	48%	—	7%	44%	43%	12%	unk.	13%
Small center	—	—	—	33%	3%	—	27%	15%	unk.	6%
Large center	—	—	—	—	—	—	—	—	unk.	—
Supraregional center	—	—	—	—	85%	—	—	—	—	65%

(continued on next page)

Table 11.3 (continued)

Settlement Type	Cuicuilco	Chalco-Xochimilco	Ixtalpalapa	Texcoco	Teotihuacán Valley	Temascalapa	Tenayuca-Cuauhtitlán	Zumpango	Tacuba	Basin
Early Toltec	—	13,500	7,539	38,280	39,262	3,198	12,010	5,500	unk.	119,200
Hamlet	—	11%	7%	2%	2%	8%	7%	30%	unk.	5%
Small village	—	11%	6%	4%	1%	6%	30%	20%	unk.	7%
Large village	—	26%	20%	9%	14%	—	25%	17%	unk.	15%
Small center	—	52%	67%	85%	83%	86%	38%	33%	unk.	45%
Large center	—	—	—	—	—	—	—	—	unk.	28%
Supraregional center	—	—	—	—	—	—	—	—	unk.	—
Late Toltec	—	10,122	2,154	7,938	33,001	5,778	15,900	16,000	unk.	90,800
Hamlet	—	36%	75%	40%	16%	28%	20%	33%	unk.	26%
Small village	—	22%	25%	26%	21%	49%	44%	33%	unk.	30%
Large village	—	18%	—	11%	25%	23%	17%	3%	unk.	17%
Small center	—	24%	—	23%	38%	—	19%	31%	unk.	27%
Large center	—	—	—	—	—	—	—	—	unk.	—
Supraregional center	—	—	—	—	—	—	—	—	unk.	—
Early Aztec	—	50,190	4,923	unk.	unk.	unk.	unk.	5,000	unk.	unk.
Hamlet	—	7%	unk.	unk.	unk.	unk.	unk.	unk.	unk.	unk.
Small village	—	10%	unk.	unk.	unk.	unk.	unk.	unk.	unk.	unk.
Large village	—	7%	unk.	unk.	unk.	unk.	unk.	unk.	unk.	unk.
Small center	—	76%	unk.	unk.	unk.	unk.	unk.	100%	unk.	unk.
Large center	—	—	—	—	—	—	—	—	unk.	—
Supraregional center	—	—	—	—	—	—	—	—	unk.	—
Late Aztec	—	99,600	16,040	140,500	110,000	16,000	62,000	41,000	350,000[c]	835,000
Hamlet	—	9%	9%	3%	3%	28%	12%	20%	7%[d]	7%
Small village	—	5%	13%	6%	27%	56%	20%	21%	7%[d]	11%
Large village	—	8%	13%	17%	30%	16%	22%	38%	8%[d]	15%
Small center	—	68%	66%	53%	31%	—	46%	21%	22%[d]	36%
Large center	—	10%[c]	?	—	—	—	—	—	6%[c]	4%
Supraregional center	—	—	21%	—	—	—	—	—	57%[c]	27%
(Documentary est.)	—	(125,000)	(22,000)	(140,000)	(110,000)	(5,000)	(100,000)	(110,000)	(350,000)	(962,000)[e]

Sources: Parsons et al. 1982:265, 270; Sanders et al. 1979:183–219; and Nichols 1980:122, 156.

Note: — = 0; unk. = not surveyed; ? = approximation.

[a] Settlement types are those used by Sanders et al. (1979:183–219) to report their population estimates.

[b] Including the site of Teotihuacán with estimated population of 3,000 (Cowgill 1974:381).

[c] Documentary-based estimates for large centers (10,000 persons each), Tenochtitlán-Tlatelolco (200,000 persons), and Tacuba region (Sanders et al. 1979: 154).

[d] Since no survey data are available for this important area, the combined percentage of population residing in hamlets and villages in the Tacuba region was assumed to be similar to that of Chalco-Xochimilco and Ixtalpalapa regions (22 percent), with the balance distributed in centers of varying size.

[e] The documentary estimate of the population in the Pachuca region is 100,000 persons (Sanders et al. 1979:218) which would bring the total estimated population of the Basin in A.D. 1519 to ca. 1,062,000 persons.

Late Formative period (Fig. 11.4), but it was accompanied by a population increase in the eastern and northeastern Basin (Parsons 1989:167, 171–173; Sanders 1981:166; Sanders et al. 1979:95–98). In the Early Terminal Formative period (Fig. 11.5), population growth slowed in the southern Basin but continued unabated in the eastern (Texcoco) and northeastern (Teotihuacán) sections, which at that time made up almost half of the Basin's population (Parsons 1989:175–177; Sanders 1981:168; Sanders et al. 1979: 98–102).

The accompanying changes in sociopolitical organization from 650 B.C. to 100 B.C. mark a shift from nonegalitarian, but minimally ranked, societies to state-ordered stratified societies (cf. Paynter 1989). This shift had been completed by 100 B.C.

LATE MIDDLE FORMATIVE PERIOD (900–650 B.C.). A shift in sociopolitical organization between 900–650 B.C. is signaled by the emergence of several settlement or site clusters (Fig. 11.3). Each consists of a "major nucleated settlement plus a number of smaller villages and hamlets" that "presumably reflect sociopolitical groupings" (Santley 1977:396). The clusters and the centers, roughly equivalent in size, suggest politically autonomous peer-polity units (Renfrew 1986a:1–2; see also Price 1977). The equivalence of these units must be qualified by the presence of two or three larger centers, possibly with public architecture. Their presence indicates that some polities were able to increase their size, and they may reflect the beginnings of a hierarchy of site clusters (Parsons 1989: 169), a pattern that becomes accentuated in subsequent periods.

Parsons has suggested that data on site size and site spacing within the Basin during the Middle Formative period hint at the beginnings of a sociopolitical hierarchy with two or three large centers, each greater than 40 hectares and probably with public architecture, representing the highest or regional level and eight to nine smaller centers covering from 10 to 30 hectares, possibly with public architecture (1989: 169). However, the regular spacing (8–9 km) between centers in the Chalco-Xochimilco area around the lake shore, according to Parsons (1989:169), argues against a single integrated hierarchical system. Instead, he proposes that each center was relatively autonomous, with its own territory and resources, and without much, if any, domination by regional centers (1989:169).

Table 11.4

Site Distributions in the Basin of Mexico and Tula Region during the Early Postclassic Period

Settlement Type	Basin of Mexico (3,500 km² survey area)	Tula Region (1,000 km² survey area)
Hamlets	555	35
Small nucleated villages	37	58
Small dispersed villages	83	18
Large nucleated villages	9	13
Large dispersed villages	10	26
Provincial centers	10	0
Supraregional centers	0	1[a]
Small ceremonial centers	2	1
Salt-making stations	5	0
Unknown	2	0

Source: Sanders et al. (1979:141, table 5.14).

[a]Estimated population size for Tula is 60,000 persons (Sanders et al. 1979:141).

Sanders et al. (1979:96–97) argue that although the Middle Formative settlement patterns present a range of sites from hamlets to large villages and the differentiated burials clearly involve ranking, "social stratification and hierarchical political dominance seem to be absent from the scene" (1979:97) until the Late Formative period. Similarly Santley notes that in the northwestern (Cuauhtitlán) region during the Middle Formative period, there were four spatially defined site clusters and that "these presumably reflect sociopolitical groupings" (1977:396).

In a related study, Earle uses nearest-neighbor analyses to determine if hierarchical relationships existed for Middle, Late, and Terminal Formative sites in the eastern (Texcoco) and southern (Ixtapalapa and Chalco) survey areas of the Basin (1976:206–212). For the Middle Formative sites, Earle concludes that "Level 2 sites (minimum size, 8 ha) do show regular spacing and probably represent focal points for competitive social units of some kind, perhaps still composed of locally based lineages, although this is not known" (1976:212).

These conclusions agree with those reached by Steponaitis, who worked with the same data but used different procedures. Steponaitis concludes that there was "village autonomy in political affairs" (1981: 341), with no evidence for any social or political ties "strong enough to allow one settlement to mobilize large amounts of surplus from another" (1981:341).

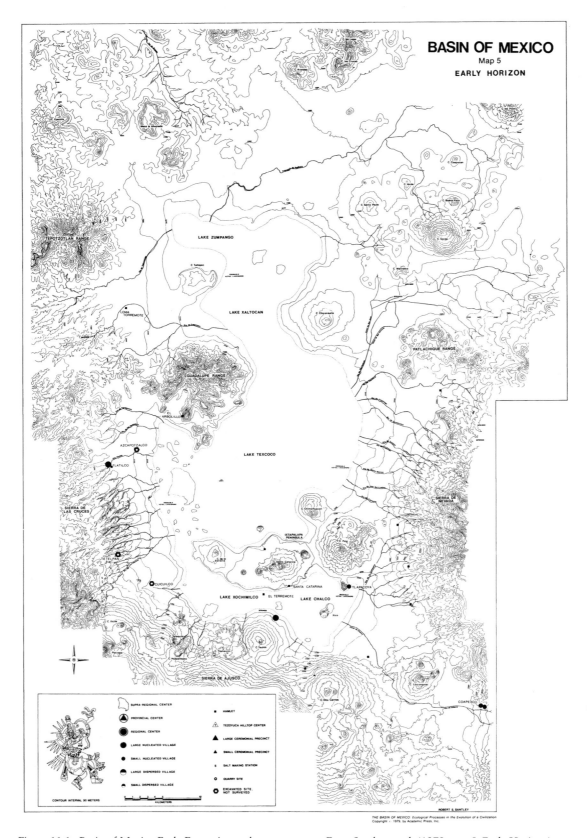

Figure 11.1. Basin of Mexico Early Formative settlement patterns. From Sanders et al. (1979:map 5, Early Horizon).
Reprinted with permission of Academic Press and the authors.

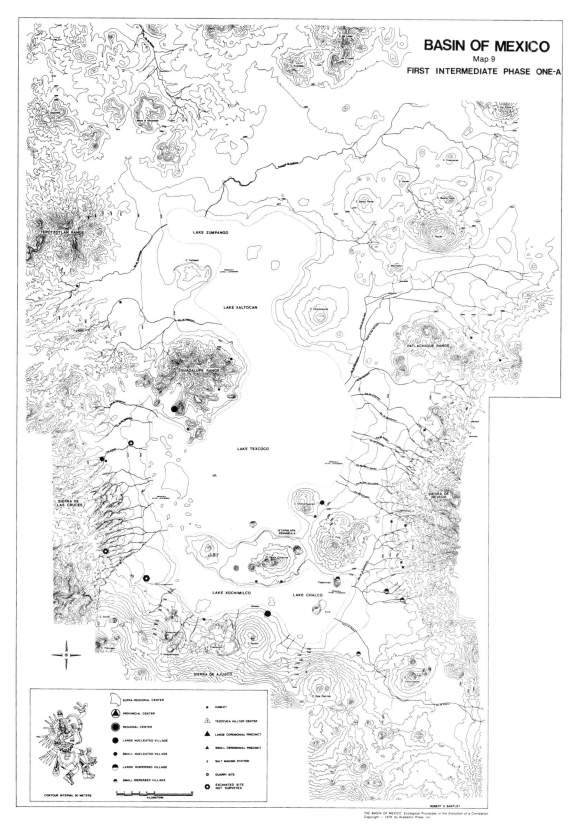

Figure 11.2. Basin of Mexico Early Middle Formative settlement patterns. From Sanders et al. (1979:map 9, First Intermediate Phase One-A). Reprinted with permission of Academic Press and the authors.

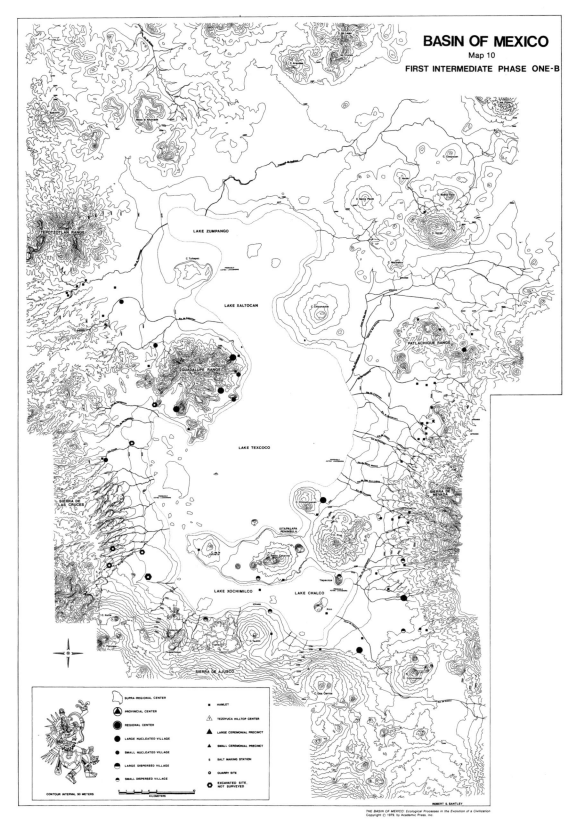

Figure 11.3. Basin of Mexico Late Middle Formative settlement patterns. From Sanders et al. (1979:map 10, First Intermediate Phase One-B). Reprinted with permission of Academic Press and the authors.

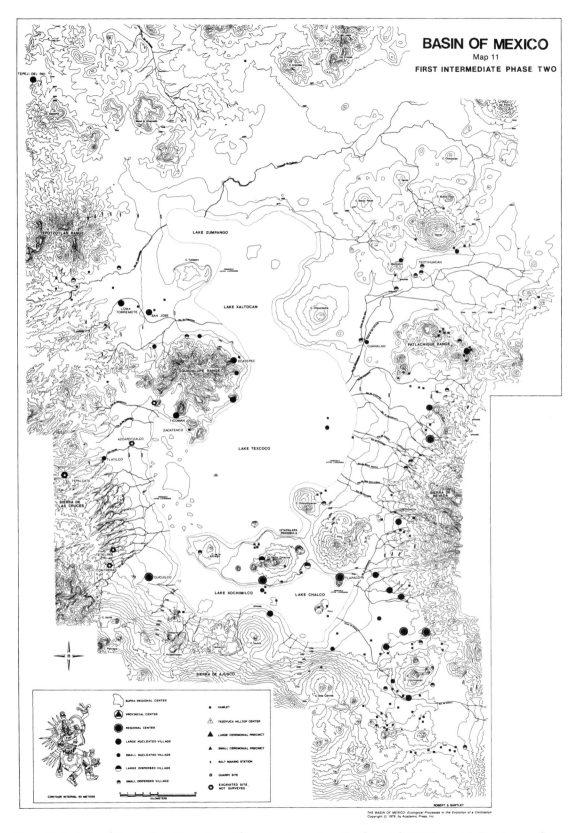

Figure 11.4. Basin of Mexico Late Formative settlement patterns. From Sanders et al. (1979:map 11, First Intermediate Phase Two). Reprinted with permission of Academic Press and the authors.

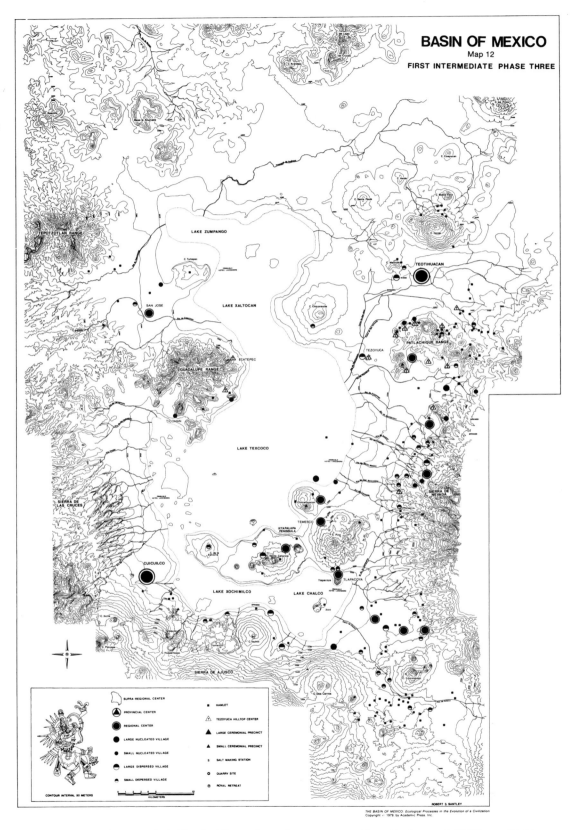

Figure 11.5. Basin of Mexico Early Terminal Formative settlement patterns. From Sanders et al. (1979:map 12, First Intermediate Phase Three). Reprinted with permission of Academic Press and the authors.

A number of problems associated with Middle Formative settlements remain unresolved, including: (1) the lack of data from Cuicuilco, (2) the large number of small sites in the Texcoco and Teotihuacán areas apparently unassociated with any major center(s) that may represent pioneering settlements, and (3) the need to demonstrate in concrete terms the interaction between a center and the dependencies within its territory (Parsons 1989:170). Nonetheless, we argue that the Middle Formative settlement pattern per se suggests the initial appearance of clusters of politically autonomous polities. Each polity probably consists of one or more landholding lineages, initially with minimal status and rank differentiation, which become increasingly economically stratified at the individual and lineage level (McAnany 1995; Price 1977; Renfrew 1986a:1–2; Sanders et al. 1979:97).

Although most centers were about the same size, the presence of two or three larger centers suggests that some polities were able to increase in size. The tendency of a few such units to be larger than the others and for most of the population to live in the regional centers persists until all are incorporated into a single state, Teotihuacán, with most of the population living in the city of Teotihuacán. However, the size differential, initially at least, probably did not denote a superior hierarchical political position for the larger sites with reference to the other polities. Essentially, the peer-polity model put forth by Renfrew (1986a) is applicable to the Basin of Mexico beginning with the Middle Formative. The peer-polity units within this matrix may have evolved from societies with minimal rank and status differentiation through economically stratified lineage-based societies to states—whose size and settlement pattern resemble Renfrew's "early state modules" or city-states (1986a:2), perhaps without passing through an intervening classic chiefdom stage (Sanders and Webster 1978:282; Santley 1984:44; but cf. Drennan 1987:317–318, 1991: 264, 282–287).

The general question of the role, if any, of chiefdoms as antecedents to state-level society in central Mexico, as well as elsewhere, is still actively discussed (e.g., Blanton et al. 1996; Creamer and Haas 1985; Earle 1987, 1991; Feinman 1991; Feinman and Neitzel 1984; Hudson et al. 1985; Marcus and Flannery 1996:155–158; Sanders and Webster 1978; Stein and Rothman 1994). Furthermore there is substantial disagreement about the definition and archaeological recognition of chiefdoms. However, a chiefdom is generally considered to represent an intermediate

form of scale and organizational complexity in non-state societies falling between tribes and states (Earle 1987:279; Feinman 1991:229; Feinman and Neitzel 1984:40).

LATE FORMATIVE PERIOD (650–300 B.C.). During the Late Formative period (Fig. 11.4), the growth in the number of sites and in site size, accompanied by the construction of monumental public architecture at some sites (usually modest, but occasionally up to 5 meters in height), permits the definition of at least a three-level hierarchy of settlements based on size and architecture (Sanders et al. 1979:97). The hierarchy includes hamlets, small and large villages, and six regional centers (Sanders et al. 1979:97). Five of the regional centers had populations between 1,000 and 3,500, while the sixth, Cuicuilco, may have had a population of 5,000–10,000 (Sanders et al. 1979:97). This disparity in population size means that there were two levels of centers—Cuicuilco as a regional center at the top in a fourth organizational level, the five other centers making up the next level down. Below them are villages and hamlets (Parsons 1989:171; Sanders et al. 1979:98).

Independent analysis of settlement data by Steponaitis (1981:342) supports the existence of a political hierarchy in the Late Formative Basin of Mexico. "In sum, the evidence . . . suggests that there were three levels of settlement hierarchy in the study area during the Late Formative" (Steponaitis 1981:346). He argues, however, that two of the six centers, Cuicuilco and CH-5, were distinctive enough to be considered regional centers by the end of the period (1981:346). Earle suggests that the five centers (not including Cuicuilco) "may represent the loosely held dominance of a central village over several neighboring and related villages" (1976:212). He proposes that the settlement patterns might reflect the presence of a chiefdom level of organization, ranked but not stratified. Similarly Sanders argues that in the Late Formative period the development of more pronounced regional settlement hierarchies suggests the possibility of a paramount chiefdom centered at Cuicuilco (1981:172, 174).

EARLY TERMINAL FORMATIVE PERIOD (300–100 B.C.). Trends noted previously continued during the Early Terminal Formative period (Fig. 11.5). The Basin's total population increased to about 125,000, expansion to the east and northeast (Texcoco and Teotihuacán) accelerated, and two regional centers, Cuicuilco and Teotihuacán, became dominant (Parsons 1989:175–179; Sanders et al. 1979:98–104). The population of each center has been estimated to be between 20,000 and 40,000 (Parsons 1989:175; Sanders et al. 1979:101). In addition to these two large urban or proto-urban regional centers with major public architecture, there were ten small regional centers (Parsons 1989:175–179; Sanders et al. 1979:99), each with 3,000–7,000 inhabitants and modest amounts of public architecture. The pattern of a large number of equivalent peer polities associated with the two larger units continues from the Middle Formative period. The difference at this time is to be found in the establishment of one of the two centers, Teotihuacán, in the northeastern area of the Basin. Cuicuilco and Teotihuacán probably headed two city-state systems, each including smaller, subordinate city-state units, represented by the smaller centers.[5]

Analyses by Brumfiel suggest that these systems of site hierarchies mark the appearance of a "state-like political organization" (1976b:247). Earle proposes that the smaller centers at this time were integrated "into a larger state organization" and that they lost their independence (1976:219). Studies by Steponaitis detail some aspects of the relationships between centers during the Early Terminal Formative period (Patlachique phase). He proposes "that Teotihuacán and Cuicuilco were political centers of roughly equivalent order and together formed the apical level of the settlement hierarchy within the Valley of Mexico" (1981:351). These would be "Primary Regional Centers" (Steponaitis 1981:252, 353) and would constitute a fourth level in the settlement hierarchy. Below this level were two secondary regional centers, one in the Texcoco region and the other in the Lake Chalco area. "Each of the two regional centers in the study areas appears to have formed the nucleus of a geographically discrete cluster of local centers and villages" (1981:352). Although these two secondary regional centers might have been independent at the beginning of the period (see also Blanton et al. 1993:115, 122–123), they were later incorporated into the increasingly powerful centers of Teotihuacán and Cuicuilco.

We would suggest that the peer-polity units, from their initial emergence in the Formative period, were characterized by a tendency, possibly ecological and/or political in origin, for a few such units to become much larger than the others. These larger units began a process of dominating and incorporating smaller units and their populations, a process that accelerated through time until one center, Teotihuacán, essen-

tially incorporated all the others and became the single state dominating the Basin and much of the central Mexican highlands (see also Marcus 1992a).

Sociopolitical organization, 900–100 B.C.

By the Early Terminal Formative period state-level sociopolitical organization had certainly emerged in the Basin of Mexico. The major problem is to determine the sociopolitical significance attached to the settlement clusters of the Late Middle Formative and Late Formative periods. As noted above, Earle proposes a chiefdom level of organization for the Late Formative clusters, as does Spencer, who suggests that the fast growth of Teotihuacán and Cuicuilco "was beginning to approach the operational limits of a chiefly political economy" and that the development of state organization during the Terminal Formative period involved a rapid change in administrative structures (1990:20). Brumfiel suggests some type of undefined pre-state organization for the larger sites (1976b:247), and Steponaitis argues for the evolution of increasingly more comprehensive forms of sociopolitical organization during the Late Formative without ever saying what they might be (1981:346). Drennan concludes that chiefdoms do not continue beyond the Late Formative period in the Basin of Mexico and that Middle and Late Formative developments represent only one of several possible trajectories of chiefdom formation (1991:272). Bennyhoff even suggests that Late Formative Cuicuilco "may well represent the first city-state in the Valley of Mexico" (1967:21).

During the late 1960s and the 1970s, the concept of the chiefdom was proposed as an intermediate stage between egalitarian societies and states/civilizations in the Basin of Mexico (e.g., Sanders and Price 1968; Sanders et al. 1979; Santley 1977). In his research at the Late Formative site of Loma Torremote, Santley concluded that the architecture, the distribution of artifacts, and the burial patterns were consistent with a model of ranked lineages, which he likened to a Polynesian *ramage* system and complex chiefdom organization (Sanders et al. 1979:328; Santley 1977:358–359). Although he noted that the sumptuary rules at Loma Torremote, as evidenced in burial goods, did not adequately isolate chiefly persons and mark their higher status (Sanders et al. 1979:330; Santley 1977:359), Santley argued that the limited mortuary data from other sites in the northern Basin did support a model of hierarchical regional polities, as indicated by the settlement-pattern data (1977:409–410).

The main problems with the application of the chiefdom concept to Late Middle Formative and Late Formative Basin of Mexico sociopolitical units are to be found in the absence, with few exceptions (Tolstoy 1989a), of the usual archaeological manifestations (funerary monuments or monumental ceremonial architecture) of a complex chiefdom's ideology and economic redistribution (cf. Sanders and Webster 1978; Santley 1984). Subsequent states in the Basin—as in Mesopotamia—do not seem to build on or incorporate antecedent chiefdom structures (Yoffee 1993a; see Wright 1994 for an alternative position). Sanders and Webster (1978) and Santley (1984, 1993) have subsequently proposed a scenario similar to that recently elaborated by Binford (1983:214–232) and Yoffee (1993a) where states in the Basin developed from stratified polities that formed in the context of tribal "big-man" organizations. Status in such organizations is based on achievement and patron-client relations; rank and status in chiefdoms are ascribed according to kinship organization.

Sanders and his colleagues argue that states can develop from stratified societies without an intervening chiefdom stage (Sanders and Webster 1978:282; Santley 1984, 1993). Stratified societies are those with economic stratification but without the institutions—social, economic, religious, or political—that maintain stratification in states (Webster, this volume). In support of their argument, Sanders and Webster note the absence of tombs and funerary cults—characteristics of complex chiefdoms elsewhere in Mesoamerica (Flannery and Marcus 1994; Sharer and Grove 1989)—at Late Formative centers such as Cuicuilco. The Late Formative regional settlement hierarchy documented by Steponaitis and Earle could be the signature of either a stratified society (cf. Bennyhoff 1967) or a complex chiefdom. Internal features of their capitals should differentiate them from each other. Unfortunately, the currently available data from the regional centers are not adequate to resolve these questions.

Drennan (1991), noting the same problems, argues that the Basin of Mexico sequence and that of the Valley of Oaxaca represent one kind of trajectory for chiefdom development, where societies mobilized "resources toward public works programs designed to create communal ritual space" and "show modest internal economic differentiation in regard to wealth and status" along with "some signs of early economic

differentiation and interdependence" (1991:272). These features are contrasted with a trajectory for chiefdom development that "mobilized resources toward fierce status competition focused on the person of the chief" (Drennan 1991:272). The Olmecs, he argues, combined the characteristics of both trajectories.

Similarly Feinman (1995:267; see also Blanton et al. 1996:7) has recently argued that although craft specialization, long-distance trade, and status competition (elements of a "network mode" of political economy) were present in Formative period polities in the Basin, their political economies by the Late Formative tended to stress a "corporate mode" or strategy. This strategy "emphasizes collective ritual and its potential manipulation, public construction, integrated social segments, the importance of kinship affiliation, and relatively suppressed economic differentiation (more egalitarian access patterns)" (Feinman 1995:267).

Even taking into consideration the caveats regarding the nature and quality of the available data, it is obvious that significant political evolution continued during the Late Formative period (Steponaitis 1981: 346), elaborating the structure and forms present in the Late Middle Formative. This evolution of political structure involved an increase in the size of the polities and a disproportionate increase in the size of two of them, Cuicuilco and CH-5, both in the southern Basin. It is probable that the settlement-pattern changes reflect the evolution of structured economic and (probably) ideological interaction within polities that were lineage-based. Such economic differentiation between lineages and between individuals probably began with the development of a food-producing economy in the Basin of Mexico and is first noted in the Early Formative period.

There is no evidence for a highly elaborated ritual veneration of apical ancestors, for a complex system of ranked lineages, or for leadership/chiefdomship positions legitimized in the idiom of ancestors. There is, however, evidence for a recurrent theme in the ideology of chiefdoms, "symbols of individual position within a society as seen most vividly in the burials" (Earle 1987:299). These symbols are often manifested in material terms in foreign objects exchanged, sometimes over great distances, among high-status individuals for "the esoteric knowledge and power they embodied" (Earle 1987:299; Helms 1993:28–51; cf. Flannery and Marcus 1994:389, referring to the Early Formative).[6]

These Late Formative period societies were directly antecedent to the city-states of the Early Terminal Formative period. Since the previously noted pattern of one or more centers being larger than the others continues, we are confronted with a matrix of polities, without complete parity between units, a kind of *primus inter pares*, in which the large centers of Cuicuilco and Teotihuacán are the *primi*. Available data do not clearly indicate the reasons for such differences, although we suspect that locational advantage for trade and agricultural intensification were important, along with political factors that encouraged nucleation (Charlton 1984b; Nichols 1980, 1987, 1989). This tendency, coupled with subsequent particularistic historical events like the eruptions of Mount Xitle and the destruction of Cuicuilco, ends with the complete dominance of the Basin by one city-state, Teotihuacán.

Cycle I, Part 3: The city-state of Teotihuacán, Late Terminal Formative and Classic periods, 100 B.C.–A.D. 650/750

The stable period of Teotihuacán's unquestioned dominance in the Basin of Mexico (Figs. 11.6 and 11.7) and adjacent areas of central Mexico began about 100 B.C. and continued through the Classic period (Millon 1973, 1981, 1988, 1992; Parsons 1989:179–189; Sanders 1981:175–176; Sanders et al. 1979:105–129). This period is approximately equal in length to the period during which complex societies in the form of city-states first developed (Cycle I, Part 2, 900–100 B.C.).

Sanders and his colleagues have suggested that after the destruction of Cuicuilco by a volcanic eruption, which left Teotihuacán as the sole powerful polity in the Basin of Mexico, the Basin's overall population might have declined from 140,000 to 100,000/120,000 at the beginning of the Late Terminal Formative period (Parsons 1989:179, 183; Sanders 1981:175–176; Sanders et al. 1979:107). After the demise of Cuicuilco, there was probably also a resettlement of 80–90 percent of the population (80,000–94,000) in the city of Teotihuacán (Millon 1981:221–222, 1988:102, 1992:344, 351; Parsons 1989:183; Sanders 1981:157, 176–178; and Sanders et al. 1979:114). The Basin's population subsequently increased to about 230,000 and remained, as far as can be ascertained, at approximately this level through the Classic period (Parsons 1989:179, 183; Sanders 1981:157,

175–176; Sanders et al. 1979:107). The city of Teotihuacán's population grew to between 125,000 and 150,000 (Millon 1988:102, 1992:344; Parsons 1989:183; Sanders 1981:157). However, the proportion of the Basin's population resident at Teotihuacán declined from 80–90 percent to 50–65 percent as a result of a very rapid, selective repopulation and resettlement of the Basin directed by Teotihuacán at the beginning of the Classic period (Parsons 1989:183; Sanders et al. 1979:114; Millon 1981:219–222, 1988:103). The dominance and power of the Teotihuacán polity is reflected, first, in the extreme nucleation of the population during the Late Terminal Formative period (Fig. 11.6) and, subsequently, by the massive reorganization of the city and the structured reoccupation of the Basin and adjacent portions of the central plateau (Figs. 11.7, 11.8; Manzanilla 1995:156; Millon 1988:103; Sanders et al. 1979:114, map 20).

Teotihuacán as a City-State

The tendencies of the proto-urban and urban components of earlier settlement patterns in the Basin of Mexico to increase disproportionately in size by incorporating people from other settlements culminate in Teotihuacán's concentration of almost all the Basin's population in the city at the beginning of the Late Terminal Formative period. This action, along with the subsequent redistribution of population at the beginning of the Classic period, reflects the extent to which the Teotihuacán state had control over people in the Basin as well as in a larger region (Millon 1988:136–142). Such control extended to inner as well as outer hinterlands in central Mexico, some 25,000 square kilometers in extent, with a total population of 300,000–500,000 (Millon 1981:219–223, 228, 1988:113–114).

The evidence for population relocation and control, the massive construction program at Teotihuacán (Millon 1973:51–54, 1988:110–113, 1992:351; Millon et al. 1965), the evidence of continued urban planning and building, and the extension of power well outside the Basin of Mexico (Millon 1981:212, 214–217, 221, 1988:1992) attest to the existence of a state system no later than the beginning of the Late Terminal Formative period and its persistence to the final collapse (Millon 1988:110–113, 136–137). We suspect that stratified state systems were probably present in the Basin of Mexico at least as early as the Late Formative period, as indicated by the two re-

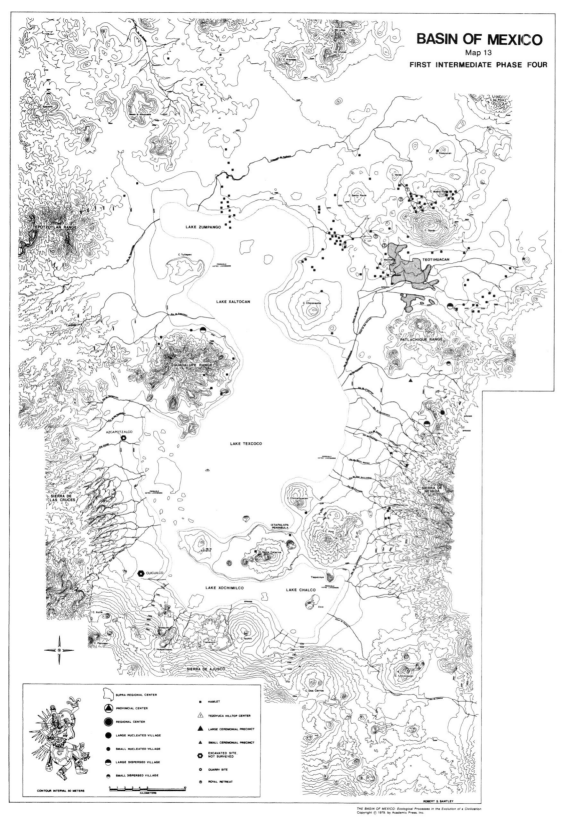

Figure 11.6. Basin of Mexico Late Terminal Formative settlement patterns. From Sanders et al. (1979:map 13, First Intermediate Phase Four). Reprinted with permission of Academic Press and the authors.

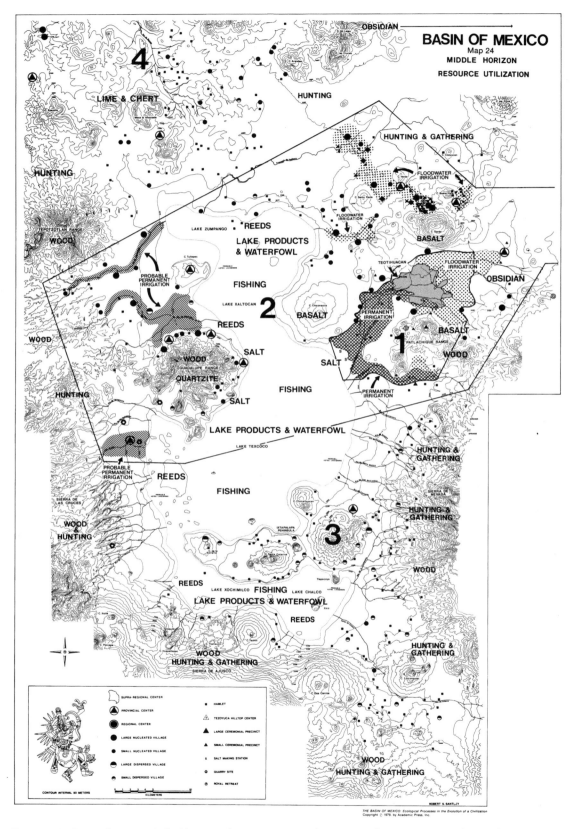

Figure 11.7. Basin of Mexico Early Classic settlement patterns and resource utilization. From Sanders et al. (1979:map 24, Middle Horizon resource utilization). Reprinted with permission of Academic Press and the authors.

Map 20
CENTRAL MEXICAN SYMBIOTIC REGION
MIDDLE HORIZON SETTLEMENT

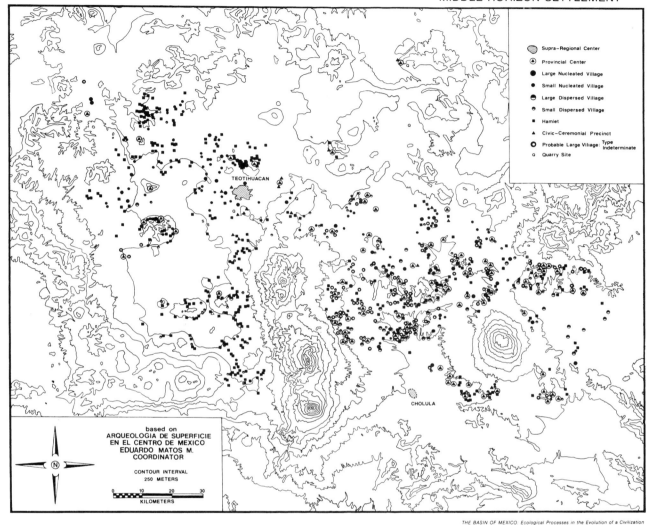

Figure 11.8. Central Mexican Teotihuacán settlement system. From Sanders et al. (1979:map 20, Central Mexican Symbiotic Region Middle Horizon settlement). Reprinted with permission of Academic Press and the authors.

gional city-state systems of Cuicuilco and Teotihuacán, which integrated between them most of the smaller polities in the Basin.

Although class stratification is documented at Teotihuacán, details on the early period and the highest and lowest classes are not well known (Cowgill 1993; Millon 1981:212–217, 1992; Sempowski 1994; Spence 1994). Recent research at the Temple of the Feathered Serpent has provided additional information on the power actualized by the top leader(s) at Teotihuacán (Cabrera Castro et al. 1989, 1991; Cabrera Castro and Cabrera 1991; Cowgill and Ca-

brera 1991; Serrano Sánchez 1993; Serrano Sánchez et al. 1991; Sugiyama 1991, 1992). However, there are no "identifiable, recognizable portraits or idealized representations of the individuals at the very top" (Millon 1981:213). Millon has proposed that, after the sacrifices in the Temple of the Feathered Serpent were made, individual rulership effectively became collective leadership, remaining so until the end of Teotihuacán (1992:340; but see also Grove 1994).

It is our argument that Teotihuacán, a single, regionally dominant city-state with enormous inner and outer hinterlands, represents the logical outcome, *reductio ad absurdum,* of the operation of basic principles of growth and integration guiding cultural evolution in the Basin of Mexico (Kroeber 1944), beginning in the Early Formative. Sanders and his colleagues state that their "model for the . . . [Classic period] is that of a single, highly evolved polity that had complete control over its immediate hinterland" (1979:127). Millon would include the outer hinterlands as well (1992:222–223). Sanders and his colleagues go on to describe this regional state as an unsound, inefficient, but long-lived primate system (1979:127–128).

All the evidence recovered to date points to a highly centralized Teotihuacán state system with effective wielders of power located in the city of Teotihuacán. The success of Teotihuacán in eliminating rivals and extending control over a large area would seem to preclude it from being considered a city-state according to Trigger's definition (1993:8–14; cf. Renfrew 1986a), which necessitates a city-state being in a network of adjacent, competitive city-states. Teotihuacán still retained some aspects of a city-state, albeit a gargantuan one, without an immediate network of independent polities within which to interact. These include a heavily urbanized, extremely large population consisting of all segments of society, food producers and nonfood producers, an emphasis on urban craft production for both rural and urban sectors of society, an intensification of agricultural production near the city, an economic system integrating rural and urban sectors, and widely shared ideological symbols (Trigger 1993). However, some other characteristics are suggestive of a territorial state, as defined by Trigger: territorial extent, early monumentality of construction, and a "hierarchy of administrative centers" (even though distorted by a disproportionately large number of people, food producers and craft specialists living at Teotihuacán, the top of the hierarchy).

In our opinion, Teotihuacán is an example of a city-state whose singular evolution continued in a context lacking significant equivalent rivals and possessing a relatively low regional population density, one that persisted until the Late Postclassic period (Sanders 1981). The mechanisms—ideological, political, economic, social structural—that underwrote Teotihuacán's centripetal integration and organization of central Mexico and the populations of its hinterlands are imperfectly known, both for Teotihuacán and for the surrounding regions. As far as we can tell, however, they persisted to the end of Classic period,

when the extreme centralization characteristic of Teotihuacán broke down, never to appear again in the same configuration.

Cycle II: Epi-Teotihuacán and Early Postclassic periods, A.D. 650/750–1150

The development of the state (Teotihuacán in central Mexico), created a precondition for later state formation (Bray 1977:394; cf. Kohl 1987:30 on the Near East). The processes of state formation in central Mexico after Teotihuacán were not identical to those leading to Teotihuacán, in part because the knowledge and memory of Teotihuacán had created a cultural context previously unknown and in part because the breakup of Teotihuacán initiated processes previously unknown or of minor importance. These processes, which included warfare and tributary-state formation, were initially strongest in areas outside of, but adjacent to, the Basin of Mexico. It is probable that the militaristic tributary state began to develop in those areas during the Epi-Teotihuacán period. Once in operation, these processes were influential in the rise of two successive macroregional states, Tula (Cycle II, Part 2) and Tenochtitlán (Cycle III, Part 2).

In many aspects, the events of Cycle II foreshadow those of Cycle III (A.D. 1150–1521). Each cycle consisted of two parts, one of multiple, small, independent polities, the other of large integrative structures (Charlton 1973:421; Sanders 1981:186). Characteristic of Part 1 (Epi-Classic or Epi-Teotihuacán) of Cycle II, following the end of Teotihuacán but prior to the rise of Tula, were population movements and the establishment of small independent sociopolitical units in the Basin of Mexico and in adjacent areas of central Mexico (Figs. 11.9 and 11.10; Diehl and Berlo 1989:3–4).

These sociopolitical units were probably equivalent to the city-states (*altepetl,* Hodge, this volume) encountered by the Spaniards in central Mexico in A.D. 1519 (Bray 1972a). The Epi-Teotihuacán period, between 200 and 250 years in length, ended with the rise of Tula as the first new major post-Teotihuacán state system in central Mexico. Over the next 200–250 years, Tula integrated much of central Mexico (Figs. 11.11 and 11.12) and influenced distant areas of Mesoamerica such as Yucatan (Charlton 1973, 1975, 1978; Diehl 1981, 1983, 1993; Healan 1989; Marcus 1989, 1992a:398–399; Sanders 1981:186; Sanders et al. 1979:129–149; Smith 1992a:55–56).

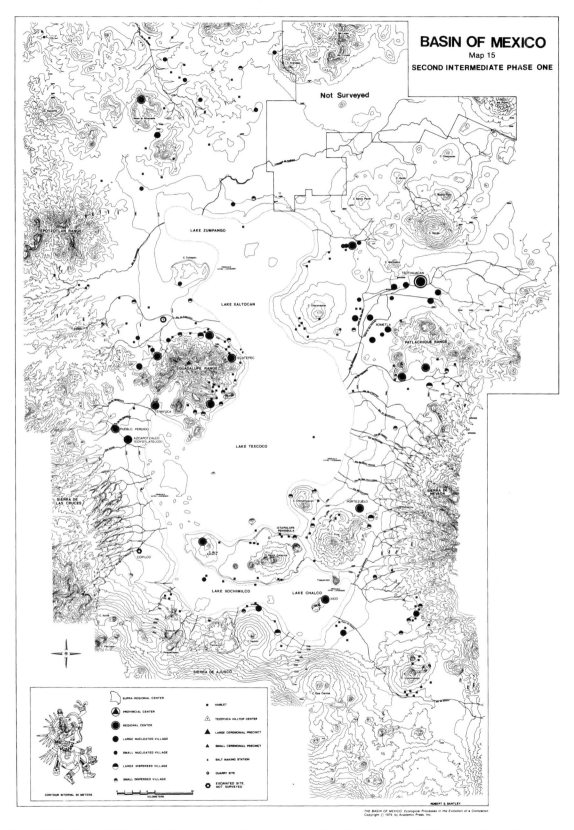

Figure 11.9. Basin of Mexico Epi-Teotihuacán settlement patterns. From Sanders et al. (1979:map 15, Second Intermediate Phase One). Reprinted with permission of Academic Press and the authors.

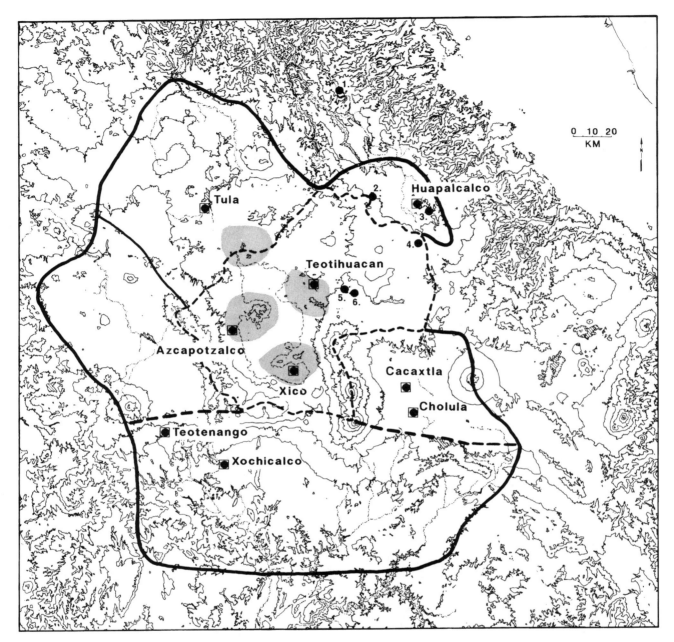

Figure 11.10. Central Mexican Epi-Teotihuacán settlement patterns. (1–6 obsidian source areas.) Contour interval 500 meters. Base map derived from the Detenal 1:250,000 Series maps NE 14–1 to NE 14–3 (1970), NE 14–4 to NE 14–6 (1976), and NF 14–10 to NE 14–12 (1970). Shaded areas in the Basin of Mexico approximate continuous settlement (Sanders et al. 1979:map 15). Drawn by Cynthia L. Otis Charlton.

Cycle II, Part 1: Epi-Teotihuacán (Early Toltec) period, A.D. 650/750–900/950

The chronological and settlement pattern frameworks we are using for the two indigenous post-Teotihuacán cycles (II and III) are ultimately based on changes in ceramic complexes. A recent series of excavations has provided an opportunity to evaluate and refine the archaeological chronology with absolute dates. Ac-

cording to Parsons and his colleagues, some of the later ceramic complexes, such as Mazapan (Late Toltec period, A.D. 900/950–1150) and Aztec I (Early Aztec period, A.D. 1150–1350/1430), may actually have begun during the Epi-Teotihuacán period (1996). A further complication is to be found in the possibility that the Coyotlatelco ceramic complex, diagnostic of occupations of the immediate post-Teotihuacán period (A.D. 650/750–900/950), may, in

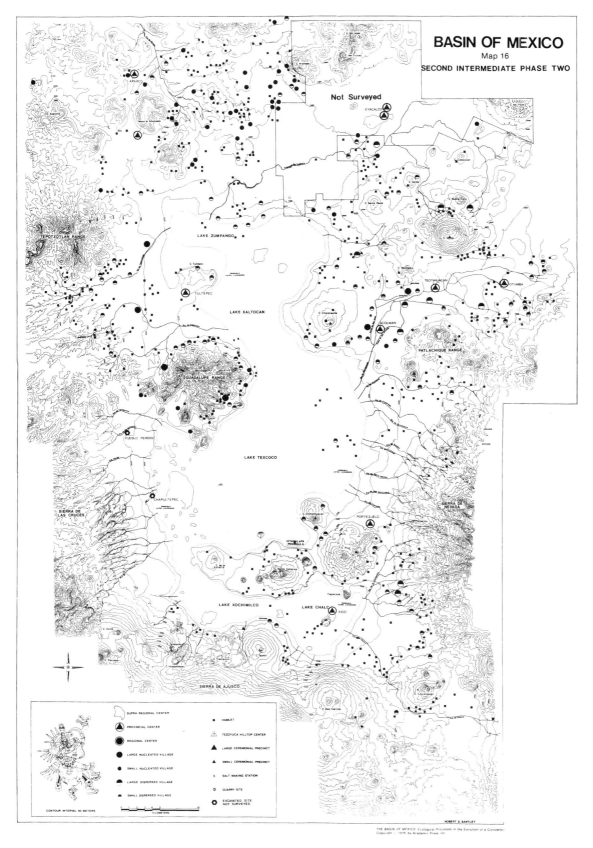

Figure 11.11. Basin of Mexico Late Toltec settlement patterns. From Sanders et al. (1979:map 16, Second Intermediate Phase Two). Reprinted with permission of Academic Press and the authors.

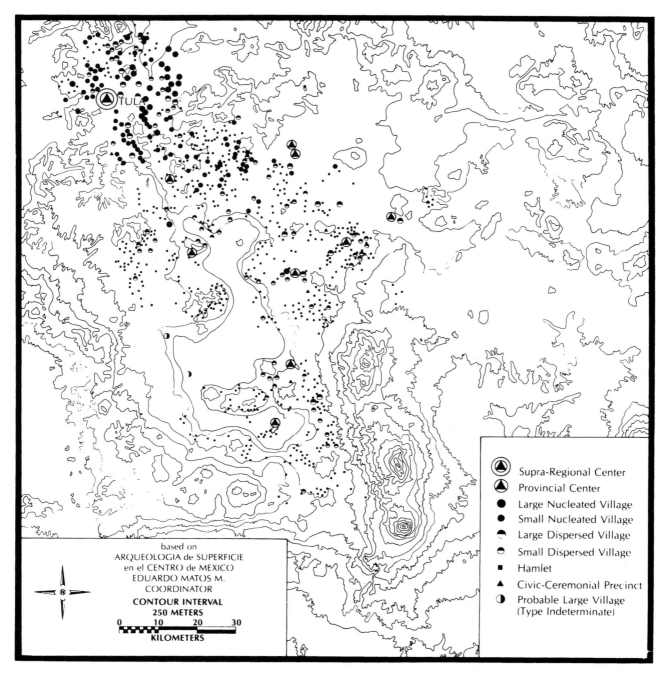

Figure 11.12. Central Mexico, Late Toltec settlement patterns. Figure 11.4, William T. Sanders and Robert Santley, "A Tale of Three Cities: Energetics and Urbanization in Pre-Hispanic Central Mexico," in Evon Z. Vogt and Richard M. Leventhal, eds., *Prehistoric Settlement Patterns: Essays in Honor of Gordon R. Willey,* University of New Mexico Press and Peabody Museum of Archaeology and Ethnology, Harvard University. Copyright 1983 by the President and Fellows of Harvard College.

some subregional contexts, be contemporary with the last century of Teotihuacán's dominance (ca. A.D. 650–750) and persist from then until the emergence of Tula. Radiocarbon dates for Teotihuacán published by Rattray suggest that this apparent contemporaneity with Teotihuacán may not exist (1991), as the Late Classic occupation (Metepec phase) at Teoti-

huacán may have ended by A.D. 650. The cycles we propose here, especially their duration and beginning and ending dates, may need modification as additional dates clarify what is apparently a most complex period.

The Epi-Teotihuacán period involved both continuity and discontinuity with Teotihuacán (Charlton

1973, 1975, 1991; Diehl and Berlo 1989:3). The continuities—in population, settlement locations, settlement patterns, and degree of urbanization—are strongest within the Basin of Mexico. Many sites continue to be occupied from the preceding period, while others appear to have been founded by migrants from Teotihuacán (Charlton 1973, 1975, 1991; Diehl 1989:16; Parsons 1970, 1971:202, 1989: 189–195; Sanders et al. 1979:130). The collapse of the Teotihuacán city-state system is marked archaeologically by an overall population decline at Teotihuacán and throughout the Basin; (1) from about 250,000 to 175,000 (Diehl 1989:13) or (2) from about 230,000 to 115,000/117,000 (Parsons 1989: 189–191; Sanders 1981:157; Sanders et al. 1979: 129–137).

Within the Basin, population is distributed in highly urbanized settlement clusters of unequal sizes within restricted zones. The realignment of population, the configuration of the settlement clusters, their environmental location, and their spatial separation, taken together, suggest the emergence of independent city-states in areas with agricultural lands having the best access to moisture (springs, streams, lake, high water table, flood water, direct rainfall) and possibly associated with the introduction of *chinampa* (raised field) agriculture in the southern Basin (Alden 1979; Blanton 1975; Charlton 1973, 1975; Diehl 1989; Parsons 1989:189–193; Sanders 1981:184, 186; Sanders et al. 1979:129–37). The relations between these new city-states may have been peaceful, with integrative economic structures responsible for the distribution of the Coyotlatelco ceramic complex. Some have suggested that mutual hostility was basic to their interrelationships, citing the spatial separation and the location of regional centers (Alden 1979; Blanton 1975; Blanton et al. 1993:138; Parsons 1989:193; and Sanders et al. 1979:133). Only one of the regional centers (Zumpango cluster), however, is located on a defensible hilltop. No additional evidence for warfare or hostilities—for example, fortresses, outposts, fortifications, and weapons—has been reported (Charlton 1973:415).

We are uncertain of the processes involved in the devolution and fragmentation of the Teotihuacán polity, the loss of population, the source(s) of new populations (if any), and the relocation of those people and the existing populations in the Basin. In the northern part of the Basin, the Teotihuacán, Cuauhtitlán and Zumpango areas, which had substantial Classic period populations, declined in population; other areas

to the south with Epi-Teotihuacán period occupations gained population after the Classic period (Charlton 1973, 1975; Diehl 1989; Parsons 1989: 189–191; Sanders 1981; Sanders et al. 1979:129).

In the northern Basin, three settlement clusters have been defined ranging in size from 5,500 to 78,000 (Fig. 11.9; Charlton 1975; Sanders et al. 1979:129–131; Parsons 1989:189, 191). These are the Teotihuacán Valley cluster, including settlements in the Texcoco area (population estimated at 78,000 [Parsons 1989:191], and 75,000–80,000 [Sanders et al. 1979: 130]), the Tenayuca-Cuauhtitlán or Guadalupe cluster (population estimate from 12,000 [Parsons 1989:191] to 20,000 [Sanders et al. 1979:131]), and the Zumpango cluster (population estimated from 5,500 [Sanders et al. 1979:131] to 6,400 [Parsons 1989:191]). These clusters are separated from each other by apparently unoccupied land, making their delineation relatively easy.

In the southern Basin, there tends to be more continuous occupation within a relatively extensive zone of Early Toltec period settlement (Charlton 1975; Parsons 1989:193), with "three or four substantial regional centers, spaced between 7 and 15 km apart" (Sanders et al. 1979:130). Sanders et al. (1979:130–132) and Parsons (1989:191) have divided this occupation into three clusters[7]—the Portesuelo cluster (population estimated at 12,000 [Sanders et al. 1979: 132]), the Cerro de la Estrella cluster (population estimated at 5,000 [Sanders et al. 1979:132]), and the Xico cluster (population estimated at 7,100–7,400 [Sanders et al. 1979:132]).

We argue that each settlement cluster, separated from other clusters by unoccupied lands or through nearest-neighbor analysis, represents an independent, separate, political unit, a city-state (Parsons 1989: 193). These clusters were of unequal size, both in terms of total population and in terms of percentage of population living in urban settlements, a situation similar to the pre-state Formative period political units and to the later Early Aztec city-states (Cycle III, Part 1). Although Teotihuacán had lost a substantial portion of its population, it remained the largest Early Toltec urban settlement and fell within the largest settlement cluster in the Basin. The Teotihuacán cluster is physically separate from the others (Fig. 11.9). The proximity of the southern clusters to each other might indicate a confederacy type of relationship such as is found among the much later Early Aztec city-states.

Outside the Basin, but in immediately adjacent

areas (Fig. 11.10), new regional centers, city-states, developed at the same time that the Basin of Mexico's settlement and political structures were changing. These new centers were frequently, but not always, located in naturally defensible positions, such as hilltops, and they were enhanced by walls, ditches, and earthworks (e.g., Xochicalco in Morelos [Hirth 1984a, 1989; Hirth and Guillén 1988], Cacaxtla in Tlaxcala [García Cook 1981:269–270], Teotenango in the Valley of Toluca [Piña Chan 1975], and various sites in the Mezquital Valley [Mastache and Cobean 1989]). Along with others such as Cholula in Puebla (Dumond and Müller 1972; Marquina 1970; McCafferty 1996) and Huapalcalco in the Tulancingo Valley (Müller 1963), they "developed local styles in ceramics, architecture, iconography, and other cultural elements, styles which suggest the presence of new ethnic groups or radical changes in the older cultural traditions" (Mastache and Cobean 1989:55; see also Jiménez Moreno 1966:59–80; Nagao 1989).

The relationships between the city-states within and without the Basin of Mexico are not clear. The Coyotlatelco ceramic complex is shared by many of the surrounding city-states but not by Xochicalco, Huapalcalco, or Cholula. The pattern of Teotihuacán-derived city-states within the Basin and the development of militaristic, warring, competitive city-states in many of the surrounding areas provided the matrix within which the new forms of state organization and expansion developed.

Cycle II, Part 2: The city-state of Tula, Early Postclassic (Late Toltec) period, A.D. 900/950–1150

The political fragmentation and economic decentralization that followed Teotihuacán throughout Central Mexico was resolved briefly, first through the militaristic state of Tula (Figs. 11.11–11.13) and then, following a second period of political fragmentation after Tula's demise (Fig. 11.14), by the expansion of the Aztecs (Figs. 11.15–11.16). During the Late Postclassic period, the Epi-Teotihuacán city-states of the Mezquital Valley and the Basin of Mexico became incorporated into the Tula macroregional city-state (Fig. 11.12). This is the first example of a macroregional city-state reconstituted within the continuum of secondary-state formation processes leading from Teotihuacán to Tenochtitlán. Developments elsewhere are less clear. Xochicalco, Cacaxtla, and Huapalcalco were abandoned. Cholula and Teote-

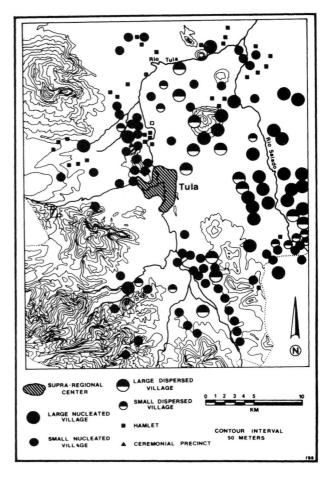

Figure 11.13. Tula Region, Late Toltec settlement patterns. From Sanders et al. (1979: 144, figure 5.10, The Tula Region, Second Intermediate Phase Two). Reprinted with permission of Academic Press and the authors.

nango continued, possibly representing state systems similar in size and complexity to that centered at Tula.

The Toltec city-state, centered at the city of Tula in the Mezquital Valley northwest of the Basin of Mexico, does not replicate Teotihuacán (Diehl 1981, 1983; Healan 1989; Matos M. 1974, 1976; Sanders et al. 1979:137–149; Sanders and Santley 1983). Tula's grandeur in size, planning, art, and architecture did not equal those of its predecessor, Teotihuacán, or its successor, Tenochtitlán (Diehl 1983:67, 118; Healan 1989:6; Healan et al. 1989:245–249). This situation may be due to Tula's short duration of 200–250 years (Sanders et al. 1979:146). Yet Teotihuacán was quite large and architecturally grand early in its history, so new factors of integration may have been at work in Tula (Blanton et al. 1993:139–142; Sanders et al. 1979:146).

The population resident in Tula has been variably

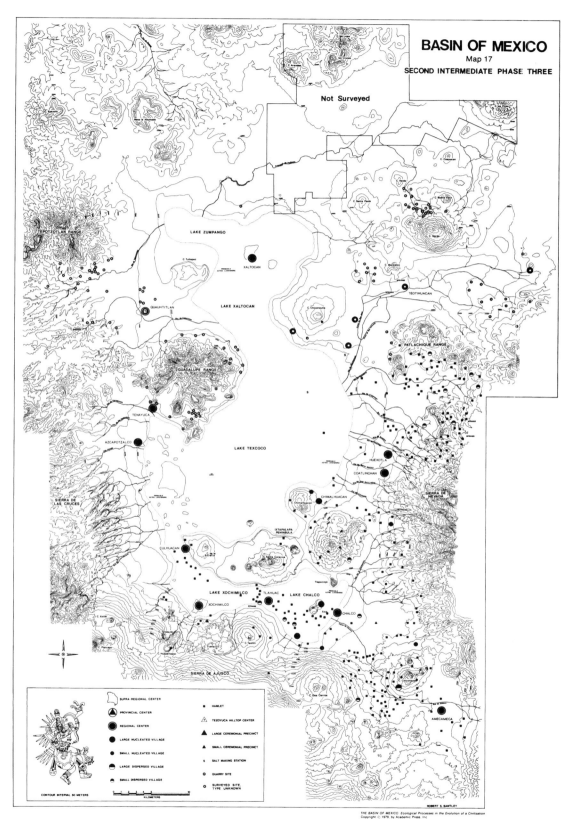

Figure 11.14. Basin of Mexico Early Aztec settlement patterns. From Sanders et al. (1979:map 17, Second Intermediate Phase Three). Reprinted with permission of Academic Press and the authors.

estimated as falling between 32,000 and 60,000 (Diehl 1981:284, 1983:58; Sanders et al. 1979: 141; Sanders 1981:186; Healan and Stoutamire 1989:235). Although the city of Tula was smaller by half than Teotihuacán, there was a substantial concentration of population within a 20-kilometer radius of Tula (Table 11.4). Sanders and his colleagues suggest that there were as many as 60,000 inhabitants in the area immediately around Tula (Figs. 11.12 and 11.13; 1979:142–143), raising the total urban and immediately adjacent population in the Mezquital Valley to about 120,000. If this were taken as Tula's urban population, then Tula had approximately the same size population as Teotihuacán (Sanders et al. 1979:144–145; Sanders 1981:186). Tula's "urban" population, according to this definition, was more widely dispersed than Teotihuacán's, although it was probably still associated with a nucleation of political and economic functions and an urban-rural settlement dichotomy (Blanton et al. 1993:142; Parsons 1989:195–200; Sanders et al. 1979:137–149).

There are four settlement and demographic trends that reflect the incorporation of the Basin into the city-state of Tula. First, the range of settlement types within the Basin, and presumably the range of state functions performed outside Tula, was reduced. Hamlets and small dispersed villages were emphasized, particularly in the south, and large nucleated communities were more common in the north (Charlton 1973:417, 420; Sanders et al. 1979:138). This resulted in the most extreme ruralization of the Basin's prehispanic population (Parsons 1989:195; Sanders et al. 1979:138).

Second, population density increases from south to north in the Basin and is highest in the northwest. Population density continues to increase to the north within the Mezquital Valley in the area around Tula (Figs. 11.11–11.13; Parsons 1989:195; Sanders et al. 1979:140). "The growth of the center of Tula apparently acted as an enormous magnet, pulling the rural population of the Basin in the northwesterly direction" (Sanders et al. 1979:141; see also Charlton 1973:420–421).

Third, within the Basin, areas previously abandoned were now populous, reflecting a redistribution of population within the Toltec state system (Sanders et al. 1979:140).

Fourth, the Basin's population, from the Epi-Teotihuacán period to the Early Postclassic period, might have undergone a slight decrease (from 115,000 to 92,000 persons [Parsons 1989:197]) or have remained level (115,000 to 120,000 persons [Sanders 1981; Sanders et al. 1979]). If the Tula-area population is added to that of the Basin, then the combined total would be equivalent to the Classic period population of the same two areas, about 250,000 within the core and immediate hinterlands (Sanders 1981:186; Sanders et al. 1979:186). This would give the Teotihuacán city-state and the Tula city-state equivalent populations of about 250,000 each within their core and immediate hinterlands. If Tula's population were symmetrically arranged around the city, then surveys in areas not examined to date could alter this apparent equivalency (Sanders and Santley 1983: 269–270).

In addition to these settlement and demographic trends, Parsons has noted some patterns of interest in regional ceramic distributions (1989:197). In the northwestern, Zumpango region, the ceramic complex is closely related to that at Tula. In the central section of the Basin, from Teotihuacán to Ixtapalapa, the complex is similar to that (defined as Mazapan) from the Teotihuacán Valley. In the south, the Chalco-Xochimilco areas, the ceramics are a simplified version of the central Basin complex. The variations in regional settlement patterns (Figs. 11.11 and 11.12) and the variations in ceramic complexes might result from differences in local organization within the Toltec state or might even be correlated with a proposed political and economic frontier within the Basin between Cholula, to the south in the modern state of Puebla, and Tula to the north (Parsons 1989:198; Sanders et al. 1979:146–149)

The extent of the area under Tula's control has not yet been defined. On the basis of Figures 11.8 and 11.12 (Sanders and Santley 1983:263, 270), we suggest that Tula's control of central Mexico extended over an area at least equivalent to that probably controlled by Teotihuacán, about 25,000 square kilometers, albeit with a different areal emphasis. This area is much less than that indicated by Diehl (1983:118–120), which extends north from Xochicalco to a point north and east of Tula to an area south of El Tajín, and from there to the southwest around Cholula to a point east of Xochicalco.

Diehl has recently reexamined the evidence for a Toltec horizon throughout Mesoamerica. He argues for the existence of such a horizon, attributes its origins to the Toltecs of Tula, Hidalgo, and its spread to Toltec merchants (1993:263, 286–287). Calnek notes that the physical evidence for imperial control over distant areas is not obvious (1978:1007). Weaver suggests that Tula had limited integrated territory but an extended sphere of influence (1993:405). From an archaeological point of view, however, the Aztec empire would seem to be equally invisible (Umberger and Klein 1993).

Tula as a City-State

Tula's preeminence as a macroregional city-state in the Mezquital Valley and the immediately adjacent Basin of Mexico (Fig. 11.12) lasted only 200–250 years, a time span approximately equal in length to the preceding period, which was dominated by smaller, multiple city-states that formed in the wake of Teotihuacán's decline (Fig. 11.9). In one sense, the Tula city-state continued earlier (Cycle I) tendencies for proto-urban and urban settlements in the Basin of Mexico to increase disproportionately in size by incorporating people from other settlements. This trend culminated in Teotihuacán, continued on a reduced scale in the small Epi-Teotihuacán period city-states, and reemerged in a modified, less incorporative form with the development of Tula. The increase in population density and site complexity near Tula demonstrates the integrative force of the city-state and its control over the Mezquital Valley and the Basin of Mexico.

At the same time, however, the settlement system of the Tula city-state reflected changes in organization that differentiated it from Teotihuacán. The construction program at Tula was short-lived and not on as massive a scale as that at Teotihuacán. Urban planning is evident but not to the same extent as at Teotihuacán. Finally, agricultural producers were located outside Tula, not within the city, as at Teotihuacán (Sanders 1981:186). Healan and his colleagues describe the arrangement of residential compounds at Tula as being "looser"—less uniform—than at Teotihuacán (1989:251). This impressionistic description applies equally to the city-state settlement system. In the Basin, settlements were much more rural in character than they were during the Classic period and the population much more dispersed. More variation in residential structures and their arrangement and in the configuration of settlements might reflect the lack of direct state controls in many areas of life. At the same time, the city-state created a "Pax Tula" in which it was safe to live outside tightly nucleated settlements, at least within the area effectively controlled by the Tula city-state.

We propose that Tula—a large, regionally domi-

nant city-state with inner and outer hinterlands and populations equivalent in size to those of Teotihuacán—integrated areas of central Mexico economically, politically, and socially following a Teotihuacán model but with a less centralized primate system characteristic of the early Postclassic world (Blanton et al. 1993:142). As was the case under Teotihuacán's rule, there were no large provincial centers in the Basin, although the proportion of the population who lived in small centers was greater (Table 11.3). All the evidence points to a city-state system with the effective wielders of power centered in the city of Tula. Yet, as at Teotihuacán, there were no unambiguous examples of representations of the elite who were at the top of the Tula city-state. The success of the city-state of Tula in eliminating or profiting from the elimination of rivals (with the exceptions of Cholula and Teotenango?) and extending control over a large area would, as in the case of Teotihuacán, seem to preclude it from being considered a city-state if one accepts Trigger's definition that a city-state must be part of a network of adjacent competitive city-states (1993:8–14; cf. Renfrew 1986a).

Further research in the Valley of Toluca and in the Cholula region may yet demonstrate the presence of large, contemporary city-states at Teotenango and Cholula. Even without such data, however, it is reasonable to say that Tula did retain some aspects of a city-state as defined by Trigger—although Tula was a very large one, without an apparent immediate network of independent polities with which to interact. The characteristics include a substantial population of food producers and nonfood producers in an urbanized zone (Tula and the immediately surrounding area), an emphasis on urban craft production for both rural and urban sectors of society, an intensification of agricultural production near the city, an economic system integrating rural and urban sectors, and widely shared ideological symbols (Trigger 1993).

However, as noted for Teotihuacán, some other characteristics are suggestive of a territorial state (again following Trigger's definition)—territorial extent, early monumentality of construction (less developed at Tula than at Teotihuacán), and a "hierarchy of administrative centers," even though distorted by a large number of nonfood producers at Tula and food producers in the immediate hinterlands around Tula at the top of the hierarchy.

In our opinion, Tula, like Teotihuacán, is an example of a city-state whose evolution may have occurred in a context where nearby equivalent rivals were eliminated, their populations integrated, and where the regional population density was relatively low until the Late Postclassic period (Sanders 1981). The mechanisms (ideological, political, economic, social structural) that supported Tula's center-focused integration and organization of the population of a large section of central Mexico are imperfectly known, both in Tula and in the surrounding regions. So far as we can tell, however, such mechanisms developed out of the Teotihuacán-writ-small city-states of the Epi-Teotihuacán period and were ultimately based on Teotihuacán, although they underwent modifications related to the reduction of political power in the Postclassic period (Blanton et al. 1993: 212–213). There are some similarities to the Teotihuacán city-state, such as a generally primate settlement system (Blanton et al. 1993:141–142; Sanders et al. 1979:137–149), but the extreme centralization characteristic of Teotihuacán had broken down and never appeared again.

Cycle III: Middle and Late Postclassic Periods, A.D. 1150/1200–1521

Recent radiocarbon dates for the Basin of Mexico suggest that the Early Aztec ceramic complexes (Aztec I and II) that define the conventional archaeological chronology for the middle Postclassic period (Cycle III, Part 1, A.D. 1150/1200–1350/1430) might, in fact, have been partly contemporaneous with Tula (Parsons et al. 1996). For present purposes, however, we will follow Mastache and Cobean (1989:39) and use the date of A.D. 1150/1200 to mark the beginning of Cycle III.

The last half of the twelfth century saw the end of Tula as a major integrative, regionally based city-state and the beginning of the final cycle of preconquest cultural evolution in Central Mexico. Tula's demise set the stage for the events that led ultimately to the rise of Tenochtitlán. We argue that the processes of state formation in central Mexico after Tula were again modified, this time to include the memory and experiences of Tula in addition to those of Teotihuacán.

Emphasized in Cycle III (as noted in ethnohistoric and archaeological data) were population movements, ethnicity, dynastic struggles, intercity warfare, the militaristic tributary city-state, the organization of alliances and confederacies, imperial expansion, and intensification of economic specialization and exchange (Bray 1977; Brumfiel 1983; Brundage 1972;

Calnek 1982; Carrasco 1971a, 1971b; Davies 1973, 1987; Gibson 1964; Nicholson 1971, 1975, 1978; Smith 1983, 1984). The general structure and pattern of Cycle II events foreshadow those of Cycle III. One factor that clearly differentiates the two cycles, however, is the major population growth that occurred in Cycle III, Part 2 (A.D. 1430–1521), where population levels far exceeded any previously known in central Mexico (Sanders 1981:190). We believe that population growth, as well as absolute population size, are directly related to innovations in macroregional city-state organization.

Cycle III (A.D. 1150/1200–1521) consisted of two parts. Part 1, A.D. 1150/1200–1430, was characterized by the familiar multiple, small, independent polities (city-states), the development of limited warfare between them (A.D. 1250–1350), and the beginning of large, but structurally fragile, tributary empires headed by the city-states of the Acolhua and the Tepaneca (A.D. 1350–1430). In Part 2 of this cycle, A.D. 1430–1521, a single major polity or city-state, Tenochtitlán—initially with the help of less powerful allies, Tlacopán and Texcoco—integrated economically, politically, ideologically, and socially, *but not demographically,* numerous other city-states of varying sizes and distances from the center. The tributary city-state empire of the Aztecs, as described by the Spaniards, may be a late city-state development designed to accommodate large numbers of subject people without resettling them into a highly centralized administrative system such as probably existed in the city-states of Teotihuacán and, to a lesser extent, Tula.

The small city-states of Cycle III, Part 2, although integrated into a major city-state tributary empire headed by Tenochtitlán, retained most of their state functions in their local setting (Charlton 1973:421; Sanders 1981:190; Sanders et al. 1979:153–155; Smith and Berdan 1996:1–3). The physical incorporation of substantial percentages of the population into the city-state center, as at Teotihuacán, or into the center and the area immediately surrounding it, as at Tula, may have occurred in the environs of Tenochtitlán-Tlatelolco, where between 33 and 50 percent of the Basin's population resided. The rest of the population of the Late Aztec period Basin was organized and administered through semiautonomous city-states, each of which had substantial freedom of action in religious, economic, political, and social matters. Thus, for about ninety years, Tenochtitlán, picking up the mantle of Tula, integrated much of central Mexico with principles of population organization and administration that often did not co-opt local administration. The development of these new principles may be related to the substantial population increase in the Basin, which was between four and five times larger than that of either the Teotihuacán or Tula city-state (Figs. 11.15 and 11.16). Tenochtitlán extended its conquests and tributary empire out of central Mexico and reached distant areas of Mesoamerica, but with very limited administrative integration (Gibson 1971; Hassig 1988, 1992). This massive, indirectly ruled city-state tributary empire system was destroyed by the Spanish conquest in A.D. 1521.

Cycle III, Part 1: Middle Postclassic (Early Aztec) period, A.D. 1150/1200–1430

The processes involved in the devolution and fragmentation of the Tula polity and the correlated population movements are not clear. We do know that the Early Aztec period involved substantial population increase and relocation in the Basin of Mexico (Fig. 11.14; Parsons 1989:200–202; Sanders et al. 1979: 149–153) and an apparent abandonment of the Mezquital Valley. The population in the Basin of Mexico increased from about 92,000/120,000 to about 250,000 (Parsons 1989:202). Within the Basin, discontinuities in population size, settlement location, and settlement patterns, including the degree of urbanization, are quite marked (compare Figs. 11.11 and 11.14). Population growth occurred throughout the Basin but was greatest in the south and central regions. The ruralization of the Late Toltec period was reversed with the establishment of numerous nucleated centers (Parsons 1989:202).

By A.D. 1250, militaristically competitive city-states were present in the Basin (Hodge, this volume). The time depth of their militaristic nature is unclear, both in the documents and in the archaeological record. There is no evidence that settlements were situated in fortified locations similar to those of Xochicalco, Cacaxtla, and Teotenango, which developed following Teotihuacán's demise. Although descriptions of conflict figure prominently in the documents, defense does not seem to have been a factor in the location of settlements unless spacing reflects defensive considerations (cf. Alden 1979). Warfare was probably on a small scale, with very limited conflicts and conquests. The labor investment in fortifications was either not effective or, more probably, not cost-effective, when the costs incurred by losing such a

conflict, as well as the probable short duration of such a loss, were calculated.

During the second century after Tula's collapse (A.D. 1250–1350) the new regional populations built up small-scale conquest "empires," ephemeral and short-lived (Caso 1966), in the Basin of Mexico (Davies 1980; Sanders et al. 1979:149–153) and in surrounding regions. They were inherently unstable, dependent on alliances and leaders, both subject to change in unpredictable ways. Brumfiel presents a detailed synthesis of such instability in the Basin of Mexico during this period (1983:268–270).

Between A.D. 1250 and 1350, warfare apparently escalated to the point where two ethnic groups, the Acolhua—centered at Texcoco, Huexotla, and Coatlinchán, on the eastern side of the central Basin of Mexico—and the Tepaneca—centered at Tenayuca and Azcapotzalco, on the western side—began to embark on more extensive but no less fragile conquests. This escalation is the hallmark of the last part of the Early Aztec period, from A.D. 1350 to 1430. Its effects on the sociopolitical structure of the late fifteenth century were critical (Brumfiel 1983:270–273; Carrasco 1984; Davies 1980:240–247; Hassig 1988: 125–140; Offner 1979). The expansion of Azcapotzalco and Texcoco, for example, affected areas outside the Basin. Although there were excursions, alliances, confederacies, and conquests, Davies is probably correct in arguing that none of the regions was able to "burst its bounds" in its quest to conquer the others (1980:176). The major result was the establishment of the conditions that gave rise to the Triple Alliance of Texcoco, Tlacopán, and Tenochtitlán, dominated by Tenochtitlán.

Sanders and his colleages argue that the Early Aztec settlement patterns, based on the distribution of Aztec I and II ceramics (Fig. 11.14), reflect the political situation around A.D. 1400, when both the Acolhua and the Tepaneca had risen to power, but before the formation and expansion of the Triple Alliance (1979:151, map 17). The presence of two large sites on the west of Lake Texcoco (Tenayuca and Azcapotzalco) and two on the east (Coatlinchan and Huexotla), each pair with a population of 10,000–15,000, they feel, reflects the existence of these two polities. The smaller centers in the southern Basin, each with a population of about 5,000, probably "functioned as small regional centers, each of which dominated small tributary regions within the southern Basin" (Sanders et al. 1979:151; Parsons 1989:203). In this interpretation, the distribution of Aztec I and II ce-

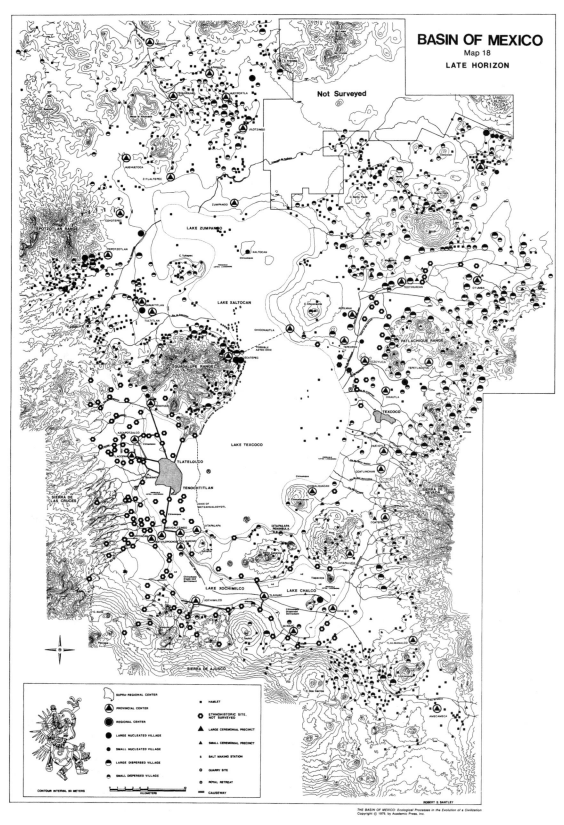

Figure 11.15. Basin of Mexico Late Aztec settlement pattern. From Sanders et al. (1979:map 18, Late Horizon). Reprinted with permission of Academic Press and the authors.

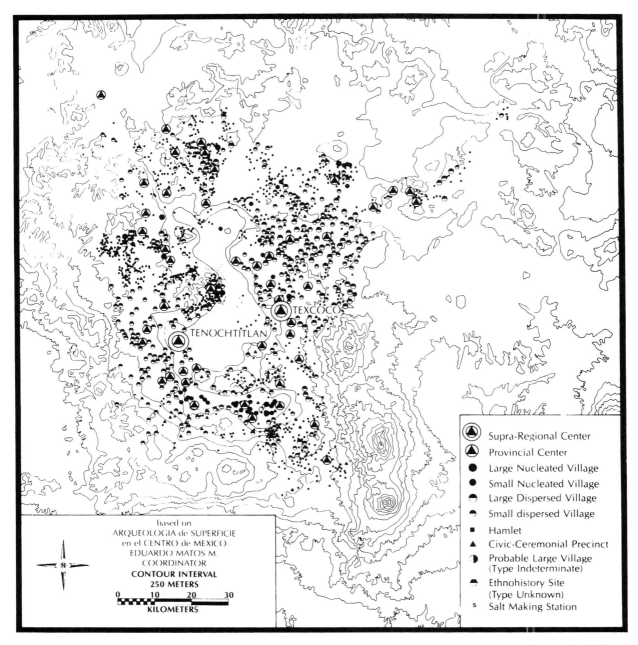

Figure 11.16. Central Mexico Late Aztec settlement system. Figure 11.5 in William T. Sanders and Robert Santley, "A Tale of Three Cities: Energetics and Urbanization in Pre-Hispanic Central Mexico," in Evon Z. Vogt and Richard M. Leventhal, eds., *Prehistoric Settlement Patterns: Essays in Honor of Gordon R. Willey,* University of New Mexico Press and Peabody Museum of Archaeology and Ethnology, Harvard University. Copyright 1983 by the President and Fellows of Harvard College.

ramics reflects the sociopolitical situation, not of A.D. 1350, prior to the rise of the Acolhua and the Tepaneca, but of about A.D. 1400, just prior to the momentous events of the first quarter of the fifteenth century. Alden's spatial analysis of some of the same settlement-pattern data from the eastern and southern Basin of Mexico also suggests that the distribution of Early Aztec ceramics reflects the sociopolitical

situation in the Basin in A.D. 1400 (1979:174–177).

Despite the obvious political fragmentation of this period, there exists good evidence for some persisting regional economic integration (Blanton 1996:62–67). This evidence includes the widespread Pachuca obsidian at Huexotla (Brumfiel 1976a, Table XXIX), near Chalco (Brumfiel 1986; Parsons et al. 1982: 155–157), and in Tenochtitlán (Reyes C. and García-

Bárcena 1979). Otumba obsidian was also widely distributed (Charlton and Spence 1983:69). In addition, the large number of cotton spindle whorls in Morelos (Norr 1987) and in the Basin at Huexotla and Xico (Brumfiel 1987:108) and Chalco (O'Neill 1962:214) may have been tied to an increase in cotton production and spinning to provide garments for newly emerging elites in the post-Tula Basin (Smith and Hirth 1988).

Smith (1983) and Hassig (1985:73) have suggested that the economic institution involved in the movement of goods at this time was the solar market, focused on each of the small city-states (see also Hodge, this volume; Blanton 1996:67). Local production and distribution within each city-state may have been the rule at this time (Nichols and Charlton 1988). Brumfiel found evidence at Huexotla for part-time nonagricultural specialization in spinning, salt production, ceramic figurines, spindle whorls, and censer decorations, all of which were distributed to regional consumers (1980:467).

Similar market systems probably occurred at this time throughout central Mexico. Goods such as obsidian, salt, and cotton entered each of these systems horizontally, and local craft and agricultural products circulated within them. Regional ratios of agricultural to nonagricultural production within each city-state varied, depending on local resources and the agricultural productivity of the land. Thus areas to the north in the Basin of Mexico, with obsidian resources and reduced agricultural potential, would have had a heavier emphasis on nonagricultural production than areas in the central and southern Basin (Nichols and Charlton 1988).

In the southern Basin of Mexico, agricultural intensification was under way with the construction of chinampas (Parsons 1989:202; Parsons et al. 1982; Parsons et al. 1985). These developments are important, for they, along with later constructions, provided a major source of food for a rapidly growing population in the Basin of Mexico and underwrote, in part, the later expansion of the Triple Alliance (cf. Parsons 1976:247–248). They may be related to the increase in population in the southern Basin at this time.

Within the Basin of Mexico, Texcoco and its allies were defeated by Azcapotzalco in A.D. 1418. During the following decade, there was a falling out between the Aztecs (Mexica) of Tenochtitlán and the Tepaneca of Azcapotzalco. When Tezozomoc, the long-lived ruler of the Tepaneca, died in A.D. 1427, war broke out. The Aztecs, allied with a Tepaneca tributary, Tlacopán, the defeated Acolhua, and the Acolhua allies, Tlaxcala and Huejotzingo, conquered the Tepaneca one year later (Brumfiel 1983:271–274; Davies 1980: 302–316; Hassig 1988:136–147).

Until the fall of Azcapotzalco, the hegemony of any city-state, large or small, rested on an "unstable complex of payoffs and alliances" (Brumfiel 1983:271). Brumfiel argues convincingly that the growth and decline of Azcapotzalco destroyed the local noble houses, causing succession crises, precluding the formation of alliances, and reducing or eliminating resistance to the Triple Alliance of Tenochtitlán, Tlacopán, and Texcoco (1983:271–273). Ability became a factor in succession, changing a strict filial system to a fraternal system (Hassig 1988:141; Rounds 1982: 83–84). Finally, the ruler and nobles acquired direct control over conquered lands and tribute rights (Brumfiel 1983:275–276; Hassig 1988:145–147). These changes, plus the ideology of war for sacrificial victims (Conrad and Demarest 1984:44), have been cited as significant for the period of expansion between A.D. 1430 and 1519.

Cycle III, Part 2: The city-state of Tenochtitlán, Late Postclassic (Late Aztec) period, A.D. 1430–1521

Historically and archaeologically this interval represents the best-known period within central Mexico, a period of conquest-based expansion and integration (Bray 1977:378). The quantity and quality of the archaeological data available for this period are impressive (as summarized by Hodge and Smith 1994; Sanders et al. 1979:153–181, maps 18–19; and Sanders and Santley 1983:271–279).

The settlement surveys of the Basin clearly demonstrate a massive population increase by the last century before the conquest (Figs. 11.15 and 11.16; Parsons 1989:205–213; Sanders 1981:189–194; Sanders and Santley 1983:271–276; Sanders et al. 1979:153–181). The population of about 250,000 during the first part of Cycle III rises to 800,000–1,200,000 in the second part of the cycle. The basic sociopolitical unit continued to be the city-state, but it was present in much greater numbers and in some instances was much larger than previously (Parsons 1989:210; Sanders et al. 1979:154). Sanders and his colleagues suggest that these city-states fell into several categories based on the size of their urbanized population from small, 3,000–4,000, to very large, 150,000–

200,000 in the case of Tenochtitlán and Tlatelolco (Sanders et al. 1979:154–155; Sanders 1981:189–190; Hodge, this volume, 1984).

Within the Basin, Tenochtitlán and its allies employed the tributary city-state model to integrate all city-states into what was essentially a single polity, but one without the massive population relocation and settlement restructuring characteristic of Tula and Teotihuacán. The occupation of the Basin was very intensive. Many new settlements, including city-state capitals, possibly as administrative centers, along with villages and hamlets, were founded in previously unoccupied areas (Sanders et al. 1979:156). Although some Early Aztec political centers continued as important centers in their respective areas, the Triple Alliance capitals—Texcoco, Tlacopán, and Tenochtitlán-Tlatelolco—were all founded in areas with little or no previous occupation, possibly denoting a break with earlier administrative models (Sanders et al. 1979:155).

The most intensive occupation of the Basin was a concentration of "between 300,000 and 400,000 people . . . in a block of 400 square kilometers along the western shores and within Lakes Texcoco and Xochimilco" (Sanders and Santley 1983:274; see also Sanders 1981:190; Sanders et al. 1979:163). Such a concentration, well beyond levels previously reached at Teotihuacán and Tula, was possible because of the canoe, which was used to supply the city (Sanders and Santley 1983:274–279; Sanders et al. 1979:176).

Unlike the settlement systems associated with Teotihuacán or Tula, which were primate in nature with clearcut evidence of the dominance of the largest urban settlement over other settlements in political, economic, social, and religious matters, the settlement system of the Late Postclassic Basin of Mexico involved neither the physical integration of the population in a settlement system focused on the dominant city-state of Tenochtitlán nor the extreme centralization of decision making characteristic of those earlier macroregional city-states (Blanton 1976:193, 1996: 67–83; Blanton et al. 1993:156–157; Charlton 1973:421; Parsons 1989:207; Sanders 1981:189; Sanders et al. 1979:176).

Tenochtitlán as a City-State

Tenochtitlán's dominance as a macroregional city-state in central Mexico and distant regions within Mesoamerica lasted approximately ninety years, cut short by the Spanish conquest. The first part of Cycle III encompassed 230–280 years, a period similar in length to that of Cycle II, Part 1. Both followed the breakup of large city-state regional systems and were characterized by small, multiple city-states. Like Tula, the Tenochtitlán city-state system marked a further break from the Cycle I and II tendencies of proto-urban and urban settlements in the Basin of Mexico to grow disproportionately by incorporating people from other settlements. This trend culminated at Teotihuacán, continued on a reduced scale in the small Epi-Teotihuacán city-states, reemerged in a modified, less incorporative form at Tula, and then continued into the Early Aztec period city-states.

However, the unprecedented size of the Late Aztec population in the Basin (Sanders 1981:190) effectively precluded use of a strong city-state settlement system with a simple urban center/rural hinterland pattern (cf. Healan et al. 1989:249) and attendant centralization of population and functions, as existed in central Mexico during the hegemony of Teotihuacán and Tula. Urbanism persisted as a major characteristic of the Basin's Late Aztec settlement system in both small and large city-states (Parsons 1989: 207). Tenochtitlán-Tlatelolco and its immediately surrounding area formed a dense urban settlement of about 400,000 within a 600-square-kilometer area (Sanders 1981:190, 194; Sanders et al. 1979:163), representing 33–50 percent of the Basin's total population. Sanders and his colleagues consider all these settlements urban parts of Greater Tenochtitlán, "a kind of single great community, economically and politically integrated at several levels, and forming a discrete component, not duplicated elsewhere, of the Late Horizon settlement system" (1979:163).

Healan and his colleagues argue that this was not an enlarged Aztec version of an urban center analogous to Tula or Teotihuacán but was similar to a "northeastern U.S. megalopolis" (1989:249). Although the increase in population density and settlement size at Tenochtitlán and the surrounding area is reminiscent of Tula and Teotihuacán, as single large urban centers dominating a city-state settlement system with a rural hinterland, when the rest of the settlement system is observed, it becomes clear that Tenochtitlán's urban dominance had not resulted in a centralization of population or of political, economic, religious, and social functions. All these remained in the subordinate, integrated, but decentralized small city-state centers throughout the Basin, as well as in the supraregional centers of Tenochtitlán-Tlatelolco and Texcoco. The distribution of mounded architecture and elite residences supports this view of decentralization (Blanton et al. 1993:157).

At the same time, however, the settlement system of the Tenochtitlán city-state reflects changes in population organization differentiating it from Teotihuacán and Tula. The construction program at Tenochtitlán was not on as massive a scale as that at Teotihuacán and more closely approximates that of Tula. Urban planning at Tenochtitlán-Tlatelolco is evident and approximates the rigidity of Teotihuacán (Umberger 1996:89–90). Most agricultural producers resided outside Tenochtitlán, not within the city as at Teotihuacán (Sanders 1981:186; Sanders and Santley 1983:274). The residential compounds at Tenochtitlán-Tlatelolco "were looser arrangements of individual houses and a central courtyard and housed far fewer individuals" (Healan et al. 1989:251) than the Teotihuacán apartment compound. Unlike the Toltec and Teotihuacán settlement systems with their emphasis on primacy, in the hinterland areas outside Tenochtitlán-Tlatelolco, there was a full range of settlements, from single houses to city-state capitals, including a second, smaller, supraregional center, Texcoco, with an emphasis on urbanism.

The Tenochtitlán settlement system differed from that of Teotihuacán and Tula in the degree of control over urban and hinterland populations. The large size of the Basin's population precluded direct control, as had been the case previously (Blanton 1976; Blanton et al. 1993:156–157; Sanders 1981:193–194; Sanders et al. 1979:153–181). Kowalewski and his colleagues discuss a similar situation in the Valley of Oaxaca (1989:307). The "market dynamic" emphasis (Blanton 1976:194, 1996:67–80; Blanton et al. 1993:156–157; Kowalewski et al. 1989:307), along with an associated commercialism and secularization, differentiate the integration of the Tenochtitlán city-state from that of Tula or Teotihuacán. Such an emphasis, we feel, came about because of the great population increase in the Basin, and it was associated with an economical form of political control practiced by the Aztecs (Gledhill 1989:116–117; Hassig 1985:101–102, 1988:19, 1992:146–147; Santley and Alexander 1992:28–29).

Tenochtitlán-Tlatelolco, a large city-state, dominant over several regions, with a heavily occupied urban center and rural hinterlands within the Basin of Mexico, integrated that area and adjacent regions of central Mexico economically, politically, and socially through an outwardly loose, militaristic, tributary city-state model, adapted to a demographic situation with populations four and five times those previously recorded for this area. Documentary and archaeological evidence indicate a city-state system with the effective wielders of political, social, economic, and religious power—with differing spheres of concern—located not only in the center, Tenochtitlán, but also throughout the city-states incorporated within the Tenochtitlán city-state system.

The success of the Tenochtitlán-Tlatelolco city-state in reducing, but not incorporating, rivals would seem to place it within Trigger's definition of a city-state (1993:8–14), which necessitates a city-state being part of a network of adjacent competitive city-states. Other characteristics present include a substantial population of food producers and non-food producers in an urbanized zone (Tenochtitlán-Tlatelolco and the immediately surrounding area), an emphasis on urban craft production for both rural and urban sectors of society, an intensification of agricultural production near the city, an economic system integrating rural and urban sectors, and widely shared ideological symbols (Trigger 1993). However, as noted for Teotihuacán and Tula, some other characteristics are suggestive of a territorial state (again following Trigger's definition): territorial extent, early monumentality of construction (less developed at Tula and Tenochtitlán than at Teotihuacán), and a clear "hierarchy of administrative centers."

In our opinion, Tenochtitlán, unlike Tula and Teotihuacán, represents an example of a city-state whose evolution occurred in a context where nearby equivalent rivals were conquered but not physically incorporated and where a relatively high regional population density persisted throughout the Late Postclassic period (Sanders 1981). The mechanisms (ideological, political, economic, social structural) that supported Tenochtitlán's control over a large population in the Basin of Mexico are relatively well known, particularly for the center. As far as we can tell, these mechanisms underwent modifications related to a trend to limit the extent of state-level power and an increase in commercial activities. The primate settlement system no longer exists (Blanton 1976, 1996). The extreme centralization characteristic of Teotihuacán and found to a lesser degree at Tula is absent from the Late Aztec period.

Cycle IV: Spanish Conquest to Nation-State, Part I: Early Colonial Period, A.D. 1521–1620

The entirety of Cycle IV is too complicated to treat in full here. Of importance is the Early Colonial period, when city-state-like units reappear or persist in modified form. Following the Spanish conquest, the city-states incorporated into the Tenochtitlán regional system as administrative and economic units reemerged (Charlton 1986:124–127; Gibson 1964; Lockhart 1991:93). Lockhart compares these units, the *altepetl* or ethnic state, to "early Mediterranean city-states" (1992:14). "They were like city-states in size, and also in their degree of independence and strong ethnic awareness" (Lockhart 1991:23). Yet they also differed; the dominance of nucleated populations in urbanized settlements (*cabeceras*) over dependencies (*sujetos*) was not "central to their manner of organization" (Lockhart 1991:23).

The growth of mercantilism and manufacturing centered in cities, beginning in the medieval period, led to greater distinctions between urban and rural dwellers in southern Europe (Chittolini 1991). The Spanish brought with them to Mexico the conception of a dominant city and subordinate countryside that significantly altered the organizational structure of indigenous city-states in central Mexico. Like early Mediterranean city-states (Finley 1977a), the Aztecs apparently had viewed city/town and hinterland as an integrated unit; the Nahuas' vocabulary, for example, did not have a word to distinguish the city from the *altepetl* (Lockhart 1992:19).

Since the Spaniards replaced Tenochtitlán's political and economic control with their own centralized system located in Mexico City, the city-state units of the sixteenth century lacked the independence characteristic of prehispanic city-states at a comparable stage in city-state cycles. The settlement pattern in the Basin was one of many low-level centers dominated by Mexico City (Charlton 1986:125). The associated population decline during the sixteenth century from an estimated population of 800,000–1,200,000 in A.D. 1521 to a total indigenous population in the Basin of 150,000–160,000 by about A.D. 1620 (Charlton 1986:125; Sanders 1970:430) meant that most of the city-state-like units lacked an adequate demographic base to support the maintenance or development of independent state institutions and complexity. Gibson (1952, 1964) and Lockhart (1991, 1992)

provide insights into the nature of indigenous communities after the conquest.

Cycle IV differs in another way from the prehispanic cycles, in that the strong central city-state power, Tenochtitlán, instead of disappearing from the scene or being significantly reduced in its influence, was replaced by a new nonindigenous urbanized power center located in the same place. The Spaniards replaced indigenous political, economic, social, and religious institutions, both in Tenochtitlán and in numerous small city-states, more rapidly and to a much greater degree in central Mexico than in other parts of Mesoamerica. Thus, when the smaller city-states reasserted themselves, they did so within the context of a structure created by the conquerors. The independence and competitiveness did not develop to the extent seen in the first part of Cycles II and III.

Comparisons and Conclusions

Any cursory examination of the sequence of settlement patterns in the Basin of Mexico and adjacent sections of the central Plateau reveals three prehispanic cycles of state development, each marked by an initial period of numerous competitive small states and followed by a period dominated by a single, large integrative city-state that subsequently dissolved into numerous small city-states, thereby beginning a new cycle. Using the settlement-pattern data, augmented whenever possible with excavated and ethnohistoric information, we have proposed that the basic social, political, economic, and ideological unit of all three cycles was the city-state.

The three cycles of prehispanic city-states are broadly similar in form and content; each represents a swing from decentralization involving numerous small, independent city-states to centralization with a single large dominant city-state. All cycles maintain high levels of urbanized populations in periods of small as well as large city-states. Yet, while there are similarities, there are also differences that clearly demonstrate the evolution of central Mexican civilization.

The first difference is that of tempo. Later cycles formed and dissolved more rapidly than the first. The earliest cycle was the longest. Certainly the development of city-states without earlier models took time. But the period of consolidation under Teotihuacán was unusually long, and Teotihuacán's position as the dominant center in the Basin was unusually stable.

The two later prehispanic cycles were much shorter in duration, although only the second cycle was completed, since the Spanish conquest truncated the third cycle. In both instances, the rapidity of development of major integrative city-states from numerous more or less independent units suggests that there had formed a substantial background of knowledge, proficiency, and expertise in state-building. In the case of the second cycle (the Epi-Teotihuacán and Early Postclassic periods), knowledge of statecraft did not translate into a lengthy hegemony for the centralizing city-state, Tula. Given the rapid demise of the Tenochtitlán city-state system, it appears that the organizational structures of the third cycle were no more permanent.

A second major difference in the three cycles is the reduction in intensity of political, social, economic, and ideological integration of settlements and people into the dominant city-state during the second part of each cycle. There is a general trend through time from the tightly integrated Teotihuacán city-state system to a slightly more loosely integrated Tula city-state system and finally to a system in which Tenochtitlán integrated very few functions and assimilated very few people but relied primarily on the administrative role of the small city-states and confederations of city-states under its control to carry out necessary political, economic, social, and ideological activities. Such decentralization was characteristic of neither Teotihuacán nor Tula (at least, not to the same degree) and probably reflects the development of production and distribution mechanisms, as well as administrative techniques, to cope with the major increase in population during the Late Aztec period.

The Late Aztec period developments in population and city-state organization represent a distinct break from earlier patterns, in terms of a more decentralized city-state system and one that was part of a larger system or network, a classic marker of city-state systems. The apparent lack of competitors to Teotihuacán, and possibly to Tula, may be the result of a lacuna in regional settlement data from other regions in central Mexico, including a nearby possible competitor, Cholula.

Notes

1. For example, Bray 1972a, 1972b; Brumfiel 1983; Calnek 1982; Charlton, in press; Diehl and Berlo 1989; Hirth 1984a, 1989; Hodge 1984, 1992, 1994, 1996, and this volume; Marcus 1989, 1992a; and Smith 1992a.

2. See Berdan et al. 1996; Berlo 1989; Brumfiel 1983; Davies 1977, 1980, 1987; Dibble 1971; Diehl and Berlo 1989; Hassig 1985, 1988; Hodge 1984:5–8; Marcus 1992c:45–57; Smith 1983, 1984; and van Zantwijk 1985.

3. For survey data see Blanton 1972; Charlton 1972, 1978; Diehl 1983; García Cook 1981; Hirth 1974, 1980; Hirth and Angulo Villaseñor 1981; Millon 1973; Millon et al. 1973; Nichols 1996; Parsons 1971, 1989; Parsons et al. 1982; Sanders 1965; and Sanders et al. 1979.

4. Intensive surveys provide complementary data on the large urban centers of Teotihuacán (Millon 1981) and Tula (Diehl 1983; Healan 1989; Matos M. 1974, 1976), on a few Formative period villages and towns (e.g., Domínguez Chávez 1979; Santley 1977; Tolstoy 1975; Tolstoy and Fish 1975; Tolstoy et al. 1977), and on several Late Postclassic regional centers (e.g., Huexotla and its rural hinterland [Brumfiel 1976a, 1980], Xico [Brumfiel 1982, 1986], Xaltocán [Brumfiel, in press], Otumba and its rural hinterland [Charlton et al. 1991; Evans 1988; Nichols 1994; Otis Charlton et al. 1993]; and Chalco [Hodge, in press]).

There are additional relevant studies of sociopolitical evolution in the Basin of Mexico (e.g., Blanton et al. 1993; Boehm de Lameiras 1986), in subregions such as Cuauhtitlán in the northwest (Nichols 1980), and on specific aspects of the settlement patterns there and in adjacent regions of central Mexico (Brumfiel 1976b; Earle 1976; Grove 1981; Hirth 1974, 1980, 1987; Santley 1977; Sarmiento 1994; Steponaitis 1981) having to do with the nature and timing of increased Formative period political complexity in the Basin. Blanton et al. (1996); Drennan (1991) and Feinman (1991) include discussions of the Formative period occupation within comparative studies of the evolution of pre-state level complex cultures. García Cook (1981), Hirth (1980), Hirth and Angulo Villaseñor (1981), and Sanders and Santley (1983) consider the impact of Teotihuacán on regional settlement patterns. Alden (1979), Blanton (1975), Charlton (1973, 1975), Mastache and Cobean (1989), and Parsons (1970) examine the Epi-Teotihuacán settlement patterns. Bell et al. (1988), Bray (1983), Evans (1980), Evans and Gould (1982), Gorenflo and Gale (1986, 1990), Ruggles (1992), Santley (1986, 1991), Saucedo (1994), and Smith (1979, 1980) evaluate various models for an understanding of Aztec settlement patterns.

5. In accordance with the dictum of Sanders and his colleagues, we have tried to sidestep the "Tezoyuca problem," the chronology and function of the Tezoyuca sites (Sanders et al. 1979:104). These sites are located primarily in defensible locations in the Patlachique Range (Fig. 11.5) and date from the Early Terminal Formative

period. It is uncertain, however, if Tezoyuca ceramics are earlier than the Patlachique phase materials that characterize this period or if they represent an elite occupation. In our opinion, these sites minimally represent a defensive development early in the Terminal Formative period, when the regional center of Teotihuacán was emerging in opposition to Cuicuilco.

6. There is another line of evidence that suggests that chiefdoms were present during the Late Formative period and the early portion of the Terminal Formative period. The highest frequencies of resist or negative painted ceramics from excavated sites in the Teotihuacán Valley are found at the Tezoyuca site (Cuanalán 2.8 percent, Tezoyuca 7.67 percent, and Patlachique 4.79 percent [Sanders 1975:136]). The same is true for polychrome designs, with the highest frequency being at the Tezoyuca site.

Another interesting pattern at Tezoyuca is to be found in the vessel forms. The Tezoyuca site has a much higher proportion of hemispherical bowls than occurs at other sites. According to Sanders and his colleagues (1975:138), "Virtually all the hemispherical bowls from Tezoyuca are small vessels that look like individual serving vessels. Most of the concave and straight-sided bowl rims found at Tezoyuca are apparently drinking goblets. Together these two make up approximately half the total sherds in the Tezoyuca sample. Virtually all of the vessels are highly decorated. The high percentage of individual, highly decorated serving vessels at Tezoyuca may relate to a pattern of public ceremonial feasting and food distributions, suggesting the possibility of a relationship to Service's definition of the chiefdom level of social structure."

It is possible, however, that the Tezoyuca ceramics are more an expression of hierarchy than of chiefdoms. The Tezoyuca sites are some kind of elite ceremonial/administrative/military centers linked to the inception of Teotihuacán and its early relationships with the Cuicuilco-dominated area of the Basin south of the Patlachique Range (cf. Parsons 1971:186–191; Sanders 1965:94–98, 168–169).

7. Compare Alden 1979:188, who defines four to five clusters with populations ranging from 7,000 to 12,000 persons.

12

When Is a City-State?

Archaeological Measures of Aztec City-States and Aztec City-State Systems

MARY G. HODGE

Administrative records and histories of the Aztec empire of central Mexico (A.D. 1430–1521) make explicit reference to political units that are in many ways equivalent to the city-state as defined by Charlton and Nichols in the first chapter of this volume: "small, territorially based, politically independent state systems characterized by a capital city or town and socially integrated adjacent hinterland ... relatively self-sufficient economically, and perceived as being ethnically distinct." City-states usually occur in groups of polities of roughly equivalent size.

This form of polity is represented in Aztec vocabularies and histories and is depicted in maps and codices. In the Aztec language, Nahuatl, this basic political unit is called *altepetl* (pl. *altepeme*), from the root terms *atl* (water) and *tepetl* (hill), referring to the principal physical attributes defining a Nahua community (Karttunen 1983:9). Place names in Nahua codices emphasize this concept, since the symbol for an *altepetl* is a stylized hill with a name glyph attached (Fig. 12.1). Sixteenth-century Nahuatl dictionaries also convey the central connotations of the *altepetl*. Molina's dictionary of 1571, for example, defines *altepetl* as *pueblo o rey* (town or king) (Molina 1970:4): the Spanish word *rey* (king) is recorded as a synonym of *vey tlatoani, altepetl* (great *tlatoani* [speaker, king]) in Molina (1970:103), suggesting that the idea of the *altepetl* is inextricably associated with the presence of a ruler. *Altepetl* thus encompasses the concepts of settlement, city, state, king, sovereign (*poblado, ciudad, estado, rey, soberano;* Siméon 1971:21).

The term *city-state* has been widely applied to the *altepetl* by anthropologists (e.g., Bray 1972a; Calnek 1978; Charlton and Nichols 1990; Hodge 1984).[1] Bray describes the Aztec city-state polity as "a Mexican city state [that] can be defined as a sovereign territory with its own government and with one or more rulers chosen from a royal lineage" (1972a:164). The Aztec city-state was ideally a defined territory containing a capital or central place and rural dependencies. The urban center or town was the seat of government; it contained the principal temple dedicated to a city-state deity and was a center for market exchange and craft production.

Our knowledge of Aztec-period polities (A.D. 1150–1520) comes from documentary reports and archaeological evidence. In textual sources, the Aztec city-state emerges clearly; an archaeological definition poses a greater challenge. This paper observes Aztec city-states from both perspectives and explores how Aztec city-states changed over time. I summarize below the central characteristics of the Aztec city-state polity, as portrayed in documentary sources. I then examine archaeological evidence, with an emphasis on the polities' territorial organization, to determine when and under what conditions the Aztec city-state can be identified in the archaeological record. I compare a selection of city-states as archaeological entities at two time periods—the preimperial period, corresponding to the Early Aztec archaeological period, and the imperial period (after A.D. 1430), which starts in the middle of the Late Aztec archaeological period (A.D. 1350–1520)—to identify change in city-states during Aztec times.[2] Finally, I assess the degree to which Aztec-period polities in the Basin of Mexico conform to the generalized definitions of a city-state polity and a city-state system, as formulated in the introduction to this volume.

Aztec City-States: The View from the Documents

Documentary descriptions of Aztec city-states come from Nahuatl chronicles written after the Spanish Conquest; copies of traditional painted books of history, taxation, genealogy, and ritual (see Cline 1973–1975); Spanish accounts by participants in the conquest of the Aztec empire (Cortés 1971; Díaz del Castillo 1956); Spanish friars' accounts (e.g., Durán 1967, 1971; Sahagún 1950–1982); and reports by colonial administrators (for example, Zorita 1963). I summarize below the characteristics of Aztec city-state urban centers based on documentary reports, including urban plans: the urban centers' functions (e.g., market exchange), rulers, political administration, state rituals, and the people and their traditional "ethnic" identities. I then present perspectives from the documentary sources on city-state territories (boundary conventions, settlement hierarchies, confederations of city-states, and the original settlement of city-states).

The Urban Design of Aztec City-State Centers: Tenochtitlán

The Aztec empire's central settlement, Tenochtitlán, nearly monopolizes textual reports. Any discussion of city-states must begin there, since Tenochtitlán's predominance in documentary reports has promoted certain assumptions about other Aztec urban centers.

By about A.D. 1500, Tenochtitlán—centered on an island in Lake Texcoco—housed 200,000–250,000

Figure 12.1. A typical place-glyph for an *altepetl*. A sixteenth-century Nahua artist designated the city-state center of Coatlinchán using a symbol for a snake ('*coatl*'), added to the image of a public building and the signs for hill water. Redrawn by R. Richard Rogers from Mapa de Coatlinchán in *Códices de México* (1979).

people and covered an area of 12–15 square kilometers. Its quadriform layout was emphasized by causeways that met at a central plaza-temple-palace complex. The four great sectors of the city were further divided into residential divisions called *tlaxillacalli,* each supporting a temple and civic officials. In the residential sectors, walled compounds composed of separate dwellings were occupied by extended families, each in its own house. Farther outside the center, *chinampa* (raised field) plots produced food for the city (Boone 1987; Calnek 1976; Rojas 1986; Sanders et al. 1979). Located on the same island as Tenochtitlán was the settlement of Tlatelolco. It was conquered by Tenochtitlán in A.D. 1473, and its economy and political organization were thereafter closely controlled by Tenochtitlán's rulers. Between A.D. 1430 and 1500, Tenochtitlán became the political and economic center of the Aztec empire. Tribute collection and its attendant bureaucracy were centered at Tenochtitlán, as was military leadership of the empire. Tenochtitlán controlled the Basin of Mexico's main marketplace at Tlatelolco, and Tlatelolco also housed the central guild of *pochteca* (traders who specialized in sumptuary and extraimperial goods, traded in behalf of the imperial ruler, and obtained information for the empire's ruler on areas where they traded; see Sahagún 1950–1982, Book 9).

Recent comparative research has revealed differences between Tenochtitlán and other Aztec urban centers (Cline 1990; Hodge 1984; Offner 1983;

Schroeder 1991). It now is clear that Tenochtitlán's city plan, its specialized political offices, and its economic complexity were not simply duplicated in other communities and that the majority of Aztec city-states cannot be understood if they are viewed simply as microcosms of Tenochtitlán (Hodge 1984, 1994).

Beyond Tenochtitlán: Documentary Evidence of Other Aztec Cities

City plans

Though each is represented less frequently than Tenochtitlán, many of the nearly forty Aztec period city-state urban centers in the Basin of Mexico are depicted by maps and described in prose documents. Maps painted by Nahua scribes indicate that the commonplace components of city-state urban centers were the central plaza, with civic buildings, temples or shrines, a marketplace, and a *tecpan,* or *tlatoani*'s residence. Residential areas surrounded the ceremonial-civic center; dependent rural communities occupied the territory outside the center. Topographic features such as hills, rivers, or hilltop shrines (Fig. 12.2) defined city-state boundaries (for examples, see the *Santa Cruz Map* [Linné 1948]; *Relaciones geográficas* maps [Acuña 1984–1987; del Paso y Troncoso 1905–1906]; AGN, *Catálogo de Ilustraciones* [1979–1981]). Some plans depict imperial administrative buildings, as in the map accompanying the *Relación de Cempoala,* which shows the imperial administrative-tribute collection building (Acuña 1984–1987). Even the urban organization of Texcoco—the second most important political center in the Basin of Mexico by A.D. 1500—did not mimic Tenochtitlán. It is clear that the palace and perhaps the entire ceremonial center followed a quadriform design (Radin 1920). With 30,000–40,000 inhabitants, Texcoco was the second most populous city in the Basin, but its urban population occupied several irregular sectors or *barrios* (Hicks 1982; Offner 1983). Outside the ceremonial center Texcoco followed a more dispersed plan and lacked the grid-like layout of Tenochtitlán. This less planned, more dispersed layout outside the ceremonial-palace zones seems typical of Aztec city-state centers.

Archaeological evidence supports the generalization based on documents that a nearly constant trait of the Aztec city-state in any period was its central settlement (Sanders et al. 1979). Only a few rich urban centers have been studied intensively by archaeol-

Figure 12.2. Portion of the *Santa Cruz Map* painted in the mid-1500s which exemplifies the layout of an Aztec community in a valley between hills. Here the community of Coatlinchán is shown to contain a public building (located by the road, a flat-topped structure identified by circular decorations and a church (which in Colonial times replaced and often covered the Aztec ceremonial structures). Houses are scattered on the landscape surrounding the public buildings. After Linné (1948). Redrawn by R. Richard Rogers.

ogists, however, since most were covered by colonial-period construction and are now overlain by modern settlements.

City-state society

A major feature of city-state organization was its hereditary ruler, called *tlatoani* (Nahuatl, "speaker"; pl. *tlatoque;* Molina [1970:140] defines *tlatoani* as "*hablador, o gran señor*"). The *tlatoani* was assisted by administrators of the elite class in his leadership, protection, and administration of the *altepetl.* Other specialists included priests and scribes (Carrasco 1977; Hodge 1984). Elites and the state were supported by the commoner class—one chronicler reports that losing the support of commoners signaled the end of a *tlatoani*'s ability to govern (Chimalpahin 1965). Rulers' attempts to attract and retain commoner populations suggest that they were concerned about commoner labor, a source of wealth (Hicks 1986; Parsons et al. 1982:86–87).

Aztec society, as described in the chronicles, consisted of nobility and commoners. The elite were organized through the "noble house" (*tecpan* or *tecalli*). The head of such a noble house was the *teuctli* ("lord"; pl. *teteuctin*), and his children were *pipiltin* ("noble people"; s. *pilli; Hicks 1986; Karttunen 1983:195). Commoners were *macehualli* ("subject"; pl. *macehualtin*), but their degree of subjugation and association with the noble houses varies greatly in documentary accounts (see Anderson et al. 1976; Carrasco and Monjarás-Ruíz 1976, 1978; Hicks 1986; Schroeder 1991). Documentary references to craft specialists and traders suggest that these groups formed intermediate social categories (Anderson et al. 1976; Carrasco 1977).

Archaeological research on Aztec-period communities contrasts with the documents' normative descriptions of Aztec social classes. A gradation in economic and perhaps social status seems to have been the case, since domestic architecture and household possessions differ only somewhat between elite and commoner residences (Evans 1988; Smith 1992b). Brumfiel's survey of the urban center of Huexotla shows spatial variation in decorated ceramics, with greater variety in the urban core and less in the rural periphery, suggesting gradations in access to crafts and therefore a gradual decline in wealth from the center to the edges of a city (1976a, 1980).

City-state marketplaces

By A.D. 1500 a regional hierarchy of economic functions created differences among city-states in the Basin of Mexico. Some exchange must have occurred in every community, but official marketplaces operated at different intervals and served different areas (Berdan 1975, 1985, 1987). Markets were held daily, or at five- or twenty-day intervals in accordance with the Nahua calendrical system (Hassig 1982; Hicks 1986:52). Of 38 city-state centers in the Basin of Mexico, 18 had official marketplaces at or near the time of the Spanish conquest (Blanton 1996). Two of these were the major marketplaces that operated daily at Tenochtitlán and Texcoco; they offered the greatest range of goods. The remainder were secondary or tertiary markets.

The relatively regular spacing of the marketplaces conforms to a central-place system, though the marketplace hierarchy's structure and locations were influenced by political contingencies (Blanton 1996;

Blanton et al. 1993). Marketplaces as a source of income motivated victorious city-states to take markets and trading specialties from defeated areas (*Anales de Cuauhtitlán* 1975:para. 155–158). Since *tlatoque* acquired income from the fees paid by merchants who traded in the markets, control of marketplaces was desirable (Anderson et al. 1976; Carrasco and Monjarás-Ruíz 1976; Chimalpahin 1965).

City-state territories

Nahuatl documents indicate that boundaries were important, known, and recorded, and Nahuatl dictionaries contain a number of terms relating to boundaries. For example, *altepequaxochtli* refers to "*terminos o mojones de pueblo o ciudad*" (limits or boundaries of a pueblo or city; Molina 1970:4), and *altepetepantli* refers to the limits or boundaries of a city ("*terminos o mojones de la ciudad*"; Molina 1970:4). *Quaxochtli* means "end" or "boundary" of lands or cities ("*termino o linde de tierras o de ciudades*"; Molina 1970:88). The *Anales de Cuauhtitlán* mentions officials called *quaxochpixque* (border keepers), who governed communities on the borders of Cuauhtitlán (1974:148–149, 180). A town official in charge of land documents within the *altepetl* is reported in colonial documents from Amecamecan in Chalco province (though referred to by the Spanish term *guardapapeles;* see Hodge 1984:41).

In Aztec chronicles, *altepetl* boundaries are denoted in several ways. One is to list communities within a city-state territory. Another convention for delineating the extent of polities is to name boundary points—the communities and topographic features on the edges of a city-state territory. Pictorial representations depict communities, rivers, hills, caves, and other topographic features defining the boundaries of a polity (see, for example, *Anales de Cuauhtitlán* 1974; *Relaciones geográficas* and their maps [Acuña 1984–1987; del Paso y Troncoso 1905–1906]). Since Aztec city-state territories lacked manmade markers that can be identified by archaeologists today, such lists are crucial for identifying city-state territories.

Supra–City-State Organizations

"Tribes" or ethnic groups

Fray Diego Durán reported that the Basin of Mexico was settled by "seven tribes of people [who] went out from Chicomoztoc, the Seven caves" on a migration into central Mexico (Durán 1964:9). He relates how the tribes (the Xochimilca, the Chalca, the Tepaneca,

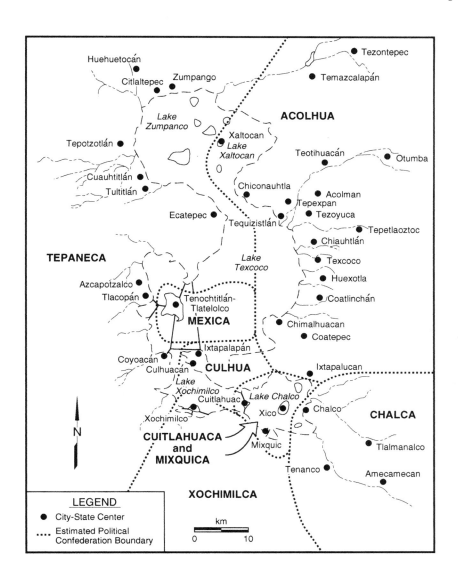

Figure 12.3. Regional city-state confederations in the Basin of Mexico that existed as independent political entities prior to incorporation in the Aztec empire. Drawing by R. Richard Rogers.

the Culhua, the Tlahuica, the Tlaxcallans, and the Mexica) settled in different portions of the Basin of Mexico and the central plateau. By the 1500s, city-state urban centers contained people of different ethnic or tribal identities. Nahuatl predominated in central Mexican city-states, and speakers of Otomí, Popoluca, Matlatzinca or Tepehua are reported in some city-states (Acuña 1984–1987).

Durán proposed a date of A.D. 820 for the Nahua migrations into the Basin of Mexico; however, later analyses of the migration myths and comparisons with dates presented in the chronicles produced a consensus that the settlement of Aztec communities in the Basin of Mexico took place between A.D. 1150–1250 (Smith 1984:170–173; see also Davies 1980; Gibson 1964). Archaeological excavations combined with radiocarbon dating now suggest that some city-states were founded much earlier than tra-

ditional histories suggest and earlier than the regional archaeological chronology had predicted (see below).

Confederations of city-states

Some attributes of Aztec city-states can be related to the political structures, history, and identity of regional political confederations (Gibson 1971; Hicks 1986; Hodge, in press). The eight geographically discrete confederations of city-states (Fig. 12.3) that occupied the Basin of Mexico in Early Aztec times became components of the Aztec empire. The Tenochca (Mexica), Acolhua, and Tepaneca confederations formed the regional states of the Triple Alliance, while other confederations (Culhua, Xochimilca, Cuitlahuaca, Mixquica, and Chalca) became provinces subject principally to Tenochtitlán within the empire (see Davies 1973, 1980; Gibson 1964; Hodge, in press; van Zantwijk 1985). Ethnic and historical traditions contributed to the identity of the regional confederations and provided an explanation for their existence, even as provinces within the empire.

Each regional confederation displayed a distinct style of political organization. The Acolhua confederation's structure was characterized by one *tlatoani* in each city-state. This tradition was institutionalized at the time the Aztec empire was formed (ca. A.D. 1430) as part of a reorganization of the Acolhua confederation by its *tlatoani* ("Chichimeca *teuctli*"), Nezahualcoyotl. In this imperial reorganization, some Acolhua-region city-states were demoted to administered territories governed by *calpixque* (administrators). In contrast, the Chalca confederation was characterized by multiple *tlatoani* offices within a single city-state. After the Chalco region's conquest by Tenochtitlán, the political structure of the Chalca confederation was altered, and *tlatoani* offices were reduced in number. Prior to its conquest by Tenochtitlán and Texcoco, moreover, the Chalca confederation had no institutionalized head city-state: *tlatoque* of different city-states provided leadership at different times. After incorporation into the empire, a provincial hierarchy was instituted in the Chalca region (see Chimalpahin 1965; Hodge 1984; Schroeder 1991).

In the Tepaneca realm, composite city-states (in which one ruler and city governed subordinate city-states and *tlatoque*) emerged prior to its conquest by the Aztec empire. In some cases, the political structure of Tepaneca polities was simplified under imperial rule (best documented in Cuauhtitlán, where regional administrative offices held by Cuauhtitlán elites were eliminated). In other Tepaneca city-states, Mexica administrators, rather than local lords, were placed in *tlatoani* offices or in other administrative positions (Hodge 1984; Hicks 1992).

City-state political organizations were also altered in areas of the Basin controlled closely by Tenochtitlán's rulers (the Culhua, Cuitlahuaca, Xochimilca, and Mixquica confederations). New *tlatoani* offices were added to city-states having a hereditary ruling house (notably Azcapotzalco and Xochimilco), and Mexica nobles were placed in these new offices (Brumfiel 1983; Hodge 1984; Rounds 1979).

Selectivity of Textual Accounts of Aztec City-States

Analyses of central Mexican city-states using community-specific documents have revealed social,

economic, and political variation (Blanton 1996; Hicks 1982, 1992; Hodge 1984, in press; Schroeder 1991). The concept of the city-state presented in capital-centric documents obscures the variation that actually existed prior to the emergence of the Aztec empire and prior to the Spanish Conquest. Each city-state, for example, can be characterized as having its own deity and ritual cycle, but city-states incorporated into the empire were required to observe Mexica calendrical rituals. Deity images were taken from conquered city-states to Tenochtitlán, and some of the rituals emblematic of conquered city-states were later performed in Tenochtitlán (Durán 1971; López Austín 1973; Umberger 1996). Diachronic analyses of specific city-state organizations have revealed a process of imperialization in central Mexico that transformed Tenochtitlán (Brumfiel 1983; Rounds 1979; van Zantwijk 1985) and suppressed distinctive characteristics of subjugated societies, as is typical of empires (Brumfiel et al. 1994; Hodge 1984). The recent documentary research on specific city-states and regions suggests that significant variation in city-state structures and development processes will be discovered through archaeological study.

Archaeological Evidence of Aztec City-States

Archaeological data serve as a source of information about aspects of Aztec city-states that are absent from documents. In keeping with this volume's theme, I explore the potential contributions of archaeological research to understanding the structure of city-states and the origins of the city-state system in central Mexico as well as lines of inquiry to which the city-state unit of analysis can contribute. The data presented below are Aztec examples of the issues that this volume compares cross-culturally:

1. City-state areal and population size, along with the methods used to determine them;
2. City-state settlement patterns, economic organization, and political systems;
3. Dates for the emergence of city-states, their persistence and termination;
4. The external relationships of city-states, including their degree of incorporation into more inclusive socio-political-economic units;
5. Observations on the factors responsible for the development of city-states.

The Territorial Organization of Aztec City-States

This section reviews the archaeological evidence of Late Postclassic city-states in the Basin of Mexico, which enables us to observe how the city-state entity—so clearly described in documents—appears archaeologically. I also present findings on how dividing archaeological settlement-pattern data into politically meaningful groups permits identification and comparison of Aztec city-states prior to and during the imperial period.

Information about Aztec city-state polities that complements and supplements the documentary sources is provided by regional surveys of the Basin of Mexico. The surveys have furnished data on settlement sizes, locations, populations, and change over time. An important contribution of the regional archaeological surveys is that they provide comparable data on all or most settlements; documents, on the other hand, do not cover all communities and usually emphasize only the most important centers. Indeed, they often omit data on small and rural settlements.

Regional surveys conducted in the 1960s and 1970s of the Basin of Mexico mapped settlements of the Early Aztec (A.D. 1150–1350) and the Late Aztec (also called the Late Horizon—A.D. 1350–1521) periods (Blanton 1972; Parsons 1971; Parsons et al. 1982; Sanders et al. 1979).[3] The Basin of Mexico presents major problems for archaeological survey because Mexico City and other large communities obscure much pre-Columbian settlement. The surveys mapped as many settlements as could be identified through complete coverage of areas not obscured by modern settlement. The data are strongest for the eastern, southern, northern, and northwestern parts of the Basin, which were less populated than the west and south. In this chapter I employ data from the eastern and southern parts of the Basin (the Texcoco, Ixtapalapa, and Chalco-Xochimilco survey regions) because data from these survey zones have been published in full (Blanton 1972; Parsons 1971; Parsons et al. 1982; Parsons et al. 1983) and because this area is the focus of a regional study of ceramic production, stylistic differences, and exchange (Hodge and Minc 1990, 1991).

The surveys identified and classified Aztec settlements according to size, density of artifact scatters, and complexity of architecture. They revealed that during the Late Aztec period the Basin of Mexico contained approximately one million people (Sanders et al. 1979:12–14, 33–40). At least 500,000 of them lived in urban centers at approximately A.D. 1500, and the other half lived in smaller settlements (Sanders et al. 1979:162).

The ubiquity of Late Aztec occupation presented problems for the archaeological survey. Identifying urban centers was possible, since they are named in documents, depicted on historical and modern maps, and are represented by heavy accumulations of artifacts and architectural remains. Smaller sites were more difficult to define, however.

We have had one outstanding problem in dealing with Late Horizon rural occupation: much of it is so dispersed that we find it difficult, and sometimes impossible, to define sites according to the same considerations we have applied to other periods—basically, delimiting a discrete spatial cluster of occupational remains, clearly separable from other clusters. . . . There is a very distinct tendency for individual houses, or small clusters of individual houses, to be broadly and continuously dispersed over the landscape. . . . Where we are faced with a sea of scattered mounds and sherd clusters, it has been extremely difficult to define objectively a coherent cluster of occupation to which the label site can reasonably be attached. (Sanders et al. 1979:163–166)

Not only are individual site boundaries indistinct, but the extreme density of Late Aztec settlements makes identification of city-state boundaries difficult as well.

Archaeologists have employed spatial models to define relationships among communities using the regional settlement-pattern data produced by the surveys, and such spatial analyses of settlements and populations have proved useful at the regional scale, if adapted to the terrain of the Basin of Mexico (e.g., Blanton 1996; Evans and Gould 1982; Gordon 1980; Gorenflo and Gale 1990; Smith 1979). However capable of revealing regional structures of economies, transport systems, and so on, such models alone do not help us discern the attributes of individual Aztec city-states. Information from documents, in conjunction with archaeological settlement data, permits Aztec political boundaries to be defined in Aztec terms. Using this direct historical approach, Early and Late Aztec city-state territories and populations can be identified, estimated, and compared.

Identifying city-state territories

I have used information from documents for identifying city-state territories (Hodge 1994) within the

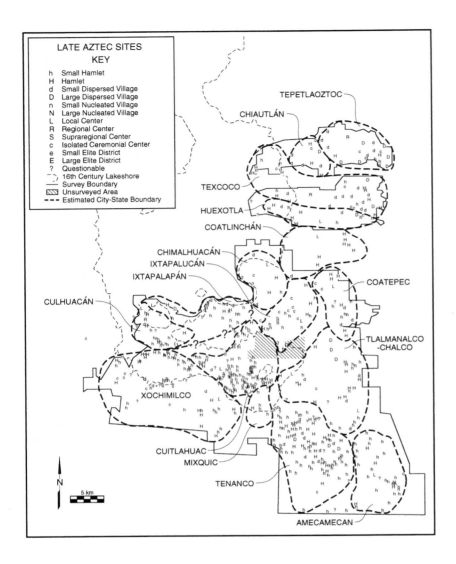

Figure 12.4. City-state territories of the Late Aztec period, identified through use of documentary sources and settlement data from the Texcoco and Chalco-Xochimilco survey regions (Parsons et al. 1983). Base map after Parsons et al. (1983:figure 9). Redrawn by R. Richard Rogers.

nearly uninterrupted expanse of Late Aztec sites in the eastern and southern parts of the Basin, from which regional survey data have been published (Parsons 1971; Parsons et al. 1982; Parsons et al. 1983). My use of the direct historical approach, combined with archaeological settlement data, for the study of Late Aztec polities provided comparable data on the sizes and internal organizations of city-states prior to and during the imperial period (Hodge 1994; the direct historical approach has also been used effectively for identifying the geographic extent of prehispanic confederations, city-states, and early colonial Mexican polities—see Gerhard 1970, 1972; Gibson 1964; Sanders 1970; Trautmann 1968).

By identifying sites that were dependencies of specific city-state urban centers from documents relating to the imperial period and early colonial times, city-state territories can be defined. When archaeological sites are assigned to a city-state, the areal extent of

sites provides an estimate of polity size, and the sum of site population estimates provides an estimate of a polity's population. This method permits estimation of the shape, size, and population of city-states. (For a map of the Late Aztec city-states in the eastern and southern part of the Basin of Mexico, see Fig. 12.4.)

Territory form

Figure 12.4 shows that Aztec city-state territories of varied sizes and shapes interlocked around the lakes, attesting to the importance of the Basin of Mexico lakes for transportation and aquatic resources. Categories of city-state territories include valley, hillside, vertical lake-to-piedmont, and lakebed/island polities. Valley systems such as Amecamecan and Tenanco occupy a river valley. A linear, vertical shape characterizes Texcoco, Huexotla, and Coatlinchán, whose territories are long strips extending west to east from the lakeshore to the highlands. Other city-states—for example, Xochimilco, Mixquic, and Chalco—contain lakeshore and highlands but are less linear. In hillside territories, the city-state center and dependent communities cluster around a slope or the top of a hill (as in Tepetlaoztoc, Ixtapalucan, and Chimalhuacán). Island settlements such as Cuitlahuac (also Tenochtitlán, Xaltocán, and Early Aztec Xico) have a clearly identifiable center, but the association of rural communities with a particular island city-state center is difficult to define, since many rural settlements are simply homesteads on small islands in the lakebed or near *chinampas*.

Chronicles reporting Early Aztec period events make it clear that city-state and confederation boundaries were fluid during the Early Aztec period because of conflicts, conquests, and fission of the communities composing confederations. Spaces between settlement clusters of the Early Aztec period (Fig. 12.5), however, define city-state territories that are similar to the Late Aztec period. Late Aztec territories fill in around Early Aztec city-state centers, suggesting that

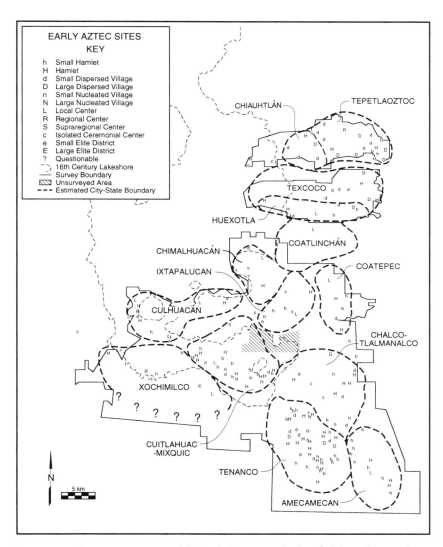

Figure 12.5. City-state territories of the Early Aztec period, identified through using documentary sources and settlement data from the Texcoco and Chalco-Xochimilco survey regions (Parsons et al. 1983). The existence of city-states of the Early Aztec period was established from documentary reports in which each polity operated as a city-state (e.g. had a *tlatoani*) during the Early Aztec period and from dates of settlements in historical chronicles. Territories were identified on the bases of reported dependencies, the location of archaeological sites mapped by the regional surveys, and buffer zones between city-state settlement clusters. Base map after Parsons et al. (1983:figure 8). Redrawn by R. Richard Rogers.

Aztec city-state units were relatively stable. Cases of instability are well documented (see below).

Figure 12.4 depicts the extent of city-state territories as estimated for the Late Aztec period. It is important to note that individual city-state boundaries relating to the imperial period cannot be distinguished everywhere in the Basin of Mexico using the method I have described. We know, for example, that city-state boundaries were changed radically in some areas by imperial and regional state rulers, who altered the territorial integrity of city-states for political purposes. The most outstanding example is the Teotihuacán Valley, where dependent communities of city-state centers were intermingled, apparently to undercut the local support base of *tlatoque* and thus reduce their ability to secede from the state (Evans 1980; Gibson 1964:46; Münch 1976). Pronounced integration of city-state centers and dependent rural areas with the regional state capital, Texcoco, typifies the Acolhua regional state. In contrast, in the Tenochca-dominated areas of the Basin, city-state rulers' control over local dependencies was diminished, with less disruption of territory boundaries. Tenochca rulers tended to assign lands in dependent city-states to support rulers and nobles in other city-states, thus putting the dependent elites' source of economic support outside their home city-state.

By defining Aztec city-state territories as described above, it has been possible to estimate the area, population size, population distribution, and settlement hierarchy of individual city-states. These estimates provide uniform, comparable data on polities in the eastern and southern parts of the Basin. Although representative of only about one-half of the Aztec polities in the Basin of Mexico, the data on this selection of polities helps to identify basic trends in Aztec city-state organization. In the future, when such data are assembled for the Cuauhtitlán-Temascalapa survey region (work in progress by Sanders and Gorenflo) and for the Zumpango region (work in progress by Parsons), a more complete picture of Aztec polities can be constructed.

Comparison of polity size, population, and settlement complexity provide perspectives on city-states not available from documentary accounts (Tables 12.1 and 12.2). I have presented in detail the methodology for identifying Late Aztec city-state territories elsewhere (Hodge 1994). I compare the archaeological evidence of Early and Late Aztec period city-states below.

The Territorial Organization of Late Aztec City-States

Late Aztec polities are compared by political rank, population, and territory size in Table 12.1. Among the fifteen city-states compared, the total polity populations average 12,000 but display a wide range, from an estimated high of 40,430 to a low of 2,026. Urban center populations average 8,000 but range from 25,000 to 1,000—although at least one city-state (Tenanco) in the study region had no urban center (it probably had only elite residential precincts). The same may be true of Chiauhtlán, in which no urban center could be found, though the data remain equivocal for this city-state, since the urban center may be obscured by modern communities.

Territory sizes average 75 square kilometers but vary greatly, from approximately 20 square kilometers to 228 square kilometers; elsewhere in the Basin there may have been city-states as large as 900 square kilometers (Hodge 1984). Territory size does not correlate with political rank, but this is not surprising, in view of documentary reports that politically dominant city-states acquired income, including subsistence goods, as tribute from polities that they conquered (Alva Ixtlilxochitl 1975–1977; Berdan and Anawalt 1992; del Paso y Troncoso 1912).

Table 12.1 shows that high political rank in the Aztec imperial hierarchy correlates with large city-state population size. Texcoco, one of the leaders of the Triple Alliance and a founder of the empire, has the largest population of the city-states compared in this study. Texcoco's ability to sustain such a large populace is credible, since documents report that some of its elites and its palace were supported by tribute received from conquered communities such as Chalco, from other city-states within the Acolhua state, and from *calpixqui*-administered territories in the Acolhua state. Rank 3 and 4 city-states had intermediate population sizes, and Rank 5 polities fall below Rank 3 and 4 in total population.

Inspection of rural-urban population distribution with the city-states shows no correlation to polity size or population (Table 12.3). Recent research by Barbara Williams in Tepetlaoztoc suggests that urban-rural population distribution may be related to land quality and land use (1994).

A significant trend in intrapolity settlement patterns is the relative absence of site-size—and presumably functional—hierarchies within the Late Aztec

Table 12.1

Ranking and Size of Late Aztec Polities in the Eastern and Southern Basin of Mexico

Polity Name and Political Rank	Population				Total Population	Territory Size (km²)
	Urban Center	Percent	Rural Sites	Percent		
Political rank 2						
Texcoco	25,000	62	15,430	44	40,430	117
Political rank 3						
Huexotla	15,000	65	8,405	35	23,405	37
Tepetlaoztoc	13,500	60	8,765	40	22,265	93
Tlalmanalco-	4,000		4,340			
Chalco[a]	12,500	76	730	24	25,570	228
Xochimilco	10,700	75	3,545	25	14,245	164
Chimalhuacán	12,000	96	560	4	12,560	37
Cuitlahuac	4,500	47	4,980	53	9,480	68
Ixtapalapa	2,800	80	2,558	20	5,358	20
Culhuacán	3,250	90	480	10	4,830	20
Mexicaltzingo[b]	1,000					
Political rank 4						
Amecameca	10,000	95	515	5	10,515	55
Tenango	150	2	6,350	98	6,500	143
Political rank 5						
Coatepec	2,500	78	710	28	3,210	46
Mixquic	2,250	82	490	18	2,740	16
Ixtapaluca	1,630	80	396	20	2,026	27

Rank 2 = Regional state center; Rank 3 = City-state center with *Tlatoani*; Rank 4 = City-state center subordinate to a level 3 center; Rank 5 = Center governed by administrator

Sources: Blanton 1972; Parsons 1971; Parsons et al. 1983.

Note: Two city-states in Figure 12.4 are omitted here. Chiauhtlán is omitted because no central settlement could be identified by the archaeological survey. Its territory was about 18 square kilometers and its archaeologically estimated population was 1,790. Coatlinchán's urban center was surveyed and estimated to have contained 5,500 to 11,000 people. Most of Coatlinchán's territory fell outside the regional survey boundaries, however, and as a result, its total population could not be estimated using the archaeological survey and ethnohistorical data.

[a]Since Chalco was governed from Tlalmanalco after the Triple Alliance conquered the Chalco region, Chalco is combined here with Tlalmanalco.

[b]Culhuacán's and Mexicaltzingo's small territories could not be distinguished from one another, so their rural and total populations are combined.

city-states (Table 12.4), suggesting that many functions were performed in the city-state center rather than intermediate administrative centers. Calculating the average distance from farthest dependent community to a city-state center supports the conclusion that city-state urban centers were the principal administrative-economic centers in their territories. The distance between the urban centers and rural communities in the city-states examined in this study averages 7.1 kilometers—a walk that could be made in a few hours—a finding that suggests that tribute payment, performing labor on public works, exchange at a

marketplace, or attendance at calendrical and religious ceremonies occurred predominantly in the city-state center. The primacy of urban centers within city-states is also clear in those having a pronounced nucleation of population (in nine polities, the urban population was greater than 75 percent of the total). In other polities, the settlement categories consisted of an urban center and small villages and hamlets. Large villages that might have housed intermediate administrative or economic functions are lacking.

The conclusion based on archaeological data that decision making and other polity functions were cen-

Table 12.2

Ranking and Size of Early Aztec Polities and Confederations in the Eastern and Southern Basin of Mexico

	Population				
Polity Name	Urban Center	Percent	Rural Sites	Percent	Total Population
Acolhua Confederation					
Huexotla	7,500	58	4,650	42	12,150
Texcoco	?	—	13,130	100	13,130
Tepetlaoztoc	6,750	62	4,880	38	11,630
Chimalhuacán	6,000	92	550	8	6,550
Coatepec	1,250	95	70	5	1,320
Ixtapaluca	375	70	160	30	535
Cuitlahuaca-Mixquica Confederation					
Cuitlahuac	3,750	83	755	17	4,500
Mixquic	1,125	85	200	15	1,325
Culhua Confederation					
Culhuacán and	1,625	79	335	21	3,060
Mexicaltzingo[a]	1,100				
Ixtapalapa	1,400	97	50	3	1,450
Chalca Confederation					
Chalco-Tlalmanalco	6,250	60	4,225	40	10,475
Amecameca	5,000	98	125	2	5,125
Tenango	350	9	3,665	91	4,025[b]

Sources: Blanton 1972; Parsons 1971; and Parsons et al. 1983.

Note: The Xochimilca Confederation is omitted because nearly all Early Aztec sites are obscured by the concrete of modern settlements. The urban center of Xochimilco is estimated at 5,000–10,000 people; surveyable areas suggest that its rural population numbered only 130. Because the data represent a restricted—and therefore unreliable—sample, they provide very inaccurate estimates.

[a]The small, closely packed territories of Mexicaltzingo and Culhuacán could not be differentiated based on current data; thus they are combined here.

[b]Total Acolhua population = 45,315; total Cuitlahuaca population = 5,825; total Culhua population = 4,510; total Chalca population = 19,625. Confederation population estimates are incomplete for Acolhua and Chalca, since they extend beyond the area under study.

tralized is supported by documentary reports of administrative personnel resident in the urban centers and people's attendance at rituals performed at the urban center by the *tlatoani* (Anderson et al. 1976; Carrasco 1977; Carrasco and Monjarás-Ruíz 1976, 1978; *Relación de Huexotla* and other *Relaciones geográficas* in Acuña 1984–1987 and del Paso y Troncoso 1905–1906). Additional support comes from reports that the complexity of intrapolity hierarchies was reduced in some city-states in Late Aztec times by the imperial rulers. For example, in Cuauhtitlán, an intermediate level of administrative offices composed of governors of dependent towns (offices filled by persons appointed by the ruler of Cuauhtitlán) was eliminated after Cuauhtitlán entered the Aztec empire (perhaps to leave more of Cuauhtitlán's income available for imperial taxation). And, as mentioned previously, in Amecamecan-Chalco multiple *tlatoani* offices were reduced in number. In the Chalco region, a provincial administrative hierarchy was created in

imperial times, probably to increase control over this rebellious part of the Basin (Hodge 1984, 1991; Schroeder 1991).

The Territorial Organization of Early Aztec City-States

The Basin of Mexico archaeological surveys identified four Early Aztec cities with populations of 10,000–15,000, two on each side of Lake Texcoco. On the eastern side of the Basin were Huexotla and Coatlinchán, balanced by Azcapotzalco and Tenayuca (unsurveyable because it is covered by Mexico City) on the west. All other city-state centers were estimated to have had closer to 5,000 occupants. Communities of various sizes surrounded the city-state centers, and in some instances, there are breaks in occupation that suggest boundaries between territories (Parsons 1974).[4]

Estimates of fourteen Early Aztec city-state territo-

Table 12.3

Percentage of Late Aztec Urban Center versus Rural Communities in the Eastern and Southern Basin of Mexico

		Population Estimates				
Rank	Polity Name[a]	Urban Center Maximum	Urban Center Minimum	Rural Maximum	Urban Maximum Percent	Urban Minimum Percent
2	Texcoco	25,000	12,500	15,430	62	44
3	Huexotla	15,000	7,500	8,405	65	47
3	Tepetlaoztoc	13,500	6,750	8,765	60	77
3	Xochimilco	10,700	5,350	3,545	75	60
3	Chimalhuacán	12,000	6,000	560	96	91
3	Cuitlahuac	4,500	2,250	4,980	47	31
3	Tlalmanalco-Chalco[b]	4,000 12,500	2,000 6,000	5,070	76	61
3	Ixtapalapa	2,800	1,400	2,558	52	35
3	Mixquic	2,250	1,125	490	82	70
3	Culhuacán and Mexicaltzingo[c]	3,250 1,100	1,650 550	480	90	82
4	Amecameca	10,000	5,000	515	95	91
4	Tenango	150	75	6,350	2	1
5	Coatepec	2,500	1,250	710	78	64
5	Ixtapaluca	1,630	862	396	80	69

Rank 2 = Regional state center; Rank 3 = City-state center with *Tlatoani;* Rank 4 = City-state center subordinate to a Level 3 center; Rank 5 = Center governed by administrator

[a]Two city-states in the study area—Chiauhtlán and Coatlinchán—are omitted from these comparisons because much of the area surrounding Coatlinchán fell between regional survey strips and because surveys were unable to detect a political center in Chiautla's territory.

[b]Combined; see Table 12.1, note a.

[c]Urban populations of Culhuacán and Mexicaltzingo are estimated separately, but their very small neighboring territories are combined. Rural population size and settlement patterns are difficult to estimate in areas like Culhuacán, Mexicaltzingo, and Ixtapalapa, where modern settlements cover many prehispanic rural sites.

ries, populations, and settlement hierarchies (Tables 12.2 and 12.5) present a contrasting view of city-states when compared to the Late Aztec data. Though difficult to measure because Early Aztec sites are in the same locations as Late Aztec sites and their remains are greatly outnumbered by Late Aztec artifacts and construction (Sanders et al. 1979), the population size of Early Aztec urban centers averaged 4,000 persons, with a range of 375 to 7,500 persons. Total city-state population size ranged between 535 and 13,130 persons, averaging 6,000. Intrapolity site-size hierarchies are slightly more pronounced during the Early Aztec period than during the Late (Tables 12.4 and 12.5). As mentioned above, there are suggestions in documents that intrapolity hierarchies existing in preimperial times were later suppressed.

Compared to the Late Aztec period, Early Aztec settlement patterns conform more closely to the definition of a city-state posed at the beginning of this chapter: "small, territorially-based . . . with a city and hinterland, . . . relatively self-sufficient" and appearing in "groups of roughly equivalent size." The balance of size, urban center population, and total population characteristic of the Early Aztec period are congruent with documentary reports that the Early Aztec period was characterized by competing polities that formed alliances and regional confederations for protection and aggression. City-states such as Texcoco in the Late Aztec period are better described as regional state centers, if not imperial centers, which achieved great size and wealth through exaction of tribute from dependent polities. In the Acolhua region, for example, former city-states such as Coatepec were reduced to administered territories, presumably releas-

Table 12.4

Settlement-Size Distribution of Late Aztec City-States in the Eastern and Southern Basin of Mexico

Rank	Polity Name	Regional Center	Local Center	Large Village	Small Village	Hamlet	Small Hamlet	Questionable
Acolhua State (core area only)								
2	Texcoco	1	0	3	12	11	7	5
3	Huexotla	0	1	0	2	1	3	0
3	Chiautlán	0	?	1	5	3	0	0
3	Tepetlaoztoc	0	1	7	5	3	2	1
3	Chimalhuacán	0	1	0	0	2	1	2
5	Coatepec	0	1	0	3	4	4	0
5	Ixtapaluca	0	1	0	0	4	13	0
Tenochca Zone (southeast area only)								
3	Cuitlahuac	0	1	1	2	13	53	3
3	Mixquic	0	1	0	1	4	8	1
3	Xochimilco	0	1	0	2	18	37	4
3	Culhuacán and	0	2	0	1	2	11	3
3	Mexicaltzingo							
3	Ixtapalapa	0	1	1	5	5	9	0
3	Tlalamanalco-	0	1	2	4	11	15	0
4	Chalco	0	1	0	1	10	15	8
4	Tenanco	0	0	3	9	22	51	3
4	Amecameca	0	1	0	0	5	21	2
	Total	1	13	15	38	100	212	28

Note: Regional survey site categories for the Late Aztec period are Supraregional Centers (with monumental public architecture and 25,000+ residents); Provincial Centers (with distinct elite architecture, well-defined public architecture, and 1,000–10,000 residents); Large and Small Nucleated Villages (concentrated populations of 500–1,000+ and 100–500, respectively, but minimal public architecture); Large and Small Dispersed Villages (with populations of 500–1,000 and 100–500, respectively, and light surface remains); Hamlets (20–100 people; no public architecture); Small Hamlets (20 or fewer residents), and Isolated Ceremonial Centers (no permanent occupants). For a more complete explanation of site-size categories, see Parsons (1971:21–25) and Sanders et al. (1979:55).

ing the labor and land that might have been used to support a *tlatoani* and his *tecalli*, thereby allowing it to be absorbed as tribute by Texcoco's elites.

Initial Emergence

> Pottery, so dismal to read about, so important in reflecting cultural patterns, tells the story of this process [spread of Aztec culture].
>
> (Vaillant 1966:100)

Although we can compare Early Aztec city-state polities to those of the Late Aztec period and infer their political organization from territory size, population size, population distribution, and internal hierarchy, one question that remains is: When can Aztec city-states be recognized archaeologically? Without the support of imperial and colonial documentation, what features characterize a city-state? Are there such

characteristics (as seen in earlier central Mexican city-state systems; see J. Marcus 1989), or like the Aztec empire (Smith and Berdan 1992), are Aztec city-states almost invisible archaeologically?

According to the Basin of Mexico survey findings, Early Aztec settlement locations generally differed from those of the preceding Late Toltec period, characterized by relatively sparse occupation and a tendency for sites to be on top of hills. The Early Aztec settlement preference is for the Basin floor (Parsons 1974), but the Early Aztec occupation nonetheless proved difficult to define because most Early Aztec sites occur in the same locations as Late Aztec sites. Even though the Early Aztec period is represented by different ceramics than Late Aztec, the Early Aztec population was also difficult to measure because Late Aztec sherds on site surfaces greatly outnumbered the Early Aztec ones. The survey found on a Basin-wide

Table 12.5

Settlement-Size Distribution of Early Aztec City-States in the Eastern and Southern Basin of Mexico

Polity Name	Regional Center	Local Center	Large Village	Small Village	Hamlet	Small Hamlet	Questionable
Acolhua Confederation							
Huexotla	0	1	0	1	2	1	0
Coatlinchan	0	1	?	?	?	?	?
Texcoco	0	?	3	6	5	0	1
Tepetlaoztoc	1	0	7	10	3	2	0
Chimalhuacán	0	1	0	0	2	0	2
Coatepec	0	1	0	2	1	2	0
Ixtapaluca	0	1	0	0	1	4	0
Total	1	5	10	19	14	9	3
Cuitlahuaca Confederation							
Cuitlahuac	0	0	2	6	7	1	1
Mixquic	0	1	0	0	1	1	0
Total	0	1	2	6	7	2	1
Xochimilca Confederation							
Xochimilco	0	1	0	1	1	2	0
Total	0	1	0	1	1	2	0
Culhua Confederation							
Culhuacán-	0	1					
Mexicaltzingo	0	1	0	1	1	1	2
Ixtapalapa	1	0	0	0	1	0	0
Total	1	2	0	1	3	1	2
Chalca Confederation							
Amecameca	0	1	0	0	1	5	0
Chalco	0	1	0	3	5	3	5
Tlalmanalco	0	1	3	3	4	6	0
Tenanco	0	0	3	7	14	16	1
Total	0	3	6	13	24	30	6

Note: Based on archaeological data from the eastern and southern Basin of Mexico (Early Aztec period).

See Table 12.4 for a discussion of site typology.

scale that the Early Aztec period sites indicate a smaller population, one estimated at half the Late Aztec population.

The remains of Aztec urban centers, mapped according to sherd scatters and architectural remains, represent material evidence of the existence of Early Aztec sites and polities. To date, the best-known Early Aztec civic-ceremonial centers are at Tenayuca, where twin pyramid-temples were excavated (Noguera 1935), and at Huexotla, where several pyramids and a massive wall are evident (Brumfiel 1976a; García García 1987). From the archaeological evidence, these centers stand out as the most monumental of city-states in Early Aztec times. The archaeological surveys identified other city-state centers of this period that are less well-preserved (Table 12.2; Fig.

12.5). A survey of documentary histories found that all the city-state centers examined in this study reportedly functioned as city-states (e.g., had *tlatoque*, participated in wars, made political alliances, or had marketplaces) by the A.D. 1200s. The exception is Chiauhtlán, which is described as a settlement in the Early Aztec period, but it may not have been a *tlatoani* center until Nezahualcoyotl's reorganization of the Acolhua regional state in the 1430s (see Alva Ixtlilxochitl 1975–1977, 2:89; Alvarado Tezozomoc 1975; *Anales de Cuauhtitlán* 1974; Chimalpahin 1960, 1965; Davies 1980; Durán 1967; Offner 1983).

The Early Aztec period in the Basin of Mexico represents a change in settlement locations from the preceding Late Toltec period. Several large communities were spaced about 20 kilometers apart around the

Basin's lakes (except for a few island cities such as Tenochtitlán, Cuitlahuac, and Xaltocán), and these urban centers were surrounded by smaller settlements (Fig. 12.5). The Aztec communities are "new," in the sense that they do not overlap with the locations of Late Toltec communities. For example, Aztec remains at Chalco are stratigraphically above Toltec remains but appear after a near-abandonment or even a hiatus in occupation, perhaps the result of displacement of the occupants during all or part of the Late Toltec period (Hodge 1993).

Aztec culture is evident in a new ceramic assemblage. According to Smith (1984:178), "In the Basin of Mexico, the Middle and Late Postclassic 'Aztec' orangeware tradition is clearly intrusive, since the component orange paste ceramics have no local antecedents (see Parsons 1966:442–445) and are quite distinct from the Early Postclassic (Tollan phase) orange ceramics of Tula (Cobean 1978)." Smith adds that Aztec occupation is manifested by

The inception of new ceramic styles or traditions in central Mexico at approximately the same time. These ceramic manifestations continue from their first appearance until the sixteenth century, at which time they are associated with Nahuatl-speaking descendants of the Aztlan migrants. Although the origins of the ceramic styles are uncertain and cannot be traced to a north Mexican hearth, the fact that they first appear in central Mexico close to the historical date of arrival of the Aztlan groups and then continued with evidence of stylistic evolution until the 16th century strongly argues for their association with the Nahuatl immigrants and supports the historical date derived above. (Smith 1984:177–178)

Recent field research has produced information on the timing of Aztec city-states' settlement (via radiocarbon dating of ceramics), based on the assumption that the initial appearance of Aztec ceramics signals the foundation of Aztec communities and city-states. At Chalco, Aztec ceramics (Aztec I Black-on-Orange, Chalco Polychrome and Aztec Red ware) appear at A.D. 1100 (calibrated intercept; uncalibrated A.D. 1010 ±100; Beta-73525), a date close to that estimated in the regional chronology. Other sites show an earlier appearance of Aztec I ceramics. At nearby Ch-Az-195, Early Aztec ceramics appear at A.D. 690 (calibrated intercept; uncalibrated A.D. 640 ±60; Beta-4458) and at Xaltocán at A.D. 880 (calibrated intercept; uncalibrated A.D. 770 ±60; Beta-50317).

Aztec II Black-on-Orange, also associated with the Early Aztec period, appears at Chalco dated ca. A.D. 1240 (calibrated intercept; uncalibrated A.D. 1190 ±90; Beta-57757). At Xaltocán, Aztec II appears at A.D. 1235 (calibrated intercept; uncalibrated A.D. 1130 ±70; Beta-14910). Also in the northern Basin, at Azcapotzalco, Aztec II appears at A.D. 1240 (calibrated intercept; uncalibrated A.D. 1140 ±90; Beta-57759) directly over Coyotlatelco (Early Toltec) ceramics, as at Chalco. At Otumba, in the northeast Basin, the initial Aztec occupation is evident in Aztec II ceramics as well (for more information on the chronology, see Brumfiel 1992; Hodge 1993; Nichols and Charlton 1996; Parsons et al. 1996; Smith and Doershuk 1991).

These dates show that some Aztec city-states are older than previously thought because the initial dating was based on excavations that lacked absolute dates (e.g., Vaillant 1962); others seem to have been founded in the 1100s–1200s, as predicted by the current regional chronology (Sanders et al. 1979).

External Relationships

It is clear that the Aztec empire altered regional confederation relationships and created a hierarchy of political power and economic strength (measured by access to land and labor) in the Basin of Mexico. Economic relationships, especially those focusing on production and exchange, constitute an important area of inquiry to which archaeological research can contribute, and such research can complement documentary reports of a marketplace economy in the Basin of Mexico and the presence of craftspeople in city-states.

Archaeological research shows that craft specialization was present in some city-state centers. Survey data suggest suppression of craft specialization in the Late Aztec period in favor of agricultural production at city-states nearest to the dominant urban centers like Texcoco and Tenochtitlán. In contrast, there is clear evidence that intensive craft production did occur at sites farther from the imperial capital—sites such as Otumba (for a discussion of ceramic, lithic, lapidary, and fiber production at Otumba, see Charlton et al. 1991; Nichols 1994; Otis Charlton et al. 1993; Otis Charlton 1994). Examples of other types of goods produced outside the imperial capitals included fine crafts and ceramic serving dishes (Brumfiel 1987; Hodge 1992; Hodge et al. 1992, 1993).

Exchange patterns shed some light on relations among city-states. Analyses of the sources and distributions of ceramics to identify regional patterns of exchange have shown that in the Early Aztec period exchange occurred with the greatest intensity among city-states in the same confederation. Less intense exchange took place between city-states of different confederations (Hodge and Minc 1990, 1991). At least one Early Aztec Black-on-Orange ceramic style (Mixquic Black-on-Orange) had a distribution sufficiently localized to characterize city-state boundaries (Minc et al. 1994), but in general, exchange occurred at the supra–city-state or confederation level. For ex-

ample, Figure 12.6 shows the sites where Chalco Polychrome was recovered at Early Aztec sites during surveys (Parsons et al. 1982) of the area examined in this paper. The greatest concentration of such sites is in the Chalco Valley, and the sites correspond to the area of the Chalco confederation. The Late Aztec exchange of ceramics occurred with greatest intensity at the confederation level despite a regional consolidation of ceramic styles, exemplified by Aztec III Black-on-Orange, which is an archaeological marker

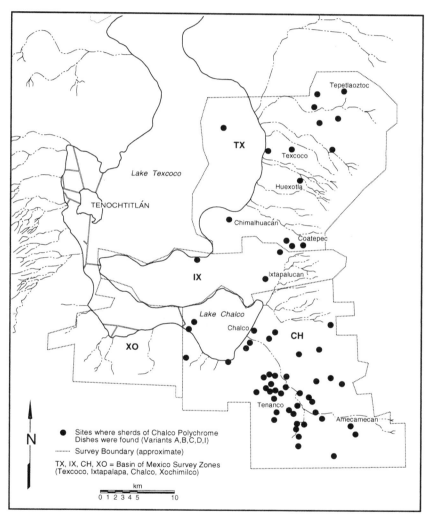

Figure 12.6. Sites in the Texcoco, Ixtapalapa, Chalco, and Xochimilco survey regions (Parsons et al. 1982) where Chalco Polychrome was recovered. Chalco Polychrome is found at nearly every site in the area corresponding to the Chalco confederation, indicating that these politically allied city-states shared a common exchange system as well. Outside this region, it is less frequent, suggesting that communities outside the Chalco confederation obtained it through (different) market systems in which this ceramic was a "trade ware." Of the sites where Chalco Polychrome was recovered, 53 percent are located in the Chalco confederation's territory, 21 percent are in the Acolhua confederation's territory, and the remaining 16 percent are in the Xochimilca, Cuitlahuaca-Mixquica or Culhua confederations. Compositional analyses indicate that Chalco Polychrome was produced in the Chalco region (Minc et al. 1994; Hodge et al. 1992, 1993). Base map after Parsons et al. (1983:figure 8). Redrawn by R. Richard Rogers.

throughout Late Postclassic Mesoamerica of contact with the Basin of Mexico (Hodge 1992; Hodge et al. 1992, 1993). Late Aztec exchange involving specialized, labor-intensive decorated ceramics made in craft workshops operated at the confederation level and sometimes on a regional scale as well.

Ceramics represent only a portion of the Aztec exchange system of course. Spence (1985) concluded that obsidian followed a noncentralized exchange system during the Late Aztec period, suggesting that this product, which had only a few sources, involved a different exchange system than that of decorated ceramic serving dishes, which were made in several cities. Research on clay figurine manufacture may result in the identification of yet another series of economic relationships between Aztec city-states (Otis Charlton 1994). Research focused on city-state economies and the classes of goods that moved through them (such as work in progress by Minc to characterize community-specific ceramic production) is necessary to characterize economic activities at the city-state level.

When Is a City-State Recognizable as an Archaeological Entity?

This comparative study of a selection of Aztec city-states has demonstrated that polities changed over time and that external relationships, including confederation affiliation and incorporation into the Aztec empire, altered their internal organizations. The city-state polity's compact scale—with a political and economic center within a day's walking distance of most communities and a political leadership composed of the *tlatoani, tecalli,* and some administrators—may have contributed to its persistence over time. Aztec city-states, founded by the A.D. 1100s, endured through the Aztec empire (A.D. 1430–1520) and became the administrative units within the Spanish colonial empire (Gibson 1964; Gerhard 1972).

Early Aztec city-states (A.D. 800–1150) were characterized by balanced population sizes, political powers, and economic strengths. Groups of them allied to form regional confederations. In contrast, Late Aztec city-states were part of the Aztec empire's regional political system, and some achieved much greater political power, population size, and wealth than others.

A new era of city-state archaeology has begun in central Mexico, one based on regional surveys that provide a context for the single city-state. Polity-focused studies are acquiring data for diachronic studies of individual city-states, as well as comparative, synchronic studies. In response to the threat to Aztec period archaeological sites near Mexico City from urban expansion, much research is now being conducted in the Basin of Mexico (Brumfiel 1976a, 1991, 1992; Charlton and Nichols 1990; Hodge 1993). In addition, in other regions of the Mesa Central, where construction is impinging on Postclassic sites, research on city-states has also been initiated (McVicker and Urquizo 1991; Neff et al. 1991; Smith and Heath-Smith 1994; de Vega Nova and Mayer Guala 1991).

Some themes in the archaeology of Aztec city-states for which comparative data would be useful to supplement existing studies are: investigation of domestic units, including rulers' houses and elite dwellings as well as commoner residences (for comparison to those by Evans 1991, 1993; Smith 1992b; Smith et al. 1994; Vaillant 1962); studies of Aztec ceremonial activities at the city-state level (following Cook de Leonard and Lemoine 1954–1955); and urban excavations (as at Tlatelolco—see, for example, Arroyo 1990; and analyses of Tenochtitlán—e.g., Aveni et al. 1988; Matos M. 1988). Economic studies at the city-state level of production, markets, exchange, and potential for self-sufficiency would also address issues raised by the comparative study of city-states. The archaeology of social organization and social change is possible at Aztec city-state sites through studies of the archaeological evidence for sociopolitical identities and/or ethnicities (e.g., Brumfiel et al. 1994; Hodge 1992; Otis Charlton 1994).

Summary: The City-State as a Unit for Archaeological Analysis of Aztec Culture

The Aztec city-state, in its different forms over time and space, is clearly evident in documentary accounts that describe the cities and their rulers' lives, actions, and dynasties and the wars and alliances among city-states. Aztec city-states and their confederations claimed distinct identities based on their historical traditions, deities, rituals, and locations. Urban centers show great continuity in location from their founding in Early Aztec times through the Aztec imperial period and on into the present day.

The archaeological picture is different. In its clearest archaeological form, the Aztec city-state is easily recognized, but many identified in documentary accounts are difficult to define from archaeological data alone. The elusive nature of Aztec city-state territorial units results from the fact that most Aztec city-state centers are difficult to study archaeologically because they are obscured by modern urban settlements and because boundaries between city-states are often not evident from either manmade markers or from the settlement patterns. Until recently, the difficulties in identifying archaeological data at the city-state level led to an emphasis on regional or site-specific studies—for example, studies of Aztec culture using broader or more restricted scales of analysis than the city-state. Combining information from documents on culturally and historically defined territories with archaeological data permits identification and measurement of political territories as the Aztecs defined them. Although the individual Aztec city-state can be an elusive archaeological unit, current research focusing on city-state units is providing new insights into Aztec life.

Notes

1. Some authors have employed terms that emphasize the rulers and political organization—for example, *kingdom* (Schroeder 1991), *petty kingdom* (Brumfiel 1987), *state* (Hicks 1986:41–45), or *town* (Gibson 1964:31).

2. The Early Aztec period is currently defined in the regional archaeological chronology as A.D. 1150–1350 (see below for new data on the beginning of this period). The Late Aztec archaeological period is defined by a regional spread of Aztec III, or Tenochtitlán Phase, Black-on-Orange ceramics, a style perhaps distributed by the short-lived expansionist Tepaneca empire and later by the Aztec empire, A.D. 1430–1521 (Vaillant 1938; Parsons 1966; Smith and Berdan 1992).

3. These time spans begin with the formation of the Aztec city-state system and go through the Aztec imperial period, A.D. 1430–1520. Since the Late Aztec ceramic period emerged prior to the empire, the two periods cannot be used to compare preimperial and imperial-period city-states precisely; however, general comparisons between preimperial and imperial-period conditions can be made and must serve until the ceramic chronology has been further refined.

4. Early Aztec territories were estimated by overlaying the Late Aztec boundaries onto those of the Late Aztec period, if no contradictory data appear in documentary sources. The Early Aztec territories may have been somewhat smaller than Late Aztec ones, but in this study, Early Aztec territory sizes are considered to be in the same locations and about the same sizes as the Late Aztec territories (in the cases where Late Aztec city-states succeed Early Aztec ones) because there is very little detail in the documents on Early Aztec polity boundaries. Documentary reports of border disputes suggest that open buffer zones may have been common. When the Basin's polities were politically unified under the empire in Late Aztec times, spaces between city-states were filled in by new communities.

13

Early State Formation on the North Coast of Peru

A Critique of the City-State Model

DAVID J. WILSON

Given the focus of this volume on the city-state as a postulated universal type of early civilization, it is appropriate to begin this paper with the assertion that most anthropological archaeologists interested in sociocultural evolution and the rise of complex societies can be divided into four more or less mutually exclusive terminological camps. The first camp, of least relevance here but important to mention nonetheless, includes a few scholars who might be called the "typological nihilists." In reacting to the variable meanings assigned to "chiefdom" and "state" and what they see as the "essentialist" nature of the whole slate of evolutionary-ecological stage terms, they make it their business to criticize the use of all such terminology but offer us no scheme of their own (e.g., Leonard and Jones 1987; see also Bawden's 1989 critique of the papers in J. Haas et al. 1987). We might say that since they don't know what a *state* is they prefer not to use the term, nor would they want to append the adjectival term *city* since no one can agree on what that means either.

The second camp consists of the "evolutionary-ecologists" themselves who, following Morgan, White, and Steward, see the theoretical utility of some sort of stage/level terminology in cross-cultural studies of human societies (e.g., Fried 1967; Flannery 1972; Johnson and Earle 1987; Sanders and Price 1967; Schreiber 1992; Service 1962, 1975; Wright and Johnson 1975; Wright 1978). In general, most members of this camp seem disinclined to divide the state into subtypes, although some replace such terms as *bands* with *family level foragers* and see "simple" and "complex" chiefdoms as two stages, or levels of integration, in the development of societal complexity (cf. Johnson and Earle 1987). This group, of which I count myself a member (e.g., Wilson 1981, 1988), thinks it knows what a state is, but is unwilling to tack on adjectival terms such as *city,* and prefers to talk about the "first-order sites," or "primary centers," that arise as a feature of such polities.

The third camp, which represents a variation of the evolutionary-ecological camp, might be termed the "multistage state typologists," in that its adherents look at the evolution of states around the world and see a profusion of distinctive stages that must be classified. Examples of this approach include the papers in Claessen and Skalník (1978), where early states are classed as "inchoate," "typical," and "transitional"; and those in Friedman and Rowlands (1978), where, using an even more elaborate scheme, early states are classed as "asiatic," "dualistic," "territorial," and "city," some or all of which exhibit varying degrees of "centrifugalism" or "centripetalism" as they develop. In a sense, the members of this group not only know what a state is, but are loathe to leave the matter simply there in their drive to classify its apparent variable forms in exquisite detail.

The fourth camp, possibly in reaction to typological excesses, postulates the existence of different types of states, but limits the number of types to two. These "modified state typologists," as represented, for example, by Trigger in his recent study of early civilizations (1993), look around the preindustrial world and see only two kinds of states: city-states and territorial states. Since the focus of this volume is the city-state and Trigger is quite specific about what he sees as the principal features of the "city-state" in contrast to the "territorial state," it is useful to outline his definitions of the two types. These will not only provide models against which the data from the Peruvian north coast can be compared and contrasted, but, in light of what these data suggest about the inapplicability of the city-state model itself in this case, will also provide grounds for a plea to utilize the universal heuristics advocated by the second camp mentioned above.

At the appropriate point I will also provide a brief rationale for my choice of data from the Central Andes (i.e., "Why the Santa and Casma Valleys, and not Wari, Chimu, and Inca?"), in part as a rejoinder. One of the discussants in the symposium that preceded this volume postulated that these later, more spectacular Andean cultures might be more relevant here than the earlier complex societies of the north coast.

Theoretical Considerations

Trigger's city-state and territorial state models

In constructing his dual model of ancient states, it is interesting that Trigger takes as his fundamental criterion in choosing examples of city and territorial states the need for detailed written documentation. This automatically limits him to two kinds of cases: first, ancient states that developed literacy at the time of their formation (Sumer, the Maya, Egypt, and the Shang); and, second, more recent states that were described by their literate conquerors (the Aztecs, the Yorubas, and the Incas). It excludes those ancient, or pristine, states which, although at least as complex as their literate counterparts, if not more so, did not develop writing. Perhaps the best example of such a state from the Central Andes is the Moche, an extensive multi-

valley polity recently made more notable by the finding at Sipán, in the Lambayeque Valley, of the richest royal tombs ever excavated in the Americas (cf. Alva and Donnan 1993; see also Benson 1972; Donnan 1973; Proulx 1973; Strong and Evans 1952; Willey 1953; Wilson 1988).

City-states, as defined by Trigger, include Sumer, the Aztecs, the Maya, and the Yorubas. They are characterized by the following features: (1) small territories covering only a few hundreds of square kilometers; (2) capital cities that contain the great majority of the total population, or as much as 80 percent of the state's inhabitants in the case of ancient Sumer; (3) a threefold hierarchy of site types, including the capital, smaller centers, and villages and hamlets; (4) the presence in the city of considerable numbers of farmers who live there for protection; (5) the frequent presence of a defensive wall around the city, due to continual war with other nearby city-state polities; (6) a highly developed economy that includes advanced craft production and technology, as well as 10 to 20 percent of the population as nonfood producers; (7) intensive farming, but small surpluses; from which it follows that city-states have (8) smaller populations; (9) smaller monumental architecture; and (10) less political unity than territorial states.

Trigger's examples of territorial states include ancient Egypt, the Inca, and the Shang. Compared to city-states, they are characterized by (1) huge territories; (2) national capitals which, although as large as "substantial city-states," must be seen as small in relation to the vast bulk of the population in rural areas; (3) the same threefold hierarchy, including the capital, administrative centers, and villages and dispersed homesteads; (4) the presence in the capital of only the ruling class, administrators, craft specialists, and retainers, with the rest of the population, including farmers, located in the rural areas; (5) no defensive wall around the capital (but, presumably, forts on the state peripheries); (6) a less developed economy since crafts in the capital served only the elite, whereas farmers were relatively more self-sufficient; (7) less intensive farming, but large surpluses; from which it follows that territorial states had (8) larger populations; (9) larger monumental architecture; and (10) greater political unity than city-states.

Aside from the criticism of the requirement that written sources be available to describe the component features of the states chosen as examples, I will make the following four points as a general theoretical critique of Trigger's models.

First of all, he does not take sufficiently into account the environmental contexts in which states arose and how this might affect their nature (e.g., some are located in lacustrine contexts, some along a single major river system, some in highland valleys, some are environmentally circumscribed, and some are not).

Second, his models fail to account for the kinds of subsistence adaptations that characterize each state in its environmental setting and how this might affect the form they took (here I am thinking of the Central Mexican Symbiotic region, Inca terracing and verticality; and coastal Peruvian canal irrigation and its extent and implications for the size of local sociopolitical units, to mention only three cases; cf. Murra [1975], Sanders and Price [1968], and Wilson [1987, 1988]).

Third, Trigger postulates that if a city-state and a territorial state ever came into direct conflict the city-state would emerge victorious because of its relative technological superiority, in spite of the far greater demographic and political clout of the territorial state. Although his argument is based on examples that include the inability of Egypt to conquer Southwest Asian city-states and the conquest by Greek city-states of the Persian Empire, I find it illogical as an a priori working principle when approaching archaeological data sets on complex societies.

Fourth, I am uncomfortable with the fact that his examples represent both pristine developments that occurred at the beginning of a long sequence of continual state formation/reformation (e.g., Egypt, Sumer, the Maya) and later states that represent the culmination of developments in statecraft many centuries, if not several millennia, after the initial rise of sociopolitical complexity (the Aztecs, the Yorubas, and the Incas).

For example, one could postulate that larger-scale territorial states might be expected to occur later in sequences and smaller-scale ("city") states to occur earlier. This certainly can be argued for Egypt, where pristine state formation occurred first at the basin, or *nome*, level in late predynastic times well prior to the unification of Upper and Lower Egypt by about 3100 B.C. (Trigger et al. 1983). As I will discuss in greater detail below, it can be argued as well for the Peruvian north coast where pristine state formation seems to have occurred at the local valley level by at least 350 B.C. (if not by 1500 B.C.; cf. Pozorski and Pozorski 1987, 1994) some centuries prior to the rise of the multivalley Moche state in the first centuries A.D. (cf.

Alva and Donnan 1993; Benson 1972; Proulx 1973; Willey 1953; Wilson 1988). One might also take issue with Trigger's assertion that the Aztecs represent a "city-state" per se, since the Aztec *state* as commonly referred to consisted of a Triple Alliance of city-states that extended its control over one of the largest territories ever conquered by a prehispanic Mesoamerican group (cf. Collier et al. 1982; Sanders et al. 1979).

A universalist approach to state origins and development

In this section I would like not only to outline briefly a few general systemic features of states that are important for archaeologists who work with nonliterate and literate complex polities around the world, but also to present an updated version of a systems model I have been developing over the past several years that attempts to take into account as many features as possible that are crucial for societal adaptations in general and state formation in particular.

With regard to the first point, I am aware that I am reinventing at least a part of a very well-worn, if not well-tested, wheel, but I think it important to do this as a reminder that it is the *systemic* features common to all states, or any other kind of society, that should be of more interest in the cross-cultural perspective advocated by Steward. In this approach the unique local features of societies are of lesser concern, although admittedly they often provide some of the main points of interest for scholars who would append the kinds of adjectival terms mentioned in the introduction to this paper. However, given the vast literature on states, and at least my general agreement with Trigger's argument about the features that characterize them, there is no need to provide a definition of a state polity here.

It is critical that if we view a state—any kind of state—as a system, then, as I have argued elsewhere (Wilson 1989), it is necessary to adopt a methodology that includes some sort of settlement-pattern approach, comprehensive or otherwise, in order to have at hand as complete a sample as possible of all the kinds of settlements that constituted its postulated hierarchical organization. Anyone who has read Wright and Johnson's (1975) classic paper on the origins of the state in the Near East will find this aspect of my argument unsurprising, although it still seems necessary to assert to some of our colleagues who would construct "states" out of excavations at single sites in the earliest part of sequences, without having any

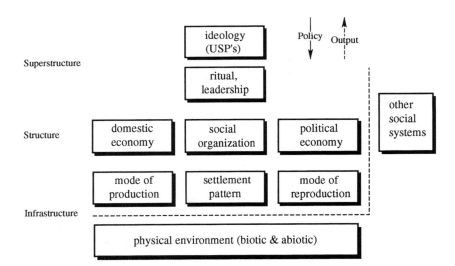

Figure 13.1. A systems-hierarchical model of societal systems.

data whatsoever on the rest of the (rural) sites in the system. In other words, following Wright and Johnson, a convincing demonstration of the presence of a chiefdom or state in a given area includes having access to settlement data that permit the identification of the number of levels of site size and function in the system, since chiefdoms classically are characterized by two levels, and states by three or more—among several other criteria such as relative territorial extent, number of sites, estimated population, size and nature of the principal center, scale of monumental architecture, and the type of subsistence system.

When we look at ancient states as systems, as opposed to types (i.e., city, territorial, Asiatic, or whatever), then it becomes important that we label the centers of these polities as such, namely *centers,* which arise in large part as a function of the adaptive need for overarching coordination of increasingly complex features both internal and external to the system in question (I speak here to some degree as an unrepentant consensual theorist, at least for the data from the Peruvian north coast). I shall return to this point in the section on the north coast data, but will confine the discussion for now to the theoretical perspective that underlies this sort of argument.

Figure 13.1 shows an updated version of a generalized systems model that I have been developing over the past several years in teaching courses on human ecology and sociocultural evolution, having applied it in arguments about the interconnectedness of variables at all systemic levels, from the ideological to the material, in dealing with a wide variety of recent and ancient societies around the world—including, in Africa, the BamButi, the Bantu, the Ik/ Teuso, the !Kung, and ancient Egypt; in North America, the

Ihalmiut, potlatching groups of the Northwest Coast, and ancient Chaco; in Polynesia, ancient Easter Island; in New Guinea, the Tsembaga Maring; in Middle America, the Aztecs; and, in South America, the Ona, the Yahgan, the Yanomamo, the Jívaro, the Tukanoan Desana, the Kogi/ Tairona, and theoretical arguments about the rise of complex society in the Central Peruvian Andes. As discussed elsewhere (Wilson 1992), I have derived most of the features of the model from the theoretical arguments of Steward (1955, 1977), Rappaport (1968, 1971, 1979), Flannery (1972), and Harris (1977, 1979).

The model's two principal characteristics are that it (1) breaks a society down into its most important features through the hierarchical ordering of a basic set of discrete component variables; and (2) attempts to make sense of the overall societal system in terms of assertions about the causal relationships among these variables. I will go so far as to risk the wrath of my postmodernist colleagues and assert that what one is doing in this sort of analysis is making a society "intelligible," first, by identifying all potential critical variables and, second, by asserting, if not demonstrating, causal relationships among selected sets of these variables (I am well aware of the epistemological difficulties represented by this argument, but do not see the "hardcore" philosophers getting much beyond philosophy per se in telling us to how to proceed here; e.g., see R. Gould 1992).

The model is *hierarchical* in that it asserts that the principal variables characteristic of all societies are ordered as follows: At the base of the system is the physical environment whose characteristics are important in defining at least some of the central features of the society in question. Above this, at the level of infrastructure, are the mode of production (subsistence), the settlement pattern, and the mode of reproduction (demography), which are intimately related at the local level to the physical environment as well as to each other, and provide further defining characteristics for higher-order levels in the system. Above this is the structure, including the domestic economy, social organization, and the political economy, which not only are derived from the infrastructural base but are equally important (or causal) in regulating and defining variables at the lower-order level. The superstructure consists of the highest-order variables that regulate, maintain, and define a society; it includes both concrete behavioral aspects (e.g., ritual and leadership) at a lower level and abstract mental aspects (ideology, cosmology, ultimate sacred postulates) at a higher level. Here, it is important to note that social organization is shown centrally positioned immediately below ritual/leadership, since, like the behavioral superstructural level, it may be considered not only as derived from lower-order levels but critically important in regulating them. Finally, the model also asserts that societies must be understood both in light of their local physical environment and their social environment (other local/regional social systems) as well.

The model is *systemic* in that it asserts that the nature and form of a society derive from the often highly complex (if not often counterintuitive) relationships that exist among multiple variables, although no "causal arrows" are shown on the basic model in Figure 13.1, since their number, direction, and positioning are considered empirical questions related to the kinds of arguments made about a particular set of data from a given society. Following Flannery (1972), the model asserts that there is a general two-way causal relationship between abstract superstructure and concrete infrastructure (Flannery calls bottom-up influences "output" and top-down ones "policy"). Thus, although Harris's (1979) contribution is clear in my inclusion of four of his societal variables (mode of production, mode of reproduction, domestic economy, and political economy), the model does not follow his premise that all causation is bottom-up, from the infrastructure to higher levels.

Although a claim for universality is made for the model—in other words, for its efficacy in dealing both with ethnographic and archaeological data sets—I make no claim that the model necessarily explains societal reality. Rather, I have found that its principal application is in the *description* of complex,

multivariate arguments, often of a highly theoretical nature, made by researchers about a particular society (e.g., Harris's and Chagnon's competing arguments about Yanomamo "reality"; cf. Chagnon 1968, 1977, 1983, 1992; Harris 1977; see also Wilson 1992).

The systems-hierarchical model is derived from logico-positivist principles, that is, from a point of view that places essentially no stock in the current idealist, if not nihilistic and antiscientific, tendencies of a postmodernist, interpretivist anthropology (e.g., see Marcus and Fischer 1986). Nevertheless, though one might agree, as I do, with many of Harris's scathing attacks on various idealist positions (e.g., 1979), this does not mean that one has to buy his brand of infrastructural determinism either. Indeed, the most convincing evidence of the causal importance of both ideology and infrastructure is to be found in the reading of ethnographic studies, not in archaeological ones. Ironically, however, in spite of the disinclination of many archaeologists to read the ethnographic literature, it is the archaeologists who have followed Harris's version of materialism more than the sociocultural anthropologists (cf. Schiffer 1983), not least because it is rather more difficult to dig up an "ultimate sacred postulate" (relegated by Harris to the status of a trivial dependent variable) than it is a "utilitarian secular pot." This does not mean that as archaeologists we should not be interested in reconstructing higher-order variables and some of the possible reasons for their nature and presence in ancient systems, a point I will return to below.

Given its strong descriptive focus, the model is intended to reproduce graphically and parsimoniously the complexities of arguments that often are book-length in their extent. I thus reject as superficial, if not naive, any critique that the model consists merely of "labels in little black boxes" (for a detailed discussion of the myriad variables that make up each of the principal subsystems that he, at least, views as important, see Harris 1979). Indeed, I have found that, no matter what its length is, any systemic textual argument that makes basic sense can easily be represented and *critiqued* once its elements are laid out in accordance with the model. For example, excessively materialistic or idealistic arguments can be exposed in detail to show their failure to invoke plausible correlated cause at the other levels in a system.

A final observation is that the model is not panglossian; that is, it does not invoke the functionalist notion that "all things work for the best in the best of all possible worlds." Thus, as Flannery's classic paper on the evolution of complexity makes clear (1972), societies not only can exhibit dynamic equilibrium over the long term (an example from South America were the Ona and Yahgan of Tierra del Fuego, who existed in stable, enduring adaptations for some 10,000 years until recent European intervention in the area), but can also exhibit both system-building stages as they grow and system-destroying pathologies as they die out. This relative volatility may well be both the blessing and the curse associated with those areas where complex societies developed.

Space does not permit further discussion of the model's features and implications here, but the model helps resolve such classic issues as (1) idealist versus materialist accounts of social reality—both are necessary and challenge the researcher to demonstrate how the two realms interrelate functionally; (2) internal versus external arguments about cause in local systems—both are important, although the precise mix must be considered an empirical question for research; and (3) quantification versus qualification in the ecological study of societies—we can quantify the material world, but, in a very real sense, find it more appropriate to qualify the abstract mental one.

The Santa and Casma Valley Cases

I have chosen to focus on the Santa and Casma Valleys rather the better-known Central Andean cultures such as the Wari (Middle Horizon, ca. A.D. 650–1100), the Chimu (Late Intermediate period, ca. A.D. 1100–1475), or the Inca (Late Horizon period, pre-A.D. 1475–1532) for two reasons (Fig. 13.2). First, the north coast south of the Moche Valley has been

THE CASMA AND SANTA VALLEY SEQUENCES IN RELATION TO CENTRAL ANDEAN CHRONOLOGY AND CULTURES

Figure 13.2. The Casma and Santa Valley sequences in relation to central Andean chronology and cultures.

Absolute Chronology	Casma Valley Period	Santa Valley Period	Central Andean Period	Major Culture
1532	Manchán	Late Tambo Real	Late Horizon	Inca
1475		Early Tambo Real	Late Intermediate	Chimú
1100	Casma	Late Tanguche	Late	Wari
			Middle Horizon	
			Early	
700	Choloque	Early Tanguche	Late	
	Nivín	Guadalupito		Moche
			Early Intermediate	
A.D.	Cachipampa	Late Suchimancillo	Beginning	
-------------		Early		Gallinazo
B.C.	Patazca	Vinzos	Late	
350			Early Horizon	
	Pallka	Cayhuamarca		Chavín
1000			Beginning	
	Moxeke	?	Initial	
1800-------			Preceramic	
	Huaynuná	Las Salinas	Preceramic	

the locus of my research. Second, and more importantly, following Trigger's definitions of city- and territorial states, Wari, Chimu, and the Inca are examples of territorial states (see also Kolata, this volume). They not only extended over many thousands of square kilometers but included great numbers of sites, apart from the main centers, where the overwhelming majority of the population of the state resided.

Based on archaeological and ethnohistoric research to date, population estimates for the Inca, Chimu, and Wari states are as follows: (1) for the Inca, greater Cuzco's population is estimated at 100,000, the empire's population at 14,000,000, and the territorial extent at 1,750,000 square kilometers (cf. Hyslop 1990); (2) for the Chimu, Chan Chan's population is estimated at 25,000, the state's population at 500,000, and the territorial extent at 75,000 square kilometers (cf. Moseley and Day 1977; Schaedel 1972); and (3) for the Wari, the population of Wari site is estimated at 30,000 (cf. Isbell and McEwan 1991; Moseley 1992), and, assuming densities of 8 persons per square kilometer, as in the case of the Inca, over some 250,000 square kilometers, the population of the state was about 2,000,000. Thus, the people residing in the primary centers were a mere 0.007 percent (Cuzco), 0.060 percent (Chan Chan), and 0.0015 percent (Wari), respectively, of the population of each state. With capitals containing far less than 1 percent of the each state's total population and vast territories that covered many tens of thousands of square kilometers, the Inca, the Chimu, and the Wari hardly qualify as city-states (see also Kolata, this volume). One therefore has to search earlier in the archaeological record in order to find such a society, if indeed city-states ever existed in the Central Andes.

Research Setting and Methods

As mentioned above, my research on Peruvian north coast state origins has involved comprehensive settlement-pattern studies (Fig. 13.3) of the following areas: the Santa Valley Project, 1979–1980, a survey of more than 750 square kilometers of the coastal sector of the valley (Wilson 1983, 1987, 1988, 1989); the Moche-Casma Road-Settlement Project, 1986–1987, a survey of all extant roads and roadside sites linking valleys across the five deserts lying between the Moche and Casma Valleys, over an area of some 3200 square kilometers (publications are in preparation); and the Casma Valley Project, 1989–1995,

a comprehensive study of all sites in a nine-period sequence from the late Preceramic (pre-1800 B.C.) through the end of the Late Horizon period (A.D. 1532), in a valley characterized by some of the earliest societal complexity in the Americas (e.g., Pozorski and Pozorski 1994). Since the nature of the Peruvian coastal environment and the research methods utilized in the above projects have been outlined in extensive detail (Wilson 1988), I will confine the discussion of these two aspects of the work to a brief overview.

With regard to the environment, no better area for the long-term preservation of even the most ancient archaeological remains exists anywhere else in the world. On the "modern" desert surface adjacent to the narrow valley floors we find sites of all periods dating back some 3,700 years and beyond, to the late Preceramic. With essentially no rainfall, there is little or no coverage of any of these remains from geological processes, except for isolated, discrete barchan dunes formed as sand blows inland off the beaches. With very little land available in these narrow, highly circumscribed valleys, I postulate that the strong tendency throughout the sequence was to locate settlements on the nonirrigable desert slopes and *pampas* that lie adjacent to the valley floors, rather than in the midst of the cultivable floors themselves (Wilson 1988). Moreover, we have found multicomponent sites all along the north and south desert margins, indicating that cultural stratification, or "tell" formation, is not a problem. In short, we are able to retrieve a sample of ancient sites far closer to a 100-percent ideal than anywhere else in the world. If this is so, then Peru is unique in its appropriateness for locating most or nearly all of the sites in ancient subsistence-settlement systems, and thus for testing theories about the origins and development of complex societal systems.

As a general example of the kind of preservation we find, it is possible to visit nearly any habitation site of a given prehistoric period and discover on the surface either (1) the excellently preserved remains of each low-walled stone dwelling that existed on the site (including main doors, rooms, stone storage pits, and doorways into rooms); or (2) the fairly well-preserved remains of organic *quincha*, or wattle-and-daub, dwellings (including wall "stubs" sticking up about 10 cm above the surface and the cordage used to lace them together). Both kinds of sites include well-preserved remains of maize cobs, cordage, shell-fish, cotton seeds, cotton fibers, textiles, wooden im-

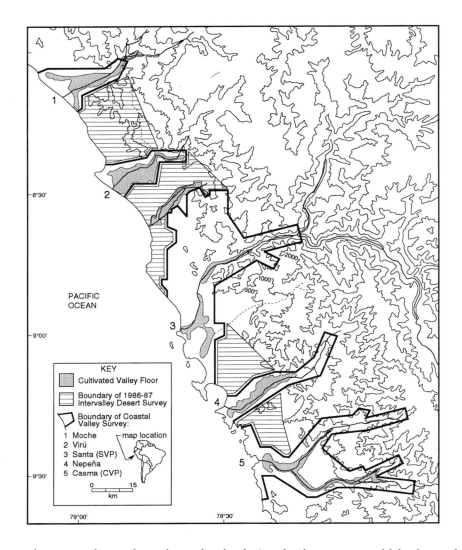

Figure 13.3. Map of the Peruvian north coast, showing the projects and valleys mentioned in the text.

plements, charcoal, and potsherds dating back at least to the earliest centuries A.D.

Thus, in making population estimates for each period in a sequence, we either can count the exact number of discrete dwellings that existed on a stone-walled habitation site or at least estimate with some accuracy the density of *quincha* structures that existed at the second type of site. Compared to other areas of the world, then, we can achieve both accurate estimates of site size in hectares and numbers/densities of habitation structures to produce, in turn, relatively accurate estimates of the numbers of people who constituted each cultural system (such estimates are of course based on the assumption of the contemporaneity of all sites in a system whose principal pottery diagnostics are the same from site to site).

As was done in the well-known settlement surveys in the Basin of Mexico that were used as a basis to devise methods appropriate for the Peruvian coastal context (Parsons et al. 1982; Sanders et al. 1979), we survey all possible areas of a valley where ancient sites

could be located, including the valley floor and the desert margins. We mark in detail all remains and associated pottery and other period diagnostics on large-scale (ca. 1:10,000) vertical aerial photographs. Each large, complex site is mapped using transit and stadia, compass and tape, or airphoto enlargements. In addition, at the end of the project we produce drawings of a large sample (ca. 60 percent, in the case of Santa) of the ceramic diagnostics that have been collected during the fieldwork. These are used for site-to-site comparisons and for comparison with materials published in the north coast literature, not only to refine chronology but to test hypotheses about intersite socioeconomic relations in the different kinds of systems (usually chiefdoms or states) that appear in the record.

The Santa Valley

In several publications I have presented the principal data and theoretical conclusions of the Santa Valley

Project, including arguments against Carneiro's internecine-coercive theory of state origins (cf. Wilson 1983, 1987, 1988; see also Carneiro 1970). Here I will confine the discussion, first, to several general features of the settlement pattern of the Late Suchimancillo period (ca. A.D. 200–400), as an example of the role of centers in the emerging complexity of the pre-state sequence; and, second, to the presentation of a systems argument about how these centers might have originated and functioned in the local and regional north coast contexts. Although it is my opinion that the subsistence-settlement system of the Late Suchimancillo period represents a chiefdom level of sociopolitical integration, it will also be instructive to examine it briefly in light of Trigger's city-state model.

As shown in Figure 13.4, the Late Suchimancillo period exemplifies the strong upvalley focus of all the pre-state settlement systems in the Santa Valley sequence. Like the preceding systems, it also features a

pronounced clustering of settlements with sites more or less continuously distributed throughout each cluster. Yet, the construction and widespread distribution of fortresses indicates that conflict was also a continual feature of the system—in other words, it is unlikely that people would have gone to the considerable trouble of building an extensive series of stone fortresses had war been a sporadic event rather than a process. The question thus arises as to what sort of warfare could have been occurring.

The first would be a highly localized kind of war, involving rampant conflict among all sites (i.e., the kind of internecine warfare we know to be characteristic of some village societies in the Amazon; e.g., Chagnon 1992; Harner 1972). Aside from being egregiously maladaptive in the coastal Peruvian setting, this can be ruled out for two reasons: (1) sites are located much too close to each other for warfare between these settlements to have been a long-term

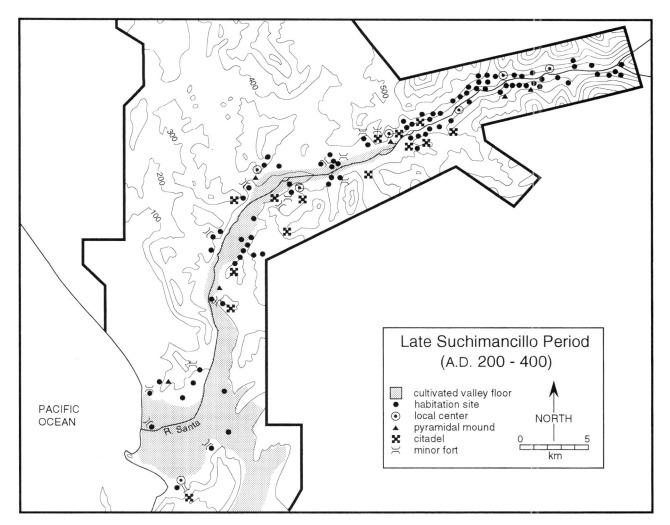

Figure 13.4. Settlement-pattern map of the Late Suchimancillo period (ca. A.D. 200–400), Santa Valley Project.

processual feature, and (2) the presence of canal irrigation networks and the consequent difficulty, if not impossibility, of building and maintaining separate canals further rules out such localized conflict.

The second possible kind of warfare would involve conflict between clusters, but this can be ruled out as well, again for two reasons: (1) the population sizes of the clusters are substantially different from one another, that is, the necessary balance of demographic power to sustain war as a longer-term process would not have existed; and (2) there is almost no land in the uppermost valley. Yet some 18,000 people apparently lived in this uppermost cluster. Surrounded by absolute desert to the north, south, and east, they must have had access to land in the downvalley area—which argues against sustained between-cluster warfare in the Late Suchimancillo system. The remaining possibility—war with other areas outside the valley—is therefore the kind that was indeed occurring here (somehow all this does not seem plausible to Carneiro and his supporters, but that is an issue I shall not delve into here; cf. Roscoe and Graber 1988).

Given the strong similarities between the pottery assemblages of Santa and those of valleys to the north, as well as the general lack of such similarities between Santa and valleys (especially Casma) to the south, I have argued for socioeconomic relations, or trade, with the northern valleys (such as Viru) and conflict with the southern valleys (Casma). In light of such differing relations, it is likely that at least part of the local ideology involved the promotion and maintenance of cooperative relations locally and with the people of the valleys to the north, as well as hostility toward those in valleys to the south. (Ceramic similarities between Santa and the Nepeña Valley during the late Early Horizon suggest possible socioeconomic ties at this time with the valley to the immediate south, so the situation is complex.)

In light of critical features of (1) the physical environment—circumscribed, with the cultivable valley floor increasingly narrow inland toward the Andes; (2) the subsistence infrastructure—canal-based agriculture; (3) the settlement pattern—with most sites located upvalley probably for defensive reasons; and (4) the political system—warfare, and the corresponding need to regulate defense and access to land and food—a likely scenario emerges for the origins and functioning of centers. They originated in the context of managing and coordinating both structural and infrastructural complexities (including redistribution of land and food since the majority of people lived upvalley as a defensive measure), construction and maintenance of forts, and organization for defense against attack.

In view of the absence of any single large center, as well as the widespread distribution of smaller local centers of roughly equal sizes, I argue that none of the pre-state systems, including Late Suchimancillo, is a clear candidate for a state level of integration. Such a level would require at least three tiers of site size and political function (Wright and Johnson 1975), but the settlement-pattern data suggest that only two such tiers are present in this and earlier systems in pre-state Santa. We can therefore rule out Late Suchimancillo period as a candidate for Trigger's version of a city-state.

Figure 13.5 summarizes the principal elements of the above argument in a systems-hierarchical model. The ceremonial-civic centers, or the local centers mentioned above, are viewed as having originated in a context that involved mutual feedback among several lower-order causal variables at the structural and infrastructural levels. Nevertheless, the ultimate "cause" of the adaptive characteristics of the local pre-state Santa Valley system was political, not infrastructural, in nature—namely, war, in the form of the continual threat of attack or actual raiding against the valley, if not both. But, in actuality, the matter of ultimate causation does not end here, at least once we examine the possible reason for the attacks from outside (which could have been either nearby Andean groups or neighboring coastal valleys, although I think it more likely to have been the latter at this early stage in the Central Andean sequence).

Comparison of the variable river regimes of north coast valleys (ONERN 1972a, 1972b, 1973), shows that the Santa is the only first-class stream in the area (i.e., it runs at high levels year-round due to continual snowmelt in the adjacent cordillera). Other nearby valleys to the north and south are either second-class (seasonal runoff) or third-class (ephemeral runoff). One of these valleys is Casma, where, in spite of the clear evidence we have for precocious complexity (see below), the regime is that of a second-class river. With different river regimes, rising populations in most areas, and the possibility of unpredictable nutritional pressures, we thus have in place the elements in some other nearby valley (e.g., Casma) of infrastructural pressures leading to the attacks on Santa as an adaptive solution. Yet, like Santa, the people of such a valley also were faced with choices of a mental, or superstructural, nature: that is, whether to limit/regulate

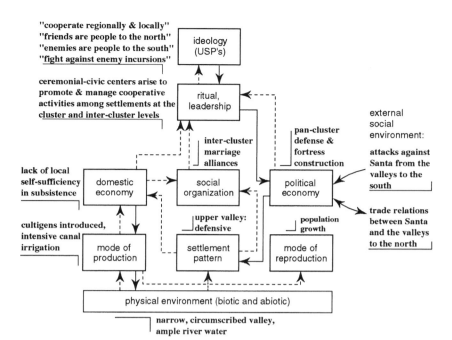

Figure 13.5. A systems-hierarchical model of the pre-state system of the Santa Valley.

population locally (perhaps in light of the constraints of early irrigation technology) or, alternatively, to solve their problem by attempting to conquer the people living to the north. Although one could argue that it was the river regimes, subsistence, and population—all at the infrastructural level—that ultimately were the driving forces in these early systems, it is difficult to imagine how such cultural variables as subsistence and population were not equally a function of higher-order policy decisions and choice at the superstructural level.

In sum, taking a systems perspective it is possible to argue that centers in this area of the north coast arose in a dynamic situation characterized by multiple, interrelated factors at the infrastructural, structural, and superstructural levels, probably as a means of ensuring definitive higher-order control and management over the increasingly complex features of developing agriculturally based societies. Certainly, it does not seem plausible to assign ultimate "cause," as Harris's cultural materialist view would have it, to the infrastructural level of these early subsistence-settlement systems (for a view similar to that of Harris, see Carneiro 1970, 1992). In any case, I will end this section by noting that although the elements of the above argument may seem rather facilely derived in a few paragraphs, it has taken several grants, some years of study across desert terrain, and not a little analysis to be able to "play" with such scenarios about the rise of complexity in this north coast setting.

The Casma Valley

As mentioned earlier, we are still carrying out the Casma Valley study so a more definitive resolution of the questions raised by the work in Santa awaits completion of the ceramic analysis in 1997 and the final analysis of the settlement patterns shortly thereafter. With this caveat in mind, I will deal here with two of the more important early periods from the Casma sequence, specifically to address the issues raised by Trigger's model of a city-state. These include the Moxeke, or Initial, period (ca. 1800–1000 B.C.) and the Patazca, or later Early Horizon, period (ca. 350 B.C.–0 A.D./B.C.). The earlier of the two periods recently has become well known in the popular press because of the pioneering excavations of Shelia and Thomas Pozorski (1987, 1994) at the Pampa de la Llama-Moxeke site (see Fig. 13.6, which shows a plan view prepared by our project). Their work and ours demonstrate that the vast majority of the architectural remains here, including Huaca A, date to the Initial period (ca. 1800–900 B.C.), which is surprisingly early for a center in the Americas with such an "urban" appearance. Indeed, according to a *New York Times* article (Stevens 1989), this site represents the earliest appearance of a "city" and "monumental architecture" anywhere in North and South America, thus making Casma exceedingly relevant to the central focus of this paper.

Based on their work at Pampa de la Llama-Moxeke and at the nearby site of Taukachi-Konkán, located

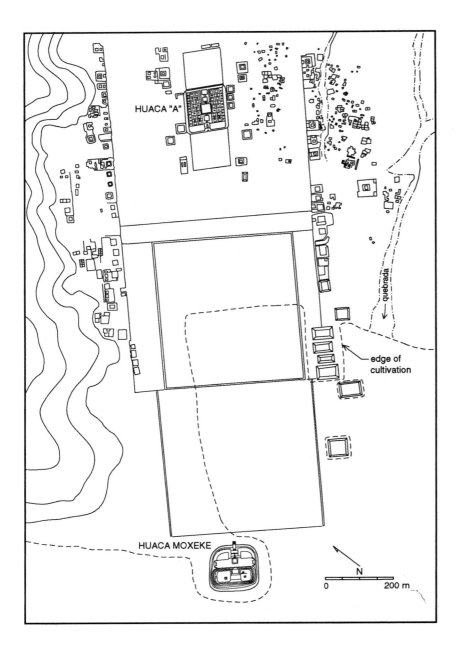

Figure 13.6. Plan view of the main site area at Pampa de la Llama-Moxeke, Casma Valley Project.

in the Sechín branch of the valley, the Pozorskis argue that "true civilization" arose in the Casma Valley far earlier than anyone would ever have suspected for the Central Andes (1994). Although surprised to find that the residential areas of the site are small in relation to the uninhabited public areas, they view Pampa de la Llama-Moxeke as a "bustling center that housed about 2,500 people within an area of two km²." Given the presence of food items and "luxury" goods in the chambers of Huaca A, they argue that the city had coercive control over the surrounding rural populace, although farmers apparently lived in the center as well. From this perspective the Moxeke system almost comes out sounding like the first major empire

in the Andes; for example, "We uncovered evidence that access to [Huaca A] was so carefully restricted and monitored that the associated bureaucratic system boggles the mind" (Pozorski and Pozorski 1994:69).

Our project's surface work at Pampa de la Llama confirms the Pozorskis' assertions about the early date of the site (indeed, our knowledge of Initial period pottery is the result of their publications from work in the 1980s at early Casma Valley sites). However, the total area covered by surface architecture and related Initial period pottery is 111.8 hectares, in other words, 1.1 square kilometers, and not 200 hectares, or 2 square kilometers, as they assert (note that the rectangular area encompassed within our plan view is about 1.3 km²). They are correct nevertheless in the argument that the residential areas are small in relation to public space (compensating polar planimeter measurements on our detailed map of the site indicate a total of only 20 hectares of residential structures, and my preliminary population estimate for the entire site is 2,000 persons, or 500 persons fewer than their estimate).

However, to date our broader focus on the system-wide settlement pattern of this period does not provide evidence supporting their assertion of a "civilization," at least in the sense of a *state*. As shown in the Moxeke settlement map (Fig. 13.7), which is a preliminary view based on our five-season project, fifty-four other habitation sites exist in the Casma and Sechín branches of the valley, most of them roughly 1 hectare or less in size. With a total inhabited area of 185 hectares, and assuming 100 persons per hectare based on the density of dwellings, I estimate the Moxeke period population in both branches of the valley to have been about 18,500 persons. Thus, our research indicates that nearly 90 percent of the Moxeke population resided well outside the main center. Indeed, it is interesting that all of the rural sites are located well up both branches from the Pampa de la

Llama site—rather far from the central site to have been "coercively" controlled by it.

Recalling Trigger's definition of a city-state, the Moxeke period thus hardly seems to fit the requirements. Given the huge areas covered by open space, plazas, and ceremonial mounds, I would argue that even the assertion that Pampa de la Llama is a "city" is open to question. Moreover, it has no defensive wall around it. The only evidence for conflict—one of Trigger's criteria for a "territorial state"—lies out in the rural hinterland in the form of nine hilltop/ridgetop forts that were found to have Moxeke period pottery diagnostics associated with them. It is impossible to deny that the site is formally laid out and impressive in its extent, but I would prefer not to see Pampa de la Llama as a "city" compared, for example, to the Chimú site of Chan Chan that covers a huge area of 16 square kilometers and includes thousands of dwellings and nine royal compounds.

At the pan-valley level, the Moxeke period system can be seen as characterized to some degree by a three-level hierarchy of site size and function—with Pampa de la Llama-Moxeke being the largest and most intensively occupied site, an additional seven sites of smaller size at the "second-tier" level, and a larger number of even smaller "third-tier" habitation

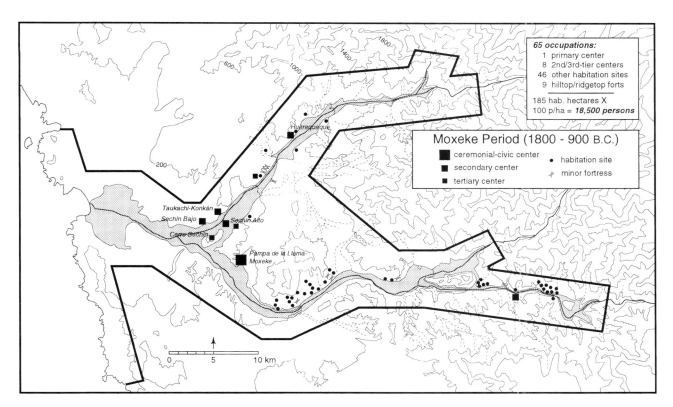

Figure 13.7. Settlement-pattern map of the Moxeke period (ca. 1800–1000 B.C.), Casma Valley Project.

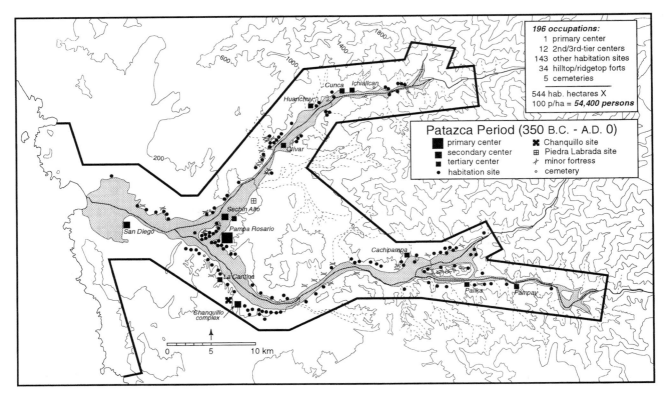

Figure 13.8. Settlement-pattern map of the Patazca period (ca. 350 B.C.–1 B.C./A.D.), Casma Valley Project.

sites scattered in several clusters in the hinterland. However, at least three features of the settlement pattern suggest that Moxeke period does not represent a system complex enough to qualify it as a state.

First, the apparently ample supply of valley bottomland associated with each of the principal site groupings suggests that each could have been self-sufficient in terms of subsistence productivity.

Second, assuming such self-sufficiency, the widespread distribution of fortresses suggests that warfare could have been occurring at the intercluster level. Indeed, to complicate this hypothetical scenario further, it is possible that the population groupings in the two branches alternated between pan-valley integration at a chiefdom level (at which point the main center was built and supported by hinterland sites) and *dis*integration to local egalitarian, or village-level, societies—a highly possible dynamic scenario for the long time period between 1800 and 900 B.C.

Third, although an additional five ceremonial-civic centers of varying size are located in the mouth of the Sechín branch, to the northwest of the Pampa de la Llama-Moxeke site, each was probably far less extensive than the principal center. But all of them—including Taukachi-Konkán, Sechín Bajo, Sechín Alto, and Cerro Sechín—also have occupations dating to

one or more later periods in the sequence, and probably reached their maximum size and architectural monumentality in these later periods. For example, although the finger-marked conical adobe bricks on the interior of the main pyramidal mound at Sechín Alto indicate a probable Initial period beginning for this mound, we found almost no Moxeke sherds on its surface as opposed to the nearly universal presence of Patazca period sherds.

In light of our research to date in the valley, a far better candidate for pristine state formation on the north Peruvian coast is the Patazca period system itself (Fig. 13.8). Compared to the 65 total sites of the preceding period, we have found 196 sites dating to the Patazca period in the area shown on the settlement map. Sites are much more continuously distributed in this system (suggesting far greater integration), and there appears to be a well-developed hierarchy of site size and function consisting of four principal tiers—with the site of Pampa Rosario (located near the confluence of the Sechín and Casma branches) at the apex of the system, five evenly distributed local centers below it (again suggesting substantial systemic integration), a number of sites at the third level, and a large number of rural sites at the lowest political level. In addition, numbers of fortresses were constructed and used, including the impressive fortress of Chanquillo (due south of the Pampa Rosario site on the map, along the south margin of the Casma branch).

Compared to any pre-state system of the Santa Valley, Patazca is far more complex, and, with a preliminary population estimate of some 55,000 people, it is far more populous than the system of any period in the Santa sequence. It is worth noting that the Pampa Rosario site covers 44 hectares, with a preliminary population estimate of less than 2,000 persons, so it constitutes a mere 4 percent of the total population and the city-state model thus does not apply here either.

Final Comments

In light of the data presented in this paper for the earliest and latest periods in the Central Andean sequence, the Moche state of the Early Intermediate period is the only remaining possible candidate for a city-state on the north coast. We can rather quickly eliminate it as a candidate, however. The primary center of the Moche state, the site of Huaca del Sol, covers a relatively small area of some 2 square kilometers (Moseley 1992). Thus, in all likelihood the vast bulk of the state's population resided in the rural hinterland. Considering the large area of the north coast occupied by this multivalley polity (Fig. 13.9), then, like its later counterparts in the Central Andes, Moche was a territorial state.

The Central Andes appears to be characterized by slowly developing differences of *scale*; complex societies that arose, first, at the local valley level in somewhat variable forms (at least in light of the data presented here) and, later, at the regional and interregional levels. At the local level it seems that a multiplicity of societal and environmental variables were mutually interrelated and causal in the rise of sociopolitical complexity, as people coped with the problems that came about because of their very success (as measured either by sheer population growth or the increasing size of polities) in adapting to one of the most challenging environments on earth. Short of arguing that these early polities developed spectacular centers simply because it was their aesthetically and technologically driven genius to do so, it seems more likely that Andean primary sites are the physical manifestation of the systemic need, in areas capable of agricultural intensification, to develop political and ideological *centrality* as the principal means of inte-

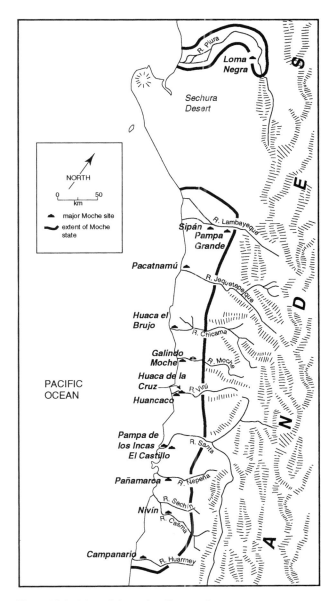

Figure 13.9. Map of the multivalley Moche state (ca. A.D. 400–650).

gration in solving adaptive problems. This, among many other things, obviously would have entailed the concomitant societal creation of powerful elites whose inherited higher-status positions became the linchpin of emerging complexity.

As I hope is clear from the arguments of this paper, we probably need to keep some of the basic stage/level terminology proposed by our principal theoretical forebears, the evolutionary-ecologists: namely, "bands, villages, chiefdoms, and states" as *stage heuristics* for dealing temporally with changes in human societal systems as a function of adaptation to population growth and subsistence intensification in a general sense; and the same types *qua* "levels of sociopolitical integration" for their utility as *level heuristics* in dealing spatially and temporally with human adaptation to the limitations and possibilities of differing physical environments. On the other hand, I do not think most other terms—especially the adjectival ones modifying the state—have such universal application. In a significant vernacular sense, these other terms are the muddy bath water we'd like to throw out and the noun terms are the theoretical baby we'd like to keep.

I am uncertain why some researchers are driven to propose universality for such polities as city-states. If the Central Andes is at all important as one of the six areas of the world where pristine states arose, then the city-state as a type, at least as defined by Trigger, is unworkable as a useful universal heuristic. If, on the other hand, it is applicable to some other societies—for example, Sumer, the Maya and the Aztecs—then, instead of trying to find it everywhere else, perhaps we should try to find out why city-state organization appears where it does. One way to do this, I propose, is by looking at some of the factors I have attempted to demonstrate as critical in the systems-hierarchical model—especially including (1) critical aspects of the local physical environment, (2) the nature of the subsistence sytem, (3) population size and the distribution of settlements, (4) higher-ordered management of the local system, (5) the highest-order ideological phenomena that sustain it, as well as (6) the consideration of the larger regional political context made up of other nearby social groups coping with their own local problems. This is the last thing the "modified," or "two-type typologists" seem inclined to do, however.

Surely, if Steward was at all correct in his theoretical assertions, then there is an intimate connection between all these variables and the differing complexity that characterizes societies at the continental and worldwide levels. The theoretical trend represented by the "multistage" and "two-type typologists," on the other hand, seems to me to run directly counter to such plausible and workable models as those proposed by Steward and his intellectual descendants. But if I am incorrect in my critique of the city-state model discussed in this paper, then going along with the trend this sort of theorizing represents, I would like to propose the following competitive models as the principal kinds of states found around the ancient world: the "pyramid state" (Egypt, the Maya, and the Aztecs) and the "platform state" (Moxeke, Moche, and Chimu). Otherwise, our only recourse will be to throw out the stage/level baby with the muddy bath water and become typological nihilists. If so, then it really will turn out that the *state* was just a state of mind.

14

Of Kings and Capitals

Principles of Authority and the Nature of Cities in the Native Andean State

ALAN L. KOLATA

Cities, and the larger political formations within which they are embedded, are dynamic congeries of political, economic, and social institutions that are shaped and reshaped by historical circumstance. This dynamism and mutability in the face of exogenous forces might suggest the impossibility of a coherent, general theory about the forms and forces of urban transformation of the archaic city. Underlying the seemingly chaotic, undirected exigencies that constitute the life cycle of cities, however, are regularities of structure and similarities in form, function, and historical evolution that provide touchstones for a such a theory. In this respect, I am in complete agreement with Charlton and Nichols (this volume) on the validity of cross-cultural analyses.

This chapter explores the structure of indigenous cities of the Andean region and evaluates them in terms of cities elsewhere in the preindustrial world. This comparative method will set the organizational principles that structured certain Andean cities in a richer context of regional and empirical variability, thereby bringing into relief potential patterns of similarity and dissimilarity. My specific focus is on the urban system of the Inca, for which documentary evidence is richest, but I will also refer to two other expansionist state societies—Tiwanaku in the Lake Titicaca basin and Chan Chan, capital of the north coast Peruvian kingdom of Chimor (Fig. 14.1). The basic lineaments of the argument I make apply to these Andean capitals as well.

Each of these Andean states was characterized by a symbolically dominant metropole, with secondary cities subordinate to the center. This configuration contrasts dramatically with other urban systems in the prehispanic Americas—for instance, that of the late fifteenth- and early sixteenth-century Basin of Mexico, where a constellation of relatively autonomous city-states was enmeshed in a complex matrix of politics and elite competition for natural and human resources (Hodge, this volume). In some sense, city-states—defined as "small, territorially based, politically independent state systems with a city and a hinterland, relatively self-sufficient economically and relatively homogeneous ethnically"—were rare in the Andean highlands. The only examples that seem to coincide with this definition are the Aymara Kingdoms of the Lake Titicaca basin (particularly the Lupaqa and Colla) prior to their incorporation into the Inca empire in the mid-fifteenth century. These kingdoms appear to be the product of the disintegration of the Tiwanaku empire during the eleventh century.

246 ALAN L. KOLATA

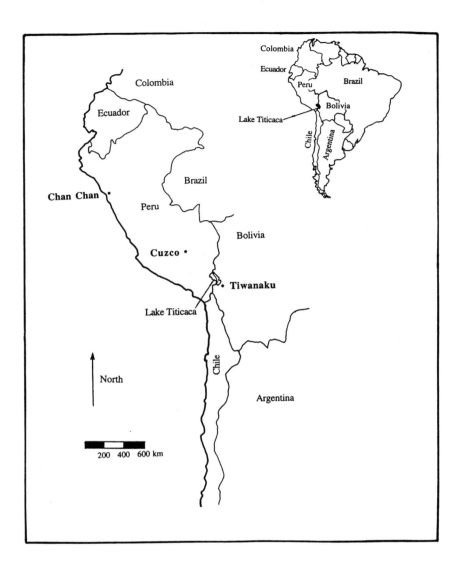

Figure 14.1. Map of the Andes showing places mentioned in the text.

In other words, the city-state phenomenon in the Lake Titicaca basin in prehispanic times may have been the result of political balkanization that followed imperial collapse—a derivative, rather than autochthonous process (similar to that envisioned by J. Marcus [1989] for the post-Teotihuacán Mesoamerican world).

Archaeological investigation in the Andean highlands is still in its infancy, and future research may reveal other instances of city-state formations, as the product of either primary or secondary developmental processes. Even so, I would argue that we can define a number of characteristics of ancient Andean capitals that distinguish them from their counterparts elsewhere in the preindustrial world. All these distinguishing characteristics are related in one degree or another to the patrimonial principles of authority that underlie the origins and structure of these cities (Weber 1978).

The first of these characteristics—the lack of either price-fixing or administered markets—is probably the single most distinguishing feature of the Andean city, one that sets it apart from other preindustrial cities. A second distinguishing feature of Andean capitals is their relative lack of social heterogeneity, a feature reflected in and flowing from two additional characteristics—low urban population size and intense development of instruments of social control within the urban environment.

Andean capitals and their secondary urban settlements were essentially regal and religious in nature. They were the seats of royal lineages and the centers of cults. The intersection of political and religious authority is expressed materially in an exaggerated form of necrolatry: many of the great temples and palaces of Cuzco, Tiwanaku, and Chan Chan were repositories for the mummified remains of deceased kings. Andean kings, in an ideological sense, never died. Thus an essential core of Andean religiosity was ancestor worship, and dead royals were at the summit of a hierarchy of deceased lineage and ethnic group ancestors.

Andean cities were centers for elite cultural definition and self-expression; a large resident population of commoners was inimical to their purpose and function. Apart from commoners incorporated into the cities in a retainer capacity, the masses rarely participated in urban culture, except on ritual occasions. Not surprisingly, several—perhaps most—Andean capitals were focal points for pilgrimages. Commoners flowed into the cities at prescribed times: in a real sense, they were religious tourists in an elite theme park that imparted a sense of emotional participation in, but social segregation from, that esoteric world. Access to Andean capitals such as Cuzco and Chan Chan was consciously restricted by soaring palace and boundary walls and tortuous pathways within the great residential and temple compounds. Instruments of social control are vividly reflected in sumptuary laws and theories of separate descent for elites and commoners.

The *raison d'être* of the Andean city was not fundamentally economic but political and ideological. Andean cities displayed an intense concern for public symbolism that connected city to hinterland and urban elites to rural commoners. Capitals such as Tiwanaku were the distilled essence of elite belief and the focal point of publicly expressed concepts of universal order. The farms and fields of the countryside provided the model for the relationship between humankind and nature and influenced the design and social order of Andean cities. The symbolic text written into the design of Cuzco and Tiwanaku, for example, attempted to identify or to harmonize the productive (yet potentially destructive) forces of nature with the culturally created order of human society. To understand the nature of Andean cities then, we must first understand the symbolic structure that shaped urban form and invested it with cultural significance and public meaning.

Politics, Religion, and Symbols in Native Andean Cities

The interpenetration of cult and command was expressed visually and conceptually in Andean capitals by the spatio-temporal organization of public shrines and their constituent social groups. The capital of the Inca empire, Cuzco, offers the best example of the interplay of politics, religion, and the built form of the Andean capital (Zuidema 1990). In Cuzco, the social instrument for conceiving and experiencing the interpenetration of cult and command was the *ceque* system, a symbolic sacred landscape of the city—and, by extension, of the Inca empire itself—organized in a complex collection of shrines arrayed along lines of sight. This sacred landscape was central to the Inca people's identity as an ethnic group and to their belief in the right to rule other nations. The system emanated from the temple of Qorikancha, which contained idols of the Inca state cults and incorporated in its interior precincts niches for housing the sacred mummy bundles of Inca royalty.

From the Qorikancha, as from the center, there went out certain lines which the Indians call *ceques*. They formed four parts corresponding to the four royal roads that went out from Cusco. On each one of those *ceques* were arranged in order the shrines which there were in Cusco and its district, like stations of holy places, the veneration of which was common to all. Each *ceque* was the responsibility of the *parcialidades* [the Spanish name for groups of people who formed related parts of a larger ethnic whole] and families of the city of Cusco, from within which came the attendants and servants who cared for the shrines of their *ceque* and saw to offering the established sacrifices at the proper times. (Bernabé Cobo, cited in Rowe 1979)

This remarkable conceptual organization of Cuzco and its environs incorporated 41 directional sight lines, or *ceques*, radiating from the Qorikancha. Along the *ceques* were 328 *huacas* (shrines), places or objects imbued with sacred power. As Cobo notes, different sets of related lineages (*ayllus*) or larger social groups (*parcialidades*) were responsible for maintaining the *huacas* along the *ceque* line designated to that group. Their responsibilities included the offering of ritually prescribed sacrifices at the sacred shrines.

Cuzco's *ceque* system bound together in multiple layers Inca concepts of geographic and symbolic space, time, history, and social organization. Perhaps the most important meaning embedded in the system was reflected in the sidereal-lunar agricultural calendar, in which each of the 328 *huacas* represented one day. Throughout the agricultural cycle, members of at least one of the *parcialidades* resident in Cuzco were engaged in communal rituals to insure abundant harvests and the fertility of the camelid herds. The ceremonies served as a trenchant reminder that the Incas' success as a people destined to rule other nations hinged on group solidarity and on their ability to sustain a concordance between the social and natural orders.

In Lefebvre's terms, the people of Cuzco conjoined spatial practice, the representation of space, and representational space (that is, space as perceived, conceived, and lived) in a cohesive system. By representational space, Lefebvre specifically means "space as directly lived through its associated images and symbols" (1991:39). Representational space, he continues, "overlays physical space making symbolic use of its objects," just as the *ceque* system and its constellation of shrines overlaid the physical space of Cuzco, investing the urban and rural landscape with cultural and historical meaning. Two salient classes of symbolic associations link the *huacas* arrayed along the ritual *ceque* paths of Cuzco and its environs—water and irrigation, on the one hand, and dynastic lore and "history," on the other (Sherbondy 1982, 1992). Each relates to distinct principles of legitimate authority, a distinction I characterize as the "inside-outside" dichotomy.

The first of these symbolic associations concerns the autochthonous people of Cuzco—the original inhabitants of the valley who were later dominated by the Inca elite. Fully one-third (109) of the *ceque* shrines relate to springs, streams, rivers, and pools that are actually or symbolically sources of flowing water for irrigating adjoining lands. These water-related shrines can be interpreted, in one sense, as markers delimiting and sectioning arable land among various social groups (Sherbondy 1992; Zuidema 1986). Sacrifices made at these shrines emphasize associations with telluric phenomena and with the fertility and genesic properties of land fed by flowing water. The principle of legitimate authority expressed by these associations emerges from the rights of the autochthonous populations as the original holders of usufruct title. This is the "inside" pole of my dichotomy—the legitimacy and authority that accrues from original possession.

The second set of symbolic associations of the *ceque* system shrines relates to the event-history of the Inca kings and queens or the royal class as a whole. This "history" includes mythical events relating to the origin accounts of the Inca as a distinct ethnic group and as a royal dynasty that derived its authority from outside the Cuzco environs. It also commemorates significant achievements in the lives of (possibly) historic kings. The commemorative shrines are usually (although not always) located along the paths in the Chinchaysuyu quarter. Various Inca origin myths, eloquently analyzed by Zuidema in a number of path-breaking papers, emphasize migration and ritualized peregrinations or movements along a vector commemorated by landscape markers.

In one version of the origin myth recorded by Juan de Santacruz Pachacuti Yamqui (cited in Zuidema 1990:71), Manco Capac, founder of the Inca dynasty, migrates from Lake Titicaca to Cuzco, conquers the two principal native lords, and appropriates their lands and irrigation waters. Another version recounts the origins of the Inca as an ethnic group and as a royal caste through the emergence of four couples—specifically, four pairs of brothers and sisters—from sacred caves at Pacariqtambo. This is the story of the brothers/sisters Ayaar (Urbano 1981; Zuidema 1990:9–10). After an extended migration north to Cuzco and the magical lithification of several brothers en route, Manco Capac establishes authority over the natives of the valley, again appropriating the lands and waters of Cuzco.

Both versions of the origin myth feature migration from a sacred landscape (Lake Titicaca and sacred caves, each with aqueous, telluric, and fertility associations) to the valley of Cuzco and the subsequent conquest and subordination of indigenous populations. The special sociological characteristic of the first Incas is that they are outsiders; their authority stems from their foreignness and aggressiveness. They are archetypal *sinchis* (warlords). They do not possess legitimate authority but appropriate authority by force. Further, they must assert and reaffirm their authority by continuing peregrinations through the conquered territory. This is the opposite, "outside" pole of my dichotomy—legitimate authority as appropriated or usurped by outsiders. This, of course, is nothing more than the Inca version of Sahlins's "stranger king." As Sahlins remarks of Polynesian kingship:

It is the remarkably common fact that the great chiefs and kings of political society are not the people they rule. By the local theories of origin, they are strangers. . . . Power is not represented here as an intrinsic social condition. It is usurpation, in the double sense of a forceful seizure of sovereignty and a sovereign denial of the prevailing moral order. Rather than a normal succession, usurpation is the principle of legitimacy. (1985:78–80)

At the risk of pushing the comparative interpretation too far, I would argue that this tension between the two poles of legitimate authority (possessed versus appropriated) lies at the core of archaic states generally, and accounts, at least in part, for the apparent fragility of these traditional state formations.

The *ceque* system was, in some sense, the Inca solution to integrating these opposing forces into a cohering, if not completely coherent, social and symbolic whole. By encapsulating or incorporating (in the case of communities granted the status of Inca-by-privilege) non-Inca groups in the *ceque* system, the Inca, via collaborative, habitual social and spatial practice, effectively glossed over the natural tensions and contradictions that arose from their usurpation of authority. That is to say, conquered and conquerors shared an ideology of worship focused on the *ceque* shrines of Cuzco and its environs. Encoded in this symbolic landscape of shrines were metaphorical and literal referents to the autochthonous inhabitants of the land, who possessed legitimate authority, and to the foreign *sinchis* who, by force-of-arms, usurped and appropriated legitimate authority. This dialectic of the inside-outside principles of authority is encoded in symbolic terms within the Inca-constructed sacred geography of Cuzco.

Although we may perceive a dialectic between opposing principles of authority, this is not a case of equivalency of power in mutual and balanced counterpoint. One of the poles of this dialectic is clearly dominant, the other subordinate. The power and de facto legitimacy of the successful usurper is, by definition, superior to authority derived from original possession, for the autochthonous groups are dislodged and dispossessed of the source of their authority—the exclusive right to irrigate and cultivate their land.

The Inca rulers, like most archaic kings, attempted to perpetuate their legitimacy by reconfiguring social space both in their capitals and in the rural reaches of their domains. They created or modified preexisting centers to publicly proclaim and make tangible the source of their legitimate right to rule. The warlords and their elite cadre of kinsmen, retainers, and clients constructed and inhabited majestic centers accoutered with monumental representations of space they had conceived. The centers were imbued with signs of sacred authority—enormous plazas for public ritual; temples, palaces, and thrones; great urban gardens— all to symbolically expressing the Inca elites' legitimacy. They became dwellers in cities of their own design, and from these cities they circulated in the hin-

terlands, in effect extending the ideological grounds of their created cosmopolitan culture. Lefebvre remarks:

The city state thus establishes a fixed centre by coming to constitute a hub, a privileged focal point, surrounded by peripheral areas which bear its stamp. From this moment on, the vastness of pre-existing space appears to come under the thrall of divine order. At the same time the towns seem to gather in everything which surrounds them, including the natural and divine, and the earth's evil and good forces. As image of the universe (*imago mundi*), urban space is reflected in the rural space that it possesses and indeed in a sense *contains*. Over and above its economic, religious, and political context, therefore, this relationship already embodies an element of symbolism, of image-and-reflection: the town perceives itself in its double, in its repercussions or echo; in self-affirmation, from the height of its towers, its gates, and its campaniles, it contemplates itself in the countryside that it has shaped—that is to say, in its work. The town and its surroundings thus constitute a *texture*. (1991:235; original emphasis)

As Lefebvre recognizes, the city of the archaic state actively shaped its countryside, constructing a fabric of social relations. This shaping proceeded conceptually, symbolically, and materially through commissioned pubic works, such as the great irrigated agricultural complexes of the Inca, Chimu, and Tiwanaku elites, and through the reorganization of autochthonous populations in the provinces.

As in most agrarian states, particularly those lacking a merchant-market complex (as was the case in the Andes), the intimate and potentially conflictive relationship between city and countryside dominates the political dynamic. This conflict recapitulates the tensions reflected in the inside-outside dichotomy, the uneasy relationship between foreign rulers and autochthonous populations. But how is power extended from city to countryside in the traditional state and in the Andes specifically? How was the principle of appropriated authority transformed into a system of governance?

The Autocratic City and the Patrimonial State

Although the intensity of this city-country relationship varied over time and space in ancient agrarian states, one feature remained constant: the city lived off the surrounding countryside by extracting tribute, both goods and labor service (the latter appears to have been emphasized in the Andean world). At the same time, the archaic city-state provided reciprocal services—most notably, security and a sense of inclusion in a greater social universe. In other words, the city interjected into the countryside distinct cultural values and opened up new cultural perspectives from those of the circumscribed social landscape of the countryside. Native Andean cities differed from most other preindustrial states in this regard, perhaps because of the lack of "democratizing" forces inherent in a market-based economy.

The cosmopolitan perspective imparted to the rural commoner on pilgrimage to native Andean capitals was limited, controlled, and framed in a discourse of religiosity. Almost certainly there was no intent to encourage migration to the cities. Indeed, there were few economic incentives for rural populations to migrate to the city except as retainers to the ruling lineage. These positions were of limited number, of course, so most of the population remained on the land as agricultural producers. The result was a notable absence of social diversity in the cities.

The Andean capitals, particularly the capitals of the expansionist states (Cuzco, Chan Chan, and Tiwanaku are three paradigmatic cases) were autocratic in terms of both politics and social composition. A brief passage from Pedro Sancho de la Hoz, one of the first Spaniards to see Cuzco before its destruction, testifies to this special character:

Cuzco, because it is the capital city and residence of the Inca nobles, is large enough and handsome enough to compare with any Spanish city. It is full of the palaces of magnates, for in it reside no poor folk. Each of these Inca magnates, as well as all the *curacas,* erect there dwellings, although they do not permanently occupy them. (cited in Brundage 1967:8)

I would argue that similar patterns were expressed at other Andean capitals such as Chan Chan and Tiwanaku.

At the same time, these capitals served as a fulcrum for mediating the conflicts between elites and commoners, city and countryside, that constantly threatened to erupt. As Lefebvre remarks, "The town—urban space—has a symbiotic relationship with that of rural space over which (often with much difficulty) it holds sway" (1991:234–235). But what was the political and economic articulation of this symbolic interconnectedness? How did the capitals "hold sway,"

however tenuously, over their tributary hinterlands in the Andean world?

First, it is important to understand that the relationship between such states and local communities is not invariably oppressive and extractive. The two entities are always counterpoised in a dynamic of mutualism. Centralized states exert directive control over regional economies and impinge on the autonomy of local communities, but they also introduce local communities into more inclusive social and economic worlds. They create dynamic interconnections among diverse communities, accelerating local economic development. In turn, by identifying themselves as the agents of development, states derive legitimacy, prestige, and intensification of their social power (Ludden 1985, in press). The centralization of authority in traditional states does not invariably imply bureaucratization, however. We can easily conceive a broad spectrum of institutional possibilities for the expression and exercise of authority operating simultaneously in early state societies, a spectrum that ran from localized relations of kinship to relations framed around consensual or coerced associations between rulers and subject populations.

In many respects, governance in the native Andean state turned on what Weber called "patrimonial" authority, which he contrasted with formal bureaucratic states:

Permanent agencies, with fixed jurisdiction, are not the historical rule but rather the *exception.* This is even true of large political structures such as those of the ancient Orient, the Germanic, and Mongolian empires of conquest, and of many feudal states. In all these cases, the ruler executes the most important measures through personal trustees, table-companions, or court-servants. Their commissions and powers are not precisely delimited and are temporarily called into being in each case. (1978:1006; original emphasis)

In the case of states like the Inca and Tiwanaku, permanent agencies with distinct jurisdictions never emerged at all or were only weakly developed in the formal network of command.

In Weber's concept of the fully modern bureaucracy, the power of the state is exercised through a system of formal rules applied without reference to the actors' social personae and statuses. This kind of abstract regulation of state affairs is alien to the native states of the Americas and probably to most archaic states of the world. But the absence of a rationalizing theory of public administration does not necessarily imply arbitrary, ad hoc exercise of power, the abrogation of power to local authorities, or less centralization of authority.

One of Weber's prime examples of patrimonial authority elaborated into an expansive state formation was Pharaonic Egypt. (He also mentions the Inca in passing.) Weber comments that all the subject territories and populations of Pharaonic Egypt might be considered "a single tremendous *oikos* ruled patrimonially by the pharaoh" (1978:1013; *oikos* here refers to the authoritarian household of a prince or manorial lord; see Weber 1978:381). As Wheatley notes, one of the characteristics of patrimonial authority conceived by Weber was that the ruler (the supreme patriarch, as it were) "treats all political administration as his personal affair, while the officials, appointed by the ruler on the basis of his personal confidence in them, in turn regard their administrative operations as a personal service to their ruler in the context of duty and respect" (1971:52). With respect to the obligations of the subject populations:

In the patrimonial state the most fundamental obligation of the subjects is the material maintenance of the ruler, just as is the case in the patrimonial household; again the difference is only one of degree. At first, this provisioning takes the form of honorary gifts and of support in special cases, in accordance with the spirit of intermittent political action. However, with the increasing continuity and rationalization of political authority, their obligations became more and more comprehensive. (Weber 1978:1014)

Thus the fundamental lineaments of patrimonial authority derive from sentiments of personal obligation reinforced by tradition. Subjects' obligations to a ruler may be either coerced or consensual, or they may derive from kinship relations. Consanguineal bonds of kinship within dynastic lines, affinal, indirect, remote, or fictive kinship ties, voluntary association or attachment to royal lineages (mutualism), or violent subjugation and incorporation of subject populations were all pathways for establishing personal obligations and social links between rulers and subjects.

Weber correctly recognized, however, that the principal strut undergirding the patrimonial authority of a ruler (originally identified with military action—i.e., the power that accrues to a warlord) was "a consensual community which also exists apart from his independent military force and which is rooted in the belief that the ruler's powers are legitimate insofar as

they are *traditional*" (1978:1020; original emphasis). The importance of this insight cannot be underestimated, for it introduces the role of ideology in the construction of authority and the emergence of hierarchically organized societies. In a similar vein, Godelier notes that "the power of domination consists of two indissoluble elements whose combination constitutes its strength: violence and consent, [but] of these two components of power, the stronger is not the violence of the dominant, but the consent of the dominated to their domination" (1978:767). Ideology as a shared belief system assumes a central position in maintaining the consent—or better, the acquiescence—of the dominated social classes to a hierarchical social order.

Given this construction, why would a dominated class consent to actively participate in a belief system that serves the interests of an elite, dominating class? Godelier's solution to this conundrum makes great sense: participation in the society-wide belief system enhanced the economic interests of the dominated class. Specifically, he hypothesized that an elite ideology that reifies hierarchical relations of dominance and exploitation could only be promoted and perpetuated if these relations were cast in the form of an exchange of services between the elite and the dominated. The precise form of the exchange may vary, but in the case of early agrarian-based states, the emerging elite class probably offered esoteric knowledge of the supernatural realm, of "invisible realities and forces controlling (in the thought of these societies) the reproduction of the universe and of life" in exchange for the supplementary labor (Godelier 1978: 767). Other, more pragmatic services that an elite class could have offered to commoners were articulation of agricultural calendars, adjudication of boundary disputes, maintenance of security, management of redistribution networks, administration of social and economic links among diverse local communities, and the like.

Still, as Godelier acknowledges, even if dominated classes share the system of political and economic ideas, beliefs, and symbols promulgated by a dominant class, the threat of coercion hovers in the background. It may be that the most successful class-stratified societies arrived at an appropriate balance of force and persuasion. Unmitigated terror leads, in time, to divisiveness, disgust, and revolt; ideological propaganda unreinforced by the potential for sanctions leads, in time, to fragmentation and dissolution of the hierarchical social order.

Hierarchy in patrimonial state offices emerges first in the context of the tightly inbred world of the king's *oikos.* In a social environment in which personal obligation and fealty are the *sina qua non* of office, the ruler turns first to his kinsmen and immediate dependents to create a body of administrative officials. These dependents, even though they may have conflicted loyalties of their own (or, for the more highly placed, strategies for usurping princely authority for themselves) are more easily manipulated because they usually reside at court (the extended household of the king). But as Weber implies, the expansion of authority beyond a local domain increases administrative burdens to a point where the ruler must recruit officials "in an extrapatrimonial fashion" (1978:1026). In this way, inner and outer circles of officials develop.

These inner and outer "courts" perform similar administrative functions on behalf of the king's expanding *oikos,* but they exhibit differential access and degrees of dependency to the ruler. The task of the king in this environment of political intrigue and competition for influence is to maintain sufficient personal contact with subordinates and clients to reinforce the bonds of personal loyalty and dependence. Personal contact and public demonstrations of reciprocity in the form of gift exchange, hosting of banquets, and the like were the life's blood of this kind of politico-administrative system.

Given that personal contact and public appearance were essential to the legitimacy of leadership, it is not surprising to learn that the king in patrimonial states was often itinerant and that his court moved with him (see, for instance, Briant [1988] on the "nomadic" Achaemenid kings and Keightley [1983a] on the itinerant kings of Shang period China). The mobile residential complexes of the kings were imposing, majestic, and infused with the symbols of earthly and divine power, but it was the traveling court that constituted the true focus of authority, a capital in motion with the king at its center. And it was explicitly from the person of the king that power emanated.

The itinerant capitals were, in a sense, simulacra of the fixed capital, consciously wrought as awe-inspiring images of sacred and secular authority. The royal capitals, fixed or itinerant, were frequently designed as microcosmic representations of the state, and cosmograms as well—condensed reflections of the order of the humanly perceived universe. The itinerant king moved with all the symbols of his power and with the images of the empire's gods: the gods, the king, and the cosmos traveled as one.

We know from sixteenth-century documentary sources that Inca kings were constantly in motion. They struck out with glittering retinues of warriors, priests, and camp followers in battle campaigns, on elaborate tours of their provinces, on ritually prescribed peregrinations to sacred shrines. Some were absent from Cuzco for years at a time, which raises an interesting question about the role of Cuzco as an administrative center. Apparently, administration of the Inca empire was effected by the coterie of kinsmen and dependents clustered around the moving court, in concert with the "patrimonial officials" resident in the provinces. As was the case with the kings of other archaic empires, however, the Inca's grasp on power was tenuous. Like the great Darius, forcefully dispossessed of kingship by Alexander, the Inca king Atahualpa, on an extended tour through his realm, lost command when the Spanish took him captive in his itinerant capital on November 16, 1532.

Predatory, expansionist patrimonial states, such as Pharaonic Egypt and the Inca, develop highly differentiated patrimonial offices, defined hierarchically by their degree of relatedness to the paramount ruler. The political coin of the realm, as it were, becomes the ability to demonstrate one's real or fictive kinship ties with the ruler. The highly differentiated offices function, in effect, as a proto-bureaucracy in which the language of authority is voiced in the idiom of kinship. This "bureaucratization" of patrimonial office leads to the emergence of new status groups—cohorts of local lords and state clients—with a common desire for recognition and representation at the court of the ruler. The local lords, in turn, operate from a politico-economic base that recapitulates the structural forms of the ruler's *oikos.* They compete to form their own independent or quasi-independent patrimonial estates, through which they extend their influence and control over local populations. They frequently seek to appropriate the religious mystique of the ruler by replicating the architecture and symbolic configuration of the ruler's capital.

The geopolitical landscape of the patrimonial state consists of congeries of petty polities coalesced around the households of local lords, linked only tenuously, if at all, but merged administratively into the *oikos* of the paramount ruler. That is to say, political, social, and administrative linkages in such a state structure are strong vertically but weak or incompletely developed horizontally. The personalized, centralizing nature of ultimate authority in such a structure results in the weakening or disintegration of "natural" affinities within ethnic and other traditional groups in favor of opportunistic gravitation toward the court of the ruler.

Inspired by Weberian categories, I have characterized this geopolitical landscape in the Andean world as a *"hyper-oikos"* (Kolata 1983:367). By this I meant that the economy and political influence of the paramount ruler's household extended far beyond the capital's circumscribed hinterland. The agents of that extension were the elites who governed the provincial settlements. These aristocratic managers were directly or symbolically related to members of the royal household, and they worked to further the economic and political ends of that household. This is the meaning behind the political device of installing "Incas by privilege." The *hyper-oikos* was a technique for building an empire by integrating an elite class in an extensive fictive kinship system. The elites were bound by a complex, elaborate network of privilege and obligation that was manipulated by the royal household.

The *hyper-oikos* was essentially an extension of the imperial household ruled through a network of client states and local lords by subtle suasion through the force of sacred tradition and by the implicit threat of physical retaliation for rebellion. Yates comes to similar conclusions with respect to archaic Chinese states such as the Shang (this volume). Webster's analysis of the Classic period Maya city-states is also consistent with this interpretation (this volume), although Maya political structure and geopolitical influence appear more fragmented and weakly integrated than that of the Inca, Tiwanaku, or—for that matter—Shang states.

Conclusions

Many, if not all, Andean states operated with patrimonial principles of authority, political systems that can be characterized as organizationally centralized but nonbureaucratic. What are the implications of these principles of authority for Andean urban structure, form, and meaning? I have already signaled some of them. Andean cities were not venues of a flourishing merchant class. There were no free artisans and craftsmen organized into guilds that could exert pressure on municipal authorities. There were no commercial transactions in the modern sense of disinterested buyers and sellers brought together in a marketplace. There was no broad-based, public participation in the political life of the city, as we see—

or imagine as an ideal—in the archetypal city-state, the *polis* of Greece, especially Athens (Morris, this volume), the exemplar of urban "democracy."

Moral, political, and military authority in the Andean capital flowed from the ruling lineages and their coterie of kin, fictive kin, retainers, and camp followers. The capitals, perhaps to a greater degree than urban centers in other parts of the preindustrial world, were autocratic, built for and dominated by a native aristocracy. In this sense, Andean capitals were truly patrician cities—places for symbolically concentrating the political and religious authority of the elites. Andean capitals boasted little in the way of pluralism and social heterogeneity, although these were not entirely absent.

The *raison d'être* of Andean capitals was servicing aristocratic lineages and their entourages. The city was an extension of the elite households and a public expression of their religious and secular authority. Its residents were attached in one way or another to the economic, political, and social needs of the royal households. The city was shaped by the religious and political mystique of the elite, wielded in premeditated self-interest, not the invisible hand of the marketplace.

Andean capitals were small by modern standards— the permanent populations of Chan Chan and Tiwanaku probably never exceeded 25,000–30,000 and may have been much smaller (Moseley 1975; Kolata 1993). Cuzco's central core held no more than 15,000–20,000 residents, although the population of the entire metropolitan district may have approached 50,000 (Agurto 1980). Chan Chan, Tiwanaku, and Cuzco were among the largest cities to emerge in the prehispanic Andean world. Secondary cities were smaller: few ever reached 10,000 inhabitants, and most were in the 3,000–5,000 range. In contrast, the hinterlands were thickly settled, reflecting the fact that the fundamental work of Andean states was rural, not urban.

In some senses, Andean society was nonurban, perhaps even antiurban, in orientation. Unlike the preindustrial metropolises of Europe, which acted as magnets for the surrounding countryfolk, there was little economic incentive and virtually no opportunity for rural dwellers to migrate to Andean cities, since the right to reside in these regal-ritual cities was tied to a relationship with patrician lineages. The inherent structural limitations of this kind of patron-client relationship, which demands face-to-face contact, limited the scale and diversity of social relations. Lacking the democracy and entrepreneurial opportunity that comes with a market, Andean capitals were essentially "company towns" catering to the interpenetrating businesses of state religion and elite politics.

Given the special role of Andean cities, it is not surprising that native Andean states exhibit a low degree of urbanization. There were never many urban settlements extant at one time. Furthermore, the cities that did emerge exhibited extremely low diversity in structural type. In many respects, Andean states were not polystructural urban cultures at all. Rather, they were polities dominated by elite cities of similar structure. This can, of course, be claimed to a lesser degree of

Rome and other preindustrial states as well, but the Andean case is notable for the recursive replication of scale, sociological composition, and cultural meaning of these cities across time and space. In contrast to the Roman case, for instance, no trading colonies grew to be self-sustaining urban settlements; no frontier garrisons emerged as politically autonomous cities. It is as if there was in the prehispanic Andean world a single social and cognitive template for urban structure and significance, and this template drew its ultimate meaning from elite self-representation poised against the socially undifferentiated masses that populated the rural reaches of this world.

15

The Obvious and the Chimerical

City-States in Archaeological Perspective

Numbers, the Homeric gods, relations, chimeras
and four-dimensional space all have being, for if
they were not entities of a kind, we could make
no propositions about them.

(Russell 1901:276)

NORMAN YOFFEE

Introduction: Unleashing the Chimera

There used to be inscribed directly beneath his name
on the office-door placard of a colleague in Tucson
the epigram "Distinguished Codifier of the Obvious."
Though this title might not seem particularly flat-
tering at first glance, it makes a very large claim indeed. There are some important ideas in every field
that describe working procedures or explain phenomena, ideas which when first stated, seem to observers
so obvious that they don't warrant being formalized
(or being published). When readers think about it,
however, they see that in fact no one has previously
brought together well-known material, which seemed
logically distinct, or named clearly evident mechanisms and processes so succinctly and lucidly. Although these "obvious" ideas and the felicitous terminology invented to refer to them are seldom in
themselves theoretical breakthroughs, they rapidly
enter professional discourse and soon become taken
for granted. Such terms as "cultural and natural
formation processes," "interaction sphere," and
"attached and independent specialist" come to mind
as theoretical codifications that make a difference in
the working lives of many archaeologists.

Analytical philosophers teach that the structure of
thought is not independent of the structure of language. Understanding entails a consideration of how
terms and categories are used for practical application
and how they may seem "natural," having emerged
from training and specialization. In archaeological
theory useful terms are especially precious, in light of
two common failures to communicate. Perhaps because archaeologists are creative people, they are keen
to develop new terms and just as ready to jettison
them in favor of still newer ones. There is, however,
the greater danger that clever terms can become "factoids"—that is, certain terms are invented as handy
labels for provisional arguments but get repeated so
often that they seem like facts (Maier 1985). These
are very hard to refute because they were never
"proved," and even when the cases against them multiply enormously, there may still be claims for their
"heuristic" value (by which is meant that many archaeologists have already used the term/idea so often
that they are unwilling to give it up). What is wanted
is a term that is not quite clever and an idea that is
beyond heuristic.

It seems to me that the idea of this volume, that
early states are often and normally city-states, brings
order to much material, and the term *city-state*,
though not created by our contributors, can be use-

fully employed in a variety of detailed and wide-ranging archaeological explanations. The properly comparative perspective afforded by archaeologists in this volume—namely the perspective of the prehistoric (and early historic) world—shows that Greeks were not the only ones to invent the city-state as a political form. There are ancient Indian (Kenoyer, this volume) and Chinese (Yates, this volume) writings on city-states; Mesopotamian city-states are the normal units of political boundary and social and economic activity; Harappan city-states, Shang and Zhou city-states, Maya city-states, imperial city-states in Mesoamerica and South America are characteristic forms of early states in their regions.

Having got this useful category of city-states, however, we must resist elevating it to an intellectual fetish. Indeed, as is the case with other "obvious" ideas and evocative labels, we must unpack the term *city-state*, trace the variability within it, and explain the significant divergences from it. Morris, for example, has shown (not unexpectedly) that Greek city-states are completely different from Mesopotamian city-states in the constitution of citizenship. His comparison of the social ideology in Greek city-states to the hunter-gatherer San, rather than to other (city-)states, is a remarkable image in its defiance of the expectations of neoevolutionary social theory. Ancient Egypt is a great exception to the evolution of city-states (Wenke, this volume), as is well known, and Teotihuacan is a city-state gone pituitary; on the north coast of Peru we find "valley-states," not city-states (Wilson, this volume); and in the central Andes (and elsewhere in Peru, perhaps at Teotihuacan, and in other places of the world; see, notably, Sinopoli and Morrison [1995]), we observe that city-states can become empires without passing through an intermediate stage of the territorial state. (In his critique of the unilinear, stage-level principle in social evolutionary theory, Churchill noted that the United States was the only example of a society that had passed from barbarism to decadence without having passed through the intervening stage of civilisation). In this concluding chapter, my aim is not to distill the essence of the ancient city-state from the considerable wisdom of the foregoing chapters but to explore how the term must live a chimerical existence if its value is to be appreciated.

Deconstructing the Obvious

In their first chapter of this volume, Charlton and Nichols recapitulate the traits of city-states listed in Griffeth and Thomas (1981a):

In general we understand city-states to be small, territorially based, politically independent state systems, characterized by a capital city or town, with an economically and socially adjacent hinterland. The whole unit, city plus hinterlands, is relatively self-sufficient economically and perceived as being ethnically distinct from other similar state systems. City-states frequently, but not inevitably, occur in groups of fairly evenly spaced units of approximately equivalent size.

As the papers in this volume show, there is a great deal of variability in city-states; indeed, there is no city-state that fits all the characteristics of city-states, and if the "ideal-typical" model of the city-state is to be employed (Pyburn, this volume, after Weber), then these variations and exceptions need to be explained. Let us consider briefly what they are.

First, there is a cankering exception to all archaeological and ancient historical rules of the ubiquity of the city-state in antiquity, ancient Egypt. Toward the end of the fourth millennium B.C., following rapidly upon the development of large cemeteries and the standardization of material culture along the entire Nile Valley from the First Cataract at Aswan to the Mediterranean, an Egyptian territorial state arose (see Baines and Yoffee in press, with copious references cited there; Wenke, this volume). This state was politically centralized, a development that can be seen in the polarization of wealth, the decline of regional centers, the growth of mortuary architecture, luxury goods, characteristic art forms, and writing. In Egypt the establishment of the unified and centralized polity was characterized more by its territorial extent than by the process of urbanization. Throughout Egyptian civilization there has been a clear definition of the extent of the country (Liverani 1990), the political state and the congruent cultural limit of Egypt extending from the Mediterranean to its southern border and hardly farther. Whereas, in some periods, Egypt conquered sections of the Middle Nile and Palestine and Syria, they were not held for long periods and were regarded as non-Egyptian. When defining their world Egyptians were more interested in their frontiers than in their center.

Government policy appears not to have favored cities, notably by relying on an estate-based system of redistribution. Strong territorial demarcation in Egypt is explained by Wenke in this volume as the result of evolutionary trends toward stratification in the ecologically similar environment of the Nile Valley, the concentrations of most important resources within Egypt's borders, and the transport link provided by the Nile. The relatively small population within this large, if linear, expanse made urbanism, which implies a form of demographic implosion (see below), less likely to accompany trends toward increasing social differentiation and hierarchization. Rather, symbols of kingship and unification are found all over the country in the Late Prehistoric period (now generally known as Dynasty 0), and these motifs supply the principal evidence of a developing territorial ideology (Baines and Yoffee in press:18; for another perspective, see Kemp 1989).

Wenke considers that urbanism (and not only in Egypt) is a response to the increasing importance of intensified economic relations, especially the formation of economic elites, who were not simply officers of government, but who interacted with the apparatus of the state. (This was also the case in Mesopotamia at least in certain periods, but the situation in Mesopotamia is complicated in that "private" economic elites also could be officers of the state [Yoffee 1995]). In Egypt the unified polity was quite able to command the production and manage the distribution of resources without an elaborate urban infrastructure. Similarly for Cuzco and Tiwanaku, the lack of an intensive and competitive set of economic behaviors, and especially the absence of an economic elite relatively autonomous from the apparatus of state, may help explain the regal-ritual nature of these polities, as described by Kolata in this volume.

The characteristics of city-states themselves, as discussed in this volume, also do not fit the Griffeth-Thomas trait-list, as can be seen from the following, briefly noted, exceptions.

Small size: the largest exception is Teotihuacan; the city alone covered over 20 square kilometers with an estimated population of 125,000 people. The large geographical size of some Maya city-states, notably Tikal, and their (intermittent) control over settlements in their regions, has led some scholars to question the city-state nomenclature altogether, or to regard Mesoamerican city-states as products of the dissolution of territorial states (J. Marcus 1989, 1993; but see discussion in Webster, this volume). Whereas Tiwanaku was not itself geographically large (by Teotihuacan standards) and had a low urban population, it was the center of a large territorial empire, the "essence of elite belief and focal point of publicly expressed concepts of universal order." The countryside was "thickly settled," and the city lived off tribute and labor from this rural population (citations from Kolata, this volume).

Politically independent: city-states can arise from the collapse of earlier states—in this volume represented by the city-states discussed by Hodge and Charlton and Nichols, which became part of the Aztec empire and thus by definition not politically independent. It is also typical, for example, in Mesopotamia and in the Lowland Maya region, that city-states do try to conquer other city-states and sometimes succeed.

Economic self-sufficiency: in the Chuzan example presented by Pearson (this volume) it is clear that not only were the fortified castle sites and their hinterlands not economically self-sufficient units but that they were economically dependent on trade, especially with China. Indeed, Pearson describes the economic relations as a classic core-periphery structure, although the form of the trade was ideologically remarkable (i.e., non-Western and non-Modern World System): Chuzan city-states gave China tribute and China returned lavish gifts. (This form of trade can also be seen in ancient Egypt and the Near East in the Late Bronze Age; see Liverani 1990). Long-distance trade was also vitally important to the Old Assyrian city-state (Larsen 1976), and traders were important members of the ruling elite in Assur. In southern Mesopotamia, entrepreneurs often contracted with temple and palace organizations to supply distant goods (e.g., van de Mieroop 1992). Pyburn argues that Maya city-states—or at least some of them—relied on trade. Neither Teotihuacan nor Tiwanaku—the former a single city administering a large region, and ranging far afield for exotic preciosities, with a (plausibly inferred) market and the latter with no market, but a large interdependent system for the exchange of goods—can be characterized as economically self-sufficient. The great trading city-states of the Italian Renaissance are obvious counterexamples to the putative trait of local economic self-sufficiency.

Fairly evenly spaced peer polities: although Teotihuacan may once have had at least one "peer," with the disappearance of Cuicuilco it dominated its region without serious rivals for centuries. According to Millon (1988), even at the time of its collapse Teotihuacan (hardly a "capital city" of a territorial state) had no inimical peers, and thus the fiery destruction of the ritual and governmental center of the city should be ascribed to internal forces. Not only may Tula, Tiwanaku, Vijayanagara, and Rome also be considered city-states without (many) peers, these examples further show that city-states can become empires. The neoevolutionist notion that city-states become territorial states (or nation-states) and eventually empires is refuted in two documented countertendencies. In Mesopotamia, city-states are never successfully absorbed into territorial states until non-Mesopotamian political systems and non-Mesopotamian ideologies of governance reformulate the social and natural landscapes of the area (Yoffee 1988). In the New World, we see that it is quite normal for city-states to be (or become centers of) empires.

Ethnically distinct: Mesopotamian city-states are notorious examples of multiethnic communities. Sumerians, Akkadians, Amorites, Kassites, Hurrians, and many other named social orientations (the names refer to languages rather than ethnic groups, *sensu stricto*) lived together in Mesopotamian city-states. Although these city-states provided identifications of citizenship, ethnic relations that transcended city-state boundaries could be mobilized to advantage in the struggle for power within city-states (Emberling and Yoffee in press; see also Murowchick 1994 for discussions of ethnic and linguistic diversity in ancient China).

Finally, the category "city-state" must be unpacked because even in a single region of city-states there are many variations on the theme, as Pyburn in this volume has enunciated: some city-states are larger than others, some are more dependent on long-distance trade than others, and some are more independent politically than others. In cross-cultural perspective, there are city-states with "egalitarian" ideologies in that elites are unable to distance themselves in access to certain resources, including political rank (Morris, this volume); city-states are company towns (the company being the governmental and ritual elite; Kolata, this volume); and city-states seem to exist without major palaces (Kenoyer, this volume), among other variations. Wherein, then, lies the utility of the category "city-state"?

Reclaiming the Obvious

In Anderson's book on the origins of nation-states and nationalism, scarcely a word needed to be devoted to the issue of *territoriality* (1983). That is, Anderson could take for granted that national consciousness could be molded through print languages into a vehicle for the exercise of state power over a delimited but relatively large expanse. Similarly, Geertz (1980), in delineating European definitions of the state in terms of monopolizing violence (among other things)—and thereby showing the lack of fit of

the term to the "theatre-state" of Bali—reckoned with states as occupying reasonably large and more-or-less easily demarcated territory. Yet in the case of many ancient states it is precisely the lack of any large territory within which there may be a number of potentially competitive urban places, but at any time only one seat of state administration, that leaves room for and justifies the category city-state. Indeed, the continuing debates of which ancient states are territorial states and which are not (Trigger 1993, 1985) assumes the existence of city-states.

In this volume, for example, Yates refutes Trigger's (1993) classification of Shang China as a territorial state. He notes that China had its own model of city-states, and the struggle of Shang and Zhou kings to "galacticize" the countryside, that is, to centralize ritual in a capital, with smaller versions being replicated in other sites, did not succeed until the Qin and Han dynasties. Although Webster begins his essay on the Lowland Maya by doubting that there were either cities or states in the area, he soon makes it clear that, of course, there were independent central places in which there was plenty of socioeconomic stratification and governmental specialization. Maya cities were, however, not like Mesopotamian ones or Teotihuacan, and the Maya "states" were quite unlike the state of Egypt. In Mesopotamia there are many city-states, each an arena of social and political struggle and hence hard to integrate on a territorial level (Stone, this volume). Kenoyer has described at least five Harappan city-states, and Morris has enumerated 750 Greek city-states, of which some possess "less stateness or cityness" than others. Whereas Kolata has delineated the regal-ritual nature of Tiwanaku, it seems that Wari, another Andean city-state, which became an empire during the same period, was a larger urban center (Isbell and McEwan 1991; Schreiber 1992) and might have been less exclusively reserved for governmental and ceremonial activities. In sum, many—although not all—ancient states were city-states, and they fit some form of "peer-polity" or parallel-development model.

Although these ancient city-states are not large territorial, quasi-national political systems, the various essays in this volume show that territoriality has considerable importance in cultural terms for the understanding of interactions among the city-states. *Civilization* is the commonly used term for a territorial culture that includes the state, and it is this territorial culture that allows Morris to speak of "classical Greece," the "Greek world" with its 750 *poleis*. Pan-

Hellenic civilization (after Small, this volume) over-arched distinctions between *polis* and *ethne,* the more compact citizen state and the larger, looser "agro-literate" state. This sense of pan-Hellenism was, of course, invented (*sensu* Anderson 1983) and reproduced institutionally, as for example in the neutrally located sanctuaries and festivals (Small, this volume). Born at the conjunction of historical developments, some originating well outside the borders of Greece, Greek city-states were fragile and flourished briefly, to be submerged within the wake of larger historical trends and also undermined by their own success. As Morris puts it, however, the idea of community born in Greek city-states did not collapse, but has lived on, transmogrified to be sure, as the basis for democratic ideologies in a quite different world.

Webster and Pyburn, in addition to stressing the many possible variations among an estimated 60–70 Maya city-states (at the end of the eighth century), describe the "Classic Maya Great Tradition" (Webster), Maya religion, rulership, and stratification within which all the various city-states interacted (see also Sharer 1991). Maya cosmology provided the logic of rule and subservience, and the need for central ritual and governmental action that led to (or in a more complex feedback process was also the result of) the existence of city-states.

Kenoyer (this volume) points to the impressive evidence for an Harrapan civilizational commonalty overlying the five or six or more politically independent Harrapan city-states. In addition to similarities in urban architectural forms, perhaps reflecting conscious governmental models that are known in much later (Maurya) times, it is striking to what extent each city-state used a common form of writing—or at least a corpus of symbols that formed a lingua franca, mainly found on seals, "chert weights for commerce and taxation, and a wide range of other artifacts indicat[ing] that the communities living in these [city-states] were integrated into a single cultural system."

This theme of politically independent city-states, which were the loci of centralized governmental systems and for social and political struggle (as will be resumed in the next section of this essay), but which were seldom brought into any lasting territorial political system, is familiar to Mesopotamianists (Stone, this volume; Yoffee 1988, 1993a, 1993b, 1995). Its widespread relevance to so many early civilizations, however, emerges only from the scale of the world afforded from this volume. In Mesopotamia the fiercely maintained political independence of city-states is matched by the overarching "civilizational" idea that there *should* be a single center for all Mesopotamia. The destiny of such city-states, therefore, included alliances with other city-states, treaties, and most frequently warfare. If the independent city-states had crystallized from an area-wide cultural "interaction sphere" and were the basic units of political life, the shared sense of being pieces in a larger cultural system was seldom out of mind of the leaders of the city-states. If this example represents interactions among other city-state systems, we can see that reclaiming the category "city-state" affords us also a valuable point of entry into the nature of the civilizations in which city-states were embedded.

The Lifestyle of a Chimera

Two interesting themes of social organization within city-states are occasioned by the chapters in the volume. The first concerns the nature of social conflict in city-states and thus the nature of political integration in them. The second, related theme pertains to the pattern and pace of change in city-states.

Kenoyer's revision of the standard descriptions of Harappan-phase urban organization emphasizes the multimound components of the city-states. These mounds do not represent functionally distinct aspects of a systemic whole, but "changing centers of power among elites and merchants." Critical evidence for various centers of power in the sites are that walls surround individual mounds, the various areas of settlement "were founded at different times and grew at different rates," vacant areas between mounds were intentionally maintained, and the 'redundancy' of artifacts and inferred function in the mounds indicates they were rival administrative/ritual centers. Later Mauryan historic writing on types of South Asian city-states delineates the kinds of elites, resident aliens, social classes and amounts of material wealth, craft and industrial specializations, and local assemblies as well as ideologies for right action in the various kinds of city-states. On the basis of the archaeological and the early historical evidence Kenoyer suggests that the "authoritarian model" of Harappan city-states must give way to the study of competing elites; Harappan city-states are interpreted to have fluctuated between being strongly centralized to being constituted by intraurban confederacies. Collapse can be explained, at least in part, by the internal forces in these structural arrangements, and the continuities in South Asian civilization in the Maurya period can be ascribed to the nature of that collapse and subsequent political reformulation.

In Stone's essay her use of the term *consensual* is actually meant to denote the accommodations among the various loci of power and authority in Mesopotamian city-states. The tripartite division of Mesopotamian society into royal, sacral, and "community" sectors (originally proposed by D'jakonov and Gelb, see Yoffee 1995), though stressing the variety of local centers of authority and power in city-states, does not adequately describe the interrelations among the sectors—in which, for example, leaders of the community in the Old Babylonian period and private entrepreneurs (van de Mieroop 1992; Stol 1982) contracted with the palace and were able to hold official ranks in the royal estate. Moreover, the relations between temple and palace and those not entirely dependent on either of these manorial organizations changed radically over time (Yoffee 1995). Stone's excavations and kite-photography/ground-truth surveys at Tell Abu Duwari/Mashkan-Shapir show the excellent archaeological evidence for the structure of Old Babylonian city-states. In addition to administrative and temple districts, Stone and Zimansky have identified neighborhoods, each containing elite and poorer structures. Workshops were found throughout these residential zones. Whereas Stone rightly emphasizes that the city-state was the scene of local political struggle in Mesopotamia and thus difficult to integrate on a larger level, one can add that basic loyalties of citizenship also inhered within city-states, which actively resisted incorporation into territorial states or empires.

This major theme of conflict within city-states is played out in every paper in the volume. In the Chuzan castle-sites, internal and external conflict leads to rival elites being forced to reside in the dominant king's community (shades of Versailles). More often, however, power was shared between the king and his councilors. In Maya city-states, the palaces and temples, greater and lesser lords and their retinues of dependents, capitals and villages that make up a city-state were possible foci for political and social struggle, according to both Webster and Pyburn. Yates cites Keightley's pithy observation that the Shang state was full of holes, like Swiss cheese, not solid, like tofu. Rivaling confederations of political control, feudal masters, roving warrior-intellectuals, and lineage centers competed for independence and hegemony prior to Qin unification. Kolata views the usurpation of power by Tiwanaku lords as leading to

a natural set of tensions that were mediated by the construction of new capitals and their sacred geography.

The structure of elites and the restraints on their power that Morris describes in classical Athens are clear examples of conflict in city-states as are the various social corporations characterizing the Mesoamerican city-states in Hodge's paper. The impression given, as vividly in imperial Aztec times as in fragmented Greece, is one of fragility, the incompleteness of political integration, and the vulnerability to external pressures. In the case of Egypt, our single example of a territorial state, internal conflict existed between rulers and priestly elite (hardly separate categories; Baines and Yoffee in press), as is most vivid in the Amarna period, and between local and centralized authority, but was largely submerged by the ideology and reality of political stability.

This fabled Egyptian stability leads Wenke to consider whether the relative unimportance of urbanism in Egypt might account for certain "ritualized qualities of Egyptian literature, arts, religion." He concludes that the "creative role of urban life," especially in "fostering inventions, accelerating cultural change, producing feelings of alienation," is largely a myth and that "there is no indication that innovations in the arts and sciences suffered . . . from the near absence of urban life" there. This problem of linking urbanism and creativity was not explored by our authors and can easily lead to a bad patch of philosophical quicksand. Nevertheless, a few observations on city-states as "hothouses of change" must suffice on this theme of cultural change in city-states.

Kung fu-tzu (Confucius) said that

It is the function of good government to civilize the countryside, civilization being the separation of administration from rural life. The natural order of the countryside is chaotic and brutish, and cities are formed to provide order and humanize those uncivilized elements that provide food and labor for centralized administration.

Many archaeological studies bear out the observation of Confucius that cities transform the countryside. Indeed, the evolution of cities entails also the evolution of the countryside, ruralization being the counterpart of urbanization. The most prominent examples in this volume are in the development of Teotihuacan and Tula (Charlton and Nichols, this volume), in Mesopotamia, and in South Asia. This process of ruralization means that the "countryside" of city-states is quite unlike the countryside of the same area in the time period before city-states. The countryside is made into "a chaotic and brutish landscape" by city-states, who fear its wildness (from their perspective), as they depend on its resources.

Whereas the "propinquity theory" of cultural change in city-states may seem logically attractive, especially if one is drawn to the type of "trait-transmission" studies cited by Wenke, the "costs" of intra–city-state competition have to be added to the balance when appraising the likelihood of accelerated social and economic change in them. Morris notes that the very struggle "to promote and defend the citizen state" tended to lead to its transformation to the "agro-literate" alternative. It is not at all clear that the "axial" changes Wenke discusses cursorily were born in city-states. For the purposes of this summary, it is the changed structure of both urban and rural landscapes, which include new kinds of elites and new possibilities of resistance to them, that may provide the source for "axially" social and ideological change on the world-historical stage.

Evolution of the Obvious

In general, city-states evolve as collecting basins for the crystallization of long-term trends toward stratification and social differentiation in a geographical region. Since the specific trends in each region differ and are not the main subject of the essays in this volume, one may attempt to infer the several leading reasons for the evolution of city-states from their central characteristics, as presented in this volume: city-states grow from important pilgrimage sites, from market sites (which are often the same as pilgrimage sites), from defensive locations (into which people flock), from geographically favorable nodes in which one might control the distribution of water and access to prime agricultural land and trade routes, or (normally) from some combination of the above.

Common to the evolution of city-states, whatever the prime reason(s) for their geographic location, is a "multiplier effect" in which economic activities spawn other economic activities (e.g., Jacobs 1969). New agricultural specializations in the storage and redistribution of crops in villages led, in turn, to new forms of planning and leadership, the erosion of wealth-leveling mechanisms (Hayden 1994), and the creation of patron-client relations. Changing interactions with those in the countryside effected new economic and social relations there, too, and the further growth of villages as they became service centers (foci of religion and defense as well as economic centers) for their hinterlands.

This outline of evolutionary developments is intended to be relatively uncontroversial. At some point in the process, there is a "phase transition" (Langton, cited in Kauffman 1993), a rapid change from the relatively small complexities of village life to the vastly more complex and intensified socioeconomic and political relations in city-states. The "moment" of phase-transition does not seem to be entirely predictable since the resulting city-state is not simply a larger version of a foregoing village (or territorial organization), with a more elaborate (centralized and specialized) form of governmental apparatus, but is a totally new kind of political and social system.

In the process of city-state formation, leaders of various co-resident social groups compete for power, and new arenas for competition are created to channel this struggle. Since these arenas are themselves products of urban interactions (which include new relations with a concomitantly ruralized countryside), John Robb has argued that the city-state can be considered an "invention of itself" (1994)—see below on the new arenas of competition that are "invented" in city-states. The important role of kinship in (city-)states, which is discussed in several chapters, can better be understood in this perspective.

Yates's chapter represents the dissatisfactions of China scholars (e.g., Chang 1980; Wheatley 1971), as well as others (Fairservis 1989; Possehl 1990; Willey 1985), who either object to the definition of states as political systems in which offices are largely divorced from the bonds of kinship (after Weber 1978) or conclude that their highly stratified, differentiated, and politically centralized societies—but which contain critical kinship relations—are not states at all, but chiefdoms. From the chapters in this volume, we see that there is no ancient (city-)state in which kinship does not play a major role: In Mesopotamia, ethnic groups, leaders of communities, and urban assemblies of notables all play leading roles (Baines and Yoffee in press; Yoffee 1995); in Greece, Morris has discussed the roles of "tribes and peoples" and high-ranking kinsmen in the formation and operation of urban institutions. In the New World, as far as I know, no one has questioned the profoundly important kin ties that are the lifeblood of territorial states and their capitals (Kolata, this volume).

As Pyburn puts it, there is no absolute dichotomy between kin-based and non–kin-based societies. Kinship "is a vocabulary that people use to talk about and negotiate social relations," and that occurs in states as well as nonstates. Following Pyburn, the questions we need to ask are how and in which ways are kin ties interpreted and transformed in (city-)states, what do these new uses of kinship tell us about politics and especially political economy, and how do these uses change over time? If kin ties exist in all societies, however, we must be prepared to see that they are more important in some societies than others and that some choices are less available or not available, according to the constellation of power relations in them (Wolf 1990).

In the new arenas for competition in (city-)states are certain ranks and offices that concern the management of social and economic relations. These offices solve problems that arise between members of different social corporations, represent the entire society in war and/or defense, and maintain the new symbols that effectively incorporate all the sectors of the (city-) state. Individuals competing for such offices do so in large measure on the basis of their leadership of social groups, and that leadership is often based on their ranking in a kinship system. However, in city-states it is typical that leaders also are able to appeal to those who are not necessarily their own kinsmen, and it is their success in doing so that may privilege them in their struggle for power.

Though the specific nature of such struggles and the ways in which kinship is negotiated as part of them must vary greatly, we may resolve the conundrum of Yates (and others). (City-)states are not defined according to the presence or absence of kin ties in political offices, but in the creation of new arenas of competition among the leaders of socially differentiated and economically stratified co-resident groups.

Summary: The Obvious Chimera

It will not have escaped the reader that in using the expression *(city-)state* in the last section I have hedged my evolutionary bets, and I have done so for a specific reason. The process of state formation is not limited to city-states, and the formation of new arenas for social and political struggle occurs in the territorial states studied by Kolata and Wenke as well as the city-states described in other essays. Indeed, Kolata's chapter shows that capital cities in territorial states are also centers of government and ritual, appropriating surplus from a restructured countryside in which it was symbolically dominant. Although the lack of

markets and economic elites distinguishes the character of the capitals of Andean territorial states (and thus the nature of social and political struggle in them) from that of most city-states, there are also many similarities between city-states and capitals of territorial states.

Further discussion of the processes of state formation, however, would have me defy the prime directive of all summarizers: "thou shallt steer a course between the Scylla of becoming the Judge Wapner of your volume and the Charybdis of ignoring the presented papers altogether in favor of writing a chapter of your own." Although there may have been a few rocky collisions in the preceding sections of this chapter, I end by returning to the major themes and accomplishments of this volume.

Charlton and Nichols conceived the idea of this volume in order to determine whether the term *city-state* clarified their research on a "system of interrelated small polities" in the Basin of Mexico, about A.D. 1350–1521, and in particular whether city-states were as common in the ancient world as they expected. The results show that, indeed, city-states are normal products of worldwide social evolutionary trajectories (and are not simply products of the dissolution of territorial states). Early territorial states, like Egypt, are quite exceptional.

No list of the essential traits of city-states, the higher and lower limits of population or areal size, however, can be produced, since city-states come in large and small packages, and they are not usually economically self-sufficient, being usually dependent on trade with near neighbors and distant lands. City-states are rarely ethnically homogeneous, some being extremely socially diverse. Nevertheless, certain, properly qualified generalizations allow us to compose a "field guide" for observing city-states. City-states usually include a hinterland consisting of other, usually smaller cities, as well as villages and agricultural lands. City-states frequently exist along with other city-states, trading with them and fighting against them for intervening arable land and access to trade routes. City-states are thus crystallizations of long-term, regional evolutionary trajectories toward increasing economic stratification and social differentiation. These trends also include the development of the idea that there should be inequality, rulers and subjects, and common purpose among city-states sharing a basically similar cosmological system, even if the reality of the political independence of city-states was a fact of life. City-states could become empires and thus be considered the capitals of empires.

The category of "city-state" is useful not because it leads to a set of correlates that afford archaeological identification, although, as I have summarized, there is a set of readily ascertainable qualities of city-states. Rather, the term *city-state* is inherently and intentionally flexible, allowing for, even expecting, important differences in major political and socioeconomic institutions, and it requires that variability be delineated and explained. In some cases, however, the variability is itself illusory since narratives of uniqueness can also result from failures of cross-cultural imagination. Use of the comparative method (which is mandated by the term *city-state*) is thus, paradoxically, the only way in which attributions of uniqueness can gain plausiblilty.

The panoply of archaeological knowledge in this volume allows significant questions about city-states (and their exceptions) to be posed that have been mooted heretofore only on a more limited basis (M. Hammond 1972; Trigger 1993). Much of the mythology of the evolution of ancient states may be ascribed to previous archaeological conceptions of the state as a territorially integrated political system—that is, the product of progressive control over expanses of territory and the political management of goods, services, and information. We can see now that the earliest states are mostly city-states, the scenes of new struggles for power and authority, the battlegrounds for independence and dominion.

Investigating the evolution of city-states, as I have described the research in this volume (importantly including the use of historic and artistic sources along with other archaeological data), avoids the trap of overdefining the city-state, since any attempt to delineate semipermanent institutions and fixed relations can only lead to a bewildering variety of traits and their exceptions. The task is not to discover or establish a new organizational essence, one that seeks to categorize and so control research, but to effect a point of entry into the processes that underlie endlessly reforming institutional commonalities among diverse phenomena (after Geertz 1973:34). Our collective research on city-states and the evolutionary trajectories that lead to them enables us to narrow our focus from large spaces, vague interconnections, and impersonal forces to the structures (gaps in structures, incomplete structures, resistance to and changes in structures) and networks of power and social actors. Archaeologists, surprisingly, are like poets, who often find truths in concision and frequently resort to a packed leanness of speech. Codifying a chimera may not seem an especially dignified labor, but it provides a welcome portion of clarity in the development of archaeological theory.

Acknowledgments

Many thanks to Bob Adams, John Baines, George Cowgill, Geoff Emberling, and Deborah Nichols for clarifying points, improving arguments, and patching holes.

References

Abdel-Nour, Antoine
1982   *Introduction à l'histoire urbaine de la Syrie ottomane (XVI–XVIIIe siecle)*. Publications de l'Université Libanaise section des Études historiques XXV. Beirut: Librarie Orientale.

Abercrombie, Nicholas, Stephen Hill, and Bryan S. Turner
1980   *The Dominant Ideology Thesis*. London: Allen and Unwin.

Abercrombie, Nicholas, Stephen Hill, and Bryan S. Turner, eds.
1990   *Dominant Ideologies*. London: Unwin Hyman.

Ackerman, James
1991   Commentary. In *City-States in Classical Antiquity and Medieval Italy*, edited by Anthony Molho, Kurt Raaflaub, and Julia Emlen, pp. 453–456. Ann Arbor: University of Michigan Press.

Acuña, René, ed.
1984–1987   *Relaciones geográficas del siglo XVI: México*, 9 vols. México, D.F.: Universidad Nacional Autónoma de México.

Adams, Richard E. W.
1974   A Trial Estimation of Classic Maya Palace Populations at Uaxactún. In *Mesoamerican Archaeology*, edited by Norman Hammond, pp. 285–296. Austin: University of Texas Press.

Adams, Richard E. W., and Richard C. Jones
1981   Spatial Patterns and Regional Growth among Classic Maya Cities. *American Antiquity* 46:301–322.

Adams, Richard N.
1981   Natural Selection, Energetics, and Cultural Materialism. *Current Anthropology* 22:603–624.

Adams, Robert McC.
1965   *Land behind Baghdad: A History of Settlement on the Diyala Plains*. Chicago: University of Chicago Press.
1966   *The Evolution of Urban Society: Early Mesopotamia and Prehispanic Mexico*. Chicago: Aldine.
1972   Settlement and Irrigation Patterns in Ancient Akkad. In *The City and Area of Kish*, edited by McGuire Gibson, pp. 182–208. Coconut Grove: Field Research Projects.
1978   Strategies of Maximization, Stability, and Resilience in Mesopotamian Society, Settlement, and Agriculture. *Proceedings of the*

American Philosophical Society
122:329–335.

1981   *Heartland of Cities: Surveys of Ancient Settlement and Land Use on the Central Floodplain of the Euphrates.* Chicago: University of Chicago Press.

1992   Ideologies: Unity and Disunity. In *Ideology and Pre-Columbian Civilizations,* edited by Arthur A. Demarest, and Geoffrey W. Conrad, pp. 205–222. Sante Fe: School of American Research.

Adams, Robert McC., and Hans Nissen
1972   *The Uruk Countryside: The Natural Setting of Urban Societies.* Chicago: University of Chicago Press.

AGN, Catálogo de Ilustraciones
1979–1981   *Catálogo de Ilustraciones.* México, D.F: Centro de Información Gráfica del Archivo General de la Nación.

Agurto, Santiago C.
1980   *Cuzco: Traza urbana de la ciudad Inca.* Cuzco: UNESCO and the Instituto Nacional de Cultura.

Alcock, Susan
1993   *Graecia Capta: The Landscapes of Roman Greece.* Cambridge: Cambridge University Press.

Alcock, Susan, John Cherry, and Jack Davis
1994   Intensive Survey, Agricultural Practice, and the Classic Landscape of Greece. In *Ancient Histories and Modern Archaeologies,* edited by Ian Morris, pp. 137–170. Cambridge: Cambridge University Press.

Alden, John R.
1979   A Reconstruction of Toltec Period Political Units in the Valley of Mexico. In *Transformations: Mathematical Approaches to Culture Change,* edited by Colin Renfrew and Kenneth L. Cooke, pp. 169–200. Academic Press, New York.

Allan, Sarah
1984   Drought, Human Sacrifice and the Mandate of Heaven in a Lost Text from the *Shang shu. Bulletin of the School of Oriental and African Studies* 47:523–539.

1991   *The Shape of the Turtle: Myth, Art, and Cosmos in Early China.* Albany: State University of New York Press.

Allen, Richard O., Hany Hamroush, and Daniel J. Stanley
1993   Impact of the Environment on Egyptian Civilization before the Pharaohs. *Analytical Chemistry* 65:36–43.

Altekar, Anant S.
1984 [1958]   *State and Government in Ancient India.* Delhi: Motilal Banarsidass.

Alva Ixtlilxochitl, Fernando de
1975–1977   *Obras históricas,* 2 vols. México, D.F.: Universidad Nacional Autónoma de México.

Alva, Walter
1988   Discovering the New World's Richest Unlooted Tomb. *National Geographic* 174:510–548.

Alva, Walter, and Christopher B. Donnan
1993   *Royal Tombs of Sipán.* Los Angeles: Fowler Museum of Cultural History.

Alvarado Tezozomoc, Hernando
1975   *Crónica Mexicana.* México: Editorial Porrúa, S.A.

Amit, M.
1973   *Great and Small Poleis: A Study in the Relations between the Great Powers and the Small Cities in Ancient Greece.* Latomus, Brussels.

Anales de Cuauhtitlán
1974 [1938]   *Die Geschichte der Königreiche von Colhuacan und Mexiko.* Translated by Walter Lehmann. Stuttgart: Kohlhammer, Quellenwerke zur alten Geschichte Amerikas aufgezeichnet in den Sprachen der Eingeborenen, 1.

1975 [1945]   *Códice Chimalpopoca: Anales de Cuauhtitlán y Leyenda de los Soles.* Translated by Primo Feliciano Velázquez. México, D.F.: Universidad Nacional Autónoma de México, Instituto de Investigaciones Históricas, Primera Serie Prehispánica 1.

Anderson, Arthur J. O., Frances F. Berdan, and James Lockhart
1976   *Beyond the Codices: The Nahua View of Colonial Mexico.* Berkeley: University of California Press.

Anderson, Benedict
1983   *Imagined Communities: Reflections on the Origin and Spread of Nationalism.* London: Verso.

Anderson, Wendy
1992   Badarian Burials: Evidence of Social Inequality in Middle Egypt during the Predynastic Era. *Journal of the American Research Center in Egypt* 29:51–66.

Andrews, Anthony P.
1983   *Maya Salt Making and Trade.* Tucson: University of Arizona Press.

Andrews, E. Wyllys, IV, and Irwin Rovner
1973   Archaeological Evidence on Social Stratifi-
            cation and Commerce in the Northern
            Maya Lowlands: Two Mason's Tool Kits
            from Muna and Dzibilchaltun, Yucatan. In
            *Archaeological Investigations in the Yuca-
            tan Peninsula,* edited by Margaret A.
            Harrison and Robert Wauchope, pp.
            81–102. Middle American Research Insti-
            tute Publication 31. New Orleans: Tulane
            University.

Andrews, E. Wyllys, V, and Barbara Fash
1992   Continuity and Change in a Royal Maya
            Residential Complex at Copan. *Ancient
            Mesoamerica* 3:63–87.

Angel, J. Lawrence
1972   Biological relations of Egyptians and East-
            ern Mediterranean Populations during Pre-
            dynastic and Dynastic Times. *Journal of
            Human Evolution* 1:307–313.

Ardeleanu-Jansen, Alexandra
1992   New Evidence on the Distribution of Arti-
            facts: An Approach towards a Qualitative-
            Quantitative Assessment of the Terra-Cotta
            Figurines of Mohenjo-Daro. In *South Asian
            Archaeology, 1989,* edited by Catherine Jar-
            rige, pp. 5–14. Madison: Prehistory Press.

Arnold, Bettina
1990   The Past as Propaganda: Totalitarian Ar-
            chaeology in Nazi Germany. *Antiquity*
            244:464–78.

Arroyo, Salvador Guillermo
1990   El templo a Ehecatl en Tlatelolco. Paper pre-
            sented at Seminario Alfonso Caso, "La
            Epoca Final del México Antiguo, Siglos XII
            a XVI." México, D.F.: Museo Nacional de
            Antropología y Instituto Nacional de Antro-
            pología e Historia.

Asato, Susumu
1980   Kokogaku ni Okeru Gusuku Ronso [The
            Gusuku Controversy in Archaeology]. In
            Nihon Jokaku Taikei [Survey of Japanese
            Castles], vol. 1: *Hokkaido and Okinawa,*
            edited by Hideo Fujimoto and Shohachiro
            Naka, pp. 331–335. Tokyo: Shin Jimbutsu
            Oraisha.
1987   Ryukyu: Okinawa no Kokogakuteki Jidai
            Kubun o Meguru Shomondai (jo) [Ryukyu:
            Some Problems Surrounding Archaeologi-
            cal Periodization, Part 1]. *Kokogaku Ken-
            kyu* 34(3):65–84.
1988   Ryukyu: Okinawa no Kokogakuteki Jidai
            Kubun o Meguru Sho Mondai (ge) [Ryu-

kyu: Some Problems Surrounding Archaeo-
            logical Periodization, Part 2]. *Kokogaku
            Kenkyu* 34(4):50–67.
1990   *Kokogaku kara Mita Ryukyu Shi (jo)* [Ryu-
            kyu History Seen from Archaeology].
            Naha: Okinawa Bunko.

Asheri, David
1963   Laws of Inheritance, Distribution of Land,
            and Political Constitutions in Ancient
            Greece. *Historia* 12:1–21.
1966   *Distribuzioni di terre nel'antica Grecia.* Tu-
            rin: Memorie dell'Accademia delle Scienze
            di Torino, ser. 4.10.
1969   Leggi greche sul problema dei debiti. *Studi
            classici e orientali* 18:5–122.

Athens, J. Stephen
1977   Theory Building and the Study of Evolution-
            ary Process. In *For Theory Building in Ar-
            chaeology,* edited by Lewis Binford, pp.
            353–384. New York: Academic Press.

Atwell, William S.
1977   Notes on Silver, Foreign Trade, and the
            Late Ming Economy. *Ch'ing-shih wen-t'i*
            [Problems in Ching History] 3(8):1–33.

Atzler, Michael
1971–72   Randglossen zur Ägyptischen Vorg-
            eschichte. *Jaarbericht Ex Oriente Lux*
            22:228–246.

Austin, M., and P. Vidal-Naquet
1977   *Economic and Social History of Ancient
            Greece.* Berkeley: University of California
            Press.

Aveni, Anthony F., Edward E. Calnek, and Horst Hartung
1988   Myth, Environment, and the Orientation of
            the Templo Mayor of Tenochtitlan. *Ameri-
            can Antiquity* 53:287–309.

Baba, Hisao, and Shuichiro Narasaki
1991   Minatogawa Man, the Oldest Type of Mod-
            ern *Homo Sapiens* in East Asia. *Daiyonki
            Kenkyu* [The Quaternary Research]
            30(2):221–230.

Badawy, Alexander
1967   The Civic Sense of Pharaoh and Urban
            Development in Ancient Egypt. *Journal of
            the American Research Center in Egypt*
            6:103–109.

Baer, Klaus
1960   *Rank and Title in the Old Kingdom.* Chi-
            cago: University of Chicago Press.

Bagley, Robert W.
1988   Sacrificial Pits of the Shang Period at San-

xingdui in Guanghan County, Sichuan Province. *Ars Asiatiques* 43:78–86.

Baines, John
1990   Restricted Knowledge, Hierarchy, Decorum: Modern Perceptions and Ancient Institutions. *Journal of the American Research Center in Egypt* 27:1–23.

Baines, John, and Norman Yoffee
in press   Order, Legitimacy, and Wealth in Ancient Egypt and Mesopotamia. In *Archaic States: A Comparative Perspective,* edited by Gary Feinman and Joyce Marcus. Santa Fe: School of American Research Advanced Seminar Series.

Bakr, Mohammad
1988   The New Excavations at Ezbet el-Tell, Kufur Nigm: The First Season (1984). In *The Archaeology of the Nile Delta: Problems and Priorities,* edited by Edwin C. M. van den Brink, pp. 49–62. Amsterdam: Netherlands Foundation for Archaeological Research in Egypt.

Ball, Joseph W., and Jenifer T. Taschek
1991   Lowland Maya Political Organization and Central-Place Analysis. *Ancient Mesoamerica* 2:149–165.

Baqir, Taha
1959   *Tell Harmal.* Baghdad: Department of Antiquities.

Bard, Katherine A.
1987   The Geography of Excavated Predynastic Sites and the Rise of Complex Society. *Journal of the American Research Center in Egypt* 24:81–93.
1992   Toward an Interpretation of the Role of Ideology in the Evolution of Complex Society in Egypt. *Journal of Anthropological Archaeology* 2:1–24.

Bard, Katherine A., and Robert L. Carneiro
1989   Patterns of Predynastic Settlement Location, Social Evolution, and the Circumscription Theory. Sociétés Urbaines en Égypte et au Soudan, *Cahiers de Recherches de l'Institut de Papyrologie et d'Égyptologie de Lille* 11:15–23.

Bargatzky, Thomas
1988   Evolution, Sequential Hierarchy, and Areal Integration: The Case of Traditional Samoan Society. In *State and Society: The Emergence of Social Hierarchy and Political Centralization,* edited by John Gledhill,
Barbara Bender, and Mogens T. Larsen, pp. 43–56. London: Unwin Hyman.

Barker, Alex, and Timothy Pauketak
1992   Introduction. In *Lords of the Southeast: Social Inequality and the Native Elites of Southeastern North America,* edited by Alex Barker and Timothy Pauketat, pp. 1–10. Washington, D.C.: Archeological Papers of the American Anthropological Association No. 3.

Bartoloni, Gilda, and Annette Rathje, eds.
1984   Aspetti delle aristocrazie fra VIII e VII secolo a. C. *Opus* 3.2:231–476.

Basham, Arthur L.
1964   *Studies in Indian History and Culture.* Calcutta: Sambodhi.

Baudez, Claude F., ed.
1983   *Introduccion a la Arqueología de Copán, Honduras* (3 vols.). Tegucigalpa: Instituto Hondureño de Antropología e Historia.

Bawden, Garth
1989   The Andean State as a State of Mind. Review of *The Origins and Development of the Andean State,* edited by Jonathan Haas, Shelia Pozorski, and Thomas Pozorski. *Journal of Anthropological Research* 45:327–332.

Belcher, William R.
1993   Fishing of the Third Millennium B.C.: Ongoing Research in the Greater Indus Valley. *Marine Reference Collection Centre Newsletter* 1 (3):2–3.

Bell, Thomas L., Richard L. Church, and Larry Gorenflo
1988   Late Horizon Regional Efficiency in the Northeastern Basin of Mexico: A Location-Allocation Perspective. *Journal of Anthropological Archaeology* 7:163–202.

Bennyhoff, James A.
1967   Chronology and Periodization: Continuity and Change in the Teotihuacan Ceramic Tradition. In *Teotihuacán, XI Mesa Redonda,* Vol. 1, pp. 19–29. México, D.F.: Sociedad Mexicana de Antropología.

Benson, Elizabeth P.
1972   *The Mochica: A Culture of Peru.* New York: Praeger Publishers.

Benson, Elizabeth, ed.
1986   *City-states of the Maya: Art and Architecture.* Denver: Rocky Mountain Institute for Pre-Columbian Studies.

Berdan, Frances F.
1975   Trade, Tribute, and Market in the Aztec Empire. Unpublished Ph.D. dissertation, Department of Anthropology, University of Texas, Austin.
1985   Markets in the Economy of Aztec Mexico. In *Markets and Marketing,* edited by Stuart Plattner, pp. 339–367. Lanham, MD: University Press of America, Lanham.
1987   The Economics of Aztec Luxury Trade and Tribute. In *The Aztec Templo Mayor,* edited by Elizabeth Hill Boone, pp. 161–183. Washington, D.C.: Dumbarton Oaks Research Library and Collection.

Berdan, Frances F., and Patricia Reiff Anawalt, eds.
1992   *The Codex Mendoza,* 4 vols. Berkeley: University of California Press.

Berdan, Frances F., Richard E. Blanton, Elizabeth Hill Boone, Mary G. Hodge, Michael E. Smith, and Emily Umberger, eds.
1996   *Aztec Imperial Strategies.* Washington, D.C.: Dumbarton Oaks Research Library and Collection.

Berger, Shlomo
1992   *Revolution and Society in Greek Sicily and Southern Italy.* Stuttgart: Historia Einzelschrift 71.

Berlo, Janet Catherine
1989   Early Writing in Central Mexico: *In Tlilli, In Tlapalli* before A.D. 1000. In *Mesoamerica after the Decline of Teotihuacan, A.D. 700–900,* edited by Richard A. Diehl and Janet Catherine Berlo, pp. 19–47. Washington, D.C.: Dumbarton Oaks Research Library and Collection.

Bernal, Martin
1987   *Black Athena: The Afroasiatic Roots of Classical Civilization, Vol. 1: The Fabrication of Ancient Greece.* New Brunswick: Rutgers University Press.

Bernhardt, Rainer
1985   *Polis und römische Herrschaft in der späten Republik, 149–31 v. Chr.* Berlin: De Gruyter.

Besenval, Roland
1992   Le Peuplement Ancien Du Kech-Makran. Travaux Récents. *Paléorient* 18:103–107.

Beyer, I.
1976   *Die Tempel von Dreros und Prinias und die Chronologie der kretischen Kunst des 8. u. 7. Jhs. v. Chr.* Freiburg.

Biagi, Paolo, and M. Cremaschi
1990   Geoarchaeological Investigations on the Rohri Hills (Sind, Pakistan). In *South Asian Archaeology, 1987,* edited by Maurizio Taddei and Pierfrancesco Callieri, pp. 31–42. Rome: IsMEO.

Binford, Lewis R.
1983   *In Pursuit of the Past: Decoding the Archaeological Record.* New York: Thames and Hudson.
1989   *Debating Archaeology.* New York: Academic Press.

Bintliff, John, and Anthony Snodgrass
1988   Off-Site Pottery Distributions: A Regional and Inter-Regional Perspective. *Current Anthropology* 29:506–513.

Bisht, R. S.
1982   Excavations at Banawali, 1974–77. In *Harappan Civilization: A Contemporary Perspective,* edited by Gregory L. Possehl, pp. 113–124. New Delhi: Oxford and IBH Publishing.
1989   A New Model of the Harappan Town Planning as Revealed at Dholavira in Kutch: A Surface Study of Its Plan and Architecture. In *History and Archaeology,* edited by Bhaskar Chatterjee, pp. 397–408. Delhi: Ramanand Vidhya Bhawan.
1990   Dholavira: New Horizons of the Indus Civilization. *Puratattva* 20:71–82.
1994   Secrets of the Water Fort. *Down to Earth* (May):25–31.

Black, Jeremy
1993   Eme-sal Cult Songs and Prayers. In *Veles Paraules: Ancient Near Eastern Studies in Honor of Miguel Civil,* edited by P. Michalowski, P. Steinkeller, E. C. Stone, and R. L. Zettle, pp. 23–36. Barcelona: Aula Orientalis.

Blackman, M. James, and Massimo Vidale
1992   The Production and Distribution of Stoneware Bangles at Mohenjo-daro and Harappa, as Monitored by Chemical Characterization Studies. In *South Asian Archaeology, 1989,* edited by Catherine Jarrige, pp. 37–44. Monographs in World Archaeology No. 14. Madison: Prehistory Press.

Blanton, Richard E.
1972   *Prehispanic Settlement Patterns of the Ixtapalapa Peninsula Region, Mexico.* Occasional Papers in Anthropology No. 6. University Park, PA: Department of Anthro-

pology, Pennsylvania State University.

1975   Texcoco Region Archaeology. *American Antiquity* 40:227–230.

1976   Comment on Sanders, Parsons, and Logan. In *The Valley of Mexico: Studies in Pre-Hispanic Ecology and Society,* edited by Eric R. Wolf, pp. 179–201. Albuquerque: University of New Mexico Press.

1996   The Basin of Mexico Market System and the Growth of Empire. In *Aztec Imperial Strategies,* by Frances F. Berdan, Richard E. Blanton, Elizabeth Hill Boone, Mary G. Hodge, Michael E. Smith, and Emily Umberger, pp. 47–84. Washington, D.C.: Dumbarton Oaks Research Library and Collection.

Blanton, Richard E., Gary M. Feinman, Stephen A. Kowalewski, and Peter N. Peregrine

1996   A Dual Processual Theory for the Evolution of Mesoamerican Civilization. *Current Anthropology* 37:1–14.

Blanton, Richard E., Stephen A. Kowalewski, Gary M. Feinman, and Laura M. Finsten

1993 [1981]   *Ancient Mesoamerica: A Comparison of Change in Three Region*s. 2nd ed. Cambridge: Cambridge University Press.

Blockmans, Wim P.

1994   Voracious States and Obstructing Cities: An Aspect of State Formation in Preindustrial Europe. In *Cities and the Rise of States in Europe, A.D. 1000 to 1800,* edited by Charles Tilly and Wim P. Blockmans, pp. 218–250. Boulder: Westview Press.

Boardman, John

1962   Archaic Finds at Knossos. *Annual of the British School at Athens* 57:8–34.

1967   The Khaniale Tekke Tombs, II. *Annual of the British School at Athens* 62:57–75.

1980   *The Greeks Overseas.* London: Penguin.

Bodman, Herbert J.

1963   *Political Factions in Aleppo, 1760–1826.* Chapel Hill: University of North Carolina Press.

Boehm de Lameiras, Brigitte

1986   *Formación del Estado en el México Prehispánico.* Zamora: Colegio de Michoacan.

Bokonyi, Sandor

1985   The Animal Remains of Maadi, Egypt: A Preliminary Report. In *Studi di Paleontologia in Onore di S. M. Puglisi,* pp. 494–504. Rome: Universita di Roma "La Sapienza."

Bongard-Levin, Giorgii M.

1986   *A Complex Study of Ancient India: A Multi-Disciplinary Approach.* Delhi: Ajanta Publishers.

Bonine, Michael E.

1980   *Yazd and Its Hinterland: A Central Place System of Dominance in the Central Iranian Plateau.* Marburger Geographische Schriften 83, Geographischen Institutes der Universität Marburg, Marburg.

Boone, Elizabeth Hill, ed.

1984   *Ritual Human Sacrifice in Mesoamerica.* Washington, D.C.: Dumbarton Oaks Research Library and Collection.

1987   *The Aztec Templo Mayor.* Washington, D.C.: Dumbarton Oaks Research Library and Collection.

Bouhdiba, Abdelwahab, and Dominique Chevallier, eds.

1982   *La Ville arabe dans l'Islam.* Paris: CNRS.

Bourdieu, Pierre

1984   *Distinction: A Social Critique of the Judgment of Tastes.* Translated by Richard Nice. Cambridge: Harvard University Press.

Bourriau, Janine

1981   *Umm el-Ga'ab: Pottery from the Nile Valley before the Arab Conquest.* Cambridge: Fitzwilliam Museum.

Boyd, Robert, and Peter J. Richerson

1985   *Culture and the Evolutionary Process.* Chicago: University of Chicago Press.

Brace, C. Loring., David P. Tracer, Lucia Allen Yaroch, John Robb, Kari Brandt, and A. Russel Nelson

1993   Clines and Clusters Versus "Race:" A Test in Ancient Egypt and Case of a Death on the Nile. *Yearbook of Physical Anthropology* 36:1–31.

Bravo, Benedetto

1974   Une lettre sur plomb de Berezan: colonisation et modes de contrat dans le Pont. *Dialogues d'histoire ancienne* 1:111–187.

Bray, Warwick

1972a   The City-State in Central Mexico at the Time of the Spanish Conquest. *Journal of Latin American Studies* 4:161–185.

1972b   Land-use, Settlement Pattern, and Politics in Prehispanic Middle America. In *Man, Settlement, and Urbanism,* edited by Peter J. Ucko, Ruth Tringham, and G. W. Dimbleby, pp. 909–926. Cambridge: Schenkman Publishing Company.

1977 Civilising the Aztecs. In *The Evolution of Social Systems,* edited by J. Friedman and M. J. Rowlands, pp. 373–398. Pittsburgh: University of Pittsburgh Press.

1983 Landscape with Figures: Settlement Patterns, Locational Models, and Politics in Mesoamerica. In *Prehistoric Settlement Patterns: Essays in Honor of Gordon R. Willey,* edited by Evon Z. Vogt and Richard M. Leventhal, pp. 167–193. Albuquerque and Cambridge: University of New Mexico Press and Peabody Museum of Archaeology and Ethnology, Harvard University.

Brewer, Douglas J.
1991 Temperature in Predynastic Egypt Inferred from the Remains of the Nile Perch. *World Archaeology* 22:288–303.

Brewer, Douglas J., and Robert J. Wenke
1992 Transitional Late Predynastic-Early Dynastic Occupations at Mendes: A Preliminary Report. In *The Nile Delta in Transition: 4th–3rd Millennium B.C.,* Proceedings of the Seminar held in Cairo, 21–24 October, 1990, edited by Edwin C. M. van den Brink, pp. 175–183. Amsterdam: The Netherlands Institute of Archaeology and Arabic Studies.

Briant, Pierre
1988 Le Nomadisme du Grand Roi. *Iranica Antiqua* 23:253–273.

van den Brink, Edwin C. M.
1988 The Amsterdam University Survey Expedition to the Northeastern Nile Delta (1984–1986). In *The Archaeology of the Nile Delta: Problems and Priorities,* edited by Edwin C. M. van den Brink, pp. 65–114. Amsterdam: Netherlands Foundation for Archaeological Research in Egypt.

Bronson, Bennet
n.d. Vacant Terrain Excavations at Tikal. Manuscript on file, University Museum, Philadelphia.

Brown, Alison
1991 City and Citizen: Changing Perceptions in the Fifteenth and Sixteenth Centuries. In *City States in Classical Antiquity and Medieval Italy,* edited by Anthony Molho, Kurt Raaflaub, and Julia Emlen, pp. 93–111. Ann Arbor: University of Michigan Press.

Brucker, Gene
1969 *Renaissance Florence.* Berkeley: University of California Press.

Brumfiel, Elizabeth M.
1976a Specialization and Exchange at the Late Postclassic (Aztec) Community of Huexotla, Mexico. Ph.D. dissertation, Department of Anthropology, University of Michigan, Ann Arbor. Ann Arbor: University Microfilms.

1976b Regional Growth in the Eastern Valley of Mexico: A Test of the "Population Pressure" Hypothesis. In *The Early Mesoamerican Village,* edited by Kent V. Flannery, pp. 234–249. New York: Academic Press.

1980 Specialization, Market Exchange, and the Aztec State: A View from Huexotla. *Current Anthropology* 21:459–478.

1982 Intensive, Systematic Surface Collection at Ch-Az-192 (Xico): A Preliminary Report. In *Late Prehispanic Chinampa Agriculture on Lake Chalco-Xochimilco, Mexico: Preliminary Report,* edited by Jeffrey R. Parsons, Elizabeth M. Brumfiel, Mary H. Parsons, Virginia Popper, and Mary Taft, pp. 195–215. Mimeographed report. Museum of Anthropology, University of Michigan, Ann Arbor.

1983 Aztec State Making: Ecology, Structure, and the Origin of the State. *American Anthropologist* 85:261–284.

1986 The Division of Labor at Xico: The Chipped Stone Industry. In *Economic Aspects of Prehispanic Highland Mexico,* edited by Barry L. Isaac, pp. 245–279. Research in Economic Anthropology, Supplement No. 2. Greenwich, CT: JAI Press.

1987 Elite and Utilitarian Crafts in the Aztec State. In *Specialization, Exchange, and Complex Societies,* edited by Elizabeth M. Brumfiel and Timothy K. Earle, pp. 102–118. Cambridge: Cambridge University Press.

1989 Factional Competition and Political Development. In *Domination and Resistance,* edited by Daniel Miller, Michael J. Rowlands, and Christopher Tilley, pp. 127–139. London: Unwin-Hyman.

1991 Agricultural Development and Class Stratification in the Southern Valley of Mexico. In *Land and Politics in the Valley of Mexico,* edited by Herbert R. Harvey, pp. 43–62. Albuquerque: University of New Mexico Press.

1992 Breaking and Entering the Ecosystem: Gender, Class, and Faction Steal the Show. *American Anthropologist* 94:551–567.

1994 Factional Competition and Political Development in the New World: An Introduction. In *Factional Competition and Political Development in the New World,* edited by Elizabeth M. Brumfiel and John W. Fox, pp. 3–13. Cambridge: Cambridge University Press.

in press   *Post-Classic Xaltocan: Ecological and Social Determinants of Production in the Northern Basin of Mexico.* Memoirs in Latin American Archaeology. Pittsburgh: Department of Anthropology, University of Pittsburgh.

Brumfiel, Elizabeth M., ed.
1992   Preliminary Report on Archaeological Investigations at Xaltocan, Mexico. Report to the National Science Foundation. Albion College, Albion, MI.

Brumfiel, Elizabeth M., and Timothy K. Earle
1987   Specialization, Exchange, and Complex Societies: An Introduction. In *Specialization, Exchange, and Complex Societies,* edited by Elizabeth M. Brumfiel and Timothy K. Earle, pp. 1–9. Cambridge: Cambridge University Press.

Brumfiel, Elizabeth M., and John W. Fox, eds.
1994   *Factional Competition and Political Development in the New World.* Cambridge: Cambridge University Press.

Brumfiel, Elizabeth M., Tamara Salcedo, and David Schaffer
1994   The Lip Plugs of Xaltocan: Function and Meaning in Aztec Archaeology. In *Economies and Polities in the Aztec Realm,* edited by Mary G. Hodge and Michael E. Smith. Albany: Institute for Mesoamerican Studies, State University of New York at Albany.

Brundage, Burr Cartwright
1967   *Lords of Cuzco: A History and Description of the Inca People in Their Final Days.* Norman: University of Oklahoma Press.
1972   *A Rain of Darts: The Mexica Aztecs.* Austin: University of Texas Press.

Bulliet, Richard
1972   *The Patricians of Nishapur.* Cambridge: Harvard University Press.

Burckhardt, Jacob
1898   *Griechische Kulturgeschichte,* Vol. 1., 4 vols. Berlin and Stuttgart: Verlag von W. Spemann.

1937 [1929, 1860]   *The Civilization of the Renaissance in Italy.* New York: Oxford University Press.
1963 [1898]   *History of Greek Culture.* Translated by Palmer Hilty. New York: Ungar.

Burford(-Cooper), Alison
1978   The Family Farm in Greece. *Classical Journal* 73:162–175.
1993   *Land and Labor in Ancient Greece.* Baltimore: Johns Hopkins University Press.

Burke, Peter
1986   City-States. In *States in History,* edited by John A. Hall, pp. 137–153. New York: Basil Blackwell.
1992   The Renaissance. In *Perceptions of the Ancient Greeks,* edited by K. J. Dover, pp. 128–146. Oxford: Basil Blackwell.

Burkert, Walter
1985   *Greek Religion.* Translated by John Raffan. Cambridge: Harvard University Press.

Butzer, Karl W.
1976   *Early Hydraulic Civilization in Egypt.* Chicago: University of Chicago Press.
1984   Long-Term Nile Flood Variation and Political Discontinuities in Pharaonic Egypt. In *From Hunters to Farmers,* edited by J. Desmond Clark and Steven A. Brandt, pp. 102–112. Berkeley: University of California Press.

Cabrera Castro, Rubén, and Oralia Cabrera
1991   El Proyecto Templo de Quetzalcoatl. *Arqueología, Segunda época* 6:19–31.

Cabrera Castro, Rubén, George Cowgill, Saburo Sugiyama, and Carlos Serrano
1989   El Proyecto Templo de Quetzalcoatl. *Arqueología* 5:51–79.

Cabrera Castro, Rubén, Saburo Sugiyama, and George L. Cowgill
1991   The Templo de Quetzalcoatl Project at Teotihuacan: A Preliminary Report. *Ancient Mesoamerica* 2:77–92.

Callaghan, Peter
1992   Archaic to Hellenistic Pottery. In *Knossos: From Greek City to Roman Colony: Excavations at the Unexplored Mansion,* II, edited by L. H. Sackett, pp. 89–136. British School at Athens Supp., Vol. 21. London: Thames and Hudson.

Calnek, Edward E.
1976   The Internal Structure of Tenochtitlan. In *The Valley of Mexico, Studies in Prehis-*

panic Ecology and Society, edited by Eric R. Wolf, pp. 287–302. Albuquerque: University of New Mexico Press.

1978   The City-State in the Basin of Mexico: Late Prehispanic Period. In *Urbanization in the Americas from Its Beginnings to the Present,* edited by Richard P. Schaedel, Jorge E. Hardoy, and Nora Scott Kinzer, pp. 463–470. The Hague: Mouton.

1982   Patterns of Empire Formation in the Valley of Mexico, Late Postclassic Period. In *The Inca and Aztec States, 1400–1800: Anthropology and History,* edited by George C. Collier, Renato I. Rosaldo, and John D. Wirth, pp. 43–62. New York: Academic Press.

Canciani, Fulvio
1970   *Bronzi orientali e orientalizzanti a Creta nell' VIII e VII secolo a.C.* Studia archeologia 12, Rome.

Caneva, Isabella, Marcella Frangipane, and Alba Palmieri
1987   Predynastic Egypt: New Data from Maadi. *The African Archaeological Review* 5:105–114.

1989   Recent Excavations at Maadi (Egypt). In *Late Prehistory of the Nile Basin,* edited by Lech Krzyzaniak and Michal Kobusiewicz, pp. 287–294. Poznan: Polish Academy of Sciences.

Carneiro, Robert L.
1970   A Theory of the Origin of the State. *Science* 169:733–738.

1990   Chiefdom-Level Warfare as Exemplified in Fiji and the Cauca Valley. In *The Anthropology of War,* edited by Jonathan Haas, pp. 190–211. Cambridge: Cambridge University Press.

1992   Point Counterpoint: Ecology and Ideology in the Development of New World Civilizations. In *Ideology and Pre-Columbian Civilizations,* edited by Arthur A. Demarest and Geoffrey W. Conrad, pp. 175–203. Santa Fe: School of American Research Press.

Carr, R. F., and J. E. Hazard
1961   *Map of the Ruins of Tikal, El Peten, Guatemala.* Tikal Reports No. 11, Museum Monograph No. 21, University Museum, University of Pennsylvania, Philadelphia.

Carrasco, Pedro
1971a   The Peoples of Central Mexico and Their Historical Tradition. In *Handbook of Middle American Indians,* Vol. 11, edited by Gordon F. Ekholm and Ignacio Bernal, pp. 459–473. Austin: University of Texas Press.

1971b   Social Organization of Ancient Mexico. In *Handbook of Middle American Indians,* Vol. 10, edited by Gordon F. Ekholm and Ignacio Bernal, pp. 349–375. Austin: University of Texas Press.

1977   Los Señores de Xochimilco en 1548. *Tlalocan* 7:229–65.

1984   The Extent of the Tepanec Empire. In *The Native Sources and the History of the Valley of Mexico,* edited by J. de Durand-Forest, pp. 73–93. 44th International Congress of Americanists, 1982. Oxford: B.A.R International Series 204.

Carrasco, Pedro, and Jesús Monjarás-Ruiz, eds.
1976   *Colección de documentos sobre Coyoacan,* Vol. 1: *Visita del Oider Gómez de Santillán al pueblo de Coyoacan y su sujeto Tacubaya en el año de 1553.* Colección Científica No. 39. México, D.F.: Instituto Nacional de Antropología e Historia.

1978   *Colección de documentos sobre Coyoacan,* Vol. 2: *Autos referentes al cacicazgo de Coyoacan que proceden del AGN.* Colección Científica No. 65. México, D.F.: Instituto Nacional de Antropología e Historia.

Carter, Elizabeth
1993   A Surface Survey of Lagash, al-Hiba, 1984. *Sumer* 46:60–63.

Cartledge, Paul
1978   Literacy in the Spartan Oligarchy. *Journal of Hellenic Studies* 98:25–37.

1983   Trade and Politics Revisited: Archaic Greece. In *Trade in the Ancient Economy,* edited by Peter Garnsey, Keith Hopkins, and C. R. Whittaker, pp. 33–49. London: Chatto and Windus.

1985   Rebels and Sambos in Classical Greece: A Comparative View. In *Crux: Essays Presented to G. E. M. de Ste. Croix on his 75th Birthday,* edited by Paul Cartledge and David Harvey, pp. 16–46. Exeter: History of Political Thought 6.

1988   Serfdom in Classical Greece. In *Slavery— And Other Forms of Unfree Labour,* edited by Léonie Archer, pp. 33–41. London: Routledge.

1990   *Aristophanes and His Theatre of the Absurd.* Bristol: Bristol Classical Press.

Caso, Alfonso
1966   La Epoca de los Señorios Independientes
        1232–1427. *Revista Mexicana de Estudios
        Antropológicos* 20:147–152.

Cavalli-Sforza, Luigi, and M. Feldman
1981   *Cultural Transmission and Evolution.*
        Princeton: Princeton University Press.

Chagnon, Napoleon A.
1992 [1968,   *Yanomamo: The Fierce People.* 4th ed.
1977, 1983]   New York: Holt, Rinehart, Winston.

Chang, Kwang-chih
1976   *Early Chinese Civilization: Anthropological
        Perspectives.* Cambridge: Harvard Univer-
        sity Press.
1980   *Shang Civilization.* New Haven: Yale Uni-
        versity Press.
1986   *The Archaeology of Ancient China.* 4th edi-
        tion. New Haven: Yale University Press.
1989   Ancient China and Its Anthropological
        Significance. In *Archaeological Thought
        in America,* edited by C. C. Lamberg-
        Karlovsky, pp. 155–166. Cambridge: Cam-
        bridge University Press.
1994a   Shang Shamans. In *The Power of Culture:
        Studies in Chinese Cultural History,* edited
        by Willard J. Peterson, Andrew H. Plaks,
        and Ying-shih Yü, pp. 10–36. Hong Kong:
        The Chinese University Press.
1994b   Ritual and Power. In *China: Ancient Cul-
        ture, Modern Land,* edited by Robert E.
        Murowchick, pp. 61–69. Cradles of Civili-
        zation, Vol. 2. Norman: University of Okla-
        homa Press.

Chang, Pin-tsun
1983   Chinese Maritime Trade: The Case of Six-
        teenth Century Fu-chien (Fukien). Ph.D. dis-
        sertation, Princeton University. Ann Arbor:
        University Microfilms.
1991   The First Chinese Diaspora in Southeast
        Asia in the Fifteenth Century. In *Emporia,
        Commodities, and Entrepreneurs in Asian
        Maritime Trade, c. 1400–1750,* edited by
        Roderich Ptak and Dietmar Rothermund,
        pp. 13–28. Beitrage zur Sudasienforschung
        Sudasien Institut, Universität Heidelberg,
        Band 141. Stuttgart: Franz Steiner Verlag.

Chang, S. T. H.
1992   Commodities Imported to the Chang-chou
        Region of Fukien during the Late Ming Pe-
        riod: A Preliminary Analysis of the Tax
        Lists Found in Tung-ha-yang-k'ao. In *Em-
        poria, Commodities, and Entrepreneurs in
        Asian Maritime Trade, c. 1400–1750,* ed-

ited by Roderich Ptak and Dietmar Rother-
mund, pp. 159–194. Beitrage zur Sudasien-
forschung Sudasien Institut, Universität Heidelberg, Band 141. Stuttgart: Franz Steiner
Verlag.

Charlton, Thomas H.
1972   Population Trends in the Teotihuacan Val-
        ley, A.D. 1400–1969. *World Archaeology*
        4:412–423.
1973   Texcoco Region Archaeology and the Co-
        dex Xolotl. *American Antiquity*
        38:412–423.
1975   From Teotihuacan to Tenochtitlan: The
        Early Period Revisited. *American Antiquity*
        30:231–235.
1978   Teotihuacan, Tepeapulco, and Obsidian Ex-
        ploitation. *Science* 200:1227–1236.
1984a   Urban Growth and Cultural Evolution
        from a Oaxacan Perspective. *Reviews in
        Anthropology* 11:197–207.
1984b   Production and Exchange: Variables in the
        Evolution of a Civilization. In *Trade and
        Exchange in Early Mesoamerica,* edited by
        Kenneth G. Hirth, pp. 17–42. Albuquer-
        que: University of New Mexico Press.
1986   Socioeconomic Dimensions of Urban-Rural
        Relations in the Colonial Period Basin of
        Mexico. In *Handbook of Middle American
        Indians, Supplement 4, Ethnohistory,* ed-
        ited by Ronald Spores, pp. 122–133. Aus-
        tin: University of Texas Press.
1991   The Influence and Legacy of Teotihuacan
        on Regional Routes and Urban Planning.
        In *Ancient Road Networks and Settlement
        Hierarchies in the New World,* edited by
        Charles D. Trombold, pp. 186–197. Cam-
        bridge: Cambridge University Press.
1994   Economic Heterogeneity and State Expan-
        sion: The Northeastern Basin of Mexico
        during the Late Postclassic Period. In *Econ-
        omies and Polities in the Aztec Realm,* ed-
        ited by Mary G. Hodge and Michael E.
        Smith, pp. 221–256. Albany: Institute for
        Mesoamerican Studies, State University of
        New York at Albany.
in press   The Aztecs and Their Contemporaries: The
        Central and Eastern Mexican Highlands. In
        *Cambridge History of the Native Peoples
        of the Americas,* edited by Murdo Mac-
        Leod and Richard E. W. Adams. Cam-
        bridge: Cambridge University Press.

Charlton, Thomas H., and Deborah L. Nichols, eds.
1990   *Los procesos del desarrollo de los estados
        tempranos: El caso del estado Azteca de*

Otumba, 4 vols. Report submitted to the Instituto Nacional de Antropología e Historia, México, D.F.

Charlton, Thomas H., Deborah L. Nichols, and Cynthia Otis Charlton
1991 Aztec Craft Production and Specialization: Archaeological Evidence from the City-State of Otumba, Mexico. *World Archaeology* 23:98–114.

Charlton, Thomas H., and Michael W. Spence
1983 Obsidian Exploitation and Civilization in the Basin of Mexico. In *Mining and Mining Techniques in Ancient Mesoamerica,* edited by Phil G. Weigand and Gretchen Gwynne, pp. 7–86. Anthropology 6, State University of New York-Stony Brook.

Charpin, Dominique
1986 *Le clergé d'Ur au siècle d'Hammurabi (XIXe–XVIIIe siècles av. J.-C.).* Paris: Librarie Droz.

Chase, Diane Z.
1985 Social and Political Organization in the Land of Cacao and Honey: Correlating the Archaeology and Ethnohistory of the Postclassic Lowland Maya. In *Late Lowland Maya Civilization: Classic to Postclassic,* edited by Jeremy A. Sabloff and E. Wyllys Andrews V, pp. 347–378. Albuquerque: University of New Mexico Press.
1988 The Cultural Dynamics of Prehistoric Maya Warfare. Paper presented at the 87th Annual Meeting of the American Anthropological Association, Phoenix.
1990 The Invisible Maya: Population History and Archaeology at Santa Rita, Corozal, Belize. In *Pre-Columbian Population History in the Maya Lowlands,* edited by T. Patrick Culbert and Don S. Rice, pp. 199–213. Cambridge: Cambridge University Press.

Chase, Diane Z., and Arlen F. Chase
1989 Caracol Update: Recent Work at Caracol, Belize. Paper presented at the Seventh Round Table of Palenque. Palenque, Chiapas, México.
1992 An Archaeological Assessment of Mesoamerican Elites. In *Mesoamerican Elites: An Archaeological Assessment,* edited by Diane Z. Chase and Arlen F. Chase, pp. 303–317. Norman: University of Oklahoma Press.

Ch'en, Ta-tuan
1968 Investiture of Liu-ch'iu Kings in the Ch'ing Period. In *The Chinese World Order: Traditional China's Foreign Relations,* edited by John K. Fairbank, pp. 135–164. Cambridge: Harvard University Press.

Cherry, John H., and Colin Renfrew
1986 Epilogue and Prospect. In *Peer Polity Interaction and Socio-Political Change,* edited by Colin Renfrew and John F. Cherry, pp. 149–158. Cambridge: Cambridge University Press.

Childe, V. Gordon
1934 *New Light on the Most Ancient East.* London: Kegan Paul.
1936 *Man Makes Himself.* London: Kegan Paul.

Chimalpahin Quauhtlehuanitzin, Diego Francisco de San Antón Muñón
1960 *Das Geschichtswerke des Domingo de Muñon Chimalpahin Quauhtlehuanitzin.* Quellenkritische Studien zur frühhindianisches Geschichte Mexikos, Beiträge zur mittelamerikanischen Völkerkunde 5. Hamburg: Hamburgishen Museums für Völkerkunde und Vorgeschichte.
1965 *Relaciones originales de Chalco Amequemecan escritas por Don Francisco de San Antón Muñón Chimalpahin Quauhtlehuaniztin.* Translated by Sylvia Rendón. México, D.F.: Fondo de Cultura Económica.

China Pictorial Publications
1989 *The Silk Road on Land and Sea.* Beijing: China Pictorial Publishing Company.

Chittolini, Giorgio
1991 The Italian City-State and Its Territory. In *City-States in Classical Antiquity and Medieval Italy,* edited by Anthony Molho, Kurt Raaflaub, and Julia Emlen, pp. 589–602. Ann Arbor: University of Michigan Press.
1994 Cities, "City-States," and Regional States in North-Central Italy. In *Cities and the Rise of States in Europe, A.D. 1000 to 1800,* edited by Charles Tilly and Wim P. Blockmans, pp. 28–43. Boulder: Westview Press.

Chun, Allen J.
1990 Conceptions of Kinship and Kingship in Classical Chou China. *T'oung Pao* 76:16–48.

Ciappelli, Giovanni
1991 Commentary. In *City-States in Classical Antiquity and Medieval Italy,* edited by Anthony Molho, Kurt Raaflaub, and Julia

Emlen, pp. 121–131. Ann Arbor: University of Michigan Press.

Claessen, Henri J. M., and Peter Skalník, eds.
1978   *The Early State*. The Hague: Mouton.
1981   *The Study of the State*. The Hague: Mouton.

Claessen, Henri J. M., and Pieter van de Velde
1987a   Introduction. In *Early State Dynamics*, edited by Henri Claessen and Pieter van de Velde, pp. 1–23. Leiden: E. J. Brill.

Claessen, Henri J. M., and Pieter van de Velde, eds.
1987b   *Early State Dynamics*. Leiden: E. J. Brill.
1991   *Early State Economics*. New Brunswick and London: Transaction Publishers.

Claessen, Henri J. M., Pieter van de Velde, and Michael Smith, eds.
1985   *Development and Decline: The Evolution of Sociopolitical Organization*. South Hadley, MA: Bergin and Garvey Publishers.

Clark, David
1982   *Urban Geography*. London: Croom Helm.

Clark, Hugh R.
1991   *Community, Trade, and Networks: Fujian Province from the Third to the Thirteenth Century*. Cambridge: Cambridge University Press.

Cliff, Maynard B.
1982   Lowland Maya Nucleation: A Case Study from Northern Belize. Unpublished Ph.D. dissertation, Department of Anthropology, Southern Methodist University, Dallas.

Cline, Howard F., ed.
1973–1975   Guide to Ethnohistorical Sources. *Handbook of Middle American Indians*, Vols. 12–15. Austin: University of Texas Press.

Cline, S. L.
1990   *Colonial Culhuacan, 1580–1600: A Social History of an Aztec Town*. Albuquerque: University of New Mexico Press.

Cobean, Robert H.
1978   The Ceramics of Tula, Hidalgo. Ph.D. dissertation, Department of Anthropology, Harvard University, Cambridge. (Published in translation in 1990 by Instituto Nacional de Antropología e Historia, México, D.F., Colección Científica, Serie Arqueología, No. 215.)

Códices de México
1979   *Los Códices de México*. Presentacion por Yolanda Mercades Martinez, prologo por Alberto Ruz Lhuiller. México, D.F.: Instituto Nacional de Antropología e Historia.

Coe, Michael
1961   Social Typologies and Tropical Forest Civilizations. *Comparative Studies in Society and History* 4:65–86.
1965   A Model of Ancient Community Structure in the Maya Lowlands. *Southwestern Journal of Anthropology* 21:97–114.

Cohen, Ronald
1978a   State Origins: A Reappraisal. In *The Early State*, edited by Henri Claessen and Pieter Skalník, pp. 31–75. The Hague: Mouton.
1978b   Introduction. In *Origins of the State: The Anthropology of Political Evolution*, edited by Ronald Cohen and Elman Service, pp. 1–20. Philadelphia: Institute for the Study of Human Issues.
1988   Introduction. In *State Formation and Political Legitimacy*, edited by Ronald Cohen and John Toland, pp. 1–21. Political Anthropology, Vol. 6. New Brunswick: Transaction Publishers.

Coldstream, John N.
1973   Knossos 1951–61: Orientalising and Archaic Pottery from the Town. *Annual of the British School at Athens* 68:33–63.
1977   *Geometric Greece*. London: Methuen.
1982   Greeks and Phoenicians in the Aegean. In *Phönizier im Westen*, edited by Hans Georg Niemeyer, pp. 261–275. Mainz: Von Zabern (Madrider Beiträge, Band 8).
1984   A Protogeometric Nature Goddess from Knossos. *Bulletin of the Institute of Classical Studies* 31:93–104.
1992   Early Hellenic pottery. In *Knossos: From Greek City to Roman Colony. Excavations at the Unexplored Mansion* II, edited by L. H. Sackett, pp. 67–87. British School at Athens Supp., Vol. 21. London: Thames and Hudson.

Collier, George A., Renato I. Rosaldo, and John D. Wirth, eds.
1982   *The Inca and Aztec States, 1400–1800: Anthropology and History*. New York: Academic Press.

Connor, W. Robert
1971   *The New Politicians of Fifth-Century Ath-*

ens. Princeton: Princeton University Press.

1984   *Thucydides.* Princeton: Princeton University Press.

Conrad, Geoffrey W., and Arthur A. Demarest
1984   *Religion and Empire: The Dynamics of Aztec and Inca Expansionism.* Cambridge: Cambridge University Press.

Cook de Leonard, Carmen, and Ernesto Lemoine Villicaña
1954–1955   Materiales para la geografía histórica de la región Chalco-Amecameca. *Revista Mexicana de Estudios Antropológicos* 14 (Part 1):289–295.

Cornell, Timothy J.
1991   Rome: The History of an Anachronism. In *City-States in Classical Antiquity,* edited by Anthony Molho, Kurt Raaflaub, and Julia Emlen, pp. 53–69. Ann Arbor: University of Michigan Press.

Cortés, Hernán
1971   *Letters from Mexico.* New York: Grossman Publishers.

Costantini, Lorenzo
1990   Harappan Agriculture in Pakistan: The Evidence of Nausharo. In *South Asian Archaeology, 1987,* edited by Maurizio Taddei and Pierfrancesco Callieri, pp. 321–332. Rome: IsMEO.

Coutellier, V., and Daniel J. Stanley
1987   Late Quaternary Stratigraphy and Paleogeography of the Eastern Nile Delta, Egypt. *Marine Geology* 77:257–275.

Cowgill, George L.
1974   Quantitative Studies of Urbanism at Teotihuacan. In *Meosamerican Archaeology: New Approaches,* edited by Norman Hammond, pp. 363–396. Austin: University of Texas Press.

1988   Onward and Upward with the Collapse. In *The Collapse of Ancient States and Empires,* edited by Norman Yoffee and George L. Cowgill, pp. 244–276. Tucson: University of Arizona Press.

1992   Teotihuacan Glyphs and Imagery in the Light of Some Early Colonial Texts. In *Art, Ideology, and the City of Teotihuacan,* edited by Janet Catherine Berlo, pp. 231–246. Washington, D.C.: Dumbarton Oaks Research Library and Collection.

1993   What We Still Don't Know about Teotihua-

can. In *Teotihuacan: Art from the City of the Gods,* edited by Kathleen Berrin and Esther Pasztory, pp. 116–125. New York: Thames and Hudson.

1996   Discussion. *Ancient Mesoamerica* 7:325–331.

Cowgill, George L., and Oralia Cabrera
1991   Excavaciones en el Frente B y Otros Materiales del Análisis de la Cerámica. *Arqueología, Segunda época* 6:41–52.

Creamer, Winifred, and Jonathan Haas
1985   Tribe versus Chiefdom in Lower Central America. *American Antiquity* 50:738–754.

Creel, Herrlee G.
1970   *The Origins of Statecraft in China. Vol. 1: The Western Chou Empire.* Chicago: University of Chicago Press.

Crone, Patricia
1989   *Pre-Industrial Societies.* Oxford: Basil Blackwell.

Crumley, Carole L.
1987a   A Dialectical Critique of Hierarchy. In *Power Relations and State Formation,* edited by Thomas C. Patterson and Christine W. Gailey, pp. 155–169. Archaeological Papers of the American Anthropological Association No. 6. Washington, D.C.

1987b   Celtic Settlement before the Conquest: The Dialectics of Landscape and Power. In *Regional Dynamics: Burgundian Landscapes in Historical Perspective,* edited by Carole E. Crumley and William T. Marquadt, pp. 283–311. San Diego: Academic Press.

1990   A Critique of Cultural Evolutionist Approaches to Ranked Society with Particular Reference to Celtic Polities. Paper presented at 55th annual meeting of the Society for American Archaeology, Las Vegas.

Crumley, Carole, and William T. Marquadt, eds.
1987   *Regional Dynamics: Burgundian Landscapes in Historical Perspective.* San Diego: Academic Press.

Culbert, T. Patrick
1988   Political History and the Decipherment of Maya Glyphs. *Antiquity* 62:135–152.

1991a   Polities in the Northeast Peten, Guatemala. In *Classic Maya Political History,* edited by T. Patrick Culbert, pp. 128–146. Cambridge: Cambridge University Press.

Culbert, T. Patrick, ed.
1991b   *Classic Maya Political History.* Cambridge: Cambridge University Press.

Culbert, T. Patrick, Laura J. Kosakowsky, Robert E. Fry, and William Haviland
1990   The Population of Tikal, Guatemala. In *Pre-Columbian Population History in the Maya Lowlands,* edited by T. Patrick Culbert and Don S. Rice, pp. 103–122. Albuquerque: University of New Mexico Press.

Culbert, T. Patrick, and Don S. Rice, eds.
1990   *Pre-Columbian Population History in the Maya Lowlands.* Albuquerque: University of New Mexico Press.

Curtin, Philip D.
1984   *Cross Cultural Trade in World History.* Cambridge: Cambridge University Press.

Dahrendorf, Ralf
1988   *The Modern Social Conflict.* Berkeley: University of California Press.

Dales, George F.
1991   Some Specialized Ceramic Studies at Harappa. In *Harappa Excavations 1986–1990: A Multidisciplinary Approach to Third Millenium Urbanism,* edited by Richard H. Meadow, pp. 61–70. Monographs in World Archaeology No. 3. Madison: Prehistory Press.

Dales, George F., and J. Mark Kenoyer
1993   The Harappa Project, 1986–1989: New Investigation at an Ancient Indus City. In *Harappan Civilization: A Recent Perspective,* edited by Gregory. L. Possehl, pp. 469–520. New Delhi: Oxford and IBH.

D'Altroy, Terrence
1994   Public and Private Economy in the Inka Empire. In *The Economic Anthropology of the State,* edited by Elizabeth M. Brumfiel, pp. 169–222. Monographs in Economic Anthropology No. 11. Lanham, MD: University Press of America.

D'Altroy, Terrence N., and Timothy Earle
1985   Staple Finance, Wealth Finance, and Storage in the Inca Political Economy. *Current Anthropology* 26:187–206.

David, Jean-Claude
1975   Alep, Dégradation et tentatives actuelles de réadaptation des structures urbaines traditionelle. *Bulletin d'Études Orientales* 28: 19–50.

Davies, John K.
1978a   Athenian Citizenship: The Descent Group and the Alternatives. *Classical Journal* 73:105–21.
1978b   *Democracy and Classical Greece.* Glasgow: Fontana.

Davies, Nigel
1980 [1973]   *The Aztecs.* Norman: University of Oklahoma Press.
1977   *The Toltecs until the Fall of Tula.* Norman: University of Oklahoma Press.
1980   *The Toltec Heritage.* Norman: University of Oklahoma Press.
1987   *The Aztec Empire: The Toltec Resurgence.* Norman: University of Oklahoma Press.

Deger-Jalkotzy, Sigrid, ed.
1983   *Griechenland, die Ägäis und die Levante während der 'Dark Ages' vom 12. bis zum 9. Jh. v. Chr.* Vienna: Osterreichische Akademic der Wissenschafer.

Delougaz, Pinhas, Harold D. Hill, and Seton Lloyd
1967   *Private Houses and Graves in the Diyala Region.* Oriental Institute Publications No. 88. Chicago: University of Chicago Press.

Demarest, Arthur A.
1978   Inter-Regional Conflict and 'Situational Ethics' in Classic Maya Warfare. In *Codex Wauchope: A Tribute Roll,* edited by Marco Giardino, Barbara Edmonson, and Winifred Creamer, pp. 101–111. Human Mosaic. New Orleans: Tulane University.
1989   Ideology and Evolutionism in American Archaeology: Looking beyond the Material Base. In *Archaeological Thought in America,* edited by Clifford C. Lamberg-Karlovsky, pp. 89–102. Cambridge: Cambridge University Press.
1991   Report on Recent Excavations at Piedras Negras. Paper presented at the 56th Annual Meeting of the Society for American Archaeology, New Orleans.
1992   Ideology in Ancient Maya Cultural Evolution. In *Ideology in Precolumbian Civilizations,* edited by Arthur Demarest and Geoffrey Conrad, pp. 135–157, Santa Fe: School of American Research Press.

Demarest, Arthur, and Geoffery Conrad, eds.
1992   *Ideology.* Cambridge: Cambridge University Press.

Derrida, Jacques
1976   *Of Grammatology.* Baltimore: Johns Hopkins University Press.

Diakanoff, Igor M.

1971   On the Structure of Old Babylonian Society. In *Beitrage zur Sozialen Struktur des alten Vorderasien,* edited by Horst Klengel, pp. 15–31. Schriften zur Geschichte und Kultur des alten Orients I. Berlin: Akademie Verlag.

1972   Socio-Economic Classes in Babylon and the Babylonian Concept of Social Stratification. In *Gesellschaftklassen im alten Zweitstromland und in den angrenzended Gebeiten—XVIII Rencontre assyriologique internationale, Munchen, 29. Juni bis 3, Juli 1970,* edited by Dietz Otto Edzard, pp. 41–52. Munich: Verlag de Bayerischen Akademie der Wissenschaften.

1974a   Slaves, Helots, and Serfs in Early Antiquity. *Acta Antiqua* 22:45–78.

1974b   *Structure of Society and the State in Early Dynastic Sumer.* Malibu: Undena Press.

1982   The Structure of Near Eastern Society before the Middle of the Second Millennium B.C. *Oikumene* 3:7–100.

Díaz del Castillo, Bernal

1956   *The Discovery and Conquest of New Spain, 1517–1521,* edited by Genaro García. Translated by A. P. Maudslay. New York: Farrar, Strauss, and Giroux.

Dibble, Charles E.

1971   Writing in Central Mexico. In *Handbook of Middle American Indians,* Vol. 10, edited by Gordon F. Ekholm and Ignacio Bernal, pp. 322–332. Austin: University of Texas Press.

Diehl, Richard A.

1981   Tula. In *Handbook of Middle American Indians, Supplement 1, Archaeology,* edited by Jeremy A. Sabloff, pp. 277–295. Austin: University of Texas Press.

1983   *Tula: The Toltec Capital of Ancient Mexico.* New York: Thames and Hudson.

1989   A Shadow of Its Former Self: Teotihuacan during the Coyotlatelco Period. In *Mesoamerica after the Decline of Teotihuacan, A.D. 700–900,* edited by Richard A. Diehl and Janet Catherine Berlo, pp. 9–18. Washington, D.C.: Dumbarton Oaks Research Library and Collection.

1993   The Toltec Horizon in Mesoamerica: New Perspectives on an Old Issue. In *Latin American Horizons,* edited by Don Stephen Rice, pp. 263–294. Washington, D.C.: Dumbarton Oaks Research Library and Collection.

Diehl, Richard A., and Janet Catherine Berlo

1989   Introduction. In *Mesoamerica after the Decline of Teotihuacan, A.D. 700–900,* edited by Richard A. Diehl and Catherine Janet Berlo, pp. 1–8. Washington, D.C.: Dumbarton Oaks Research Library and Collection.

Dikshit, K. N.

1984   The Harappan Levels at Hulas. *Man and Environment* 7:99–102.

Dionisotti, A. C.

1992   The Medieval West. In *Perceptions of the Ancient Greeks,* edited by A. J. Dover, pp. 100–127. Oxford: Basil Blackwell.

Domínguez Chávez, Humberto

1979   *Arqueología de Superficie en San Cristobal Ecatepec, Estado de México: Un Estudio del Desarrollo de las Fuerzas Productivas en el México Prehispánico.* México, D.F.: Biblioteca Enciclopédica del Estado de México.

Dong Qi

1995   Zhongguo XianQin chengshi fazhan shi gaishu [Survey of the History of the Development of Cities in Pre-Qin China]. *Zhongyuan wenwu* 1:73–78.

Donlan, Walter

1994   Chief and Followers in Pre-State Greece. In *From Political Economy to Anthropology: Situating Economic Life in Past Societies,* edited by Colin M. Duncan and David W. Tandy, pp. 34–51. Critical Perspectives on Historic Issues, Vol. 3. Montréal and New York: Black Rose Books.

Donnan, Christopher B.

1973   *Moche Occupation of the Santa Valley, Peru.* University of California Publications in Anthropology, Vol. 8. Berkeley: University of California Press.

Dover, K. J., ed.

1992   *Perceptions of the Ancient Greeks.* Oxford: Basil Blackwell.

Drennan, Robert D.

1987   Regional Demography in Chiefdoms. In *Chiefdoms in the Americas,* edited by Robert D. Drennan and Carlos A. Uribe, pp. 307–324. Lanham, MD: University Press of America.

1988   Household Location and Compact versus Dispersed Settlement in Prehispanic Mesoamerica. In *Household and Community in the Mesoamerican Past,* edited by Richard R. Wilk and Wendy Ashmore, pp. 273–294. Albuquerque: University of New Mexico Press.

1991   Pre-Hispanic Chiefdom Trajectories in Mesoamerica, Central America, and Northern South America. In *Chiefdoms: Power, Economy, and Ideology,* edited by Timothy Earle, pp. 263–287. Cambridge: Cambridge University Press.

1996   One for All and All for One: Accounting for Variability without Losing Sight of Regularities in the Development of Complex Societies. In *Emergent Complexity: The Evolution of Intermediate Societies,* edited by Jeanne E. Arnold, pp. 25–34. Archaeological Series 9. Ann Arbor: International Monographs in Prehistory.

Dumond, Don E., and Florencia Müller
1972   Classic to Postclassic in Highland Central Mexico. *Science* 175:1208–1215.

Dunnell, Robert
1980   Evolutionary Theory and Archaeology. In *Advances in Archaeological Method and Theory,* Vol. 3, edited by Michael B. Schiffer, pp. 35–99. New York: Academic Press.

1989   Aspects of the Application of Evolutionary Theory in Archaeology. In *Archaeological Thought in America,* edited by Clifford C. Lamberg-Karlovsky, pp. 35–49. Cambridge: Cambridge University Press.

1992   Is a Scientific Archaeology Possible? In *Metaarchaeology,* edited by L. Embre, pp. 73–97. The Netherlands: Kluver.

Dunning, Nicholas
1991   Ancient Anthrosols of the Maya Lowlands. Paper presented at the Conference on Ancient Maya Agriculture and Biological Resource Management, University of California, Riverside.

Durán, Fray Diego
1964   *The Aztecs: The History of the Indies of New Spain.* Translated by Doris Heyden and Fernando Horcasitas. New York: Orion Press.

1967   *Historia de Las Indias de Nueva España,* 2 vols., edited by Angel M. Garibay. México, D.F.: Editorial K. Porrúa.

1971   *Book of the Gods and Rites and the Ancient Calendar.* Translated by Fernando Horcasitas and Doris Heyden. Norman: University of Oklahoma Press.

Durkheim, Émile
1964 [1893]   *The Division of Labor in Society.* Glencoe, IL: The Free Press.

Durrani, Farzand Ali
1988   Excavations in the Gomal Valley: Rehman Dheri Excavation Report 1. *Ancient Pakistan* 6:1–232.

Durrani, Farzand Ali, Ihsan Ali, and George Erdosy
1991   Rehmandheri Excavations, 1991. *Ancient Pakistan* 7:63–151.

Earle, Timothy
1976   A Nearest-Neighbor Analysis of Two Formative Settlement Systems. In *The Early Mesoamerican Village,* edited by Kent V. Flannery, pp. 195–223. New York: Academic Press.

1978   *Economic and Social Organization of a Complex Chiefdom.* Museum of Anthropology Anthropological Papers No 63. University of Michigan, Ann Arbor.

1987   Chiefdoms in Archaeological and Ethnohistorical Perspective. *Annual Review of Archaeology* 16:279–308.

1989   The Evolution of Chiefdoms. *Current Anthropology* 30:84–88.

1991   The Evolution of Chiefdoms. In *Chiefdoms, Power, Economy, and Ideology,* edited by Timothy Earle, pp. 1–15. Cambridge: Cambridge University Press.

Early China
1989   Forum. *Early China* 14:77–172.

Edens, Christopher
1992   Dynamics of Trade in the Ancient Mesopotamian 'World System.' *American Anthropologist* 94:118–139.

Eder, Walter
1991   Who Rules? Power and Participation in Athens and Rome. In *City States in Classical Antiquity and Medieval Italy,* edited by Anthony Molho, Kurt Raaflaub, and Julie Emlen, pp. 169–196. Ann Arbor: University of Michigan Press.

Ehlers, Eckart
1992   The City in the Islamic Middle East. In *Modelling the City: Cross-Cultural Perspectives,* edited by Eckart Ehlers, pp. 89–107. Ferd. Bonn: Dúmmlers Verlag.

Ehrenberg, Victor
1969   *The Greek State.* 2nd ed. London: Methuen.

Ehrenreich, Robert M.
1992   Metalworking in Iron Age Britain: Hierarchy or Heterarchy? In *Metals in Society: Theory beyond Analysis,* edited by Robert M. Ehrenreich, pp. 69–80. University Museum of Archaeology and Anthropology, University of Pennsylvania.

Eisenstadt, Shmuel N., ed.
1986   *The Origins and Diversity of Axial Age Civilizations.* Albany: State University of New York Press.

Eisenstadt, Shmuel N., Michel Abitbol, and Naomi Chazan
1988   *Early State in African Perspective.* Leiden: E. J. Brill.

Eiwanger, Josef
1987   Die Archäologie der späten Vorgeschichte: Bestand und Perspektiven. In *Problems and Priorities in Egyptian Archaeology,* edited by Jan Assmann, Gunter Burkard, and Vivian Davies, pp. 81–104. London: Routledge.

Ellis, John R.
1976   *Philip II and Macedonian Imperialism.* Princeton: Princeton University Press.

Emberling, Geoff, and Norman Yoffee
in press   Thinking about Ethnicity in Mesopotamian Archaeology and History. In *Standortsbestimmung der Vorderasiatischen Archäologie,* edited by Hartmut Kühne, Karin Bartl, and Reinhard Beinbeck.

Engels, Friedrich
1972 [1884]   *The Origin of the Family, Private Property, and the State.* Edited with an Introduction by Eleanor Burke Leacock. London: Lawrence and Wishart.

Erdosy, George
1988   *Urbanization in Early Historic India.* Oxford: B.A.R. International Series 430.

Evans, Geoffrey
1958   Ancient Mesopotamian Assemblies. *Journal of the American Oriental Society* 78: 1–11, 114–115.

Evans, Susan T.
1980   A Settlement System Analysis of the Teotihuacan Region, Mexico. Ph.D. dissertation, Department of Anthropology, Pennsylvania State University, University Park. Ann Arbor: University Microfilms.
1991   Architecture and Authority in an Aztec Village: Form and Function of the Tecpan. In *Land and Politics in the Valley of Mexico: A Two-Thousand Year Perspective,* edited by Herbert R. Harvey, pp. 63–92. Albuquerque: University of New Mexico Press.
1993   Aztec Household Organization and Village Administration. In *Prehispanic Domestic Units in Western Mesoamerica: Studies of the Household, Compound, and Residence,* edited by Robert S. Santley and Kenneth G. Hirth, pp. 173–189. Boca Raton: CRC Press.

Evans, Susan T., ed.
1988   *Excavations at Cihuatecpan: An Aztec Village in the Teotihuacan Valley.* Vanderbilt University Publications in Anthropology No. 36. Nashville: Department of Anthropology, Vanderbilt University.

Evans, Susan T., and Peter Gould
1982   Settlement Models in Archaeology. *Journal of Anthropological Archaeology* 1:275–304.

Fairservis, Walter A., Jr.
1975   *The Roots of Ancient India.* Chicago: University of Chicago Press.
1984   Harappan Civilization according to Its Writing. In *South Asian Archaeology, 1981,* edited by Bridget Allchin, pp. 154–161. Cambridge: Cambridge University Press.
1986   Excavation of the Archaic Remains East of the Niched Gate: Season of 1981. Hierakonpolis Project Occasional Papers in Anthropology III, Poughkeepsie.
1989   An Epigenetic View of the Harappan Culture. In *Archaeological Thought in America,* edited by C. C. Lamberg-Karlovsky, pp. 205–217. Cambridge: Cambridge University Press.
1991   A Revised View of the *Na'rmr* Palette. *Journal of the American Research Center in Egypt:* 28:1–20.

Fallers, Lloyd A.
1956   *Bantu Bureaucracy: A Study of Integrating Conflict in the Political Institutions of an East African People.* Cambridge: Heffer.

Falola, Toyin
1984   *The Political Economy of a Pre-Colonial African State: Ibadan 1830–1900.* Ibadan: African Press.

Fash, Barbara
1992   Late Classic Architectural Themes in Copan. *Ancient Mesoamerica* 3:89–104.

Fash, William L.
1982   Deducing Social Organization from Classic
        Maya Settlement Patterns: A Case Study
        from the Copan Valley. In *Civilization in
        the Ancient Americas,* edited by Richard
        M. Leventhal and Alan L. Kolata, pp. 261–
        288. Albuquerque and Cambridge: Univer-
        sity of New Mexico Press and Peabody Mu-
        seum of Archaeology and Ethnography,
        Harvard University.
1988   A New Look at Maya Statecraft from Co-
        pan, Honduras. *Antiquity* 62:157–169.
1989   The Sculptural Facade of Structure 9N-82:
        Content, Form, and Significance. In *The
        House of the Bacabs, Copan, Honduras,* ed-
        ited by David Webster, pp. 41–72. Washing-
        ton, D.C.: Dumbarton Oaks Studies in Pre-
        Columbian Art and Archaeology No. 29.
1991   *Scribes, Warriors and Kings.* Cambridge:
        Cambridge University Press.

Fash, William L., and David Stuart
1991   Dynastic History and Cultural Evolution at
        Copan, Honduras. In *Classic Maya Politi-
        cal History,* edited by T. Patrick Culbert,
        pp. 147–179. Cambridge: Cambridge Uni-
        versity Press.

Fattovich, Rodolfo
1979   Trends in the Study of Predynastic Social
        Structure. *First International Congress of
        Egyptology, Cairo, Actes* (Berlin): 17–39.

Fedak, Janos
1990   *Monumental Tombs of the Hellenistic Age.*
        Phoenix Supp., Vol. 28, Toronto.

Fedick, Scott L.
1989   The Economics of Agricultural Land Use
        and Settlement in the Upper Belize River
        Valley. In *Prehistoric Maya Economies of
        Belize,* edited by Patricia A. McAnany and
        Barry L. Isaac, pp. 215–253. Research in
        Economic Anthropology Supplement No.
        4. Greenwich, CT: JAI Press.
1994   Land Evaluation and Ancient Maya Land
        Use in the Upper Belize River Area, Belize,
        Central America. *Latin American Antiquity*
        6:16–34.

Feinman, Gary M.
1991   Demography, Surplus, and Inequality: Early
        Political Formations in Highland Meso-
        america. In *Chiefdoms: Power, Economy,
        and Ideology,* edited by Timothy Earle, pp.
        229–261. Cambridge: Cambridge Univer-
        sity Press.

1995   The Emergence of Inequality: A Focus on
        Strategies and Processes. In *Foundations of
        Social Inequality,* edited by T. Douglas
        Price and Gary M. Feinman, pp. 255–280.
        New York: Plenum Press.

Feinman, Gary, and Jill Neitzel
1984   Too Many Types: An Overview of Seden-
        tary Prestate Societies in the Americas. *Ad-
        vances in Archaeological Method and The-
        ory,* Vol. 7, edited by Michael B. Schiffer,
        pp. 39–102. New York: Academic Press.

Ferguson, Yale H.
1991   Chiefdoms to City States: The Greek Expe-
        rience. In *Chiefdoms: Power, Economy,
        and Ideology,* edited by Timothy Earle, pp.
        169–192. Cambridge: Cambridge Univer-
        sity Press.

Finkelstein, Jacob
1972   *Late Old Babylonian Documents and Let-
        ters.* Yale Oriental Series 13. New Haven:
        Yale University Press.

Finley, Moses I.
1977a   The Ancient City: From Fustel de Cou-
        langes to Max Weber and Beyond. *Compar-
        ative Studies in Society and History*
        19:305–327.
1977b   *The World of Odysseus.* New York:
        Viking.
1978   The Fifth-Century Athenian Empire: A Bal-
        ance Sheet. In *Imperialism in the Ancient
        World,* edited by Paul Garnsey and C. R.
        Whittaker, pp. 103–126. Cambridge: Cam-
        bridge University Press.
1981   *Economy and Society in Ancient Greece,* ed-
        ited by Brent Shaw and Richard Saller. Lon-
        don: Chatto and Windus.
1982   *Economy and Society in Ancient Greece,* ed-
        ited by Brent Shaw and Richard Saller. New
        York: The Viking Press.
1985a   *Democracy Ancient and Modern.* 2nd ed.
        London: Hogarth.
1985b   *Ancient History: Evidence and Models.*
        London: Chatto and Windus.

Fish, Suzanne K., and Stephen A. Kowalewski, eds.
1990   *The Archaeology of Regions: A Case for
        Full Coverage Survey.* Washington, D.C.:
        Smithsonian Institution Press.

Fisher, N. R. E.
1992   *Hybris.* Warminster: Aris and Philips.

Flam, Louis
1981   *The Paleography and Prehistoric Settle-
        ment Patterns in Sind, Pakistan (ca. 4000–*

2000 B.C.). Unpublished Ph.d. dissertation, University of Pennsylvania, Philadelphia.

1986   Recent Explorations in Sind: Paleography, Regional Ecology, and Prehistoric Settlement Patterns. In *Studies in the Archaeology of India and Pakistan,* edited by Jerome Jacobson, pp. 65–89. New Delhi: Oxford and IBH.

1991   Fluvial Geomorphology of the Lower Indus Basin (Sindh, Pakistan) and the Indus Civilization. In *Himalayas to the Sea: Geology, Geomorphology and the Quaternary,* edited by John F. J. Shroder. London: Routledge Press.

1993   Excavation at Ghazi Shah, Sindh, Pakistan. In *Harappan Civilization: A Recent Perspective,* edited by Gregory. L. Possehl, pp. 457–467. New Delhi: Oxford and IBH.

Flannery, Kent V.
1968   The Olmec and the Valley of Oaxaca: A Model for Inter-Regional Interaction in Formative times. In *Dumbarton Oaks Conference on the Olmec,* edited by Elizabeth Benson, pp. 79–110. Washington, D.C.: Dumbarton Oaks Research Library and Collection.

1972   The Cultural Evolution of Civilizations. *Annual Review of Ecology and Systematics* 3:399–426.

Flannery, Kent V., and Joyce Marcus
1994   *Early Formative Pottery of the Valley of Oaxaca, Mexico.* Museum of Anthropology Memoir No. 27. Ann Arbor: University of Michigan.

Flannery, Kent V., and Joyce Marcus, eds.
1983   *The Cloud People: Divergent Evolution of the Zapotec and Mixtec Civilizations.* New York: Academic Press.

Ford, Anabel
1986   *Population Growth and Social Complexity: An Examination of Settlement and Environment in the Central Maya Lowlands.* Anthropological Research Papers No. 35. Tempe: Arizona State University.

1990   Maya Settlement in the Belize River Area: Variations in Residence Patterns of the Central Maya Lowlands. In *Precolumbian Population History in the Maya Lowlands,* edited by T. Patrick Culbert and Don Rice, pp. 167–181. Albuquerque: University of New Mexico Press.

1991a   Critical Resource Control and the Rise of the Classical Period Maya: The Hydraulic

Hypothesis Revisited. Paper presented at the Conference on Ancient Maya Agriculture and Biological Resource Management, University of California, Riverside.

1991b   Economic Variation of Ancient Maya Residential Settlement. *Ancient Mesoamerica* 2:35–46.

Forge, Anthony
1972   Normative Factors in the Settlement Size of Neolithic Cultivators (New Guinea). In *Man, Settlement and Urbanism,* edited by Peter J. Ucko, Ruth Tringham, and G. W. Dimbleby, pp. 363–376. London: Unwin.

Fornara, Charles W.
1983   *Translated Documents of Greece and Rome: I. Archaic Times to the End of the Peloponnesian War.* 2nd ed. Cambridge: Cambridge University Press.

Fortes, Meyer
1953   The Structure of Unilineal Descent Groups. *American Anthropologist* 55:17–41.

Fortes, Meyer, and E. E. Evans-Pritchard
1940   *African Political Systems.* London: Oxford University Press.

Foucault, Michel
1986   *The Foucault Reader,* edited by P. Rabinow. Harmondsworth: Penguin.

Fowler, William Warde
1893   *The City-State of the Greeks and Romans.* London: Macmillan.

Fox, Richard G.
1977   *Urban Anthropology: Cities in Their Setting.* Englewood Cliffs, NJ: Prentice-Hall.

Foxhall, Lin
1992   The Control of the Attic Landscape. In *Agriculture in Ancient Greece,* edited by Berit Wells, pp. 155–159. Stockholm: Skrifter Utgivna i Svenska Institutet i Athen.

Foxhall, Lin, and Hamish Forbes
1982   *Sitometreia:* The Role of Grain as a Staple Food in Classical Antiquity. *Chiron* 12:41–89.

Frank, Andre Gunder
1993   Bronze Age World System Cycles. *Current Anthropology* 34:383–430.

Franke-Vogt, Ute
1992   Inscribed Objects from Moenjo-daro: Some Remarks on Stylistic Variability and Distribution Patterns. In *South Asian Archaeol-*

ogy, 1989, edited by Catherine Jarrige, pp. 103–112. Madison: Prehistory Press.

Frankfort, Henri
1956   *The Birth of Civilization in the Near East.* Bloomington: University of Indiana Press.

Freidel, David
1983   Political Systems in Lowland Yucatan: Dynamics and Structure in Maya Settlement. In *Prehistoric Settlement Patterns: Essays in Honor of Gordon R. Willey,* edited by Evon Z. Vogt and Richard M. Leventhal, pp. 375–386. Albuquerque and Cambridge: University of New Mexico Press and Peabody Museum of Archaeology and Ethnology, Harvard University.
1986   Maya Warfare: An Example of Peer-polity Interaction. In *Peer-Polity Interaction and Sociopolitical Change,* edited by Colin Renfrew and John Cherry, pp. 93–108. Cambridge University Press, London.

Freidel, David, and Linda Schele
1988   Kingship and Power in the Late Preclassic Maya Lowlands. *American Anthropologist* 90:547–567.

Freter, AnnCorinne
1988   The Classic Maya Collapse at Copan, Honduras: A Regional Settlement Perspective. Ph.D. dissertation, Department of Anthropology, Pennsylvania State University, University Park. Ann Arbor: University Microfilms.
1992   Chronological Research at Copán: Methods and Implications. *Ancient Mesoamerica* 3:117–134.

Frézouls, Edmond
1991   Commentary on Urban and Architectural Forms. In *City States in Classical Antiquity and Medieval Italy,* edited by Anthony Molho, Kurt Raaflaub, and Julia Emlen, pp. 447–452. Ann Arbor: University of Michigan Press.

Fried, Morton H.
1967   *The Evolution of Political Society: An Essay in Political Anthropology.* Random House, New York.
1978   The State, the Chicken, and the Egg: Or, What Came First? In *Origins of the State: The Anthropology of Political Evolution,* edited by Ronald Cohen and Elman Service, pp. 35–48. Philadelphia: Institute for the Study of Human Issues.

Friedman, Jonathan
1982   Catastrophe and Continuity in Social Evolution. In *Theory and Explanation in Archaeology,* edited by Colin Renfrew, Michael Rowlands, and Barbara Seagraves, pp. 175–196. New York: Academic Press.
1992   The Past in the Future: History and the Politics of Identity. *American Anthropologist* 94:837–859.

Friedman, Jonathan, and Michael Rowlands
1977   Notes towards an Epigenetic Model of the Evolution of 'Civilisation.' In *The Evolution of Social Systems,* edited by Michael Rowlands and Jonathan Friedman, pp. 201–276. London: Duckworth.

Friedman, Jonathan, and Michael Rowlands, eds.
1978   *The Evolution of Social Systems.* Pittsburgh: University of Pittsburgh Press.

Fujimoto, Hideo, and Shohachiro Naka, eds.
1980   *Nihon Jokaku Taikei* [Outline of Japanese Castles], Vol. 1: *Hokkaido and Okinawa,* pp. 235–345. Tokyo: Shin Jimbutsu Oraisha.

Fung, Christopher
1994   The Beginnings of Settled Life. In *China: Ancient Culture, Modern Land,* edited by Robert E. Murowchick, pp. 51–59. Cradles of Civilization, Vol. 2. Norman: University of Oklahoma Press.

Funke, Peter
1980   *Homonoia und Arche: Athen und die griechische Staatenwelt vom Ende des peloponnesischen Krieges bis zum Königsfrieden.* (Historia Einzelschrift 19.) Wiesbaden: Steiner.

Gagarin, Michael
1986   *Early Greek Law.* Berkeley: University of California Press.

Gailey, Christine
1985   The State of the State in Anthropology. *Dialectical Anthropology* 9:65–91.

Gailey, Christine, and Thomas Patterson
1987   Power Relations and State Formation. In *Power Relations and State Formation,* edited by Thomas Patterson and Christine Gailey, pp. 1–26. Washington, D.C.: Archaeology Section, American Anthropological Association.
1988   State Formation and Uneven Development. In *State and Society,* edited by John Gledhill, Barbara Bender, and Mogens

Trolle Larsen, pp. 77–90. London: Unwin Hyman.

Gallant, Thomas W.

1985   *A Fisherman's Tale: An Analysis of the Potential Productivity of Fishing in the Ancient World.* Ghent: Miscellanea Graeca 7.

1989   Crisis and Response: Risk-Buffering Behavior and Subsistence Crises in Hellenistic Greek Communities. *Journal of Interdisciplinary History* 19:393–413.

1991   *Risk and Survival in Ancient Greece: Reconstructing the Rural Domestic Economy.* Cambridge: Polity Press.

Gamito, Theresa J.

1988   *Social Complexity in Southwest Iberia, 800–500 B.C.* Oxford: B.A.R. International Series 359.

García Cook, Angel

1981   The Historical Importance of Tlaxcala in the Cultural Development of the Central Highlands. In *Handbook of Middle American Indians, Supplement, Vol. 1, Archaeology,* edited by Jeremy A. Sabloff, pp. 244–276. Austin: University of Texas Press.

García García, María Teresa

1987   *Huexotla: Un sitio del Acolhuacan.* Colección Científica No. 65. México, D.F.: Instituto Nacional de Antropología e Historia.

Garnsey, Peter

1988   *Famine and Food Supply in the Graeco-Roman World: Responses to Risk and Crisis.* Cambridge: Cambridge University Press.

1992   Yield of the Land. In *Agriculture in Ancient Greece,* edited by Berit Wells, pp. 147–153. Stockholm: Skrifter Utgivna i Svenska Institutet i Athen.

Garnsey, Peter, Thomas W. Gallant, and D. Rathbone

1984   Thessaly and the Grain Supply of Rome during the Second Century B.C. *Journal of Roman Studies* 74:30–44.

Garnsey, Peter, and Ian Morris

1989   Risk and the Polis: The Evolution of Institutionalized Responses to Food Supply Problems in the Ancient Greek State. In *Bad Year Economics: Cultural Responses to Risk and Uncertainty,* edited by Paul Halstead and John O'Shea, pp. 98–105. Cambridge: Cambridge University Press.

Gauthier, Philippe

1985   *Les cités grecques et leurs bienfaiteurs.* Bul-

letin de correspondance hellénique supp., vol. 15, Paris.

Gawantka, Wilfried

1985   *Die Sogenannte Polis: Entstehung, Geschichte, und Kritik der modernen althistorischen Grundbegriffe der griechische Staat, die griechische Staatsidee, die Polis.* Stuttgart: Franz Steiner.

Geertz, Clifford

1963   *Agricultural Involution: The Process of Ecological Change in Indonesia.* Berkeley: University of California Press.

1973   *The Interpretation of Culture.* New York: Basic Books.

1980   *Negara: The Theater State in Nineteenth-Century Bali.* Princeton: Princeton University Press.

Gehrig, Ulrich, and Hans Georg Niemeyer, eds.

1990   *Die Phönizier im Zeitalter Homers.* Mainz: Von Zabern.

Gehrke, Hans-Joachim

1985   *Stasis: Untersuchungen zu den inneren Kriegen in den griechischen Staaten des 5. und 4. Jhs. v. Chr.* Munich: Vestigia 35.

1986   *Jenseits von Athen und Sparta: das dritte Griechenland und seine Staatenwelt.* Munich: C. H. Beck.

Gelb, Ignace J.

1967   Approaches to the Study of Ancient Society. *Journal of the American Oriental Society* 87:1–8.

1972   The Arua Institution. *Revue d'Assyriologie* 66:1–32. Paris: CNRS, Éditions Recherche sur les Civilisations 83.

Gellner, Ernest

1983   *Nations and Nationalism.* Oxford: Blackwell.

1988   *Plough, Book, and Sword.* Chicago: University of Chicago Press.

Gerhard, Peter

1970   A Method for Reconstructing Precolumbian Political Boundaries in Central Mexico. *Journal de la Société de Américanistes* n. s. 59:27–41.

1972   *A Guide to the Historical Geography of New Spain.* Cambridge: Cambridge University Press.

Gibson, Charles

1952   *Tlaxcala in the Sixteenth Century.* Stanford: Stanford University Press.

1964   *The Aztecs under Spanish Rule.* Stanford: Stanford University Press.

1971   Structure of the Aztec Empire. In *Handbook of Middle American Indians,* Vol. 10, edited by Gordon F. Ekholm and Ignacio Bernal, pp. 376–394. Austin: University of Texas Press.

Gibson, D. Blair, and Michael Geselowitz
1988   The Evolution of Society in Late Prehistoric Europe: Toward a Paradigm. In *Tribe and Polity in Late Prehistoric Europe,* edited by D. Blair Gibson and Michael Geselowitz, pp. 3–37. New York: Plenum.

Gibson, McGuire
1972   *The City and Area of Kish.* Coconut Grove: Field Research Projects.
1973   Population Shift and the Rise of Mesopotamian Civilization. In *The Explanation of Culture Change: Models in Prehistory,* edited by Colin Renfrew, pp. 445–463. London: G. Duckworth.

Giddens, Anthony
1980   *The Class Structure of the Advanced Societies.* 2nd ed. London: Hutchinson.

Gilman, Antonio
1991   Trajectories toward Social Complexity in the Later Prehistory of the Mediterranean. In *Chiefdoms, Power, Economy, and Ideology,* edited by Timothy Earle, pp. 146–168. Cambridge: Cambridge University Press.

Glatz, August
1960   Die Freie Reichsstadt und Ihre Bürger. In *Gengenbach: Vergangenheit und Gegenwart,* pp. 107–140. Jan Thorbecke Verlag, Constance (im Auftrage der Stadt Gengenbach).

Gledhill, John
1988   Introduction: The Comparative Analysis of Social and Political Transitions. In *State and Society,* edited by John Gledhill, Barbara Bender, and Mogens Trolle Larsen, pp. 1–29. London: Unwin Hyman.
1989   The Imperial Form and Universal History: Some Reflections on Relativism and Generalization. In *Domination and Resistance,* edited by Daniel Miller, Michael Rowlands, and Christopher Tilley, pp. 108–206. London: Unwin Hyman.

Gledhill, John, and Michael Rowlands
1982   Materialism and Socio-Economic Process in Multi-Linear Evolution. In *Ranking, Resource and Exchange,* edited by Colin Renfrew and Stephen Shennan, pp. 144–150. Cambridge: Cambridge University Press.

Godelier, Maurice
1978   Infrastructure, Societies, and History. *Current Anthropology* 19:763–771.

Gonlin, Nancy
1993   Rural Household Archaeology at Copan, Honduras. Ph.D. dissertation, Department of Anthropology, Pennsylvania State University, University Park. Ann Arbor: University Microfilms.

Gordon, Connie
1980   A Spatial Analysis of the Late Prehistoric Basin of Mexico. Ph.D. dissertation, Department of Anthropology, Columbia University, New York. Ann Arbor: University Microfilms.

Gorenflo, Larry, and Nathan Gale
1986   Population and Productivity in the Teotihuacan Valley: Changing Patterns of Spatial Association in Prehispanic Central Mexico. *Journal of Anthropological Archaeology* 5:199–228.
1990   Mapping Regional Settlement in Information Space. *Journal of Anthropological Archaeology* 5:241–274.

Gould, Russell T.
1992   Is There Such a Thing as Archaeological Knowledge? A Critique of Empiricism and Idealism. *Haliksa'i* 8:37–47.

Gould, Stephen J.
1989   *Wonderful Life.* New York: W. W. Norton.
1992   Mozart and Modularity. *Natural History* February:8–16.

Graffam, Gray
1992   Beyond State Collapse: Rural History, Raised Fields, and Pastoralism in the South Andes. *American Anthropologist* 94:882–904.

Grafton, Anthony
1991   *Defenders of the Text.* Princeton: Princeton University Press.
1992   Germany and the West, 1830–1900. In *Perceptions of the Ancient Greeks,* edited by K. J. Dover, pp. 225–245. Oxford: Basil Blackwell.

Graham, Elizabeth A.
1987   Resource Diversity in Belize and Its Implications for Models of Lowland Trade. *American Antiquity* 52:753–767.

Granet, Marcel
1968   *La Pensée Chinoise.* Paris: A. Michel.

Grant, Michael
1987   *The Rise of the Greeks.* History of Civiliza-
              tion. New York: Charles Scribner's Sons.

Griffeth, Robert, and Carol G. Thomas
1981a   Introduction. In *The City-State in Five Cul-
              tures,* edited by Robert Griffeth, and Carol
              G. Thomas, pp. xiii–xx. Santa Barbara,
              CA: ABC-Clio.
1981b   Five City-States Compared. In *The City-
              State in Five Cultures,* edited by Robert
              Griffeth and Carol G. Thomas, pp. 181–
              207. Santa Barbara, CA: ABC-Clio.

Griffeth, Robert, and Carol G. Thomas, eds.
1981c   *The City-State in Five Cultures.* ABC-Clio,
              Santa Barbara, CA.

Griffiths, Gordon
1981   The Italian City-State. In *The City-State in
              Five Cultures,* edited by Robert Griffeth
              and Carol G. Thomas, pp. 71–108. ABC-
              Clio, Santa Barbara, CA.

Grove, David
1981   The Formative Period and the Evolution of
              Complex Culture. In *Handbook of Middle
              American Indians, Supplement, Vol. 1, Ar-
              chaeology,* edited by Jeremy A. Sabloff, pp.
              373–391. Austin: University of Texas Press.
1987   Chalcatzingo in a Broader Perspective. In
              Ancient Chalcatzingo, edited by David C.
              Grove, pp. 434–442. Austin: University of
              Texas Press.
1994   Review of Art, Ideology, and the City of
              Teotihuacan. *American Anthropologist*
              96:215–216.

Grubb, James S.
1988   *Firstborn of Venice: Vicenza in the Early
              Renaissance State.* The Johns Hopkins Uni-
              versity Studies in Historical and Political
              Science, Series 105, No. 3, Baltimore.
1991   Diplomacy in the Italian City-State. In
              *City-States in Classical Antiquity and Medi-
              eval Italy,* edited by Anthony Molho, Kurt
              Raaflaub, and Julia Emlen, pp. 603–617.
              Ann Arbor: University of Michigan Press.

Grube, Nikolai
1990   A Reference to Water-Lily Jaguar on Cara-
              col Stela 16: Copan Note 68. On file at the
              Instituto Hondureño de Antropología e
              Historia, Tegucigalpa.

Guy, John
1984   Trade Ceramics in Southeast Asia and the
              Acculturation Process. *Trade Ceramics
              Studies* 4:117–126.

Haas, Herbert, J. Devine, Robert J. Wenke, Mark Lehner,
W. Wolfli, and G. Bonani
1987   Radiocarbon Chronology and the Histori-
              cal Calendar in Egypt. In *Chronologies in
              the Near East,* edited by O. Aurenche,
              J. Evin, and P. Hours, pp. 585–606. Ox-
              ford: B.A.R. International Series 379.

Haas, Jonathan
1982   *The Evolution of the Prehistoric State.*
              New York: Columbia University Press.

Haas, Jonathan, Shelia Pozorski, and Thomas Pozorski,
editors
1987   *The Origins and Development of the An-
              dean State.* New York: Cambridge Univer-
              sity Press.

Hägg, Robin, ed.
1983   *The Greek Renaissance of the Eighth Cen-
              tury* B.C. Stockholm: Skrifter Utgivna i Sven-
              ska Institutet i Athen.

Hall, Edith
1989   *Inventing the Barbarian: Greek Self-
              Definition through Tragedy.* Oxford: Ox-
              ford University Press.

Halliday, W. R.
1967 [1923]   *The Growth of the City State: Lectures on
              Greek and Roman History.* Chicago:
              Argonaut.

Halperin, David
1990   *One Hundred Years of Homosexuality.* Lon-
              don: Routledge.

Halstead, Paul
1981   From Determinism to Uncertainty: Social
              Storage and the Rise of the Minoan Palace.
              In *Economic Archaeology: Towards an
              Integration of Ecological and Social Ap-
              proaches,* edited by Alison Sheridan and
              Geoff Bailey, pp. 187–213. Oxford: B.A.R.
              International Series 96.
1987   Traditional and Ancient Rural Economy in
              Mediterranean Europe: *Plus ça change?
              Journal of Hellenic Studies* 107:77–87.
1988   On Redistribution and the Origin of Mi-
              noan-Mycenaean Palatial Economies. In
              Problems in Greek Prehistory, edited by
              E. B. French and K. A. Wardle, pp. 519–
              529. Bristol: Bristol Classical Press.
1989   The Economy Has Normal Surplus: Eco-
              nomic Stability and Social Change among
              Early Farming Communities of Thessaly,
              Greece. In *Bad Year Economics,* edited by
              Paul Halstead and John O'Shea, pp. 68–80.
              Cambridge: Cambridge University Press.

Halstead, Paul, and Glynis Jones
1989   Agrarian Ecology in the Greek Islands:
            Time Stress, Scale, and Risk. *Journal of Hel-
            lenic Studies* 109:41–55.

Halstead, Paul, and John O'Shea
1982   A Friend in Need Is a Friend Indeed: Social
            Storage and the Origins of Social Ranking.
            In *Ranking, Resource, and Exchange*, ed-
            ited by Colin Renfrew and Stephen Shen-
            nan, pp. 92–99. Cambridge: Cambridge
            University Press.

Hammond, Mason
1972   *The City in the Ancient World*. Cambridge:
            Harvard University Press.

Hammond, Nicholas G. L.
1990   *The Macedonian State*. Oxford: Oxford
            University Press.

Hammond, Norman
1972   Locational Models and the Site of Lubaan-
            tun, a Classic Maya Centre. In *Models in
            Archaeology*, edited by David L. Clark, pp.
            757–800. London: Methuen.
1991a   Inside the Black Box: Defining Maya Polity.
            In *Classic Maya Political History*, edited by
            T. Patrick Culbert, pp. 253–284. Norman:
            University of Oklahoma Press.

Hammond, Norman, ed.
1985   *Nohmul: A Prehistoric Maya Community
            in Belize, Excavations 1973–1983*. Oxford:
            B.A.R. International Series 250(i).
1991b   *Cuello: An Early Maya Community in
            Belize*. Cambridge: Cambridge University
            Press.

Hammond, Norman, K. Anne Pyburn, John Rose, Justine
Staneko, Debra Muyskens, T. Addyman, Arthur Joyce,
Cynthia Robin, Colleen Gleason, and Mark Hodges
1988   Excavation and Survey at Nohmul, Belize,
            1986. *Journal of Field Archaeology*
            15:1–15.

Hannerz, Ulf
1980   The Search for the City. In *Exploring the
            City*, edited by Ulf Hannerz, pp. 59–118.
            New York: Columbia University Press.

Hansen, Mogens
1985   *Demography and Democracy*. Copen-
            hagen: Herning.
1988   *Three Studies in Athenian Demography*.
            Royal Danish Academy of Science and Let-
            ters, Historisk-filosofiske Meddelelser 56,
            Copenhagen.
1989   *The Athenian Ecclesia II*. Copenhagen: In-
            stitute Tusculanum.

1991   *The Athenian Democracy*. Translated by
            John Crook. Oxford: Blackwell.

Hansen, Richard D.
1991   The Road to Nakbe. *Natural History*
            May:8–14.

Harner, Michael J.
1972   *The Jívaro: People of the Sacred Waterfalls*.
            New York: Anchor Books.

Harris, Marvin
1977   *Cannibals and Kings: The Origins of Cul-
            tures*. New York: Vintage Books.
1979   *Cultural Materialism: The Struggle for a Sci-
            ence of Culture*. New York: Vintage Books.

Harris, William V.
1989   *Ancient Literacy*. Cambridge: Harvard Uni-
            versity Press.

Harrison, Peter
1986   Tikal: Selected Topic. In *City-states of the
            Maya: Art and Architecture*, edited by Eliza-
            beth Benson, pp. 45–71. Denver: Rocky
            Mountain Institute for Pre-Columbian
            Studies.
1990   The Revolution in Ancient Maya Studies. In
            Vision and Revision in Maya Studies, ed-
            ited by Flora S. Clancy and Peter D. Har-
            rison, pp. 99–114. Albuquerque: University
            of New Mexico Press

Harvey, F. David
1965   Two Kinds of Equality. *Classica et Medi-
            evalia* 26:101–146.

Hasebroek, Johannes
1933   *Trade and Politics in Ancient Greece*. Lon-
            don: Bell.

Hassan, Fekri A.
1986   Desert Environment and Origins of Agricul-
            ture in Egypt. *Norwegian Archaeological
            Review* 19:63–76.
1988   The Predynastic of Egypt. *Journal of World
            Prehistory* 2:135–185.
1992   Primeval Goddess to Divine King: The
            Mythogenesis of Power in the Early Egyp-
            tian State. In *The Followers of Horus: Stud-
            ies Dedicated to Michael Allen Hoffman*,
            edited by Renée Friedman and Barbara
            Adams, pp. 307–321. Oxford: Oxbow.
1993   Town and Village in Ancient Egypt: Ecol-
            ogy, Society, and Urbanization. In *The Ar-
            chaeology of Africa*, edited by Thurstan
            Shaw, Paul Sinclair, Bassey Andah, and
            Alex Okpoko, pp. 551–569. London:
            Routledge.

Hassan, Fekri A., and S. W. Robinson
1987   High-Precision Radiocarbon Chronometry of Ancient Egypt and Comparisons with Nubia, Palestine, and Mesopotamia. *Antiquity* 61:119–135.

Hassig, Ross
1982   Periodic Markets in Precolumbian Mexico. *American Antiquity* 47:46–51.
1985   *Trade, Tribute, and Transportation.* Norman: University of Oklahoma Press.
1988   *Aztec Warfare: Imperial Expansion and Political Control.* Norman: University of Oklahoma Press.
1992   *War and Society in Ancient Mesoamerica.* Berkeley: University of California Press.

Haviland, William A.
1981   Dower Houses and Minor Centers at Tikal, Guatemala: An Investigation into the Identification of Valid Units in Settlement Hierarchies. In *Lowland Maya Settlement Patterns,* edited by Wendy Ashmore, pp. 89–117. Albuquerque: University of New Mexico Press.
1992   Status and Power in Classic Maya Society: The View from Tikal. *American Antiquity* 94:937–940.

Hayden, Barbara
1983   New Plans of the Early Iron Age Settlement of Vrokastro. *Hesperia* 52:367–387.

Hayden, Brian
1994   Aggrandizers as Great Attractors. Paper presented in a symposium, "Prehistoric Cultures as Complex Adaptive Systems," at the 59th Annual Meeting of the Society for American Archaeology, Anaheim.

Hayes, William C.
1955   *A Papyrus of the Late Middle Kingdom in the Brooklyn Museum (35.1446).* Brooklyn: The Brooklyn Museum.

Healan, Dan M., ed.
1989   *Tula of the Toltecs: Excavations and Survey.* Iowa City: University of Iowa Press.

Healan, Dan M., and James W. Stoutamire
1989   Surface Survey of the Tula Urban Zone. In *Tula of the Toltecs: Excavations and Survey,* edited by Dan M. Healan, pp. 203–236. Iowa City: University of Iowa Press.

Healan, Dan M., Robert H. Cobean, and Richard A. Diehl
1989   Synthesis and Conclusions. In *Tula of the Toltecs: Excavations and Survey,* edited by

Dan M. Healan, pp. 239–251. Iowa City: University of Iowa Press.

Helck, H. Wolfgang
1974   *Die altägyptische Gaue.* Weisbaden: Harrassowitz.

Helms, Mary W.
1993   *Craft and the Kingly Ideal: Art, Trade, and Power.* Austin: University of Texas Press.

Henan sheng wenwu yanjiusuo
1993   Zhengzhou Sandeli Huayuan xincun kaogu fajue jianbao. [Brief Archaeological Excavation Report of Huayuan New Village, Sandeli, Zhengzhou.] *Zhengzhou: Zhongzhou guji chuban she:* 228–241.

Henan sheng wenwu yanjiusuo Zhoukou diqu wenhua qu wenwuke
1983   Henan sheng Huaiyang Pingliangtai Longshan wenhua chengzhi shijue jianbao. [Brief Report of the Trial Excavations of the Longshan Culture Remains at Pingliangtai, Huaiyang, Henan Province.] *Wenwu* 3:21–36.

Hendon, Julia
1987   The Uses of Maya Structures: A Study of Architecture and Artifact Distribution at Sepaltura, Copan, Honduras. Ph.D. dissertation, Department of Anthropology, Harvard University, Cambridge. Ann Arbor: University Microfilms.
1991   Status and Power in Classic Maya Society: An Archaeological Study. *American Anthropologist* 93:894–918.
1992   The Interpretation of Survey Data: Two Case Studies from the Maya Area. *Latin American Antiquity* 3:22–42.

Herlihy, David
1991   The Rulers of Florence, 1282–1530. In *City-States in Classical Antiquity and Medieval Italy,* edited by Anthony Molho, Kurt Raaflaub, and Julia Emlen, pp. 197–221. Ann Arbor: University of Michigan Press.

Herman, Gabriel
1987   *Ritualised Friendship and the Greek City.* Cambridge: Cambridge University Press.

Herodotus
1972   *Books I and II.* Translated by A. D. Godley. London: Loeb Classical Library.

Hesiod
1982   *Hesiod: Theogeny, Works and Days; Theognis: Elegies.* Translated by D. Wender. London: Penguin.

Hester, Thomas R., and Harry J. Shafer
1994   The Ancient Maya Craft Community at
            Colha, Belize, and Its External Relation-
            ships. In *Archaeological Views from the
            Countryside: Village Communities in Early
            Complex Societies,* edited by Glenn M.
            Schwartz, and Steven E. Falconer, pp. 48–
            63. Washington, D.C.: Smithsonian Institu-
            tion Press.

Hester, Thomas, Harry J. Shafer, and Jack D. Eaton
1982   *Archaeology at Colha, Belize, 1981: In-
            terim Report.* Center for Archaeological Re-
            search, University of Texas at San Antonio.

Hicks, Frederic
1982   Tetzcoco in the Early 16th Century: The
            State, the City, and the *Calpolli. American
            Ethnologist* 9:230–249.
1986   Prehispanic Background of Colonial Politi-
            cal and Economic Organization in Central
            Mexico. In *Handbook of Middle American
            Indians, Supplement, Vol. 4 Ethnohistory,*
            edited by Ronald Spores, pp. 35–54. Aus-
            tin: University of Texas Press.
1992   Subject States and Tribute Provinces: The
            Aztec Empire in the Northern Valley of
            Mexico. *Ancient Mesoamerica* 3:1–10.

Hirschman, Albert
1991   *The Rhetoric of Reaction: Perversity, Futil-
            ity, Jeopardy.* Cambridge: Harvard Univer-
            sity Press.

Hirth, Kenneth G.
1974   Precolumbian Population Development
            along the Rio Amatzinac. Ph.D. disserta-
            tion, Department of Anthropology, Univer-
            sity of Wisconsin, Milwaukee. Ann Arbor:
            University Microfilms.
1980   *Eastern Morelos and Teotihuacan: A Settle-
            ment Survey.* Publications in Anthropology
            No. 25. Nashville: Department of Anthro-
            pology, Vanderbilt University.
1984   Xochicalco: Urban Growth and State For-
            mation in Central Mexico. *Science*
            255:579–586.
1987   Formative Period Settlement Patterns in the
            Rio Amatzinac Valley. In *Ancient Chalcat-
            zingo,* edited by David C. Grove, pp. 343–
            367. Austin: University of Texas Press.
1989   Militarism and Social Organization at
            Xochicalco, Morelos. In *Mesoamerica after
            the Decline of Teotihuacan, A.D. 700–900,*
            edited by Richard A. Diehl and Catherine
            Janet Berlo, pp. 69–81. Washington, D.C.:
            Dumbarton Oaks Research Library and
            Collection.

Hirth, Kenneth G., ed.
1992   *Trade and Exchange in Early Mesoamerica.*
            Albuquerque: University of New Mexico
            Press.

Hirth, Kenneth, and Jorge Angulo Villaseñor
1981   Early State Expansion in Central Mexico:
            Teotihuacan in Morelos. *Journal of Field
            Archaeology* 8:135–150.

Hirth, Kenneth G., and Ann Cyphers Guillén
1988   *Tiempo y Asentamiento en Xochicalco.* Se-
            rie Monografías 1. México, D.F.: Universi-
            dad Nacional Autónoma de México.

Hisao Fujii
1995   *Chusei no Shiro to Kassen* [Castles and
            Battlefields of the Middle Ages]. Tokyo:
            Asahi Shimbunsha.

Hodder, Ian
1982   *The Present Past.* London: Batsford.
1993   *Theory and Practice in Archaeology.* Lon-
            don: Routledge.

Hodge, Mary G.
1984   *Aztec City States.* Museum of Anthropol-
            ogy Memoir No. 18. Ann Arbor: University
            of Michigan.
1991   Land and Lordship: The Politics of Aztec
            Provincial Administration in the Valley of
            Mexico. In *Land and Politics in the Valley
            of Mexico: A Two-Thousand Year Perspec-
            tive,* edited by H. R. Harvey, pp. 113–139.
            Albuquerque: University of New Mexico
            Press.
1992   The Geographical Structure of Aztec
            Imperial-Period Market Systems. *National
            Geographic Society Research & Explora-
            tion* 8:428–445.
1993   Exploring Aztec Urban Life: An Archaeo-
            logical Study of Prehispanic Chalco. En-
            glish version of Interim Report to Consejo
            de Arqueología, Instituto Nacional de An-
            tropología e Historia, México, D.F.
1994   Polities Composing the Aztec Empire's
            Core. In *Economies and Polities in the
            Aztec Realm,* edited by Mary G. Hodge
            and Michael E. Smith, pp. 43–72. Albany:
            Institute for Mesoamerican Studies, State
            University of New York at Albany.
1996   Political Organization of the Central Prov-
            inces. In *Aztec Imperial Strategies,* edited
            by Frances F. Berdan, Richard E. Blanton,
            Elizabeth Hill Boone, Mary G. Hodge, Mi-
            chael E. Smith, and Emily Umberger. pp.
            17–45. Washington, D.C.: Dumbarton
            Oaks Research Library and Collection.

Hodge, Mary G., ed.
in press   *Place of Jade: Society and Economy in Ancient Chalco.* Department of Anthropology Memoirs in Latin American Archaeology. Pittsburgh: University of Pittsburgh.

Hodge, Mary G., and Leah D. Minc
1990   The Spatial Patterning of Aztec Ceramics: Implications for Prehispanic Exchange Systems in the Valley of Mexico. *Journal of Field Archaeology* 17:415–437.
1991   Aztec-Period Ceramic Distribution and Exchange Systems. Final Report to the National Science Foundation for Grant #BNS-8704177, Washington, D.C.

Hodge, Mary G., Charles D. Frederick, and Carlos A. Cordova
1994   Prehispanic Sites and the Changing Environment: Investigating Human-Environmental Interaction in the Basin of Mexico 1500 B.C.–A.D. 1520. Report to H. John Heinz Charitable Trust.

Hodge, Mary G., and Hector Neff
1994   Xaltocan in the Economy of the Basin of Mexico: A View from Ceramic Tradewares. Paper presented at the 59th Annual Meeting of the Society for American Archaeology, Anaheim.

Hodge, Mary G., Hector Neff, M. James Blackman, and Leah D. Minc
1992   A Compositional Perspective on Ceramic Production in the Aztec Empire. In *Chemical Characterization of Ceramic Pastes in Archaeology,* edited by Hector Neff, pp. 203–220. Monographs in World Archaeology No. 7. Madison: Prehistory Press.
1993   Black-on-Orange Ceramic Production in the Aztec Empire's Heartland. *Latin American Antiquity* 4:130–157.

Hodge, Mary G., and Michael E. Smith, eds.
1994   *Economies and Polities in the Aztec Realm.* Albany: Institute for Mesoamerican Studies, State University of New York at Albany.

Hodkinson, Stephen
1983   Social Order and the Conflict of Values in Classical Sparta. *Chiron* 13:239–281.
1986   Land Tenure and Inheritance in Classical Sparta. *Classical Quarterly* 36:378–406.
1988   Animal Husbandry in the Greek *Polis.* In *Pastoral Economies in Classical Antiquity,* edited by C. R. Whittaker, pp. 35–74. Proceedings of the Cambridge Philological Society Supp., Vol. 14, Cambridge.

1989   Inheritance, Marriage, and Demography: Perspectives upon the Success and Decline of Classical Sparta. In *Classical Sparta: Techniques behind Her Success,* edited by Anton Powell, pp. 79–121. Norman: University of Oklahoma Press.
1992   Sharecropping and Sparta's Economic Exploitation of the Helots. In *Philolakon: Lakonian Studies in Honour of Hector Catling,* edited by Jan Sanders, pp. 123–134. London: British School at Athens.

Hoepfner, Wolfram
1989   Die frühen Demokratien und die Architekturforschung. In *Demokratie und Architektur,* edited by Wolfgang Schuller, Wolfram Hoepfner, and Ernst-Ludwig Schwandner, pp. 9–16. Munich: Deutscher Kunstverlag.

Hoepfner, Wolfram, and Ernst-Ludwig Schwandner
1986   *Haus und Stadt im klassischen Griechenland.* Munich: Deutscher Kunstverlag.

Hoffman, Michael A.
1982   *The Predynastic of Hierakonpolis: An Interim Report.* Cairo: Egyptian Studies Association.
1989   A Stratified Predynastic Sequence from Hierakonpolis (Upper Egypt). In *Late Prehistory of the Nile Basin and the Sahara,* edited by Lech Krzyzaniak and Michal Kobusiewicz, pp. 317–324. Poznan: Muzeum Archeologicznew Poznaniu.

Hoffman, Michael A., Hany A. Hamroush, and Ralph O. Allen
1986   A Model of Urban Development for the Hierakonpolis Region from Predynastic through Old Kingdom Times. *Journal of the American Research Center in Egypt* 23:175–187.

Hohman, Hasso, and Annegrete Vogrin
1982   *Die Architektur von Copan.* Graz, Austria: Akademische Druck Verlagsanstalt.

Hommon, Robert J.
1986   Social Evolution and Ancient Hawaii. In *Island Societies: Archaeological Approaches to Evolution and Transformation,* edited by Patrick Kirch, pp. 55–68. New York: Cambridge University Press.

Houby-Nielsen, Sanne
1992   Interaction between Chieftains and Citizens? Seventh Century B.C. Burial Customs in Athens. *Acta Hyperborea* 4:343–74.
1995   "Burial Language" in Archaic and Classical

Kerameikos. *Proceedings of the Danish Institute at Athens* 1:129–191.

Hourani, Albert H., and Samuel M. Stern, eds.
1970   *The Islamic City.* Philadelphia: University of Pennsylvania Press.

Houston, Stephen D.
1992   Classic Maya Polities. In *New Theories on the Ancient Maya,* edited by Elin C. Danien and Robert J. Sharer, pp. 65–70. University Museum Monograph No. 77. University Museum Symposium Series, Vol. 3. Philadelphia: The University Museum, University of Pennsylvania.

Hsu, Cho-yun
1965   *Ancient China in Transition: An Analysis of Social Mobility 722–222 B.C.* Stanford: Stanford University Press.

Hubei sheng bowuguan
1982   Chu du Jinan cheng de kancha yu fajue (shang). [Exploration and Excavation of the Chu capital, Jinan City (Part 1).] *Kaogu xuebao* 3:325–349.

Huber, Louisa G. Fitzgerald
1988   The Bo Capital and Questions concerning Xia and Early Shang. *Early China* 13:46–77.

Hudson, Charles, Marvin Smith, David Hally, Richard Polhemus, and Chester DePratter
1985   Coosa: A Chiefdom in the Sixteenth-Century Southeastern United States. *American Antiquity* 50:723.

Humphreys, S. C.
1978   *Anthropology and the Greeks.* London: Routledge and Kegan Paul.

Hunter, Virginia
1994   *Policing Athens.* Princeton: Princeton University Press.

Huot, Jean-Louis, ed.
1989   *Larsa: Travaux de 1985.* Paris: CNRS, Éditions Recherche sur les Civilisations.

Huot, Jean-Louis, Axelle Rougelle, and Joël Suire
1989   La structure urbaine de Larsa. In *Larsa: Travaux de 1985,* edited by Jean-Louis Huot. Paris: CNRS, Éditions Recherche sur les Civilisations.

Hyslop, John
1990   *Inka Settlement Planning.* Austin: University of Texas Press.

Isager, Signe, and Jan Erik Skydsgaard
1992   *Ancient Greek Agriculture.* London: Routledge.

Isbell, William, and Gordon McEwan, eds.
1991   *Huari Administrative Structure: Prehistoric Monumental Architecture and State Government.* Washington, D.C.: Dumbarton Oaks Research Library and Collection.

Jacobs, Jane
1969   *The Economy of Cities.* New York: Random House.

Jacobsen, Thorkild
1970   *Towards the Image of Tammuz.* Cambridge: Harvard University Press.
1982   *Salinity and Irrigation Agriculture in Antiquity: Diyala Basin Archaeological Projects: Report on Essential Results, 1957–58.* Malibu: Undena Press.

Jameson, Michael H.
1978   Agriculture and Slavery in Classical Athens. *Classical Journal* 73:122–46.
1992   Agricultural Labor in Classical Greece. In *Agriculture in Ancient Greece,* edited by Berit Wells, pp. 135–146. Stockholm: Skrifter Utgivna i Svenska Institutet i Athen.

Jameson, Michael H., Curtis Runnels, and Tjeerd van Andel
1994   *A Greek Countryside.* Stanford: Stanford University Press.

Jansen, Michael
1978   City Planning in the Harappa Culture. In *Art and Archaeological Research Papers* No. 14, edited by Dalu Jones and George Michell, pp. 69–74. London.
1980   Public Spaces in the Urban Settlements of the Harappa Culture. In *Art and Archaeological Research Papers,* edited by Dalu Jones and George Michell, pp. 11–19. London.
1984a   Preliminary Results of Two Years' Documentation at Mohenjo-Daro. In *South Asian Archaeology, 1981,* edited by Bridgit Allchin, pp. 135–153. Cambridge: Cambridge University Press.
1984b   Architectural Remains in Mohenjo-Daro. In *Frontiers of the Indus Civilization,* edited by Brij Bhushan Lal and S. P. Gupta, pp. 75–88. Delhi: Books and Books.
1985   Mohenjo-daro HR-A, House I, a Temple? Analysis of an Architectural Structure. In *South Asian Archaeology, 1983,* edited by Maurizio Taddei, pp. 157–206. Naples: Istituto Universitario Orientale.
1987   Preliminary Results on the "Forma Urbis" Research at Mohenjo-Daro. In *Interim Re-*

ports, Vol. 2: *Reports on Field Work Carried out at Mohenjo-Daro, Pakistan, 1983–84, by IsMEO-Aachen University Mission,* edited by Michael Jansen and Gunter Urban, pp. 9–21. Aachen: IsMEO/RWTH.

1989   Some Problems regarding the *Forma Urbis* Mohenjo-Daro. In *South Asian Archaeology, 1985,* edited by Karen Frifelt and Per Sørensen, pp. 247–254. London: Curzon Press.

1991   Mohenjo-Daro: A City on the Indus. In *Forgotten Cities on the Indus,* edited by Michael Jansen, M. Mulloy, and Gunter Urban, pp. 145–165. Mainz am Rhein: Phillip von Zabern.

1993   Mohenjo-daro: Type Site of the Earliest Urbanization Process in South Asia. In *Urban Form and Meaning in South Asia: The Shaping of Cities from Prehistoric to Precolonial Times,* edited by Howard Spodek and Doris M. Srinivasan, pp. 35–52. Washington, D.C.: National Gallery of Art.

Jansen, Michael, and Maurizio Tosi
1988   *Interim Reports, Vol. 3: Reports on Field Work Carried Out at Mohenjo-Daro, Pakistan, 1983–86, by IsMEO-Aachen University Mission.* Aachen: IsMEO/RWTH.

Jansen, Michael, and Gunter Urban
1984   *Interim Reports, Vol. 1: Reports on Field Work Carried Out at Mohenjo-Daro, Pakistan, 1983–84, by IsMEO-Aachen University Mission.* Aachen: IsMEO/RWTH.

1987   *Interim Reports, Vol. 2: Reports on Field Work Carried Out at Mohenjo-Daro, Pakistan, 1983–84, by IsMEO-Aachen University Mission.* Aachen: IsMEO/RWTH.

Jarrige, Jean-François
1986   Excavations at Mehrgarh-Nausharo. *Pakistan Archaeology* 22:62–131.

1988   Excavations at Nausharo. *Pakistan Archaeology* 23:149–203.

1990   Excavation at Nausharo, 1987–88. *Pakistan Archaeology* 24:21–67.

Jeffery, Lilian H.
1976   *Archaic Greece: The City-States c. 700–500* B.C. New York: St. Martin's Press.

1990   *The Local Scripts of Archaic Greece,* 2nd ed., edited by Alan Johnston. Oxford: Clarendon Press.

Jeffreys, David G.
1985   *The Survey of Memphis I.* London: The Egypt Exploration Fund.

Jiménez Moreno, Wigberto
1966   Mesoamerica before the Toltecs. In *Ancient Oaxaca: Discoveries in Mexican Archaeology and History,* edited by John Paddock, pp. 1–82. Stanford: Stanford University Press.

Joffe, Alexander
1991   Early Bronze I and the Evolution of Social Complexity in the Southern Levant. *Journal of Mediterranean Archaeology* 4:3–58.

n.d.   Parallelisms and Divergences in a Third Millennium Periphery: The Case of the Northern and Southern Levant. Manuscript on file with the author.

Johnson, Allen W., and Timothy Earle
1987   *The Evolution of Human Societies: From Foraging Group to Agrarian State.* Stanford: Stanford University Press.

Johnson, Andrew L., and Nancy C. Lovell
1994   Biological Differentiation at Predynastic Naquada, Egypt: An Analysis of Dental Morphological Traits. *American Journal of Physical Anthropology* 93:427–433.

Johnson, Curtis
1990   *Aristotle's Theory of the State.* New York: St. Martin's Press.

Johnson, Gregory A.
1977   Aspects of Regional Analysis in Archaeology. *Annual Review of Anthropology* 6:479–508.

1978   Information Sources and the Development of Decision-Making Organizations. In *Social Archaeology: Beyond Subsistence and Dating,* edited by Charles Redman, Mary Jane Berman, Edward V. Curtin, William T. Langhorne, Jr., Nina M. Versaggi, and Jeffery C. Wanser, pp. 87–112. New York: Academic Press.

1981   Monitoring Complex System Integration and Boundary Phenomena with Settlement Size Data. In *Archaeological Approaches to the Study of Complexity,* edited by Sander E. van der Leeuw, pp. 144–188. Amsterdam: Albert Egges van Giffen Instituut voor Prae- en Protohistorie, CINGVLA VI, University of Amsterdam.

1982   Organizational Structure and Scalar Stress. In *Theory and Explanation in Archaeology,* edited by Colin Renfrew, Michael J. Rowlands, and Barbara A. Seagraves, pp. 389–421. New York: Academic Press.

1983   Decision-Making Organization and Pastoral Nomad Camp Size. *Human Ecology* 11:175–199.

1989   Dynamics of Southwestern Prehistory: Far Outside Looking In. In *Dynamics of Southwest Prehistory*, edited by Linda S. Cordell and George J. Gumerman, pp. 371–389. Washington, D.C.: Smithsonian Institution Press.

Jones, Christopher
1991   Cycles of Growth at Tikal. In *Classic Maya Political History*, edited by T. Patrick Culbert, pp. 102–127. Norman: University of Oklahoma Press.

Jones, Grant D.
1982   Agriculture and Trade in the Colonial Period Southern Lowlands. In *Maya Subsistence*, edited by Kent Flannery, pp. 275–293. New York: Academic Press.
1983   The Last Maya Frontiers of Colonial Yucatan. In *Spaniards and Indians in Southeastern Mesoamerica: Essays on the History of Ethnic Relations*, edited by Murdo J. MacLeod and Robert Wasserstrom, pp. 64–91. Lincoln: University of Nebraska Press.

Jones, Nicholas
1987   *Public Organization in Ancient Greece*. Memoirs of the American Philosophical Society 176, Philadelphia.

Jones, P. J.
1965   Communes and Despots: The City-State in Late Medieval Italy. *Transactions of the Royal Historical Society* (Series 5) 15:71–96.

Joshi, Jagat Pati
1973   Excavations at Surkotada. In *Radiocarbon and Indian Archaeology*, edited by D. P. Agrawal and A. Ghosh, pp. 173–181. Bombay: Tata Institute for Fundamental Research.

Joshi, Jagat Pati, and Madhu Bala
1982   Manda: A Harappan Site in Jammu and Kashmir. In *Harappan Civilization*, edited by Gregory. L. Possehl, pp. 185–196. New Delhi: Oxford and IBH.

Just, Roger
1989   *Women in Athenian Law and Life*. London: Routledge.

Kaiser, Werner
1964   Einige Bermerkungen zur ägyptische Frühzeit. *Zeitschrift ägyptische Sprache Altertumskunde* 91:86–125.

1985   Zur Sudausdehnung der vorgeschichtlichen Deltakulturen und zur frühen Entwicklung Oberägyptens. *Mitteilungen des Deutschen Archäologischen Instituts Abteilung Kairo* 41:61–87.

Kanawati, Naguib
1977   *The Egyptian Administration in the Old Kingdom: Evidence of Its Economic Decline*. Warminster: Aris & Phillips.

Kardulias, P. Nick
1994   Towards an Anthropological Historical Archaeology in Greece. *Historical Archaeology* 28:39–55.

Karetsou, Alexandra
1973   Domkimastiki erevna eis Agian Pelagian Irakleiou Kritis. *Praktika tis en Athinais Arkhaiologikis Etaireias*: 200–212.

Karttunen, Frances
1983   *An Analytical Dictionary of Nahuatl*. Austin: University of Texas Press.

Kauffman, Stuart
1993   *The Origins of Order: Self-Organization and Selection in Evolution*. New York: Oxford University Press.

Kaye, Harvey
1984   *The British Marxist Historians*. Oxford: Polity.

Keightley, David N.
1978   The Religious Commitment: Shang Theology and the Genesis of Chinese Political Culture. *History of Religions* 17:211–235.
1979–80   The Shang State as Seen in the Oracle-Bone Inscriptions. *Early China* 5:25–34.
1982   Shang China Is Coming of Age: A Review Article. *Journal of Asian Studies* 41.3:549–557.
1983a   The Late Shang State: When, Where, and What? In *The Origins of Chinese Civilization*, edited by David N. Keightley pp. 523–564. Berkeley: University of California Press.

Keightley, David N., ed.
1983b   *The Origins of Chinese Civilization*. Berkeley: University of California Press.

Keith, Donald
1980   A Fourteenth Century Shipwreck at Sinangun. *Archaeology* 30(2):33–43.

Kemp, Barry J.
1977   Early Development of Towns in Egypt. *Antiquity* 51:185–200.

1983 Old Kingdom, Middle Kingdom, and Second Intermediate Period c. 2686–1552 B.C. In *Ancient Egypt: A Social History,* edited by Bruce Trigger, Barry J. Kemp, David O'Connor, and Alan Lloyd, pp. 71–182. Cambridge: Cambridge University Press.

1989 *Ancient Egypt: Anatomy of a Civilization.* London: Routledge.

Kenoyer, J. Mark

1989 Socio-Economic Structures of the Indus Civilization, as Reflected in Specialized Crafts and the Question of Ritual Segregation. In *Old Problems and New Perspectives in the Archaeology of South Asia,* edited by J. Mark Kenoyer, pp. 183–192. Wisconsin Archaeological Reports No. 2. Department of Anthropology, University of Wisconsin, Madison.

1991a The Indus Valley Tradition of Pakistan and Western India. *Journal of World Prehistory* 5:331–385.

1991b Urban Process in the Indus Tradition: A Preliminary Model from Harappa. In *Harappa Excavations, 1986–1990: A Multidisciplinary Approach to Third Millenium Urbanism,* edited by Richard H. Meadow, pp. 29–60. Monographs in World Archaeology No. 3. Madison: Prehistory Press.

1992 Harappan Craft Specialization and the Question of Urban Segregation and Stratification. *Eastern Anthropologist* 45 (1–2):39–54.

1994 The Harappan State: Was It or Wasn't It? In *From Sumer to Meluhha: Contributions to the Archaeology of West and South Asia, in Memory of George F. Dales,* edited by J. Mark Kenoyer, pp. 71–80. Department of Anthropology, Madison.

1995 Interaction Systems, Specialized Crafts and Culture Change: The Indus Valley Tradition and the Indo-Gangetic Tradition in South Asia. In *Language, Material Culture, and Ethnicity: The Indo-Aryans in Ancient South Asia,* edited by George Erdosy. Mouton, pp. 213–257. Berlin: DeGruyter.

Kenoyer, J. Mark, and Heather M. L. Miller

in press Metal Technologies of the Indus Valley Tradition in Pakistan and Western India. In *The Emergence and Development of Metallurgy,* edited by Vincent C. Pigott. Philadelphia: University Museum Press.

Kepinski-Lecomte, Christine

1992 *Haradum I: Une ville nouvelle sur le Moyen-Euphrate (XVIIIe–XVIIe av. J.-C.).* Paris: CNRS, Éditions Recherche sur les Civilisations.

Kerferd, George B.

1984 The Concept of Equality in the Thought of the Sophistic Movement. In *Equality and Inequality of Man in Ancient Thought,* edited by Iiro Kajanto, pp. 7–15. Helsinki: Societas Scientiarum Fennica 75.

Kerr, George

1958 *Okinawa: History of an Island People.* Rutland, VT: Tuttle Publishers.

Kessler, Adam T.

1994 *Empires beyond the Great Wall: The Heritage of Genghis Khan.* Natural History Museum of Los Angeles County, Los Angeles.

Keuls, Eva

1985 *The Reign of the Phallus.* Berkeley: University of California Press.

Kin, Shouki, Masayuki Tana, Isamu Chinen, and Shiichi Toma

1988 *Gusuku Rodo: Okinawa no Gusuku Monogatari* [On the Road to the *Gusuku:* The Story of Okinawa *Gusuku* (Castles)]. Naha: Mugisha.

King, Eleanor, and Daniel Potter

1994 Small Sites in Prehistoric Maya Socioeconomic Organization: A Perspective from Colha, Belize. In *Archaeological Views from the Countryside: Village Communities in Early Complex Societies,* edited by Glenn M. Schwartz and Steven E. Falconer, pp. 64–90. Washington, D.C.: Smithsonian Institution Press.

Kinjo, Seitoku

1971 Min dai sho, chuki ni okeru kaigai boeki ni tsuite [Concerning Overseas Trade of the Early and Middle Ming Period]. *Ryukyu Daigaku Bungakubu Hogakubu Kiyo, Rekishi, Chirigaku, Shakaigaku* [Contributions of the Faculties of Arts and Law: History, Geography, and Sociology] 15:111–128.

Kirch, Patrick

1984 *The Evolution of the Polynesian Chiefdoms.* Cambridge: Cambridge University Press.

Kitto, Humphrey D. F.

1970 *The Greeks.* Baltimore: Penguin Press.

Klapisch-Zuber, Christiane

1991 Commentary. In *City-States in Classical An-*

tiquity and Medieval Italy, edited by Anthony Molho, Kurt Raaflaub, and Julia Emlen, pp. 241–247. Ann Arbor: University of Michigan Press.

Knapp, A. Bernard
1988   *The History and Culture of Ancient Western Asia and Egypt.* Chicago: Dorsey.

Kochakova, Natalia B.
1978   Yoruba City-States (at the Turn of the Nineteenth Century). In *The Early State,* edited by Henri J. Claessen and Peter Skalník, pp. 495–510. The Hague: Mouton.

Kohl, Philip L.
1978   The Balance of Trade in Southwestern Asia in the Mid-Third Millennium, B.C. *Current Anthropology* 19:463–492.
1984   Force, History, and the Evolutionist Paradigm. In *Marxist Perspectives in Archaeology,* edited by Malcolm Spriggs, pp. 127–134. Cambridge: Cambridge University Press.
1987   State Formation: Useful Concept or Idée Fixe? In *Power Relations and State Formation,* edited by Thomas C. Patterson and Christine W. Gailey, pp. 27–34. Washington, D.C.: Archaeology Section, American Anthropological Association.

Kolata, Alan L.
1983   Chan Chan and Cuzco: On the Nature of the Ancient Andean City. In *Civilization in the Ancient Americas,* edited by Richard M. Levanthal and Alan L. Kolata, pp. 345–371. Albuquerque and Cambridge: University of New Mexico Press and Peabody Museum Press, Harvard University.
1993   *The Tiwanaku: Portrait of an Andean Civilization.* Oxford: Basil Blackwell.

Kowalewski, Stephen A.
1990   Merits of Full Coverage Survey: Examples from the Valley of Oaxaca, Mexico. In *The Archaeology of Regions: A Case for Full Coverage Survey,* edited by Suzanne K. Fish and Stephen A. Kowalewski, pp. 33–86. Washington, D.C.: Smithsonian Institution Press.

Kowalewski, Stephen A., Gary M. Feinman, Laura Finsten, Richard E. Blanton, and Linda M. Nicholas
1989   *Monte Albán's Hinterland, Part II: Prehistoric Settlement Patterns in Tlacolula, Etla, and Ocotlan, the Valley of Oaxaca, Mexico.* Museum of Anthropology Memoir No. 23. University of Michigan, Ann Arbor.

Krapf-Askari, Eva
1969   *Yoruba Towns and Cities.* Oxford: Oxford University Press.

Kristiansen, Kristian
1991   Chiefdoms, States, and Systems of Social Evolution. In *Chiefdoms: Power, Economy, and Ideology,* edited by Timothy Earle, pp. 16–43. Cambridge: Cambridge University Press.

Kroeber, Alfred L.
1944   *Configurations of Culture Growth.* Berkeley and Los Angeles: University of California Press.

Kroeper, Karla
1988   The Excavations of the Munich East-Delta Expedition in Minshat Abu Omar. In *The Archaeology of the Nile Delta: Problems and Priorities,* edited by Edwin C. M. van den Brink, pp. 11–46. Amsterdam: Foundation for Archaeological Research in Egypt.
1989   Settlement in the Nile Delta to the End of the Old Kingdom. Ph.D. dissertation. Uniwersytet Warszawski Wydzial Historcyczny, Warsaw.
1990   Tell Ibrahim Awadæ North-eastern Delta. *Bulletin de Liaison* 14:6–8.

Kroeper, Karla, and Dieter Wildung
1985   *Minshat Abu Omar.* Munich: Staatliche Ägyptischer Kunst.

Kroll, John H., and Nancy M. Waggoner
1984   Dating the Earliest Coins of Athens, Corinth, and Megara. *American Journal of Archaeology* 88:325–340.

Kromer, Karl
1978   Siedlungsfunde aus dem frühen Alten Reich in Giseh. *Denkschriften, Öesterreichische Akademie der Wissenschaften, Philosophisch-historische Klasse* 136:1–130.

Krzyzaniak, Lech
1977   *Early Farming Cultures on the Lower Nile: The Predynastic Period in Egypt.* Warsaw: Polish Academy of Sciences.
1988   Research on the Location of the Predynastic Settlement at Minshat Abu Omar. Paper presented at the Fifth International Congress of Egyptology, Cairo.

Kurjack, Edward B.
1974   *Prehistoric Lowland Maya Community and Social Organization: A Case Study at Dzibilchaltun, Yucatan, Mexico.* Middle American Research Institute Publication No. 38. New Orleans: Tulane University.

Kurke, Leslie
1991　　　*The Traffic in Praise: Pindar and the Poet-
　　　　　ics of Social Economy.* Ithaca: Cornell Uni-
　　　　　versity Press.
1992　　　The Politics of *Habrosyne. Classical Antiq-
　　　　　uity* 11:91–120.

Kurtz, Donald V.
1981　　　The Legitimation of Early Inchoate States.
　　　　　In *The Early State,* edited by Henry J. Claes-
　　　　　sen and Peter Skalník pp. 177–200. The
　　　　　Hague: Mouton.

Kutzbach, John E., and COHMAP Members
1988　　　Climatic Changes of the Last 18,000 Years:
　　　　　Observations and Model Simulations. *Sci-
　　　　　ence* 241:1043–1052.

Kwan, K. K., and Jean Martin
1985　　　Canton, Pulau Tioman, and Southeast
　　　　　Asian Maritime Trade. In *A Ceramic Leg-
　　　　　acy of Asia's Maritime Trade,* edited by
　　　　　Southeast Asian Ceramic Society, pp. 49–
　　　　　63. Singapore: Southeast Asian Ceramic So-
　　　　　ciety (West Malaysian Chapter) and Oxford
　　　　　University Press.

Kyle, Donald G.
1987　　　*Athletics in Ancient Athens.* Leiden: E. J.
　　　　　Brill.

Laffineur, Robert, and Wolf-Dieter Niemeyer, eds.
1995　　　*Politeia: State and Society in the Aegean
　　　　　Bronze Age.* Liège: Aegaeum 6.

Lal, Brij Bhushan
1979　　　Kalibangan and the Indus Civilization. In
　　　　　Essays in Indian Protohistory, edited by
　　　　　D. P. Agrawal and Dilip K. Chakrabarti,
　　　　　pp. 65–97. Delhi: B. R. Publishing.

Lal, Makkhan
1986　　　Iron Tools, Forest Clearance, and Urbaniza-
　　　　　tion in the Gangetic Plains. *Man and Envi-
　　　　　ronment* 10:83–90.

Lambrick, H. T.
1964　　　*Sind: A General Introduction.* Hyderabad:
　　　　　Sindhi Adabi Board.

Lambrinoudakis, Vassilis G.
1988　　　Veneration of Ancestors in Geometric
　　　　　Naxos. In *Early Greek Cult Practice,* edited
　　　　　by Robin Hägg, Nanno Marinatos, and
　　　　　Gullog Nordquist, pp. 235–246. Stock-
　　　　　holm: Skrifter Utgivna i Svenska Institutet i
　　　　　Athen.

de Landa, Diego
1941　　　*Landa's Relación de Las Cosas de Yucatan,*
　　　　　edited and annotated by Alfred M. Tozzer.

Papers of the Peabody Museum, Vol. 17.
Cambridge: Harvard University.

Landé, Carl H.
1977　　　Introduction: The Dyadic Basis of Clientism.
　　　　　In *Friends, Followers, and Factions,* edited
　　　　　by Steffen Schmidt, Laura Gausti, Carl
　　　　　Landé, and James Scott, pp. xiii–xxxvii.
　　　　　Berkeley: University of California Press.

Langdon, Susan H.
1987　　　Gift Exchange in the Geometric Sanctuar-
　　　　　ies. In *Gifts to the Gods: Proceedings of
　　　　　the Uppsala Symposium, 1985,* edited by
　　　　　Tullia Linders and Gullog Nordquist, pp.
　　　　　107–113. Uppsala: Academia Ubsaliensis.

Langley, James C.
1992　　　Teotihuacan Sign Clusters: Emblem or Ar-
　　　　　ticulation? In *Art, Ideology, and the City
　　　　　of Teotihuacan,* edited by Janet Catherine
　　　　　Berlo, pp. 247–280. Washington, D.C.:
　　　　　Dumbarton Oaks Research Library and
　　　　　Collection.

Lapidus, Ira
1984　　　*Muslim Cities in the Later Middle Ages.*
　　　　　Cambridge: Cambridge University Press.

Lapidus, Ira, ed.
1969　　　*Middle Eastern Cities.* Berkeley: University
　　　　　of California Press.

Laporte, Juan Pedro, and Vilma Fialko C.
1990　　　New Perspectives on Old Problems: Dynas-
　　　　　tic References for the Early Classic at Tikal.
　　　　　In *Vision and Revision in Maya Studies,* ed-
　　　　　ited by Flora S. Clancy and Peter D. Har-
　　　　　rison, pp. 33–66. Albuquerque: University
　　　　　of New Mexico Press.

Larsen, Jakob A. O.
1968　　　*Greek Federal States.* Oxford: Clarendon
　　　　　Press.

Larsen, Mogens Trolle
1976　　　*The Old Assyrian City-State and Its Colo-
　　　　　nies.* Copenhagen: Akademisk Forlag.
1987　　　Commercial Networks in the Ancient Near
　　　　　East. In *Centre and Periphery in the An-
　　　　　cient World,* edited by Michael Rowlands,
　　　　　Mogens T. Larsen, and Kristian Kristi-
　　　　　ansen, pp. 47–56. Cambridge: Cambridge
　　　　　University Press.

Lebessi, Angeliki
1981　　　I synekheia tis kritomykinaikis latreias.
　　　　　Arkhaiologiki Ephemeris: 1–24.

Lebra, William
1966　　　*Okinawan Religion.* Honolulu: University
　　　　　of Hawaii Press.

Lee, Richard
1979   *The !Kung San.* Cambridge: Cambridge
            University Press.
1990   Primitive Communism and the Origin of So-
            cial Inequality. In *The Evolution of Politi-
            cal Systems: Sociopolitics in Small-Scale
            Sedentary Societies,* edited by Steadman
            Upham, pp. 225–246. Cambridge: Cam-
            bridge University Press.

Lefebvre, Henri
1991   *The Production of Space.* Translated by
            D. Nicholson-Smith. Cambridge: Basil
            Blackwell.

Le Goff, Jacques
1980   The Symbolic Ritual of Vassalage. In *Time,
            Work, and Culture in the Middle Ages,*
            translated by Arthur Goldhammer, pp.
            237–287. Chicago: University of Chicago
            Press.

Lehner, Mark
1992   Excavations on the Giza Plateau, 1989–91.
            Paper presented at the 57th Annual Meet-
            ing of the Society for American Archaeol-
            ogy, Pittsburgh.

Leonard, Robert D., and George T. Jones
1987   Elements of an Inclusive Evolutionary
            Model for Archaeology. *Journal of Anthro-
            pological Research* 6:199–219.

Leonardi, Giovanni
1988   New Problems of Surface Archaeology:
            Sampling in HR East Area of Moenjodaro
            (Pakistan). In *Interim Reports,* Vol. 3:
            *Reports on Field Work Carried Out at
            Mohenjo-Daro, Pakistan, 1983–86, by
            IsMEO-Aachen-University Mission,* edited
            by Michael Jansen and Maurizio Tosi, pp.
            7–70. Aachen: IsMEO/RWTH.

Levy, Thomas E.
1993a   Production and Social Change in the South-
            ern Levant. In *Spatial Boundaries and So-
            cial Dynamics: Case Studies from Agrarian
            Societies,* edited by A. F. C. Holl and
            Thomas E. Levy, pp. 63–82. Ann Arbor:
            International Monographs in Prehistory.
1993b   Regional Interaction in the Southern Le-
            vant. Paper presented at the 58th Annual
            Meeting of the Society for American Ar-
            chaeology, St. Louis.

Lewenstein, Susan, and Bruce Dahlin
1990   The Albion Island Transect Survey: Coming
            to Terms with the Belizean Second Growth.

In *Ancient Maya Wetland Agriculture: Ex-
            cavations on Albion Island, Northern Be-
            lize,* edited by Mary Pohl, pp. 339–356.
            Boulder: Westview Press.

Lewontin, Richard C.
1979   Sociobiology as an Adaptationist Program.
            Behavioral Science 24:5–14.

Li Chi, Liang Ssu-yung, Tung Tso-pin, Fu Ssu-nien,
Lin Chin-ting, Kuo Pao-chiin, and Lin Yü-hsia
1956   *Ch'eng-tzu-yai: The Black Pottery Culture
            Site at Lung-shan-chen in Li-ch'eng-hsien,
            Shantung Province.* Translated by Kenneth
            Starr. New Haven: Yale University Publica-
            tions in Anthropology No. 52.

Li Xiandeng
1984   Wangchenggang yizhi chutu de tongqi can-
            pian ji qita. [Fragments of Bronze Vessels
            and Other Items Excavated from the Ruins
            of Wang chenggang.] *Wenwu* 11:73–75.

Lin Yun
1986   Guanyu Zhongguo zaoqi guojia xingshi de
            jige wenti. [A Few Questions concerning
            the Form of the Early Chinese State.] *Jilin
            daxue shehui kexuebao* 6:1–12.

Link, Stefan
1991   *Landverteilung und sozialer Frieden im
            archaischen Griechenland.* Stuttgart: His-
            toria Einzelschrift 69.

Linné, Sigvald
1948   *El valle y la ciudad de México en 1550.*
            Publication No. 9, n. s. Stockholm: The Eth-
            nographical Museum of Sweden.

Lintott, Andrew
1982   *Violence, Civil Strife, and Revolution in the
            Classical City.* Baltimore: Johns Hopkins
            University Press.

Lipinski, Edward, ed.
1987   *Phoenicia and the East Mediterranean in
            the First Millennium* B.C. Leuven: Peeters,
            Studia Phoenicia 5.

Liu Li
1994   Development of Chiefdom Societies in the
            Middle and Lower Yellow River Valley in
            Neolithic China: A Study of the Longshan
            Culture from the Perspective of Settlement
            Patterns. Unpublished Ph.D. dissertation,
            Department of Anthropology, Harvard Uni-
            versity, Cambridge.

Liverani, Mario
1990   *Prestige and Interest: International Rela-*

tions in the Near East, ca. 1600–1000 B. C. History of the Ancient Near East, Studies, Vol. 1. Padua: Sargon sri.

Lloyd, Peter C.
1954   The Traditional Political System of the Yoruba. *Southwestern Journal of Anthropology* 10:366–384.
1971   *The Political Development of Yoruba Kingdoms in the Eighteenth and Nineteenth Centuries.* London: Royal Anthropological Institute.

Lockhart, James
1991   *Nahuas and Spaniards: Postconquest Central Mexican History and Philology.* Nahuatl Studies Series 3. Stanford: Stanford University Press and UCLA Latin American Center.
1992   *The Nahuas after the Conquest.* Stanford: Stanford University Press.

López Austín, Alfredo
1973   *Hombre-Dios: Religión y política en el mundo Náhuatl.* México, D.F.: Instituto de Investigaciones Históricas, Universidad Nacional Autónoma de México.

Loraux, Nicole
1991   Reflections of the Greek City on Unity and Division. In *City-States in Classical Antiquity and Medieval Italy,* edited by Anthony Molho, Kurt Raaflaub, and Julia Emlen, pp. 33–51. Ann Arbor: University of Michigan Press.
1993   *The Children of Athena.* Translated by Caroline Levine. Princeton: Princeton University Press.

Ludden, David
1985   *Peasant History of South India.* Princeton: Princeton University Press.
1992   India's Development Regime. In *Colonialism and Culture,* edited by Nicholas B. Dirks, pp. 247–288. Ann Arbor: University of Michigan Press.

Ma Shizhi
1981   Guanyu Chunqiu Zhanguo cheng de tantao. [Inquiries regarding Cities of the Springs and Autumns and Warring States Periods.] *Kaogu yu Wenwu* 4:93–98.
1984   Shi Lun woguo gucheng xingzhi de jiben moshi. [A Preliminary Hypothesis of the Basic Pattern of the Shape of Ancient Chinese Cities.] *Zhongyuan wenwu* 4:59–65.
1987   Zai lun woguo gucheng xingzhi de jiben moshi—Du HeYunao xiansheng 'Du Ma Shizhi xiansheng wen yougan.' [Another Discussion of the Basic Pattern of the Shape of My Country's Ancient Cities—A Reaction to Reading Mr. He Yunao's "A Reaction to Reading Mr. Ma Shizhi's Article."] *Zhongyuan wenwu* 1:65–69.

MacDowell, Douglas
1986   *Spartan Law.* Edinburgh University Press, Edinburgh.

Mackay, Ernest J. H.
1938   *Further Excavations at Mohenjodaro.* New Delhi: Government of India.

MacKinnon, Carol
1989   *Toward a Feminist Theory of the State.* Cambridge: Harvard University Press.

Maier, Franz Georg
1985   Factoids in Ancient History: The Case of Fifth-Century Cyprus. *Journal of Hellenic Studies* 105:32–39.

Mainichi Shimbunsha Bunka Kikaku Kyoku Daiichi Bu [Mainichi Newspapers Cultural Planning Division, Tokyo Planning Section No. 1], ed.
1993   *Harukanaru Toji no Kaido Ten* [Exhibition: Distant Sea Routes of Ceramics]. Tokyo: Mainichi Shimbunsha.

Mair, Lucy
1977   *Primitive Government.* London: Scholar Press.

Maisels, Charles Keith
1987   Models of Social Evolution: Trajectories from the Neolithic to the State. *Man* 22:331–359.
1990   *The Emergence of Civilization.* London: Routledge.

Manzanilla, Linda
1995   La zona del Altiplano central en el Clásico. In *Historia Antigua de México. Volumen II El Horizonte Clásico,* edited by Linda Manzanilla and Leonardo López Luján, pp. 139–173. México, D.F.: Instituto Nacional de Antropología e Historia.

Marcus, Abraham
1989   *The Middle East on the Eve of Modernity: Aleppo in the Eighteenth Century.* New York: Columbia University Press.

Marcus, George E., and Michael M. J. Fischer
1986   *Anthropology as Cultural Critique: An Experimental Moment in the Human Sciences.* Chicago: University of Chicago Press.

Marcus, Joyce

1976   *Emblem and State in the Classic Maya Low-
        lands: An Epigraphic Approach to Territo-
        rial Organization.* Washington, D.C.:
        Dumbarton Oaks Research Library and
        Collection.

1983   On the Nature of the Mesoamerican City.
        In *Prehistoric Settlement Patterns: Essays
        in Honor of Gordon R. Willey,* edited by
        Evon Z. Vogt and Richard M. Leventhal,
        pp. 195–242. Albuquerque and Cambridge:
        University of New Mexico Press and Pea-
        body Museum of Archaeology and Ethnol-
        ogy, Harvard University.

1989   From Centralized Systems to City-States:
        Possible Models for the Epiclassic. In *Meso-
        america after the Decline of Teotihuacan,
        A.D. 700–900,* edited by Richard A. Diehl
        and Janet Catherine Berlo, pp. 201–208.
        Washington, D.C.: Dumbarton Oaks Re-
        search Library and Collection.

1992a   Political Fluctuations in Mesoamerica: Dy-
        namic Cycles of Mesoamerican States. *Na-
        tional Geographic Research & Exploration*
        8:392–411.

1992b   Royal Families, Royal Texts: Examples
        from the Zapotec and Maya. In *Mesoameri-
        can Elites: An Archaeological Assessment,*
        edited by Diane Z. Chase, and Arlen F.
        Chase, pp. 221–241. Norman: University
        of Oklahoma Press.

1992c   *Mesoamerican Writing Systems.* Princeton:
        Princeton University Press.

1993   Ancient Maya Political Organization. In
        *Lowland Maya Civilization in the Eighth
        Century A.D.,* edited by Jeremy A. Sabloff
        and John S. Henderson, pp. 111–184.
        Washington, D.C.: Dumbarton Oaks Re-
        search Library and Collection.

1995   Maya Hieroglyphs: History or Propaganda?
        In *Research Frontiers in Anthropology,* ed-
        ited by Carol Ember, Mark Ember, and Pe-
        ter Peregrine, pp. 1–24. Englewood Cliffs,
        NJ: Prentice Hall.

Marcus, Joyce and Kent V. Flannery

1996   *Zapotec Civilization: How Urban Society
        Evolved in Mexico's Oaxaca Valley.* New
        York: Thames and Hudson.

Marquina, Ignacio

1970   Pirámide de Cholula. In *Proyecto Cholula,*
        edited by Ignacio Marquina, pp. 31–46.
        Serie Investigaciones No. 19. México, D.F.:
        Instituto Nacional de Antropología e
        Historia.

Martin, Simon, and Nikolai Grube

1996   Maya Superstates. *Archaeology* 48:41–46.

Martines, Lauro

1979   *Power and Imagination: City-States in
        Renaissance Italy.* New York: Alfred A.
        Knopf.

Marx, Karl

1932 [1852]   *Capital and Other Writings.* New York:
              Modern Library.

Mastache, Alba Guadalupe, and Robert H. Cobean

1989   The Coyotlatelco Culture and the Origins
        of the Toltec State. In *Mesoamerica after
        the Decline of Teotihuacan, A.D. 700–900,*
        edited by Richard A. Diehl and Janet Cath-
        erine Berlo, pp. 49–67. Washington, D.C.:
        Dumbarton Oaks Research Library and
        Collection.

Matheny, Raymond

1986   Early States in the Maya Lowlands during
        the Late Preclassic Period: Edzna and Mira-
        dor. In *City-States of the Maya: Art and Ar-
        chitecture,* edited by Elizabeth Benson, pp.
        1–44. Denver: Rocky Mountain Institute
        for Pre-Columbian Studies.

Mathews, Peter

1985   Maya Early Classic Monuments and Inscrip-
        tions. In *A Consideration of the Maya
        Early Classic Period in the Maya Low-
        lands,* edited by Gordon R. Willey and Pe-
        ter Mathews, pp. 5–54. Institute for Meso-
        american Studies Pub. 10. Albany: State
        University of New York.

1991   Classic Maya Emblem Glyphs. In *Classic
        Maya Political History,* edited by T. Patrick
        Culbert, pp. 19–29. Norman: University of
        Oklahoma Press.

Mathews, Peter, and Gordon Willey

1991   Prehistoric Polities of the Pasion Region: Hi-
        eroglyphic Texts and Their Archaeological
        Settings. In *Classic Maya Political History,*
        edited by T. Patrick Culbert, pp. 30–72.
        Cambridge: Cambridge University Press.

Mathieu, Rémi

1987   Chamanes et chamanisme en Chine An-
        cienne. *L'Homme* 101 (28.1):10–34.

Matos Moctezuma, Eduardo

1988   *The Great Temple of the Aztecs.* New
        York: Thames and Hudson.

Matos Moctezuma, Eduardo, ed.

1974   *Proyecto Tula, 1a Parte.* Colección Científica 15. México, D.F.: Instituto Nacional de Antropología e Historia.

1976   *Proyecto Tula, 2a. Parte.* Colección Científica 33. México, D.F.: Instituto Nacional de Antropología e Historia.

Maudslay, Alfred P.
1974 [orig.   *Biologia Centrali-Americana: Archaeology,*
1889–1902]   Vol. V. New York: Milpatron Publishing.

Mazarakis-Ainian, Alexandros
1985   Contribution à l'étude de l'architecture grecque religieuse des âges obscurs. *L'Antiquité Classique* 54:5–54.

1987   From Ruler's Dwellings to Temples: A Study of the Origins of Greek Religious Architecture in the Protogeometric and Geometric Periods. Unpublished Ph.D. dissertation, University of London, London.

1988   Early Greek Temples: Their Origin and Function. In *Early Greek Cult Practice,* edited by Robin Hägg, Nanno Marinatos, and Gullog Nordquist, pp. 105–119. Stockholm: Skrifter Utgivna i Svenska Institutet i Athen.

McAnany, Patricia
1990   Economic Foundations of Prehistoric Maya Society: Paradigms and Concepts. In *Prehistoric Maya Economies of Belize,* edited by Patricia McAnany and Barry Isaac, pp. 347–372, Research in Economic Anthropology Supplement No. 4. Greenwich, CT: JAI Press.

1995   *Living with the Ancestors: Kinship and Kingship in Ancient Maya Society.* Austin: University of Texas Press.

McCafferty, Geoffrey G.
1996   Reinterpreting the Great Pyramid of Cholula, Mexico. *Ancient Mesoamerica* 7:1–17.

McClung de Tapia, Emily, and Judith Zurita Noguera
1994   Las primeras sociedaes sedentarias. In *Historia Antigua de México. Volumen I El México Antiguo, Sus áreas Culturales, los orígenes y el Horizonte Preclásico,* edited by Linda Manzanilla and Leonardo López Luján, pp. 209–246. México, D.F.: Instituto Nacional de Antropología e Historia.

McGuire, Randall
1983   Breaking Down Cultural Complexity: Inequality and Heterogeneity. *Advances in Archaeological Method and Theory* 6:91–142.

1992   *A Marxist Archaeology.* New York: Academic Press.

McGuire, Randall, and Robert Paynter, eds.
1991   *The Archaeology of Inequality.* Oxford: Blackwell.

McKillop, Heather
1989   Coastal Maya Trade: Obsidian Densities at Wild Cane Cay. In *Prehistoric Maya Economies of Belize,* edited by Patricia McAnany and Barry Isaac, pp. 17–56. Research in Economic Anthropology Supplement No. 4. Greenwich, CT: JAI Press.

McVicker, Donald, and Laurene Urquizo
1991   Report on the Aztec Presence at Tlacotepec. Unpublished manuscript, Department of Anthropology, North Central College, Napierville, IL.

Meadow, Richard H.
1991a   Faunal Remains and Urbanism at Harappa. In *Harappa Excavations, 1986–1990: A Multidisciplinary Approach to Third Millenium Urbanism,* edited by Richard H. Meadow, pp. 89–106. Monographs in World Archaeology No. 3. Madison: Prehistory Press.

1993   Animal Domestication in the Middle East: A Revised View from the Eastern Margin. In *Harappan Civilization: A Recent Perspective,* edited by Gregory. L. Possehl, pp. 295–320. New Delhi: Oxford and IBH.

Meadow, Richard H., ed.
1991b   *Harappa Excavations, 1986–1990: A Multidisciplinary Approach to Third Millenium Urbanism.* Monographs in World Archaeology No. 3. Madison: Prehistory Press.

Meadow, Richard H., and J. Mark Kenoyer
1994   Excavations at Harappa, 1993. In *South Asian Archaeology, 1993,* edited by Asko Parpola and Pasko Koskikallio. Helsinki: Suomalainen Tiedeakatemia.

Meiggs, Russell, and David M. Lewis
1969   *A Selection of Greek Historical Inscriptions.* Oxford: Clarendon Press.

van de Mieroop, Marc
1992   *Society and Enterprise in Old Babylonian Ur.* Berliner Beitraege zum Vorderen Orient 12. Berlin: Reimer Verlag.

Miller, Daniel
1985   Ideology and the Indus Civilization. *Journal of Anthropological Archaeology* 4:34–71.

1991   *Material Culture and Mass Consumption.* Oxford: Basil Blackwell.

Miller, Daniel, Michael Rowlands, and Christopher Tilley, eds.
1989   *Domination and Resistance.* London: Unwin Hyman.

Miller, Mary E.
1986   *The Murals of Bonampak.* Princeton: Princeton University Press.

Millet, Nicholas B.
1990   The Narmer Macehead and Related Objects. *Journal of the American Research Center in Egypt* 27:53–59.

Millett, Paul
1983   Maritime Loans and the Structure of Credit in Fourth-Century Athens. In *Trade in the Ancient Economy,* edited by Peter Garnsey, Keith Hopkins, and C. R. Whittaker, pp. 36–52. Berkeley: University of California Press.
1989   Patronage and Its Avoidance in Classical Athens. In *Patronage in Ancient Society,* edited by Andrew Wallace-Hadrill, pp. 15–48. London: Routledge.
1991   *Lending and Borrowing in Ancient Athens.* Cambridge: Cambridge University Press.

Millon, René
1973   *The Teotihuacan Map, Part 1: Text, Vol. 1, Urbanization at Teotihuacan, Mexico.* Austin: University of Texas Press.
1981   Teotihuacan: City, State, and Civilization. In *Handbook of Middle American Indians, Supplement, Vol. 1, Archaeology,* edited by Jeremy A. Sabloff, pp. 198–243. Austin: University of Texas Press.
1988   The Last Years of Teotihuacan Dominance. In *The Collapse of Ancient States and Civilizations,* edited by Norman Yoffee and George L. Cowgill, pp. 102–164. Tucson: University of Arizona Press.
1992   Teotihuacan Studies: From 1950 to 1990 and Beyond. In *Art, Ideology, and the City of Teotihuacan,* edited by Janet Catherine Berlo, pp. 339–429. Washington, D.C.: Dumbarton Oaks Research Library and Collection.

Millon, René, R. Bruce Drewitt, and James A. Bennyhoff
1965   The Pyramid of the Sun at Teotihuacan: 1959 Investigations. *Transactions of the American Philosophical Society* n.s. 55. Philadelphia.

Millon, René, R. Bruce Drewitt, and George L. Cowgill
1973   *The Teotihuacan Map, Part 2, Vol. 1, Urbanization at Teotihuacan, Mexico.* Austin: University of Texas Press.

Minc, Leah D., Mary G. Hodge, and M. James Blackman
1994   Stylistic and Spatial Variability in Early Aztec Ceramics: Insights into Pre-Imperial Exchange Systems. In *Economies and Polities in the Aztec Realm,* edited by Mary G. Hodge and Michael E. Smith, pp. 133–174. Albany: Institute for Mesoamerican Studies, State University of New York at Albany.

Misra, Virendra Nath
1984   Climate, A Factor in the Rise and Fall of the Indus Civilization: Evidence from Rajasthan and Beyond. In *Frontiers of the Indus Civilization,* edited by B. B. Lal and S. P. Gupta, pp. 461–490. New Delhi: Books and Books.

Molho, Anthony, Kurt Raaflaub, and Julia Emlen
1991a   Preface. In *City-States in Classical Antiquity and Medieval Italy,* edited by Anthony Molho, Kurt Raaflaub, and Julia Emlen, pp. 9–17. Ann Arbor: University of Michigan Press.

Molho, Anthony, Kurt Raaflaub, and Julia Emlen, eds.
1991b   *City States in Classical Antiquity and Medieval Italy.* Ann Arbor: University of Michigan Press.

Molina, Fray Alonso de
1970   *Vocabulario en Lengua Castellana y Mexicana y Mexicana y Castellana.* México, D.F.: Porrúa.

Molloy, John P., and William L. Rathje
1974   Sexploitation among the Maya. In *Mesoamerican Archaeology: New Approaches,* edited by Norman Hammond, pp. 431–444. Duckworth, London.

de Montmollin, Oliver
1989   *The Archaeology of Political Structure.* Cambridge: Cambridge University Press.

Morgan, Catherine
1990   *Athletes and Oracles: The Transformation of Olympia and Delphi in the Eighth Century B.C.* Cambridge: Cambridge University Press.
1991   Ethnicity and Early Greek States: Historical and Material Perspectives. *Proceedings of the Cambridge Philological Society* n.s. 37:131–163.

Morgan, Lewis H.
1877   *Ancient Society.* Cleveland: World Publishing Society.

Morley, Sylvanus G., and George W. Brainerd (revised by Robert Sharer)
1983   *The Ancient Maya.* Palo Alto: Stanford University Press.

Morris, Ian
1986   Gift and Commodity in Archaic Greece. *Man* 21:1–17.
1987   *Burial and Ancient Society: The Rise of the Greek City-State.* Cambridge: Cambridge University Press.
1989   Circulation, Deposition, and the Formation of the Greek Iron Age. *Man* 23:502–519.
1991   The Early Polis as City and State. In *City and Country in the Ancient World,* edited by Andrew Wallace-Hadrill, pp. 25–57. London: Routledge.
1992   *Death-Ritual and Social Structure in Classical Antiquity.* Cambridge: Cambridge University Press.
1993   The Origins of Pan-Hellenism. In *Greek Sanctuaries, New Approaches,* edited by Nanno Marinatosa and Robin Hägg, pp. 18–44. London: Routledge.
1994a   Archaeologies of Greece. In *Classical Greece: Ancient Histories and Modern Archaeologies,* edited by Ian Morris, pp. 8–47. Cambridge: Cambridge University Press.
1994b   The Athenian Economy: Twenty Years after *The Ancient Economy. Classical Philology* 89:351–366.
1996   The Strong Principle of Equality and the Archaic Origins of Greek Democracy. In *Demokratia: A Conversation about Democracies Ancient and Modern,* edited by Josiah Ober and Charles Hedrick, pp. 19–48. Princeton: Princeton University Press.
1997   The Art of Citizenship. In *New Light on a Dark Age: Exploring the Culture of Geometric Greece,* pp. 9–43. Columbia: University of Missouri Press.
in prep.   *Darkness and Heroes: Manhood, Equality, and Democracy in Iron Age Greece.* Oxford: Blackwell.

Moseley, Michael E.
1975   Chan Chan: Andean Alternative of the Preindustrial City. *Science* 187:219–225.
1992   *The Incas and Their Ancestors: The Archaeology of Peru.* London: Thames and Hudson.

Moseley, Michael E., and Kent C. Day
1977   *Chan Chan: Andean Desert City.* Albuquerque: University of New Mexico Press.

Mueller, Gerhard
1991   *Wohlwollen und Vertrauen: die Investiturgesandtschaft von Chen Kan im Jahr 1534 vor dem Hintergrund der Politischen und Wirtschaftlichen Beziehungen des Ming Reiches zu den Ryukyu Inseln Zwischen 1372 und 1535.* Heidelberg: Wurzburger Sinologische Schiften, Ed Forum.

Mughal, Mohammad Rafique
1990a   Further Evidence of the Early Harappan Culture in the Greater Indus Valley, 1971–90. *South Asian Studies* 6:175–200.
1990b   The Harappan 'Twin Capitals' and Reality. *Journal of Central Asia* 13:155–162.
1990c   The Protohistoric Settlement Patterns in the Cholistan Desert. In *South Asian Archaeology, 1987,* edited by Maurizio Taddei, pp. 143–156. Rome: IsMEO.
1991   The Harappan Settlement Systems and Patterns in the Greater Indus Valley (circa 3500–1500 B.C.). *Pakistan Archaeology* 25:1–72.
1992   The Geographical Extent of the Indus Civilization during the Early, Mature, and Late Harappan Times. In *South Asian Archaeology Studies,* edited by Gregory. L. Possehl, pp. 123–143. New Delhi: Oxford and IBH.

Muhly, James
1992   The Crisis Years in the Mediterranean World: Transition or Cultural Disintegration? In *The Crisis Years: The Twelfth Century B.C. from Beyond the Danube to the Tigris,* edited by William Ward and Martha Joukowsky, pp. 10–26. Dubuque, IA: Kendall Hunt.

Mukerji, Chandra
1983   *From Graven Images.* New York: Columbia University Press.

Mulhall, Stephen, and Adam Swift
1992   *Liberals and Communitarians.* Oxford: Blackwell.

Müller, Florencia Jacobs
1963   Exploración Arqueológica en Huapalcalco, Hgo. Quinta Temporada, 1959. *Anales de Antropología,* 6a XV:75–97.

Münch G., Guido
1976   *El cacicazgo de San Juan Teotihuacán durante la colonia, 1521–1821.* Colección Científica, No. 32. México, D.F.: Instituto Nacional de Antropología e Historia.

Murowchick, Robert, ed.
1994   *China: Ancient Culture, Modern Land.* Cradles of Civilization, Vol. 2. Norman: University of Oklahoma Press.

Murra, John V.
1975   *Formaciones económicas y políticas del mundo andino.* Lima: Instituto de Estudios Peruanos.

Musti, Domenico, ed.
1991   *La transizione dal miceneo all' alto arcaismo, dal palazzo alla città.* Rome: Consigli Nazionale di Ricerche.

Nagao, Debra
1989   Public Proclamation in the Art of Cacaxtla and Xochicalco. In *Mesoamerica after the Decline of Teotihuacan, A.D. 700–900,* edited by Richard A. Diehl and Janet Catherine Berlo, pp. 83–104. Washington, D.C.: Dumbarton Oaks Research Collection and Library.

Nakahara, Kotetsu
1984   Hokuzan (Nakijin) no Rekishi [The History of Hokuzan (Nakijin)]. *Chiiki to Bunka* 27:16–21.

Nassaney, Michael S.
1992   Communal Societies and the Emergence of Elites in the Prehistoric American Southeast. In *Lords of the Southeast: Social Inequality and the Native Elites of Southeastern North America,* edited by Alex W. Barker and Timothy R. Pauketat, pp. 111–143. Washington, D.C.: Archaeological Papers of the American Anthropological Association No 3.

Naumann, Ute
1976   *Subminoische und protogeometrische Bronzeplastik aus Kreta.* Mainz: Von Zabern.

Needham, Joseph
1959   *Science and Civilisation in China,* Vol. 3, Mathematics and the Sciences of the Heavens and Earth. Cambridge: Cambridge University Press.

Needham, Joseph, and Robin D. S. Yates
1994   *Science and Civilisation in China,* Vol. 5, Part 6. Cambridge: Cambridge University Press.

Neff, Hector, Michael Glascock, Donald McVicker, and Laurene Urquizo
1991   Aztec Colonial Presence at Tlacotepec in the Valley of Toluca, Mexico. Final Report on Neutron Activation Analysis. Missouri University Research Reactor, University of Missouri, Columbia.

Neff, Hector, and Mary G. Hodge
in press   Serving Vessel Production at Chalco: Evidence from Neutron Activation Analysis. In *Place of Jade: Society and Economy in Ancient Chalco,* edited by Mary G. Hodge. Department of Anthropology Memoirs in Latin American Archaeology. Pittsburgh: University of Pittsburgh.

Negbi, Ora
1992   Early Phoenician Presence in the Mediterranean Islands. *American Journal of Archaeology* 96:599–616.

Ng, Chin-keong
1971   The Fukienese Maritime Trade in the Second Half of the Ming Period: Government Policy and Elite Groups' Attitudes. *Nanyang University Journal, Vol. 5, Part II: Social Sciences and Humanities,* pp. 81–100.
1983   *Trade and Society: The Amoy Network on the China Coast, 1683–1735.* Singapore: Singapore University Press, National University of Singapore.

Nichols, Deborah L.
1980   Prehispanic Settlement and Land Use in the Northwestern Basin of Mexico, the Cuautitlan Region. Ph.D. dissertation, Department of Anthropology, Pennsylvania State University, University Park. Ann Arbor: University Microfilms.
1987   Risk and Agricultural Intensification during the Formative Period in the Northern Basin of Mexico. *American Anthropologist* 89:596–616.
1989   Reply to Feinman and Nicholas: There Is No Frost in the Basin of Mexico? *American Anthropologist* 91:1023–1026.
1994   The Organization of Provincial Craft Production and the Aztec City-State of Otumba. In *Economies and Polities in the Aztec Realm,* edited by Mary G. Hodge and Michael E. Smith, pp. 175–193. Albany: Institute for Mesoamerican Studies, State University of New York at Albany.
1996   An Overview of Regional Settlement Pattern Survey in Mesoamerica. In *Arqueología Mesoamericana: Homenaje a William T. Sanders,* 2 vols., edited by A. Guadalupe Mastache, Jeffrey R. Parsons, Mari Carmen Serre Puche, and Robert S. Santley, Vol. 1:59–96. México, D.F.: Insituto Nacional de Antropología e Historia.

Nichols, Deborah L., and Thomas H. Charlton
1988   Processes of State Formation: Core versus Periphery in the Late Postclassic Basin of Mexico. Paper presented at the 53rd Annual Meeting of the Society for American Archaeology, Phoenix.
1996   The Postclassic Occupation at Otumba: A Chronological Assessment. *Ancient Mesoamerica* 7:231–244.

Nicholson, Henry B.
1971   Prehispanic Mexican Historiography. In *Investigaciones Contemporáneas sobre Historia de México,* pp. 38–81. Memorias de la Tercera Reunión de Historiadores Mexicanos y Norteamericanos. Austin: University of Texas Press.
1975   Middle American Ethnohistory: An Overview. In *Handbook of Middle American Indians,* Vol. 15, edited by Howard F. Cline, pp. 487–505. Austin: University of Texas Press.
1978   Western Mexico: A.D. 900–1250. In *Chronologies in New World Archaeology,* edited by R. E. Taylor and Clement W. Meighan, pp. 285–329. New York: Academic Press.

Niederberger, Christine B.
1976   *Zohapilco, Cinco Milenios de Ocupación Humana en un Sitio Lacustre de la Cuenca de México.* Colección Científica No. 3. México, D.F.: Instituto Nacional de Antropología e Historia.
1979   Early Sedentary Economy in the Basin of Mexico. *Science* 203:131–142.
1987   *Paleopaysages et Archeologie Pre-Urbaine du Bassin de Mexico (Mexique),* 2 vols. Études Mésoaméricaines, Vol. XI. México, D.F.: Centre D'Études Mexicaines et Centraméricaines.

Nissen, Hans J.
1988   *The Early History of the Ancient Near East, 9000–2000 B.C.* Chicago: University of Chicago Press.

Nissen, Nils
1982   Die 'Tempelstadt': Regierungform der fruh-dynastischen Zeit in Babylonien? In *Gesellschaft un Kultur im alten Mespotamien,* edited by Horst Klengel, pp. 195–200. Berlin: Akademie Verlag.

Nivison, David
1989   The 'Question' Question. *Early China* 14:115–125.

Noguera, Eduardo
1935   *Tenayuca.* México, D.F.: Secretaría de Educación Pública, Departamento de Monumentos.

Norr, Lynette
1987   The Excavation of a Postclassic House at Tetla. In *Ancient Chalcatcingo,* edited by David C. Grove, pp. 400–408. Austin: University of Texas Press.

Nowicki, Kreysztof
1987   The History and Setting of the Town at Karphi. *Studi Micenei ed Egeo-Anatolici* 26:235–256.

Ober, Josiah
1989   *Mass and Elite in Democratic Athens: Rhetoric, Ideology, and the Power of the People.* Princeton: Princeton University Press.
1991   Aristotle's Political Sociology: Class, Status, and Order in the *Politics.* In *Essays on the Foundations of Aristotelian Political Science,* edited by Carnes Lord and David O'Connor, pp. 112–135. Berkeley: University of California Press.
1996   *The Athenian Revolution. Essays on Ancient Greek Democracy and Political Theory.* Princeton: Princeton University Press.
in press   *The Athenian Critics of Popular Rule.* Princeton: Princeton University Press.

O'Connor, David
1989   New Funerary Enclosures (*talbezirke*) of the Early Dynastic Period at Abydos. *Journal of the American Research Center in Egypt* 26:51–86.

Offner, Jerome A.
1979   A Reassessment of the Extent and Structuring of the Empire of Techotlalatzin, Fourteenth-Century Ruler of Texcoco. *Ethnohistory* 26:231–242.
1983   *Law and Politics in Aztec Texcoco.* New York: Cambridge University Press.

Ojo, G. J. Afolabi
1966   *Yoruba Culture: A Geographical Analysis.* London: University of London Press.

Okinawa Kenritsu Hakubutsukan
1992   *Gusuku—Gusuku ni Katarasetai Chiiki no Rekishi* [Gusuku: The Local History Which the Castles Tell]. Naha: Okinawa Kenritsu Hakubutsukan.

O'Neill, George C.
1962   Postclassic Ceramic Stratigraphy at Chalco in the Valley of Mexico. Unpublished Ph.D. dissertation, Department of Anthropology, Columbia University, New York.

ONERN (Oficina Nacional de Evaluación de Recursos Naturales)

1972a   *Inventario, evaluación y uso racional de los recursos naturales de la costa: cuencas de los Ríos Casma, Culebras y Huarmey.* 3 vols. Lima: ONERN.

1972b   *Inventario, evaluación y uso racional de los recursos naturales de la costa: cuencas de los Ríos Santa, Lacramarca y Nepeña.* 3 vols. Lima: ONERN.

1973   *Inventario, evaluación y uso racional de los recursos naturales de la costa: cuencas de los Ríos Virú y Chao.* 2 vols. Lima: ONERN.

Oppenheim, A. Leo
1964   *Ancient Mesopotamia: A Portrait of a Dead Civilization.* Chicago: University of Chicago Press.

Oren, Eliezer D.
1989   Early Bronze Age Settlement in Northern Sinai: A Model for Egypto-Canaanite Interconnections. In *L'Urbanisation de la Palestine a l'age du Bronze Ancien: Bilan et Perspectives des Recherches Actuelles: Actes du Colloque d'Emmaus,* edited by Pierre de Miroschedji, pp. 389–405. Oxford: B.A.R. International Series 527.

Osborne, Michael J.
1983   *Naturalization in Athens III/IV.* Brussels: AWLSK.

Osborne, Robin
1985   Buildings and Residence on the Land in Classical and Hellenistic Greece. *Annual of the British School at Athens* 80:119–128.

1987   *Classical Landscape with Figures.* London: George Philips.

1988   Social and Economic Implications of the Leasing of Land and Property in Classical and Hellenistic Greece. *Chiron* 18:279–323.

1991   Pride and Prejudice, Sense and Subsistence: Exchange and Society in the Greek City. In *City and Country in the Ancient World,* edited by John Rich and Andrew Wallace-Hadrill, pp. 119–46. London: Routledge.

1992   Is It a Farm? The Definition of Agricultural Sites and Settlements in Ancient Greece. In *Agriculture in Ancient Greece,* edited by Berit Wells, pp. 21–27. Stockholm: Skrifter Utgivna i Svenska Institutet i Athen.

Oshiro, Kei
1983   Okinawa ni Okeru Tetsu Kanren Iseki to Tekki Shiryo ni Tsuite-Gusuku seki Shutsudo no Shiryo o Chushin to Shite [Okinawan Sites with Iron Artifacts—In Particular, Materials concerning *Gusuku* (Castle) Sites]. *Nanto Koko* 8:5–18.

Otis Charlton, Cynthia
1994   Plebeians and Patricians: Contrasting Patterns of Production and Distribution in the Aztec Figurine and Lapidary Industries. In *Economies and Polities in the Aztec Realm,* edited by Mary G. Hodge and Michael E. Smith, pp. 195–220. Albany: Institute for Mesoamerican Studies, State University of New York at Albany.

Otis Charlton, Cynthia, Thomas H. Charlton, and Deborah L. Nichols
1993   Aztec Household-Based Craft Production: Archaeological Evidence from the City-State of Otumba, Mexico. In *Prehispanic Domestic Units in Western Mesoamerica: Studies of the Household, Compound, and Residence,* edited by Robert S. Santley and Kenneth G. Hirth, pp. 147–171. Boca Raton: CRC Press.

Owens, E. J.
1991   *The City in the Greek and Roman World.* London: Routledge.

Parrot, André
1958   *Mission archéologique de Mari II: Le Palais: Architecture.* Institut Français d'Archéologie de Beyrouth, Bibliothèque et historique LXVIII. Paris: Paul Guethner.

Parsons, Jeffrey R.
1966   The Ceramic Sequence in the Teotihuacan Valley, Mexico. Ph.D. dissertation, Department of Anthropology, University of Michigan. Ann Arbor: University Microfilms.

1970   An Archaeological Evaluation of the Codice Xolotl. *American Antiquity* 35:431–440.

1971   *Prehistoric Settlement Patterns in the Texcoco Region, Mexico.* Museum of Anthropology Memoir No. 3. Ann Arbor: University of Michigan.

1974   The Development of a Prehistoric Complex Society: A Regional Perspective from the Valley of Mexico. *Journal of Field Archaeology* 1:81–108.

1976   The Role of Chinampa Agriculture in the Food Supply of Aztec Tenochtitlan. In *Cultural Change and Continuity: Essays in Honor of James Bennett Griffin,* edited by Charles E. Cleland, pp. 233–257. New York: Academic Press.

1989   Arqueología Regional en la Cuenca de México: Una Estrategia para la Investigación Futura. *Anales de Antropología* 26:157–257.

1990   Critical Reflection on a Decade of Full-Coverage Regional Survey on the Valley of Mexico. In *The Archaeology of Regions: A Case for Full-Coverage Survey,* edited by Suzanne K. Fish and Stephen A. Kowalewski, pp. 7–32. Washington, D.C.: Smithsonian Institution Press.

Parsons, Jeffrey R., Elizabeth Brumfiel, and Mary Hodge

1996   Earlier Dates for Early Aztec in the Basin of Mexico. *Ancient Mesoamerica* 7:217–230.

Parsons, Jeffrey R., Elizabeth Brumfiel, Mary H. Parsons, and David J. Wilson

1982   *Prehispanic Settlement Patterns in the Southern Valley of Mexico: The Chalco-Xochimilco Region.* Museum of Anthropology Memoir No. 14. University of Michigan, Ann Arbor.

Parsons, Jeffrey R., Keith W. Kintigh, and Susan A. Gregg

1983   *Archaeological Settlement Pattern Data from the Chalco, Xochimilco, Ixtapalapa, Texcoco, and Zumpango Regions, Mexico.* Research Reports in Archaeology, Contribution No. 9, Technical Reports No. 14. Museum of Anthropology, University of Michigan, Ann Arbor.

Parsons, Jeffrey R., Mary H. Parsons, Virginia Popper, and Mary Taft

1985   Chinampa Agriculture and Aztec Urbanization in the Valley of Mexico. In *Prehistoric Intensive Agriculture in the Tropics,* edited by I. S. Farrington, pp. 49–96. Oxford: B.A.R. International Series 232.

del Paso y Troncoso, Francisco, ed.

1905–1906   *Papeles de Nueva España.* Segunda Serie, Geografía y Estadística, 7 vols. Madrid: Sucesores de Rivadeneyra.

1912   *Códice Kingsborough. Memorial de los Indios de Tepetlaoztoc.* Madrid: Hauser y Menet.

Patterson, Orlando

1982   *Slavery and Social Death.* Cambridge: Harvard University Press.

Patterson, Thomas

1986   Ideology, Class Formation, and Resistance in the Inca State. *Critique of Anthropology* 6:75–85.

1991   *The Inca Empire: The Formation and Disintegration of a Pre-Capitalist State.* New York: Berg.

Patterson, Thomas C., and Christine W. Gailey, eds.

1987   *Power Relations and State Formation.* Washington, D.C.: Archaeology Section, American Anthropological Association.

Paynter, Robert

1989   The Archaeology of Equality and Inequality. *Annual Review of Anthropology* 18:369–399.

Paynter, Robert, and Randall McGuire

1991   The Archaeology of Inequality: Material Culture, Domination, and Resistance. In *The Archaeology of Inequality,* edited by Randall McGuire and Robert Paynter, pp. 1–27. Oxford: Blackwell.

Pearson, Richard

1990   Chiefly Exchange between Kyushu and Okinawa, Japan, in the Yayoi Period. *Antiquity* 64:912–922.

1992   *Ancient Japan.* Washington and New York: Arthur Sackler Gallery and George Braziller.

Peebles, Christopher S., and Susan M. Kus

1977   Some Archaeological Correlates of Ranked Societies. *American Antiquity* 42:421–448.

Pei Mingxiang

1991   Zhengzhou Shangdai wangcheng de buju ji qi wenhua neihan. [The Layout of the Royal City of the Shang Dynasty at Zhengzhou and Its Cultural Signficance.] *Zhongyuan wenwu* 1:265–302.

Peirce, Neal R.

1993   *Citistates: How Urban America Can Prosper in a Competitive World.* Washington, D.C.: Seven Locks Press.

Pendergast, David M.

1992   *Noblesse Oblige:* The Elites of Altun Ha and Lamanai, Belize. In *Mesoamerican Elites: An Archaeological Assessment,* edited by Diane Z. Chase and Arlen F. Chase, pp. 61–79. Norman: University of Oklahoma Press.

Peng Bangjiong

1982   Buci 'Zuoyi' lice. [The Scope of the Term 'Create a Town' in the Oracle Inscriptions.] In *Jiagu tanshilu,* edited by Hu Houxuan, pp. 265–302. Beijing: Sanlian shudian.

Perlman, Paula

1992   One Hundred-Citied Crete and the 'Cretan *politeia.*' *Classical Philology* 87:193–205.

Peters, Heather A.

1983   The Role of the State of Chu in Eastern

Zhou Period China: A Study of Interaction and Exchange in the South. Unpublished Ph.D. dissertation, Yale University, New Haven.

Petrie, William M. F.
1900   *The Royal Tombs of the First Dynasty, Part 1.* Egypt Exploration Fund Memoir 18. London.

Phelps Brown, Henry
1988   *Egalitarianism and the Generation of Inequality.* Oxford: Oxford University Press.

Piggott, Stuart
1952   *Prehistoric India.* Baltimore: Penguin Books.

Piña Chan, Román
1975   *Teotenango: El Lugar de la Muralla.* Toluca: Dirección de Turismo, Gobierno del Estado de México.

Pleket, Henry W.
1975   Games Prizes, Athletes, and Ideology. *Stadion* 1:49–89.

Plutarch
1932   *The Lives of the Noble Grecians and Romans.* Translated by John Dryden, revised by Arthur Clough. New York: Modern Library.

Pohl, Mary D.
1991   Review of *Canal Irrigation in Prehistoric Mexico* by William E. Doolittle. *American Antiquity* 56:738–739.
1994   The Economics and Politics of Maya Meat Eating. In *The Economic Anthropology of the State,* edited by Elizabeth M. Brumfiel, pp. 119–148. Monographs in Economic Anthropology No. 11. Lanham, MD: University Press of America.

Pohl, Mary D., ed.
1990   *Ancient Maya Wetland Agriculture: Excavations on Albion Island, Northern Belize.* Boulder: Westview Press.

Pokora, Timoteus
1978   China. In *The Early State,* edited by Henri J. M. Claessen and Peter Skalník, pp. 191–212. The Hague: Mouton.

de Polignac, François
1995   *Cults, Territory, and the Origins of the Greek City-State.* Translated by Janet Lloyd. Chicago: University of Chicago Press.

Pollock, Susan
1992   Bureaucrats and Managers: Peasants and

Pastoralists, Imperialists and Traders: Research on the Uruk and Jemdet Nasr Periods in Mesopotamia. *Journal of World Prehistory* 6:297–336.

Porten, Bezalel, and Ada Yardeni
1993   *Textbook of Aramaic Documents from Ancient Egypt,* (2 vols.). Jerusalem: The Hebrew University; Winona Lake: Eisenbrauns.

Possehl, Gregory L.
1990   Revolution in the Urban Revolution: The Emergence of Indus Urbanism. *Annual Review of Anthropology* 19:281–282.

Postgate, Nicholas
1990   Excavations at Abu Salabikh, 1988–89. *Iraq* 52:95–106.
1992   *Early Mesopotamia.* New York: Routledge.

Pounds, Norman J. G.
1969   The Urbanization of the Classical World. *Annals of the Association of American Geographers* 59:135–157.

Powell, Marvin
1985   Salt, Seed, and Yields in Sumerian Agriculture: A Critique of the Theory of Progressive Salinization. *Zeitschift für Assyriologie* 75:7–38.

Poyck, Augustus P. G.
1962   Farm Studies in Iraq. *Mededelingen van de Landbouwhogeschool te Wageningen* 62, Nederland.

Pozorski, Shelia, and Thomas Pozorski
1987   *Early Settlement and Subsistence in the Casma Valley, Peru.* Iowa City: University of Iowa Press.
1994   Early Andean Cities. *Scientific American* 270:6 (June):66–72.

Pracchia, Stephano, Maurizio Tosi, and Massimo Vidale
1985   On the Type, Distribution, and Extent of Craft Industries at Mohenjo-daro. In *South Asian Archaeology, 1983,* edited by Janine Shotsmans and Maurizio Taddei, pp. 207–247. Naples: Istituto Universitario Orientale.

Preucel, Robert W., ed.
1992   *Processual and Postprocessual Archaeologies.* Center for Archaeological Investigations, Occasional Paper No. 10. Carbondale: Southern Illinois University.

Price, Barbara J.
1977   Shifts in Production and Organization: A

Cluster Interaction Approach. *Current Anthropology* 18:209–233.

Proulx, Donald A.
1973   *Archaeological Investigations in the Nepeña Valley, Peru.* Research Report No. 13, Department of Anthropology, University of Massachusetts, Amherst.

Puleston, Dennis E.
1977   The Art and Archeology of Hydraulic Agriculture in the Maya Lowlands. In *Social Process in Maya Prehistory,* edited by Norman Hammond, pp. 449–479. New York: Academic Press.
1978   Terracing, Raised Fields, and Tree Cropping in the Maya Lowlands: A New Perspective on the Geography of Power. In *Prehispanic Maya Agriculture,* edited by Peter D. Harrison and B. L. Turner, II, pp. 225–246. Albuquerque: University of New Mexico Press.

Pyburn, K. Anne
1988   The Settlement of Nohmul: Development of a Prehistoric Maya Community in Northern Belize. Unpublished Ph.D. dissertation, Department of Anthropology, University of Arizona, Tucson.
1989   *Prehistoric Maya Community and Settlement at Nohmul, Belize.* Oxford: B.A.R. International Series 509.
1990a   Nohmul Demography, A Report on Four Excavation Seasons. In *Pre-Columbian Population History in the Maya Lowlands,* edited by T. Patrick Culbert and Don S. Rice, pp. 183–197. Albuquerque: University of New Mexico Press.
1990b   Report on the 1990 Archaeological Field Season on Albion, Island, Northern Belize. Paper presented at the 57th Annual Meeting of the American Anthropological Association, New Orleans.
1991a   Chau Hiix: A New Archaeological Site in Northern Belize. *Mexicon* 8:84–86.
1991b   Prehispanic Maya States: The Evidence for Absence? Paper presented at the 1991 Annual Meeting of the Society for Economic Anthropology, Bloomington, Indiana.
1992   The Archaeologist and the Sacred Text: Political Consciousness and the Direct Historic Approach. Paper presented at the 57th Annual Meeting of the Society for American Archaeology, Pittsburgh.
1993   Policies from High Places: New Perspectives on the Maya Collapse. Paper presented

at the Annual Meeting of the Society for Economic Anthropology, New Hampshire.
1994   The Origin of Ancient Maya Pottery: Specialist Products and Specialist Production. In *Terre Cuite Société Maya: La Céramique, Document Technique, Économique, Cultural.* XIVe Recontres Internationales d'Archeologie et d'Histoire d'Antibes. Juan-les-Pins, France: Édicions APDCA.
1996   The Political Economy of Ancient Maya Land Use: The Road to Ruin. In *The Managed Mosaic: Ancient Maya Agriculture and Resource Use,* edited by Scott Fedick, pp. 236–247. Salt Lake City: University of Utah Press.

Qi Wenxin
1991–92 An Inquiry into the Original Meaning of the Chinese Character for King *(wang). Chinese Studies in History: A Journal of Translations* 25.2:3–16.

Qiu Xigui
1989   An Examination of Whether the Changes in Shang Oracle-Bone Inscriptions are Questions. *Early China* 14:77–114.

Quaglioni, Diego
1991   The Legal Definition of Citizenship in the Late Middle Ages. In *City-States in Classical Antiquity and Medieval Italy,* edited by Anthony Molho, Kurt Raaflaub, and Julia Emlen, pp. 155–168. Ann Arbor: University of Michigan Press.

Quanzhou Songdai Haichuan Fajue Baogao Banxiezu [Excavation Report Compilation Committee for the Song Dynasty Sunken Ship in Quanzhou]
1975   Quanzhouwan Songdai Haichuan Fajue Jianbao [Brief Report on the Excavation of the Song Dynasty Sunken Ship in Quanzhou Bay]. *Wen Wu* 10:1–10.

Quiller, B.
1981   The Dynamics of the Homeric Society. *Symbolae Osloenses* 56:109–155.

Quirke, Stephen
1990   *The Administration of Egypt in the Late Middle Kingdom: The Hieratic Documents.* New Malden: Sia.
1992   *Ancient Egyptian Religion.* London: British Museum Press.

Raaflaub, Kurt
1991   City-State, Territory, and Empire in Classical Antiquity. In *City-States in Classical Antiquity and Medieval Italy,* edited by Anthony Molho, Kurt Raaflaub, and Julia

Emlen, pp. 565–588. Ann Arbor: University of Michigan Press.

Radin, Paul, ed.
1920   Mapa Quinatzin. In *Sources and Authenticity of the History of the Ancient Mexicans*, pp. 38–41. University of California Publications in American Archaeology and Ethnology 17(1):1–150.

Rae, Donald
1981   *Equalities*. Cambridge: Harvard University Press.

Ragaranjan, L. N.
1992 [1987]   *Kautilya: The Arthashastra*. New Delhi: Penguin Books.

Raikes, Robert L., and Robert H. Dyson
1961   The Prehistoric Climate of Baluchistan and the Indus Valley. *American Anthropologist* 63:265–281.

Ramachandran, R.
1989   *Urbanization and Urban Systems in India*. Delhi: Oxford University Press.

Rappaport, Roy A.
1968   *Pigs for the Ancestors*. New Haven: Yale University Press.
1971   The Sacred in Human Evolution. *Annual Review of Ecology and Systematics* 2:23–44.
1979   *Ecology, Meaning, and Religion*. Richmond, CA: North Atlantic Books, Richmond.

Rathje, William L.
1970   Socio-Political Implications of Lowland Maya Burials: Methodology and Tentative Hypotheses. *World Archaeology* 1:359–374.
1971   The Origin and Development of Lowland Classic Maya Civilization. *American Antiquity* 36:275–285.
1972   Praise the Gods and Pass the Metates: A Hypothesis of the Development of Lowland Rainforest Civilizations in Mesoamerica. In *Contemporary Archaeology*, edited by Mark P. Leone, pp. 365–392. Carbondale: Southern Illinois University Press.
1975   The Last Tango in Mayapan: A Tentative Trajectory of Production Distribution Systems. In *Ancient Civilization and Trade,* edited by Jeremy A. Sabloff and C. C. Lamberg-Karlovsky, pp. 409–448. Albuquerque: University of New Mexico Press.
1977   The Tikal Connection. In *The Origins of*

Maya Civilization, edited by Richard E. W. Adams, pp. 373–382. Albuquerque: University of New Mexico Press.

Rattray, Evelyn C.
1991   Fechamientos por Radiocarbono en Teotihuacán. *Arqueología, Segunda época* 6:3–18.

Redding, Richard W.
1992   Egyptian Old Kingdom Patterns of Animal Use and the Value of Faunal Data in Modeling Socioeconomic Systems. *Paleorient* 18:99–107.

Reddy, Seetha N.
1991   Complementary Approaches to Late Harappan Subsistence: An Example from Oriyo Timbo. In *Harappa Excavations, 1986–1990: A Multidisciplinary Approach to Third Millenium Urbanism,* edited by Richard H. Meadow, pp. 127–136. Madison: Prehistory Press.

Redford, Donald B.
1989   Prolegomena to Archaeological Investigations of Mendes. Manuscript on file with the author, Seattle.
1992   *Egypt, Canaan, and Israel in Ancient Times*. Princeton: Princeton University Press.

Rehak, Paul, ed.
1995   *The Role of the Ruler in the Prehistoric Aegean*. Liège: Aegaeum 7.

Renfrew, Colin
1975   Trade as Action at a Distance: Questions of Integration and Communication. In *Ancient Civilizations and Trade*, edited by Jeremy A. Sabloff and C. C. Lamberg-Karlovsky, pp. 3–60. Albuquerque: University of New Mexico Press.
1982   Polity and Power: Interaction, Intensification, and Exploitation. In *An Island Polity: The Archaeology of Exploitation in Melos*, edited by Colin Renfrew and Malcom Wagstaff, pp. 64–90. Cambridge: Cambridge University Press.
1984   *Approaches to Social Archaeology*. Edinburgh: Edinburgh University Press.
1986a   Introduction: Peer Polity Interaction and Sociopolitical Change. In *Peer Polity Interaction and Sociopolitical Change.*, edited by C. Renfrew, and John F. Cherry, pp. 1–18. Cambridge: Cambridge University Press.
1986b   Peer Polity Interaction and Socio-Political

Change. In *Interaction by Design: The Greek City State.* In *Peer Polity Interaction and Socio-political Change,* edited by Colin Renfrew and John F. Cherry, pp. 1–18. Cambridge: Cambridge University Press.

1989   Comments on Archaeology into the 1990s. *Norwegian Archaeological Review* 22:33–41.

Renfrew, Colin, and John F. Cherry, eds.
1986   *Peer Polity Interaction and Socio-political Change.* Cambridge: Cambridge University Press.

Reyes Cortés, Manuel, and Joaquín García Bárcena
1979   Estratificación en el Area de la Catedral. In *El Recinto Sagrado de México-Tenochtitlán, Excavaciones 1968–1969 y 1975–1976,* edited by Constanza Vega Sosa, pp. 17–28. México, D.F.: Instituto Nacional de Antropología e Historia.

Rice, Don S.
1986   The Peten Postclassic: A Settlement Perspective. In *Late Lowland Maya Civilization,* edited by Jeremy A. Sabloff and E. Wyllys Andrews, V, pp. 301–344. Albuquerque: University of New Mexico Press.

1993   Eighth-Century Physical Geography, Environment, and Natural Resources in the Maya Lowlands. In *Lowland Maya Civilization in the Eighth Century A.D.,* edited by Jeremy Sabloff and John Henderson, pp. 11–63. Washington, D.C.: Dumbarton Oaks Research Library and Collection.

Rice, Don S., and T. Patrick Culbert
1990   Historical Contexts for Population Reconstruction in the Maya Lowlands. In *Pre-Columbian Population History in the Maya Lowlands,* edited by T. Patrick Culbert and Don S. Rice, pp. 1–36. Cambridge: Cambridge University Press.

Rice, Don S., and Dennis Puleston
1981   Ancient Maya Settlement Patterns in the Peten, Guatemala. In *Lowland Maya Settlement Patterns,* edited by Wendy Ashmore, pp. 121–156. Albuquerque: University of New Mexico Press.

Rice, Don S., and Prudence M. Rice
1984   Lessons from the Maya. *Latin American Research Review* 19:7–34.

1990   Population Size and Population Change in the Central Peten Lakes Region: Guatemala. In *Precolumbian Population History of the Maya Lowlands,* edited by T. Patrick Culbert and Don S. Rice, pp. 123–148. Albuquerque: University of New Mexico Press.

Rice, Michael
1990   *Egypt's Making: The Origins of Ancient Egypt.* London: Routledge.

Rice, Prudence
1986   The Peten Postclassic: Perspectives from the Central Peten Lakes. In *Late Lowland Maya Civilization: Classic to Postclassic,* edited by Jeremy A. Sabloff and E. Wyllys Andrews, V, pp. 251–300. Albuquerque: University of New Mexico Press.

1987   Economic Change in the Lowland Maya Late Classic Period. In *Specialization, Exchange, and Complex Societies,* edited by Elizabeth Brumfiel and Timothy Earle, pp. 76–85. Cambridge: Cambridge University Press.

Rickett, W. Allyn, trans.
1985   *Guanzi: Political, Economic, and Philosophical Essays from Early China,* Vol. 1. Princeton: Princeton University Press.

Riese, Berthold
1989   The Inscription on the Sculptured Bench of the House of the Bacabs. In *The House of the Bacabs,* edited by David Webster, pp. 82–87. Washington, D.C.: Dumbarton Oaks Research Library and Collection.

Riesenberg, Peter
1992   *Citizenship in the Western Tradition.* Chapel Hill: University of North Carolina Press.

Rihll, T. E., and A. G. Wilson
1991   Modelling Settlement Structures in Ancient Greece: New Approaches to the Polis. In *City and Country in the Ancient World,* edited by John Rich and Andrew Wallace-Hadrill, pp. 58–95. London: Routledge.

Rindos, David
1984   *The Origins of Agriculture.* New York: Academic Press.

1985   Darwinian Selection, Symbolic Variation, and the Evolution of Culture. *Current Anthropology* 26:65–88.

Ringle, William M., and E. Wyllys Andrews, V
1990   The Demography of Komchen, an Early Maya Town. In *Precolumbian Population History in the Maya Lowlands,* edited by T. Patrick Culbert and Don Rice, pp. 215–244. Albuquerque: University of New Mexico Press.

Rissman, Paul C.
1989   The Organization of Seal Production in the Harappan Civilization. In *Old Problems and New Perspectives in the Archaeology of South Asia*, edited by J. Mark Kenoyer, pp. 159–170. Wisconsin Archaeological Reports No. 2. Department of Anthropology, University of Wisconsin, Madison.

Robb, John
1994   The Evolution of the State as Invention of Itself. Manuscript, Museum of Anthropology, University of Michigan, Ann Arbor.

Robertson, Robin A., and David Freidel, eds.
1986   *Archaeology at Cerros, Belize, Central America, Vol. 1: An Interim Report.* Dallas: Southern Methodist University Press.

de Rojas, José Luis
1986   *México Tenochtitlán: Economía e Sociedad en el Siglo XVI.* México, D.F.: Fondo de Cultura Económica.

Röllig, Wolfgang
1982   Die Phönizier des Mutterlandes zur Zeit der Kolonisierung. In *Phönizier im Westen*, edited by Hans Georg Niemeyer, pp. 15–30. (Madrider Beiträge 8) Mainz: Von Zabern.

Romano, Dennis
1987   *Patricians and Popolani: The Social Foundations of the Venetian Renaissance State.* Baltimore: Johns Hopkins University Press.

de Romilly, Jacqueline
1977   *The Rise and Fall of States according to Greek Authors.* Jerome Lectures 11. Ann Arbor: University of Michigan Press.

Roscoe, Paul B., and Robert B. Graber, eds.
1988   Circumscription and the Evolution of Society. *American Behavioral Scientist* 31:4.

Rosen, Ralph
1988   *Old Comedy and the Iambographic Tradition.* Atlanta: American Classical Studies 19.

Rounds, J.
1979   Lineage, Class, and Power in Aztec History. *American Ethnologist* 6:73–86.
1982   Dynastic Succession and the Centralization of Power in Tenochtitlan. In *The Inca and Aztec States, 1400–1800: Anthropology and History,* edited by George A. Collier, Renato I. Rosaldo, and John D. Wirth, pp. 63–89. New York: Academic Press.

Roux, Georges
1980   *Ancient Iraq.* New York: Penguin Books.

Rowe, John Howland
1965   The Renaissance Foundations of Anthropology. *American Anthropologist* 67:1–20.
1979   An Account of the Shrine of Ancient Cuzco. *Ñawpa Pacha* 5:59–76.

Roys, Robert
1943   *The Indian Background of Colonial Yucatan.* Carnegie Institution of Washington Publication 548.
1957   *The Political Geography of the Yucatan Maya.* Carnegie Institution of Washington Publication 613.

Rubin, Vitaly
1965   Tzu-ch'an and the City-state of Ancient China. *T'oung Pao* 52:8–34.
1976   *Individual and State in Ancient China.* New York: Columbia University Press.

Ruggles, Amy J.
1992   An Analysis of Late-Horizon Settlement Patterns in the Temascalapa-Teotihuacan Basins: The Creation of Idealized Settlement Patterns through Location-Allocation Models and GIS. Unpublished M.A. thesis, Department of Geography, University of California, Santa Barbara.

Runciman, Walter G.
1989   *A Treatise on Social Theory*, II. Cambridge: Cambridge University Press.
1990   Doomed to Extinction: The *Polis* as an Evolutionary Dead-End. In *The Greek City from Homer to Alexander,* edited by Oswyn Murray and Simon Price, pp. 347–367. Oxford: Oxford University Press.

Ruschenbusch, Eberhard
1978   *Untersuchungen zu Staat und Politik in Griechenland vom 7. bis 4. Jh. v. Chr.* Bamberg: Fotodruck Verlag.
1984a   Die Bevölkerungszahl Griechenlands im 5. und 4. Jh. v. Chr. *Zeitschrift für Papyrologie und Epigraphik* 56:55–57.
1984b   Modell Amorgos. In *Aux origines de l'hellénisme, la Crète et la Grèce. Hommage à Henri van Effenterre,* edited by Henri van Effenterre, pp. 265–271. Paris: Centre Gustave Glotz.
1985   Die Zahl der griechischen Staaten und Arealgrösse und Bürgerzahl der 'Normalpolis.' *Zeitschrift für Papyrologie und Epigraphik* 59:253–263.
1989   Zur Verfassungsgeschichte Griechenlands. In *Demokratie und Architektur,* edited by Wolfgang Schuller, Wolfram Hoepfner, and Ernst-Ludwig Schwandner, pp. 53–61. Munich: Deutscher Kunstverlag.

Russell, Bertrand

1993 [1901]   Is Position in Time and Space Absolute or Relative? In *Toward the "Principles of Mathematics" 1900–02. Collected Papers of Bertrand Russell,* Vol. 3, edited by Gregory H. Moore, pp. 259–282. London: Routledge.

Rutter, Jeremy

1990   Some Comments on Interpreting the Dark-Surfaced Handmade Burnished Pottery of the 13th and 12th Century B.C. Aegean. *Journal of Mediterranean Archaeology* 3:29–49.

1992   Cultural Innovations in the Post-Palatial Aegean. In *The Crisis Years: The Twelfth Century B.C. From Beyond the Danube to the Tigris,* edited by William Ward and Martha Joukowsky, pp. 61–78. Dubuque, IA: Kendall Hunt.

Ryukyu Shikki Jigyo Kyodo Kumiai

1991   *Ryukyu Shikki: Rekishi to Gijutsu, Giho* [Ryukyu Lacquer: History, Techniques, Methods]. Naha: Ryukyu Shikki Jogyo Kyodo Kumiai.

Sabloff, Jeremy A.

1975   *Excavations at Seibal, Department of the Peten, Guatemala: The Ceramics.* Memoirs of the Peabody Museum of Archaeology and Ethnology 13(2), Harvard University, Cambridge.

1990   *The New Archaeology and the Maya.* New York: Scientific American Library.

1996   Settlement Patterns and Community Organization in the Maya Lowlands. *Expedition* 38:3–13.

Sahagún, Bernardino de

1950–1982   *General History of the Things of New Spain,* 13 vols. Translated by Arthur J. O. Anderson and Charles E. Dibble. Santa Fe and Salt Lake City: School of American Research and the University of Utah Press.

Sahlins, Marshall

1972   *Stone Age Economics.* Chicago: University of Chicago Press.

1985   *Islands of History.* Chicago: University of Chicago Press.

Said, Edward

1978   *Orientalism.* 1st ed. New York: Pantheon Books.

Sakai, Robert

1968   The Ryukyu (Liu Ch'iu) Islands as a Fief of Satsuma. In *The Chinese World Order: Traditional China's Foreign Relations,* edited by John K. Fairbank, pp. 112–134. Cambridge: Harvard University Press.

Sakamaki, Shunzo

1963   *Ryukyu: A Bibliographical Guide to Okinawan Studies.* Honolulu: University of Hawaii Press.

1964   Ryukyu and Southeast Asia. *Journal of Asian Studies* xxiii:383–389.

Sakellariou, M. B.

1989   *The Polis-State Definition and Origin.* Research Centre for Greek and Roman Antiquity, National Hellenic Research Foundation, Athens.

Sakihara, Mitsugu

1987   *A Brief History of Okinawa Based on the Omoro Soshi.* Tokyo: Honpo Shoseki Press.

Salkever, Stephen

1986   Tragedy and the Education of the *Demos.* In *Greek Tragedy and Political Theory,* edited by Peter J. Euben, pp. 222–251. Berkeley: University of California Press.

Sallares, Robert

1991   *The Ecology of the Ancient Greek World.* London: Duckworth.

Salmon, Claudine, and Denys Lombard

1979   A Thirteenth Century Vessel Found with its Cargo in the Anchorage at Zaitun. *Research on Maritime Shipping and Traditional Networks in Southeast Asia.* Workshop Final Report No. 15, Southeast Asian Ministers of Education Organization Regional Centre for Archaeology and Fine Arts, Bangkok.

Sanders, William T.

1965   *The Cultural Ecology of the Teotihuacan Valley.* Department of Sociology and Anthropology, Pennsylvania State University, University Park.

1970   The Population of the Teotihuacan Valley, the Basin of Mexico, and the Central Mexican Symbiotic Region in the 16th Century. In *The Natural Environment, Contemporary Occupation, and 16th Century Population of the Valley,* edited by William T. Sanders, Anton Kovar, Thomas Charlton, and Richard A. Diehl. Occasional Papers in Anthropology No. 3. Department of Anthropology, Pennsylvania State University, University Park.

1981   Ecological Adaptation in the Basin of Mexico: 23,000 B.C. to the Present. In *Hand-*

book of Middle American Indians, Supplement 1, Archaeology, edited by Jeremy A. Sabloff, pp. 147–197. Austin: University of Texas Press.

1989   Household, Lineage, and State in Eighth-Century Copan, Honduras. In *The House of the Bacabs*, edited by David Webster, pp. 89–105. Studies in Pre-columbian Art and Archaeology No. 29. Washington, D.C.: Dumbarton Oaks Research Library and Collection.

1992   Ranking and Stratification in Prehispanic Mesoamerica. In *Mesoamerican Elites: An Archaeological Assessment*, edited by Diane Z. Chase and Arlen F. Chase, pp. 278–291. Norman: University of Oklahoma Press.

Sanders, William T., and Deborah L. Nichols

1988   The Valley of Oaxaca and Ecological Theory. *Current Anthropology* 29:33–80.

Sanders, William T., Jeffrey R. Parsons, and Robert S. Santley

1979   *The Basin of Mexico: Ecological Processes in the Evolution of a Civilization.* New York: Academic Press.

Sanders, William T., and Barbara J. Price

1968   *Mesoamerica: The Evolution of a Civilization.* New York: Random House.

Sanders, William T., and Robert S. Santley

1983   A Tale of Three Cities: Energetics and Urbanism in Prehispanic Central Mexico. In *Prehistoric Settlement Patterns: Essays in Honor of Gordon R. Willey*, edited by Evon Z. Vogt and Richard M. Leventhal, pp. 243–291. Albuquerque and Cambridge: University of New Mexico Press and Peabody Museum of Archaeology and Ethnology, Harvard University.

Sanders, William T., and David Webster

1978   Unilinealism, Multilinealism, and the Evolution of Complex Societies. In *Social Archeology: Beyond Subsistence and Dating*, edited by Charles L. Redman, Mary Jane Berman, Edward V. Curtin, Jr., William T. Langhorne, Nina M. Versaggi, and Jeffrey C. Wanser, pp. 249–302. New York: Academic Press.

1988   The Mesoamerican Urban Tradition. *American Anthropologist* 90:521–546.

1989   The Mesoamerican Urban Tradition: A Reply to Smith. *American Anthropologist* 91:460–461.

Sanders, William T., Michael West, Charles Fletcher, and Joseph Marino

1975   *The Formative Period Occupation of the Valley: Part 1, Texts and Tables.* Occasional Papers in Anthropology No. 10. Department of Anthropology, Pennsylvania State University, University Park.

Santley, Robert S.

1977   Intra-Site Settlement Patterns at Loma Torremote and Their Relationship to Formative Prehistory in the Cuautitlan Region, State of Mexico. Ph.D. dissertation, Department of Anthropology, Pennsylvania State University, University Park. Ann Arbor: University Microfilms.

1984   Obsidian Exchange, Economic Stratification, and the Evolution of Complex Society in the Basin of Mexico. In *Trade and Exchange in Early Mesoamerica*, edited by Kenneth G. Hirth, pp. 43–86. Albuquerque: University of New Mexico Press.

1986   Prehispanic Roadways, Transport Network Geometry, and Aztec Politico-Economic Organization in the Basin of Mexico. In *Economic Aspects of Prehispanic Highland Mexico*, edited by Barry L. Isaac, pp. 223–244. Research in Economic Anthropology, Supplement No. 2. Greenwich, CT: JAI Press.

1991   The Structure of the Aztec Transport Network. In *Ancient Road Networks and Settlement Hierarchies in the New World*, edited by Charles D. Trombold, pp. 198–210. Cambridge: Cambridge University Press.

1993   Late Formative Period Society at Loma Torremote: A Consideration of the Redistribution vs. the Great Provider Models as a Basis for the Emergence of Complexity in the Basin of Mexico. In *Prehispanic Domestic Units in Western Mesoamerica: Studies of the Household, Compound, and Residence*, edited by Robert S. Santley and Kenneth G. Hirth, pp. 67–86. Boca Raton: CRC Press.

Santley, Robert S., and Rani T. Alexander

1992   The Political Economy of Core Periphery Systems. In *Resources, Power, and Interregional Interaction*, edited by Edward M. Schortman and Patricia Urban, pp. 23–50. New York: Plenum Press.

Sarmiento, Griselda

1994   La Creación de los primeros centros de poder. In *Historia Antigua de México. Volumen I El México Antiguo, Sus áreas Cul-*

turales, los orígenes y el Horizonte Preclásico, edited by Linda Manzanilla and Leonardo López Luán, pp. 247–277. México, D.F.: Instituto Nacional de Antropología e Historia.

Saucedo, Eric D.
1994   Identifying City-State Polities in the Southern and Eastern Basin of Mexico: A Central Place Analysis of Aztec Settlement Types. Unpublished M.A. thesis, Department of Anthropology, University of Iowa, Iowa City.

Sasaki, Komei
1991   Nihon no Rekishi Tanjo [The Birth of Japanese History]. *Nihon no Rekishi* [History of Japan], Vol. 1. Tokyo: Shueisha.

Sauvaget, Jean
1941   *Alep.* Bibliothèque archéologique et historique 36. Paris: Paul Guethner.

Schaedel, Richard P.
1972   The City and the Origin of the State in America. *Actas y memorias, XXXIX Congreso Internacional de Americanistas,* 1970, Vol. 2:15–33. Lima.

Schaps, David
1979   *Economic Rights of Women in Ancient Greece.* Edinburgh: Edinburgh University Press.

Scharfe, Hartmut
1989   *The State in Indian Tradition.* Leiden: E. J. Brill.

Schele, Linda
1978   Genealogical Documentation on the Tri-Figure Panels at Palenque. In *Third Palenque Round Table, 1978,* edited by Merle Greene Robertson and Donnan C. Jeffers, pp. 41–70. Palenque Round Table Series No. 4. Monterey: Pre-Columbian Art Research Center.
1991   The Owl, Shield, and Flint Blade. *Natural History* November:6–11.

Schele, Linda, and David A. Freidel
1990   *A Forest of Kings: The Untold Story of the Ancient Maya.* New York: William Morrow and Co.

Schele, Linda, and Peter Mathews
1991   Royal Visits and Other Inter-Site Relationships among the Classic Maya. In *Classic Maya Political History: Hieroglyphic and Archaeological Evidence,* edited by T. Patrick Culbert, pp. 226–252. Albuquerque: University of New Mexico Press.

Schele, Linda, and Mary Ellen Miller
1986   *The Blood of Kings: Dynasty and Ritual in Maya Art.* Fort Worth: Kimbell Art Museum.

Schiffer, Michael
1983   Review of *Cultural Materialism: The Struggle for a Science of Culture,* by Marvin Harris. *American Antiquity* 48:190–194.
1988   The Structure of Archaeological Theory. *American Antiquity* 53:461–85.

Schilcher, Linda Schatkowski
1985   *Families in Politics.* Berlin Islamstudien 2. Stuttgart: Franz Steiner.

Schortman, Edward M., and Patricia A. Urban
1992   Current Trends in Interaction Research. In *Resources, Power, and Interregional Interaction,* edited by Edward M. Schortman and Patricia A. Urban, pp. 235–256. New York: Plenum Press.

Schreiber, Katharina
1992   *Wari Imperialism in Middle Horizon.* Museum of Anthropology Anthropological Papers No. 87. Ann Arbor: University of Michigan.

Schroeder, Susan
1991   *Chimalpahin and the Kingdoms of Chalco.* Tucson: University of Arizona Press.

Schwartz, Glenn M., and Steven E. Falconer, eds.
1994   *Archaeological Views from the Countryside: Village Communities in Early Complex Societies.* Washington, D.C.: Smithsonian Institution Press.

Sealey, Raphael
1976   *A History of the Greek City-States 700–338 B.C.* Berkeley: University of California Press.

Seidlmayer, Stephan
1987   Wirtschaftliche und gesellschaftliche Entwicklung im Übergang vom Alten zum Mittleren Reich: Ein Beitrag zur Archäologie der Gräberfelder der Region Qau-Matmar in der Ersten Zwischenzeit. In *Problems and Priorities in Egyptian Archaeology,* edited by Jan Assman, Gunter Burkhard, and Vivian Davies, pp. 175–218. London: Routledge.

Sempowski, Martha L.
1994   Mortuary Practices at Teotihuacan. In *Mortuary Practices and Skeletal Remains at*

Teotihuacan, edited by René Millon, pp. 1–314. Urbanization at Teotihuacan, Mexico, Vol. 3. Salt Lake City: University of Utah Press.

Sen, Amartya
1992   *Inequality Reexamined.* Cambridge: Harvard University Press.

Serjeant, Robert B., ed.
1980   *The Islamic City.* Paris: UNESCO.

Serrano Sánchez, Carlos
1993   Funerary Practices and Human Sacrifice in Teotihuacan Burials. In *Teotihuacan: Art from the City of the Gods,* edited by Kathleen Berrin and Esther Pasztory, pp. 108–115. New York: Thames and Hudson.

Serrano Sánchez, Carlos, Martha Pimienta Merlín, and Alfonso Gallardo Velázquez
1991   Los Entierros del Templo de Quetzalcoatl. *Arqueología, Segunda época* 6:53–67.

Service, Elman R.
1962   *Primitive Social Organization.* New York: Random House.
1971   *Cultural Evolutionism: Theory in Practice.* New York: Rinehart and Winston.
1975   *Origins of the State and Civilization.* New York: W. W. Norton.
1978   Classical and Modern Theories of the Origins of Government. In *Origins of the State: The Anthropology of Political Evolution,* edited by Ronald Cohen and Elman Service, pp. 21–34. Philadelphia: Institute for the Study of Human Issues.

Shafer, Byron E., ed.
1991   *Religion in Ancient Egypt: Gods, Myths, and Personal Practice.* Ithaca: Cornell University Press.

Shafer, Harry J., and Thomas R. Hester
1983   Ancient Maya Workshops in Northern Belize, Central America. *American Antiquity* 48:519–543.

Shaffer, Jim G.
1982   Harappan Culture: A Reconsideration. In *Harappan Civilization,* edited by Gregory. L. Possehl, pp. 41–50. New Delhi: Oxford and IBH.
1991   The Indus Valley, Baluchistan, and Helmand Traditions: Neolithic through Bronze Age. In *Chronologies in Old World Archaeology,* edited by Robert Ehrich, pp. 441–464. Chicago: University of Chicago Press.
1993   Reurbanization: The Eastern Punjab and Beyond. In *Urban Form and Meaning in South Asia: The Shaping of Cities from Prehistoric to Precolonial Times,* edited by Howard Spodek and Doris M. Srinivasan, pp. 53–67. Washington, D.C.: National Gallery of Art.

Shandong sheng wenwu kaogu yanjiusuo
1982   *Qufu Luguo gucheng.* [The Ancient City of the State of Lu, Qufu]. Vol. 1. Jinan: QiLu shushe.

Shanks, Michael, and Christopher Tilley
1987a   *Social Theory and Archaeology.* Oxford: Polity Press.
1987b   *Reconstructing Archaeology.* Cambridge: Cambridge University Press.
1989   Archaeology into the 1990s. *Norwegian Archaeological Review* 22:1–12.

Shansi sheng kaogu yanjiusuo Houma gongzuo zhan
1988   Shansi Houma Jinguo yizhi Niucun gucheng de shijue. [Trial Excavations of the Ancient City of Niucun at the Remains of the Jin Capital, Houma, Shansi.] *Kaogu yu wenwu* 1:57–60.

Sharer, Robert J.
1991   Diversity and Continuity in Maya Civilization: Quirigua as a Study Case. In *Classic Maya Political History,* edited by T. Patrick Culbert, pp. 180–198. Cambridge: Cambridge University Press.
1994   *The Ancient Maya.* Palo Alto: Stanford University Press.

Sharer, Robert J., and David C. Grove, eds.
1989   *Regional Perspectives on the Olmec.* Cambridge: Cambridge University Press.

Sharer, Robert, Julia C. Miller, and Loa B. Traxler
1992   Evolution of Classic Period Architecture in the Eastern Acropolis: A Progress Report. *Ancient Mesoamerica* 3:145–160.

Sharma, Jagdish P.
1968   *Republics in Ancient India: c. 1500 B.C.–500 B.C.* Leiden: E. J. Brill.

Shaughnessy, Edward L.
1989   Historical Geography and the Extent of the Earliest Chinese Kingdoms. *Asia Major,* third series, 2:1–22.

Shaw, Joseph
1989   Phoenicians in Southern Crete. *American Journal of Archaeology* 93:165–183.

Sherbondy, Jeanette
1982   The Canal System of Hanan Cuzco. Unpub-

lished Ph.D. dissertation, Department of Anthropology, University of Illinois at Urbana.

1992   Water Ideology in Inca Ethnogenesis. In *Andean Cosmologies through Time: Persistence and Emergence,* edited by Robert V. Dover, Katharine E. Seibold, and John H. McDowell, pp. 46–66. Bloomington: Indiana University Press.

Shipley, Graham
1992   *Perioikos:* The Discovery of Classical Lakonia. In *Philolakon: Lakonian Studies in Honour of Hector Catling,* edited by Jan Sanders, pp. 211–226. London: British School at Athens.

Shuri Jo Fukugen Kiseikai, Naha Shuppansha Henshubu
1987   *Shashinshu Shuri Jo* [A Photo Album of Shuri Castle]. Naha: Naha Shuppansha.

Siemens, Alfred H.
1982   Prehispanic Agricultural Use of the Wetlands of Northern Belize. In *Maya Subsistence: Studies in Memory of Dennis E. Puleston,* edited by Kent Flannery, pp. 205–225. New York: Academic Press.

Silverblatt, Irene
1988   Women in State. *Annual Review of Anthropology* 17:427–460.

Siméon, Rémi
1971 [1885]   *Dictionnaire de la Langue Nahuatl ou Mexicaine.* Imprimerie National, Paris. Graz, Austria: Akademische Druck-und Verlagsanstalt.

Simon, Christopher
1986   The Archaic Votive Offering and Cults of Ionia. Unpublished Ph.D. dissertation, University of California, Berkeley.

Sinclair, R. K.
1988   *Democracy and Participation in Athens.* Cambridge: Cambridge University Press.

Sinopoli, Carla, and Kathleen Morrison
1995   Dimensions of Imperial Control: The Vijayanagara Capital. *American Anthropologist* 97:83–96.

Sismondi, J. C. L. Simonde de
1826   *Histoire des Républiques Italiennes du Moyen Age.* Bruxelles: A. Whalen.

Sjoberg, Gideon
1960   *The Preindustrial City: Past and Present.* Glencoe, IL: The Free Press.

Skalník, Peter
1989   Outwitting the State: An Introduction. In *Outwitting the State,* edited by Peter Skalník, pp. 1–21. Political Anthropology, Vol. 7. New Brunswick: Transaction Publishers.

Slotkin, J. S.
1965   *Readings in Early Anthropology.* Viking Fund Publications in Anthropology No. 40, Sol Tax, general editor. New York: Wenner-Gren Foundation for Anthropological Research.

Small, David
1987   Social Correlations to the Greek Cavea in the Roman Period. In *Roman Architecture in the Greek World,* edited by Sarah Macready and F. H. Thompson, pp. 85–93. London: Society of Antiquaries.

1990   Handmade Burnished Ware and Prehistoric Aegean Economics. *Journal of Mediterranean Archaeology* 3:3–25.

1992   Incomplete Formations: A Comparison of the Classical Greek and Maya. Paper presented at the 57th annual meeting of the Society for American Archaeology, Pittsburgh.

1994   A Different Distinction: The Case of the Greek State. In *The Economic Anthropology of the State,* edited by Elizabeth Brumfiel, pp. 287–314. Monographs in Economic Anthropology No. 11. Lanham, MD: University Press of America.

1995   Heterarchical Paths to Evolution: The Role of External Economies. In *Heterarchy and the Analysis of Complex Societies,* edited by Robert Ehrenreich, Carole Crumley, and Janet Levy, pp. 55–70. Washington, D.C.: Archaeological Papers of the American Anthropological Association No. 6.

Smith, Bruce
1992   Mississippian Elites and Solar Alignments: A Reflection of Managerial Necessity, or Levers of Social Inequality? In *Lords of the Southeast: Social Inequality and the Native Elites of Southeastern North America,* edited by Alex Barker and Timothy Pauketat, pp. 11–30. Washington, D.C.: Archeological Papers of the American Anthropological Association No. 3.

Smith, David H.
1958   Zaitun's Five Centuries of Sino Foreign Trade. *Journal of the Royal Asiatic Society,* October 1958:163–177.

Smith, Harry S., and David G. Jeffreys
1986   A Survey of Memphis, Egypt. *Antiquity* lx:88–95.

Smith, Michael E.
1979   The Aztec Marketing System and Settlement Pattern in the Valley of Mexico: A Central Place Analysis. *American Antiquity* 44:110–124.
1980   The Role of the Marketing System in Aztec Society and Economy: Reply to Evans. *American Antiquity* 45:876–883.
1983   Postclassic Culture Change in Western Morelos, Mexico: The Development and Correlation of Archaeological and Ethnohistorical Chronologies. Ph.D. dissertation, Department of Anthropology, University of Illinois, Urbana. Ann Arbor: University Microfilms.
1984   The Aztlan Migrations of the Nahuatl Chronicles: Myth or History? *Ethnohistory* 31:153–156.
1989   Cities, Towns, and Urbanism: Comment on Sanders and Webster. *American Anthropologist* 91:454–458.
1992a   Rhythms of Change in Postclassic Central Mexico: Archaeology, Ethnohistory, and the Braudelian Model. In *Archaeology, Annales, and Ethnohistory,* edited by A. Bernard Knapp, pp. 51–74. Cambridge: Cambridge University Press.
1992b   *Archaeological Research at Aztec-Period Rural Sites in Morelos, Mexico,* Vol. 1: *Excavations and Architecture.* Department of Anthropology Memoirs in Latin American Archaeology No. 4. Pittsburgh: University of Pittsburgh.

Smith, Michael E., and Frances F. Berdan
1992   Archaeology and the Aztec Empire. *World Archaeology* 23:353–367.
1996   Introduction. In *Aztec Imperial Strategies,* edited by Frances F. Berdan, Richard E. Blanton, Elizabeth Hill Boone, Mary G. Hodge, Michael E. Smith, and Emily Umberger, pp. 1–12. Washington, D.C.: Dumbarton Oaks Research Library and Collection.

Smith, Michael E., and John F. Doershuk
1991   Late Postclassic Chronology in Western Morelos, Mexico. *Latin American Antiquity* 2:291–310.

Smith, Michael E., and Cynthia Heath-Smith
1994   Excavations of Aztec-Period Houses at Yautepec, Morelos, Mexico. Paper presented at the 59th annual meeting of the Society for American Archaeology, Anaheim.

Smith, Michael E., Cynthia Heath-Smith, Ronald Kohler, Joan Odess, Sharon Spanogle, and Timothy Sullivan
1994   The Size of the Aztec City of Yautepec: Urban Survey in Central Mexico. *Ancient Mesoamerica* 5:1–12.

Smith, Michael E., and Kenneth G. Hirth
1988   The Development of Prehispanic Cotton-Spinning Technology in Western Morelos, Mexico. *Journal of Field Archaeology* 15:349–358.

Smith, Robert
1988   *Kingdoms of the Yoruba.* Madison: University of Wisconsin Press.

Snead, Rodman E.
1968   Weather Patterns in Southern West Pakistan. *Archiv für Meteorologie, Geophysik, und Bioklimatologie,* Series B (16):316–346.

Snodgrass, Anthony
1971   *The Dark Age of Greece.* Edinburgh: Edinburgh University Press.
1977   *Archaeology and the Rise of the Greek State.* Cambridge: Cambridge University Press.
1980   *Archaic Greece: The Age of Experiment.* Berkeley: University of California Press.
1983   Heavy Freight in Archaic Greece. In *Trade in the Ancient Economy,* edited by Peter Garnsey, Keith Hopkins, and C. R. Whittaker, pp. 16–26. Berkeley: University of California Press.
1986   Interaction by Design: The Greek City State. In *Peer Polity Interaction and Sociopolitical Change,* edited by Colin Renfrew and John F. Cherry, pp. 47–58. Cambridge: Cambridge University Press.
1987   *An Archaeology of Greece.* Berkeley: University of California Press.
1990a   Survey Archaeology and the Rural Landscape of the Greek City. In *The Greek City From Homer to Alexander,* edited by Oswyn Murray and Simon Price, pp. 113–136. Oxford University Press, Oxford.
1990b   The Economics of Dedication at Greek Sanctuaries. *Scienze dell' antichità* 3–4:287–294.
1991   Archaeology and the Study of the Greek City. In *City and Country in the Ancient World,* edited by John Rich and Andrew Wallace-Hadrill, pp. 1–24. London: Routledge.

1994   Response: The Archaeological Aspect. In *Classical Greece: Ancient Histories and Modern Archaeologies,* edited by Ian Morris, pp. 197–200. Cambridge: Cambridge University Press.

Spence, Michael W.

1985   Specialized Production in Rural Aztec Society: Obsidian Workshops of the Teotihuacan Valley. In *Contributions to the Archaeology and Ethnohistory of Greater Mesoamerica,* edited by William J. Folan, pp. 76–125. Carbondale: Southern Illinois University Press.

1994   Human Skeletal Material from Teotihuacan. In *Urbanization at Teotihuacan,* Vol. 3, edited by René Millon, pp. 315–427. Salt Lake City: University of Utah Press.

Spencer, Charles S.

1987   Rethinking the Chiefdom. In *Chiefdoms in the Americas,* edited by Robert D. Drennan and Carlos A. Uribe, pp. 369–389. Lanham, MD: University Press of America.

1990   On the Tempo and Mode of State Formation: Neoevolutionism Reconsidered. *Journal of Anthropological Archaeology* 9:1–30.

Spencer, Herbert

1896   *Principles of Sociology,* Vol. 1. New York: D. Appleton.

Srinivas, Mysore N.

1962   *Caste in Modern India and Other Essays.* Bombay: Asia Publishing House.

Starr, Chester G.

1977   *The Economic and Social Growth of Early Greece 800–500 B.C.* New York: Oxford University Press.

de Ste. Croix, Geoffrey E. M.

1966   The Estate of Phaenippus (Ps.-Dem., xlii). In *Ancient Society and Institutions,* edited by Ernst Badian, pp. 109–114. Macmillan, London.

1981   *The Class Struggle in the Ancient Greek World: From the Archaic Age to the Arab Conquests.* Ithaca: Cornell University Press.

Stein, Gil, and Mitchell S. Rothman, eds.

1994   *Chiefdoms and Early States in the Near East: The Organizational Dynamics of Complexity.* Monographs in World Archaeology No. 18. Madison: Prehistory Press.

Steinkeller, Piotr

1987   The Foresters of Umma: Toward a Definition of Ur III Labor. In *Labor in the An-*

cient Near East, edited by Marvin J. Powell, pp. 73–115. Winona Lake: Eisenbrauns.

1993   Early Political Development in Mesopotamia and the Origins of the Sargonic Empire. In *Akkad—The First World Empire: Structure, Ideology, Traditions,* edited by Mario Liverani, pp. 107–129. Padova: Sargon.

n.d.   The City of Umma ca. 2,000 B.C.: Towards a Sumerian Urban Demography. Manuscript.

Steponaitis, Vincas P.

1981   Settlement Hierarchies and Political Complexity in Nonmarket Societies: The Formative Period of the Valley of Mexico. *American Anthropologist* 83:320–363.

Stevens, William K.

1989   Andean Culture Found to Be as Old as the Great Pyramids. *The New York Times,* Science Times, Tuesday, October 3, pp. 17, 20.

Steward, Julian H.

1949   Cultural Causality and Law: A Trial Formulation for the Development of Early Civilization. *American Anthropologist* 51:1–27.

1955   *Theory of Culture Change.* Urbana: University of Illinois Press.

1977   *Evolution and Ecology: Essays on Social Transformation,* edited by Jane C. Steward and Robert F. Murphy. Urbana: University of Illinois Press.

Stol, Marten

1982   State and Private Business in the Land of Larsa. *Journal of Cuneiform Studies* 34:127–230.

Stone, Elizabeth

1987   *Nippur Neighborhoods.* Studies in Ancient Oriental Civilization 44. Chicago: Oriental Institute Press.

1990   The Tell Abu Duwari Project, 1987. *Journal of Field Archaeology* 17:141–162.

1993   The Spatial Organization of Mesopotamian Cities. In *Veles Paraules: Ancient Near Eastern Studies in Honor of Miguel Civil,* edited by Piotr Michelowski, pp. 235–242. Barcelona: Aula Orientalis.

Stone, Elizabeth, and Paul Zimansky

1992   Mashkan-shapir and the Anatomy of an Old Babylonian City. *Biblical Archaeologist* 55, 1:212–218.

1994   The Second and Third Seasons at Tell Abu Duwari, Iraq. *Journal of Field Archaeology* 21:437–456.

1995   The Tapestry of Power in a Mesopotamian
               City. *Scientific American* April, pp. 117–123.

Storey, Glenn
1992   Preindustrial Urban Demography. Ph.D. dis-
               sertation, Department of Anthropology,
               Pennsylvania State University, University
               Park. Ann Arbor: University Microfilms.

Strong, William D., and Clifford Evans, Jr.
1952   *Cultural Stratigraphy in the Virú Valley,
               Northern Peru: The Formative and Flor-
               escent Epochs.* New York: Columbia Uni-
               versity Press.

Strudwick, Nigel
1985   *The Administration of Egypt in the Old
               Kingdom: The Highest Titles and Their
               Holders.* London: KPI.

Stuart, David
1992   Hieroglyphs and Archaeology at Copan.
               Ancient Mesoamerica 3:169–185.
1993   Historical Inscriptions and the Maya Col-
               lapse. In *Lowland Maya Civilization in the
               Eighth Century A.D.*, edited by Jeremy
               Sabloff and John Henderson, pp. 321–354.
               Washington, D.C.: Dumbarton Oaks Re-
               search Library and Collection.

Sugiyama, Saburo
1991   El Entierro Central de la Pirámide de la Ser-
               piente Emplumada. *Arqueología, Segunda
               época* 6:33–40.
1992   Rulership, Warfare, and Human Sacrifice at
               the Ciudadela: An Iconographic Study of
               Feathered Serpent Representations. In *Art,
               Ideology, and the City of Teotihuacan,* ed-
               ited by Janet Catherine Berlo, pp. 205–230.
               Washington, D.C.: Dumbarton Oaks Re-
               search Library and Collection.

Tambiah, Stanley Jeyaraja
1977   The Galactic Polity: The Structure of Tradi-
               tional Kingdoms in Southeast Asia. In *An-
               thropology and the Climate of Opinion,* ed-
               ited by Stanley Freed, pp. 69–97. New
               York: New York Academy of Sciences.
1985   *Culture, Thought, and Social Action: An
               Anthropological Perspective.* Cambridge:
               Harvard University Press.

Taylor, Timothy
1992   The Gundestrup Cauldron. *Scientific Ameri-
               can* 266(3):84–89.

Thapar, B. K.
1975   Kalibangan: A Harappan Metropolis be-
               yond the Indus Valley. *Expedition*
               17(2):19–32.

Thapar, Romila
1984   *From Lineage to State: Social Formations
               in the Mid-First Millennium B.C. in the
               Ganga Valley.* Bombay: Oxford University
               Press.

Thomas, Carol G.
1981   The Greek Polis. In *The City-State in Five
               Cultures,* edited by Robert Griffeth and
               Carol G. Thomas, pp. 31–69. Santa Bar-
               bara: ABC-Clio.

Thomas, Rosalind
1992   *Literacy and Orality in Ancient Greece.*
               Cambridge: Cambridge University Press.

Thompson, J. Eric S.
1954   *The Rise and Fall of Maya Civilization.*
               Norman: University of Oklahoma Press.

Thorp, Robert L.
1985   The Growth of Early Shang Civilization:
               New Data from Ritual Vessels. *Harvard
               Journal of Asiatic Studies* 45.1:5–75.
1991   Erlitou and the Search for the Xia. *Early
               China* 16:1–38.

Tian An
1988   Archaeological Exploration of the Lu City at
               Qufu. Translated by David D. Buck. *Chinese
               Sociology and Anthropology* 19.1:9–34.

Tilly, Charles, and Wim P. Blockmans, eds.
1994   *Cities and the Rise of States in Europe, A.D.
               1000 to 1800.* Boulder: Westview Press.

Tolstoy, Paul
1975   Settlement and Population Trends in the Ba-
               sin of Mexico (Ixtapaluca and Zacatenco
               Phases). *Journal of Field Archaeology*
               2:331–349.
1989a   Coapexco and Tlatilco: Sites with Olmec
               Materials in the Basin of Mexico. In *Re-
               gional Perspectives on the Olmec,* edited by
               Robert J. Sharer and David C. Grove, pp.
               85–121. Cambridge: Cambridge University
               Press.
1989b   Western Mesoamerica and the Olmec. In
               Regional Perspectives on the Olmec, edited
               by Robert J. Sharer and David C. Grove,
               pp. 275–302. Cambridge: Cambridge Uni-
               versity Press.

Tolstoy, Paul, and Suzanne Fish
1975   Surface and Subsurface Evidence for Com-
               munity Size at Coapexco, Mexico. *Journal
               of Field Archaeology* 2:97–104.

Tolstoy, Paul, Suzanne K. Fish, Martin W. Boksenbaum,
Kathryn Blair Vaughn, and C. Earle Smith
1977   Early Sedentary Communities of the Basin

of Mexico. *Journal of Field Archaeology* 4:92–106.

Tolstoy, Paul, and Louise I. Paradis
1970   Early and Middle Preclassic Culture in the Basin of Mexico. *Science* 167:344–351.

Toma, Shiichi
1985   Kokogakujo yori mita Okinawa no gusuku [Okinawa Castles as Seen from Archaeology]. *Okinawa Ken Kyoiku Cho Bunka Ka Kiyo* [Contributions of the Culture Section, Board of Education, Okinawa Prefecture] 2:1–23.

Trautmann, Wolfgang von
1968   *Untersuchungen zur indianischen Siedlungs- und Territorialgeschichte im Becken von Mexico bis zur frühen Kolonialzeit.* Hamburgi;hcen Museums für Völkerkunde un Vorgeschichte, Beitrage fur Mittleamerikanischen Völkerkunde 7.

Trigger, Bruce G.
1978   Inequality and Communication in Early Civilizations. In *Time and Traditions: Essays in Archaeological Interpretation,* edited by Bruce G. Trigger, pp. 194–215. New York: Columbia University Press.
1983a   The Rise of Egyptian Civilization. In *Ancient Egypt: A Social History,* edited by Bruce Trigger, Barry J. Kemp, David O'Connor, and Alan B. Lloyd, pp. 1–70. Cambridge: Cambridge University Press.
1983b   Archaeology at the Cross-roads: What's New? *Annual Review of Anthropology* 13:275–300.
1985   The Evolution of Pre-Industrial Cities: A Multilinear Perspective. In *Mélanges Offerts à Jean Vercoutter,* edited by Francis Geus and Florence Thill, pp. 343–353. Paris: CNRS Éditions Recherche sur les Civilisations.
1989a   *A History of Archaeological Thought.* Cambridge: Cambridge University Press.
1989b   Comments on Archaeology into the 1990s. *Norwegian Archaeological Review* 22:28–31.
1990a   Monumental Architecture: A Thermodynamic Explanation of Symbolic Behavior. *World Archaeology* 22:119–132.
1990b   Maintaining Economic Equality in Opposition to Complexity: An Iroquoian Case Study. In *The Evolution of Political Systems: Sociopolitics in Small-Scale Sedentary Societies,* edited by Steadman Upham, pp. 119–145. Cambridge: Cambridge University Press.

1993   *Early Civilizations: Ancient Egypt in Context.* Cairo: The American University in Cairo Press.
1995   Expanding Middle Range Theory. *Antiquity* 69:449–458.

Trigger, Bruce G., Barry J. Kemp, David O'Connor, and Alan B. Lloyd
1983   *Ancient Egypt: A Social History.* New York: Cambridge University Press.

Tu Cheng-sheng
1986   Guanyu Zhoudai guojia xingtai lice—'Fengjian chengbang' shuo chuyi. [The 'Feudal City-state' in Ancient China: An Analysis of Chou Dynasty State Formation.] *Zhongyang yanjiuyuan lishi yuyan yanjiusuo jikan* 57.3:465–498.
1987   Cong kaogu ziliao lun Zhongyuan guojia de qiyuan ji qi zaoqi de fazhan. [Discussion from Archaeological Materials of the Origins of the State in the Central Plains and the Development of Early States in that Region.] *Zhongyang yanjiuyuan lishi yuyan yanjiusuo jikan* 58.1:1–81.
1992   *Gudai shehui yu guojia.* [Ancient Society and the State.] Taibei: Yunchen wenhua chuban.

Tu Wei-ming
1985   *Confucian Thought: Selfhood as Creative Transformation.* Albany: State University of New York Press.

Turner, Bryan S.
1986   *Equality.* London: Macmillan.

Turner, Frank M.
1981   *The Greek Heritage in Victorian Britain.* New Haven: Yale University Press.

Turner, Sue Ellen, Norman I. Turner, and R. E. W. Adams
1981   Volumetric Assessment, Rank Ordering, and Maya Civic Centers. In *Lowland Maya Settlement Patterns,* edited by Wendy Ashmore, pp. 71–88. Albuquerque: University of New Mexico Press.

Umberger, Emily
1996   Art and Imperial Strategy in Tenochtitlan. In *Aztec Imperial Strategies,* edited by Frances F. Berdan, Richard E. Blanton, Elizabeth Hill Boone, Mary G. Hodge, Michael E. Smith, and Emily Umberger, pp. 85–106. Washington, D.C.: Dumbarton Oaks Research Library and Collection.

Umberger, Emily, and Cecelia F. Klein
1993   Aztec Art and Imperial Expansion. In *Latin American Horizons,* edited by Don Stephen

Rice, pp. 295–336. Washington, D.C.: Dumbarton Oaks Research Library and Collection.

Underhill, Anne P.

1990   Archaeological Evidence for Evolution of the Xia State: A Discussion. Paper Presented at the International Symposium on Xia Culture, University of California, Los Angeles.

1991   Pottery Production in Chiefdoms: The Longshan Period in Northern China. *World Archaeology* 23.1:12–27.

1992   Regional Growth of Cultural Complexity during the Longshan Period of Northern China. In *Pacific Northeast Asia in Prehistory: Hunter-Fisher-Gatherers, Farmers, and Sociopolitical Elites,* edited by C. Melvin Aikens and Song Nai Rhee, pp. 173–177. Pullman: Washington State University Press.

Upham, Steadman

1990   Decoupling the Processes of Political Evolution. In *The Evolution of Political Systems: Sociopolitics in Small-Scale Sedentary Societies,* edited by Steadman Upham, pp. 1–17. Cambridge: Cambridge University Press.

Urbano, Henrique

1981   *Wiracocha y Ayar: Heroes y Funciones en las Sociedades Andinas.* Cuzco: Centro de Estudios Rurales "Bartolomé de las Casas."

Vaillant, George

1938   A Correlation of Archaeological and Historical Sequences in the Valley of Mexico. *American Anthropologist* 40:535–573.

1966   *The Aztecs of Mexico: Origin, Rise, and Fall of the Aztec Nation.* Harmondsworth, Middlesex: Penguin Books.

van der Vliet, E. Chl. L.

1987   Tyranny and Democracy: The Evolution of Politics in Ancient Greece. In *Early State Dynamics,* edited by Henri Claessen and Pieter van de Velde, pp. 70–90. Leiden: E. J. Brill.

Vatin, Claude

1984   *Citoyens et non-citoyens dans le monde grec.* Paris: Enseignement supérieur.

Vats, Mahdo Sarup

1940   *Excavations at Harappa.* Delhi: Government of India Press.

de Vega Nova, Hortensia, and Pablo Mayer Guala

1991   Proyecto Yautepec. *Boletín, Consejo de Ar-*
queología, Instituto Nacional de Antropología e Historia (1991):79–84, México D.F.

Vernant, Jean-Paul

1980   *Myth and Society in Ancient Greece.* Translated by Janet Lloyd. Brighton: Harvester.

Vidal-Naquet, Pierre

1986   *The Black Hunter.* Translated by Andrew Szegedy-Maszak. Johns Hopkins University Press, Baltimore.

Vidale, Massimo

1990   On the Structure and the Relative Chronology of a Harappan Industrial Site. In *South Asian Archaeology, 1987,* edited by Maurizio Taddei and Pierfrancesco Callieri, pp. 203–244. Rome: IsMEO.

Vidale, Massimo, and J. Mark Kenoyer

1992   La civiltà della Valle dell'Indo. *ARCHEO* Anno VII (9[91]):54–99.

Viel, René

1983   Evolución de la Cerámica en Copán: Resultados Preliminares. In *Introducción a la Arqueología de Copán, Honduras,* edited by Claude F. Baudez, pp. 471–549. Tegucigalpa: Instituto Hondureño de Antropología e Historia.

Vilatte, Sylvie

1995   *Espace et Temps: La Cité Aristotélicienne de la "Politique".* Annales Littéraires de l'Université de Besançon No. 552. Paris: Les Belles Lettres.

Vinogradov, I. V.

1991   The Predynastic Period and the Early and the Old Kingdoms in Egypt. In *Early Antiquity,* edited by I. M. Diakonoff, pp. 137–157. Chicago: University of Chicago Press.

von der Way, T.

1987   Tell el-Fara'in - Buto, 2 Bericht mit einem Beitrag von Klaus Schmidt zu den lithischen Kleinfunden. *Mitteilungen des Deutschen Archäologischen Instituts Abteilung Kairo* 3:241–250.

1988   Investigations concerning the Early Periods in the Northern Delta of Egypt. In *The Archaeology of the Nile Delta: Problems and Priorities,* edited by Edwin C. M. van den Brink, pp. 245–249. Amsterdam: Netherlands Foundation for Archaeological Research in Egypt.

1992   Indications of Architecture with Niches at Buto. In *The Followers of Horus. Studies Dedicated to Michael Allen Hoffman,* edited by Renee Friedman and Barbara Adams, pp. 217–226. Oxford: Oxbow.

Wada Hisanori
1975   Ryukyu Koku no Sanzan Toitsu ni Tsuite Shin Kosatsu (A New Interpretation on the Unification of Sanzan [The Three Principalities in the Fifteenth Century into the Ryukyu Kingdom]). *Ochanomizu Jimbun Kagaku Kiyo* [Ochanomizu Studies in Arts and Culture] 28:2:13–39.

Waldrop, M. M.
1992   *Complexity.* New York: Touchstone.

Waley, Daniel
1988   *The Italian City-Republics.* 3rd ed. London; Longman.

Wallace-Hadrill, Andrew
1989   *Patronage in Ancient Society.* London; Routledge.

Wallerstein, Immanuel
1974   *The Modern World System: Capitalist Agriculture and the Origins of the European World Economy in the Sixteenth Century.* New York: Academic Press.

Walzer, Michael
1983   *Spheres of Justice: A Defense of Equality and Pluralism.* New York: Basic Books.

Wang Guimin
1983   Jiu Yinxu jiaguwen suijian shushuo 'Sima' zhiming de qiyuan. [A Trial Explanation of the Origin of the Administrative Term 'Sima' on the Basis of Its Appearance in the Oracle Bone Inscriptions from the Wastes of Yin.] In *Jiaguwen yu Yin Shang shi,* edited by Hu Houxuan, pp. 173–190. Shanghai: Guji chuban she.

Wang, Gungwu
1990   Merchants without Empires: The Hokkien Sojourning Communities. In *The Rise of Merchant Empires: Long-Distance Trade in the Early Modern World, 1350–1750,* edited by J. D. Tracy, pp. 400–421. Cambridge: Cambridge University Press.

Wang Zhenzhong
1992   Zhongguo wenming qiyuan de bijiao yanjiu. [Comparative Researches into the Origins of Chinese Civilization.] Unpublished Ph.D. dissertation, Zhongguo shehui kexueyuan yanjiusuo.

Watson, Richard A.
1990   Ozymandias, King of Kings: Postprocessual Radical Archaeology as Critique. *American Antiquity* 55:673–689.

Watt, James C., and Barbara B. Ford
1991   *East Asian Lacquer: The Florence and Herbert Irving Collection.* New York: The Metropolitan Museum of Art.

Wattenmaker, Patricia
1994   Household Economy in Early State Society: Material Value, Productive Context, and Spheres of Exchange. In *The Economic Anthropology of the State,* edited by Elizabeth M. Brumfiel, pp. 93–118. Monographs in Economic Anthropology No. 11. Lanham, MD: University Press of America.

Weaver, Muriel Porter
1993   *The Aztecs, Maya, and Their Predecessors,* 3rd ed. San Diego: Academic Press.

Weber, Steven A.
1992   South Asian Archaeobotanical Variability. In *South Asian Archaeology, 1989,* edited by Catherine Jarrige, pp. 283–290. Monographs in World Archaeology No. 14. Madison: Prehistory Press.

Weber, Max
1949   *The Methodology of the Social Sciences.* Translated by Edward Shils and Henry A. Finch. Glencoe, IL: The Free Press.
1958   *The City.* Glencoe, IL: The Free Press.
1978   *Economy and Society: An Outline of Interpretive Sociology.* Translated by E. Fischoff et al., edited by Guenther Roth and Claus Wittich. Berkeley: University of California Press.

Webster, David
1976   *Defensive Earthworks at Becan, Campeche, Mexico.* Middle American Research Institute Publication No. 41. New Orleans: Tulane University.
1988   Copan as a Classic Maya Center. In *The Southeast Classic Maya Zone,* edited by Elizabeth Hill Boone and Gordon Willey, pp. 5–50. Washington, D.C.: Dumbarton Oaks Research Library and Collection.
1992   Maya Elites: The Perspective from Copan. In *Mesoamerican Elites: An Archaeological Assessment,* edited by Diane Z. Chase and Arlen F. Chase, pp. 135–156. Norman: University of Oklahoma Press.

Webster, David, ed.
1989   *The House of the Bacabs.* Washington, D.C.: Dumbarton Oaks Studies in Precolumbian Art and Archaeology No. 29.

Webster, David, and Elliot Abrams
1983   An Elite Compound at Copan, Honduras. *Journal of Field Archaeology* 10:285–296.

Webster, David, and AnnCorinne Freter
1990   The Demography of Late Classic Copan. In *Precolumbian Population History in the Maya Lowlands,* edited by T. Patrick Culbert and Don Rice, pp. 37–62. Albuquerque: University of New Mexico Press.

Webster, David, and Nancy Gonlin
1988   Household Remains of the Humblest Maya. *Journal of Field Archaeology* 15:169–190.

Webster, David, and Jennifer Kirker
1995   Too Many Maya, Too Few Buildings: Investigating Construction Potential at Copán, Honduras. *Journal of Anthropological Research* 51:363–387.

Webster, David, William T. Sanders, and Peter van Rossum
1992   A Simulation of Copan Population History. *Ancient Mesoamerica* 3:185–198.

Webster, David, Alfred Traverse, David Rue, and William T. Sanders
1996   Vegetational and Settlement History at Copán, Honduras. Final Report to the National Oceanic and Atmospheric Association, Washington, D.C.

Webster, Gary S.
1990   Labor Control and Emergent Stratification in Prehistoric Europe. *Current Anthropology* 31:337–366.

Weintraub, Karl
1988   Jacob Burckhardt: The Historian among the Philologists. *American Scholar* 57:273–282.

Weiss, Harvey, ed.
1986   *The Origins of Cities in Dry-Farming Syria and Mesopotamia in the Third Millennium B.C.* Guilford, CT: Four Quarters Publishers.

Weissleder, Wolfgang
1978   Aristotle's Concept of Political Structure and the State. In *Origins of the State: The Anthropology of Political Evolution,* edited by Ronald Cohen and Elman Service, pp. 187–203. Philadelphia: Institute for the Study of Human Issues.

Wenke, Robert J.
1981   Explaining the Evolution of Cultural Complexity: A Review. In *Advances in Archaeological Method and Theory,* Vol. 4, edited by Michael B. Schiffer, pp. 79–127. New York: Academic Press.
1986   Old Kingdom Community Organization in the Western Egyptian Delta. *Norwegian Archaeological Review* 19:15–33.
1989a   Egypt: Origins of Complex Societies. *Annual Review of Anthropology* 18:129–155.
1989b   Comments on Archaeology into the 1990s. *Norwegian Archaeological Review* 22:31–33.
1991   The Evolution of Egyptian Civilization: Issues and Evidence. *Journal of World Prehistory* 5:279–329.

Wenke, Robert J., Richard Redding, Paul Buck, Michal Kobusiewicz, and Karla Kroeper
1988   Kom el-Hisn: Excavations of an Old Kingdom West Delta Community. *Journal of the American Research Center in Egypt* 25:5–34.

Wheatley, Paul
1971   *The Pivot of the Four Quarters: A Preliminary Enquiry into the Origins and Character of the Ancient Chinese Society.* Chicago: Aldine.
1977   Review of Chang (1976). *Journal of Asian Studies* 36:543–545.

Wheeler, R. E. Mortimer
1947   Harappa, 1946: The Defenses and Cemetery R-37. *Ancient India* 3:58–130.
1968   *The Indus Civilization.* Cambridge: Cambridge University Press.
1972 [1966] *Civilizations of the Indus Valley and Beyond.* New York: McGraw Hill.

White, Christine, and Henry B. Schwarcz
1989   Ancient Maya Diet as Inferred from Isotopic and Elemental Analysis of Human Bone. *Journal of Archaeological Science* 16:451–474.

White, Hayden
1973   *Metahistory: The Historical Imagination in Nineteenth-Century Europe.* Baltimore: Johns Hopkins University Press.

White, Joyce
1992   Prehistoric Roots of Heterarchy in Early Southeast Asian States. Paper presented at 57th annual meeting of the Society for American Archaeology, Pittsburgh.

White, Leslie
1949   *The Science of Culture.* New York: Grove.

Whitehead, David
1977   *The Ideology of the Athenian Metic.* Cambridge Philological Society Supp., Vol. 4, Cambridge.

1991   Norms of Citizenship in Ancient Greece. In *City States in Classical Antiquity and Medieval Italy,* edited by Anthony Molho, Kurt Raaflaub, and Julia Emlen, pp. 135–154. Ann Arbor: University of Michigan Press.

Whitley, James
1991   *Style and Society in Dark Age Greece.* Cambridge: Cambridge University Press.
1994   Protoattic Pottery: A Contextual Approach. In *Classical Greece: Ancient Histories and Modern Archaeologies,* edited by Ian Morris, pp. 51–70. Cambridge: Cambridge University Press.

Wickham, Chris
1989   *Early Medieval Italy: Central Power and Local Society 400–1000.* Ann Arbor: University of Michigan Press.

Wicks, Robert S.
1992   *Money, Markets, and Trade in Early Southeast Asia: The Development of Indigenous Money Systems to A.D. 1400.* Studies on Southeast Asia, Cornell University, Ithaca, NY.

Wildung, Dietrich
1984   Terminal Prehistory of the Nile Delta: Theses. In *Origins and Early Development of Food-Producing Cultures in North-Eastern Africa,* edited by Lech Krzyaniak and Michal Kobusiewicz, pp. 265–269. Poznan: Museum Archeologicznew Poznaniu.

Wilhemy, Herbert
1969   Das Urstromtal am Ostrand der Iduse bene und das Sarasvati Problem. *Zeitschrift für Geomorphologie,* sup. bund 8:76–91.

Wilk, Richard R., and Robert M. Netting
1984   Households: Changing Forms and Functions. In *Households: Comparative and Historical Studies of the Domestic Group,* edited by Robert M. Netting, Richard R. Wilk, and Eric J. Arnould, pp. 1–28. Berkeley: University of California Press.

Wilk, Richard R., and H. Wilhite
1991   The Community of Cuello: Patterns of Household and Settlement Change. In *Cuello: An Early Maya Community in Belize,* edited by Norman Hammond, pp. 118–133. Cambridge: Cambridge University Press.

Wilkinson, Tony, and David Tucker
1995   Settlement Development in the North Jezira, Iraq: A Study of the Archaeological Landscape. *Iraq Archaeological Reports* 3.

Wiltshire and Baghdad: British School of Archaeology in Iraq and Department of Antiquities and Heritage.

Willetts, Ronald
1967   *The Law Code of Gortyn.* Kadmos Supp., Vol. 1, Berlin.

Willey, Gordon R.
1953   *Prehistoric Settlement Patterns in the Viru Valley, Peru.* Bureau of American Ethnology Bulletin 155. Washington, D.C.: Smithsonian Institution.
1973   *The Altar de Sacrificios Excavations: General Summary and Conclusions.* Papers of the Peabody Museum of American Archaeology and Ethnology No. 64(3). Cambridge: Harvard University.
1985   Ancient China—New World and Near Eastern Ideological Traditions: Some Observations. *Symbols,* Spring:14–17, 22. Cambridge: Peabody Museum, Harvard University.
1991   Horizontal Integration and Regional Diversity: An Alternating Process in the Rise of Civilization. *American Antiquity* 56:197–215.

Willey, Gordon R., William R. Bullard, John B. Glass, and James C. Gifford
1965   *Prehistoric Maya Settlements in the Belize Valley.* Papers of the Peabody Museum of American Archaeology and Ethnology No. 54. Cambridge: Harvard University.
1990   The Classic Maya Sociopolitical Order: A Study in Coherence and Instability. In *New World Archaeology and Culture History,* edited by Gordon R. Willey, pp. 316–329. Albuquerque: University of New Mexico Press.

Willey, Gordon R., and Richard Leventhal
1979   Prehistoric Settlement at Copan. In *Maya Archaeology and Ethnohistory,* edited by Norman Hammond and Gordon R. Willey, pp. 75–102. Austin: University of Texas Press.

Willey, Gordon R., Richard Leventhal, and William Fash
1978   Maya Settlement in the Copan Valley. *Archaeology* 31:32–43.

Williams, Barbara J.
1994   Ethnohistorical Rural Settlement Data Compared with Archaeological Surface Remains: A Test of Preservation from Contact Period Tepetlaoztoc. In *Economies and Polities in the Aztec Realm,* edited by Mary G. Hodge and Michael E. Smith, pp. 73–88.

Albany: Institute for Mesoamerican Studies, State University of New York at Albany.

Wilson, David J.

1981   Of Maize and Men: A Critique of the Maritime Hypothesis of State Origins on the Coast of Peru. *American Anthropologist* 83:93–120.

1983   The Origins and Development of Complex Prehispanic Society in the Lower Santa Valley, Peru: Implications for Theories of State Origins. *Journal of Anthropological Archaeology* 2:209–276.

1987   Reconstructing Patterns of Early Warfare in the Lower Santa Valley, Peru: New Data on the Role of Conflict in the Origins of Complex North-Coast Society. In *The Origins and Development of the Andean State*, edited by Jonathan Haas, Shelia Pozorski, and Thomas Pozorski, pp. 56–69. New York: Cambridge University Press.

1988   *Prehispanic Settlement Patterns in the Lower Santa Valley, Peru: A Regional Perspective on the Origins and Development of Complex North Coast Society.* Washington, D.C.: Smithsonian Institution Press.

1989   Full-Coverage Survey in the Lower Santa Valley: Implications for Regional Settlement Pattern Studies on the Peruvian Coast. In *The Archaeology of Regions: The Case for Full-Coverage Regional Survey*, edited by Suzanne K. Fish and Stephen A. Kowalewski, pp. 117–145. Washington, D.C.: Smithsonian Institution Press.

1992   Modeling the Role of Ideology in Societal Adaptation: Examples from the South American Data. In *Ideology and Pre-Columbian Culture Change*, edited by Arthur A. Demarest and Geoffrey W. Conrad, pp. 37–63. Santa Fe: School of American Research Press.

Wilson, John A.

1951   *The Culture of Ancient Egypt.* Chicago: University of Chicago Press.

1960   Egypt through the New Kingdom: Civilization without Cities. In *City Invincible,* edited by C. Kraeling and Robert McC. Adams, pp 124–164. Chicago: University of Chicago Press.

Wingard, John

1992   The Role of Soils in the Development and Collapse of Classic Maya Civilization at Copan, Honduras. Ph.D. dissertation, Department of Anthropology, Pennsylvania State University, University Park. Ann Arbor: University Microfilms.

Winkler, John

1990   Laying Down the Law: The Oversight of Men's Sexual Behavior in Athens. In *Before Sexuality,* edited by David Halperin, John Winkler, and Froma Zeitlin, pp. 171–210. Princeton: Princeton University Press.

Winkler, John, and Froma Zeitlin, eds.

1990   *Nothing to Do with Dionysos?* Princeton: Princeton University Press.

Wittfogel, Karl

1957   *Oriental Despotism: A Comparative Study of Total Power.* New Haven: Yale University Press.

Wohlleben, Joachim

1992   Germany 1750–1830. In *Perceptions of the Ancient Greeks,* edited by K. J. Dover, pp. 170–202. Oxford: Basil Blackwell.

Wolf, Eric R.

1982   *Europe and the People without History.* Berkeley: University of California Press.

1990   Facing Power: Old Insights, New Questions. *American Anthropologist* 92:586–96.

Wong, Grace

1979   A Comment on the Tributary Trade between China and Southeast Asia, and the Place of Porcelain in This Trade, during the Period of the Song Dynasty in China. In *Chinese Celadon and Other Related Wares in Southeast Asia,* edited by Southeast Asian Ceramic Society, pp. 73–100. Singapore: Ars Orientalis.

Wood, Ellen M.

1988   *Peasant-Citizen and Slave: The Foundations of Athenian Democracy.* London: Verso.

Woolley, Leonard

1974   *Ur Excavations VI: The Buildings of the Third Dynasty.* London: British Museum.

Woolley, Leonard, and Max Mallowan

1976   *Ur Excavations VII: The Old Babylonian Period.* London: British Museum.

Wright, Henry T.

1977   Recent Research on the Origin of the State. *Annual Review of Anthropology* 6:379–398.

1978   Toward an Explanation of the Origin of the State. In *The Origins of the State: The An-*

thropology of Political Evolution, edited by Ronald Cohen and Elman Service, pp. 49–68. Philadelphia: Institute for the Study of Human Issues.

1981 The Southern Margins of Sumer. In *Heartland of Cities,* edited by Robert McC. Adams, pp. 295–345. Chicago: University of Chicago Press.

1986 The Evolution of Civilizations. In *American Archaeology, Past and Future,* edited by David J. Meltzer, Donald D. Fowler, and Jeremy A. Sabloff, pp. 323–368. Washington, D.C.: Smithsonian Institution Press.

1994 Prestate Political Formations. In *Chiefdoms and Early States in the Near East: The Organizational Dynamics of Complexity,* edited by Gil Stein and Mitchell S. Rothman, pp. 67–84. Monographs in World Archaeology No. 18. Madison: Prehistory Press.

Wright, Henry T., and Gregory A. Johnson
1975 Population, Exchange, and Early State Formation in Southwestern Iran. *American Anthropologist* 77:267–289.

Wright, Rita P.
1989 The Indus Valley and Mesopotamian Civilizations: A Comparative View of Ceramic Technology. In *Old Problems and New Perspectives in the Archaeology of South Asia,* edited by J. Mark Kenoyer, pp. 145–156. Wisconsin Archaeological Reports No. 2. Madison: Department of Anthropology, University of Wisconsin.

Wylie, Alison
1989 Archaeological Cables and Tacking. *Philosophy of the Social Sciences* 19:1–18.

1992 On 'Heavily Decomposing Red Herrings': Scientific Method in Archaeology and the Ladening of Evidence with Theory. In *Metaarchaeology,* edited by Lester Embree, pp. 269–288. Dordrecht: Kluwer.

Yan Wenming
1994 Longshan shidai chengzhi de faxian yu Zhongguo wenming qiyuan de tansuo. [The Discovery of the Remains of City Walls of the Longshan Period and an Exploration of the Origins of Chinese Civilization.] Paper presented at the International Symposium on the Integration of Chinese Archaeology and History.

Yates, Robin D. S.
1990 War, Food Shortages, and Relief Measures in Early China. In *Hunger in History: Food Shortage, Poverty, and Deprivation,* edited

by Lucile Newman, William Crossgrove, Robert W. Kates, Sarah Millman, and Robley Mathews, pp. 128–157. New York: Basil Blackwell.

1994 Body, Space, Time, and Bureaucracy: Boundary Creation and Maintenance in Early Imperial China. In *Boundaries in Chinese Culture,* edited by John Hay, pp. 56–80. London: Reaktion.

Yoffee, Norman
1979 The Decline and Rise of Mesopotamian Civilization: An Ethnoarchaeological Perspective on the Evolution of Social Complexity. *American Antiquity* 44:5–35.

1981 *Explaining Trade in Ancient Western Asia.* Malibu: Undena.

1988 The Collapse of Ancient Mesopotamian States and Civilization. In *The Collapse of Ancient States and Civilizations,* edited by Norman Yoffee and George Cowgill, pp. 44–68. Tucson: University of Arizona Press.

1991 Maya Elite Interaction: Through a Glass Sideways. In *Classic Maya Political History,* edited by T. Patrick Culbert, pp. 285–310. Cambridge: Cambridge University Press.

1993a Too Many Chiefs? (or Safe Texts for the 90s). In *Archaeological Theory: Who Sets the Agenda?* edited by Norman Yoffee and Andrew Sherratt, pp. 60–78. Cambridge: Cambridge University Press

1993b Mesopotamian Interaction Spheres. In *Early Stages in the Evolution of Mesopotamian Civilization: Soviet Excavations in Northern Iraq,* edited by Norman Yoffee and Jeffrey Clark, pp. 257–269. Tucson: University of Arizona Press.

1995 Political Economy in Early Mesopotamian States. *Annual Review of Anthropology* 24:281–311.

Yoffee, Norman, and George Cowgill, eds.
1988 *The Collapse of Ancient States and Empires.* Tucson: University of Arizona Press.

Zagarell, Allen
1986 Trade, Women, Class, and Society in Ancient Western Asia. *Current Anthropology* 27:415–430.

van Zantwijk, Rudolf
1985 *The Aztec Arrangement: The Social History of Pre-Spanish Mexico.* Norman: University of Oklahoma Press.

Zheng Ruokui
1995 Yinxu 'Dayi Shang' zuyi buju chutan. [A

Preliminary Exploration of the Layout of Lineage Settlements at Dayi Shang, Wastes of Yin.] *Zhongyuan wenwu* 3:84–93.

Zhongguo shehui kexueyuan kaogu yanjiusuo Luoyang Han Wei gucheng gongzuodui
1984   Yanshi Shang cheng de chubu kantan he fajue. [Preliminary Explorations and Discoveries of the Shang City at Yanshi.] *Kaogu* 6:488–504, 509.

Zhu Fenghan
1990   *Shang Zhou jiazu xingtai yanjiu.* [Researches on the Form of Shang and Zhou Clans.] Tianjin: Guji chuban she.

Zimmermann, Hans-Dieter
1975   Frühe Ansätze zur Demokratie in den griechischen Poleis. *Klio* 57:293–299.

Zinn, Howard
1990   *The Politics of History.* 2nd ed. Urbana: University of Illinois Press.

Zou Heng
1980   Shi lun Xia wenhua. [A Trial Discussion of Xia Culture.] In *Xia Shang Zhou kaoguxue lunwen ji.* [Collected Essays on Xia, Shang, and Zhou Archaeology.] Beijing: Wenwu chuban she: 129–137.

Zorita, Alonso de
1963   *Life and Labor in Ancient Mexico: The Brief and Summary Relation of the Lords of New Spain.* Translated by Benjamin Keen. New Brunswick: Rutgers University Press.

Zuidema, Tom
1986   The Social and Cosmological Replication of the Upriver-Downriver Dichotomy in Incaic Cuzco. Paper presented at the 48th Annual Meeting of the Society for American Archaeology, Philadelphia.
1990   *Inca Civilization in Cuzco.* Austin: University of Texas Press.

Index

Index prepared by Deborah Hodges